TRANSITIONS IN SOCIETY

THE CHALLENGE OF CHANGE

Colin Bain • Jill Colyer • Dennis DesRivieres • Sean Dolan

OXFORD
UNIVERSITY PRESS

OXFORD
UNIVERSITY PRESS

70 Wynford Drive, Don Mills, Ontario M3C 1J9
www.oup.com/ca

Oxford University Press is a department of the University of Oxford.

It furthers the University's objective of excellence in research, scholarship, and education by publishing worldwide in

Oxford   New York
Auckland Bangkok Buenos Aires Cape Town
Chennai Dar es Salaam Delhi Hong Kong Istanbul
Karachi Kolkata Kuala Lumpur Madrid Melbourne Mexico City
Mumbai Nairobi São Paulo Shanghai Taipei Tokyo Toronto

Oxford is a registered trade mark of Oxford University Press
in the UK and in certain other countries

Published in Canada
By Oxford University Press

Copyright © Oxford University Press Canada 2002

The moral rights of the author have been asserted

Database right Oxford University Press (maker)

First published 2002

National Library of Canada Cataloguing in Publication Data

Bain, Colin M.
Transitions in society: the challenge of change

Includes bibliographical references and index.

ISBN 0-19-541768-2

1. Sociology. I. Title.

HM586.B36 2002   301   C2002-900647-3

Printed and bound in Canada
This book is printed on permanent (acid-free) paper ∞

4—05 04

Acquisitions editor: Patti Henderson
Text design: Brett Miller
Formatting: VISU*TronX*
Developmental editors: Tracey MacDonald, Margaret Hoogeveen
Copy editor: Susan McNish
Photo researcher: Maria DeCambra
Cover design: Joan Dempsey
Permissions editor: Ann Checchia

Acknowledgements

The authors would like to acknowledge the many people who have assisted us in the complex and challenging task of producing this book.

At Oxford University Press Canada we have been impressed with the depth of advice and support we have received. We wish to thank MaryLynne Meschino (Director, Education Division), Patti Henderson (Acquisitions Editor) for initially giving us the vote of confidence to go ahead with this project. Vince Morgan (Production Manager) and Brett Miller (Design Manager) turned our manuscript dreams into finished reality.

We wish to thank Developmental Editors Margaret Hoogeveen and Tracey MacDonald for their constant prodding to make additional improvements to the manuscript, and the positive suggestions they made for doing it. Maria DeCambra (Photo Researcher) and Susan McNish (Copy Editor) added their own vital contributions behind the scenes. To the many others we have not named, we thank you sincerely.

Our spouses have greatly assisted us, as they always do. Your love, advice, and support have eased our task. Thank you to Vi Bain, Scott Grondin, Shirley DesRivieres and Sharon Goodland. Baby Sam Grondin-Colyer is especially mentioned for his co-operation in allowing his mummy time to work on the project!

Colin Bain
Jill Colyer
Dennis DesRivieres
Sean Dolan

Cover Art: Élaine Boily, Atlas or Projection I, 2000
Mixed media on canvas, 91 x 122 cm
Collection of the artist.

This book is dedicated to the memory of

Herbert Arthur Seifert
(April 1923 to May 1989)

&

Ruth Louise (Nilson) Seifert
(January 1923 to November 1989)

TABLE OF CONTENTS

FEATURES

Groundbreakers

Skill Builders

Competing Perspectives

FOREWORD

Does human society and social change interest you? Good! The author/editor team of *Transitions in Society* would like to welcome you to the study of social science.

As you make your way through this course, you will learn about human behaviour and how and why it changes in both individuals and society at large. You will learn the fundamentals of the social sciences, wrestle with the issues raging in social science circles, and learn the skills and methods scientists use to study social change. You will be introduced to social scientists who explain their research techniques. You will encounter examples of academic writing that demonstrate what you can expect should you choose to pursue an education in the social sciences. You will conduct your own social science project, using the skills and methods used by scientists in the field.

A new course is always a challenge. By using the tools in this resource, you will succeed.

Features in *Transitions in Society*

As you flip through the book, you will notice a variety of features. Every chapter, for example, opens with a feature called **Focusing on the Issues**. The study of human behaviour almost always involves issues, some of which are not easy to solve. The subject of the Focusing on the Issues feature allows you to get a taste of what's to come. You'll also find the following features in just about every chapter.

- **Case Studies** are the authors' opportunity to give you detailed information about a topic that they believe you'll find interesting.
- In the **Competing Perspectives** features, you'll find articles with two opposing opinions about a contentious topic. Questions are provided to help you make up your own mind.
- **Groundbreaker** features tell you about the individuals whose foundational ideas and forward-looking research carved new avenues into the study of human society and social change.
- Watching movies can be more than just Friday-night entertainment. Our **Film Society** feature will help you choose classic films that throw light on your study of human behaviour.
- Check out the **Internet Resources** features to identify Web sites of particular use in social science research.
- While taking this course, you're going to learn skills used by social scientists, including everything from developing a hypothesis to structuring your research report according to American Psychological Association guidelines in the **Skill Builder** features. You'll find these in both the chapters and the skills appendix.

If you're particularly interested in one of the social sciences featured in the book, watch for the **icons** used to indicate the focus of major subsections. The icons are as follows:

 Anthropology

 Psychology

 Sociology

Don't forget the **index** at the back of the book to help you find information quickly. The **glossary** provides definitions for any difficult social science terms. You'll discover, however, that difficult and important words are highlighted in bold and defined right on the chapter pages. When researching a

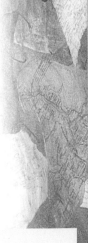

particular topic, you might want to check out the chapter-by-chapter bibliography at the back of the book. This section lists the sources the authors used to conduct their research.

Summative Project

You may be asked to complete a three-stage Summative Project over the course of the term or year. This book is structured to allow you to complete one or more or the following project types: Research Essay, Survey, or a Field Observation.

Whichever project type you choose, it will be broken down into three major stages (explained at the end of each unit). Each of the three major units in this book contains Skill Builder features that will help you develop the particular skills you will need to complete your Summative Project. The Skill Builder features and the particular chapters they appear in are listed below.

At each stage, you will also be asked to provide a submission that relates to your specific project type, as outlined below.

Materials for Submission, by Project Type

	For Research Paper	For Survey	For Field Observation
Stage 1: Conceptualizing Your Project	• proposal for research paper	• proposal for survey	• proposal for field research project
Stage 2: Processing and Interpreting Your Research	• research notes • rough outline of paper	• research notes • list of survey questions • completed survey	• research notes • raw data collected for field research
Stage 3: Creating a Finished Product	• completed research paper with sources	• completed survey report	• completed field observation report

By applying the techniques demonstrated in the Skill Builder features to your own work on the Summative Project, you should be able to develop your researching and reporting skills.

CHAPTER 1

AN INTRODUCTION TO THE SOCIAL SCIENCES

INTRODUCTION

The social sciences comprise a broad field of study that focuses exclusively on one area of interest: human behaviour. Social scientists study human beings to find out what we tend to have in common, and how we are distinct both as individuals and as groups. In this chapter, you will begin to explore the topics examined by social scientists from three disciplines:

anthropology, psychology, and sociology. You will learn about the methods they use to study humans, some of the major differences of opinion and viewpoint that exist within their ranks, and the work of some current Canadian social scientists. You will also become familiar with some of the basic terminology used by practitioners in the three disciplines.

Social scientists such as the linguistic anthropologist at left, devote themselves to learning more about human society. How might the information they gather be useful to others trying to learn more about human society?

Focusing on the Issues

Children Learn What They Live
By Dorothy Law Nolte

If children live with criticism, they learn to condemn.
If children live with hostility, they learn to fight.
If children live with ridicule, they learn to feel shy.
If children live with shame, they learn to feel guilty.
If children live with encouragement, they learn confidence.
If children live with tolerance, they learn patience.
If children live with praise, they learn appreciation.
If children live with acceptance, they learn to love.
If children live with approval, they learn to like themselves.
If children live with honesty, they learn truthfulness.
If children live with security, they learn to have faith in themselves and those about them.
If children live with friendliness, they learn the world is a nice place in which to live.

Source: Excerpted from the book CHILDREN LEARN WHAT THEY LIVE, © 1998 by Dorothy Law Nolte and Rachel Harris, The poem "Children Learn What They Live," © Dorothy Law Nolte. Used by permission of Workman Publishing Co., Inc., New York, All Rights Reserved.

THINK ABOUT IT

1. As you reflect on your own experiences, which lines in this poem are meaningful to you?
2. Summarize the main ideas contained in the poem.
3. What is your opinion of the main message of this poem? Explain your reasoning.
4. Can we know from our own experiences whether or not the main ideas are valid? Would we be better to suspend our judgment until we have researched the findings of social scientists who have investigated the subject? Explain your reasoning.

■ Learning Expectations

By the end of this chapter, you will be able to

- define and correctly use anthropological, psychological, and sociological terms and concepts
- demonstrate an understanding of the main areas of study in anthropology, psychology, and sociology
- demonstrate an understanding of various methods for conducting research
- describe and apply to real-life contexts the theories that are central to anthropology, psychology, and sociology
- demonstrate an understanding of a variety of research methods and approaches used in anthropology, psychology, and sociology

Section 1.1   What Social Scientists Examine

Key Concepts

social science

behaviour

discipline

anthropology

culture

psychology

sociology

What are the social sciences? Perhaps you took a social science course in Grade 11 and have some idea. Even if you did, chances are that you're more familiar with the contents and methods of the natural sciences such as chemistry and biology.

Unlike the natural sciences, which involve the study of the physical world, the **social sciences** use research and analysis to explain human **behaviour**. Unlike the humanities, which involve the study of the products of human culture (such as literature and art), the social sciences are concerned with what people think and how they act. They include economics, political science, history, human geography, family studies, anthropology, psychology, and sociology. Economics, for example, can show us the types of decisions that people make in times of high unemployment, rapid inflation, or

growing international competition. Whatever the social science **discipline**, or branch of study, it focuses on some aspect of human behaviour.

To the social scientist, human behaviour consists of anything humans do that is observable and measurable. Human behaviour, therefore, consists of the things that humans say, do, think, buy, avoid, support, demonstrate against, and so on. People's buying habits represent one form of behaviour, while the pattern of our sports participation shows another. Each behaviour requires different measurement techniques. A researcher can identify and tabulate a person's buying habits, for example, by examining his or her credit card receipts. What a person thinks, however, is less easily determined. The researcher might interview the subject, or might design a questionnaire for the person to fill out. Social scientists have techniques for observing and measuring all types of behaviours.

This book focuses on three social sciences: anthropology, psychology, and sociology. **Anthropology** examines the development of the human species and human **cultures** throughout the world. (A human culture consists of the ways of living of a group of people, including their traditions, inventions, and conventions.) Especially in recent times, many anthropologists try to live with the cultural group they are studying, often for extended periods. **Psychology** is the study of people's feelings, thoughts, and personality development. The goal of this social science is to discover the underlying triggers or causes of human behaviours. Many psychologists are interested in incidents in people's past experience that influence them. One branch of psychology emphasizes animal experiments in laboratory situations, believing that

Figure 1.1 A Canadian Alliance leadership convention. Political science, one of the social sciences, is concerned with politics and systems of government. Political scientists can show us, for example, whether people support the party they believe will do the most for them personally, or the party they think will do the best job for society as a whole. How might researchers gather this information?

these experiments lead to greater understanding of the human mind. **Sociology** looks at the development and structure of human society, and how it works. Where psychology focuses more on individual behaviour, sociology examines how people act in group situations. Sociologists use statistical analysis as one of their basic research tools to explain human behaviour.

Look again at the poem "Children Learn What They Live" on page 3. The three social science disciplines that are the subject of this book would each bring a different focus to a study of the issues raised by the poem. Can you identify which discipline would take each of the following approaches? (The answers are at the bottom of page 6.)

Identify-the-Discipline Quiz

Discipline 1: Practitioners of this social science would ask how accurately this poem reflects what we know about the development and functioning of human society. They might conduct a statistical analysis to find out whether children do in fact tend to develop into the kind of adults that the poem suggests they do. Alternatively, they might track a sample of people from childhood to adulthood to find out what links, if any, connect childhood experiences with adult personality.

Discipline 2: These social scientists would ask how accurately this poem reflects what we know about human culture. They might participate as observers in a number of cultures in different countries to see how children are treated and to try to establish a possible link in each culture between childhood experiences and the resulting adult behaviours.

Discipline 3: Social scientists from this discipline would consider people's feelings about how they were treated as children. They would examine how these feelings affect the development of the individuals' adult personalities. These social scientists might focus on a manageable number of individual subjects, recording in detail their experiences as children and adults. In this way, they would try to understand how the minds of their subjects work.

It is important to understand that the three disciplines are not entirely separate. For example, the work of some social anthropologists is not that different from that of some sociologists. Both look at the overlapping areas of cultural beliefs and social institutions among humans. Similarly, psychologists and sociologists have both put great effort into explaining criminal behaviour, and their methods and findings sometimes overlap. Anthropology, psychology, and sociology are perhaps best described as disciplines that largely support one another. Although they are different in emphasis, they are not three conflicting disciplines.

Figure 1.2 Sally Boysen from Ohio State University conducts an experiment to study chimps' intelligence. Would an anthropologist, psychologist, or sociologist be more likely to conduct this experiment? Why?

Pause and Reflect

1. What is the major difference between the humanities and the social sciences? Give an example of each.
2. To the social scientist, what are the characteristics of a human behaviour? What are some examples of such behaviours?
3. What are the main focus and typical methods used by each of the three social science disciplines examined in this section?
4. In your own words, explain why anthropology, psychology, and sociology are not entirely separate disciplines.
5. Pretend that you are applying to a university program in the social sciences. Complete the paragraph beginning with these words in your letter of application: "The social sciences interest me because…" You can write about the social sciences in general or a specific social science of your choice.

Section 1.2   Anthropology

Key Concepts

participant-observation

Gross Domestic Product (GDP) per capita

intuition

kinship

patrilineal

fictive kinship

ethnography

school of thought

institution

binary opposite

materialism

determinism

How Anthropologists Conduct Their Work

In the previous section, you read that one of the central tools of anthropology is the detailed observation of subject groups. Anthropologists commonly live with their subjects for a long time, participating as a group or community member and recording their observations. This technique is known as **participant-observation**. Practitioners of this technique believe that, by living and participating in a group such as a small village, the researcher will be totally accepted by the group members. These researchers believe, further, that the behaviours they observe will be more or less the same as if the researcher were not present—in other words, that the group members will not put on a show of unusual behaviours. Using this technique, anthropologists have recorded the lives of various communities, originally in more isolated parts of the world, but increasingly within developed nations. In the case study on page 7, one anthropologist looks at the social problems that resulted from poverty in a community in Brazil.

Identify-the-Discipline Answers

- **Discipline 1:** Sociology
- **Discipline 2:** Anthropology
- **Discipline 3:** Psychology

Poverty in Brazil

During the 1980s, anthropologist Nancy Scheper-Hughes participant-observed women living in a squatter town in northeast Brazil. Since the 1950s, giant, mechanized sugar plantations had forced subsistence farmers off their lands. To survive, many former farmers became day labourers on the plantations. Male labourers were paid $10 per week, and female labourers $5, while a family of four needed $40 per week to meet basic food needs. In addition, sugar cane had displaced other crops such as beans, making it difficult to obtain a balanced diet with locally grown foods. Widespread malnutrition resulted. Many rural men eventually left their wives and families behind and moved to cities in search of work, sending money home and visiting occasionally. The structure of local communities was severely disrupted.

During the same period, the national statistics for Brazil did not reflect the local experience. Brazil experienced a tremendous economic expansion. Its **Gross Domestic Product (GDP) per capita** (the total wealth produced by a country's economy divided by total population) had risen from $648 in 1971 to $4508 in 1993. Moreover, figures published by the Brazilian government showed that, in 1993, for every 1000 live births, 57 died in the first year of life. (For comparison, Canada's infant mortality rate at this time was 7.1 per thousand live births.) Although high by comparison with other industrialized nations, the rate was falling, and Brazil began to enjoy an international reputation as a nation rising to "developed" status.

But what, Scheper-Hughes wondered, was life like for the subsistence families whose livelihoods had been destroyed by the sugar plantations? To what extent did national statistics hide the grim reality of their lives? Scheper-Hughes participant-observed a northeastern community she called Bom Jesus. (Note: "Bom Jesus" is a fictitious name. Anthropologists rarely reveal the

Figure 1.3 Brazil's proudest export, an Embraer Regional Jet, illustrates the high degree of technological and industrial expertise that has developed in parts of this formerly poor country. What groups in Brazilian society might benefit from new high-tech industries like this one? Which groups would be largely unaffected?

identity of the communities they observe. Anthropologists believe that giving participant communities anonymity will encourage participants to be more open and frank with observers.)

Because many of the adult males lived outside the community, Scheper-Hughes was able to enjoy a closer relationship with the women than would otherwise have been possible. They told her about their married lives, and she discovered that they had endured much worse conditions than the national statistics implied. A study of the complete reproductive lives of 100 post-menopausal women showed that, on average, each had seen 4.7 of her offspring die. Scheper-Hughes visited cemeteries and consulted local registry books and church records to find out how many babies had died. As mentioned earlier, the national infant mortality rate was 57 per 1000. For the northeastern region, the rate was 116 per 1000. In 1987, through her analysis, Scheper-Hughes discovered that the rate in Bom Jesus was 211 and had risen to 493 during the worst year.

Scheper-Hughes also discovered that—like some unemployed and impoverished workers in developed countries—the residents of Bom Jesus used tranquilizers to help them cope with the stress of their lives.

Scheper-Hughes concluded that the overall influence of "global financialization" had led to malnutrition and impoverishment as well as substance abuse for the residents of Bom Jesus. Her work shows that social scientists must probe behind the figures published by governments to discover whether the picture they present matches real people's lives.

Questions

1. What specific circumstances caused the problems that developed in Bom Jesus? What overall influence does Scheper-Hughes believe led to these problems?
2. Compare the infant mortality figures of Bom Jesus with the Brazilian national figures. Explain the difference.
3. How did Scheper-Hughes collect her statistics?
4. Suggest three methods used in the Bom Jesus study that are typical of the methods used by anthropologists.

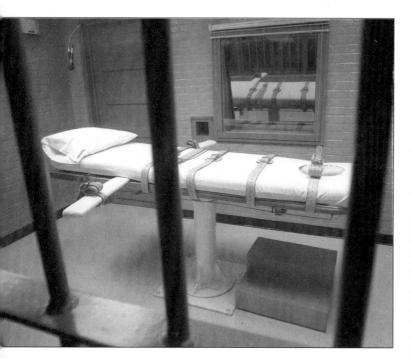

Figure 1.4 The Texas death chamber, May 2000, in Huntsville, Texas. Texas executes more people than any other jurisdiction in North America. Do you think this means that Texas has a low murder rate? Only careful study can determine whether or not what we "know" to be true is indeed true.

Testing Our Intuition

When you read the poem "Children Learn What They Live" on page 3, you may have been tempted to agree or disagree with each statement based on your experience. You may have been tempted to think you know the truth of something through your **intuition**—your own emotions and logic.

Similarly, after reading the case study on page 7, you might think that the work of Scheper-Hughes was unnecessary because you already "know" intuitively that there is a link between poverty and health and social problems. This, of course, leads us to ask the following question: Why do we need social scientists to research assumptions that we know intuitively to be true? To find the truth, we must first acknowledge that intuitions are beliefs, not facts. What proof do you have, after all, to back up your intuitions? Let's try replacing the word "know" with the word "think" in the same question: Why do we need social scientists to research assumptions that we think intuitively to be true? Now try answering the question.

In many cases, social scientists have demonstrated that what the majority, or a significant number of people, might believe to be true cannot be verified by evidence; it therefore cannot be accepted as true. Many people might say, "I know intuitively that when a society brings in the death penalty, the murder rate declines." However, the social scientists who researched this issue found contradictory evidence. The murder rate in fact does not decline. By doing their research and testing our intuitive beliefs, anthropologists and other social scientists play a valuable role. In testing the commonly held beliefs of a population, they help us see whether or not what we "know intuitively" is in fact true.

Comparing Cultures

A major function of anthropologists is to increase our knowledge of what it is to be human by noting and comparing cultural differences. For example, anthropologists are interested in the question of **kinship**. Kinship is a family relationship based on what a culture considers a family to be. Almost every culture considers that you have a kinship relationship with your sister or brother. Other sibling relationships raise questions, however. Is a half-sister or half-brother your kin? A stepsister or stepbrother? A half-brother or half-sister born to one of your parents outside marriage? Different cultures have different rules about which of these relationships are truly kinship. Most Western cultures would accept that two children with the same mother but different fathers are kin. The Lakher people of Myanmar (formerly known as Burma), however, believe that two such children are not relatives at all.

Kinship is therefore based on cultural concepts. Anthropologists have concluded that human cultures define the concept of kinship in three ways: mating (marriage), birth (descent), and nurturance (adoption).

We acquire kin through our parents, through our marriage partners, and through those we choose to bring into our families. But within these three broad categories, most cultures are fairly selective regarding who fits, and who does not. In many societies, children whose parents are not married by religious, legal, or accepted social definitions may be rejected as kin by some of their biological relatives. Marriage and mating are not, therefore, identical principles in kinship definition. Similarly, adopted children enjoy the same rights as their non-adopted siblings in most cultures, because nurturance and descent are equally regarded as definitions of kinship. Foster children, however, do not receive the same rights, because their foster parents are not considered real kin. Kinship is a complex matter, subject to great differences of interpretation.

Most human societies are **patrilineal**. This means that members organize their families through their father's line. Characteristics of this approach include women taking their husband's family name on marriage, and all children taking their father's family name. Other cultures are matrilineal, with the mother's line being pre-eminent. Among the Navajo people of the American Southwest, for example, the traditional family unit consists of the head-mother, her husband, and some of their children together with their spouses. Although the head-mother's husband is normally chief livestock herder and spokesperson for the family in dealing with outsiders, the head-mother's opinions usually prevail. She is identified with the land, and all residence rights are traced through her.

Anthropologists use the term "**fictive kinship**" to describe the practice of acknowledging as kin people who are not biologically related. Godparents are a form of fictive kinship, in which parents choose an individual to take a parental interest in the child's religious upbringing.

Kinship principles define a number of important rules in a culture. These include where people live (residence rules), how generations are linked to each other (descent rules), how people pass on positions of authority (succession), and how they pass on their physical possessions (inheritance rules).

You will read more about the work of anthropologists in later chapters. What is the key role of anthropologists? Perhaps their most important contribution is in illustrating the enormous variety of human ways of living, which they accomplish by focusing on different cultures around the world. What is considered normal, rude, funny, beautiful, romantic, and dastardly can vary enormously from culture to culture. Not only may we be impressed with the vast differences in beliefs, values, and practices that anthropologists

reveal, we may also be surprised by the many similarities between cultures that seem, at first glance, to be quite different.

The Skills and Methods of Anthropologists

All anthropologists use similar methods, including participant-observation, the collection of statistics, field interviews, and the rigorous compilation of detailed field notes. The fieldwork of anthropologists is known as **ethnography**, the scientific study of human races and cultures. In the boxed feature on this page, you can read about the skills and methods used by an anthropologist studying Muslim women in Canada.

Skills and Methods

A STUDY OF MUSLIM WOMEN
By Anthropologist Parin Dossa

The Researcher: Parin Dossa, Associate Professor of Anthropology, Simon Fraser University
The Study: Ethnographic Study of Muslim Women in Canada

My Research Project and Its Goals

If you were an anthropologist doing field research on immigrant Muslim women in Canada, you would encounter two scenes: (a) exclusion and discrimination of Muslim women as the Other (not like us/different) and (b) Muslim women's engaged and creative response to this exclusion. For example, Muslim women are rarely asked about their views on the September 11 tragedy and its backlash on immigrant Muslim communities. Nonetheless, these women have much to offer because they can provide an important and useful perspective from their position on the margins of society.

As an anthropologist, your critical response to the discrepancy between these two scenes would make you realize that, ultimately, you are dealing with questions of social justice, equality, and human dignity. Examining the discrepancy constitutes the core of my research project (April 1997 to April 2001) on Iranian Muslim women in metropolitan Vancouver. My goal has been to encourage

Figure 1.5 Associate Professor Parin Dossa

dialogue and conversations at multiple levels: among people as well as across cultural, gender, and ethnic boundaries.

The Steps I Went Through to Set Up the Research

My encounter with the two "scenes" outlined above brought to the fore one question: How do we conduct socially accountable research that takes into consideration participants' voices and life experiences? My anthropological response to this question was to conduct bottom-up research accomplished through the ethnographic methods of participant-observation and open-ended conversations.

My conviction that we should first know the participants as people rather than "research subjects" led me to do four months of volunteer work in an English-as-a-Second-Language program. It was here that I met the first few participants, who facilitated more contacts.

Ethical Considerations

During the course of my research I followed the university's ethical guidelines. I explained my research focus to the participants and assured them that their identities would be kept anonymous. I also informed them of their rights to withdraw from the study at any time, and that a copy of the findings would be made available to them on request. I took care to explain both the benefits and the limitations of research, highlighting my focus on accountability: to undertake collaborative work and encourage dialogue.

How We Carried Out the Research

Forty women and ten service providers participated in this team-based study involving two community-based researchers and two student researchers. The ethnographic research consisted of four components:

*   engaging in semi-structured interviews
*   participant observation of daily life and special occasions
*   listening to stories
*   socializing to gain empathy and cultural sensitivity

How We Collated and Interpreted the Results

My research focused on linking the words and worlds of women with two notable issues: justice and equality. This goal led me to use the stories and life narratives of the participants as primary data. Narratives can show how a life is shaped by and also shapes societal norms and practices. Speaking from the margins, Iranian women's stories revealed the potential for change. To link the narratives to the issues of justice and equality, I organized their stories along four interrelated themes: being a refugee, looking for work, being a senior, and being a caregiver to a disabled child. Each of these themes revealed insights that had policy as well as service-provision implications.

My research showed that Iranian Muslim women are actively engaged in giving new meanings to words such as "refugee," "citizenship," "women," and "justice." By examining these ideas with new eyes, these women are engaged in drawing the attention of other people to positive change.

How I Communicated the Results

The primary means of communicating anthropological research results is to publish articles about the study in scholarly journals—publications read by anthropologists and other scholars throughout the academic world. In addition, I presented my work to colleagues at academic conferences, to community-based workers, and by speaking with participants. This challenging task requires the use of multiple "languages" for different audiences.

Note: To read an excerpt from Parin Dossa's research project, please see page 262.

1. What (a) personal and (b) academic skills would Parin Dossa have needed to conduct her research? Which do you think was most crucial?
2. Make a list of the steps that she used through the course of her research project.

Schools of Thought in Anthropology

So far, we have looked at anthropology as though it were a single, unified discipline. In fact, as is the case for sociology and psychology as well, anthropology covers a wide range of subject interests. When a certain way of interpreting a discipline's subject matter gains widespread credibility, it is considered a school of thought. Anthropology is divided into a number of **schools of thought**. At conferences, academics vigorously debate the relative strengths of the competing approaches. New schools of thought usually emerge as offshoots of existing approaches.

Functionalism

According to functionalists, all cultures are set up to deal with the universal problems that human societies face. These problems are all connected with trying to meet either physical or psychological needs. Consequently, every custom or practice in a culture serves a purpose, particularly in providing stability. Established laws, practices, and customs within a society can be called **institutions**. To understand a culture, it is necessary to investigate the social functions of these institutions.

At the core of functionalism is a belief that society is itself a logical institution that functions in the best interests of the majority. Culture, the system of kinship, beliefs, and practices that holds society together, must

therefore be equally logical. Although a society's practices may at first seem strange to the outsider, functionalists believe that the role of anthropologists is to explain, not to judge.

Critics charge that functionalists present cultures and societies as being more stable than they are. Additionally, since functionalists believe that every practice serves a purpose, critics accuse them of downplaying the negative results of some practices.

Structuralism

According to structuralists, the human mind functions on the principle of **binary opposites**. This means that humans tend to see things in terms of two forces that are opposite to each other, such as night and day, good and evil, female and male. All cultures, Bronislaw Malinowski observed, distinguish between people born "here" and outsiders, normal days and holy or feast days, boys' clothing and girls' clothing. These binary opposites are defined in a particular culture in a way that is logical to its members. Items are not inherently good or bad, but become so when placed in the right or wrong element. For example, your shoes are "good" when you wear them outside or place them on a boot mat, but "bad" when you place them on the dining room table.

All cultures develop complex rules about where items are good and where they are bad. The set of rules in each culture is different, however. Structuralists believe that anthropologists

Schools of Thought in Anthropology

School of Thought	Famous Practitioners	Time Period	Typical Questions	Central Approach
Functionalism	Bronislaw Malinowski, Margaret Mead, Ruth Benedict	1930s to 1960s	• What purpose in society does this institution serve? • How does this institution contribute to the overall stability of society?	To understand a culture, it is necessary to investigate the social functions of institutions.
Structuralism	Claude Levi-Strauss, Mary Douglas	1940s to 1970s	• What are the main principles that govern the way the human mind works? • How are these principles reflected in the way human cultures work?	All cultures develop complex rules that are logical structures, based on binary opposites. Anthropologists must seek out and explain these rules.
Cultural Materialism	Marvin Harris, Carol Ember, Stephen Sanderson	1970s to present	• How do population and economic factors influence the type of culture that develops? • What are the laws of development that apply to all cultures?	The true explanation of a culture can only be derived by examining members' decisions regarding human reproduction and economic production.

Figure 1.6 Anthropologists generally fall into three categories, each group advocating one of the approaches shown in this table. How are these schools of thought different, and how are they similar?

must seek out and explain these rules. Only by understanding the operation of the human mind can anthropologists analyze cultures and societies. With a full understanding of the human mind, anthropologists will see that human cultures are logical structures trying to meet human needs.

Critics charge that structuralists overemphasize logic and stability in human societies. Why do cultures sometimes die out, critics ask, if they always meet the needs of their members?

Cultural Materialism

According to cultural materialists, technological and economic factors are the most important ones in moulding a society. This theory is known as **materialism**. Cultural materialists also believe in a theory called **determinism**, which says that the types of technology and economic methods that are adopted always determine (or act as deciding factors in forming) the type of society that develops.

Figure 1.7 What is the boy at right doing that Western society considers "bad"? Structuralists say that every culture has a complex set of rules about what is "good" and "bad." These rules vary dramatically from culture to culture.

Anthropologists have long debated the relationship between social and cultural factors within a society, and the economic structure that goes with it. Marvin Harris (1927–2001) began the cultural materialist school with the publication of his book *The Rise of Anthropological Theory* (1968). He argued that material factors are the starting point to understanding a culture. Also known as a society's infrastructure, these material factors include the ways in which goods are produced, and the methods used to reproduce the population at what is considered an acceptable rate. The infrastructure determines a society's structure (social classes, distribution of wealth) and also its superstructure (music, recreation, and the arts).

Harris saw all human societies as having three levels, as shown in Figure 1.8. Level 1 determines Levels 2 and 3. Harris acknowledged that Levels 2 and 3 can affect each other and Level 1. Level 1, however—infrastructure—is the major determinant of the other two levels; the other levels can have only a minor effect on Level 1. Therefore, cultural materialists believe that anthropologists must find the root causes of this behaviour by analyzing the society's decisions regarding technology (especially human reproduction) and economic production (Level 1).

Like other determinists, cultural materialists have been criticized for trying to establish laws that apply to all cultures and their development. Many anthropologists believe that their role is to observe and explain, not to try to create a subject based on scientific laws. Other critics believe that cultural materialists observe cultures through biased eyes. That is, they try to find the ways that the cultures reflect the laws of cultural materialism rather than listening to the subject cultures explain themselves.

Cultural Materialists' Levels of Society

Level 3: Superstructure (music, recreation, arts)	1. Members' behaviour 2. Members' mental processes
Level 2: Structure (social classes, distribution of wealth)	1. Domestic economy 2. Political mechanisms
Level 1: Infrastructure (material factors)	1. Methods to produce goods and services needed to survive and prosper 2. Methods to ensure human reproduction at a satisfactory rate

Figure 1.8 According to cultural materialists, Infrastructure (Level 1) determines both structure (Level 2) and superstructure (Level 3). Give an example of your behaviour being determined by the ways that goods and services are produced in your society.

Pause and Reflect

1. What is participant-observation, and how does it facilitate the research of anthropologists?

2. What dimensions of human behaviour most interest anthropologists?

3. What are schools of thought?

4. Create a chart to show the similarities and differences among the various schools of thought in anthropology. Explain the main criticisms of the three schools of thought.

5. Suggest a study of some aspect of your community that would be of interest to an anthropologist. Explain how the research would be conducted, being sure that the research techniques match the skills and methods of anthropologists.

Section 1.3 Psychology

 ### How Psychologists Conduct Their Work

Like other social scientists, psychologists study how and why humans act as they do. They tend to focus, however, on factors that are unique to the individual. Whereas anthropologists and sociologists study how humans function in cultures or societies, psychologists look more toward the individual, and the personal and unique experiences that influence how that individual will act and think.

Experimental psychology is the branch of the discipline that sets up experiments to see how individuals act in particular situations. (You will read about such an experiment in the case study on page 16.) From these experiments, psychologists hope to identify the normal range of human behaviours and the reasons for them. But psychology is more than that. **Clinical psychology** is a branch of the discipline that develops programs for treating individuals suffering from mental illnesses and behavioural disorders. For example, psychologists treat dangerous sex offenders in federal prisons in an attempt to prevent them from reoffending on release.

Let us look at a specific example of research in psychology. If you were walking along the street and came across a hostile confrontation between two people, what would you do? Would you help a stranger who was being threatened with violence from another person? We might like to think that we would assist a helpless person in such a situation, but we might not come through as we would hope. Strong forces are at work encouraging us to stay out of private dis-

putes. The case of Kitty Genovese in New York City is a case in point. In 1964, Ms. Genovese was murdered in the street outside her apartment building, after loud shouting was heard. Evidence showed that 38 people in various apartment buildings witnessed the murder, but no one made any attempt to prevent it. (You can find a detailed examination of this case in Bain and Colyer, 2001, pages 328 to 329.)

Psychologists have long been interested in our unwillingness to get involved in uncomfortable situations, even if someone's personal safety is at risk. We have a tendency to see ourselves as bystanders in such situations, rather than as **actors** (what social scientists call people who become active participants in given situations.) In the wake of the Kitty Genovese murder, psychologists carried out a number of experiments to try to understand why no one helped her. In the case study on page 16, we look at one such experiment.

The Skills and Methods of Psychologists

Research psychologists use a variety of methods in their studies. They conduct experiments, frequently with animals such as mice or dogs. They create studies of individuals over long periods of time. They organize surveys and engage in reviews of scholarly literature. In the boxed feature on page 17 you can read about the skills and methods used by a psychologist studying the strategies people use when they play games.

Key Concepts

experimental psychology

clinical psychology

actor

confederate

variable

conscious/ unconscious

id

superego

ego

neurotic

stimulus-response

When Bystanders Join In

Four years after Kitty Genovese was murdered, two psychologists, John Darley and Bibb Latane, wanted to identify the factors that influence bystanders' decisions to get involved in public situations. They set up an experiment to find out what would affect whether or not people would get involved in a Frisbee game with strangers.

To begin, they hired three young women to participate as **confederates**, meaning they were members of the experimental team. Two of the young women began a Frisbee game in the waiting room at Grand Central Station—the main train terminal in New York City. They threw the Frisbee to a third confederate. She either joined the game, laughing and smiling, or let the Frisbee fall to the floor and kicked it away, telling the other two that they were silly and behaving

dangerously. Whether she reacted positively or negatively was the most important **variable** (factor that had an influence on the experiment's outcome) in determining the bystanders' response. The times she responded negatively, no one else in the waiting room joined the game. If she responded positively, however, 86 per cent of the people in the waiting room joined in. Occasionally, people would come into the waiting room just to join the game!

Darley and Latane's experiment suggests that whether or not we intervene in a situation depends on the cues we get from the participants and other bystanders. If this conclusion is extended to the Kitty Genovese case, it suggests that if just one bystander had joined in to try to help her, others might well have come forward too.

Figure 1.9 Friends of Ray Saikkonen, a mechanical engineering student at Ryerson Polytechnic University in Toronto, mourn his loss outside a police station. On June 12, 1996, Saikkonen tried to stop thieves who had just robbed the restaurant where he worked. He was shot twice and killed. This outcome highlights the primary reason why people are reluctant to get involved in potentially dangerous situations, including other people's fights. Why else might people be reluctant to get involved?

Questions

1. What was the most important variable in the experiment described here?
2. According to this experiment, why might the 38 people who witnessed Kitty Genovese's murder have been unwilling to assist her?

Skills and Methods

A STUDY OF GAME THEORY
By Psychologist Robert West

The Researcher: Robert West, Assistant Professor, Department of Psychology, Carleton University, Ottawa

The Study: Simple Games as Dynamic, Coupled Systems

My Research Project and Its Goals

Mathematicians have developed a method, called Game Theory, for calculating the best strategy for playing games, including video games, sports games, and financial games, such as playing the stock market. People, however, do not always use the best strategy, so game theory cannot fully account for people's behaviour. This is not surprising because most people do not calculate ideal strategies before starting to play a game. Instead, they learn and adapt to their opponents as they play. To explain this aspect of game playing, a psychological theory of how people play games is needed. The goal of my research study was to develop such a theory.

Figure 1.10 Professor Robert West

The Steps I Went Through to Set Up the Research

A research team consisting of me and four other researchers at Carleton University (Ottawa) and Carnegie Mellon University (Pittsburgh) began our preparations by reviewing past psychological findings related to how people predict what will happen next. We then developed a theory to explain how people learn and adapt to their opponents by using their opponents' past behaviours to predict what they will do next.

We chose to test our theory using the game Paper, Rock, Scissors (PRS) as our model game. In this simple game, the opponents make hand signals at exactly the same moment. The hand signals symbolize one of paper (flat hand), rock (fist), or scissors (a V shape made from the index and middle finger). One opponent will win each "round," based on the following relationships:

- scissors wins over paper (scissors can cut paper)
- rock wins over scissors (rock can break scissors)
- paper wins over rock (paper can cover rock)

Should the two opponents present the same hand signal in a round, it's a tie. Results are tabulated by counting up the wins for each player.

We chose PRS for two reasons. First, PRS is a very simple game, so it is relatively easy and inexpensive to study. Second, PRS involves the same basic skills as more complex games such as boxing, tennis, various video games, and playing the stock market. Specifically, in all of these games you have an advantage if you can guess correctly what the opponent will do next.

The next step of our preparations involved creating a computer simulation of a person playing PRS according to the theory we developed. After that was done, we played the simulation against a variety of imaginary opponents that were also simulated on the computer. Following this, we tabulated the results to examine the pattern of wins and losses for our model player. We predicted that, if our theory was correct, human players should produce the same pattern of results as the model player when playing against the simulated opponents. To test this, we created a simple PRS video game with simulated opponents and arranged for people to play against it.

Ethical Considerations
Because people tend to enjoy playing video games, there were no ethical concerns other than the need for anonymity of results. We informed participants that their individual results would be kept confidential.

How We Carried Out the Research
Our research involved having people play against the simulated opponents on the PRS video game we developed, and tabulating the results for comparison against the simulation results mentioned above.

How We Interpreted the Results
After the results were collected, we found that the human players produced the same pattern of wins and losses as our model, thereby indicating that our theory was correct. We also employed statistical tests to verify that our results were not a result of chance. These tests indicated that there was less than a 1 per cent probability that the results could have occurred by chance.

How We Communicated the Results
To communicate our findings we first presented the results at several academic conferences. In addition to being of interest to psychologists, the results were also of interest to academics working on game theory, and to developers of video games. After getting feedback at the conferences, we published our findings as a journal article (co-authored with C. Lebiere in 2001).

Note: To read excerpts from a journal article Robert West wrote about this research project, please see page 113.

1. Decide what skills Robert West would have needed to conduct his research. Which skill do you think was most crucial?
2. List the methods he used through the course of his research project.

Schools of Thought in Psychology

Like its social science counterparts, psychology has been divided into a number of schools of thought. These divisions took place right from the birth of the discipline toward the end of the nineteenth century.

Psychoanalytic Theory

Fundamental to psychoanalytic theory is a particular way of picturing the mind and how it works. According to psychoanalysts, the mind is divided into two parts: the **conscious** (the part we are aware of) and the **unconscious** (the part we are not aware of). The unconscious mind has more influence than the conscious has on our personality and behaviour. The unconscious is further divided into three parts. The **id** encourages us to seek physical (sexual, nutritional, etc.) satisfaction. The **superego** prompts us to do the moral thing, not the one that feels best. The **ego** referees between the two and deals with external reality. Personality development and individual behaviour are governed by how the three parts of the unconscious mind interact.

Sigmund Freud, the founder of psychoanalytic theory, believed that our early childhood experiences, usually involving our relationships with parents and family, are stored in our unconscious mind. Although we are normally unaware of these memories, they have a powerful influence on the way we function. These early relationships, for example, may have given us a general sense of frustration that has stayed with us throughout our lives. Luckier individuals may have gained a general sense of satisfaction with life, or of well-being.

If we live with a general sense of frustration, our behaviour may become **neurotic**, or abnormal, usually connected with anxiety or obsessiveness. Psychoanalysts believe that criminal behaviour is caused by frustration

stemming from early childhood experiences.

Particular to psychoanalytic theory is the belief that treating the unconscious mind can alleviate neuroses. Using dream analysis and hypnosis, Freud and his followers attempted to unlock the unconscious mind and purge deep-seated frustrations. They developed techniques to identify memories stored in the unconscious mind and to interpret their effect on the patient's behaviour. Many criminals and people with neuroses can be treated successfully in this manner.

Freud felt that individual sexual satisfaction or frustration was the key element in personality development. Other psychologists, originally supporters of Freud, later modified his ideas. Alfred Adler (1870–1937) and Carl Jung (1875–1961) felt that the sexual component was only one among many important factors in human personality development.

Schools of Thought in Psychology

School of Thought	Famous Practitioners	Time Period	Typical Questions	Central Approach
Psychoanalytic Theory	Sigmund Freud	1890s to 1930s	• How does the unconscious mind affect our actions? • How can we unlock the secrets of the unconscious mind?	The unconscious mind can be unlocked through dream analysis and hypnosis.
Behaviourism	John B. Watson, Benjamin Spock	1910s to 1950s	• How can animal experiments assist us to explain human behaviour? • Do children respond better to strict or flexible rules during their upbringing?	By identifying the factors that motivate human behaviour, psychologists can predict and control it—they can treat patients with problem behaviours.
Learning Theory	Ivan Pavlov, B.F. Skinner, Albert Bandura	1880s to present	• What mechanisms do humans use to learn proper behaviour? • Are animal experiments a true predictor of human behaviour?	By controlling the way in which humans learn behaviour, society can have a great influence on their ultimate personalities.

Figure 1.11 Psychologists generally fall into three categories, each group advocating one of the approaches shown in this table. How are these schools of thought different, and how are they similar?

Figure 1.12 Psychologists help patients recognize the childhood sources of the frustrations they experience in the present. How might this process help people?

The techniques of psychoanalytic theory, however, have been highly influential in psychology. They emphasize individual counselling, in which a trained practitioner leads the patient to explore critical prior experiences, frequently those from childhood. This method of allowing patients to explore and explain their understanding of self and others formed the basis of modern clinical psychology.

Behaviourism

Like the psychoanalysts, behaviourists believe that psychologists can predict and control or modify human behaviour by identifying the factors that motivate it in the first place. Behaviourists placed particular stress on the early childhood years, and the rules or practices parents use to raise their children. These psychologists believe that child-rearing methods have a huge influence on the character of individuals even into adulthood.

John B. Watson, the founder of behaviourism, used animal experiments to determine whether strict or flexible learning patterns are more effective. His *Psychological Care of the Infant and Child* concluded that children should be brought up using a "scientific," strictly scheduled, rules-based model. One of Watson's sons committed suicide, while the other—to Watson's annoyance—became a psychoanalyst.

In his book *Baby and Child Care*, Benjamin Spock recommended a different approach. He believed in behaviourism but viewed it from a different perspective. He believed that a permissive approach to child rearing, rather than a strict one, would result in successful, well-adjusted adults. He encouraged parents to be loving, flexible, and supportive.

The underlying theory of both approaches was that correct child-rearing methods would result in well-adjusted adults.

It has been difficult to substantiate the results claimed by Watson and Spock through experiments or other evidence. Watson's regime was probably too tough, Spock's too permissive. Later theorists concluded that every child is unique, and that the methods used in children's upbringing should be tailored to meet individual needs. Additionally, Watson and Spock largely ignored the influence of heredity in human development and on the type of adult that emerges from childhood.

Learning Theory

Learning theory is a vast area of study rather than a close-knit school of thought in which most practitioners have come to the same conclusions. Learning theorists do agree that humans are born with little instinct but much learning potential. They believe that most human behaviour is learned, especially in childhood and youth. By controlling the way in which humans learn behaviour, society can have a great influence on their ultimate personalities.

Experimenters such as Ivan Pavlov (1849–1936) and B.F. Skinner (1904–90) conducted experiments to see how animals learned best. Pavlov's experiments with dogs showed that it was possible to get a dog to associate the sound of a bell with the imminent arrival of food. At the sound of the bell, the dog would salivate in anticipation. Skinner showed that pigeons could be trained to peck at a particular coloured disk to get food rewards. Rats received food rewards for pressing a bar in a complicated sequence. These experiments led theorists to believe that learning was a **stimulus-response** effect—that if the subject is correctly stimulated it will give the appropriate response.

From this principle, learning theorists proposed that children who were brought up in loving families would grow up to become secure and loving adults, but only if parents provided clear and consistent expectations for good behaviour, and swift but fair consequences for bad behaviour. These ideas became more significant when psychologists began examining the lives of career criminals. The childhood experiences of many hardened criminals stood in sharp contrast to the ideal childhood as conceived by the learning theorists.

Alfred Bandura (b. 1925), however, showed that learning is more complicated than a mere stimulus-response effect. In his most famous experiment, young children were shown films of people hitting or petting a balloon-like doll painted like a clown, called Bobo. The children were then placed alone in a room with Bobo, where they were monitored through one-way glass. The children's behaviour closely resembled what they had seen in the film. Bandura concluded that learning is largely a modelling experience. When humans observe behaviour—either acceptable or unacceptable—they are more likely to practise it.

Figure 1.13 Benjamin Spock, a behaviourist, believed that the way we bring up children determines what they will be like as adults. He particularly encouraged mothers to have an emotional relationship with their children. What do you think is more influential: our genes (heredity) or our upbringing?

Because learning theory is such a vast field, any experimenter who argues that it may be summarized neatly into one package is open to criticism. Psychologists have argued among themselves about whether learning consists of one or a few elements, or a complicated interplay of a large number of factors. The debate continues.

Pause and Reflect

1. According to psychologists, strong forces are at work influencing our behaviour and the way we lead our lives. Identify three examples of these forces.

2. Create a chart to illustrate the similarities and differences among the various schools of thought in psychology.

3. Are the criticisms of the schools made by their opponents fair and helpful?

4. Explain the main criticisms of the three schools of thought. Suggest a way that one of these criticisms had a positive outcome.

5. Suggest a study of some group within your community that would be of interest to a psychologist. Explain how the research would be conducted, being sure that the research techniques match the skills and methods of psychologists.

Section 1.4   Sociology

Key Concepts

institution

status

hierarchy

role

role conflict

value

norm

deviance

rehabilitation

retribution

dysfunctional

capitalist

patriarchy

assimilationist

How Sociologists Conduct Their Work

Do you live your life in a vacuum? Sociologists don't believe that anyone does. Instead, we develop our beliefs and values as well as our individual personalities while interacting with the complex social system that surrounds us. Our families, our friends, and the **institutions** of society—organizations and establishments such as places of worship, schools, charitable agencies—act to mould us into the individuals we are. Our concepts of such things as freedom, love, the most desirable lifestyle, and the ideal spouse are greatly influenced by the history and current structure of the society in which we live. For example, we might come to believe that a good friend is someone who stands up for us in tough times, something we might learn from the television shows we watch, our place of worship, and our peer groups at school. Sociologists further believe that the causes of human behaviour are complex. Unlike psychologists, who focus largely on the individual, sociologists believe that we can only understand human behaviour by

undertaking systematic research and analysis of the structures of society and how these influence individual and group behaviour. Without such academic study, sociologists believe, a full explanation of human behaviour is impossible.

Considering the Roles We Play

Sociologists use a number of key concepts to analyze society. **Status** is the term used to describe our position in an institution. Think of the typical high school. Among the positions it contains are, in alphabetical order, administrative assistant, cafeteria worker, caretaker, principal, student, teacher, teaching assistant, and vice-principal. Within the school exists a **hierarchy** (or ranking) of authority and power, and each of the positions mentioned has a place on the hierarchy. Each position requires expertise in particular areas, and the **role** of each position often has a perceived status based on the assumptions and values of the society. To distinguish these roles, people are expected to dress, talk, and act in a distinctive manner, according to their status. Individual caretakers and principals may not necessarily conform to the ideal image of their roles; status does not necessarily determine behaviour. For example, particular caretakers may demonstrate qualities of leadership, and particular principals may behave inappropriately. Nonetheless, a cafeteria worker and a principal will probably dress and behave quite differently while performing their duties. Sociologists have observed that how individuals interact is greatly influenced by whether they see

Figure 1.14 A Malaysian mosque. The institutions of society, such as organized religions, help mould us as individuals. Think of an institution that has influenced who you have become.

themselves as having similar status, or different status. We learn through experience to act according to the unwritten rules of society.

On any given day, we can play a number of roles. As adults, we can play the role of child to a parent, and parent to our own children. We can act as friend, employee, spouse, and team member, as well as taking many other roles. The various roles, and the time required to play them all effectively, can cause difficulties. Sometimes the roles conflict. For example, imagine that you are responsible for supervising a friend at work, and that the friend's job performance is unsatisfactory. You are in a position of what sociologists call **role conflict**, because your roles as supervisor and friend pull you in different directions.

Breaking the Rules

Each role in society carries with it a system of **values**. Society assigns a particular set of values to each role, and the practitioners of each role are expected to accept and internalize these values as they act the role. These values relate to what is good and bad, desirable and undesirable, appropriate and inappropriate, etc. For example, men who take on the role of father are considered good fathers if they help support their children. As well, people who take on a particular role are required to follow **norms**, or specific rules that outline what is considered to be standard behaviour for a role. It is a norm of Roman Catholic priests, for example, that they remain celibate. Breaking a significant norm can render us unable to continue playing a role. For example, many marriages may be unable to survive when there is evidence that one or both partners have been unfaithful. It is important to remember that norms are arbitrary rules developed by cultures. In one culture, it may be the norm that men maintain short hair, whereas in another culture it may be the norm for men to keep their hair long and to wear it tied in a turban.

A good deal of sociological inquiry has gone into the study of **deviance**, which is any behaviour that is different from the societal norm. While some people may be labelled "deviant" simply because they display eccentric but harmless behaviours, society singles out some deviants because their behaviour is generally considered disreputable. It violates the norm and offends society. Much sociological study of deviant behaviour focuses on individuals who commit criminal acts. To understand the sociologist's approach to deviance, we must remember the general principle that guides their judgment of all behaviours: everything occurs within a social context. Similarly, sociologists believe that deviance can be explained only within the social context. Many sociologists have studied the role that society has played in creating deviant behaviour. Emile Durkheim (1858–1917), regarded as one of the founders of sociology as a discipline, wrote on this subject:

> We must not say that an action shocks the common conscience because it is criminal, but rather that it is criminal because it shocks the common conscience. We do not reprove [denounce] it because it is a crime, but it is a crime because we reprove it.
> – Emile Durkheim (1895, 1964, p. 81)

The link between deviance theory and sociology was established early in the discipline's history, and a great number of studies have been undertaken to further explain and understand criminal behaviour. One such study was conducted by Talcott Parsons and Edward Shils, two sociologists at Harvard University in Cambridge, Massachusetts, in 1952. They studied a range of people who had been convicted of serious crimes. They compared this group of people with another group that had never been in trouble with the law. They discovered that individuals who fully accepted, or internalized, most of society's values are likely to be successfully integrated into the social system. In other words, they are able to take on a role in society successfully because their behaviour will fall within the boundaries of the usual norms. Individuals who fail to internalize most of society's values, however, are likely to withdraw and experience feelings of underachievement or rebellion. They are unable to adopt a successful role in society because their behaviour lies outside accepted norms.

Sociology has formed a strong link with the criminal justice system. Extreme penalties such as corporal punishment (physical punishment) and capital punishment (execution) have been abolished in Canada and some other countries because many criminologists no longer believe that they discourage people from committing crimes. A fundamental component of modern imprisonment is **rehabilitation**, or trying to re-educate and resocialize inmates so that they grow to accept society's values and norms. While such attempts are not always successful, they have arguably led to the development of a more humane society.

Some criminologists see a troubling trend at work in the early twenty-first century. They believe that policy-makers are de-emphasizing rehabilitation as a correctional goal. The public policy debate talks of tougher sentencing, zero tolerance for an expanded range of anti-social behaviours, and "boot camps" (military-like prisons with tough regimens) for young offenders. Criminologists see **retribution** becoming a more significant force, with society punishing the guilty more forcefully. (For more on this issue, see the Competing Perspectives feature for Chapter 2, on page 56.)

The Skills and Methods of Sociologists

All sociologists use similar methods, including the collection and analysis of statistics, subject interviews, and the examination of trends in society. Their overall purpose is to engage in systematic and scientific investigation of the structures, relationships, and interactions within society in order to explain their impact on members' thoughts and actions. In the boxed feature on this page, you can read about the skills and methods used by a sociologist studying the factors that discourage black students from succeeding in school.

Skills and Methods

A STUDY OF EQUITY IN EDUCATION
By Sociologist George Dei

The Researcher: George J. Sefa Dei, Sociology and Equity Studies, OISE, University of Toronto
The Study: Learning or Leaving: Understanding the Dilemma of Black Students' Disengagement from School

My Research Project and Its Goals
Between 1992 and 1995 I worked with a number of graduate students at the Ontario Institute for Studies in Education of the University of Toronto (OISE/UT) on a research project about Black students and Black youth who had dropped out of school—school dropouts. The main

research objective was to investigate what students could tell us about the dropout problem, and particularly about the influence of race and ethnicity, class, gender, power, and social structures.

The Steps I Went Through to Set Up the Research

In any scholarly research there is a need to set out the research objectives carefully. To accomplish this we took several steps. First, we ascertained the expertise and knowledge base of the researchers. Second, we reviewed the existing literature. There already exists a vast literature on school dropouts. So how would the proposed study be different? Third, we identified some of the issues of schooling by consulting with parents, guardians, and community workers. Finally, we communicated with other academics and researchers.

Figure 1.15 Professor George Dei

Ethical Considerations

Every research and researcher must grapple with pertinent ethical and political questions.

*   What is my academic and political purpose for undertaking the study?
*   What are the benefits of my research for research subjects?
*   What are my responsibilities to my academic profession or community?
*   How do I address the power issues and differences between myself as a researcher (supported by an academic institution) and my study participants, who may feel vulnerable?
*   How will the research give voices to the study participants themselves? Research takes up a lot of people's time!

I had to wrestle with these questions because minority communities, for too long, have borne the brunt of academic research. A number of past educational research studies have focused on failures and underachievement among students from racial minority backgrounds and particularly Black students. Not many studies have dealt with the successes of students from these groups.

How We Carried Out the Research

We approached this study by regularly visiting four selected schools and some community sites. We interviewed students, students who had left school, educators, parents, and community workers both individually and in focus-group discussions. All interviews were tape-recorded and later transcribed. We ensured anonymity and confidentiality by assigning pseudonyms to study participants and codes to schools and community groups.

We asked students about what they liked and disliked about school. Who were their favourite teachers and why? And why did they stay in school? We asked dropouts why they left school. We asked teachers, educators, and parents to respond to what we had heard from students and those who had "dropped out." We asked teachers for their reasons why they felt some students left school prematurely. We also interviewed non-Black students to cross-reference what Black students and youth were saying.

This study utilized a team approach to educational research. The team approach has been effective as it has allowed the graduate students and myself to learn from each other and to debate and discuss the complexity of the issue of students' disengagement from school.

How We Collated and Interpreted the Results

Research information was analyzed on computer using specialized software, both qualitatively and quantitatively, for general trends about the school experiences of youth and the implication of these practices for educational change in Canada. Through triangulation, we compared individual narratives between and among students and teachers at selected school sites. The research information was also compared with other studies of school dropouts.

Among the study's major findings is the knowledge that the teaching, learning and administration of education are not inclusive enough to make all students feel engaged at school. Four primary concerns were expressed in Black students' and dropouts' narratives about their school experiences: (a) differential treatment according to race, (b) the absence of Black teachers, (c) the absence of Black/African-Canadian history in the classroom, and (d) struggles over individual and collective identities.

How I Communicated the Results

Through presentations at local and scholarly international conferences, published articles, papers, monographs, and books, we have been able to share the research knowledge gained with scholars in the fields of school dropouts, anti-racism, and minority/inclusive education. We presented some of our findings to local community groups, parents, and school boards. Research information was also communicated through Canadian and international newspapers, magazines, and appearances on radio and television shows.

Note: To read an excerpt from an article about George Dei's research project, please see page 320.

1. What (a) personal and (b) academic skills would George Dei have needed to conduct his research? Which do you think was most crucial?
2. Make a list of steps he used through the course of his research project.

Schools of Thought in Sociology

Sociologists have debated among themselves about the real nature of society. To some extent, this debate has been raised by the changing nature of society that sociologists observed during the course of the twentieth century. In the early decades, most Western societies had comparatively little ethnic diversity, and they did not acknowledge the ethnic diversity that did exist. It was assumed that all social classes subscribed to more or less the same unchanging beliefs and values.

By the end of the century, societies such as Canada had become more multicultural and had begun to recognize and respect the tremendous variety in lifestyles and cultural values within their populations. As society—and society's values—changed before sociologists' eyes, it was natural that their view of its essential nature should be adjusted, sometimes in different directions.

Because sociology and anthropology overlap in their field of study, the issues among the schools of thought in the two disciplines have some similarities.

Schools of Thought in Sociology

School of Thought	Famous Practitioners	Time Period	Typical Questions	Central Approach
Structural-Functionalism (also called Functionalism)	Bronislaw Malinowski, A.R. Radcliffe-Brown, Talcott Parsons	1930s to 1960s	• What systems in society provide stability? • How effectively do specialized institutions meet the overall needs of society?	To understand a society, we must study how the society works to meet the needs of its members, not how it is changing.
Neo-Marxism	Bertell Ollman, Ben Fine	1950s to 1990s	• In whose interests do the institutions of society work? • What are the causes of alienation among society's members?	Economic power, which is the basis of political power, is the key to understanding societies.
Symbolic Interactionism	George H. Mead, Charles Cooley, Herbert Blumer	1950s to present	• Why do individual people act as they do? • How do they interpret their own actions and learn from them?	The human brain intervenes between what we observe and how we act. To understand human society, we must understand how the human mind works.
Feminist Theory	Betty Friedan, Jessie Bernard (Liberal), Rosemarie Tong, Josephine Donovan (Marxian), Shulamith Firestone, Sandra Burt, Lorraine Code, Lindsay Dorney (Radical), Heidi Hartmann, Michèle Barrett. (Socialist)	1960s to present	• Why have most human societies historically undervalued women's work? • Can all people reform social institutions together, or must women act single-handedly to create greater equity?	Most societies' value systems are sexist and therefore dysfunctional. To change this, social institutions must admit that gender issues exist within them.
Inclusionism	Peter Li, Kathy Megyery, Monica Boyd	1980s to present	• What barriers prevent ethnic minorities from playing a complete role in Canadian political and economic life? • What policies need to be changed to ensure that they do?	Sociologists must recognize the ethnic diversity within societies by studying the experiences of all ethnic groups and rejecting the urge to judge through the eyes of the majority.

Figure 1.16 Sociologists generally fall into five categories, each group advocating one of the approaches shown in this table. How are these schools of thought different, and how are they similar?

Structural-Functionalism

The human body has basic needs for such things as air, water, food, clothing, and shelter. Without these you would die. Similarly, any human society will die if it does not satisfy the basic needs of its people. According to structural-functionalism, each society should provide its members with system prerequisites, the fundamental requirements for functioning. A society must have a way of satisfying material needs, a system for socializing and educating the young, a means for regulating human reproduction (usually marriage), a system for co-ordinating society's overall needs, and so on. Just as the human body has specialized systems (like the digestive system to recover nutrition from food), all human societies have specialized systems (like the family or schools) to fulfill particular needs, although these systems vary from society to society. Structural-functionalists believe that the role of the sociologist is to try to explain these systems in terms of their role in enabling human society to function.

Structural-functionalists do not concentrate on change in society. They are more interested in how society works to meet the needs of its members than in how it is changing. They believe that society functions best when its members possess a shared set of values, norms, beliefs, etc. Consequently, they see a human tendency to exist in a state of equilibrium and consensus, rather than in conflict and competition. Structural-functionalists do not tend to examine social conflict, believing that harmony among people is the more natural condition. While it is true, they believe, that some institutions can become **dysfunctional**, failing to perform their intended purpose and having a destructive effect, the human tendency toward consensus and stability makes such institutions easier to reform.

Opponents state that this school of thought places too much emphasis on stability and not enough on change. Structural-functionalists downplay the forces that divide people within a society, dismissing important negative factors such as poverty, crime, and disenfranchisement (unequal access to the vote and other social rights).

Neo-Marxism

Neo-Marxism is based on ideas originally proposed by Karl Marx (1818–1883). Marx proposed that economic power, which leads to political power, is the key to understanding societies. The struggle for economic power means that society is not static, but ever-changing. Social change results from changes made to the economic system. (To find out more about Marx's theories, please see Bain and Colyer, 2001, pages 18 and 21.)

According to neo-Marxists, if we want to understand society we must understand the

FILM SOCIETY

Title: *The Glass Menagerie* (1987)
Rating: PG
Director: Paul Newman

This movie, based on Tennessee Williams's 1944 play of the same name, explores the dynamics within a dysfunctional (impaired) family. It examines the relationships among the narrator, Tom Wingfield, a young man yearning to flee responsibilities he never wanted; his mother, Amanda, a woman deserted by her husband and yearning for another era; and Tom's sister, Laura, who is afraid of life. Frustration, guilt, and betrayal create a powerful mix of unrealized dreams and hopeless aspirations. The movie is a powerful examination of the forces that can destroy ordinary families.

economic system ("forces of production"), which creates a rich class of owners and a poor class of workers. Because of the great divisions of wealth in a **capitalist** (free market) society, conflict becomes a natural condition. Neo-Marxists believe that institutions in society (places of worship, schools, prisons, etc.) have been created to perpetuate the division between the powerful and powerless. As a result, the poor and powerless become frustrated with their inability to share in society's overall wealth. They begin to feel alienated from their society, or left out and isolated. Until a new method of wealth creation and distribution is developed and embraced, the problems of alienation will not go away.

Most neo-Marxist writing is fixed on how the economic power of the few influences all social institutions. Because neo-Marxists regard social class as the key to any explanation of a capitalist society, they give much attention to the way that one class exploits another.

Opponents believe that the neo-Marxist explanation of society is too limited. While it is true that the goal of economic success is a powerful motivating force, the neo-Marxist approach ignores the redeeming qualities of many people living in capitalist societies. By viewing all humans as being in competition with one another, neo-Marxists downplay people's attempts to achieve greater harmony.

Symbolic Interactionism

Symbolic interactionists hold very different opinions about human society than do other sociologists. According to this school of thought, humans have complex brains, and little instinctive behaviour. They can therefore interpret for themselves the stimuli they receive in daily life and attach their own meanings to them. Accordingly, one person might value and pursue fame and fortune, while a sibling might dedicate his or her life to charitable work in a developing country. It

Figure 1.17 According to neo-Marxists, the institutions of society all serve to benefit the very rich. Do you agree with this? Why or why not?

is how we as individuals process and interpret what we observe in society, not society's institutions, that form the core of our value system.

It is this faith in the importance of human thought and the reasoning process that leads symbolic interactionists to focus their research on the human mind rather than on structures in society. They believe that the human brain intervenes to interpret what we observe and then translates that into action. In order to understand human society, we must therefore understand how the human mind works.

Structural-functionalists would argue that this approach ignores the role of society's central institutions in moulding the way individuals interpret what they experience. Neo-Marxists would ask how we can be sure that the meanings we attach to our observations are not manipulated by the social institutions, such as the media, that are designed to protect the influence of the rich and powerful.

Feminist Theory

Feminist theorists focus on sex and gender issues, believing that women have traditionally been disadvantaged in society because men have discriminated against them. Most feminist theorists agree that men have made the decisions in society, and that those decisions have tended to favour the interests of men. They also agree that much of society's value system is sexist and therefore dysfunctional. Feminists disagree, however, on how much this is a problem today, and on how we can go about fixing the problem. Most social institutions are reluctant to admit that gender issues exist within them, and they resist change.

---

www.canadiansocialresearch.net

The social sciences constitute a vast area of academic inquiry. The site listed above will quickly give you an idea of the scope and diversity of the subject. The site is privately maintained by Gilles Séguin, an employee of Human Resources Development Canada, a department of the federal government. Séguin maintains the site from home, on his own time, so it is not an official government site. Click on "About this site" and you will see how he describes its purpose and functions.

Go to Themes and click on some of the hotlinks, such as "Social Statistics," "Welfare Reforms in Canada," and "Women's Social issues." These will quickly take you to sites that can provide all kinds of research material.

Although the site contains links to organizations from all across the political spectrum, note that Séguin identifies his own bias by stating that he favours the left. As with all sites, especially privately maintained ones, you should evaluate it for bias. Does Séguin's personal bias show through, perhaps in the selection of sites? Is the site a valid source of information? (A procedure for examining the validity of Web sites is illustrated in Bain and Colyer, 2001, pages 134 to 136.)

If the Web address does not connect you with the site, do a Web search using "Canadian Social Research Links" as a search string. This should bring you to the home page, where you can begin to explore the site by using the hotlinks.

This enormously varied school of thought looks at society through a number of lenses.

- *Liberal feminists* believe that the basic social institutions of society need to be made more welcoming to women and more accessible to women's influence.
- *Marxian feminists* believe that women's unpaid and undervalued domestic work has made it possible for industrial owners to pay lower wages to male workers. This situation has bolstered the power of the capitalist class. They also believe that the continuation of lower-paid jobs for women has contributed to the domination of the capitalist class.
- *Radical feminists* state that men have exploited women because of women's natural child-bearing role, which has led to systematic oppression of women. They believe that society is a **patriarchy**, in which men dominate most institutions and use this position to oppress women. They believe that the patriarchy is so entrenched in current social institutions that these institutions cannot be reformed to allow women equal standing with men and access to the same opportunities that men enjoy.
- *Socialist feminists* try to separate issues of oppression that are the result of the patriarchy and those that are a result of capitalism. If capitalism were overthrown, they ask, to what extent would female oppression continue?

Some critics have charged that the feminist approach overemphasizes gender as the key determinant in society. Issues of race and social class also affect equity in society, they note. While gender is a key factor regarding who has power and who has not, it is not the only one. In response, many feminist organizations have attempted to represent the interests of women from all backgrounds. At one point feminist writers were divided about whether feminists should focus their work on obtaining new freedoms for heterosexual women, or if they should expand their work to fight for the rights of lesbian women. Similarly, feminists needed to work through a debate about expanding their work to fight for the rights of people of colour.

Inclusionism

Early sociologists, such as Durkheim, Weber, and Marx, regarded race as one of several factors that could play a role in forming human identity. Weber, for example, recognized that conflict could take place in society between ethnic, racial, and religious groups, as well as between economic classes. However, these theorists focused almost wholly on economic differences among people; other factors tended to get left behind.

Reflecting this focus, until World War II most sociologists took an **assimilationist** view of race and ethnicity. This means that they believed that the culture of the majority would gradually absorb racial and ethnic minorities through public institutions such as schools (Park, 1950). Well into the 1960s, sociologists continued to conclude that immigrant minorities would be first culturally assimilated, and then structurally assimilated, into mainstream culture and society (Gordon, 1964).

But changes to immigration policies in many countries, including Canada, came into effect in the late 1960s. Visible minorities grew as a percentage of total population in most Western nations. Over time, it became clear that individuals could theoretically retain their racial and ethnic identities while participating fully in the life of their country. In practice, however, there were serious barriers to the full acceptance of visible minorities in Canadian life. A 1988 study showed, on average, that visible minorities earned less than did the majority, and less than their educational qualifications could be expected to demand (Li, 1988).

In the 1990s, a number of studies showed that more work needed to be done to obtain fair representation for visible minorities in Canada's political life (Megyery, 1991) and to obtain racial equity in the workplace (Boyd, 1992). The thrust of such inquiry is that modern, multicultural nations must create an environment where all people, regardless of their particular ethnic, social, or gender characteristics, can contribute to the well-being of society.

Pause and Reflect

1. Define the term "role" as used in this chapter. Give three examples of roles that you play or have played.

2. Some social institutions, such as religious institutions, promote what they believe to be appropriate behaviour among their followers. Parents may use religion to encourage some behaviours in their children (for example, tolerance) and discourage others (for example, stealing). What is your opinion on the effectiveness of religion as a deterrent to deviant behaviour? Explain your reasoning.

3. Create a chart to illustrate the similarities and differences among the various schools of thought in sociology.

4. Explain the main criticisms of the neo-Marxist, structural-functionalist, and feminist schools of thought.

5. Suggest a study of some aspect of your community that would be of interest to a sociologist. Explain how the research would be conducted, being sure that the research techniques match the skills and methods of sociologists.

COMPETING
PERSPECTIVES

Responding to September 11

At the beginning of this chapter, you learned that social scientists study human behaviour. Sometimes they find points of commonality, and sometimes they find huge differences.

On 11 September 2001, hijackers turned two Boeing jetliners into flying bombs, crashing them into the twin towers of the World Trade Center in New York City. The towers collapsed, killing about 3500 people. Another plane crashed into the Pentagon, killing about 200, and a fourth crashed into an open field, killing all on board.

Huge events like this have the capacity to bring together peoples around the world in common cause and common sympathy. The first set of extracts, below, captures just a handful of the many expressions of sympathy sent to the United States, and especially to the many family and friends who lost loved ones in the attack. These came from all over the world, from people of different cultures, political systems, faiths, and traditions.

Although the majority opinion was that this was a diabolical and unprovoked act, some groups saw it as the logical outcome of American foreign policy, which has led to much anti-Americanism around the world. You can read some of these opinions on the opposite page.

Talking Point
Letters to an online BBC forum

The perpetrators of this horrendous atrocity apparently claim to have done it for Muslims and Islam. Islam prohibits the killing of non-combatants, children, and women and those who have taken shelter in places of worship even during a war. This horrible action cannot be justified at all. Our tears are with the unfortunate victims of this calamity and their relatives.
(Dr) Muhammad Siddique, Sri Lanka

I condemn such a terrorist attack. We can understand how Americans feel right now, because we know what terror is—we lost too many of our citizens because of terror. My heart is with those innocent Americans.
Eda, Istanbul, Turkey

This was a barbaric attack. This is not the right way to show the vengeance towards a nation or an individual. I convey my heartfelt condolences for the loss of lives in this incident. Life is much more precious.
Abdul Qaiyum Nagoori, Manama, Bahrain

Dear American brothers and sisters. Please, do accept our deepest sympathies and let us express our sorrow on Tuesday's dreadful terrorist acts. People of Ukraine feel great anguish and pain. We live in one small world. Never must this happen again! Let God keep you safe.
Olga and Aram, Dnipropetrovsk city, Ukraine

It is terrorism to the core. No reason on this earth will justify these dastardly acts. The culprits, whoever they are and wherever they are, should be apprehended and brought to book. One would not have expected such a security lapse in the United States—how was it that such a large-scale, well-planned and unprecedented terrorist act went undetected?
Raja Chandran, Jeddah, Saudi Arabia

Source: Talking Point. BBC News. [Online] Available <http://newsvote.bbc.co.uk/hi/english/talking_point/newsid_1550000/1550327.stm> 2 November, 2001.

COMPETING PERSPECTIVES

Talking Point
Letters to an online BBC forum

This bombing bring back my childhood memory when US Air Force did carpet bombing in South East Asia. The taste of pain and suffering is so great that only the person who experience the real thing by himself can understand. Now the same bitter taste and despair come back again. I would say it should be a wake up call for Bush and the American people — instead of go out raining the terror all over the world again, put your foot in someone else's shoes for a change and pray hard for peace.
Sompone, Kent, WA, USA

If only a fraction of the compassion shown for America as the recipient of terrorism would have been extended to those who were exposed to terrorism in other parts of the world during the past ten years, then, maybe, we would not have to lament now.
Juergen Dudek, Australia

What happened last week in New York and Washington was horrible, beyond words, and my heart goes out to the victims and their families. But I do think that the US and the whole "civilized world" need to consider where the anger behind these attacks comes from, and have a close look at the consequences of their own foreign policies during the twentieth century. A part of the reason must lie in US policy in the Middle East, where they have manipulated their power to the best of their own economical and political advantage, and shown little regard for the lives and well being of ordinary citizens. Western superpower games must end, and that will be one way to tackle the threat of extremist terrorism.
Ingibjorg, Iceland

Source: Talking Point. BBC News. [Online]. Available <http://newsvote.bbc.co.uk/hi/english/talking_point/newsid_1550000/1550327.stm> 2 November, 2001.

Questions
1. What arguments are presented in each of the two groups of extracts?
2. What are some of the assumptions each makes about good and evil, and right and wrong in the world?
3. What factors might (a) anthropologists, (b) psychologists, and (c) sociologists suggest would influence how a person felt about this subject? How might they explain the fact that opinions on the subject could be so wide-ranging?
4. Describe a social science research project that you might conduct to study the reasons for the differences of opinion shown in these excerpts.

▶ ▶ ▶ **Chapter Activities**

Show Your Knowledge

1. a) Create a glossary of new vocabulary by listing and defining or explaining the terms and phrases you learned in this chapter.

   b) Create four questions to ask a classmate. Make each question more difficult than the previous one. Follow the four categories used for these activities: Show Your Knowledge, Practise Your Thinking Skills, Communicate Your Ideas, and Apply Your Knowledge.

2. Create a three-circle Venn diagram that illustrates what aspects of human life are of particular interest to each of anthropology, psychology, and sociology, and what aspects are of interest to all three.

3. What methods of conducting research are used in (a) anthropology, (b) psychology, and (c) sociology?

4. What are "schools of thought" in social science? List the schools of thought in (a) anthropology, (b) psychology, and (c) sociology, including a description of the major approach of each one.

Practise Your Thinking

5. Imagine that you are a social scientist, observing and recording the major "events" in a typical social science class.

   a) Record five observations in your notes. For example, "Students record homework assignment in their personal agendas."

   b) For each observation, suggest the most accurate form of measurement. For example, "For the best measurement, check all student agendas."

6. Which of the three social science disciplines described in this chapter do you think (a) examines the most interesting aspects of human beings, and (b) would be the most useful to lawmakers to help them decide what laws to make for the regulation of society? Explain your reasons for both answers.

7. In which discipline—anthropology, psychology, or sociology—do you think the schools of thought give the most varied explanations of human behaviour? Explain your answer.

8. The three social science practitioners that explained the skills and methods they used in a research project all described a number of ethical considerations. Speculate on what would happen if they did not abide by these "rules" that they set for their research. Create a comparison organizer to show, in one column, what each ethical practice accomplishes, and, in another column, what might happen if the practitioner did not abide by the practice.

Communicate Your Ideas

9. Tell a classmate which social science discipline you think will be the most interesting to study in this course, giving your reasons. Listen to your classmate's views on this matter. Discuss any similarities and differences in your answers. In your notes, write a summary of your discussion. If you were convinced by your partner to change your opinion, explain why.

10. One argument for studying the social sciences is that they can help prove or disprove what we believe to be true.

   a) Work with a partner. One of you role-plays a person who believes that society's beliefs about humans need to be backed up by social science evidence. The other role-plays a person who believes that we do not need academic research to tell us whether our beliefs are correct or not. The scene you create will take place as you stand in line at a coffee shop.

   b) Step out of your roles. Discuss with your partner what your personal opinion is on this issue and what you have learned during this role-play.

11. Pick one of the social science disciplines being studied in this course. Make a visual (poster, collage, etc.) incorporating what you consider to be the most important practitioners, key terms, main ideas, and schools of thought of the discipline. Incorporate both text and illustration on your visual. Explain to the class what the visual means to you.

12. Look at the three features about social science skills and methods written by anthropologist Parin Dossa (page 10), psychologist Robert West (page 17), and sociologist George Dei (page 24). Review the ways in which they communicated their findings. Pick one of the three studies, and imagine that you have been given the job of finding a way to communicate the findings of this study to a broader audience than just an academic one. Design your plan to do this, keeping in mind that academic institutions work on fairly tight budgets. Create an outline of the various steps of your plan on chart paper and post it in the classroom. Hold a class discussion on the most practical ways of communicating social science findings to the general public

Apply Your Knowledge

13. Identify three jobs or professions that a knowledge of each social science discipline would help a person to perform well. (Nine jobs total.) Provide reasons for what you have decided.

14. Review the material in this chapter about the types of things that researchers in the three social science disciplines study. Imagine that you were going to undertake a social science study in your local community.

   a) By adapting something that you already see in this chapter, or by creating something new, suggest a study that would be useful in learning more about your local community.

   b) Briefly explain how you would conduct the study, and what you might expect to learn from it.

15. a) Pick one of the three disciplines and describe how a practitioner of this discipline would explain your personal relationships with your family or friends.

   b) Do you think this discipline could provide you with useful insights into these relationships? Why or why not?

16. Pick one of the schools of thought outlined in this chapter. Identify a social issue or problem in Canadian society that interests you, for example, welfare cuts, violence in the media, teenage smoking, and the increasing cost of a post-secondary education. Explain what the school of thought might say about the causes of the problem or issue, and what solutions it might offer.

SOCIAL CHANGE

Focus Questions

1. Fifty years ago Gwen Boniface would have been excluded from her current position. Why?

2. Name four other occupations from which either women or men were generally excluded until recent times.

3. Why is it necessary to understand the phenomena of technological and social change?

This picture shows Gwen M. Boniface, Commissioner of the Ontario Provincial Police (with former premier Mike Harris). Until fairly recently, senior policing positions were filled exclusively by men—perhaps due to a mistaken belief that women were not "tough enough" for such jobs. Women have also entered many other historically male-dominated occupations, becoming commercial airline pilots and firefighters, although, as yet, their numbers are small. This is one of the many examples of social change that have taken place in Canada in recent years.

In this unit, you will look at how social scientists examine social change, what forces cause it, and how technological developments have altered our lifestyles and created enormous social change for most Canadians. Since the rate of technological and social change appears to be accelerating, it is necessary to understand these phenomena in order to have control over our own lives.

■ Unit Learning Goals

Overall Expectations

- appraise the differences and similarities in the methodologies and strategies of anthropology, psychology, and sociology applied to the study of change
- describe key features of major theories from anthropology, psychology, and sociology that focus on change
- analyze patterns of technological change from the perspectives of anthropology, psychology, and sociology
- analyze the ways in which the theories of early social scientists have influenced subsequent social-scientific thinking (e.g., anthropology: Franz Boaz; psychology: Ivan Pavlov; sociology: Emile Durkheim)

Skill Expectations

- define and correctly use anthropological, psychological, and sociological terms and concepts
- demonstrate an understanding of the main areas of study in anthropology, psychology, and sociology, and of the similarities and differences among them
- demonstrate an understanding of the different research methods used by anthropology, psychology, and sociology to investigate questions of importance within each field, and apply relevant skills correctly and ethically
- communicate the results of their inquiries effectively

Unit Contents

Chapter 2 Explanations of Social Change

Chapter 3 Forces that Influence Social Change

Chapter 4 Technology and Social Change

EXPLANATIONS OF SOCIAL CHANGE

INTRODUCTION

As you grow older and look around, you notice that things aren't the way they were when you were a youngster. Some changes are hard to define. Life probably seems more complicated. But is it really? And how is it different? Other changes are easy to pin down. The 11 September 2001 terrorist attacks on America, for example, shook the world and changed society irrevocably.

This photograph captures the Manhattan skyline moments before the World Trade Center falls to the ground. What social changes resulted from this event?

■ Learning Expectations

By the end of this chapter, you will be able to

- appraise the differences and similarities in the methodologies and strategies of anthropology, psychology, and sociology applied to the study of change
- describe key features of major theories from anthropology, psychology, and sociology that focus on change
- identify a major question about social change posed by anthropology, psychology, and sociology
- define different theories of change in anthropology, psychology, and sociology
- evaluate the major contribution to understanding social change made by leading practitioners in the social sciences

Focusing on the Issues

Ten Commandments for Changing the World

Changing the world [rocks]. Here are our ten commandments for changing the world. But first, some inspiration from Noam Chomsky: "If you go to one demonstration and then go home, that's something, but the people in power can live with that. What they can't live with is sustained pressure that keeps building, organizations that keep doing things, people that keep learning lessons from the last time and doing it better the next time."

1. **You gotta believe**. Have hope, passion, and confidence that valuable change can and does happen because individuals take bold initiative.
2. **Challenge authority**. Don't be afraid to question authority. The "experts" are often proven wrong (they used to believe that the earth was flat!).
3. **Know the system**. Learn how decisions are made. How is the bureaucracy structured? Who are the key players? Where do they eat lunch? Go there and talk with them. Get to know their executive assistants. Attend public meetings.
4. **Take action**. Do something—anything is better than nothing. Bounce your idea around with friends, and then act.
5. **Use the media**. Letters to the editor of your local newspaper are read by thousands. Stage a dramatic event and invite the media—they love an event that gives them an interesting angle or good photo.
6. **Build alliances**. Seek out your common allies. The system wins through "divide and conquer" tactics, so do the opposite!
7. **Apply constant pressure**. Persevere—it drives those in power crazy. Be as creative as possible in getting your perspective heard. Use the media, phone your politicians, send letters and faxes with graphics and images. Be concise. Ask specific questions and give a deadline for when you expect a response. Stay in their faces.
8. **Teach alternatives**. Propose and articulate intelligent alternatives to the status quo.
9. **Learn from your mistakes**. You're gonna make mistakes; we all do. Critique—in a positive way—yourself, the movement, and the opposition.
10. **Take care of yourself and each other**. Maintain balance. Eat well and get regular exercise. Avoid burnout by delegating tasks, sharing responsibility, and maintaining an open process. Have fun. Remember: you're not alone!

So there you have it: tools for the evolution. You can easily join the millions of people around the world working towards ecological health and sustainability just by doing something. With a bit of effort, and some extraordinary luck, a sustainable future may be assured for us and the planet.

Go forth and agitate.

Adapted from: Bischoff, Angela and Tooker Gomberg. 2001. "Ten Commandments for Changing the World." [Online]. Available <http://www.greenspiration.org/Article/Ten Commandments.html> 11 January 2002.

THINK ABOUT IT

1. Which of the above techniques would you use to try to persuade the government to increase funding for universities?
2. What are the authors of this piece trying to communicate to you? Is it convincing? Inspiring? Why?
3. Do you think that people using these techniques for achieving social change are likely to succeed or fail? Explain your reasoning.
4. Many social activists struggle to solve serious problems and eliminate human suffering. Yet this piece of writing takes a lighthearted approach. Do you think that humour and lightheartedness are effective ways of getting across serious matters such as how to achieve social change? Explain your answer.

Section 2.1   Questions About Social Change

Key Concepts

social change

developed/
developing
countries

invention

discovery

diffusion

enculturation

attitudes

behaviours

cognitive
consistency

cognitive
dissonance theory

reductionist

determinist

patriarchy

norms

exogenous/
endogenous

What sorts of questions could you ask to find out more about changes in Canadian society? Consider these:

- Which area of Canadian life has changed the most?
- What factors caused these changes?
- Have the changes, on the whole, been beneficial or detrimental?

Generate some more questions of your own that would help you learn about change in Canadian society over the past few decades.

Now think of the changes that will take place by the time you're 85 years old. Add to the following list with a few questions of your own.

- What areas of life will change more rapidly than others?
- Will the amount of change in Canada be less, more, or the same as in other countries?
- How will you be affected as an individual?

Figure 2.1 In 2000, 283 110 Ontario residents used a food bank. Will this number rise or fall in future? Social scientists studying social change try to answer many questions like this. What would you like to know about the future of your society?

These questions fascinate social scientists because they centre on social change. **Social change** refers to changes in the way society is organized, and in the beliefs and practices of the people who live in it. A narrower definition describes it as a change in the social structure and the institutions of society. Each of the social science disciplines further defines the term, reflecting the particular focus that it adopts when studying humans.

You can expect enormous political, economic, and social changes to take place in Canada during your lifetime. Some changes can be predicted with reasonable certainty. The population will continue to increase, from nearly 32 million (2002) to about 43 million (2031). It is more difficult, however, to predict the nature of the social change that will accompany these changes. Will the influence of organized religion grow or diminish? Will acceptance of alternative lifestyles such as common-law marriage increase or decline? Will our civil liberties be curtailed further?

Questions like these are extremely difficult to answer with any degree of certainty. Instead of attempting to predict the future, social scientists try to understand the nature of social change and what forces drive it. The article "Ten Commandments for Changing the World" on page 39 suggests that, with concerted effort, activists can alter the course of social change. This may be true, but very little social change occurs as a result of people's conscious efforts. Most change occurs almost naturally, as a result of a multitude of factors operating within society. This makes the study of social change a great challenge.

You learned in Chapter 1 about the differences in approach taken by the three social science disciplines studied in this book. These differences can be illustrated by examining the questions they ask about social change.

The Anthropological Questions

Anthropologists regard cultures, the focus of their studies, as constantly changing organisms (an organism is a whole with interdependent parts). The change process is normally gradual, and cultures normally do not change suddenly and completely unless they are destroyed by another culture. With this frame of reference in mind, anthropologists ask questions such as these:

1. What are the known basic mechanisms of social change?
2. What ideas or explanations can we use to describe what causes cultures to change?
3. How adequate are these ideas or explanations when we apply them to the modern world?
4. What are the implications for anthropology? Are the findings for one period valid in another?

   (Based on Oliver, 1981, p. 364)

Ultimately, anthropologists tend to see cultural change as being caused by a limited number of factors. They try to identify which factor is most significant at any particular time.

- Was a cultural change caused by a change in the society's leadership?
- Was it caused by a shift in the values and norms of the culture's members?
- Is technological change a factor in an observed cultural change?
- Have changes to the environment resulted in changes to the culture?

Change in Various Countries

Because of the nature of their discipline, anthropologists have had much contact with cultures and peoples in less wealthy countries in the world. Originally, anthropologists studied cultures that were comparatively isolated, with little or no influence from the out-

side world. An example is the Yanomamo of the Amazon basin in South America. Isolated cultures no longer exist, however, because all peoples have had at least some contact with the outside world. Anthropologists have broadened their scope to study cultural groups in mainstream society in both rich and poor nations.

Anthropologists consider the roughly 30 industrialized nations of the world to be **developed countries**. They call the remaining 180 nations **developing countries**. These nations have little or no industry, and most of the population survives by farming the land. Low incomes and a lack of infrastructure such as hospitals and transportation links characterize these less-advantaged nations. The gap in incomes, education levels, and life expectancies between developed and developing countries has increased in the past 50 years. This has prompted anthropologists to ask questions about why this shift is occurring and how international aid from developed to developing countries is affecting the situation. What factors make international aid programs effective? Is change necessarily desirable? What can developed and developing nations learn from each other? Given their focus, anthropologists are particularly well situated to suggest ways of bridging the gap between rich and poor nations.

Sources of Cultural Change

Cultures are constantly changing. Think, for example, of the changes that have taken place in methods of child rearing in your own or your parents' lifetimes. Did your parents go to daycare when they were children? Did you? Did your parents receive physical punishment (for example, the strap)? Did you? What caused these changes?

Anthropologists have concluded that there are three major sources of cultural

Figure 2.2 These Karaoke singers croon their hearts out to an appreciative audience. Karaoke, which originated in Japan, spread through diffusion to North America. Think of a food, hobby, sport, technology, or social custom that has spread from one region of the world to another.

change. The first source is **invention**—new products, ideas, and social patterns that affect the way people live. The invention of the portable stereo headset in the 1980s, for example, changed the way in which many young people listen to music. The second source is **discovery**, finding something that was previously unknown to a culture. The discovery of intelligent life on a distant planet might change the way humans think about themselves. The third source is **diffusion**, or the spreading of ideas, methods, and tools from one culture to another. The importation of herbal remedies and treatments such as acupuncture from Asia into Canada has changed the way in which some people view the treatment of medical illnesses. Although usually not harmful, diffusion can sometimes become overwhelming, to a point where it can overpower other cultures. Quebec's language laws are an attempt to prevent English (largely, American) culture from overwhelming it.

Anthropologists focus on the process of **enculturation**, by which members of a culture learn and internalize shared ideas, values, and beliefs. To understand the nature of cultural change, they classify the various aspects of culture. According to one system of classification, culture is made up of four interrelated parts.

1. *Physical environment.* The physical environment influences a culture. The length of winter in Canada, for example, affects how many winter outfits Canadians will buy in the fall.

2. *Level of technology.* The degree of technology available, together with the physical limitations of the environment, determines how receptive a culture will be to the need for change. A culture that possesses crowded multi-lane highways can realistically improve light-rail transit systems in its cities. People will be thankful for any solution that helps reduce traffic congestion. In contrast, a culture in which most people travel on foot cannot realistically expect its population to see the need for a light-rail transit system; nor could they afford this technology.

3. *Social organization.* How is the culture organized? What is its kinship system? How is labour divided and allocated? Are social rules flexible or tightly regulated? The answers to these questions help determine how readily a given culture can change. If the government of a society arrests people who chew gum, for example, as is the case in Singapore, people are not likely to take up the practice.

4. *Systems of symbols.* All cultures have symbols. Brand name clothing and hip music are significant symbols of teen culture in Canada. To an anthropologist, however, symbols include not only physical objects, but also gestures (such as the two-finger V symbol for peace), dance trends, hairstyles, or anything else that identifies a person as a member of a particular culture.

By examining the four parts of culture, anthropologists seek answers to the fundamental questions of social change.

The Psychological Questions

While anthropologists focus on culture in their investigation of social change, psychologists focus on people's behaviours and attitudes. For example, they might consider the social problem of drinking and driving. They might narrow an investigation to consider the individuals who have been convicted three times for driving while intoxicated. Clearly, the people in this group have an alcohol problem. The five-year driving ban and the prison sentence that result from conviction of this offence in Canada will perhaps protect society from such people for some time. But what happens after that? Can society successfully design programs to help people change problem behaviours like this one? Psychologists would ask the following:

• What must people do to successfully change their behaviours?

• What factors make behaviour-modification programs successful?

• Do most people need help changing behaviour, or can they be self-changers?

Much of this research involves the strong links between people's **attitudes** (what they think) and their **behaviours** (what they do). Psychologists want to know if it is necessary to change individuals' attitudes before their behaviour can be changed. In the case cited above, is it necessary to change a person's attitude about drinking before he or she will stop drinking and driving? A number of studies have looked at whether or not it is possible to persuade people to practise behaviour that is inconsistent with their attitudes. You can read about one such study in the Case Study feature on page 44.

Psychologists have discovered that it can be difficult to change people's attitudes and behaviours. They have looked at the whole question of persuasion. Are friends more effective than strangers in changing a person's attitudes? How effectively do the media mould and change our attitudes? If society considers a behaviour unacceptable, and imposes sanctions against it, are individuals more likely to stop this behaviour? What personal qualities make it easy or difficult to persuade an individual to change? Are people generally more receptive to logical or emotional arguments? Questions such as these are of particular importance to advertisers.

Changing Our Minds

Why and how do we change our minds? Through their studies, social psychologists have discovered that most individuals desire **cognitive consistency** in their beliefs. This means that we want to avoid attitudes that conflict with each other, and we tend to live more satisfying lives when this is the case. What makes us change our attitudes is the discomfort we experience when two attitudes

Figure 2.3 What makes this print ad effective? Not surprisingly, many psychologists work for advertising companies designing marketing campaigns that work.

On Changing Behaviour

Can people be persuaded to do something they don't agree with? Intuitively, you might say yes, sometimes. This question perplexed two psychologists, Leon Festinger and James M. Carlsmith. In 1959, they conducted a study to determine whether people can be persuaded to practise behaviours that run counter to their beliefs.

Sixty male undergraduates from Stanford University in California volunteered for the study. They were given a boring, repetitive task to do for one hour. None of them was supposed to enjoy the task. They were then divided into three random groups. Each individual was asked to talk to a person who hadn't done the task and to tell him or her how interesting and enjoyable the task was, something none of them would have agreed with. (Each of the 60 subjects spoke individually to the same female researcher about the task. They did not know she was part of the research team—a confederate.) The three groups were offered three different incentives: Group A was offered $20 per person; Group B, $1 per person; and Group C was offered nothing. Remember that $20 was a considerable sum of money, at least the value of a day's

work, to these students in 1959. Which group do you think registered the most excitement about the experiment?

You might be surprised. The group that registered the most excitement was Group B, the $1 group. Next came Group A, the $20 group, and lastly, Group C, the $0 group. The $20 reward was not enough for the students in Group A to overcome their belief that the task had been boring.

The researchers concluded that if we want to encourage behaviour change in subjects, a reward is a good idea. The researchers discovered, however, that a bigger reward is not necessarily a bigger incentive. If the behaviour change the reward is intended to produce (persuading someone that the task was interesting and enjoyable) conflicts with the person's beliefs (it was a drag), then making the reward larger will not yield better results. So, if you offer $1000 to entice a person to quit drinking and driving, and that person really doesn't want to quit, the reward is likely to be no more effective than a $5 reward. On its own, the money is not enough.

Questions

1. What were Festinger and Carlsmith trying to find out?
2. Describe the experiment. What was the variable?
3. Explain in your own words the conclusions of the researchers.

conflict. Our desire to regain cognitive consistency forces us to change one of the two conflicting attitudes.

The most favoured theory of attitude change is called the **cognitive dissonance theory**. It works like this: Suppose you smoke, but you also believe that smoking causes cancer and other serious diseases. You are experiencing dissonance, meaning that what you do conflicts with what you think. In your desire to regain cognitive consistency, you will probably try to avoid facing the con-

flict. You may avoid smoking in front of a friend who is strongly opposed to smoking (thereby avoiding a lecture). You may avoid reading articles in newspapers about the latest studies on smoking and health (thereby avoiding thinking about the ways that smoking can kill you). If a relative who is a smoker gets lung cancer, however, your dissonance will unavoidably increase. In a sense, the volume of your inner conflict would rise.

Ultimately, the only way you can effectively reduce the dissonance you feel is to do one of two things. You can change your behaviour to make it consistent with your attitudes—you can stop smoking. Alternatively, you can reinforce your attitudes. You can tell yourself it won't happen to you; that Grandmother was a heavy smoker and lived to be 93; or that it's actually a benefit to smoke because it makes you look "grown-up." Perhaps you'll be able to fool yourself for a while. As long as you live in a state of dissonance, however, you will probably experience anxiety and be very uncomfortable—even hostile—if someone criticizes your behaviour.

Did you ever do something that you knew was wrong—like shoplifting a candy bar—and then a friend chastised you, and you boiled over with anger? This feeling of anger results from the dissonance between what you do and what you think. How did you resolve the dissonance?

Later in this chapter you will read more about where our attitudes come from, how we change them, and what type of person can influence us to change.

 ## The Sociological Questions

While psychologists look at why and how individuals change their attitudes and behaviours, sociologists tend to focus on the massive shifts in the behaviours and attitudes of groups and whole societies. They see change as an inevitable process. The major issue for them is whether social change is patterned and predictable, or arbitrary and irregular.

Early Approaches

The major question that has always fascinated sociologists is, How does social change come about? In its earlier development as a discipline, sociology developed three main ways of explaining social change.

1. *From decay.* First, social change was seen as being caused by decline or degeneration. Early Judeo-Christian sociologists associated this with the Genesis story of Adam and Eve, who fell from grace for disobeying God's commands. It was believed that all societies began in an ideal state. As societies inevitably became more materialistic

Figure 2.4 Before its initial voyage, the *Titanic* was boastfully described as the epitome of technological progress. People thought that technological advancements could do nothing but benefit society. What effect do you think the sinking of this ocean liner might have had on people's frame of mind?

(concerned with material things) and less spiritual, they declined, becoming less able to provide for and protect their citizens.

2. *From cycles of growth and decay.* A second early sociological explanation of social change was a variation on the first. Unlike the first approach, sociologists believed that societies do not head inevitably toward destruction, but instead go through cycles of growth and decay.

3. *From progress.* A third approach believed that social change occurred as a result of the phenomenon of continuous progress. Each new society builds on the experiences of its predecessors, and social institutions change as a result.

In the late nineteenth century, when the first three approaches were becoming less popular, sociologists debated whether social change was caused by a single factor or by the interplay of many factors. The theories of those who believed that a single factor was at work are called **reductionist**, (meaning that the cause can be reduced to a specific factor.) Such theories are also called **determinist**, (meaning that a specific factor will determine the nature of the social change that takes place.) Karl Marx was perhaps the most famous sociological determinist. You may remember from Chapter 1 that he believed that the struggle for economic power between competing social groups determined the nature of social institutions and the way in which they would inevitably change. But this approach raises other questions. Why, if all societies must develop and change along determinist lines, are there such vast differences among human societies in the world?

Marx believed that those with power would fight to the death, if necessary, to retain it. Although some of Marx's original ideas have been rejected by modern social scientists, they have had considerable influence. Some sociologists examining inequalities of wealth and incomes, such as E.O. Wright and Nicos Poulazantas, built their theories on Marxist assumptions about the nature of society. They consider such factors as social class, ethnicity, and gender, and the relationship of these factors to the distribution of economic and political power in society.

Another way in which Marx retains influence is in feminist writings. Many feminist social scientists use a Marxist analysis. They see men as the group with power, and women as the group trying to capture it. They call society a **patriarchy**, a place historically designed for the convenience of men, and structured according to rules that men find comfortable. They ask, How can society be restructured to serve the needs of women as well? Betty Friedan and Gloria Steinem are two famous pioneers of feminist sociology. Along with other feminists, they have tried to answer questions such as whether men can work together with women to engineer this social change, or whether women must rely on themselves to secure it. We will return to such questions later in the chapter. Next, we will look at the primary questions asked by modern sociologists.

Analyzing Patterns of Behaviour

All sociologists believe that human behaviour is generally patterned and therefore potentially predictable. All you have to do is identify the patterns. People within societies tend to behave according to societal **norms** (customary types of behaviour). Therefore, the extent to which a society will accept social change should also be predictable. To the sociologist, social change might be defined as "any observable difference or modification in social organization or patterns of behaviour over time" (Meloff and Pierce, 1994, p. 67). Sociologists tend to look at one or more of four aspects of social change in their studies, as shown below.

1. *Direction of change.* Is it positive or negative change, and who says so? Consider the following question: Are Canadian pollution emission laws sufficient to protect the

environment? If you asked the chief executive officer of a major oil and gas company and a member of Greenpeace Canada, you would probably get different answers. Sociologists consider it vital, therefore, to consider whose opinions are being sought in the measurement of change.

2. *Rate of change.* Is the degree of change slow, moderate, or fast? Is it radical change over a short period, or slow change that will continue for decades? Is the rate of change slowing, staying steady, or increasing? What factors are affecting this rate? After identifying the forces that facilitate and oppose change, sociologists try to estimate which side has the greater influence both now and in the future.

3. *Sources.* What factors are behind the influences of change in a society? They might be **exogenous** influences, coming from another society into this one, or **endogenous** influences, coming from within the society itself. Such factors as population change, technological innovation and development, and the condition of the physical environment all influence the norms and values in a society. Changes to any of these will result in social change.

4. *Controllability.* Many sociologists are interested in the degree to which social change can be controlled or engineered. In Hutterite society, for example, the community tightly controls personal behaviour. Hutterite communities have changed relatively little in the last century, so it is obvious that exogenous influences have been largely shut out. To what degree is it possible to engineer or restrict social change in the diverse society of Canada at large? How successfully can we eliminate racism, spousal abuse, or teenage smoking? Questions like these are at the forefront of the modern sociological approach.

The three social science disciplines, as you have seen, all regard social change as an important phenomenon. Each discipline, however, uses distinct methods and comes to different conclusions about the nature of social change and its causes.

www.usi.edu/libarts/socio/chapter/socialchange/causes.html

To learn more about sociological studies on social change, visit the Web site of the Sociology Department at the University of Southern Indiana. You'll find lots of links to examples of the ideas mentioned in this section. For example, you can find out more about inventions such as the telephone, electricity, and clocks.

If the Web address does not connect you with the site, do a Web search using "University of Southern Indiana" as a search string. Then connect through the following links to reach the specific page: Departments > School of Liberal Arts > Sociology > Search > (enter "Causes").

Pause and Reflect

1. How do anthropologists regard cultures? What causes cultures to change?

2. According to the system of classification presented on page 42, anthropologists view culture as composed of four parts. Another system lists five aspects of culture: religion, social organization, language, technology, and values. Compare the two systems to assess their relative value.

3. On what do psychologists studying change concentrate? How can change be obtained?

4. What is the focus of sociologists studying social change?

5. Create a comparison organizer, and list and compare the questions about social change asked by experts in each of the three social sciences.

Section 2.2   Anthropological Theories About Social Change

Key Concepts

hunter-gathering

interaction

diffusion

acculturation

incorporation

directed change

cultural evolution

ideology

longitudinal studies

So far in this chapter, we have examined some of the major questions and the various focuses that form the basis of social science investigation about social change. We must now look more specifically at the theories social scientists bring to their study, and recount some of the famous theories dealing with the issue of social change.

Among the ways in which anthropology and the other social science disciplines resemble other sciences is in the theoretical nature of their inquiry. Social scientists propose theories, which are developed, tested, published, evaluated by other members of the discipline, and then accepted or modified as necessary. In the course of this process, people who develop widely accepted theories become known within the discipline and attract a fair degree of academic fame. Such practitioners of the discipline generally find it easier to obtain positions in prestigious universities or colleges, and to obtain the funds they need to continue their research. Some become known outside academic life through exposure to the general public on television talk shows and as authors of magazine articles. In this and the following sections of this chapter, we will consider some practitioners to understand their importance to their respective disciplines.

A famous study conducted in the 1960s illustrates anthropological theories about social change. In 1963, Richard B. Lee and Irven DeVore began to study the San of southern Africa, then known as the Bushmen of the Kalahari Desert. San means "Aboriginal people," or "first people," in the Sans' native language. You can read about a radical transformation in San culture in the following case study.

The San of Southern Africa

Traditionally, the San were a **hunter-gathering** people who lived in central southern Africa. As hunter-gatherers, they obtained their food by hunting wild animals and gathering fruit and wild vegetables. Because wild animals roam over wide areas, and because different areas offer different wild fruits and vegetables at various times of the year, the San were a nomadic people who travelled extensively over the course of the year. At the time of the anthropological study conducted by Richard B. Lee and Irven DeVore, the San had not developed a system of growing and cultivating fruit and vegetables.

The San had been in southern Africa longer than any other Aboriginal group. Over time they had adapted to the presence of other peoples that had come to live in the region. The San traded for goods such as metal cooking utensils, and some even worked on huge cattle farms run by settlers who had arrived from Europe in the seventeenth century. Nonetheless, in the 1960s the San still resembled an ancient society. They used poisoned arrows to kill their prey. They had a deep understanding of animals and their ways, and could predict weather from changes in animal behaviour. They practised techniques of water conservation that allowed them to live comfortably in the harsh climate of the Kalahari Desert, something that no other group of people was able to do.

In the mid-1960s, the countries of Botswana and Namibia were created out of colonies run by Britain and South Africa. The borders between the two nations were fenced to provide them with security. Unfortunately, the fences ran right through the territory over which the San roamed in their nomadic migrations. Land laws were instituted recognizing private ownership of land and the right of owners to keep others off their property. The San, like many Aboriginal people, had no concept of private land ownership, regarding all land as common property to be shared among everyone. Further, extensive fencing had been added to enclose Botswana's cattle ranches. In a few short years, the livelihood of the San was destroyed, and many were forced to give up their traditional lifestyle, as its foundations had likewise been destroyed. Many travelled to South Africa, where they could get work in the gold mines that were booming at the time.

Lee and DeVore detailed much of this story of the San in their book *Man the Hunter*, which they published in 1968. They raised troubling questions for anthropologists. Could Aboriginal peoples who lived traditional lifestyles hope to survive in the rapidly changing world of the late twentieth century? Was the influence of the outside world too great on these peoples? If anthropologists knew of traditional lifestyles that were dying, was their role merely to record these changes, or should they intervene to try to protect these cultures? The research group that developed out of the original study by Lee and DeVore turned over all royalties from its publications to the San to assist them as their traditional way of life declined.

Figure 2.5 The San have lived a nomadic lifestyle for thousands of years, following migrating animals. How could fences, constructed to enclose Botswana's cattle ranches, threaten this livelihood?

Questions

1. What was the San culture like before the 1960s?
2. How did it change subsequently? What factors caused it to change?
3. What ethical questions did this raise for the anthropologists studying this people?

Theories of Cultural Change

In many ways, the story of the San, as described in the case study on page 48, can be used to illustrate a number of anthropological theories about cultural change. All the changes that were forced on the San came from **interaction**, or contact with other cultures. Although it is possible for cultural change to develop from within a culture, most anthropologists believe that the most far-reaching changes come from contact with other cultures. Sometimes cultures enthusiastically adapt what they regard as beneficial changes from other cultures. In many cases, however, cultures do not want to accept change but are forced to do so by another, more powerful culture, as happened in the case of the San. The changes that took place in the cultures of the Aboriginal peoples in Canada and the United States after the arrival of Europeans represent a similar process.

Figure 2.6 Students at the St. Joseph Residential School, also known as the Crowfoot School, near Cluny, Alberta, 1890. Early in the twentieth century, the Canadian government made Aboriginal cultures change by forcing Aboriginal children such as these into residential schools. In what ways could this change Aboriginal culture? How is this an example of directed change? How is racism involved?

Adaptation can take place in a number of ways, although the results can be similar no matter which pattern of adaptation is followed. The first way is through **diffusion**, which occurs when one culture borrows cultural symbols from another. The San, for example, smoked tobacco, although it was not part of their original culture. The tobacco plant, originally a North American product, had been imported into Europe in the seventeenth century. The Europeans embraced the Aboriginal practice of smoking tobacco. Later, they brought the habit to Africa. The North American Aboriginal peoples similarly borrowed from other cultures. There were no horses in what later became Canada until the French explorers and traders brought them across the Atlantic Ocean in ships in the mid-seventeenth century. The Aboriginal peoples welcomed the horse, recognizing that it would be of enormous advantage to their lifestyle. Of course, adapting their day-to-day activities to make use of horses changed Aboriginal cultures immensely. In addition, using the horse dramatically increased the distances the people could travel. This brought various Aboriginal groups into contact with other groups that would previously have been out of range.

A second process through which cultural change can take place is through **acculturation**. This process results from prolonged contact between two cultures, during which time they interchange symbols, beliefs, and customs. This may occur in one of two ways. One people may freely borrow selected elements from the culture of another, as the Navajo did as a result of their contact with the Spanish in eighteenth-century North America. Similarly, Canadian society has borrowed the canoe from the First Nations, incorporating it as an element of Canadian culture. Such free borrowing is called **incorporation**. The second kind of acculturation takes place when one culture defeats or otherwise controls another and forces it to change aspects of its culture, or even to change the entire culture. Anthropologists call this process **directed change**, and it can often involve racist policies in which the weaker people are subjected to the wishes of the stronger power. Examples of directed change include the South African law of 1976 that required all schools to teach children in Afrikaans (the language of the white minority), even though virtually all black families spoke a variety of native languages and English in their daily lives.

The third way in which acculturation can take place is through **cultural evolution**. This view proposes that cultures evolve according to common patterns. They move from hunter-gathering cultures to industrialized states in predictable stages. Writers like Karl Marx popularized the idea of cultural

GROUNDBREAKERS
SHERRY ORTNER (B. 1941)

Sherry Ortner is a professor of anthropology at Columbia University in New York City. As a student, she was exposed to the theories of Claude Levi-Strauss and Karl Marx. (Levi-Strauss was a Belgian-born cultural anthropologist from France whose work examined the role of supernatural beliefs as a part of culture. For an explanation of Karl Marx's views, see pages 28 to 29.) Ortner's main academic interests are cultural anthropology, social theory, the importance of class and gender in understanding cultures, and **ideology**. (An ideology is a structured philosophy against which all actions are judged.)

Figure 2.7 Anthropologist Sherry Ortner

Ortner's 1974 article "Is Female to Male as Nature Is to Culture?" established her as a feminist writer. In it, she theorizes that men are more associated with culture, while women are more aligned with nature. She states that a woman's body, with its child-bearing and child-rearing functions, keeps her closely tied to the natural world. On the other hand, men are less restricted in this way and have more time to develop and participate in cultural functions. As a result, many cultural institutions, such as religion or family law, have traditionally come to reflect the input and needs of men rather than women. If social change is to come about, Ortner theorizes, men and women will have to work together to rectify the social imbalance stemming from women's inferior role in defining and developing culture.

In *Reading America: Preliminary Notes on Class and Culture* (1991), Ortner helped widen the focus of anthropology to include studies of modern industrialized cultures such as in the United States. Ortner states that too many social scientists have tried to explain problems such as income disparity as differences among peoples of different ethnic origins. She argues that, in fact, these problems stem largely from differences of social class.

Ortner has long supported **longitudinal studies**. In one of these, a group of people is tracked over a long period of time, even incorporating the study group's children into the study as they come along. In *Reading America* and *Anthropologists in a Media-Saturated World* (1997),

Ortner documented the experiences of 100 of her high-school classmates (then in their fifties) and 50 of their children. She discovered a major change in the expectations and options of the parents' generation and the children's. She illustrated how people born between 1966 and 1986 were facing greatly reduced life prospects in comparison with their parents.

Another important aspect of Ortner's research is her work studying the Sherpa people of the Himalayan region. In *Sherpas Through Their Rituals* (1978), she noted that the people of the Sherpa culture faithfully practise all the rituals of Tibetan Buddhism, out of a sense of tradition and to prevent the world from becoming unstable. In *High Religion: A Cultural and Political History of Sherpa Buddhism* (1989), she argues that widespread performance of cultural rituals is important because it means that all problems that a culture experiences—including problems stemming from social change—can be solved both to the individual's satisfaction and for the community's benefit. The Sherpa people have experienced major social change since the People's Republic of China took over Tibet in the 1950s. Many traditional Sherpa institutions, including their religion, have been persecuted, with the complete destruction of a vast majority of old temples, the imprisonment and execution of many monks, and a ban on possession of even a picture of the Tibetan spiritual leader, His Holiness the Dalai Lama. The Sherpa culture has suffered greatly. Ortner has documented the impact these changes have had on the Sherpa way of life.

Questions

1. What are the four areas of special interest to Sherry Ortner?

2. What conclusions does she come to about social change?

3. What role does religion play in Tibetan society? How is this similar to or different from the role religion plays in Canadian society?

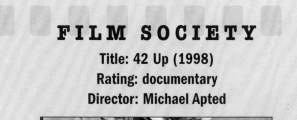

FILM SOCIETY

Title: 42 Up (1998)
Rating: documentary
Director: Michael Apted

Michael Apted's extraordinary series began with *7 Up*, a documentary made for television in 1964. He interviewed 14 British seven-year-olds from varying backgrounds about their lives and their goals. Every seven years, he interviewed the subjects again and produced a new film, the latest being *42 Up* (1998). This series is an excellent example of a longitudinal study, in which the viewer can observe changing lives and values over time, and how individuals cope with change. (*42 Up* stands alone, and includes flashbacks to the earlier films.)

evolution. Most modern anthropologists believe that the process of adaptation is too complicated to be reduced to a pattern.

As you have seen, there are a number of anthropological theories about social change. What they have in common is that they focus on how cultures change, what changes them, and how the changes affect people.

For other examples of groundbreaking anthropologists, read about Jane Goodall, Biruté Galdikas, and Dian Fossey in *The Human Way* (Bain and Colyer, Oxford University Press. Toronto, 2001, pp. 36–39).

Pause and Reflect

1. Explain how each of the three processes of cultural adaptation works.

2. Describe how the story of the San illustrates the anthropological theory of social change through interaction.

3. In a small group, brainstorm 10 examples of cultural adaptation. For example, the Europeans adopted corn, which was first grown as an agricultural crop in Central America. Your answers can be historical or contemporary.

4. History contains numerous examples of one culture using force to impose change on another. Think of, or do research to identify, an example of this form of directed change, and give your opinion on who benefited from the change, and why.

5. Which of Sherry Ortner's studies applies most directly to you and your life? Explain.

Section 2.3   Psychological Theories About Social Change

As you have already learned, the focus of much psychological investigation is on how humans change their attitudes and behaviours. Psychology is divided into two broad fields. **Experimental psychology** deals with measuring and explaining human behaviour. **Clinical psychology** focuses on the treatment of problem human behaviours.

Behaviour Modification

According to one theory, we must move through a number of stages before we can successfully change. Suppose an individual has a problem behaviour, such as excessive absenteeism from school or an over-reliance on alcohol developed as a response to personal difficulties. How can such an individual change the problem behaviour? Psychologists James Prochaska, John C. Norcross, and Carlo C. DiClemente suggest that we must go through six specific stages to achieve such a behaviour change successfully. You can see a model illustrating their theory in Figure 2.8.

The Stages of Change model is typical of the **behaviour modification** theories of psychologists. These social scientists have spent much research time attempting to determine the methods that can successfully change, or modify, human behaviour. This aspect of psychologists' work has been of special importance for people working with individuals who display criminal behaviour. How can society get criminals to change their behaviour and to stop committing criminal acts? Some politicians run for office promising that, if elected, they will "get tough on criminals." Increased prison sentences and harsher conditions in jails often go along with this approach, which psychologists call

Key Concepts

experimental psychology

clinical psychology

behaviour modification

negative/positive reinforcement

neurosis

psychosis

paranoia

schizophrenia

anti-social personality disorder

operant conditioning

personal/ collective unconscious

introverts/ extroverts

self-actualization

Stage	Characteristics
1. Precontemplation	Denial ("I don't have a problem.") Refusal ("I like myself the way I am.")
2. Contemplation	Questioning ("Do you think I should do something about the problem?")
3. Preparation	Investigation ("What is my problem doing to my health? How does my problem affect those who love me?")
4. Action	Commitment ("I've got to keep doing this, or I'll never change.")
5. Maintenance (begins about six months after Action stage begins)	Transition ("I must find alternative ways to deal with my problems. I must avoid people who are going to drag me back into my old habits.")
6. Termination (Only about 20 per cent of changers reach this stage.)	Completion. ("I don't have to work at this any more. I just don't want to go back to my old ways.")

Source: Adapted from Prochaska, Norcross, and DiClemente, 1995, pp. 10–50.

Figure 2.8 If you know someone who has made a major effort to change a particular behaviour, or if you have done so yourself, you will be in a position to judge how accurate this six-stage model is. Why would it be so hard to reach Stage 6?

negative reinforcement. In other words, if you do something of which society disapproves, society will punish you or remove a privilege so you won't do it again. For example, you might lose the privilege of going out in the evening if you miss your curfew. This is the opposite approach to **positive reinforcement**, in which people are rewarded for good behaviour. For example, prisoners are treated humanely and rewarded when they display reformed, "better" behaviours. Although neither approach is effective in all cases, many psychological studies have concluded that positive reinforcement is a more effective method of modifying behaviour.

Treating Mental Disorders

So far, we have been considering how to modify the behaviour of mentally healthy people. But psychology also studies the treatment of people with mental disorders. Psychologists classify mental disorders into three categories.

The first is **neuroses** (singular neurosis), in which sufferers experience high levels of anxiety or tension in managing their daily lives. Examples of neuroses are panic attacks, phobias, and obsessive-compulsive disorders.

The second category of mental disorders is **psychoses** (singular psychosis), in which the patient has lost touch with the real world, may suffer from delusions or hallucinations, and needs treatment before he or she can live a life with any degree of normality. Examples include **paranoia**, in which the person suffers from irrational thoughts of persecution or foreboding, and **schizophrenia**, a complex disorder that leads to feelings of distress and social isolation.

The third category is called **anti-social personality disorder**, a habitual pattern of rule-breaking and harming others. Symptoms include pathological lying; absence of empathy toward others, deliberately causing them pain; and a lack of feelings of guilt for the damage caused. Serial murderers like Paul Bernardo and Karla Homolka are examples of people who have anti-social personality disorder.

Foundational Psychologists

Burrhus Frederick (B.F.) Skinner (1904–1990)

B.F. Skinner was an American behavioural psychologist who conducted learning experiments on a variety of creatures, especially rats and pigeons. He believed that the results of these experiments could be applied to human behaviour. His experiments allowed him to develop the theory of **operant conditioning**. According to this theory, learning can be programmed by whatever consequence follows a particular behaviour. People tend to repeat behaviours that are rewarded, and to avoid behaviours that are punished. He summarized his research in *The Behavior of Organisms* (1938).

In his experiments, Skinner designed what he is most remembered for: the "Skinner box." Rats were placed in metal cages containing a number of levers that they eventually learned to press for food and

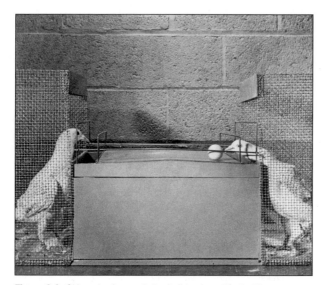

Figure 2.9 Skinner's pigeons bat a ball back and forth. When one pigeon misses, its opponent gets the reward! How does this experiment illustrate operant conditioning?

GROUNDBREAKERS
CARL JUNG (1875–1961)

Carl Jung was a Swiss psychologist who went to Vienna to study under Sigmund Freud. Initially, he strongly supported Freud's techniques and the theory of psychoanalysis. Eventually, however, he split with Freud over the latter's insistence that sexuality was the root of the human personality.

Jung argued that we are conditioned by a **personal unconscious** and a **collective unconscious**. Each of us, Jung believed, possesses a number of mythic symbols that are a product of our own unique history. As an example, he wrote, think of someone who almost drowned in the sea as a young child. To this individual's personal unconscious, the sea would represent a symbol of danger and foreboding. To the collective unconscious of the larger human community, established over centuries, the sea is a powerful symbol of sustenance—it gives us fish—and adventure—it allows us to travel to far-off places. To the individual described in Jung's example, the sea will represent a problematic symbol, as the personal and collective unconsciouses collide. Of the two, Jung believed that the collective unconscious is the more significant factor in the development of human personality. To change people's personalities and behaviours, particularly when they prevent the people from living normal lives, Jung, like Freud, believed that it was necessary to

Figure 2.10 Carl Jung believed that humans possess four major psychological functions: sensation, intuition, thinking, and feeling.

explore and treat the unconscious mind.

Jung suggested that some people use their psychological power to look inward, becoming emotionally self-sufficient. Their sense of well-being comes from within; they like being alone and may have few close friends. Jung called such people **introverts**. People in a second group, called **extroverts**, are outgoing. They use their psychological power to draw closer to other people, and they rely on these others for much of their sense of well-being.

Jung believed that it was possible to treat a person suffering from a personality disorder only if the therapist correctly understood the way the person's personality had been formed in the human mind. Jung's theories still have support among therapists today, three-quarters of a century after they were first proposed.

Questions

1. According to Carl Jung, on what is the personality dependent?

2. In what two ways, according to Jung, can humans use the four major psychological functions?

3. What crucial step must be taken before a personality disorder can be treated?

water. Initially, the rats would nose around their cages and accidentally press one of the levers, an action that would cause food or water to drop into a dish. Repeating the action brought more food or water. Eventually the rats learned to press the appropriate lever whenever they were hungry or thirsty. They had food and water on demand!

Skinner believed that people could be conditioned to behave in certain ways by giving them rewards when they displayed good

behaviours, and withholding the rewards when they displayed bad behaviours. Critics have accused him of developing a theory that is too simplistic, charging that human behaviour is a complex phenomenon that cannot be modified by a simple punishment-reward program. But behaviour modification programs are still largely based on operant conditioning. These programs, which are designed for young people or adults with problem behaviours or criminal histories,

COMPETING PERSPECTIVES

Competing Perspectives on Boot Camp

What is the best way to discourage young people from committing crimes against property and persons? Is it to treat convicted offenders to harsh regimes in special prisons? Ontario's experiment with "boot camp" for young offenders—dubbed "Project Turnaround" by the provincial government—is testing that question. At this "shock treatment" facility, 16- and 17-year-old young offenders live through a tough regime of military-like drills, physical challenges, and no frills. It's the ultimate example of negative reinforcement behaviour modification. Does it work? Read the following two articles to get two different perspectives on this issue.

Ontario's First Young Offender Boot Camp a Success
Press Release By Ministry of Correctional Services

TORONTO – March 24, 2001 – Project Turnaround, Ontario's first boot camp, works in lowering the re-offending rate of young offenders, [the] Minister of Correctional Services…said today.

[He] was commenting on the results of a three-year review of the pilot project, which showed that young offenders who completed the program at Project Turnaround were one-third less likely to re-offend than those who served their sentence in a traditional young-offender correctional institution.

"One of the first promises the [provincial government] kept was to establish a boot camp for young offenders, to teach them respect and responsibility….After three and a half years of operation and detailed study of this program [comparing it with] our traditional programs, I am very pleased to report that this model works."

The evaluation…shows that, "recidivism [relapsing into crime] rates for Project Turnaround participants were consistently lower than the rates observed for a comparable sample of youth who were not exposed to the program." In particular, the study indicates that the program works better for young offenders who are at higher levels of risk.

One year after completing the program, 50 per cent of comparison offenders re-offended compared [with] 33 per cent among Project Turnaround participants. Project Turnaround offenders also showed more positive changes in behaviour, self-esteem, and respect for the law.

"It's clear," said [the Minister], "that Project Turnaround is turning lives around. These results tell us that Ontario's no-nonsense, structured environment for young offenders is working. They also tell us that more work needs to be done in certain areas. We will continue to evaluate and improve all of our young offender programming to ensure public safety is protected by lowering youth crime."

"This is a proud day for my community," said [the Member of the Provincial Parliament] for Simcoe North. "Project Turnaround is changing the lives of young people to create law-abiding, responsible individuals."

The cost of operating the privately run Project Turnaround for the 1999/2000 fiscal year was approximately $214.00 per day per offender. This is less than the average daily rate of $331.00 for four government-operated youth centres. The per diem rates for those centres range from $294.00 to $424.00.

Established in July 1997, and operated by Encourage Youth Corporation, Project Turnaround is designed for 16- and 17-year-old young offenders who are at high risk to re-offend. The project also marked the introduction of the province's first public-private partnership in the operation of a secure-custody, young offender institution.

Source: Ministry of Correctional Services. 2001. "Ontario's First Young Offender Boot Camp a Success." [Online] Available <http://www.corrections.mcs.gov.on.ca/english/cservices/PT_nr.html> 12 October 2001.

COMPETING PERSPECTIVES

The Shine is Off Boot Camps
News Article By Nate Hendley

The rules are strict: up at 6, school from 8 until noon, then vocational training all afternoon. Physical exercise or drill three times a day, and no television allowed.

Such is life for the 32 young offenders at Project Turnaround, Ontario's debut "boot camp" for juvenile criminals. As popularized in the US, such camps aim to instill discipline and respect for authority by making delinquents wear uniforms, learn marching steps, and run around obstacle courses.

Opened in July 1997, near Barrie, Project Turnaround has hosted 191 kids so far. It represents the [Ontario government's] answer to fears about teenage criminals. As...MPP Allan McLean (Simcoe East) assured the legislature two years ago, "Ontarians called for tougher sanctions against youth crime, and Project Turnaround is answering the call."

On Nov. 18, 1999, Management Board Chairman Chris Hodgson announced that the government wants to build more boot camps—or "strict discipline facilities," as the government prefers to call them.

Before they start building, the [government] would be wise to check out recent reports from the United States that indicate boot camps do more harm than good. American states have learned that boot camps have little impact on recidivism [the rate at which criminals commit new crimes]. A series of scandals over mistreatment and even deaths of juvenile inmates has further wrecked the reputation of pseudo-military juvenile institutions. It seems that the only benefit these programs offer is more physically fit, happier juvenile criminals.

At year's end, officials in Maryland and Georgia scaled back and shut down juvenile boot camps in their states. After the *Baltimore Sun* revealed [that] guards in Maryland boot camps routinely beat and bloodied their teenage charges, state officials closed one camp in December and suspended paramilitary drills at two others....

A paper published by the US Office of Juvenile Justice and Delinquency Prevention in 1997 found "similar recidivism rates for those who completed boot camps and comparable offenders who spent long periods of time in prison."

Considering the record of American boot camps, it's no wonder Ontario politicians and officials seem eager to distance themselves from the US model. Gerry Martiniuk,...MPP for Cambridge and co-chair of the Ontario Crime Control Commission, concedes that "boot camps in the United States have gotten mixed reviews." Project Turnaround, he says, is less a carbon copy of American boot camps than a "made-in-Ontario solution" to the problem of youth crime....

For all that, the camp remains "very militaristic," says Walter Podilchak, who teaches sociology at the University of Toronto.

He points to an internal document, obtained by *The National Post* in October, which reported that nearly 40 per cent of cadets leaving Turnaround committed new crimes within one year....

Source: Hendley, Nate. 2000. "The shine is off boot camps." *Eye.* 20 January, 2000. [Online] Available <http://www.eye.net/eye/issue/issue_01.20.00/news/boot camp.html> 27 October 2001.

Questions
1. What reasons are cited in the press release to explain why boot camps are a good idea? What counter-arguments does the newspaper article offer? Present your answers in a chart.
2. Who wrote each piece? Can you detect any possibility of bias?
3. What assumptions do you think the writer of each article might be making about the causes of youth crime?
4. From what you have read about behaviour modification in this chapter, do you think that boot camps for young offenders are likely to prove successful in the long run? Why or why not?

owe much of their research backing to Skinner's experiments.

Abraham Maslow (1908–1970)

Abraham Maslow was an American psychologist best known for his analysis of human needs. He organized them into a hierarchy, which he laid out in *Motivation and Personality* (1954) and *Toward a Psychology of Being* (1962). These human needs, which we all try to satisfy, range from basic survival needs (food, clothing, and shelter), through the need for security, love, and esteem.

Maslow argued that when we have satisfied the need at one level of the hierarchy, rather than becoming satisfied overall, we tend to move on and try to satisfy the need at the next level. Picture, for example, a person who has insufficient food, clothing, and shelter. If this person should suddenly be able to satisfy those needs through some change of circumstances, he or she will then become more focused on issues of personal safety. If personal safety is assured, the person will then try to satisfy the need for love and esteem.

At the highest level, which Maslow called **self-actualization**, a person integrates the self, making the personality whole. These are secure, loved, and loving individuals who are able to dedicate themselves to serving others, believing that all humans share common bonds. Mother Teresa was a good example of a self-actualizer. In practice, most people never reach this level of psychological development. People who have been unable to satisfy the need for esteem are unable to focus on the common nature of humanity. They therefore cannot integrate, or make whole, their personalities.

Maslow's theories have perhaps had their greatest impact in industrial psychology, which focuses on changing the workplace to make work a more satisfying experience. Many organizations want to raise morale among employees in order to improve their work performance and prevent their seeking work elsewhere. (It is less expensive for employers to retain employees than to train new ones.) Such employers recognize that competitive wages allow the employees to satisfy their survival and security needs. Nonetheless, good wages alone will not retain employees if their other needs are disregarded. Managers who show appreciation for good work and who solicit their employees' opinions tend to have a more effective workforce.

Marion Woodman

Marion Woodman is a psychologist who has written extensively about the relationships between women and men, and the relationships between science and faith.

In *Leaving My Father's House* (1992), she writes that all adults have been brought up in a patriarchal system. Therefore, their attitudes about families and society are out of date. Woodman believes that women and men must free themselves from patriarchal thinking before their personal relationships can be fulfilling and before people can change the nature of society. If we can free ourselves from this old-style thinking, she concludes, we can bring a new energy to our personal relationships that will give us a new creativity for solving personal and societal problems (problems within society).

Woodman has been influenced by the psychoanalytical school of thought (see pages 18 to 20 in Chapter 1), but tempers this with a belief in a strong spiritual dimension to individual human beings. She states, "There is some place where psychology and religion meet, and where religion becomes more essential than psychology." There is a tendency in modern society to place too much faith and emphasis on science and research, and to underestimate the power of the spiritual force.

Woodman believes that professions such as medicine must change the ways in which they operate, to incorporate a spiritual as well as a scientific dimension. Medicine has adopted a model that is too specialized. Doctors tend to regard the body as a machine that can be treated with mechanical processes when it needs repairs. Woodman argues that medicine must take a more holistic approach, utilizing broader, alternative techniques, including spiritual ones. When the body is ill, doctors must consider the soul's illness as well as the physical symptoms. Woodman supports the approach of the shamans, spirit doctors in Aboriginal societies. These individuals have no scientific knowledge, but are still able to cure illnesses by tending the soul.

Pause and Reflect

1. What are the main principles of behaviour modification as outlined in this section?

2. Into what three categories do psychologists classify mental disorders? What are the main features of each?

3. Think of a time when you tried to change your behaviour. Which stage did you reach? Which one was the most difficult. Why?

4. In a comparison organizer, compare the work of the four featured psychologists. How is their work similar? How is it different?

5. What is the difference between positive and negative reinforcement? Think of an example in your life when positive reinforcement worked, and another in which negative reinforcement worked. Compare the long-term effectiveness of each technique of behaviour modification.

Section 2.4   Sociological Theories About Social Change

Sociology came comparatively late to the study of social change. For much of the early part of the twentieth century, the structural-functionalist school of thought dominated sociological inquiry. You will remember from Chapter 1 that the structural-functionalists focused more on social structure than on social change. They tried to identify which social institutions were influential in society and what characteristics gave these institutions influence.

 Seeking Equilibrium

The structural-functionalists of the early twentieth century believed that where social change did occur, it was the result of a process of **tension and adaptation**. They argued that when one part of the social system changes, tension arises between that part and the rest. This tension cannot continue indefinitely. Members of society will invariably seek to reduce or eliminate the tension by adapting other aspects of society. With adaptation, equilibrium is restored to society.

During the 1930s, when structural-functionalism was popular among sociologists, a tremendous economic depression hit North America and much of the industrialized world. High unemployment led to economic disaster for millions of families. Religious institutions, until then the major

Key Concepts

tension and adaptation

accumulation

diffusion of innovations

pluralistic societies

elite groups

capitalism

core

periphery

Key Concepts (continued)

semi-periphery

private sphere

discourse

textual discourse

source of charitable aid, were unable to cope with the massive scale of this problem. The prevailing social attitude had been that people were responsible for taking care of themselves, and that the state should not directly assist those in need of help. Social assistance programs financed by government simply did not exist. It was the enormity of the Depression disaster that caused people to rethink this position. In both Canada and the United States, governments adapted by intervening to assist distraught families and to try to restart the economy to provide work for everyone. The modern welfare state was born. (In a welfare state, the government runs programs to protect the health and welfare of its citizenry.) Society, the structural-functionalists stated, had returned to equilibrium. Social change had taken place, through the tension-adaptation model. The sociological theories described below have largely displaced structural-functionalist explanations of social change.

Figure 2.11 Since the terrorist attacks in 2001, security has increased dramatically in airports all over North America, including Edmonton International, shown above. What tension emerged after the attack? What adaptation attempted to decrease this tension?

Theoretical Models

By the 1960s, the attention of sociologists began to shift toward a consideration of social change. It quickly became a subject of primary interest, and many sociologists began studying social change and formulating theories to explain it.

Some sociological theoretical models see change as a process of **accumulation**, through which the growth of human knowledge from generation to generation allows society to develop new ways of doing things. As economic or technical changes take place in this manner, social change inevitably follows. Think, for example, about the advancements in television technology. In the 1950s, when television first became available in Canada, televisions were relatively expensive, and the whole family would sit down to watch the one set in the household. Families tended to communicate with each other about which programs to watch on the one or two channels that were available, and about what they thought of them.

With the technical advances that have taken place since the 1950s, production costs have gone down, making televisions relatively inexpensive. More people can now afford a television set. Improved economic conditions even allow some children and teenagers to have their own television in their bedrooms. With the technology improvements, viewers can choose from hundreds of stations and countless television programs, movies, sports events, game shows, and news programs. In some families, television watching has become a solitary pursuit. Family members do not talk as much among themselves about what they see. Family communication patterns have thereby been affected through the accumulation of technical and economic processes. Some sociologists would suggest that this has led to significant social change and has contributed to the weakening of the family structure.

Another model favoured by sociologists is the **diffusion of innovations** model. According to this theory, a new development—an innovation—emerges in society. It might be a technical invention or a piece of scientific knowledge; it could be a new belief, a new fashion, or one of a thousand other developments. According to sociologists, two things can affect the spread (the "diffusion") of the innovation throughout society: who adopts it and who speaks in its favour. Think of bell-bottom pants, Chicago Bulls sweaters, the Spice Girls, body piercing, and recycling. What has made such innovations popular at given times? Why do some disappear, almost overnight? Many sociological studies conclude that, in a country like Canada, innovations are likely to become widespread if they are adopted by young, urban, educated people with high-status occupations. If the young host of a music program wears a new style of jacket, chances are that others will follow his or her example. This explains why so much advertising for new products is geared to this group.

Accumulation of human knowledge and diffusion of innovations are just two of the leading causes of social change. Sociological theorists have identified other factors, including the six that are summarized in Figure 2.12.

Selected Sociological Factors That Can Cause Social Change

Factor	Example Theory	According to
Geography	Capitalism developed in northwest Europe because river systems led to the development of independent city-states and the growth of a strong merchant class.	Max Weber, 1930, *The Protestant Ethic and the Spirit of Capitalism* (New York: Charles Scribner's Sons).
External events	The growth of industrialism in Europe occurred after Europeans sailed across the Atlantic. Europeans used their colonies in North and South America as a source of raw materials and as a market for manufactured products.	Karl Marx, [1867] 1967, *Capital: A Critique of Political Economy* (New York: International Publishers).
Human factors	The American Revolution succeeded in the 1770s because, although the British should have won the war, their commanders were divided. The American commanders were united.	S.E. Morrison and H.S. Commager, [1930] 1962, *The Growth of the American Republic,* Vol. 1 (New York: Oxford University Press).
Cultural pluralism	In modern, culturally **pluralistic societies** (societies in which minorities maintain their cultural traditions), it is necessary to find consensus on basic values and beliefs in order to find a collective will to take action on social issues.	R. Bibby, 1990, *Mosaic Madness* (Toronto: Stoddart).
Technology	The creation of Canada in 1867 and the spread of European immigrants throughout Canada would not have been possible without the availability of railways.	D. Chirot, [1994] 2000, *How Societies Change* (Thousand Oaks, CA: Pine Forge Press).
Aboriginal communities	To understand the type of social change that Aboriginal communities in Canada would like to see, we must appreciate that they see themselves as autonomous nations within the Canadian state, not as ethnic groups within Canada.	James Frideres, 1988, *Native Peoples in Canada: Contemporary Conflicts* (Scarborough, ON: Prentice-Hall Canada).

Figure 2.12 Social change occurs as the result of innumerable interacting factors. Can you think of a single social change that resulted from only one influencing factor?

Leading Early Sociologists

Immanuel Wallerstein

Sociologist Immanuel Wallerstein has written much about the nature of international trade and economics. He is director of the Fernand Braudel Center at Binghamton University in New York State.

Economists and historians have long pondered the reasons why there are relatively few industrialized and rich nations in the world, and a much larger number of non-industrialized nations in which average living standards are low. At one point, many economists believed some countries remained poor because of the local conditions, including deficiencies in the quality and energy of **elite groups**. (Elite groups are skilled and educated people who have access to development funds, and who are in a position of influence.) Many historians concluded that the situation stemmed from the time period in which European nations colonized and exploited the other regions of the world. Colonies supplied cheap raw materials, which were manufactured into finished products in the colonizing countries and sold on world markets. The bulk of the wealth from this exchange accumulated in industrialized nations, while the colonies remained relatively poor. Even after the colonial empires broke up after World War II, this pattern of trade remained, with the industrialized West becoming far richer than other regions.

Wallerstein's 1974 work, *The Modern World-System*, challenges the idea that many regions remained poor because of a lack of effective leadership. Wallerstein also challenges the idea outlined above that Europe and the West became rich because of colonialism. He claims that, instead, capitalism predated European colonialism. It would have made the West rich even if colonialism had not existed, although the pace and direction of the process would have been different.

Wallerstein states that the causes of the West's success lie in the nature of **capitalism**, an economic system dependent on private investment and profit-making. Western nations that did not have extensive colonial holdings, such as Sweden, still became rich. Why was this so? Wallerstein believes it benefited because of its location, which happened to be at the **core** of the capitalist system, at the centre of international trade. This country had access to and could participate in banking, finance, and industrial production, so it flourished. Conversely, the sources of raw materials, the colonial countries, experienced little investment in important capitalist functions. As a result, these regions could only supply the most basic economic facilities, and the local populations remained poor. Wallerstein calls these regions that are far from the capitalist core the **periphery**. He writes of one additional region, which he calls the **semi-periphery**. This includes nations such as Mexico and Brazil, originally described as peripheral nations. Over time, however, these countries developed enough capitalist functions to be reclassified.

Wallerstein has been criticized for developing a model that is rigid, and that implies that there is little individual nations can do over the course of even a couple of generations to improve their economic status. Only two outcomes are possible, Wallerstein argues. An individual nation can move from one classification to another over time, or the entire world trade system can be destroyed and replaced by another structure.

The debate about Wallerstein's findings is important to international development specialists. Is it possible for a nation to become rich by adopting a unique path to growth? If world trade is becoming increasingly globalized, can the benefits be shared more widely than in the past? Writers like Wallerstein and his critics are important in setting the background for the debate about the relationship between capitalism and colonialism.

GROUNDBREAKERS

THELMA McCORMACK

Thelma McCormack, a professor of sociology at York University in Toronto, is a leading figure in Canadian sociological circles. McCormack's main field of interest is feminist studies. She believes that major social change cannot be achieved unless society re-evaluates its position on many of the issues that are important to women.

Some of Thelma McCormack's research has been devoted to the way in which women vote in the political system. Her 1975 article "Towards a Non-sexist Perspective on Social and Political Change" disproved (proved wrong) the stereotype that women tend to vote as a block. It is true, she noted, that women and men as groups show different voting patterns. The

Figure 2.13 Sociologist Thelma McCormack

difference comes about, however, because women have been differently socialized and do not have the same opportunities to participate in politics as men do.

Sociologists use the term **"private sphere"** to describe the parts of our lives that are generally out of the public light. These include matters such as our religion, our families, and our domestic lives. McCormack notes that, historically, women have been more firmly rooted in the private sphere than men, because women's family roles have demanded so much time. In her 1991 paper, *Politics and the Hidden Injuries of Gender*, she argues that this reality has impeded the progress of women in public life. The compensation, she continues, is that women have been able to develop a distinct perspective on society. Women tend to be more liberal than men in deciding what social policies to institute, and less inclined to use

force to get their opponents to comply. Indeed, modern elections are often characterized by a "gender gap," in which a majority of men support more conservative candidates and a majority of women support more liberal ones.

Another issue that McCormack has investigated is the impact of media violence on everyday life. Laboratory experiments with young children have tended to show that television violence increases real-life violence no matter how the results are classified—by age, gender, social background, or personality type. McCormack's 1994 paper, "Codes, Ratings, and Rights," cast doubt on such experiments. McCormack believes that it is impossible to duplicate in a laboratory experiment the real conditions under which children normally watch television. Further, it seems that children begin to distinguish between what is real and what is make-believe around the age of five. McCormack concluded that the link between fake violence on television and real violence in children's lives is not straightforward.

Questions

1. What are two areas of special interest for Thelma McCormack?

2. Describe the ways that men and women vote differently. How does McCormack explain these patterns?

3. What conclusions does she reach about media violence and everyday violence?

W.E.B. Du Bois (1868–1963)

William Edward Burghart Du Bois, born in Massachusetts, US, was a gifted historian and sociologist. By the time he obtained his Ph.D. from Harvard in 1895 (he was the first African-American to do so), he had devoted his research efforts to the historical background and sociological conditions of African-Americans.

Among other achievements, he helped found the National Association for the Advancement of Colored People (NAACP) in 1909. Du Bois wrote 20 books, including *Africa—Its Place in History* (1930) and *The*

Figure 2.14 Du Bois, at centre, challenged other African-American leaders to cease compromising with governments and become tougher in their struggle to advance the rights of their people. His efforts helped African Americans claim their civil rights.

Worlds of Color (1961). He contributed enormously to social science by showing that academics need to adopt a broad focus and examine the experiences of all peoples. A victim of prejudice himself, he showed its destructive impact on other African-Americans.

Dorothy Smith

Dorothy Smith is a sociologist and a specialist in communication patterns and the technologies on which they rely.

It has been known for a long time that people tend to communicate best when they are with individuals or groups with whom they share a common interest and outlook. Smith has observed the major differences that exist in the way we communicate, depending on the group we are with. In particular, she has studied the importance of **discourses**, the topics and the ways of exchanging information about them that are used by groups of people with common interests. Members of each group understand the meaning of the terms commonly used within their group. They share a strong interest in certain subjects and

like to exchange opinions about them. For example, the discourse of financial analysts includes exchanges about price/earnings ratios. Baseball fans discuss RBIs (runs batted in), and feminist sociologists write about inclusion and the patriarchy.

It is the discourse on gender that interests Smith the most. In her 1990 book, *Texts, Facts, and Femininity*, she argues that the effects of certain discourses have limited women's position in society. Images such as the traditional Hollywood image of females as beautiful, vulnerable, and available, contribute to a discourse that tells women they are incomplete without a husband. To achieve social change for women, Smith argues, it is necessary to understand and counteract discourses that limit women's choices in life.

Many of the discourses in which we participate, including the ones described in the previous paragraph, are not conducted face to face. In most discourses, people communicate ideas and values through symbols such as written words, movie roles, paintings, and photographs. Smith has coined the term **"textual discourse"** to describe these. Because discourses play an important part in our lives by influencing the way we think and act, Smith believes we must take them into consideration when trying to engineer social change.

You can see that the social sciences generally, and sociology in particular, abound with theories about social change. Some theories focus on its causes. Other theories focus on the factors that make people receptive or resistant to change. Still others look at the effects of social change and how they can be managed for the general benefit of the community. Because change seems to be prevalent in virtually all communities in the twenty-first century, we can expect that even more social scientists will be developing new theories about social change to try to explain the processes that will take us into the future.

Pause and Reflect

1. How does the rising wealth of some families and the cheaper television technology that developed after 1950 illustrate the sociological theory of social change through accumulation?

2. Define "diffusion of innovations." Identify three examples (not in the text) of innovations that have come and gone in Canadian society. What factors led to the adoption and disappearance of these innovations?

3. Select five factors that may cause or influence social change according to sociologists. Which one do you think will affect your life most? Why?

4. In a comparison organizer, summarize the main theories of the sociologists featured in this section, and show the similarities and differences in the sociologists' work.

5. So far, what social science interests you most? In a paragraph, clearly explain your choice.

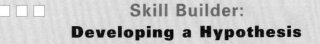

Skill Builder:
Developing a Hypothesis

Before you can begin systematic senior-level research, you have to have a working hypothesis. Whether you're a first-year undergraduate or a senior social scientist, you must be able to write a hypothesis. This feature will lead you through the steps you need to take to develop a working hypothesis of your own.

First, we need a good definition of the term. A hypothesis may be defined as "a proposition or principle put forth or stated merely as a basis for reasonable argument, or as a premise from which to draw a conclusion" (*Shorter Oxford English Dictionary*, Vol. 1, 1991, p. 1010). In other words, you don't have to be certain that your hypothesis is correct. Instead, think of it as a statement you want to prove true. After you have begun your research and learned more about the subject, you may well modify your hypothesis.

A good hypothesis will aid you in your academic research because it helps provide focus as you begin your inquiry.

Step One: Do your preliminary review

Let us suppose you have chosen to write a hypothesis about a topic covered in this chapter. Your preliminary review would consist of reading through the chapter.

Step Two: Write your hypothesis

What you write might look like one of the items below, all of which are based on information contained in this chapter. Look them over and note the characteristics that are common to all of them.

a) Cultural change is caused by a limited number of factors, and it is possible to identify which factor is most significant at any particular time.

b) Social change occurs as a result of the phenomenon of continuous progress, with each new society building on the experiences of its predecessors.

c) Positive behaviour-modification programs are more effective than negative behaviour-modification programs.

d) To win greater influence in society, women must rely on themselves to break the patriarchy.

e) The reductionist theories of Karl Marx cannot correctly explain social change because there are such vast differences among human societies.

Check each example to see which of the following criteria apply to *all* of the above examples.

i. It is written in the form of a concise statement.

ii. It reflects a position being taken by the writer.

iii. It is arguable, and a contrary position can be taken.

iv. It requires research to determine whether or not it is true.

v. It is a significant matter to social scientists.

vi. It is a complex notion, dealing with a number of variables.

vii. It is not written in the first person.

viii. It can be tested.

Step Three: Check your hypothesis
Before you finally settle on your hypothesis, check it against the characteristics of hypotheses, as listed above, to see if it meets all the criteria required of a hypothesis. Try it out—Which of the examples below contain all the characteristics listed in Step Two? What's wrong with the ones that don't?

a) Unless international aid programs respect the cultural traditions of the recipient nations, they are destined to fail in their attempts to create social change by building infrastructure.

b) If a person is displaying a harmful behaviour or attitude, are trusted friends and respected figures most likely to succeed in assisting the person to change his or her behaviour?

c) Cultures are always changing, and within that process, invention, discovery, and diffusion are the most important sources of cultural change.

d) So-called reality TV programs, like *Survivor*, are the most interesting and exciting form of entertainment available.

e) The social changes experienced by the San are typical of those experienced by Aboriginal hunter-gatherer societies when they encounter industrialized, expansionist societies.

Practise It!
To practise writing hypotheses, try writing two based on the material in this chapter. Following Step One, look through the chapter to review the material that is presented. Following Step Two, create two hypotheses that contain all the correct characteristics listed there. For Step Three, work with a partner. Together, examine the examples that each of you has created. Do they contain all the characteristics of a hypothesis? Would each hypothesis provide you with a framework as you began your research, assuming that this was your topic? Modify your hypotheses where necessary.

▶ ▶ ▶ Chapter Activities

Show Your Knowledge

1. a) Add to your glossary of new vocabulary by defining or explaining the terms and key phrases you learned in this chapter.

    b) Use these terms to create four questions to ask a classmate. Make each question more difficult than the previous one. Follow the four categories used for these activities (Show Your Knowledge, Practise Your Thinking Skills, Communicate Your Ideas, and Apply Your Knowledge).

2. How do social scientists define the term "social change"? Create an organizer to list and compare the questions about social change asked by (a) anthropologists, (b) psychologists, and (c) sociologists.

3. Identify five different areas of study relating to social change to show the diverse nature of social scientists' investigations in this area. What is the special focus of (a) anthropology, (b) psychology, and (c) sociology?

4. What do the following theories state? (a) acculturation, (b) behaviour modification, and (c) diffusion of innovations. How does each one illustrate the focus of the discipline from which it comes?

Practise Your Thinking

5. Make a list of 10 questions relating to social changes that you can reasonably expect will occur during your lifetime. (Example: Will family ties grow stronger or weaker?) Beside each question, write an A, P, or S to indicate which social science discipline would be most likely to ask this question. (You may have to write down more than one letter for some questions.) Explain your choices.

6. Look at Section 2.1. Which of the three disciplines focuses on those aspects of social change that you find the most interesting? Why do you find those aspects so interesting?

7. In which discipline—anthropology, psychology, or sociology—do you think the theories about social change show the most variety in explaining human behaviour? Explain your answer.

8. After reading the Focusing on the Issues feature on page 39, create your own 10 commandments for social change.

Communicate Your Ideas

9. Ask someone from your parents' generation to identify five of the most significant social changes that have taken place since he or she was a teenager. Take some time to decide on the focus that each social science discipline would adopt in trying to study or explain these changes. Communicate these ideas to your informant. Does your informant find these explanations convincing? Why or why not?

10. Work with two classmates. Each of you chooses one of the social science disciplines. Imagine that you are participating in a panel discussion to explain how and why your generation is different from your parents' generation. Role-play what a representative of each discipline might say. Which discipline has the most plausible explanation? Why?

11. Pick one theory of social change described in Sections 2.2 to 2.4. Do some additional research about the theory, and explain it in some detail to classmates in a small group. Explain why you chose the theory you did, and state whether you find it convincing, giving your reasons.

12. Pick one of the practitioners described in this chapter whose theories and findings interest you. You don't have to agree with the findings. Write a letter to this person stating why you agree or disagree with his or her theories and findings. If there is another practitioner, not mentioned in this text, whose work interests you, write to him or her instead. Discuss your letter with a classmate. Does your classmate agree or disagree with what you wrote in the letter? Explain. (Note: You are not expected to mail this letter.)

Apply Your Knowledge

13. Research the social conditions in Canada a century ago. Identify five major social changes that have taken place since that time. Explain these changes from the perspective of one of anthropology, psychology, or sociology.

14. Some jobs or professions can be performed better if the holder has academic knowledge in a particular field. For example, a museum curator would do well to have a degree in anthropology. For each of anthropology, psychology, and sociology, pick one job or profession that could be performed better with the benefit of expertise in the discipline. How and why does knowledge of the particular discipline result in better job performance?

15. Identify a social change taking place in Canada today.
    a) What are some of the questions that each social science discipline would ask about it?
    b) Which discipline's questions do you think would lead to the best explanation of the change? Why?

16. The Focus on the Issues feature on page 39 provides 10 strategies for changing the world through social activism. Choose one strategy that you think would be effective. Describe how you would use it to support a cause that you feel strongly about. Then do so.

CHAPTER 3

FORCES THAT INFLUENCE SOCIAL CHANGE

INTRODUCTION

Social change occurs in a multitude of different ways and at different rates. What are the conditions required for social change, both positive and negative, to occur? How does our position within society affect how we influence social change as individuals? How do the values we hold as a society influence the change? In this chapter, we will examine all of these questions, looking specifically at examples within Canadian society.

Certified nurse-midwife Becky Bruns looks over six-seek-old Trevin, whom she helped bring into the world. Midwifery became legal in Ontario in 1993, and is now funded by the provincial government. Now any woman can have a midwife provide care for her during a pregnancy. What forces do you think drove this change?

■ Learning Expectations

By the end of this chapter, you will be able to

- identify conditions for change, and impediments to change, as revealed in studies of anthropology, psychology, or sociology
- explain the relationship among conformity, alienation, and social change
- demonstrate an understanding of how social change is influenced by poverty and affluence
- explain the impact of evolving roles of individuals or groups and values on social change in Canada

Focusing on the Issues

Social change very slow in Qatar, a small Islamic country

A social transition is clearly underway in Qatar [east of Saudi Arabia], where strict allegiance to the fundamentalist Wahabi Muslim faith and to local custom has for centuries required that women be largely invisible outside the home. As many as 30 per cent of Qatari women now work, local officials say. Some of them drive cars of their own, although they must prove that they have a need to do so....

Qatar's undersecretary of education is a woman, the first to hold a prominent government position. More firsts are expected later this year, when women have been promised a right to vote in the country's first municipal elections. About 6000 Qatari women graduate each year from the University of Qatar, which educates 90 per cent of female high-school graduates, and more and more of them are going on to work, even side by side with men, something that until recently was widely regarded as un-Islamic....

But in the Middle East, Qatar still probably ranks behind only Saudi Arabia in the limits it imposes on what women may do or wear. Most marriages are still arranged, with most social contact between unrelated men and women forbidden under unwritten codes of conduct.

The university is strictly segregated, and it became clear during the group discussion...that change has become a source of confusion and debate among women as well as men....

Under its new Emir, Hamad bin Khalifa al-Thani, who took power two years ago, Qatar is rushing to reshape itself, and one of the Emir's three wives, Sheika Moza hint Nasser al-Misned, has already begun to assume a persona of her own, even as the other two remain virtually invisible. But both the country's leaders and its people are plainly determined to balance the modern with the traditional....

Working and studying is not forbidden by Islam, but going to mixed parties and having contact with foreign men cannot be done. Most women nevertheless made [it] clear [that] they yearn to play a more prominent role in Qatar society.

Those in their 20s said they would not tolerate being one among several wives, even though Islamic law permits men to have as many as four wives. All expressed relief that a woman's right to refuse a marriage proposal is now widely accepted, something they said was not true five years ago....

In the course of the discussion, each of the women...said [she was] concerned by a trend toward Islamic orthodoxy that all agreed has left their brothers more conservative in their views than their fathers.

Source: *The New York Times*. 20 July 1997. Quoted from *Women's International Network News*. Autumn 1997, Vol. 23, Issue 4. Copyright © 1997. The New York Times Company.

THINK ABOUT IT

1. What evidence is presented to suggest that women are expected to play a traditional role in Qatar? What changes have some women made to the roles that they are expected to play?

2. What factors are (a) mentioned, and (b) not mentioned in the extract that might inhibit Qatari society's acceptance of a less traditional role for women? What factors are encouraging change?

3. Social change can be considered positive or negative depending on your point of view. The women interviewed in this article tended to welcome recent changes. What might be the opinion of more traditionally minded men and women?

4. Think of an example of social change that has taken place within Canadian society that some people welcome and others oppose.

Section 3.1   Conditions for and Impediments to Social Change

Key Concepts

charisma, charismatic

value-free

modernizing elite

everyday forms of peasant resistance

worldview

modernity

traditional worldview

participatory research

advocacy research

Margaret Mead wrote that everyone over the age of 40 is an immigrant. What she meant by that was that all people over 40 find themselves living in a society that is different from the one in which they grew up. They may have moved to a new street, city, or continent, or they may still live in the house in which they were born. All are immigrants. The society that they knew as children—complete with its beliefs, values, and symbols—no longer exists. Mead concluded that all human beings have to adapt to the social changes that take place after childhood, just as immigrants do when they move to a new country.

Perhaps nowhere in the world has social change taken place so rapidly as in China. Consider the following 1998 report from the American magazine Newsweek.

In 1980 proper wedding attire consisted of his-and-hers army greatcoats; today it is white lace, accompanied by wedding consultants and mobile phones. Many educated city dwellers are now firmly plugged into

the global village. In a roomful of Chinese university students…, I discover that the only person who has not seen the movie "Titanic" is me. Western culture has long seeped into the big cities. At a nightclub in Beijing, I listen to a Hungarian jazz band and chat up the proprietor, a former Chinese Army officer who happens to be the first prominent mainlander to have undergone a sex-change operation.
(Liu and Macleod, 1998, p. 40)

Of course, a majority of Chinese citizens do not enjoy the standard of living that would pay for the gadgets, fashions, and entertainments mentioned in this article. Nonetheless, life for millions of Chinese city dwellers has changed drastically. In Canada, we also experience social change, but generally not at such a fast pace. Examples might be the massive shifts in public opinion regarding smoking, domestic violence, and equal rights for gays and lesbians. The amount of social change that took place in China over the past 20 years, however, was far more extensive. And it raises the question, What are the factors that lead to such massive social changes?

Conditions for Social Change

Some societies experience greater social change than others. In some countries, social institutions, such as a monarchy, enjoy great reverence among the population. In other nations, social institutions have lost both their popular support and their stabilizing influence on society. In such nations, popular opinion can change suddenly, with great swings in prevailing ideas.

Between these two extremes come nations like Canada. Social institutions hold a fair degree of respect as long as they fulfill the

Figure 3.1 A mass wedding in Beijing, 1999. Just 20 years ago, a sight like this would have been unthinkable in China. Instead of being considered decadent and foreign, Western white wedding dresses are now considered quite chic.

needs of most people, and the institutions themselves recognize that they must change over time as conditions and prevailing popular opinions change. The monarchy, for example, enjoys much support in Canada, although its direct impact on Canadian life is limited.

Social change itself can be positive or negative, depending on your perspective. For example, government cutbacks that reduce social services and reduce taxes will be seen by some as positive and by others as negative. Some would see the government's policies as impediments to social change because they would be eliminating what many consider to be progressive social programs. Others would view the government's policies as conditions suitable for encouraging social change because, in their view, it would encourage a better business environment.

Leadership

Sociologist Max Weber identified one of the most important components of social change: the emergence of a leader with **charisma**. Originally, this term had an exclusively religious meaning. Christians used the term "**charismatic**" to describe a person who was inspired by the Holy Spirit and chosen by God to act as a leader. Weber broadened the meaning of the term and incorporated it into the language of sociology. According to Weber, such a leader is characterized by large vision, magnetic style, and strong popular support, and has aspects of extraordinary, superhuman, and supernatural character.

A charismatic leader places great demands on his or her followers, promises them rewards for their support, yet maintains a distance between the leader and the led. Mao Zedong, the leader of the Chinese communist revolution, is a perfect example of a charismatic leader. He demanded that party members follow the difficult path of communism, giving up ownership of personal goods and businesses to the state. Mao promised the benefits of a communist life, including freedom from

poverty and exploitation. He maintained a distance between himself and the people by allowing them to glorify his image and to view his writings as the pinnacle of wisdom.

It is important to remember that social scientists who speak of charismatic leaders are trying to engage in **value-free** inquiry. By according a leader this status, they are not stating their support or even admiration for the person. Instead, they are making a statement about the leader's ability to sway people and change society, be it for good or ill.

Let us consider a charismatic leader who is universally regarded as changing society for ill. Adolf Hitler is a good example of the phenomenon of charisma because he swayed

Figure 3.2 Through the force of his personality and vision, Pierre Elliott Trudeau inspired Canadians with a vision of their country as a great nation. How did he effect social change?

the people of his country by virtue of his vision and personality. Hitler briefly imposed massive social change on Germany and most of Europe. Yet there is no doubt that he committed atrocities. To a certain extent, the influence of some leaders can be credited to their military power.

Charismatic leaders may be people of whom we approve or disapprove. What they have in common is that they personally affect the course of history and are remembered for centuries after their deaths.

The Role of Elites

On many occasions in the life of a society, no single charismatic leader appears. This does not mean, however, that the process of

Figure 3.3 The media, especially television, can create significant changes in social attitudes. Government advertisements against driving while intoxicated, like the billboard ad shown here, have done much to change public opinion on this topic. Think of another example of the media affecting social values.

change stops. Change itself does not necessarily follow a single pattern, for there are many ways in which it can come about. In most societies, there exists what sociologist Samuel N. Eisenstadt calls one or more "**modernizing elites**" (Eisenstadt, 1973, p. 33). These are groups of people who create significant social change and influence the direction in which it goes. Social changes in Saudi Arabia, for example, have developed through the efforts of an elite political group of princes (sheiks), with the assistance of increasing wealth from oil reserves. It is important to remember that social change is usually achieved through the interplay of the various modernizing elites, and not a single charismatic leader.

A Populace Ready for Change

We have seen that a charismatic leader has the potential to redirect a society down a particular path. Let's look at the flip side of the coin. If a population is not ready for the kind of social change the leader proposes, nothing will happen. For this relationship to work, the vision has to match the "mood" of the public. Otherwise, no one will listen, and the potential leader will be quickly forgotten.

What makes a public ready for certain types of change? As you have already learned, one of the topics that social psychologists study is how humans form and change their attitudes over time. A number of longitudinal studies (see Chapter 2) have been performed to discover when people's basic attitudes are formed and what factors make them supportive of, or hostile to, social change.

Theodore M. Newcomb began one of the earliest studies in the mid-1930s (Edelson, 1992, p. 12). He questioned 500 women at Bennington College, a liberal college in Vermont, about their political and social views. These young women would have been taught about liberal values such as a belief in the need for a significant role for government in matters of social welfare and social justice. Newcomb discovered that the liberal environment at Bennington moved the students' values toward a belief in the responsibility of government and society generally to care for the less fortunate.

Would the women lose their liberal views as they became older? Newcomb surveyed them again in 1961. They were now in their mid- to late forties, but their liberal values seemed intact. In 1984, a study was done of the surviving students, who were by then around the age of 70. The research team found that, if anything, the women were more liberal in their views than they had been in middle age, or even in their youth. In each of the three survey years, almost 70 per cent of the women reported that they considered themselves to be liberals, and a greater proportion of this group were politically active compared to their peer group throughout the United States.

What is intriguing about the Bennington studies is that they indicate that values acquired early in life may stay with us throughout our lives. If the values we learn in our adolescence and early adulthood are likely to stick with us throughout our lives, will the climate of debate in schools, colleges, universities, and workplaces eventually form the core of the political landscape? If so, then perhaps we can predict future social attitudes based on our observations of the present.

Impediments to Change

Traditional Cultural Values

Anthropologists who have studied the factors underlying social change have reached similar conclusions to those of sociologists. Their emphasis on culture, however, has allowed them to achieve some different insights. Much research has been undertaken into the impact of changing environmental or technical conditions on peoples and their cultures.

James Scott participant-observed an agricultural community in Malaysia, which he called Sedaka. (Its true identity was never revealed.) He observed that the poor labourers employed on the rice farms were kept in place by routine repression (Scott, 1985, p. 274).

In the late 1970s, the rich owners of the rice farms wanted to create a social change that would benefit them. Specifically, they wanted to introduce mechanical rice harvesters, a technology that would lower their labour expenses. The labourers, of course, were unhappy about this proposal because it would throw many of them out of work. In the climate of repression, how could the labourers slow this change that would make the rich richer but take away the labourers' livelihood?

Armed rebellion was clearly out of the question because the government, police, and army would have suppressed it ruthlessly. The labourers instead developed what Scott called **everyday forms of peasant resistance**, which included such things as desertion, sabotage, theft, slow working, etc. Both sides were, in anthropological terms, constructing their own **worldview**, or picture of reality. The rich were pushing the idea of **modernity**, the notion that all social change is inevitable and of benefit because it leads to an improved society. They suggested that the new technology was more efficient, easier on the land, and able to raise Malaysian international competitiveness, which would lead to increased wealth for the nation. The labourers constructed an alternative, **traditional worldview**, pushing an adherence to old practices, particularly those of charity and consideration for the poor. They argued that their ability to find work, however poorly paid, was key to their economic and cultural survival. They claimed that the machines might produce bigger harvests at first, but that they would damage the rice paddies in the long run.

The clash of the two worldviews took place at the local level. The farm owners were supported by international agricultural equipment manufacturers and banks, which would make the harvesters and finance their sale. But the local Malaysian rice farmers were rooted in their culture and were ultimately unable to suspend their cultural training that taught them that they had traditional obligations to the poor. Compromise and locally engineered solutions to the dilemma were developed. In the end, some mechanical processes were introduced, and many labourers kept their employment but were assigned different jobs. The factors that were being used to push social change (modernity) and those that were being used to resist it (traditional values), in this example, were balanced in a solution that appeared to benefit—or at least avoid harming—most of society.

The Expense

Other factors can act to slow social change. In Canada, much social change has been engineered by governments that have responded to the pressure of societal values and demands. A great deal of taxpayers' money has been invested in programs to achieve particular social goals. The introduction of government health plans across the nation in the 1960s, for example, was designed to ensure that all Canadians had access to medical care. The introduction in 2001 of up to one full year's parental leave from work, with payments from Canada's employment insurance program, is another.

Such programs are costly, however, and the demand for new programs to target other social problems outstrips the ability or willingness of governments to support them all. Ultimately, it is the taxpayer who is paying the bill, and the government can only offer as many programs as the taxpayer is able to finance. Many social programs, such as a national childcare system, have not gone forward, primarily because of the expenses involved.

Social Science Inquiry

Another important factor that can be either a support or impediment to social change is the nature of the social science inquiry itself. For example, sociologists sometimes use a method, known as **participatory research**, to produce knowledge to help stimulate social change and to empower an oppressed group. The subject group itself participates in deciding what the goals and methods of the study should be, and how the findings should be used. Groups such as sewing-machine operators who work out of their homes, stitching together clothing at piece rates, can make good subjects for participatory research.

Participatory research may not work, however, with severely marginalized groups such as illegal immigrants. Many illegal immigrants are illiterate, do not speak the same language as the researcher, are scattered geographically, and are busy trying to put food on the table.

As a result of the limitations of participatory research, a slightly different form of research began to develop in the 1980s, known as **advocacy research**. It also aims to highlight and change social inequality, but it does not require that the subject group participate to the same degree. Whereas participatory research integrates the subjects into the research process to identify and publicize the social changes that they require, advocacy research assumes that these functions will remain with the researcher, who becomes the advocate.

In the case study on page 75, sociologist Pierrette Hondagneu-Sotelo at the University of California at Los Angeles (UCLA) describes her advocacy research in a community of illegal immigrant women from Mexico living in the Los Angeles area.

It is important to remember that the pace of social change is not constant. Some periods, such as the 1960s for example, have produced massive social upheaval in Canada. Other decades, such as the 1980s, produced less far-reaching social change.

Why Advocacy Research?

Sociologist Pierrette Hondagneu-Sotelo wrote an article for the journal *American Sociologist* to explain why advocacy research may work better than participatory research in some communities. Social scientists regularly submit articles about their work to journals dedicated to their field of study. This allows them to communicate with their colleagues, who are scattered all over the world, and to learn about the work of other social scientists.

In the following excerpt from the article, Hondagneu-Sotelo introduces the subject group of her research project, the problems that would have emerged had she attempted participatory research, and the benefits of the advocacy research she did employ. Here are definitions for some of the more difficult terms she uses:

premise: opening assumption
collaborative research: research in which two or more social scientists work together on a project
subcontracted domestic work: an employment situation in which the domestic worker (usually a cleaner) hired to do a job pays another domestic worker (the subcontractor) to do the work
benign: harmless
altruism: unselfishness
stipend: a fixed payment
consciousness raising: increasing awareness
outreach materials: pamphlets and other materials produced to educate, advise, or contact members of a community

Reflections on Research and Activism with Immigrant Women

Participatory research begins with the *premise* that *collaborative research* projects must collect data that will later be useful in promoting social change, but it is difficult to know in advance what exactly will be useful. The example of *subcontracted domestic* work illustrates my inability to foresee how research findings might be useful at some later date. Since securing the initial domestic work job is difficult, many newly arrived immigrant women first find themselves subcontracting their services to other more experienced and well-established immigrant women who have steady customers for their services. While subcontracting arrangements can be beneficial to both parties—as the more *benign* case presented in the movie "El Norte" suggests—the relationship is not characterized by *altruism* or harmony of interests. In an apprentice/subcontracting arrangement the pay can be so low as to render a very exploitative and demeaning experience. One woman related having taken a job as a "helper" to an

Figure 3.4 Many immigrants who come to the United States illegally must work as subcontracted domestic workers because they do not have work permits. Many other immigrants, such as the hotel maid shown above, came to the United States legally and could therefore find jobs with better conditions. Why would this group be better able to avoid exploitation?

acquaintance. After working seven hours cleaning on one of the hottest days of the year, she received only 25 dollars, an amount reflecting less than four dollars an hour pay; other women stayed in this type of work arrangement for months and received only a small *stipend* or the promise of later being passed their own list of clients.

As I listened to these accounts of abuse and exploitation that occur among paid [subcontracted] domestic workers, I was struck by the inequality within the occupation, but I did not see this observation as particularly useful in changing this arrangement. I did not envision a forum where newly arrived undocumented immigrant women could be alerted to these types of abuses. As I look back now, I believe that if I had just entered the field determined to quickly amass data to be harnessed in the service of social change [which is the process of participatory research], I probably would have implemented methods—perhaps a survey questionnaire or structured interviews—that would not capture the arrangements that occur in subcontracted relations among paid domestic workers.

Ideally, political action and the transformation of existing power structures and economic inequities constitute a vital part of participatory research. But...many [participatory research] projects succeed only in *consciousness raising*, changing the behaviour of individuals, or solidifying community networks, but not altering the structures of established institutions [such as the standard relationship between contractors and subcontractors]. There are many practical obstacles to the implementation of political action.... Among them is the researcher's exit from the community once the data is collected.

In my case, I left the community of research in May 1988. The political action in which I used the research findings occurred in another city, Los Angeles, when I joined a group specifically designed to improve the working conditions for Latina immigrant domestic workers. When I began working with this group in Los Angeles, I told people who had initially participated in my study about the project, and later, after I had drafted the text for the some of the *outreach materials*, I solicited feedback on the text from some of the domestic workers. [Their] comments...were especially valuable, allowing me to recognize the significance of mobility within paid domestic work.

Source: Hondagneu-Sotelo, Pierrette. 1993. "Why advocacy research? Reflections on research and activism with immigrant women." *American Sociologist*, Vol. 24, Issue 1 (Spring 1993).

Hondagneu-Sotelo continued her work with various groups, thereby increasing her knowledge of the subject and becoming a better-informed advocate.

Questions

1. What are the major differences between participatory and advocacy research? (See page 74.)
2. What problems did Hondagneu-Sotelo identify in the use of participatory research?
3. In what way did she end up using the knowledge she gained from her study?
4. In your opinion, does Hondagneu-Sotelo's argue her case convincingly? Explain.

Pause and Reflect

1. What evidence did the Bennington study reveal to support Newcomb's hypothesis that our main social beliefs and values are laid down by the time we are young adults?

2. Make a table to list some conditions and impediments for social change. For each, give an example.

3. According to Weber, what are the three qualifications of a charismatic leader? From the following famous figures, choose one with whom you are familiar: Nellie McClung, John F. Kennedy, Osama bin Laden, Josef Stalin, Mahatma Gandhi, Joan of Arc, Pope John Paul II, Malcolm X, and Mother Teresa. Decide if your chosen figure is or was a charismatic leader, and justify your decision.

4. How did traditional values play a role in slowing social change in "Sedaka," Malaysia? Suggest a way that they play a similar role in your community.

5. Is social change always a good thing? Explain, using examples.

Section 3.2   Conformity and Alienation

Alienation

Adapting to change can be an extremely difficult process. Some people adapt quickly and well. Others do not fare so well and are left behind. The early sociologists, including Emile Durkheim (1859–1917) and Karl Marx (1818–1883), lived in a time of extensive change, as society adapted to urban life and industrial processes. They identified a social condition they observed among many in society who had difficulty adapting. Durkheim used the term "**anomie**" to describe the condition of the industrial workers who seemed to be without any roots or norms as they struggled daily to survive. Marx wrote about the **alienation** of the **proletariat** (or working people) and the **lumpenproletariat** (or unemployed people). They could not reach their full human potential, Marx believed, when so many aspects of their lives, such as their ability to find reasonably paid employment and decent housing, were controlled and exploited by others.

Since Marx's time, the definition of "alienation" has been broadened. The term is now applied to anyone who does not share the major values of society and feels like an outsider. The reasons for people's alienation vary, from discrimination that excludes a member of a visible minority from participating in society, to the general dissatisfaction of an unhappy teenager. Sometimes such people form groups such as gangs, or they join cults that reject society's values. A few even set about trying to destroy the society in which they live through armed struggle, hoping to build a purer society on the ruins of the old one. These extremely alienated individuals are known as **anarchists**. Such people are, of course, extremists in modern Canadian society. Most of us tend to feel alienated at some time from some aspects of our society. For example, during a period of unemployment, we might feel alienation toward a society that seems to value material wealth and professional success over other types of success. Alienation is a real factor in society.

Key Concepts

anomie

alienation

proletariat

lumpenproletariat

anarchist

subjective validity

informational influence

normative influence

 Conformity

Just as there are forces that drive us to reject society's values, there are pressures that encourage us to accept them. People tend to adopt the values of the society in which they live. The great majority of people in Canadian society have adopted fairly similar ways of thinking and acting. Even though we may disagree on which political party would do the best job of running the country, for example, most of us believe in the fundamentals of our political system, such as freedom of speech.

Similarly, virtually all people believe that their attitudes are right and proper, what social psychologists call having a **subjective validity**. Belonging to a group of people with similar views serves to reinforce this subjective validity, and that may be a key reason why we generally enjoy being among groups of like-minded people. Without subjective validity, most of us would experience uncertainty, a feeling that most people do not welcome.

Roots of Conformity

The pressures to conform to society's norms come in a number of forms. M. Deutsch and H.B. Gerrard (1955) identified two types. **Informational influence** is the human desire to accept information that another, admired person tells us is valid. Our parents may tell us that smoking is bad for us, and our teachers may tell us that working too many hours at our part-time jobs will affect our marks. Especially as our own uncertainty increases on a given subject, the pressure of this influence can become irresistible. **Normative influence** is the pressure to conform to the positive expectations of others. Some people take the same job as one or both of their parents because it has always been expected that they would, even if the topic has never been fully discussed in explicit terms.

CASE STUDY

Investigating the Desire to Conform

Psychologist Stanley Milgram designed an experiment to gauge people's reactions when the normal social rules for lineups and subway ridership are broken. He arranged for a number of accomplices to barge into lineups at ticket offices, bank machines, and similar locations in New York City. Alone, or working with a colleague, each researcher would push into the lineup, saying "Excuse me, I'd like to get in here." In a related experiment, clearly able-bodied researchers approached people seated in crowded subway trains and simply asked them if they would give up their seats, as the researchers said they wanted to sit down. In both experiments, the researchers were clearly not conforming to the expected norms of behaviour. How would the people in the lineups and on the subways react? Among the many results of the experiments, Milgram found out the following:

Figure 3.5 What would you do if an able-bodied youth asked you for your seat on the subway?

- Lineup members defended the normal rules less than 50 per cent of the time.
- They were generally unwilling to go beyond icy stares and mild grumbling to indicate their displeasure with the researchers' behaviour.
- People farther back in the line were more likely to indicate hostility than those immediately behind the intruders.
- Close to 50 per cent of subway riders gave up their seats, perhaps because they were simply surprised and confounded by the requests.
- Many of the researchers were unable to approach someone and request their seat, because violating the norms of subway ridership proved too stressful. They were unable to overcome the pressures to conform to normal behaviour.

This experiment helps us understand that people can become very uncertain when normal behaviours are suspended. We conform to certain unwritten rules in society, and we take it for granted that everyone else does, too. So when these rules are broken, to what do we then conform? Do we vigorously defend the established norms of lineups or subways, or do we obey the unwritten rule that we should not get into arguments with strangers? Clearly, whichever route the violated people chose, they experienced great discomfort.

Questions

1. What does Milgram's experiment tell us about (a) the human desire to conform, and (b) conventional behaviour?
2. Why would the people farther back in the lineup be more vocal than the people immediately behind the researcher who butted into line?
3. What is the purpose of the unwritten rules of social behaviour? What would society be like without these conventions?

Alienation and Conformity as Forces of Social Change

We can conclude that the pressures of alienation and conformity are built into the society around us. How these pressures play themselves out in a society in which social change is evolving is complex. Alienation can be so severe that people simply give up, and accept life in the margins of society, in crime or dire poverty. Instances of teenage suicide and substance abuse can frequently be explained in terms of alienation.

On the other hand, alienation can be an extremely positive force, spurring reformers into action. Women in the 1960s and earlier experienced significant alienation from society because of the prevailing social attitudes about women and their role. This alienation led some individuals to struggle to challenge the status quo. These individuals became the leaders of the women's movement—they fought for and achieved legal, financial, and political reforms to benefit women. Their alienation was a powerful motivator to change the nature of society.

Conformity generally has a tendency to discourage social change. The desire to conform can act like inertia—people tend to do the same thing the same way year after year, and resist the temptation to do things differently. Think, for example, of the day someone comes to school wearing a new style of jacket. At first, we're a little nervous; the fashion looks a little odd; we don't change our habits. Perhaps a little later, after a handful of other people start wearing similar jackets, we decide we like the new look and finally head out to the store to find the same type of jacket for ourselves. It can take a lot for us to overcome our desire to fit in—our desire to conform.

The pressure to conform can have more serious ramifications. It can, for example, encourage people to accept practices that they know, or suspect, are wrong. The racist riots against the Japanese and Chinese in British Columbia in the first decade of the twentieth century were facilitated by the fact that prominent people were discouraged from speaking out against them. Everyone was afraid of speaking out against what everyone else in society seemed to be doing.

In another example, for many years serious discussion of gay and lesbian issues was taboo because the societal norm was heterosexuality. The situation changed in the 1980s and 1990s only after a number of prominent Canadians resisted the pressure to conform outwardly to the societal norm and publicly acknowledged that they were gay or lesbian.

By 2002, gays and lesbians had won many legal victories, and discrimination against them had become illegal in most Canadian jurisdictions.

Must the struggle against conformity always occur before social change can take place? Is alienation always the force that encourages leaders to struggle against the norm? The story of South Africa under apartheid is instructive in considering these questions. Under apartheid, a strict system of laws limited the rights and benefits of nonwhites, and allowed whites to exploit others within society. Whites were accorded a position of great privilege over all others within their society. (For a powerful account of the truly awful conditions in which most black families lived under South African apartheid, see Mathabane, 1994.)

Figure 3.6 Alienation can be a positive force by encouraging us to take action against situations with which we disagree. Here, young Canadians try to pull down a perimeter fence to protest globalization at the Summit for the Americas held in Quebec City in April 2001.

Strong conformity pressures among whites encouraged them to accept the status quo and resist fighting the system, even when they believed the apartheid laws to be unjust. In the end, however, the apartheid system was overcome. One of the conditions that made this happen lay in the person of Nelson Mandela, the first president of the new multiracial South Africa. People both inside and outside South Africa were amazed that he seemed to feel no bitterness toward his oppressors, even after spending 26 years in prison (from 1964 to 1990) for opposing apartheid. It appeared that alienation had not inspired his struggle. His actions suggested to the world that it is possible to achieve social change in desperate circumstances without falling victim to alienation and the anger that usually accompanies it.

As we have seen in this section, the relationship among conformity, alienation, and social change is a complex one. Because the rate of social change appears to be increasing in Canada, the study of these phenomena is also likely to expand.

Figure 3.7 Nelson Mandela waves as he leaves Nelson Mandela Park Public School in Toronto. He resisted the debilitating effects of alienation that might well have resulted from his experiences at the hands of white South Africans. How might his lack of bitterness have made easier his task as the first post-apartheid president of South Africa?

Pause and Reflect

1. What were the main findings of (a) Durkheim about anomie and (b) Marx about alienation? Give a definition of the term "alienation" that is in keeping with how sociologists use it today.

2. What is conformity? What would society be like without conformity?

3. Create an organizer to show how conformity can be good or bad for society, and how alienation can be good or bad for society.

4. How does each of conformity and alienation encourage or slow social change?

5. Identify two examples of alienation encouraging positive social change in Canada.

Section 3.3   Poverty and Affluence in Canada

Key Concepts

income inequality

quintile

public policy question

relative income inequality

absolute income inequality

low-income cut-off line (LICO)

disincentive

functional repercussion

Karl Marx was the first to point sociology toward in-depth study of inequality in society. He demonstrated the lack of economic power, and hence social and political power, held by the working class in industrial societies. Sociology has always maintained a significant interest in inequality in society.

The balance of this chapter will focus on **income inequalities**—or the gap between what the rich and the poor earn—in Canadian society, and the various efforts of social scientists to explain or address the resulting problems.

Income Inequality in Canada

In Canada, from 1920 to the 1970s, the gap between the richest **quintile**, or fifth of the population, and the poorest quintile narrowed. The politicians of this era did not view economic inequality as a severe social problem. Structural-functionalism was in vogue among sociologists. Most held the view that, because inequality existed in all societies, it

must therefore be an inherent part of human structures. They therefore regarded inequality as a characteristic of society that they should try to understand rather than eliminate. As long as there was fluidity within society, allowing people to move up the income scale over time, inequality could be considered beneficial to society.

Opinions about income inequality changed drastically as a result of changes in the economy and in society during the 1970s. During this decade, a number of factors caused severe economic dislocation in Canada. International oil prices quadrupled, resulting in increased production costs for all sectors of the economy. A severe worldwide recession led to rising unemployment, particularly in the manufacturing sector. In the academic field, structural-functionalism lost its widespread support, and new research began to take a more hard-hitting approach to the phenomena of unemployment and income inequality. Sociologists began examining the disparities more closely and discovered, among other things, that some groups seemed consistently at a disadvantage.

Comparing Percentage Distribution of Income

The most basic method of understanding income inequality is to examine total family income by quintiles. Each quintile contains the same number (20 per cent) of families, but families in the highest quintile have family incomes that are significantly higher than families in the lowest.

Statisticians collect data and sociologists analyze them to determine social trends. In the course of their analyses, sociologists and others identify **public policy questions**. These are social questions of such significance that

Percentage Distribution of Total Income of Canadian Families by Quintiles, 1974, 1984, and 1996

Quintile	1974 (%)	1984 (%)	1996 (%)
Lowest	6.3	6.1	6.1
Second	13.1	12.3	11.9
Middle	18.2	18.0	17.4
Fourth	23.6	24.1	24.0
Highest	38.8	39.5	40.6

Source: Canadian Council on Social Development. 2001. Cat. 13-207. [Online] Available <http://www.ccsd.ca/factsheets/quin.96.htm> 26 October 2001.

Figure 3.8 Calculate a ratio to compare the income earned by families in the lowest quintile with that earned by families in the highest quintile.

politicians and social agencies have an obligation to take part in public discussions to determine whether the population wishes them to intervene to try to change the situation. If some families are poor, for example, does society have an obligation to help them try to become richer by providing them with support programs such as subsidized daycare and free medical prescriptions? Does providing such programs reduce such families' desire to improve their conditions for themselves? How can society reverse the trends?

Comparing Absolute Incomes

If we relied on the above figures alone, we might easily be tempted to accept the status quo without further investigation because all we see is a general disparity—some Canadians are getting richer while others are getting poorer. The statistics in the above section show **relative income inequality**, comparing the percentage of total income that each quintile enjoys. It would be theoretically possible for every person to enjoy an adequate income if the society and economy were rich enough.

You may know by intuition that this is not the case in Canadian society. Intuition is not enough for social scientists or public policy analysts, however, who need more specific information to identify a problem. In this particular instance, they would be assisted by finding out what groups in society tend to be rich or poor. Indeed, when we look at **absolute income inequality**, or the amount of money earned by different groups in Canada, in Figure 3.9, it is apparent that significant disparities exist based on family type.

These absolute income figures, rather than the relative ones in the quintile table, make it easier to identify some public policy questions. It is obvious that two-earner and two-parent families have the highest incomes, and that female lone-parent families have among the lowest. Does society have

Average Family Income After Tax, by Selected Family Type, Canada, 1999

Type of Family	Annual Income ($)
Elderly couples	38 038
Non-elderly couples	49 912
Two-parent families	57 665
One-earner families	40 997
Two-earner families	56 048
Male lone-parent families	37 147
Female lone-parent families	24 874
Total families	**53 507**
Elderly unattached	Male: 22 577
	Female: 18 427
Non-elderly unattached	Male: 24 446
	Female: 21 037
Total unattached	**22 046**

Source: Statistics Canada. 2001. *Highlights: Family Income After Tax.*

Figure 3.9 The figures in this table reflect the biggest single-year gain for a decade, but only for employed people. Which family type has the highest family income? Which has the lowest? Is this what you expected? Why?

Annual Household Income by Race, USA, 1997–1999*

Race	Households	Average Income (American dollars)
All races	103 702 000	$39 657
White	86 996 000	$41 591
Black	12 634 000	$26 608
Native people	815 000	$30 764
Asian	3 257 000	$48 614
Hispanic	8 990 000	$29 110

* The figures given are the average annual incomes during the three years studied.

Source: U.S. Census Bureau. 1999. [Online] Available <http://www.alliance2k.org/asian/PowerPoint/2001/sld023.htm>

Figure 3.10 Which racial groups have the highest family income? Which groups have the lowest? What might be the root causes of these differences?

a role to play in trying to make up for the effects of income inequality? Other things being equal, the children of two-parent families will have an advantage over those of female lone-parent families, over half of whom live in poverty. Does society have an obligation—to individuals in poverty and to society generally—to try to introduce social changes that would assist those most in need, or should this be a matter for the families themselves to deal with?

Figure 3.9 analyzes income by family type, illustrating major differences between the incomes among males and females, and between different family types. Significant differences also exist among the incomes of different ethnic groups. Visible minorities have lower median incomes than the rest of society. The information in Figure 3.10, based on US figures, clearly illustrates this point.

Canadian statistics show a similar imbalance in income distribution by race. You will read later in this chapter about Canada's Employment Equity Act of 1986 and its goal of ensuring a more equitable distribution of income by race, gender, and physical or mental ability.

Defining Poverty

So far, we have not adequately defined what "poverty" or "low income" mean. Statistics Canada, the statistical agency maintained by the federal government, establishes every year what it calls the **low-income cut-off line (LICO)**. On average, Canadians spend 36 per cent of their after-tax incomes on basic necessities such as food, shelter, and clothing. Statistics Canada adds 20 per cent to this figure, so that any family spending more than 56 per cent of its total income on these necessities is below the LICO, what the media usually refer to as "the poverty line." Based on income data for 1999, Statistics Canada set the LICO line as shown in Figure 3.11.

The LICO is a crude measurement tool—obviously some families can budget better than others. Nonetheless, by establishing how much money is required to live a decent life in rural areas and cities, we can better compare levels of poverty from region to region.

In Figure 3.12, we see that some groups are statistically more likely to be poor (live under the LICO) than others. In every

Low-Income Cut-off Line Settings for Selected Family Sizes and Locations, 1999

Family Size	Community 500 000+	Community 30 000 – 99 999	Rural Areas
1	$17 886	$15 235	$12 361
2	$22 357	$19 044	$15 450
3	$27 805	$23 683	$19 216
4	$33 658	$28 669	$23 260
5	$37 624	$32 047	$26 002
6	$41 590	$35 425	$28 743
7+	$45 556	$38 803	$31 485

Source: Canadian Council for Social Development. 2001.

Figure 3.11 A Canadian living in a family that takes in less than the amount indicated in this table is considered to be living in poverty. Speculate on what accounts for the difference between the amounts recommended for those living in cities and those living in rural areas.

category, females experience a higher incidence of living below the LICO than males do. Perhaps the most shocking figure is that 45.1 per cent of lone-parent families headed by a female live in poverty. Other figures show that, among families where a female lone-parent has less than a high school education, about 90 per cent are living below the LICO.

There is a saying that knowledge is power. Social scientists provide people with information that can help them make sensible decisions in life. For example, a teenager thinking of quitting school might think twice after seeing the tables in this section. Social scientists would certainly say that data are essential in effecting social change. Governments and individuals are always more likely to work toward positive social change when they see figures that support action.

The Wage Gap Between Men and Women

In the previous section, we learned that women as a group earn less than men as a group. This fact becomes particularly relevant when considering the number of single-earner families headed by women with low incomes. In 1998, for example, unattached employed women earned on average $31 388, compared with $47 077 for men. Can we account for these differences? Statistics Canada studied the wage gap and concluded that half the difference can be accounted for by differences in the following areas:

- work experience
- education
- major field of study
- occupation
- industry of employment
- supervisory responsibilities
- administrative decision-making responsibilities
- seniority

Despite this long list of factors, researchers could not account for the remaining difference. What is responsible for the remaining wage gap? The researchers did not offer any explanation. Can you think what might account for the rest of the differences in earnings?

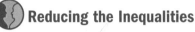 **Reducing the Inequalities**

The persistent income inequalities illustrated above continue to frustrate social policy activists trying to introduce social change. Various organizations, both public and private, have successfully lobbied for changes to remove these inequalities, or at least address the problems created by poverty. These include everything from employment and

Percentage of Selected Groups Below LICO, Canada, 1999

Type	Percentage
(1) People in an economic family*	
Males	8.2
Females	9.4
(2) People under 18 years of age (in an economic family)	
In two-parent families	8.3
In female lone-parent families	45.1
In all other economic families	18.8
(3) Unattached individuals	
Males	27.6
Females	32.1
(4) People over 65 years of age (unattached)	
Males	16.6
Females	23.3

*Note: An economic family is a group of individuals sharing a common dwelling unit who are related by blood, marriage (including common-law relationships), or adoption.

Source: Statistics Canada. 2000. *People With Low Income After Tax.*

Figure 3.12 What figures in this table strike you as most significant? Why?

training programs to affirmative action hiring policies and boys' and girls' clubs.

One final matter remains to be considered in this discussion of poverty and affluence and their impact on social change. This is the politically highly charged matter of welfare payments. The easiest short-term tool for raising the income level of the poorest people in our society is money. Money is required for survival, and some people, for a variety of reasons, are not able to earn any. The severely disabled readily spring to mind. What duty does society owe to such people, and how many other groups is it responsible for? The mentally ill? The physically incapacitated? The able-bodied who have enormous family responsibilities, such as a woman who has left

Figure 3.13 In Canadian cities, poverty has become more visible, with more people begging on the streets, sleeping outdoors, and eking out a living by scrounging in garbage bins. Canadians have long held the value that society should help its destitute through welfare. The questions lie in how much to give, and to whom. Who do you think should get help?

an abusive husband and who has three children under the age of five? The middle-aged single parent trying to upgrade his skills and make himself more marketable in the economy by attending community college? And what about the person who just can't hold a job? Or someone trying to get off drugs?

For politicians, the topic of welfare has proved to be contentious. Ever since the Depression years, all provinces and territories in Canada have offered welfare payments to the poorest people in society. A re-examination of the policy began in the 1980s.

Welfare in Ontario

The Ontario government reduced the level of welfare payments by 21.6 per cent in 1995, believing that payments were too high and that they created a **disincentive**; that is, they discouraged some recipients from finding employment. In other words, the government believed that the **functional repercussion**— or logical outcome—of the "high" payments was that people receiving welfare benefits didn't feel a need to look for work. The government's interpretation of the situation can be disputed. Some would say that welfare recipients—generally the most powerless individuals in society—made convenient targets for cuts, whether or not the cuts made sense. Either way, the expense of this social program prevented its continuation at the same level. Municipalities in Ontario became responsible for administering the cuts. The tables in Figure 3.14 illustrate welfare payments available in Toronto for qualifying persons in 2001.

Using the tables in Figure 3.14, one can easily calculate the basic needs and shelter allowance available to a given family. A single parent with two children, one aged 11 and one aged 14, would receive $572 for basic needs and $554 for shelter, giving a total of $1126/month, or $13 512/year. Is this enough? Too much? Consider that the LICO

Welfare Payments for Selected Persons and Families, Toronto, 2001
Table 1. Basic Needs Monthly Allowance

No. of Dependants Other than a Spouse	Dependants 13 Years and Over	Dependants 0–12 Years	Recipient	Recipient and Spouse
0	0	0	$195.00	$390.00
1	0	1	$446.00	$476.00
	1	0	$486.00	$512.00
2	0	2	$532.00	$576.00
	1	1	$572.00	$612.00
	2	0	$608.00	$648.00

Note: For each additional dependant over 13 years of age, $136 is added. For each additional dependant 0–12 years of age, $100 is added.

for a family of three in Toronto in 1999 (the last year currently available) was $29 373. According to this measure, then, the welfare family in the example receives less than half (about 46 per cent) of the amount necessary to avoid living in poverty.

As evidence that lower welfare payments encourage people to find jobs, the Ontario government points to the fact that 601 554 people left the welfare rolls between June 1995 and October 2001, "many to paid employment" (Ministry of Community and Social Services, 2001, p. 1). But not everyone is sure that there is so much to celebrate. A 1999 study of welfare policies across Canada by the University of Western Ontario concluded that some provinces emphasized training for long-term jobs as part of their welfare programs, while others went for the "quick fix." It accused Ontario and Alberta of pushing people into any job that came along, regardless of whether it suited the client's needs or skills. Others, the study said, were simply forced off the welfare rolls without having any visible means of support (Bailey, 1999, p. 1). This is a highly sensitive political issue, which is likely to dominate discussions about public policy for the foreseeable future. To read more on this issue, see the

Table 2. Shelter Monthly Allowance

Number of Persons In Family	Maximum Shelter Allowance
1	$325.00
2	$511.00
3	$554.00
4	$602.00
5	$649.00
6 or more	$673.00

Source: City of Toronto. 2001. *Social Services Policy*.

Figure 3.14 Welfare payments are calculated to address basic needs and shelter, as shown in these two tables. Calculate how much you would receive in a month if you were a single parent of a two-year-old child. How much would you receive in a year?

Competing Perspectives feature on page 88.

The causes of and solutions to the income disparities that exist in society are hotly debated. Some progress in reducing these disparities has been made from time to time. There is no disputing the fact that the 1990s have widened the gap between the poor and the rich in Canada. New strategies are required and much work remains to be done in the first decade of the twenty-first century if these gaps are to be reduced.

COMPETING PERSPECTIVES

Does welfare discourage people from looking for work? Or is this a myth put forward by people unfamiliar with the reality of life on welfare? This issue has been debated as governments around the world have tried to reduce spending. Consider the two points of view shown here, both typical of this international debate.

Massive welfare cuts invite more drug problems
Report in an American drug policy newsletter By Bob Curley

The fallacy behind welfare reform and underlying welfare itself is that most welfare recipients could get off the dole if only they would pull themselves up by their bootstraps. The truth is that the welfare population has very few legitimate social advancement opportunities, despite the occasional rags-to-riches story....

Throwing people off welfare if they don't get jobs would be a sound policy if there were jobs to be had. Unless the issue of economic opportunity is carefully considered and addressed in the welfare-reform debate, you can bet on a rise in drug-related crime concurrent with cuts in welfare spending. Desperate people in America's impoverished communities, like the poverty-stricken coca farmers in South America, will seek out the only growth industry around.

Knocking the chocks out from under the poor will send many careening down a road of despair, with increased substance abuse an inevitable side effect.

Welfare, like so much other social spending (including drug treatment and prevention funding) is a classic case of "Pay me now, or pay me later." Americans are so reluctant to admit that society as a whole is bolstered by the welfare state that we blindly follow conservatives whose social experiments are as radical as the ones that created welfare in the first place.

Welfare is not simply a manifestation of the largess of a compassionate and generous society. A central function of welfare is to placate a portion of the population that has been deemed unemployable. Welfare creates stability in our society by ensuring that even [those on the lowest rung] can fall just so far. The consequences of removing this safety net cannot be measured simply in terms of the suffering it will cause, or the dollars it will save. We also must consider what will take the place of welfare in our poorest communities.

Will it be jobs for everyone? If not, destroying welfare is an invitation to anarchy. Congress last week proposed to cut welfare spending by $80 billion. The impact of such a cut on drug use and drug policy would be profound.

Source: Curley, Bob. 1995. "Massive welfare cuts invite more drug problems." *Alcoholism and Drug Abuse Weekly*, Vol. 7, Issue 20. 15 May 1995.

COMPETING PERSPECTIVES

Homeless by choice or necessity?
Alberta-based magazine article By Les Sillars

The City of Calgary this summer released the results of a "snap-shot" census of homeless people conducted in May. City workers tallied 461 itinerants [homeless people] (including 37 children under the age of 14) by surveying crisis shelters and roaming the streets counting homeless-looking people. A similar 1992 survey found 447 at-large residents. Welfare advocates were quick to cite this rise as "evidence" that Social Services Minister Mike Cardinal's cuts were throwing more people onto the streets, but a ministry spokesman argues otherwise. Plenty of resources are available for those who need them, Mr. Cardinal insists, and those without homes have problems other than a [meagre] dole....

Susanna Koczkur, director of Calgary's Connection Housing, estimates the number of homeless at around 900, including families with children. However, [she did not] offer concrete evidence that the overall numbers of homeless have signifi-cantly risen, and that the cause was welfare cuts.

For his part, Social Services spokesman Bob Scott insists that the welfare system continues to provide shelter assistance to all in legitimate need. Welfare rolls have been reduced by 38 per cent since April 1993, he reports, but one-third of the 36 000 removed have returned to school and actually receive more benefits. As for the rest, he notes, "you have to do a few things to qualify. Perhaps some people don't want to do those things."

Mr. Scott adds that provincial levels of assistance for food and shelter, ranging from $394 a month for singles to $1173 for a family of four, adequately support people. "There's no lack of community or government programs," Mr. Scott insists. "There's lots."

There are enough shelters so that "nobody sleeps on the street in Calgary unless it's a choice," concurs Roy Woodbridge, manager of the Calgary Drop-In Centre.

Nearly 90 per cent of the Drop-In Centre clients, primarily single males, have mental or behavioural problems which will probably keep them out of mainstream society, explains Mr. Woodbridge. Thus, it's questionable whether last year's welfare cuts are a significant factor.

However, Mr. Woodbridge also believes there are cases where people who honestly cannot support themselves are cut off from welfare and end up either on the streets or in shelters. "With any tightening of the rules you take off some who deserve to go, some who are questionable, and some who shouldn't." Cuts had to be made, he acknowledges, but "the big question is how you tighten the rules humanely, accurately, and with sensitivity."

Source: Sillars, Les. 1994. "Homeless by choice or necessity?" *Alberta Report*, Vol. 21, Issue 38. 5 September 1994.

Questions
1. What view of welfare and welfare recipients is expressed in the report on the opposite page? What view about homelessness and the homeless is expressed in the article above?
2. Which author views welfare cutbacks as a positive social change? Which views them as negative? Explain your choices.
3. Which view do you think is more likely to have common support in your community? Explain.
4. What do you think causes people to (a) go on welfare and (b) become homeless? What solutions do you favour to the problems described here? Explain your answers.

Pause and Reflect

1. How did the lowest and highest income quintiles fare in the period examined in Figure 3.8?

2. Compare the types of information we can gather from percentage distributions of income and measures of absolute incomes.

3. What is LICO and how is it calculated?

4. What factors did the Statistics Canada study identify that partially explain why men, on average, earn more than women? Speculate on what else may be a factor.

5. In 2001, a Toronto family of two on welfare would receive $511 each month to provide them with shelter. Check out the classified ads at a Toronto Web site (for example, at <www.thestar.com>), and find out the general price range for rental apartments. Are the amounts higher or lower than $511? What conclusion can you draw from this difference? What options does a family on welfare have in the face of the problem you have identified?

Section 3.4   Values and Social Change in Canada

Key Concepts

singularity

pluralism

inclusiveness

participation rate

systemic discrimination

equal pay for work of equal value

dominant paradigm

alternative environmental paradigm

bargaining for reality

 Pluralism in Canada

The social changes that are introduced into a society at any particular time reflect its prevailing values. In Iran, until 1979, Western-educated officials who controlled the government, encouraged the nation to adopt many Western values. Following a revolution in 1979, a new government, led by the charismatic Ayatollah Khomeini, introduced laws based on a strict interpretation of Islamic religious texts. Alcohol consumption is outlawed, and the public role of women has been reduced. The government's aim is to produce a nation operating on the principles of strict spiritual faith. These social changes in Iran reflect the value of **singularity**—a belief that everyone in society should act and think the same way.

Current Canadian society is founded on a different principle, being structured to reflect the prevailing values of **pluralism** and **inclusiveness**. Pluralism means that there should be widespread acceptance of differences in culture, religion, values, and lifestyle. Inclusiveness implies that all law-abiding people, regardless of their particular background or circumstances, should be able to play a constructive role in the life of the nation.

One of the earliest struggles for inclusiveness sought to obtain for women a role similar in importance and dignity to that traditionally played by men. As you read in the previous section, there still exists a wage gap between what men and women earn. Here, you will read about a strategy used by the various levels of government to address this inequality.

Making Gains for Women

Historically, women in Canada had lower **participation rates** in the workforce. The participation rate is calculated as the percentage of a particular group, 16–64 years of age, available for paid work who are actively employed in the paid economy at any given time (either as employees or self-employed).

Typically, over 80 per cent of men participate in the paid economy. The remainder are in school, unemployed, in prison, not looking for work, at home caring for children, and so on. Female participation rates in Canada have climbed from 38 per cent (1970), to 50.4 per cent (1980), and to 57.6 per cent (1992). Sociologists have concluded that the worldwide increase in female participation rates has been caused by higher education levels among women, smaller families, higher divorce rates, a shift in attitudes toward working women, and the opening of more jobs to women. Some 1998 participation rates are contained in the bar graph in Figure 3.15.

The Employment Equity Act

Women have been through many struggles along the way toward a more equitable participation rate, particularly those who entered what were previously all-male job categories. In addition there has been a parallel and simultaneous struggle in Canada by other groups to win equity in the workplace. These groups include visible minorities that have experienced discrimination through labour practices.

Discrimination in the workplace often results from **systemic discrimination**, whereby a system exists that favours one or some groups over others in terms of hiring, benefits, promotions, and pay increases. One obvious example is a hiring requirement that rules out people from particular groups, even though the requirement may not have any relevance to the person's ability to perform the job. Height or strength requirements, for example, have often accomplished this end by preventing women or members of particular visible minorities from qualifying for jobs as police officers or firefighters.

While racial minorities, Aboriginal people, and people physically or mentally challenged continue to encounter barriers

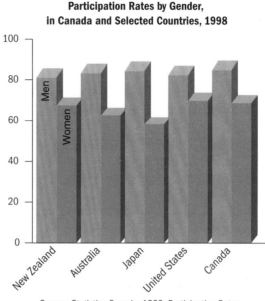

Participation Rates by Gender, in Canada and Selected Countries, 1998

Source: Statistics Canada. 1999. *Participation Rates*

Figure 3.15 In more conservative societies, more women stay out of the paid workforce. By this simple measure, which of the five countries in the table is most conservative? In which country do men and women participate at the most similar rate?

Figure 3.16 Although many Canadian women who have the opportunity still choose to stay at home with their young children, many more are working outside of the home, either through choice or because of economic necessity. What changes in values have encouraged this shift?

associated with discrimination, white women have gained some headway. A significant step forward was realized in 1986, when the federal Employment Equity Act was passed. This act affected all employees of the federal government and all federally regulated industries (for example, the armed forces, the health care system, the postal service). Its purpose was to tackle systemic discrimination. The act identifies four target groups: women, Aboriginal people, members of visible minorities, and people with mental or physical disabilities. It requires that employers develop policies to provide the target groups with workplace equity by setting hiring goals for each target group.

By using data from the 1996 census, the Treasury Board, which is the federal government department responsible for implementation of the Employment Equity Act, developed the target numbers shown in Figure 3.17. These show the percentage of the total population available for employment that each target group constitutes.

Two points should be borne in mind regarding the data in Figure 3.17. First, they represent the percentages of people available for employment, not the overall percentages in society. Women accounted for 50.3 per cent of the total population in 2000, but the Treasury Board makes statistical adjustments to subtract those who, for a variety of reasons, are considered unable to take employment. Second, an individual can be counted in more than one category.

Like all employers covered by the 1986 act, the Treasury Board is required to have a program to target, for hiring, members of the various equity groups throughout the government. By March 2000, it had achieved the results shown in Figure 3.19.

Some progress has been made since 1986 in meeting the goals of the act. The data in Figure 3.19 provide a snapshot of target groups' participation in federal employment in 2000. Participation is only part of the picture, however. Consider, for example, that in 1999–2000 women in federal service received only 40.6 per cent of promotions to executive positions (the most highly paid category) but 84.8 per cent of promotions to administrative support posi-

Percentage of Total Population Available for Employment, by Target Group, Canada, 2000

Equity Group	Availability Estimate
Women	48.7%
Aboriginal Persons	1.7%
Persons in a Visible Minority	8.7%
Persons with Disabilities	4.8%

Source: PSAC. 2000. *Analysis*.

Figure 3.17 Using these figures, employers can see what percentage of their workforce would be made up of various groups if they achieved a workplace population reflective of the Canadian workforce. Note that women are represented in the figures for all four groups.

Figure 3.18 For years, people of various groups have not been fairly represented in the workforce. How does society benefit by changing this situation?

Equity Targets and Actual Employment Situation, Government of Canada, 2000

Equity Group	Employed	Percentage of All Employees	Numerical Target	Percentage Target	Gap
Women	72 549	51.4%	68 790	48.7%	+3,759
Aboriginal Persons	4 639	3.3%	2 401	1.7%	+2,238
Persons in a Visible Minority	7 764	5.5%	6 780	4.8%	+984
Persons with Disabilities	6 687	4.7%	9 181	6.5%	-2,494

Source: PSAC. 2000. *Analysis*.

Figure 3.19 What figure in this table most surprises you? For help in reading and analyzing statistics, see the Skill Builder on page 98.

tions (the lowest-paid category). When we recall that women comprise 51.4 per cent of all federal employees, it is obvious that there is a way to go. The overall promotion figures for the other equity groups for 1999–2000 were as follows: Aboriginal persons 0.8 per cent, persons in a visible minority 2.3 per cent, and persons with disabilities 2.7 per cent, all well below their total federal employment figures.

Another feature of the 1986 Employment Equity Act was that it required employers to provide **equal pay for work of equal value**. This means that job classifications must be compared for the skills they require, the responsibilities they involve, their working conditions, and the effort required. All jobs scoring equally according to these categories must be paid at the same rates. The purpose of the legislation was to end discriminatory hiring and pay practices. One group of employees, for example warehouse workers, might be all men, and another group, for example office assistants, might be all women. Even though the work of the two groups would be essential-

ly of the same value, the warehouse workers would typically be paid at a higher rate than the office assistants.

It is ironic that the body that passed the legislation in the first place, the federal government, has been one of the last employers

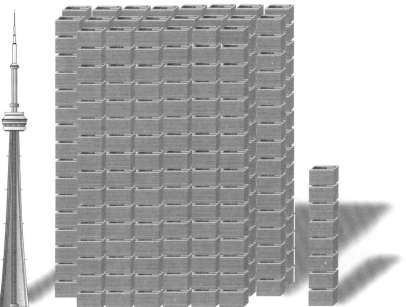

Figure 3.20 The federal government underpaid its workers by $5 billion by not giving equal pay for work of equal value between 1986 and 1999. Five billion dollars in $10 bills stacked one on top of the other would be approximately 12 500 m high. This stack is equivalent to approximately 22.6 times the height of the CN Tower (553 m).

to meet the terms of the act and then only after legal action by its employees. After passage of the Act in 1986, employee groups tried to negotiate with the Treasury Board to institute equal pay for work of equal value. After 13 years, no agreement had been reached, with the result that for this time over 200 000 mainly female employees continued to be underpaid. The matter was referred to a legal tribunal and, in July 1999, this body awarded $5 billion, or about $25 000 per eligible employee, in back pay to the underpaid workers. The amount of money involved illustrates the degree of discrimination that had prevailed for years within the wage structure of the government.

"The federal government thought that because we are women, we'd roll over and be quiet," said Colette Gervais, who expects $40 000 compensation for being underpaid as a payment clerk for 40 years. "I hope that they've learned that we are more than second-class citizens." (Jobsearch Canada, 1999)

The federal government felt that the award was too high, but to avoid costly court litigation, reached a deal for a slightly lower amount with PSAC in the fall of 1999.

Although it is a difficult process, the Employment Equity Act has allowed us to achieve social change in the workplace, reflecting the changing values of Canadians. As various groups struggle to achieve equity in the workplace, with the accompanying improvements to their finances and dignity, they are individually able to play a more complete role in society. In this way, the collective Canadian cause of inclusiveness is advanced.

The Environment and Social Change

Another Canadian value that is increasingly resulting in social change is concern for the environment. Early sociologists, such as Durkheim, downplayed physical and biological factors in society, concentrating solely on social factors. By the 1970s, however, people in industrialized societies felt a growing concern that pollution of the environment constituted a real danger to the health and future of the human race. Reflecting this general concern, sociologists began to investigate the trade-off between economic expansion and environmental damage. Today, environmental sociology is a huge and diverse field of study.

One of the most useful approaches to understanding the nature of the conflict that has emerged between the industrial and environmental lobbies is to look at the **dominant paradigm** and the **alternative environmental paradigm** (Cotgrove, 1982). (A paradigm is an underlying way of viewing the world.) The dominant paradigm, favoured by many in business and industry, holds that humans have a duty to create material wealth to make this and future generations richer, and a right to dominate, change, or even corrupt the natural world in order to do so. The alternative environmental paradigm rejects both of these principles. It holds that society must place a higher importance on non-material values, encourage stronger communities built on better personal relationships, and act with a greater respect for nature. According to this paradigm, we can only achieve this ideal through economic development that respects nature for its own sake and that refrains from exploiting the natural world for short-term economic gain, while ultimately destroying it.

Sociological surveys have repeatedly discovered that the environment ranks lower as a concern in most Canadians' consciousness than does the need for jobs and continued economic security. Surveys have found that concern for the environment is greatest among people who have a number of the following characteristics: a post-secondary education, younger than 35 years, generally liberal social attitudes, and live in a city (Brym, 1995, Ch. 16, p. 7).

Nightmare on Frederick Street

Sydney, Nova Scotia, is home to North America's largest toxic waste dump. Over 700 000 t of toxic sludge sit in what are usually called the Sydney tar ponds. (They are not ponds at all, as the waste sits in a tidal basin, and with every tidal cycle more of it is washed out to the ocean.) The toxic sludge is the result of years of waste dumping by the Sydney Steel Company, which ran a steel-making facility at this location.

Frederick Street consists of 17 homes, separated from the site by a small stream and a three-metre-high chain-link fence bearing a sign, "HUMAN HEALTH HAZARD, CONTAMINATED AREA, ABSOLUTELY NO TRESPASSING." But this fence cannot contain the poisons that lurk on the site, as wind and runoff from rain leach chemicals into the surrounding area.

Figure 3.21 Residents of the neighbourhood near the Sydney Tar Ponds arrive at the Nova Scotia legislature to register their discontent. Why do the tar ponds elicit such strong emotions in local citizens?

In 1989, the federal and Nova Scotia governments began a project to clean up the tar ponds. Finding that this would be far more complicated and expensive than first imagined, the governments abandoned it. For years, nothing was done to contain or clean up the tar ponds, until the residents became angry and began to demand action and to demonstrate against the conditions in which they were living.

In the summer of 1997, the Frederick Street Brook, as the stream is known, started to ooze a yellow sludge. Tests showed that it contained high levels of toxic chemicals like arsenic, molybdenum, benzopyrene, antimony, naphthalene, lead, toluene, kerosene, copper, and polyaromatic hydrocarbons (PAHs). Every chemical was present in concentrations higher than permitted by appropriate health guidelines. Arsenic was 18.5 times higher than the permissible level, naphthalene was 8.9 times, molybdenum and benzopyrene were 6 times the recommended limits. These chemicals are known to cause various cancers, heart and kidney disease, birth defects, brain damage, immune deficiencies, and skin problems. In July 1998, tests confirmed that soil in the yards of the Frederick Street houses had become contaminated by toxic waste.

Yet there was little response from the governments to the residents' concerns. Dr. Jeff Scott, Nova Scotia's chief medical officer, issued releases stating that residents were not at risk. Dr. Scott lives in Halifax. The Sierra Club of Canada, which took up the residents' cause, called for Dr. Scott's resignation in July 1998, and the appointment of a medical officer "who acts in the interest of public health, not toxic chemicals." Dr. Scott did not resign.

In July 2001, residents of the area around the tar ponds blockaded a highway, handing out literature to motorists trying to pass. A public meeting was organized to listen to all sides with an interest in the matter. This meeting turned into a wild skirmish, as police used pepper spray to arrest three environmental activists who, some attendees claimed, were disrupting the meeting.

Frederick Street residents are caught in a bind. They cannot realistically expect to sell their houses and move, for the houses are almost worthless. Sydney is a depressed economic area, and most residents cannot afford just to walk away from their houses. Nova Scotia has the highest cancer rates in Canada, and Cape Breton Island, where Sydney is located, has the highest lung, breast, and stomach cancer rates in the province. Yet the governments seem unwilling or unable to address the problem by cleaning up the site and providing compensation to families to assist their moving. Sydney Steel, the corporation that caused the problem in the first place, is bankrupt, so there is no one to sue for damages. The problem so far has defied a solution.

Sources: Written with information from Cox, Kevin. 2001. "Public meeting over tar ponds turns violent." *Globe & Mail.* 2 August 2001. Sierra Club of Canada. *Nightmare on Frederick Street.* [Online]. Available <http://www.sierraclub.ca/stp/stp-factsheet.html> 28 July 2001.

Questions
1. Describe how the tar ponds came into existence.
2. Why are local residents and environmental activists so angry about the situation connected with the tar ponds?
3. How would a supporter of (a) the dominant paradigm and (b) the alternative environmental paradigm explain the causes of and solutions to the current situation at the Sydney tar ponds?

It is usually when there is some sort of environmental catastrophe, such as a major oil spill or runoff from a toxic waste dump, that Canadians become alarmed about environmental concerns. The case study on page 95 is one such situation that raised the alarm of many Canadians.

Bargaining for Reality

The Sydney tar ponds case study perfectly illustrates the anthropological concept that Lawrence Rosen (1984) calls **bargaining for reality**. Power can be acquired and maintained by groups and organizations if they are able to convince others that their view of the situation is the correct one. In the tar ponds case, the governments took the position that, although the site is clearly polluted, the health risks are not fully known. They claimed that the cleanup would be hazardous and exceedingly costly, requiring them to cancel other worthwhile projects if they had to devote all their resources to this effort. Their reality featured uncertain risks and a huge public cost.

The environmentalists and residents took the position that if the risks were not entirely known, they were at least fully understood. They argued that a clean up of the site and compensation for various losses should begin at once. If the governments did not have the money to pay for the project, they should raise additional taxes from those people and businesses that could afford it. Their reality featured understood risks and human suffering. Rosen concludes that, in order for a reality to have a chance of popular support, it must be coherent, relevant, and understandable.

Some public issues regarding Canada's relationship with the United States involve competing realities. For example, President George W. Bush of the United States announced in the summer of 2001 that he wanted to obtain natural gas supplies from Alaska and the Northwest Territories, to supply the American hunger for natural resources. Such projects would require the construction of above-ground pipelines though the Northwest Territories and Alberta, pipelines that environmentalists charge will interfere with caribou migrations and create great potential for environmental catastrophe. Mr. Bush was trying to frame the issue as an energy-security matter, his opponents as an environmental matter.

However this issue is resolved, it is apparent that concern for the environment is a factor that is having a growing influence on public policy, and that social change must deal with it if it is to succeed. As the twenty-first century unfolds, it seems likely that environmental considerations will increasingly affect debates about social change.

Pause and Reflect

1. What is systemic discrimination? Who is disadvantaged by it? What Canadian value demands social change to address the problem of discrimination?

2. Formulate a question to help you analyze the statistics in the table in Figure 3.19 or the promotion figures on page 92. See the Skill Builder about reading and analyzing statistics on page 367 for ideas and assistance. Trade with another student and complete each other's question.

3. In point form, list the developments that led to back payments from the federal government to its employees to achieve employment equity. Why do you think it took so long to reach an agreement?

4. What is "bargaining for reality"? What is necessary for a reality to have a chance of popular support?

5. Think of an issue over which there are major differences of opinion, and in which the sides are trying to persuade the public that their interpretation of the facts is correct—bargaining for reality. Using your example, explain what social changes might take place should one reality win out over the other.

□ □ □   **Skill Builder:**   □ □ □
Developing Research Questions

To obtain useful research information, and to come to satisfactory conclusions about controversial issues in the early stages of a scholarly research project, it is necessary to ask a series of informed questions—questions that get you the right answers.

Definitions

Let's look at some of the different types of questions that academics try to ask when they conduct research.

a) *Factual questions.* These questions have right and wrong answers that are normally accepted by all people. Many begin with "who," "what," "when," or "where." (Example: "What toxic substances have been detected in the Sydney Tar Ponds?")

b) *Clarification questions.* These questions try to narrow the focus of the research, or eliminate misunderstandings about the meaning of terms being used. Individual researchers will tend to have similar answers to these questions. (Example: "What is 'charismatic leadership'?")

c) *Interpretive questions.* Researchers use these questions to focus on the meaning of what is being said. When answering an interpretive question, a researcher may have to take a position on the subject. Two different researchers could answer a question like this differently, with minor or major variations. Nonetheless, academics are expected to justify, with evidence, why they think they have the correct answer. (Example: "Is advocacy research more effective than participatory research in achieving social change?")

d) *Inquiry questions.* Researchers frequently develop these complex questions to look for related factors within research. These questions have more than one correct answer, and normally require considerable research to answer properly. (Example: "What are the major factors that contribute to conformity in society?") It is often possible to develop a useful hypothesis from such a question, for example, by taking the position that one factor is more important than others.

Recognizing Question Types

Look at the questions below. Identify which type of question each example represents.

1. Does the dominant paradigm or the alternative environmental paradigm represent a better way of viewing the world?

2. What was the participation rate of women in the paid labour force in Canada in 1998?

3. What are the most important factors that contribute to income inequality in Canada today?

4. How do anthropologists explain the term "worldview"?

Explain how each of the examples represents the particular question type. Be sure to review the definitions presented above and to incorporate key terms from them in your answers.

Step One: Review your material

Before a researcher attempts to compose questions about a topic, he or she must become familiar with the topic. Practise this by reviewing the information contained in this chapter.

Step Two: Create your questions

Make a list of two questions of each type (eight questions total) based on the information contained in this chapter. (It is not necessary to answer the questions.)

Step Three: Check with a partner

Work with a partner. Examine the questions and what type you chose for each one. Modify any questions as necessary.

Practise It!

Consider the following hypothesis: "The values that people form in early life tend to stay with them throughout their adult lives."

Follow the three steps outlined above to develop a list of questions that you think would help you test the validity of this hypothesis. Make sure that you include questions of all types mentioned in this Skill Builder feature. You don't have to answer the questions.

Conclusion

Developing good research questions, especially inquiry questions, at an early stage in the research process is important because they provide focus. They help you focus your research into what you will study, and what you will not. (This latter point is important because you have to set limits on your topic, and good inquiry questions help you to do this.) In practice, you will probably change or adjust some of the questions you have posed as you proceed with your research.

Chapter Activities

Show Your Knowledge

1. a) What did Newcomb's longitudinal Bennington College studies show about attitude formation?

   b) How might the studies help us understand what political debates might be like 20 years from now?

2. a) What is subjective validity?

   b) How can belonging to a group of like-minded people reinforce our subjective validity?

3. a) Describe the distribution of income, by quintile, in Canada. Refer to Figure 3.8 on page 82.

   b) What changes took place in income distribution between 1974 and 1996?

4. a) How have Canadian women's participation rates in the workforce changed over the course of the past three decades?

   b) What factors have contributed to the worldwide rise in female participation rates since the 1970s?

Practise Your Thinking

5. a) Identify some of the evidence that suggests that Canadian society is becoming more equitable in the workplace.

   b) Identify some of the evidence that suggests that barriers to equity still exist.

6. a) What factors might encourage teenagers to conform to the norms of their peer group?

   b) What factors might cause some young people to be alienated from the society in which they live?

   c) Overall, do you think that pressures of conformity and alienation are likely to increase or decline as you get older? Explain.

7. Imagine you have been asked by the federal government to make recommendations to secure a more equal income distribution in Canada, without providing major disincentives to people's desire to find paid employment. What recommendations will you make? Provide an explanation for each recommendation.

8. Look at Figure 3.19, focusing particularly on the gaps between those employed and the numerical targets.

   a) What conclusions can you draw from these figures? Explain, distinguishing between groups if necessary.

   b) What further steps do you think are needed to ensure full job equity for the target groups in the immediate future?

Communicate Your Ideas

9. Make sure you understand the meaning of "worldview." (page 73)

   a) Work with a partner to create a list of features of the worldviews of (i) students and (ii) teachers in your school.

   b) Solicit information so you can list the features of another pair of worldviews (for example, parent-teenager; boss-employee).

   c) Discuss with your class ways of understanding someone else's worldview.

   d) With your partner, choose one pair of worldviews. Act out a scene in which two people having different worldviews clash. In the end, the two characters find common ground and learn to appreciate each other on some level.

10. Imagine that you are a political prisoner under a brutal regime, sentenced to 30 years' imprisonment.

   a) Make a list of "do" and "don't" items that could help prevent you personally from becoming alienated.

   b) In groups, explain your ideas and the reasons behind them.

11. Read the section dealing with income distribution and LICO on pages 84 to 86.

   a) Make a list of public policy questions that you think emerge from the information in this section.

   b) Give an answer for each of the questions you have raised.

   c) Conduct a class debate on the following statement: "Welfare payments should be reduced from their present level to encourage welfare recipients to get jobs."

12. One of Canada's most pressing environmental problems is what to do with the garbage produced by our homes and businesses. Do some research to find out your community's plans for dealing with garbage collection and disposal in the future.

   a) Does it appear to be looking for a cheap solution or an environmentally responsible one?

   b) How do people in your community feel about the subject? Do a straw poll on the topic by asking three individuals this question: "Are you willing to do more to reduce garbage production and to pay more for its disposal if that is necessary to protect the environment?"

   c) On a chart at the front of the class, add your results to a tally of the class's findings. Add up the totals. What do the results of the class's research tell you about the type of paradigm (dominant or alternative environmental) most common in your community?

Apply Your Knowledge

13. Look at the extract from Pierrette Hondagneu-Soleto's writing in the case study on page 75.

    a) What are the major differences between advocacy and participatory research?

    b) In what ways might a studied community, such as the Latina domestic workers in Los Angeles, benefit from being the subject of an advocacy research study?

14. Research Nelson Mandela's life, focusing on his resistance to apartheid and how his approach evolved over the years. (Alternatively, you can research another political prisoner, using your own questions. Visit the Web site of Amnesty International Canada at <www.amnesty.ca> to find out more about political prisoners.)

    a) What do you think are the major features of Mandela's worldview?

    b) What do you think are the main factors that contributed to his alienation from the South African government, yet prevented his alienation from its peoples?

15. Visit the Statistics Canada Web site at <www.statcan.ca>.

    a) Find out more about income distribution, unemployment, and LICO in your region.

    b) Does it appear that the situation has changed since 1998–2000, the period from which the figures for this chapter were taken? Describe any changes you identify.

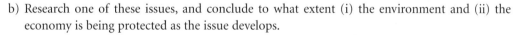

www.ccsd.ca/factsheets/fs_lic99.htm

Are you interested in some of the statistical information about poverty in Canada? Visit the above site, maintained by the Canadian Council on Social Development. If you go back one step to <http://ccsd.ca/factsheets>, you will find a large menu of statistical fact sheets. If the Web address does not connect you with the site, do a Web search using "Canadian Council on Social Development" as a search string. Then connect through the following links to reach the specific page: Free Statistics > Poverty Lines 1999 (LICOs)

WEB LINK

16. Visit the Web site of an environmental organization like the Sierra Club of Canada at <www.sierraclub.ca>.

    a) What environmental issues or public policy questions appear to be currently under debate?

    b) Research one of these issues, and conclude to what extent (i) the environment and (ii) the economy is being protected as the issue develops.

    c) Make a presentation to the class that outlines the issue and then offers and supports the conclusion you reached in part (b).

CHAPTER 4

TECHNOLOGY AND SOCIAL CHANGE

INTRODUCTION

With each technological step forward it is inevitable that society makes adjustments to accommodate the change. Many academics, including social scientists, philosophers, and scientists, wonder if society is currently placing too much emphasis on technological advancement and not enough emphasis on the changes brought about by these innovations.

Sociologists, anthropologists, and psychologists are still trying to measure the impact of technology on humanity. However, strong theories are beginning to take shape that indicate that technological development is having, and always has had, a profound effect on the way we live our lives. It is for this reason that we will focus our attention on the effects of technology on the individual, the family, and societies.

■ Learning Expectations

By the end of this chapter, you will be able to

- identify strategies for coping with the psychological stress of technological change on the individual and society
- evaluate the social impact of new technologies on family structures and dynamics
- analyze the ways in which ecological and agricultural knowledge resulting from advances in technology influences indigenous approaches to resource management and land tenure

Focusing on the Issues

Paying the Price of Progress

"Progress has never been a bargain…you have to pay for it. Sometimes I think there's a man who sits behind a counter and says, 'You can have a telephone but you lose privacy and the charm of distance. Madame, you may have the vote but at a price. You lose the right to retreat behind your powder puff and your petticoat. Mister, you may conquer the air but the birds will lose their wonder and the clouds will smell of gasoline.'"

– From the play
Inherit the Wind,
by Jerome Lawrence and
Robert E. Lee

Spencer Tracy played the role of Henry Drummond in the film version of *Inherit the Wind*. In this scene, Drummond is challenging the assumptions of Matthew Harrison Brady, the lawyer who opposes the teaching of evolution in schools.

The insights that emerged from the play *Inherit the Wind* were inspired by an actual event: the Scopes Trial of 1925. Shortly after World War I, the government of the US state of Tennessee passed the Butler Law, which banned the teaching of Darwin's theory of evolution in schools. The law was supported by Christian fundamentalists who believed that the theory was diametrically opposed to the faith message of the Bible. John T. Scopes, a 24-year-old biology teacher, was charged under the Butler Law and was eventually found guilty in one of the most famous court cases in United States history.

About 30 years after the trial, Jerome Lawrence and Robert E. Lee wrote the play *Inherit the Wind*. While not making any claims to historical accuracy, the play does manage to capture the essence of the battle between the two opposing points of view: the position of the modernist versus the position of the fundamentalist. In the end, Lawrence and Lee provide a timeless, theatrical classic that addresses the theme of societal change.

The above quote deals specifically with technological and ideological change. Henry Drummond, the lawyer defending evolution, speaks of the costs of progress and society's duty to assess those costs. Whether progress involves the emergence of telephones and airplanes or the granting of the vote to women, society must ask two questions: How does change affect the individual, the family, and society? and, Do the benefits outweigh the costs? The answers to these questions are open for debate.

THINK ABOUT IT

1. Why do you think the granting of the vote to women is listed alongside the invention of the telephone and the airplane in the *Inherit the Wind* quote?

2. Do you think about the benefits and costs of specific technologies when you use them? For instance, do you ever ask yourself what effect an invention such as the television has on the way you live your life?

3. What do you think motivated lawmakers to pass the Butler Law?

Section 4.1   Technology: An Agent of Social Change

Key Concepts

technology

social change theory

technological determinism

conspicuous consumption

pecuniary emulation

Technology Brings Change

The introduction of any new technology into a society brings with it some degree of change. In fact, technology itself is an instrument of change. A classic example of technology causing social change can be seen with the invention of the printing press in Europe. Johnannes Gutenberg's technology took the process of reading from a handful of monks and academics and extended it to the masses. Over time, every person trained in the skill of reading would have the opportunity to read a variety of mass-produced books. In other words, technology brought with it change

Figure 4.1 The printing press changed the world, opening new opportunities for learning, and creating the potential for mass literacy.

and opportunity. The eventual result was the replacement of limited learning (because previously there were so few manuscripts to read) with mass learning.

The invention of the printing press also resulted in a number of what some people may regard as negative consequences. The skill of memorization and oral recitation would rapidly begin to lose favour. The Roman Catholic Church would lose its hold on some of its congregation as the Bible became mass produced and individual readers could analyze and assess the text for themselves. During the 1500s, a Roman Catholic priest named Martin Luther used his knowledge of the printed word to challenge the authority of the Church and generate the impetus for a rift between Christian denominations that lasts to this day. The technology of the printing press initiated change—for better or worse—with new institutions surfacing while others either died out or were forced to adjust.

What Is Technology?

Before proceeding with a study of technology and corresponding social change, it is necessary to come to terms with the word **"technology."** What is technology? For some, it is the invention or creation of new tools that make the process of living a little easier. For others, it can be anything—a method of communication, an invention, an object—that is embraced by people for practical use in their everyday lives. In this case, anything from a coffee cup to a computer could be seen as technology. Marshall McLuhan, a Canadian scholar and social commentator, claimed that any technology or "medium" is the extension of some human quality; for instance, the book is the extension of the eyes, the wheel is the extension of the foot, and the computer is the extension of the brain and the central nervous system.

For the purposes of our study, we will combine these ideas into one definition. *Technology is the creation of tools or objects that both extend our natural abilities and alter our social environment.* It should be noted that the introduction of new technology brings with it the possibility for both positive and negative consequences. The key to coming to terms with technology is to consider both sides of the equation.

Does Change Begin with the Individual or the Technology?

Social change theory looks at the factors contributing to change within the structure of society. Generally, sociologists, anthropologists, and psychologists look at changes in the way people think, feel, and act and try to generate reasonable hypotheses to explain why change has taken place. As noted in Chapter 2, traditional theories of social change can be divided into a number of simple categories: sociological theories (see pages 59 to 65), anthropological theories (see pages 47 to 52), and psychological theories (see pages 53 to 59). However, since the focus of our study is technology specifically, we have to come to terms with the relationship between social change theory and technological development.

The following traditional theories take the position that change within society is brought about by a myriad of interactions within a society's framework that begin with the individual person. In other words, societal change is initiated by an individual person who shares an idea with his or her community. If that idea is accepted, society changes to adapt to the new idea. These ideas could take the shape of a new technology. Remember, earlier we defined technology as the creation of tools or objects that both extend our natural abilities and alter our social environment. From the perspective of the traditional theo-

ries of social change, we can infer that technology accompanies changes in society. Some of the potential effects of social and technological change can be seen in chart 4.2 on page 106.

In opposition to the traditional theories, there is another theory that suggests social change is not necessarily initiated by the individual, but by another force: technology. While the idea of **technological determinism** is vigorously debated among scholars, it does have particular relevance to this discussion.

The theory of technological determinism was first put forth by American economist and social theorist Thorstein Veblen (see the Groundbreaker feature on page 107). It achieved elevated status as succeeding generations of scholars from the University of Toronto—namely Harold Innis, Marshall McLuhan, and Walter Ong—put forward the idea that technology has much more of an impact on us than we are willing to admit. McLuhan said, "We shape our tools, and our tools shape us."

The position of the Toronto School effectively challenges the positions taken by the traditional theories of social change. Technological determinists see the invention of a particular tool, such as a computer, as taking on a life of its own after it has been introduced, with society simply reacting to the new technology. The traditional schools claim that a change in human thinking and communicating is accompanied by technological innovation—the technology being simply a natural and complementary partner in the process. The disparity between these two positions is the source of a heated and ongoing debate.

People prefer to see themselves as masters of their own destiny and not to see technology as their master. However, there is validity in the stance taken by technological determinists. Take, for instance, the fact that Canadians commonly gather around the television at different times of the day. Did you ever

Traditional Theories of Social Change and the Role of Technology

Theory	Explanation	Impact on Technology
Sociological Theory	• Social change arises from the decline of certain civilizations, from cycles of growth and decay, and from progress. • Change occurs as society moves in the direction of progress. • Factors affecting social change include survival, conflict, and the quest for progress. • Developmental schools include Evolutionary, Social Darwinism (Herbert Spencer), and Conflict (Karl Marx).	• Civilizations rise and fall based on their ability to create and adapt to new ideas and situations. • Technology can be instrumental in the rise or fall of a civilization, e.g., Roman military technology contributed to its rise and, it could be argued, its fall. • Despite some periods of regression, society continually improves. • Technology, along with ideology, is instrumental is societal change.
Anthropological Theory	• Cultural change and adaptation are accompanied by diffusion and acculturation. Anthropologists see acculturation occurring in three ways: through incorporation, direct change, and cultural evolution. • Structural-functionalists take the approach that change occurs gradually rather than dramatically because societies thrive on stability and equilibrium.	• As societies interact, a process of cultural sharing occurs. This often involves the sharing of technology—which in turn causes social change through the anthropological model indicated on page 49. • While society thrives on stability, technology tends to destabilize society. • New technology forces society to find a way to overcome instability and create a new equilibrium.
Psychological Theory	• Social change is brought about by the change in the mental states of individuals. Experts such as B. F. Skinner and Carl Jung have different opinions regarding the changes that individuals will experience before social change takes place. • One psychological theory is called the Social-Psychological Theory. This theory states that change occurs when individuals, driven by a need for achievement, create theories and inventions that improve the ability of society to function.	• The more mental stability is achieved by an individual, the more that stability is exhibited in society. • In social-psychological theory, technology arises out of the human need to achieve. • Innovation is based on the efforts of individuals to leave their mark on society.

Figure 4.2 Describe the main differences between how sociologists, psychologists and anthropologists view the role of technology in social change.

wonder what people did before television or radio? Certainly they worked and socialized, but instead of sitting in front of a television they sat around the hearth. With the fireplace as the family meeting place, people gathered news and entertained each other by storytelling, talking, and singing as opposed to tacitly watching television programs. The technology, in this case television, has modified people's behaviour.

Although the scholarly debate between traditional schools of social change and technological determinism is ongoing, many academics try to combine the two views by taking the position that social change is initiated by both societal ideals and the introduction of new technology. In this way, technology is neither discounted nor elevated in a balanced theory of social change.

GROUNDBREAKERS
THORSTEIN VEBLEN, (1857–1929)

Thorstein Veblen was an American sociologist and economist who coined the phrases "technological determinism," "conspicuous consumption," and "pecuniary emulation."

One of Veblen's most noteworthy books is *The Theory of the Leisure Class* wherein he applied the theory of Darwinian evolution to the economic institutions of capitalism. According to Veblen, society evolves through the invention and acceptance of new technologies. Technology forms the material base of society and subsequently determines the status of a society in comparison to other societies. Technology also dictates the pace of progress for a society—hence the label "technological determinism".

In terms of the overall structure of society, Veblen claimed that there are those who make goods and those who make money. Many societies are ruled by business leaders who seek to display their wealth as evidence of their superiority in the realm of economics. Subsequently, these institutions represent the "fittest" groups in society and rise to the ruling position in the capitalist system.

Veblen took great delight both in unveiling his Darwinian approach to the capitalist economic system and examining the leisure activities of the ruling class. He claimed that the accumulation of wealth led to the formation of a "leisure class" where wealthy members of society—more interested in making money than bettering the state of affairs within the greater community—take up

Figure 4.3 Thorstein Veblen

leisure activities such as "government, war, sports, and devout observances." The accumulation of wealth is characterized by **conspicuous consumption** (publicly demonstrating excessive wealth by purchasing luxury items) and **pecuniary emulation** (clearly demonstrating one's monetary worth). Veblen believed that the leisure class could damage the progress of society because of their competitive approach to gaining capital and the subsequent withdrawal from constructive labour in favour of leisure.

Finally, Veblen believed that progressive change is technologically grounded. Society tends to change for the better with technological development because new inventions tend to increase society's sense of efficiency. In other words, technological advancement makes good economic sense because it appeals to a large group within society while simultaneously eroding the power base of the leisure class.

Questions

1. Explain Veblen's Darwinian approach to the economic system and technological progress.

2. What effects does technological innovation have on society, according to Veblen?

3. Is Veblen's critique of capitalism fair? Explain your answer.

Pause and Reflect

1. What changes did the introduction of the printing press cause?

2. Define technology in your own words. Make a list of 8–10 technologies that play a role in your life, and briefly describe that role.

3. What is meant by the statement, "technology extends our natural abilities and alters our social environment."

4. Do traditional theories of social change tend to undervalue or overvalue technology? Explain your answer.

5. Do you agree with the traditional schools of social change or the position of technological determinism? Explain your answer.

Section 4.2   Coping with Technological Change

Key Concepts

future shock

hyperculture

technostress

technosis

theory of cultural lag

Luddite

Earlier it was noted that technology is the creation of tools or objects that both extend our natural abilities and alter our social environment. It has also been noted that periods of intense technological change can cause a revolution or dramatic change in the structure of society. The outstanding question is, How do the individual and society cope with technological change? To address this question we will look at some social scientists' views on the stresses that may result from the dramatic new information technologies of the twenty-first century. Then we will look at some suggestions for dealing with modern technological change.

 New Technology Equals New Stresses for the Individual

In a sense, the jury is still out on the psychological impact of the technologies of the information age. Research takes time and money, and the technologies are evolving so quickly that social scientists have difficulty keeping up. In the meantime, what we do have are some expert opinions on stresses brought on by new technology.

• **Technologies Can Have Negative Side Effects**

Like many people around the world, Canadians have been eager to embrace new technologies. From the cellphone and the pager to the computer and the Internet, Canadians have demonstrated a strong desire to get connected and stay connected. This eagerness has been accompanied by an almost nonchalant attitude to the introduction of new technologies. Canadians often embrace new technologies without really considering the consequences of the technology itself. For example, while the Internet allowed many people instant access to enormous amounts of useful information, it also allowed young children access to pornographic sites, hate propaganda, and detailed instructions on how to make pipe bombs.

• **Keeping Up with the Speed of Technological Change**

A second source of stress is the rate of change that people are forced to endure as a result of current technological changes. Author and futurist Alvin Toffler warned of the implications of rapid change being driven by technology in his classic book *Future Shock*. Toffler described the term **"future shock"** as the "dizzying disorientation brought on by the premature arrival of the future." He went on to say that until people learned to control the rate of change in their own lives, as well as in society in general, they are destined for a "massive adaptational breakdown."

Stephen Bertman of the University of Windsor expands on this theme in his book *Hyperculture: The Human Cost of Speed*. Bertman claims that societal change is occurring at such a staggering rate—largely driven by new technologies—that the fundamental values of society are being blurred. Bertman claims that technology has brought with it acceleration. Take the Internet as an example; we have only to type in a few keywords and the information arrives almost immediately. This rapidity often comes at the expense of our patience. This impatience is then transferred into our basic value structure. Bertman states, "…we quickly lose patience with those we might otherwise love if they do not respond swiftly, or obey as readily, as the machines we know" (Bertman, 2000, p. 5). He goes on to say that living in a society of **"hyperculture"** results in the deterioration of the family where "the virtues of sacrifice and long term commitment, so essential to effective parenthood, become rare" (Bertman, 2000, p. 5).

• Overdependence on Technology

A third source of stress is caused by our dependence on technology. According to American social scientists Michelle M. Weil and Larry Rosen, authors of *Technostress*, we tend to rely so heavily on our machines that, when they don't do what we want them to do, we experience tremendous anxiety.

The term that Weil and Rosen use to describe an overblown dependency or attachment to technology is **technosis**. People demonstrate technosis when they feel "out of touch" if they don't check their e-mail messages, or when they have their cellphone or pager on at all times. Weil and Rosen are concerned with the psychological implications of dependency on technology to the extent that it can cause both phobias and addiction.

Psychologist Kimberly Young of the University of Pittsburgh has posted a study of "cyber-disorders" on the Center for Online and Internet Addiction Web site in which she states the following:

> ...the term addiction *has extended into the psychiatric lexicon to identify problematic Internet use associated with significant social, psychological, and occupational impairment. Symptoms include a preoccupation with the Internet, increased anxiety when off-line, hiding or lying about the extent of on-line use, and impairment to real-life functioning. (Young, et al., 1999)*

Young concludes by stating, "Addictive use of the Internet directly leads to social isolation, increased depression, familial discord, divorce, academic failure, financial debt and job loss."

One of the key points made by Weil, Rosen, and Young is that technology can cause acute stress within the psyche of an individual. This problem is so significant that, if it is not dealt with effectively, the person risks losing his or her sense of stability and identity. This point is reinforced by Stanley Rothman of Smith College in the United States. On the development of computers, and especially the Internet, Rothman notes:

> *The technology is still too new to be fully evaluated, and most of the writing on the subject is quite speculative. Some things, however, are clear. Many individuals can now remain at home alone and complete much of their work there. Second, the Internet itself provides opportunity (via interactive games) to create a virtual reality in which one takes on any role one wishes to take on and creates virtual "communities" if one wishes to call them that, of computer related individuals. The potential for increasing the isolation of the individual from other "real" individuals has been greatly heightened... (Rothman, 1997, p. 12)*

Learning to Cope with Technological Change

William Ogburn is an American social scientist who examined the behaviour of society and summarized his conclusions in his **theory of cultural lag**. While widely disputed and viewed as a doctrine of technological determinism, his theory demonstrates a possible explanation of how individuals in society deal with technological change.

Ogburn's theory states that the acceptance of a new technology follows a three-phase process of invention, discovery, and diffusion. If all three phases can be verified, then a new technology has been successfully integrated into society. The acceptance of the new technology is hindered by one behavioural aspect of society: a resistance to change. Technology introduces change that temporarily destabilizes society and, until society adapts, a period of transition occurs. This transition is exacerbated by members of society who oppose the new technology, thus creating what Ogburn calls a "cultural lag." Figure 4.4 outlines this process.

Two methods of coping with technological change follow from Ogburn's cultural lag theory. Members of one school of thought accept technology and become active in its implementation. Members of another school vehemently oppose the new technology and do everything they can to halt its progress. Members of the latter group are often referred to as Luddites. According to some sources, the term **"Luddite"** is derived from the secret society whose goal it was to destroy the new textile machines introduced into England in the 1810s during the early years of the Industrial Revolution. The society's name came from Ned Ludd, who organized the machine-smashing raids in Nottingham in a desperate attempt to preserve the skilled weavers' way of life. Today, "Luddite" refers to a person who opposes technological advancement.

While most people are not Luddites, there is often a suspicion and concern over new technology based on the fact that it brings with it corresponding change and a demand for adaptation. This is the process that Ogburn suggests creates cultural lag.

Recognizing The Process

So how do we cope with technological change? One method of coping with new technology is to recognize the processes involved in the introduction and eventual acceptance of innovations. Two things should be considered before moving on: first, it is important to keep in mind that not all technological developments are accepted. New technology is accepted only when the timing is right and society demonstrates a willingness to embrace whatever it has to offer. Second, knowledge and analysis are the keys to understanding the impact of technology on our daily lives. Ogburn analyzed the effects of technology on society and came to some theoretical conclusions. Whether we agree with his conclusions or not, he made the effort to use his mind to see what happens when a new technology is introduced and society changes. Acquiring knowledge and analyzing trends is the most effective way to deal with the impact of technology on each of us, as well as on our families and our society.

Canadian scholar and author Marshall McLuhan is another example of someone who dealt with certain technological advancements by studying them and analyzing their impacts

---

Cultural Lag Theory
Theorist: William Ogburn

Process #1: Invention
- combining elements and materials to form new ones
- can be material inventions (e.g., the computer) or social inventions (e.g., capitalism)

Process #2: Discovery
- discovering a new way of viewing reality
- the combination of the discovery and the right timing initiate social change

Process #3: Diffusion
- the spread of a discovery from one area to another
- this is accompanied by acceptance of the discovery by different societies

Source: Henslin, James M. and Adie Nelson. 1996. Sociology: *A Down-to-Earth Approach*. Toronto: Allyn and Bacon Canada.

Figure 4.4 A key component of Ogburn's theory of social change is that, while some members of society adapt to the technological innovation, others lag behind the new discovery.

on society. McLuhan taught English at the University of Toronto from 1946 to 1979 and attained international recognition as an expert on media technology in the late 1960s and early 1970s. He encouraged people to consider the effects of new media on the individual and the community.

McLuhan believed that any medium is the extension of some human quality. For instance, the radio is the extension of the ear, and the book is the extension of the eye. It is the human desire to extend our collective capabilities that inspires the invention of new technologies. Based on this premise, McLuhan claimed that the introduction of a new medium or technology followed four laws, as outlined in Figure 4.5 (on page 112).

Although McLuhan's methods were considered unconventional by some academics, through his research and analysis, it was clear that McLuhan got people thinking about the effects of media on their everyday lives.

Although the general population would not have the time or the resources to study technology to the extent that McLuhan and Ogburn did, it would still be possible for the average person to make a simple mental analysis of the effects that a certain technology had on his or her everyday life.

Evaluating the Impacts of Technology on Our Lives

Often, society studies problems extensively but provides little in terms of solutions to these problems. This can sometimes create a sense of hopelessness as people conclude that the problems are too big to solve. Studies in technological change are no exception to this rule. The volume of work exposing problems associated with technology is much greater than that which suggests solutions. However, in our discussion, the theorists who brought us the terms "hyperculture" and "technostress" do suggest possible coping mechanisms.

In his book *Hyperculture*, Stephen Bertman calls on people to resist the powerful

FILM SOCIETY

Title: Metropolis (1926)
Rating: not rated
Director: Fritz Lang

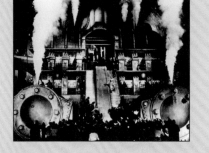

This classic film looks at the dehumanization of work and the polarization of society. An original, cutting-edge film, *Metropolis* offers an excellent introduction to a deeper study of Luddism.

pull of technology by intelligently evaluating the impact of technology on their lives. People can do this by focusing on their own sense of mental health. Bertman encourages people to step back from technology—taking what he calls a weekly sabbatical—so that they can recharge and see the role it plays in their lives. He also encourages people to actively preserve their sense of history. Whether we are referring to family, national, or world history, the danger of the information age is the possibility that real history will become lost in a mass of information that results in the creation of a virtual history. Bertman claims that things like family traditions need to be promoted, especially among the young, in order to preserve a sense of cultural and personal identity.

Similarly, Michelle Weil and Larry Rosen conclude that, while the pull of technology is almost irresistible, the key is to avoid becoming slaves to the machines. Instead, both social scientists encourage people to step back thoughtfully every once in a while and intro-

McLuhan's Four Laws of Media

Key Question	Law	Examples
What does the new medium *enhance*?	#1 Any major medium enhances or accelerates a certain process or thing.	• Money enhanced trade. • The computer enhanced information processing. • The telephone enhanced person-to-person communication.
What does the new medium *make obsolete*?	#2 The new medium *tends* to render obsolete another process or thing.	• Money made barter obsolete. • The computer made the typewriter obsolete. • The telephone and cheap communication eventually made the personal letter obsolete.
What does the new medium *retrieve* from the past?	#3 Any major medium retrieves some process or thing that had been previously obsolete.	• Money revived the spirit of conspicuous consumption. • The computer revived reading and writing *en masse*. • The telephone revived person-to-person communication for people who had been separated by distance.
What does a new medium *reverse* or flip into?	#4 Any major medium, when pushed to its extreme, flips into something entirely new.	• Money flipped into credit cards. • The desktop computer flipped into the laptop computer, which flipped into the palm pilot. • The telephone flipped into the cellular phone.

Source: Marchand, Philip. 1989 The Medium and the Messenger

Figure 4.5 How do the four laws of media serve as useful tools for anyone who chooses to analyze trends and assess the impact of technology on our everyday lives?

spectively assess their thoughts and feelings. Humans need rest and separation from things like work and technology. Those boundaries have to be built by each individual. Without boundaries, people lose their sense of security, their peace of mind, and the opportunity for downtime.

Figure 4.6 Many new "dot com" companies in Canada and around the world are run by young professionals who design their office spaces to include cafes and pool tables. This allows their computer programmers some relaxation time away from their computer screens, which, they claim, results in happier, more productive employees. Would you like to work in an office environment like this?

Pause and Reflect

1. What does Ogburn mean by "cultural lag"?

2. How can the average person cope with technological change?

3. Define "future shock," "hyperculture," and "technosis." Do you believe that these phenomena exist? Give three statements of evidence to support your answer.

4. What are the three approaches to technology suggested by Weil and Rosen? Which approach do you take? Explain your answer.

5. What impact does current computer technology have on the way you live your life? Are you governed by technology or do you govern technology?

Technology Use by Social Scientists

While social scientists investigate the effects of technology on people and societies, they also use technology to conduct those important studies. **High technologies**, such as computers and sophisticated communication devices, are invaluable tools in many professions. The following case study illustrates an example of how psychologist Robert West and his team used computer technology to study human behaviour in ways that were previously impossible.

West and his research methods were introduced in Chapter 1 (see page 17). This case study will provide a more in-depth look at his work and at the same time allow you to become familiar with the writing and presentation style of actual social science journals.

CASE STUDY

Investigating Game-Playing Behaviour

Psychologist Robert West worked with a research team to investigate opponents' behaviours when playing certain video games (for example, kung-fu fighting games, sports games) and financial games (for example, playing the stock market). (You can read about the skills and methods he used in the feature on page 17.)

According to the team's theory, players' decisions are considerably influenced by their opponents' past behaviour. To test their theory, West and the other researchers worked with a simple game called paper, rock, scissors (PRS). Both excerpts in this case study come from a journal article West wrote with a colleague, Christian Lebiere, to present their findings.

The Roots of Game-Playing Behaviour

In terms of real world behaviours, PRS can be considered to represent the elemental game-playing skill of guessing what your opponent will do next. From an evolutionary perspective, this skill would have been crucial for survival. For example, consider a cheetah chasing a gazelle. The gazelle can leap forward, to the right, or to the left. Therefore, in order to catch the gazelle, the cheetah must correctly choose whether to pounce straight ahead, to the right, or to the left. Similarly, in PRS you must guess what your opponent will do next in order to win. PRS is also a "repeated game." That is, except for the first move, the player has access to the opponent's previous moves (i.e., through memory). More generally, this is usually the case when animals and/or humans square off against each other in predator/prey competitions or in disputes over resources or mates (also in sports such as boxing or basketball). For example, in mammalian mating competitions, when two males face each other there is usually some preliminary movement, seemingly aimed at feeling out the opponent. Aside from ambushes, attacks rarely occur in the absence of some recent history of movement. Thus, although simple, PRS embodies basic and important game-playing skills.

To prove their psychological theory about the way people play games, the researchers developed a computer program designed to respond as a human being does within certain parameters. The researchers, using the computer program called lag2, represented individual players in a computerized game of PRS. After testing their theory on the computer-simulated games, the researchers tested the human subjects against the computer program.

Method

9.1.1. Subjects

Eighteen subjects from the University of Hong Kong volunteered to play against the lag2 network [one version of the neural network]. Eight of these were tested on a one-by-one basis (similar to Experiment 2), while the other 10 were tested as a group. For the group test a computer lab was used so that each subject had his or her own PC.

9.1.2. Procedure

The conditions, instructions, and apparatus were the same as in Experiment 2, except that the individually tested subjects were asked to play until either they or the lag2 network reached a score of 50, and the group tested subjects were asked to play until either they or the lag2 network reached a score of 100. As in the previous experiments, ties were treated as losses by the network. Subjects were told to play at their own pace and after approximately 20 minutes subjects were stopped, regardless of how far they had gotten. Also, subjects were told that the computer was programmed to play quite well and that if they won only by a little it would demonstrate considerable ability on their part. This was done to avoid subjects becoming discouraged and losing concentration if they failed to gain a decisive advantage.

Source: West, R.L. and C. Lebiere. 2001. "Simple games as dynamic coupled systems: Randomness and other emergent properties." *Cognitive Systems Research*. Vol. 1, No. 4.

Questions

1. How was technology used in the psychologists' experiment? How could this experiment have been conducted without the use of computer technology?
2. Who might have use for the findings of West's study? Explain your answer.
3. In the final portion of the second excerpt, West describes a step he took to prevent players from becoming discouraged. Why would West be concerned about the players' frame of mind?

Section 4.3   The Impact of Technology on the Family

In the previous section, we studied the effects of technological change on the individual. But what of its impacts on society's building block—the family? Using the examples of domestic technologies and computer communication technology, we will examine some of the impacts of technology on society in general, and specifically on the family unit.

◐ The Influence of Technology in the Home

Technological innovation in the domestic sphere in Canada following World War I brought about dramatic effects on the family dynamic. This era was characterized by a new **mass culture** in which people of all social classes in Canada could participate. For example, radios became more affordable as did music records, and these new technologies became popular ways for people of most income levels to enjoy forms of entertainment that had not previously been available to them.

The introduction of electricity into the family home brought with it a whole host of new technologies that were supposedly meant to help women manage the housework. However, it seemed to have a different impact on a woman's duties.

Gas stoves first appeared in 1919, electric refrigerators in 1920. Hot-water and warm-air heating systems, enamelled bathtubs and flush toilets, the replacement of gas-lighting with electricity, and the increasing affordability of telephones and radios did much to support the ideal of the private family in its cosy home, independent from neighbours and protected against the outside world. The long-term effects of modern domestic science and technology were elevated standards of hygiene and comfort, but also elevated expectations of women. Reduced physical labour, therefore, did not necessarily mean less housework. For many women, it simply meant the reordering of an intensive workday. (Comaccio, 1999, pp. 80–81)

Fast-forward to the 21st century and we can see how technology continues to affect the ways family members communicate and interact, not just in Canada, but around the globe. Take, for example, the introduction of the satellite television into homes in an Asian country that had previously had little experience with cultures and technological progress outside its own borders. The example in the case study on the next page gives us an idea of the power and lure of television, as well as television's potential effect on the family.

Figure 4.7 Discuss some of the positive and negative impacts that radio may have had on the family dynamic in the 1930s and 1940s.

Key Concepts

mass culture

computer communication technology

infomated household

Satellite Television in Bhutan

Located in the remote mountain ranges of the Himalayas, Bhutan is a country that has fought to remain faithful to its Tibetan Buddhist traditions. However, as the world moves further and further into the information and communication age, Bhutan has felt compelled to allow its citizenry the opportunity to see more of the world than what could be offered by Buddhist monks.

Things changed in Bhutan in mid-1999 when the king lifted the government's ban on television. He did so with a few strings attached. Television would reach the people via the Bhutan Broadcasting Service (BBS). Established by the government to provide the people with a sense of local programming and news, the BBS would air programming for several hours each evening to a captive national audience. Or were they captive?

Figure 4.8 The emergence of television effectively transformed the lives of the people of Bhutan. Evenings of discussing Tibetan Buddhism were suddenly replaced by family gatherings around the television. What are the pros and cons of this change?

Several months after the ban on television had been lifted, satellite dishes began appearing on the rooftops of Bhutanese homes, reflecting the desire of the people to experience more than national programming. Suddenly, instead of the local news of the BBS, Bhutan was subject to the wild drama of the World Wrestling Federation (WWF) and the musical styling of MTV. The impact of the WWF was of particular concern to Bhutanese parents and government officials. It seemed that some young viewers were practicing the wrestling moves demonstrated by WWF wrestlers in backyards and in open sandlots.

Television has done more than invade the living rooms of Bhutan. It has also rearranged the way people sit in them. No longer do children and parents face each other across the table or on a floor mat, discussing Buddhist teachings such as how to earn merit with good deeds. Now, family members gather around the TV set.

"Family customs are now being gradually marginalized," says Sonam Kinga, a researcher at the Centre for Bhutan Studies who is studying the impact of television here.

"People used to have a continuous interaction with their families, but they are no longer looking at each other, they're looking at the TV screen. TV has taken on the role of mediating between family members."

Bhutan's tradition of folklore, transmitted through the generations, may not survive the daily satellite transmissions, according to Kinga. He fears the slow erosion of the country's monastic tradition, making Bhutan ever more vulnerable to the television juggernaut. It's not just that teenagers are mesmerized by MTV videos and Indian movies featuring scantily clad women. Kinga frets about the story content that stresses endless love stories. Apart from the sexual innuendo, the obsession with romance risks distracting young people from traditional Buddhist themes such as repaying parents for their kindness, honouring teachers and cultivating merit.

Source: Cohn, Martin. 2001. "Lost Horizon" The Toronto Star.

Questions

1. Speculate on why the king wanted the BBS to be the only television station in Bhutan?
2. What effect did television have on family activities in Bhutan? Be specific.
3. a) Make a list of three questions sociologists might want to investigate in regard to this situation.
   b) Make a list of three questions anthropologists might ask about the introduction of satellite television in Butan.

Measuring the Impact of Computer Communication Technology

Canadians are well aware of the growing presence of the computer in society. Whether one is doing banking online, using a calculator, driving a car, or listening to a compact disc, a computer is involved, to varying degrees somewhere in the process. The computer has significantly improved information processing. It has dramatically reduced the amount of time spent gathering and accessing information to such an extent that, theoretically, we should have more free time. Recent Statistics Canada information indicates that 35.9 per cent of Canadians use **computer communication technology** for a variety of activities both at home and at work.

This demonstrates a fundamental shift in the way Canadians gather information, find entertainment, and conduct their affairs. Consider the following quotation from Aboriginal folk singer Buffy Sainte-Marie on the use of computer technology by members of the First Nations in Canada.

On an airplane, my Powerbook is singing to me in Lakota, while the words to the song appear onscreen in both Lakota and English.

In the Canadian Rockies, Indians carrying portable computers trudge through a herd of elk and into the Banff Centre for the Arts where the "Drumbeats to Drumbytes"

thinktank confronts the reality of online life as it affects Native artists...

Across Canada, thousands of First Nations children network their observations and life experiences into mainstream education, as the Cradleboard Teaching Project–Kids from Kanata partnership provides both Native content and connectivity to schools as far away as Hawaii and Baffin Island.

I make a commercial record in a tipi on the Saskatchewan plains, and CBC television films the event for international broadcast...

...The reality of the situation is that we're not all dead and stuffed in some museum with the dinosaurs: we are Here in this digital age. (Sainte-Marie, 1997)

Internet and the Family

The impact of the computer and the Internet on the family is still being determined and measured by social scientists. What is clear is that Canadians are becoming more computer- and Internet-dependent (see Figure 4.9). Now evenings at home with your family may involve reading e-mail, browsing the Internet, playing a game, or purchasing something online. Thus, as time passes, improved computer capabilities will lead to further changes to the family dynamic as family members adapt to new innovations and changes.

Computer Communications Use at Home

Purpose of use	% of all households		% of regular home user household		% of households spending <10% of their time on this activity		% of households spending <50% of their time on this activity	
	1997	1998	1997	1998	1997	1998	1997	1998
e-mail	13.3	19.3	83.1	85.6	39.8	36.8	78.1	80.5
electronic banking	3.1	5.5	19.6	24.4	66.0	67.0	89.5	90
purchasing	1.5	2.5	9.2	10.9	88.1	91.6	98.3	99.3
search for medical info	-	9.6	-	42.5	-	74.8	-	97.2
education training	-	6.8	-	30.0	-	32.3	-	79.9
look for government info	-	8.2	-	36.4	-	75.9	-	97.9
look for other info	-	15.3	-	67.9	-	28.5	-	80.1
general browsing	-	17.6	-	78.1	-	29.9	-	80.0
playing games	-	7.8	-	34.4	-	48.4	-	90
chat groups	-	5.7	-	25.4	-	52.4	-	88.4
other Internet service	2.2	2.6	13.7	11.6	66.1	71.1	90.5	95.5

Source: Dickinson, Paul and Jonathan Ellison. 1999. "Getting Connected and Staying Unplugged: The Growing Use of Computer Communications Services." Ottawa. Statistics Canada / Ministry of Industry.

Figure 4.9 Which of the above activities listed do you personally use computers to accomplish? Do you think the percentages of people using computer communications technology will continue to increase indefinitely? Explain your answer.

Transformation of Social Relationships

Social relationships have been transformed by the instant availability of information either through computer programs or the Internet. E-mail, chat rooms, and teleconferencing make instant communication available to anyone at any time. The problem is that the communication occurs via the computer itself. Sociologists wonder about the effect on social relationships when interactions are devoid of the human touch. What about body language and eye contact? Can we get an accurate impression of what someone is thinking or feeling when we cannot see him or her in person? The cues that are available to us in live encounters are absent to varying degrees when we use computer communication technologies. This, in turn, has an impact on the way family members relate to others and the ways in which they interact with each other.

Figure 4.10 The computer has affected the way children and parents spend their time together. Now parents have the option of playing on the computer with their children.

In the following case study, anthropologist Dr. Jan English-Lueck examines in detail some of the characteristics of family members who use a lot of high technology. She observed that computers have such a pronounced impact on dynamics in the home that it leads, in her opinion, to change in how we will define "family." See if you agree with her.

Information Technology and the Family

Dr. Jan English-Lueck, an associate professor of anthropology at San Jose State University, has focused some of her research on the effect of technology on families living in Silicon Valley, the information technology capital of the world. Working with colleagues Charles Darrah and James M. Freeman, English-Lueck compiled the results of 450 detailed interviews and drew several compelling conclusions.

English-Lueck focused her research on **"info-mated households"**—that is, homes with at least five information technologies, including devices such as fax machines, voice mail, pagers, TVs, VCRs, CDs, computers, and cellular phones. She was curious to see the impact of these technologies on the daily lives of the families that used them. Early on, English-Lueck concluded that infomated households revolve around work—both the paid and unpaid varieties. Paid work would be the jobs that family members held to provide them with material and professional gratification. Unpaid work included a series of tasks ranging from managing the household, doing chores, taking part in sports and other recreational activities, and "working on" one's family. In fact, the interviews demonstrated that infomated families were consumed with work.

This initial observation led to several other conclusions. For instance, parents working to support their families demonstrated three striking characteristics:

- First, they spent a lot of time thinking about their paid jobs. Therefore, even when they were not working, they were thinking about their jobs.
- Second, they were bringing a lot of work home. English-Lueck calls this the colonization of home time by work. Working parents could get more reading, writing and reflecting done in the family home than at the office. English-Lueck tells the story of a man who set up access to his work e-mail account from his home computer. His hope was that he would be able to get ahead and maybe free up some time for an afternoon or two off work down the road. Instead, the man found that this remote access allowed him to simply keep up with his work as his company placed more and more demands on him.
- Third, many parents approached their family life from a work perspective. In other words, besides thinking a great deal about their paying jobs, parents (and by extension their children) assumed task-oriented roles in the household. English-Lueck claims that families often "view themselves as management problems to be solved, just as they do at work, with technology." For instance, she cites the case of a software engineer who assumed the role of at-home mom for several years. She had each day carefully planned with activities clearly delineated so everyone knew what was going on. She also worked with other mothers to prepare a database of food

recipes and parenting articles. English-Lueck also talks of people using palm pilots to organize the home/work division of labour. Also, certain family members (usually fathers) took on "expert" roles when it came to dealing with information technologies in the home.

These characteristics of family life point to a basic redefinition of the family. English-Lueck states that in an infomated home:

> ...the family is not a natural unit that simply exists, but one defined by action. Families watch TV, camp, travel, eat and talk together. The devices that facilitate that action or talk— phones, networked computers, pagers, answering machines—take on a serious purpose for these people. Paging your children to let them know you are concerned that they arrived home safely from school demonstrates parental responsibility. Sharing an evening of movies or technology talk provides an opportunity for doing something together.

English-Lueck claims that her interviews with the families of Silicon Valley have led to five important assumptions:

1. Infomated families do not simply use technology—they live in ecosystems of technology. She says, "Pagers, faxes, cell phones, telephone answering systems and computers are used together to serve the goals of individuals and families."

2. Family use of technology is indicative of important cultural work being done by its members. Using technology can be seen as the medium by which a family can do things together—a key component of the definition of an infomated family.

3. Technology does not transform families into something new. Instead, it allows families to practise old traditions in new contexts.

4. Technology plays an important symbolic role in the life of a family. As family activity becomes more task-oriented, as is also the case of life at work, the home tends to become a place of production, with a reinvented product emerging. That reinvented product is the family unit itself.

5. Technology has blurred the line between paid work and life at home. The length of the workweek is no longer determined by time spent at the office. Instead, it is a combination of time spent working at the office and at home.

Thus, the infomated family represents a new kind of family dynamic. This new family utilizes technology to such a degree that a new definition of family has emerged. English-Lueck concludes that this is neither a good nor a bad thing. Instead she simply recognizes it as a new development, one that goes to the very heart of what it means for some people to be part of a family.

Source: English-Lueck, J.A. "Technology and Social Change: The Effects on Family and Community." Consortium of Social Science Associations Congressional Seminar, June 1998.

Questions

1. What types of communication and information technology are present in your home?

2. What impact, if any, does this technology have on the way your family members interact? Give some examples.

3. Choose one piece of recently acquired technology in your home and make a chart outlining the pros and cons of its effect on your family.

4. Are infomated families too reliant on technology and not connected enough with each other?

Skill Builder:
Developing Research Strategies

In this, the age of Internet technology and well stocked libraries, vast amounts of information are ours for the asking. The key to successfully researching a subject is to go from the general to the specific, weeding out all the extraneous sources of information along the way. It is by examining general information sources such as a textbook or an encyclopedia that you can gain a basic understanding of your topic. This is followed by a more comprehensive search for sources that will allow you to refine your hypothesis and discover information that will support or refute your initial stance. Solid research follows this process. A well-researched project makes a steady movement from the general to the specific.

Step One: Consult general information sources

First, you should approach your topic or hypothesis by reviewing sources that present information in a clear, concise fashion. For instance, let's say you are working with the following hypothesis: "Computer video games are having an adverse effect on the behaviour of children."

A good place to begin your examination of the topic would be an encyclopedia or textbook. These sources provide you with the opportunity to define the terms that are most relevant to your hypothesis. For instance, you probably want to look up the following keywords in an encyclopedia or the index of a textbook: "computer video games," "children," "families," "psychology."

Taking a general look at these topics will give you the necessary background information that you will need to proceed with your project.

Step Two: Identify content-specific sources

Once you have defined the terms that are included in your hypothesis, you are ready to proceed with a more comprehensive investigation of your topic. At this point, you will need to consult new and varied sources of information. These sources can include print sources such as newspapers, magazines, scholarly journals, and books; and electronic sources such as educational videos and Web sites.

Once again, the thrust of this stage of your inquiry is to gain more general information that will aid you in understanding the main components of your topic. Your reading should allow a degree of content mastery.

Using your hypothesis, you can conduct a search for sources at the school or public library, or on the Internet. Use the keywords mentioned in Step One as a guide to beginning your more in-depth research. These keywords should guide you to books and articles that provide you with the background that you need.

Locating these sources can be aided by the use of the following tools:

Library catalogue–Do a subject search of your topic and see what books are available.

Indexes/databases–Many journals and magazines are indexed to make it easier to find articles. Often these indexes and databases come in an electronic form that you can either access over the Internet or through a school or public library. It is a very good idea to work with a librarian in acquiring sources for your project.

Literature reviews–Sometimes current research is summarized in abstracts and reviews. These reviews summarize the conclusions presented in some articles. Once again, work with your librarian to locate reliable sources for literature review.

Web sites—Conduct your own search over the Internet, using the keywords as search strings. (See the section "E-Source Search String," on page 122 for more information.)

Step Three: Select the most appropriate sources

Now that you have a general understanding of your topic, you are ready to conduct a more thorough academic investigation. At this point you will need to evaluate the information and the sources that you have found to determine which are the most appropriate.

Reliable Print Sources

Here are a few important points regarding print information:

Books: Use books that are written by experts in the field under investigation. These authors may be scholars, journalists, or freelance writers with a clear mastery of the topic. Textbooks should be used only to gain a cursory understanding of your topic. After the initial stages of your research, you should focus on authoritative print materials that deal either directly or indirectly with your hypothesis.

Magazines and newspapers: Use articles written by reporters who interview experts for their articles.

Scholarly journals: Scholarly journals are a very reliable source of information. They are written by experts from specific academic disciplines.

Books and scholarly journals are the most reliable sources of print information. While magazine and newspaper articles are effective in highlighting certain issues, they often lack the expertise of academic work completed by experts in the field.

E-Source Search Strings

It is very important that you assess the reliability of your Internet sources. Generally, if a Web site has "edu" or "org" in its address, the site is associated with a reliable organization such as a university. Make sure you check on this. An unfortunate drawback of researching on the Internet is that anyone can post information there. That is why it is important to establish the reliability of the source.

Once again, a good starting point is to work with a school librarian to find out where the reliable Web sources are located. Librarians tend to distinguish between

- **directories:** Web sites that are arranged and categorized by topics to make searching easier and more directed, for example, <www.lii.org> Librarians' Index to the Internet
- **search engines:** databases of all items on the Internet; addresses gathered by the search engine providers, for example, <www.google.com> , <www.altavista.com>, <www.yahoo.com>

Librarians tend to prefer directories because they are arranged by people who are specifically assigned to the task. Search engines have no real filtering process. Interested parties simply register their pages with the search engine company, and then anyone searching via their site can find the Web pages posted if they type in associated keywords.

When searching for electronic sources, you should focus on certain keywords. For example, many Web search sites allow you to conduct a Boolean search. A Boolean search involves including or excluding certain information by using the words AND, OR, and NOT. For instance, if we were to conduct a Boolean search regarding our topic, we would need to follow these guidelines:

AND (and) Use the AND operator between any two search terms to find documents containing both terms.	computer video games AND psychology AND children
OR (or) Use the OR operator between any two search terms to find documents containing either of the two terms.	computer video games OR computer games OR violent computer games
AND NOT Use the AND NOT operator between any two search terms to find documents that do not include the term immediately following the NOT. In the case listed to the right, we have narrowed our search to include violence and not educational games.	Computer video games AND psychology AND children AND violence AND NOT educational games

These search techniques should help lead you to information that is specific to your topic. This, in turn, will help give focus and direction to your project.

Practise It!
1. Conduct an Internet search on the topic "Internet addiction and its effect on relationships between family members." List the three best sites you found and give a short summary of the types of information contained on each.
2. Research the broad topic "Advances in domestic technologies from the 1920s to the present day." Choose one of these technologies and narrow your research scope by finding sources that focus on its development and social impact. List three of these sources.

Section 4.4   Changes in Land Use and Agriculture

So far we have studied the impacts of technological change from a psychological perspective, when we focused on the individual, and from a sociological perspective, when we focused on the family. Now we are going to look at the anthropologist's view on how technological changes affect the broader society in terms of culture. We will do this by examining the ways in which different societies exploit their natural environments, and by looking at the role technology plays in this.

Adaptation and Technology

Our habitat is constantly changing. This change can take three different forms: it can be **abiotic** (meaning it involves non-living factors such as weather or climate), **biotic** (which involves living factors such as vegetation and animal populations), or human (involving changes in population, war, trade, etc.) (Peoples and Bailey, 1991, p. 111). Environmental change is a reality for all people, no matter where in the world they live. However, the ways in which different peoples adapt to these changes have a strong influence on how societies operate.

Humans mainly adapt to change in our environment through the use of new technologies or through changes in our behaviours. To examine this topic further, we will focus on some technological changes that influenced agricultural practices and land use. After all, agriculture helped transform the world, says professor of anthropology Daniel Vasey:

> Agriculture and people have evolved on a path that can be neatly summarized. First people were few, and farmers non-existent. Then there were many more people and most of them were farmers. Now we are billions. Most of us no longer farm, but those of us who do support the rest. (Vasey, 1992, p. vii)

Resources and Means of Production

Our planet provides a huge number of resources that vary according to climate and geographical location. For example, the wet climate of the coastal areas of British Columbia produces rain forests of immense cedar trees. The Aboriginal peoples of this region used this resource to meet many of their needs. Some tree trunks were hollowed out and used as canoes, while others were carved into totem poles. The trees were also burned to provide heat, and their bark was stripped and used for clothing and for building homes. The methods by which people extract a resource from their habitat, and then exploit that resource to meet their

Key Concepts

abiotic change

biotic change

production

hunter-gatherer

nomadic

domestication

horticulture

extensive/
intensive

pastoralism

irrigation

flood irrigation

draft plough

genetically
modified (GM)
food

needs, is called **production**. Means of production are so important that they can often have a great impact on the way people live their everyday lives. Thus when a method of resource exploitation or land use changes—either because of advancing ecological knowledge or the introduction of a new technology—this can affect a society's culture.

Production involves three components: the resource itself, the people who will use their time and energy getting the resource ready for consumption, and the technology used by these people to extract or exploit the resource. Some anthropologists define this technology as either physical tools or cultural knowledge. Physical tools can be described this way:

> Some tools reduce the amount of human time and energy needed to produce goods, and this saves labour (e.g., hoes, plows). Others allow more goods or a greater variety of goods to be produced from a given area of land (e.g., fertilizer). Still other tools allow people to produce goods that human labour alone could not provide (e.g. the saw used to take down large trees). (Peoples and Bailey, 1991, p. 114)

Cultural knowledge, on the other hand, is described as methods or knowing used by a people to exploit a resource to its full potential, or to recognize an object as being a useful resource. For example, the spear used to kill a wild horse is a physical technology, while recognizing the horse as a possible means of transportation is cultural knowledge. It follows that change in either type of technology will influence indigenous approaches to resource management and land use.

Early Anthropological Theory

Early anthropological theorists studied the different ways societies used tools, tech-niques, and cultural knowledge to produce the goods they needed to survive. Lewis Henry Morgan (1818–1881) called these activities the "arts of subsistence" (Lavenda, Schultz, 2000, p.116). Morgan categorized societies according to the level of sophistication of the technologies they employed. The more complex the tools and methods, the more evolved the society, in his estimation. Although this theory was rejected by later theorists, such as Franz Boas, Morgan's research, which linked certain arts of subsistence to particular types of social organization, remained important.

Up until the 1950s, anthropologists continued to collect data about the technologies used by various peoples, but they began to classify them into broader categories, which were not arranged in a progressive sequence of evolution as Morgan's system was. The divisions were generally identified as hunter-gatherers (or foragers), horticulturists, pastoralists, and agriculturists. Modern times have brought additional categories, as shown in Figure 4.11. We will look briefly at each group, while stopping to explore the impact of selected technologies on resource management and land use along the way.

Hunter-Gatherers

All cultures have emerged from a **hunter-gatherer** tradition. The hunter-gatherers, or foragers as they are sometimes called, subsist by travelling across a given territory and collecting wild plants and hunting animals as they go. Their ecological knowledge is extensive, and this allows them to recognize the most beneficial foods and also to predict with confidence when and where these foods will come into season. As a result, they are necessarily **nomadic**, moving from region to region in pursuit of their food supply.

Vast tracts of land are needed for this type of subsistence since the plants and ani-

The Social Transformation of Society

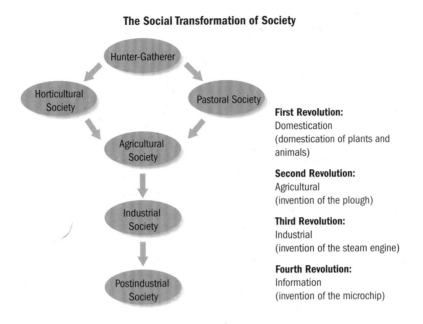

First Revolution:
Domestication
(domestication of plants and animals)

Second Revolution:
Agricultural
(invention of the plough)

Third Revolution:
Industrial
(invention of the steam engine)

Fourth Revolution:
Information
(invention of the microchip)

Source: Henslin, James M. and Adie Nelson. 1996. *Sociology: A Down-to-Earth Approach.* Toronto: Allyn and Bacon Canada.

Figure 4.11 Societies have evolved from the early stages of hunting and gathering to the complex information processing of the post-industrial age. Where we go next is anybody's guess.

mals are spread out and the people must search over large areas to collect enough food to meet their needs. As a result, foraging societies can support only small populations in relation to the amount of land used. In such societies, land ownership was unheard of, as this resource was shared.

Until about 10 000 years ago, foraging was the only type of subsistence practised. Then, a change took place in certain locations around the globe that had a major impact on the way that some peoples managed their resources and used the land—the technology of domestication became common.

Horticultural Societies

Domestication refers to the "taming" of plants and animals in order to control their availability for human use. We will refer to the domestication of plants as **"horticulture."**

The technology of domestication allowed early human groups to shed their nomadic ways and stay close to the farms where their crops were being grown and cultivated. The original horticulturists in what is now called Canada were the Iroquois who lived in the southern Great Lakes area. All Aboriginal peoples hunted, fished, and collected plants as a means of subsistence at one time, but when certain nations learned to cultivate food by planting seeds, they changed from being a nomadic people to a farming people, living in larger communities with stationary homes and fields of crops. The Iroquois used hand tools made from moose antlers to till the earth and plant such crops as peas, corn, squash, and beans.

Horticulture had a dramatic effect on the amount of land used. Instead of roaming over vast tracks of territory collecting food wherever it happened to grow, farmers could concentrate the desirable plants in a chosen area, and they could control when the plants grew and to what density. As a result, enough food could be produced to support a greater number of people on a much smaller area of land.

of land by cutting down the trees with the use of hand tools and then burning the logs and underbrush. Crops are then planted between the stumps in soil that has benefited from the addition of nutrient-rich ashes. Once the soil has been depleted of nutrients (usually a couple of years after the first planting) the farmers move to a new plot and repeat the process of clearing and planting, while the past plots are allowed to regenerate. Slash-and-burn farming is called **extensive horticulture** because it requires so much land as the farmers continue to create more plots.

Intensive horticulture uses less land because it involves the use of other technologies that allow farmers to concentrate crops in a smaller area. Early on, these technologies included irrigation, fertilizers, and simple ploughs, the use of which meant that the same plot of land could be used year after year while producing consistently high yields. These technologies are discussed later under the section subtitled Agricultural Societies.

Pastoral Societies

The domestication of animals is called **pastoralism**. Pastoralists, or herders as they are also called, are nomadic peoples who move their animals (usually sheep, cattle, horses, goats, reindeer, camels, llamas, or yaks, depending on the part of the world they inhabit) from area to area as seasons change or as pasture vegetation becomes scarce. Because the herd animals rely on naturally occurring pastures, pastoral societies need vast tracks of land for survival, just as hunter-gatherer societies do. However, the pastoralists are different from the hunter-gatherers because they get a constant supply of food and other goods necessary for survival from their animals.

Many horticultural societies also keep domesticated animals, such as chickens or pigs, to supplement their diets, just as many

Figure 4.12 The crops grown by the Huron—supplemented by wild game—could support villages of 800 to 1000 people. Examine the painting carefully and describe the way of life of the people depicted in the 15th Century.

Horticulturists can be divided into two categories: extensive and intensive. The "slash-and-burn" style of farming, common to many tropical rain forest regions, is an example of extensive horticulture. This type of farming involves the clearing of a portion pastoralists have small gardens or trade animal products to obtain vegetables. The difference between the two societies lies in their main area of dependence. Horticulturists do not depend on animals for subsistence to the extent that pastoralists do, and vice versa.

Agricultural Societies

Agricultural societies are characterized by intensive agriculture that results in the increased frequency and yield of cultivated crops. This is accomplished through the use of various technologies.

Irrigation Technologies

Irrigation is the practice of supplying water to plants that would otherwise not receive any due to lack of rain or proximity to an adequate natural water source. People who maintain flower beds or small kitchen gardens today probably still practise the earliest form of irrigation—the carrying of water to plants in handheld containers. However, because this method is very labour-intensive and impractical for use on field crops, another technology, called **flood irrigation**, was used. This method involves diverting rivers so that the water flows through an artificial ditch and onto the fields.

Irrigation allowed people to farm areas of land that had previously been too arid to sustain life. It also gave farmers more control over the problems caused by seasonal cycles. For example, crops that required sufficient water year round could now be planted in areas characterized by alternating dry and rainy seasons.

As the case study on page 128 illustrates, the introduction of irrigation technology can have an enormous impact on indigenous farming methods and on the types of crops grown.

Figure 4.13 These two Tibetan girls belong to a family of sheep herders, living in the Himalayas. Discuss the ways the pastoral lifestyle of these people might affect their culture.

Agricultural Change in Guayape Valley

David Casco is back in business. While the Honduran farmer lost most of his crop to Hurricane Mitch, it did not dampen his entrepreneurial spirit. It didn't take long before he began to rebuild his seven-hectare farm, planting vegetables and other crops for market.

Casco is convinced his farm still has a future. Before the hurricane that devastated parts of the Central America country in late October 1998, he had increased his income level through expanding the amount of land under cultivation, introducing irrigation, and diversifying crops.

The Casco family is one of more than 5000 farm families supported by a five-year CIDA (Canadian International Development Agency) initiative, called the Guayape project, intended to remove roadblocks to the creation of a dynamic and productive economy for small-scale food producers.

"New and diversified crops are key to a more dynamic agricultural sector," says Frank Schneider, Canadian director of the Guayape project. It is competitive, but farmers can generate higher incomes.

It was the higher profit from plantains, onions, green peppers, and passion fruit that first attracted David Casco to diversify his crops. "I've had bad luck with traditional crops such as corn and beans," says Casco. "Passion fruit is a new crop with less competition, so the early years could be profitable."

But diversification quickly runs into roadblocks because it requires investments in new technology such as irrigation. It is generally beyond the financial abilities of many farmers with limited or no money savings.

"I had tried going to the bank for a loan," says Casco, "but their interest rates were too high." Through a credit program supported by the Guayape project, Casco was able to obtain loans for irrigation and then introduced new crops.

While the Guayape project works with the credit sector, it also provides guides to diversify and improve production says Schneider. "Of the package of sup-

port, irrigation is probably the most important," because farmers can produce beyond the crop cycle defined by the rainy season.

The Guayape project has supported 150 irrigation systems that have helped people such as David Casco to go beyond traditional grains to include cabbage, tomatoes, watermelon, onions, plantain, and passion fruit.

Irrigation has proven popular among other producers, says Schneider, since the approach is often copied even without the support of the Guayape project. "For every irrigation system we put in, two others are added by farmers copying the system: one in the same community and another in a nearby community."

While the Guayape project has increased production of crops not traditionally produced in the area, it has also worked to find new markets. For example, it has supported a marketing co-operative to obtain contracts with major regional and international buyers. These contracts can only be obtained if producers are organized and produce sufficient volumes of any

Figure 4.14 David Casco feels that he has a bright future now that he has learned how to diversify his crops and maintain an advanced irrigation system on his Honduras farm.

commodity. If they can, the farmers are provided with a firm price and therefore are not subject to the ups and downs of the market.

This new and dynamic economy that is evolving in the Guayape Valley has benefited families such as the Cascos. David's wife, Lesly Calix de Casco, says, "Our life is a little more comfortable now, even though we still have a ways to go. We can now look forward to providing our four children with a better education, and our family has better food. We are buying important inputs for farming. Little by little, we are making progress."

Source: Canadian International Development Agency. 2001. "Guay Valley Agricultural Development Project." [Online] Available <w3.acdi-cida.gc.ca/home> November 2001.

Questions

1. Describe the Casco family's traditional approach to agricultural. Were there any disadvantages associated with this approach? Explain.
2. Describe the technological changes that were instituted on the Cascos' farm.
3. What was the impact of these new technologies on the Cascos' farm, family, and nearby communities?

The Draft Plough

The hand-held tillage tools that had been used by early horticulturists since about 3000 B.C.E. in Mesopotamia and Egypt were important in preparing the earth for crops by breaking up soil, bringing nutrients to the surface of the field, and getting rid of weeds and the residue of previous crops. The early version of this tool worked in lighter soils but could not penetrate the denser soils of areas such as in northwestern Europe.

The introduction of the sturdy **draft plough** allowed people to cultivate areas that had previously been considered too challenging to farm. When strong animals like the ox and the horse began being used to drive ploughs, much more land could be tilled much faster than was previously possible through human labour alone. The efficiency created by the advanced plough meant fewer farmers had to work the fields, while actual food production increased.

Food Surpluses and the Rise of Cities

The ultimate result of technologies such as irrigation and the draft plough was a surplus of food; that is, more food was produced than was actually needed by the farmer's family. Food surpluses led to a whole range of dramatic socio-cultural changes. For example, crops could support a much greater number of people. This resulted in the growth of larger and larger communities. Because fewer people were needed to produce the food, other community members were freed to specialize in other types of work such as weapon-making, jewellery production, and tool-making. Commerce also grew because farmers had extra food, which could be sold or traded for other types of goods. Increased leisure time and disposable income also allowed for some people to pursue cultural interests such as painting and writing.

In essence, it can be said that intensive agriculture set the stage for the socially and politically sophisticated organization we call civilization.

Farming in Canada—Twentieth Century to Present

One key development in the twentieth century in Canada and in other countries around the world directly relates to the third great social revolution as shown in Figure 4.11 on page 125. Industrialization led to increased mechanization of the farming industry. Mechanization, in turn, led to a marked decrease in the number of small family farms as large corporate farms emerged to dominate the agricultural sector. Essentially, as the animal-driven plough was replaced by the tractor, farm jobs were eliminated and a new, highly technical approach to farming emerged.

Canadian farmers were quick to adopt mechanization as an extension of the industrialization of the world. Farm machinery makes the scientific approach to farming mentioned above more practical. In fact, the industrialization of farming has made its way indoors in the form of factory farming (for example, giant chicken barns, automated cow milking assembly lines), greenhouses and hydroponics (growing plants in nutrient solutions without soil). Farmers have also demonstrated a willingness to adopt computer technology that monitors watering of crops and weather patterns to guarantee successful crop planting and harvesting.

Although mechanization has had an enormous impact on the size, number, and operations of Canadian farms, the most innovative area of the agriculture industry is evident in the emergence of biotechnology.

The Emergence of Genetically Modified Foods

Biotechnology is playing a key role in the agricultural sector of the economy. Experimenting with the genetic composition of livestock and plants has been going on for some time in the form of animal husbandry, crossbreeding, and cross-pollination.

Figure 4.15 Some worry that cows treated with rBST may be subject to undue physical stress because of the new demands to produce more milk. Do you think the costs of this particular technology outweigh the gains?

However, indigenous agricultural processes are being radically altered with the advent of new technologies that use genetic engineering to produce new foods.

Biotech scientists claim that, with the population estimated to grow to over 10 billion by the middle of the twenty-first century, new methods of producing food must be found. In short, according to some analysts, there is simply not enough farmland to feed such a huge population. It is for this reason that the biotech industry argues it must pursue genetic engineering as an option for creating a sustainable and more productive agricultural sector.

Canadians are already consuming foods that have been subject to genetic engineering. These are called **genetically modified (GM) food** products. Forty-two types of genetically modified crops have been approved by Health Canada for food use in Canada. Some of the crops approved so far include: corn, including strains resistant to corn borers and herbicides; potatoes including strains resistant to Colorado potato beetles; and tomatoes including strains that ripen slowly. (Health Canada, 2002)

Although Canada has rejected its use, some countries use a genetic supplement called recombinant bovine somatotropin (rbST) to increase milk production in cows by 10-20 per cent. Although studies have shown rbST milk is the same as milk derived from untreated animals, the supplement has been shown to cause various diseases in the cows.

Questions are being raised by concerned citizens, scientists, social scientists, and environmental lobby groups around the world as to the potential consequences of growing GM crops. Because GM technology is new and evolving so quickly, no conclusive research has been done on the long-term effects of these foods on human health, on the health of other plants and animals, the environment, local and national economies, and cultural traditions.

Some opponents of GM technology say that the introduction of such crops into developing countries will disrupt indigenous land-use practices and possibly have negative impacts on the environments of those countries. Others claim that use of the technology will create an even greater disparity between the rich and the poor the world over because farmers from developing countries will become dependent on GM seeds that are manufactured and sold by only a handful of large companies, which are based in relatively rich countries. There are plenty of questions about the possible consequences of genetically modified crops, but not enough absolute answers, it seems, to quell global fears about this new technology.

The Competing Perspectives feature on the next page addresses this debate.

www.ecojustice.net/biotechnology/index.htm

This site contains numerous quality articles on biotechnology and environmental justice. It is supported in part by Harvard University in the United States. The introduction to the site says that while numerous promising biotechnologies are being developed, important questions must be asked about their potential impacts. To quote the site's authors:

"This technology—like any other powerful technology—raises important ethical and equity questions stemming from the manner in which the technology is designed, developed and implemented in a wide range of societies around the world. Some questions that occur include: Who will be the primary beneficiaries of this technology? What are its costs? Who will bear those costs? What alternatives will be foreclosed if this technology is adopted?"

Read through some of the articles on this site and choose one which you believe raises an especially important question from an anthropological perspective.

COMPETING
PERSPECTIVES

Do the Benefits of GM Technology Outweigh the Risks?

Norman Borlaug, author of "Biotechnology Will Save the Poorest," was awarded the Nobel Prize in 1970 and is distinguished professor of international agriculture at Texas A&M University. Dr. Mae-Wan Ho, who wrote the second article, representing the "no" side of this argument, is a reader in biology at the Open University in the UK, and is the author of a best-selling book titled *Genetic Engineering—Dream or Nightmare? The Brave New World of Bad Science and Big Business.*

Yes: Biotechnology Will Save the Poorest
By Norman Borlaug

Science and technology are under attack in affluent nations, where misinformed environmentalists claim that the consumer is being poisoned by high-yielding systems of agricultural production, including genetically modified crops.

I often ask the critics of modern agricultural technology what the world would have been like without the technological advances that have occurred. For those whose main concern is "protecting the environment," let's look at the positive impact that the application of technology has had on the land.

Were Asia's 1961 average cereal yields of 930 kilograms per hectare to still prevail today, nearly 600 million hectares of additional land of the same quality would have been needed to equal the 1997 cereal harvest. Obviously, such a surplus of land was not available in Asia. Moreover, even if it were, think of the soil erosion, loss of forests and grasslands, wildlife species that would have occurred had we tried to produce these larger harvests with low technology.

There is a debilitating debate between agriculturalists and environ-mentalists over what constitutes so-called sustainable agriculture in the Third World....[and] this deadlock must be broken. We cannot lose sight of the enormous job before us to feed a global population of 10 or 11 billion people. Many of these people, probably most, will begin life in abject poverty. Only through dynamic agricultural development will they have a chance to alleviate their poverty and improve their health and productivity.

Farmers need to be motivated to adopt many of the improvements in efficiency, including irrigation water, fertilizers, and crop protection chemicals. This will require a two-pronged strategy, in which reductions in subsidies are linked to aggressive and effective education programs. Universal primary education in rural areas is imperative. Ways must be found to improve access to information and technology for farmers.

...The world has the technology—either available or well advanced in the research pipeline—to feed a population of 10 billion people. The more pertinent question today is whether farmers and ranchers will be permitted to use this new technology.

Extreme environmental elitists seem to be doing everything they can to stop scientific progress. Small, well-financed, vociferous, anti-science groups are threatening the development and application of new technology, whether it is developed from biotechnology or more conventional methods of agricultural science.

While the affluent nations can certainly afford to adopt elitist positions, and pay more for food produced by so-called natural methods, the 1 billion chronically undernourished people of the low-income, food-deficit nations cannot. Access to new technology will be the salvation of the poor, not, as some would have us believe, keeping them wedded to outdated, low-yielding, and more costly production methods. Global food insecurity will not disappear without the effective application of new technology. To ignore this reality will make future solutions all the more difficult to achieve.

Source: Borlaug, Norman. 2000. "Biotechnology Will Save the Poorest." Texas A&M University.

COMPETING PERSPECTIVES

No: Say No to GMO
By Dr. Mae-Wan Ho

Genetically Modified (GM) crops are neither needed nor beneficial. They are a dangerous diversion from the real task of providing food and health around the world.

The promises to genetically engineer crops to fix nitrogen, resist drought, improve yield and to "feed the world" have been around for at least 30 years. Such promises have built up a multibillion-dollar industry now controlled by a mere handful of corporate giants.

But the miracle crops have not materialised. So far, two simple characteristics account for all the GM crops in the world. More than 70 per cent are tolerant to broad-spectrum herbicides…, while the rest are engineered with bt-toxins to kill insect pests. A total of 65 million acres were planted in 1998 within the US, Argentina and Canada. The latest surveys on GM crops in the US, the largest grower by far, showed no significant benefit. On the contrary, the most widely grown GM crops—herbicide-tolerant soya beans—yielded on average 6.7% less and required two to five times more herbicides than non-GM varieties.

The same GM crops have already given rise to herbicide-tolerant weeds and bt-resistant insect pests. Worse still, the broad-spectrum herbicides not only decimate wild species indiscriminately, but are toxic to animals. One of them, glufosinate, causes birth defects in mammals, while another, glyphosate, is now linked to non-Hodgkin's lymphoma. GM crops with bt-toxins kill beneficial insects such as bees and lacewings, and pollen from bt-maize is lethal to monarch butterflies.

Corporations already control 75 per cent of the world trade in cereals. The new patents on seeds will intensify corporate monopoly by preventing farmers from saving and replanting seeds, which is what 85 per cent of the farmers still do in [developing countries]. Christian Aid, a major charity working with the [developing countries], concludes that GM crops will cause unemployment…, threaten sustainable farming systems and damage the environment. It predicts famine for the poorest countries.

What about GM crops with enhanced nutritional value, such as putting soya protein into rice, or incorporating genes to increase iron content? The major cause of malnutrition worldwide is the substitution of industrial monocultures for the varied diet provided by traditional farming/foraging systems. Moreover, intensive agricultural practices deplete and leach nutrients from the soil, thereby changing the nutritional values of all food crops for the worse within the past 40 years. No amount of genetic engineering can reverse this trend, which can be achieved only by re-introducing sustainable farming methods and recovering agricultural biodiversity.

Excerpted from: Ho, Mae-Wan. "Say No to GMO." *Sovereign Magazine* [Online]. Available <http://www.twnside.org.-sg/title/mwho2-cn.htm> 2001.

Questions

1. In your own words, state Norman Borlaug's position regarding the emergence of biotechnology in agriculture. Be specific.

2. What are Mae-Wan Ho's main arguments against GMO crops? With whom do you agree, and why?

3. If it is completely accepted, outline some major impacts you think GM technology will have on farming and land use in Canada.

Pause and Reflect

1. What is the significance of the invention of the plough?

2. Why did food surpluses lead to the creation of new occupations within a community?

3. How did technological change affect peoples' land use practices throughout the various subsistence categories discussed in this section?

4. In Canada, a debate is raging about wether or not GM foods should be labelled as such. Research this issue and write a report. Outline the various stances.

5. How do you think society should respond to new genetic technologies? Should they be eagerly embraced or cautiously evaluated? Support your position with specific examples.

▶ ▶ ▶ ## Chapter Activities

Show Your Knowledge

1. What are the differences between traditional theories of social change and technological determinism?

2. What contributions have Thorstein Veblen, William Ogburn, and Marshall McLuhan made to our understanding of the impact of technology on our lives?

3. Why does changing technology cause psychological stress? How can people cope with these new stresses?

4. From an anthropological perspective, how has our approach to gathering food changed over the past 12 000 years?

Practise Your Thinking

5. Identify what you consider to be the three most important technological developments from among those discussed in this chapter. Explain why you have chosen them, and describe what you consider to be their most significant impact on human societies.

6. Is "technosis" real ●r is it just a term dreamt up by a couple of psychologists? Write a one-paragraph response to this question.

7. Look at Figure 4.2, "Traditional Theories of Social Change" on page 106. Which of the three social science disciplines has the most convincing explanation of how social change affects technology. Give your reasons.

8. a) Make a list of things that computer communication technology allows you to do that would have been impossible for your grandparents to do at your age.

   b) Make a list of things that you are expected to do at school, at home, and at work (if you have a job) that your grandparents would not have been expected to do.

   c) Do you think that the increased opportunities that technology gives you are worth the extra pressure that it places on you to get things done? Explain your answer.

9. a) Identify the things that the following society types can do well, and some of the problems asso-
      ciated with them: hunter-gatherer, horticultural, pastoral, agricultural, and modern industrial
      society.

    b) Overall, do you think that technology has had a beneficial or detrimental effect on the devel-
      opment of human societies? Explain.

10. a) How is the debate over genetically modified foods adversarial in nature?

    b) What are the drawbacks of a debate where scientists on both sides of the issue are claiming to
      be correct?

Communicate Your Ideas

11. Think about how schools have changed since the days when your grandparents attended. Using
    McLuhan's Four Laws of Media, identify current technologies that have (a) enhanced, (b) made
    obsolete, (c) retrieved, and (d) reversed past technologies in schools.

12. Interview two or three people. Ask them about the role of technology in their lives and how they
    cope with technological change.

13. Imagine that you are the publications director for either (a) an international corporation that pro-
    duces GM food, or (b) an international aid agency that believes that GM foods are potentially
    harmful. Create a 300-word news release outlining what your organization believes and why.

    a) Partner with someone who represented the other organization. Discuss with each other what
      you have written.

    b) Stepping out of your roles, discuss what each of you believes, and why.

Apply Your Knowledge

14. Write a 300- to 500-word reflective essay that demonstrates whether or not you come from an
    "infomated" household.

15. Prepare and hold a class debate on the following topic: "Overall, technology allows Canadians to
    lead healthier, happier, and more challenging lives than was the case a century ago." Make sure you
    follow established rules of procedure for debates, and co-ordinate what the members of each side
    in the debate will say.

16. Examine "The Social Transformation of Society" flow chart on page 125. Do some research about
    the four revolutions that are outlined there. Which revolution do you think would have caused the
    most stress for people living though it? Why?

17. Research the following topic on the Internet: "Health risks associated with genetically modified
    foods." Be sure to examine different shades of opinion on the subject.

18. Pick the largest community in your province or territory. Investigate details about its population
    today, 50 years ago, 100 years ago, 150 years ago. Find information about agricultural production
    levels and overall population in Canada at these same times.

    a) How effectively can you establish a link between surplus agricultural production and the rise of
      big cities?

    b) What other technological developments, besides agricultural ones, would have been necessary
      to create large cities supplied with food from far away?

SUMMATIVE PROJECT

STAGE ONE: CONCEPTUALIZING YOUR PROJECT

■ Your Assignment

Your summative project is a key component of your course work. Completing an effective project will require a considerable amount of time, thought, and energy, so make sure you give yourself the time you need to perform at your best.

The first phase in the completion of this project involves using the skills you learned in Chapters 2, 3, and 4 to choose a topic, investigate the issues surrounding that topic, and conduct a preliminary search for resources. This phase gives you the chance to determine if the topic you chose is doable, or if you will have to choose a new topic before you can progress. By effectively conceptualizing your project at this stage, the next two phases will become much more straightforward.

■ The Three Steps

In Unit 1 you were introduced to three skills and given an opportunity to practise them. Now you are going to put each of those skills into action by approaching them as a series of steps. For this phase of your summative project, all three steps apply equally, no matter if you have chosen to do a research paper, survey, or a participant observation.

1. *State your hypothesis*— The first step you must take in developing a hypothesis is choosing a topic. You can pick from any of the topics covered in this book, or any other social science topic that interests you. The "interest" factor is key since it is always easier to investigate a subject that you care about, or can personally relate to. So, flip through the entire book to see what catches your eye. If nothing in this text strikes your fancy, go to the social sciences section of a library and flip through books there until you find something that does. (Tip: the bibliographical lists in this book contain many social science titles that you may want to consult in your search.)

Once you have chosen a topic, review the Skill Builder feature on page 65, and follow the steps outlined in it to develop your hypothesis.

The work you submit for assessment must include the following:
- a list of five topics that are of interest to you
- identification of one topic for your Summative Project
- development of your hypothesis

2. *Develop inquiry questions*—Now that you have chosen your topic and have stated your hypothesis, it is time to gain a better understanding of the issues surrounding that subject. This

is done by asking focused and informed questions. Review the Skill Builder feature on page 97, and follow the steps in it to draft a series of questions designed to put your hypothesis to the test.

The work you submit for assessment must include the following:

- eight to ten inquiry questions
- modification (if necessary) of your hypothesis.

3. *Develop research strategies*—You should now have a good understanding of the issues surrounding your hypothesis. The next step involves doing some in-depth research to determine if there are enough sources of information available for you to continue with your investigation. Review the Skill Builder feature on page 121, and follow the steps outlined in it to develop and employ research strategies appropriate for your topic.

The work you submit for assessment must include the following:

- a list of three general sources (encyclopedias or text books)
- a list of three more specific information sources (magazines or newspaper articles)
- a list of four scholarly sources (books or scholarly journals)
- a list of four Web sites

■ Taking Your Project Through Stage One

Although research papers, surveys, and field observations are three very different types of summative projects, they all begin the same way—with research. At this phase all students, no matter which type of project they chose, will pick a topic and research it to familiarize themselves with the issues and history surrounding it (as per the "Three Steps," previously outlined).

Once this has been completed, every student must write a **proposal** outlining what they have chosen to do, and how they will do it. You will hand this proposal in to your teacher for evaluation.

Research Paper	Survey	Field Observation
For your proposal, include:	For your proposal, include:	For your proposal, include:
• the title of your project	• the title of your project	• the title of your project
• an introductory paragraph in which you identify your topic and explain why you chose it	• an introductory paragraph in which you identify your topic and explain why you chose it	• an introductory paragraph in which you identify your topic and explain why you chose it
• a paragraph in which you state and explain your hypothesis	• a paragraph in which you state and explain your hypothesis	• a paragraph in which you state and explain your hypothesis
• one or more paragraphs outlining how you plan to use the resources you gathered to support your hypothesis.	• one or more paragraphs outlining how you will conduct your survey and what you expect the outcome to be.	• one or more paragraphs outlining how you plan to conduct your experiment and how the resources you uncovered influenced your expectations for the outcome.

■ Completed Information Form

At this point, your teacher may ask you to hand in a Completed Information Form. Make sure you double check with your teacher to see if you are required to do so at this stage of your summative project.

■ Presenting Your Ideas

Once you have finished the three steps, your teacher may ask you to present your proposal to the class. The choice of either a collage or an oral report before the class will depend in part on the subject matter of your investigation and on your personality and preferred style of learning.

Collage

You've heard the expression "a picture's worth a thousand words." It's true. The use of photographs can be extremely effective in communicating thoughts, emotions, and ideas quickly and powerfully. For this phase of your project, you can choose to present the social issue you will be investigating to the class visually in the form of a collage.

Collages are imaginative arrangements of photos, paintings, drawings, and/or other materials attached to a common background of cardboard or poster paper. Review the skill "Using Visuals to Represent and Present Your Ideas" on page 316 to learn how to choose the items for your collage wisely. Keep in mind the following criteria as you create your collage:

- Choose items from a wide variety of sources, which could include magazines, newspapers, personal photos, scraps of material, hand-drawn illustrations, etc.
- Make sure each item has a significant connection to the theme or idea you are trying to convey. Every image must be relevant and meaningful.
- Before attaching any of the images to the backboard, carefully consider their arrangement. How you place the images and items can be just as important as the images themselves.
- When it is finished, your collage should need no further explanation than what the title states. Its message should be self-evident.

Oral Presentation

If you choose to prepare an oral presentation for phase one of your project, you will need to organize your work effectively to convey to your audience a sense of preliminary content mastery.

The key to an effective oral presentation is to speak clearly and succinctly. Make your point, provide an example, and move on to your next point. You should follow the same basic structure you would use for a written report:

Format	Main Points
Introduction	• Identify your topic and hypothesis
Developing Inquiry Questions	• This section of your presentation attempts to connect inquiry questions to your hypothesis
Developing Research Strategies	• This section looks at the movement from general to specific information designed to address the issues raised by your hypothesis
Your Proposal	• Explain to the class how you expect to execute your project.
Conclusion	• Recap your main points and present the potential outcomes of your summative project.

Notes:

You may want to use visual aids such as overhead transparencies, or bristol board displays during your presentation. Essentially, visual aids take the focus of attention away from you and places it on the items you are highlighting through the media you have selected. Keep in mind that the use of visual aids should not require so much attention that your audience stops listening to you and starts reading your information. There is a tendency among some presenters to provide wordy displays that are simply distracting. Summary sentences or points are the key to effective use of visual aids.

■ Meeting the Criteria

In the end, you must demonstrate that you have successfully met the criteria for completion of the first phase of your summative project.

To meet the criteria for completing the Three Steps, make sure you
- list five topics that are of interest to you
- identify one topic for your Summative Project
- outline the issue(s) or question(s) surrounding that topic
- clearly and concisely state your hypothesis
- list eight to ten inquiry questions
- modify (if necessary) the hypothesis
- list three general sources (encyclopedias or text books)
- list three more specific information sources (magazines or newspaper articles)
- list four scholarly sources (books or scholarly journals)
- list four Web sites

To meet the criteria for writing your proposal, make sure you
- Give a title
- Write an introductory paragraph explaining the topic you have chosen
- Give a clear outline on how you plan to write your paper or execute your survey or field observation.

Collage	Oral presentation
• include a title	• speak clearly and confidently
• use a variety of visuals from a variety of sources	• make eye contact with those in your audience
• use only items that have a significant connection to the social issue you have chosen for your summative project	• use proper grammar when speaking
	• use other media forms such as posters, overheads, computer software, video, or handouts to present information
• arrange visuals in a creative and meaningful manner	
• pay careful attention to neatness and overall presentation	• make sure the visuals used do not distract the audience from what you are saying

SOCIAL TRENDS

Focus Questions

1. How have family size and composition changed in Canada over the past five decades?

2. In what ways do these changes reflect shifts in the global economy, fertility rates, immigration patterns, cultural attitudes, and gender roles?

3. How have these changes affected consumer culture, housing trends, medical technology, employment trends, and relationships among men and women?

When would the family shown above have been typical in Canadian society? Would you consider it typical now? Why or why not?

The shift in the composition of the typical Canadian family is an example of a **social trend**. Social trends are large-scale changes in our society such as an increase in immigration, a decrease in fertility rates, or a growth in the number of older, first-time parents. The exploration and evaluation of social trends is conducted by **demographers**, social scientists who study human populations and provide population data and statistics. Anthropologists, sociologists, and psychologists get involved in the action as well: anthropologists by studying the ways that social trends affect cultures; sociologists by exploring the impact on families, social institutions, and other groups; and psychologists by examining how these changes affect individuals. In the second part of this course, you will find out what some of these social scientists have discovered about social trends in Canadian society.

■ Unit Learning Goals

Overall Expectations

- appraise the differences and similarities in the approaches taken by anthropology, psychology, and sociology to the study of trends relating to the baby boom, fertility and fecundity, and the life cycle
- assess the importance of demography as a tool for studying social trends
- demonstrate an understanding of the social forces that influence and shape trends

Skill Expectations

- demonstrate an ability to select, organize, and interpret information gathered from a variety of print and electronic sources
- analyze for bias, accuracy, and relevance articles or programs on issues related to anthropology, psychology, and sociology
- demonstrate an understanding of the purpose and use of the stylistic guidelines set by the American Anthropological Association, the American Psychological Association, and the American Sociological Association
- using ethical guidelines, appropriate methodology, and a range of primary and secondary sources, develop a position on a social issue of importance to anthropology, psychology, or sociology; and, using a research design appropriate to the issue and discipline, carry out a research project in at least one of the disciplines

Unit Contents

CHAPTER 5

THE BABY BOOM AND ECHO

INTRODUCTION

During the past half century, two population cycles have dramatically affected Canadian society. The so-called baby boom and its "echo" are important forces shaping social trends today. Professionals from the fields of psychology, sociology, and anthropology view these trends from different perspectives. However, they agree that Canadian population patterns since World War II have had a strong impact on many aspects of life. In education and employment, in recreation and business, and in retirement and health care, our society has been powerfully influenced by the baby boom and echo.

The Echo Boom, the generation to which you belong, is seen by many social scientists as already having significant economic and political might. Do you agree? Why?

■ Learning Expectations

By the end of this chapter, you will be able to

- evaluate the anthropological significance of war and the impact of returning soldiers on individuals, families, and communities
- assess the psychological importance of the baby boom to other generations
- demonstrate an understanding of the social impact of the baby boom and echo boom on educational facilities, pensions, health care, and entrepreneurial and employment opportunities

142

Focusing on the Issues

Today's youth do more than echo the past
By Darrell Tan

"Guess what—we have a name!" It was a weekday evening at our university residence and the group of us at the table looked up bemusedly from our daily grub. "We're the Echo Generation," our friend continued, setting down her tray. "A researcher speaking at my mom's conference talked about us being the 'echo' of the Baby Boomers because when we get out there, there's supposed to be another boom in the economy."

I thought about this, but wasn't quite sure whether I liked the idea. We were being named in relation to another generation, on the assumption that the future will conveniently provide us with an economic revival.

But shouldn't we be defined by our own actions? Don't today's youth have the right to an identity of their own? …

Puzzling over our identity soon found me with a quintessentially Canadian crisis on my hands. A few generalized statements about today's youth came to mind:

- Today's youth face unprecedented challenges in an increasingly competitive society.
- Youth do face a difficult situation. Those starting to look for work walk into an unfriendly and uncertain job market. Those still in school are told that a Bachelor's degree isn't enough any more, that we need a Master's—all at a time when tuition fees are rising and student loans are disappearing.
- Today's youth hold incredible promise to reshape our nation. Indeed, the inspiring philosophy of every youth organization today is that youth must be given an opportunity to develop their potential, instead of being treated as a problem to be solved.

- Today's youth are the victims of negative stereotypes. There is hardly a young person today who has completely escaped the stereotype of the "obnoxious teenager"—the word "youth" seems forever linked with suspicion and disrespect.
- Today's youth really are no different from any other age's youth, and there is little sense in inventing artificial labels. In other words: They're all true.

This last one actually seems about right. What characterizes today's youth is exactly what characterized yesterday's—the thought of tomorrow.

Every generation has had the potential to go out there and "make a difference"; but each does this in a different way as it encounters new challenges and circumstances.

Now it's our turn, and though the world we're living in may seem more complex and unstable than ever, the energy of youth is no less than that of past generations. It is in the future that we finally will enter "the real world" when the scholars and athletes, leaders and supporters, all converge on society and create a present….

We are the future. Call us the Echos if you'd like, but pretty soon, we'll be creating resonances of our own.

Darrell Tan was a student at McGill University in Montreal when he wrote this article to mark Canada's first annual National Youth Week, May 1–7.

Source: Tan, Darrell. 1995. "Today's youth do more than echo the past." *The Toronto Star*. 1 May 1995.

THINK ABOUT IT

1. Why is Darrell Tan not pleased with the term "Echo Generation"? Do you agree with him?

2. Identify the difficulties faced by young people outlined by the author, then think of two or three more. Which problem do you feel is the most difficult one that your generation faces?

3. Do you view the future of your generation in a positive or a negative way? Explain your opinion.

Section 5.1   Demographic Groups in Canada

Key Concepts

demography

baby boom

echo boom

Generation Z

Generation X

Twentysomethings

baby bust

materialism

natural increase

natural decrease

net migration

youthquake

 Demographic Groups

Have you ever filled out a product survey at a shopping mall or answered market research questions over the telephone? If so, you were probably asked to give your age group. Companies want to know which consumers use their products. Also, they want to know how to make their products more appealing to these buyers. Age has a great deal to do with our interests and habits, our tastes and our spending. It is also a very important part of **demography**, the study of human populations.

Demographers provide many useful services for a nation and lots of useful data for anthropologists and sociologists. By using population statistics, they identify different age segments and make recommendations about the social and economic needs of various groups. More importantly, demographers project population growth rates into the future. Governments use demographic forecasts to plan ahead, for example, on school construction projects, health care budgets, and job creation programs targeted to certain socio-economic groups. Population data also shape immigration policies, helping to determine how many people will be allowed into a country in a particular year. Anthropologists use demographic information to study the reasons for changing patterns in population growth within countries and within specific groups. This chapter will use demographic information to identify major Canadian population groups and weigh their impact, both in the recent past and into the new millennium.

Demographers have identified several different generations born during the past half century in Canada, notably, the **baby boom** (the largest by far), the **echo boom**, and **Generation Z**. The media have invented more demographic subgroups for this era, based largely upon income, lifestyle, and values. Well-to-do early baby boomers became known as "yuppies" (short for *young-urban-professionals*), and their children were sometimes termed "puppies." A special class of yuppies was also identified, the sometimes-envied "dinks," an acronym formed from the phrase, *double-income-no-kids*. Younger than the yuppies and the dinks are two other groups, **Generation X** and the **Twentysomethings**, the latter characterized in the long-running television series *Friends*. Figure 5.1 should help you to understand these terms, and to see the number of Canadians who fit into each demographic group.

You likely see yourself as a member of a circle of friends, part of a team, or linked to a network of people with shared interests. Demographers, on the other hand, see you as an "echo boomer," part of a group that has steadily growing power in the Canadian marketplace. You may have little sisters or brothers who were born after 1995—to demographers, they are "millennium kids," a population group expected to be much smaller than yours. Your parents are most likely baby boomers, but they may even be part of the "**baby bust**," a comparatively small group born during a period of declining births between 1967 and 1979. This demographic group falls between the peaks of the baby boom and the echo boom, two very large clusters within Canada's population. Finally, your grandparents are likely part of a group that is loosely termed "pre-boomers," those people born before 1946 (though it is possible that your grandparents were born early in the baby boom).

Demographic groups born in Canada after 1945

Demographic Era	Subgroups/Nicknames	Born	Population, 1996
baby boom	Boomers	1946 to 1966	9.8 million
	Yuppies	early baby boom	
	Dinks (yuppie subgroup)	same as above	—
	Generation X (Gen-Xers)	1960 to 1966	(2.6 million)
baby bust	Twentysomethings	1967 to 1979	5.4 million
echo boom	Generation Y	1980 to 1995	6.9 million
	Echo Kids	same as above	
	Puppies (Yuppie children)	early echo boom	
un-named	Generation Z	1996 to 2010 (est.)	No data
	Millennium Kids	same as above	

Figure 5.1 Not all demographers and social scientists define each generational group by the same age boundaries. However, the parameters set out above are accepted by many experts in Canada.

A Demographic Group: Generation X

This demographic group takes its name from the title of a 1991 novel by Vancouver author Douglas Coupland. With his first novel, *Generation X: Tales for an Accelerated Culture*, Coupland was labelled the spokesperson for a new generation. His major characters were in their mid-twenties to early thirties (that is, born between 1960 and 1966). They grew up surrounded by **materialism** (a way of life that revolves around material possessions) and high technology. They rejected this society as meaningless and boring. They refused to conform to society's values, and sought "real" lives by moving to an uninhabited desert. In their escape, the characters lived by their own rules—those of a new generation.

Interestingly enough, Douglas Coupland claims that he had no intention of speaking for a whole new generation in the book. Instead, he wrote on a more personal level, expressing issues important to himself and his friends. Although some literary critics slammed the book, it proved popular with Canadian readers, as well as those in the United States and Europe, particularly because many people could relate to its theme. The use of cartoons to underscore important ideas added appeal to the novel.

Figure 5.2 Explain how this cartoon relates to the real-life experiences of people born between 1960 and 1966.

Generally speaking, life for Gen-Xers has not been easy. Canadian demographer Daniel Foot explains:

Gen-Xers' life experience has led them to distrust any sort of large institution, whether in the public or private sector. It didn't take them long to learn that, in an overcrowded world, they had no choice but

to 'look out for number one.' On their first day in kindergarten, the Gen-Xers discovered there weren't enough seats for them. In elementary school, many of them were squeezed into portables. They have been a part of a crowd ever since. Whether it was trying to enroll in a ballet class, get into a summer camp, or find a part-time job, waiting lists have been a way of life for Generation X.
(Foot and Stoffman, 1996, p. 25)

This group has often found it difficult to move into careers already dominated by older baby boomers. Until recent years, Gen Xers were frequently underemployed, working in jobs at levels lower than their education prepared them for. On top of that problem, yuppie demand for real estate forced the Gen Xers to face high rents and soaring house prices, with the result that many had to live with their parents for a longer time.

How Population Changes

You have seen that Canada has several different demographic groups. This has happened because of two factors: the natural balance of births and deaths, and the movement of people. If the number of babies born is greater than the number of people who die during a certain period of time, then population rises in what is called a **natural increase** (or **natural decrease**, when deaths exceed births).

Also, if more people come to live in a country (immigrants) than the number who depart to live elsewhere (emigrants), population increases further. This difference is termed **net migration**, expressed as a negative number when emigration is larger. Demographers combine natural increase (or decrease) and net migration to calculate a nation's population change.

High levels of births and immigration combined to drive Canada's population from about 12 million in 1946 to 20 million in 1966, an increase of almost 8 million people in just 20 years. This was an average growth rate of 3.3 per cent per year, as high as that in any of the fastest-growing developing countries today.

During the two decades after 1945, the populations of Canada, the United States, Australia, and New Zealand grew rapidly. But Canada's growth rate was the highest of all. While some of that growth was caused by immigration, the greater part of it was due to a very large number of births. In fact, so many children were born during this period that by 1966 about half of all Canadians were 24 years of age or younger! (The fraction is closer to one-quarter in 2001.)

Thirty-five years ago, Canada was a young society of people eager for rapid social change—what observers called the **youthquake**, a culture of protest. These people were the baby boomers, the large demographic group that has strongly influenced the society, economy, culture, and politics of the past half century.

Formula:
A. Births − Deaths = Natural Increase (or Decrease)
B. Immigration − Emigration = Net Migration:
C. Natural Increase (or Decrease) + Net Migration = Population Change

Sample problem: Xanidu
Population on January 1, 2001:   20 943 791
Changes during 2001:   Births: 190 880
                         Deaths: 65 987
                         Immigration: 133 256
                         Emigration: 48 712

Figure 5.3 Use the formula given to calculate the population for Xanidu in 2002.
[Answer: Natural Increase = 124 893; Net Migration = 84 544; Population Change = 209 437 (1 per cent); Population January 1, 2002 = 21 153 228.]

Pause and Reflect

1. Make a list of three ways in which demography can be useful. Think of two more to add to the list.

2. Summarize three economic and three social characteristics typical of Generation X.

3. Give an example of how the size of the baby boom generation might have had an impact on the psyche of individual members of Generation X.

4. As a retailer, brainstorm a list of six products that might be popular with the average Gen-X consumer. Explain your choices.

5. Suppose that you had the opportunity to take a part-time job conducting consumer surveys of shoppers at a nearby shopping mall. Would you be interested in this type of work? How is this market-research job connected to the ideas discussed in this section?

Section 5.2   Causes of the Baby Boom

World War II and the Baby Boom

Between 1939 and 1945, Canada was a member of the Allied Powers fighting against the Axis countries, Germany, Italy, and Japan. Population increased slowly during these war years. "Total war" required the population to focus on defeating the Axis Powers, and as a result, a million Canadians went overseas with the armed forces. On the home front, just as many Canadians worked long hours at farm and factory jobs to produce food and weapons for the war effort. Government propaganda and news reports made war a grim reality in which many people put their plans for the future on hold. Marriage rates were also low during World War II, so during this time, Canada's population increased at a rate of just over 1 per cent per year. But, in 1945, Allied victory over the Nazis and the Japanese unleashed a pent-up demand for normal life in North America and elsewhere.

Anthropologists have studied the impacts of these returning soldiers on their communities and on Canada as a whole. They noted that many soldiers didn't wait long to resume their lives. About one

Canadian bachelor in five serving overseas came home with a European **war bride** and, in many cases, with children born abroad. Almost 50 000 women and their children followed servicemen back to Canada in 1945 and 1946. Other veterans returned to rekindle relationships that had been put on hold for several years. In both cases there was often disappointment and breakup caused by too much distance or too much time apart.

Often, Canadian wives and girlfriends found that soldiers had been psychologically and socially marked by their wartime experiences. To ease the transition into peacetime life, war vets were given first priority by those hiring for government jobs. Laws were also passed to allow veterans to return to their pre-war jobs, with military service counted toward their workplace seniority. Furthermore, veterans qualified for low-cost home mortgages and loans to upgrade their education.

Demobilization of the armed forces moved slowly, and often young men continued in the services until 1946 or 1947. They looked gallant in their decorated uniforms, an envied advantage when it came to meeting

Key Concepts

war bride

birth rate

immigration

population pyramid

cohort

Figure 5.4 The young Canadian woman in this photograph was married shortly after the war. "I was a government secretary in Ottawa. In the winter of 1945–46, my friends and I were enjoying a hay-ride, when Bob and some of his Air Force pals jumped onto the wagon. I was with somebody else that night, but that's how I met him. I was 18 years old, and he had just come back from Europe where he'd been a radio operator. We married in October 1946, and had our son the following summer and our daughter in 1950."

filled with photographs of people celebrating their Golden Anniversary, including the woman in Figure 5.4.

Sociologists and psychologists have identified strong social forces that were at work in the post-war era. Marriage was considered the norm, and the young adults of the 1940s were "the most domestically oriented generation of the twentieth century" (Owram, 1996, p. 12). Some psychologists and sociologists reinforced the notion that marriage and family offered the best route to respectability and contentment. In fact, anyone who did not marry was considered suspect. Henry Bowman, author of many marriage manuals popular in the US and Canada at the time, claimed that failure to marry proved a range of personality problems such as immaturity, parental fixation, inferiority complex, or narcissism (being extremely self-centred).

In addition, sex outside marriage was socially condemned in this era; therefore, marriage was seen as a moral necessity. Marriage confirmed one's sexual identity, and society routinely saw the failure to marry as a confirmation of homosexuality (Owram, 1996, p. 15). Marriage, family, and home were the main personal goals of most young adults after World War II.

young women. Courtships were often short, resulting in marriage rates in Canada in 1946 that were almost double those of the pre-war era and still remain the highest in Canadian history. Fifty years later, in 1996, the social pages of newspapers across Canada were

Birth Rates and Births in Canada, 1921–1971

Year	Birth Rate*	Live Births	Year	Birth Rate	Live Births
1921	29.3	265 000	1946	27.2	344 000
1926	24.7	240 000	1951	27.2	381 000
1931	23.2	247 000	1956	28.0	451 000
1936	20.3	227 000	1961	26.1	476 000
1941	22.4	263 000	1966	19.4	388 000
			1971	16.8	362 000

*average number of births per 1000 people (both sexes, all ages) in the nation

Figure 5.5 What effect did World War I (1914–1919) and World War II (1939–1945) have on the **birth rate** and Canada's population?

Immigration and the Baby Boom

The end of World War II had a second important effect on demography. It marked the beginning of a rising tide of **immigration** to Canada, most of it from war-torn Europe. More than two million people came to start a new life in Canada between 1945 and 1960. At that time, Canadian immigration policy gave top priority to applicants from Britain and the Commonwealth.

Europeans and Americans were welcome too, continuing policies from the early twentieth century, which held that such people would be compatible with the prevailing climate and culture of Canada. Large numbers of immigrants came to Canada from Great Britain, the Netherlands, Italy, and Ukraine. Most took work in Canada's booming mining frontier, on Prairie and Ontario farms, or in big-city construction and manufacturing jobs. Immigration policy in Canada was racist at this time. For example, in 1957, the peak immigration year, only about 2 per cent of all immigrants were accepted from Asia, Africa, and South America.

Immigration accelerated the baby boom in Canada. Crossing the ocean to begin a new life in a foreign country is generally more appealing to the young than to the old. Young people have less attachment to the "old world," particularly when they have seen it ravaged by war. In addition, there were few opportunities for young people in the Europe of 1945, but in Canada there was the promise of work, land, and a chance to build a life. Thus, the majority of post-war immigrants were less than 35 years of age—in the prime of their lives. Marriage, family, and a home were as important to them as to returning Canadian war veterans. Consequently, the average age of marriage in Canada fell steadily between 1941 and 1956. For women it dropped from 23.2 years in 1941 to 21.6 in 1956, while for men it went from 26.4 years

to 24.5. By marrying earlier, people tended to have more children since the women were married for a greater portion of their prime child-bearing years.

Immigration to Canada, 1945–1960

Year	Immigrants	Year	Immigrants
1945	22 722	1953	168 868
1946	71 719	1954	154 227
1947	64 127	1955	109 946
1948	125 414	1956	164 857
1949	95 217	1957	282 164
1950	73 912	1958	124 851
1951	194 391	1959	106 928
1952	164 498	1960	104 111

Source: Statistics Canada. 1983. *Historical Statistics of Canada.*

Figure 5.6 Plot these data on a scattergraph and identify the general trend you see.

Figure 5.7 Netherlands Ambassador Dr. J. H. van Roijin and Mrs. van Roijin greet Dutch immigrants arriving by ship in Montreal in 1947.

www.statcan.ca/english/kits/animat/pyone.html

WEB LINK

This excellent Statistics Canada Web site provides animated population pyramids for Canada and for every province and territory for the period 1971 to 2004 (projected). This will allow you to compare the baby boom and echo boom in different years and different regions of Canada. If the Web address does not connect you with the site, do a Web search using "Government of Canada" as a search string. Then follow the links to Statistics Canada.

Population Pyramids

Photographs or videotape allow you to look back and see what you were like at different times in your life. You can see certain things about yourself that have changed and other characteristics that remain the same. Demographers use a special type of graph called a **population pyramid** to illustrate population patterns by age and sex. Examining a series of these pyramids from different years provides demographers with "snapshots" of the changing character of Canada's population.

Population pyramids compare the proportion of males and females by age category at five-year intervals. Each population group is called a **cohort**; for example in Figure 5.8, the youngest cohort is the group below 5 years of age. In that group there are more males than females. The oldest cohort is 70 years of age or more, a group with more females than males. Look for evidence of the baby boom generation in the pyramids of 1956 and 1971. (You can refresh your pyramid-graph-making skills by following the steps outlined on page 388 of the Skills Appendix.)

Population by Age and Sex, Canada

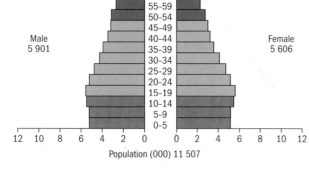

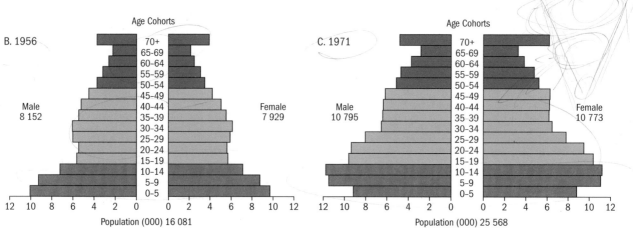

Source: Leacy, F.H. ed. 1983. *Historical Statistics of Canada*, Second Edition. Statistics Canada. Series A78-93.

Figure 5.8 Population pyramids give us snapshots that show the growth and development of the post-war baby boom in Canada. The 1941 population graph looks like a triangular spruce tree, but by 1956, the tree has grown very wide in the bottom three cohorts. Fifteen years later, the end of the baby boom is signalled by the narrower base of the tree.

Pause and Reflect

1. Suggest three difficulties war veterans would have had in readjusting to civilian life. How did Canada try to ease this transition?

2. Why were marriage rates high after World War II? How did this affect demography?

3. Explain how both immigration and societal values accelerated the baby boom.

4. Compare the population pyramids of 1941, 1956, and 1971 by identifying similarities and differences among them. Point out the following cohorts: pre-boomers, early boomers, Generation X.

5. A great many Canadian marriages from the 1940s and 1950s lasted for a long time. Develop a list of five good reasons that could be used to account for this.

Section 5.3   Nurturing the Baby Boom

Bringing Up the Boomers

Great changes in Canada after World War II affected how children were raised. Canada had become a vitally important source of natural resources and manufactured goods during the war, triggering an economic boom, which continued in peacetime. American companies invested almost $12 billion in Canada between 1945 and 1960. The northern mining frontier expanded and Alberta oil wells gushed. New manufacturing plants and the construction of the St. Lawrence Seaway created jobs in southern Ontario and Quebec. Canadians enjoyed greater prosperity than they had ever known. This prosperity changed not only the way babies were delivered and nurtured, but also the way the family functioned. The effects of economic factors in changing a society reflects the Cultural Materialist school of thought in anthropology, pioneered by Marvin Harris. (See page 14.)

Suburban Culture

The rapid population growth of the baby boom era contributed to a new suburban culture in Canada and the United States. There had been very limited construction of new housing during both the Great Depression of the 1930s and wartime. As a result, there was a severe shortage of accommodation in the immediate post-war years, and many newly married couples had to live with their parents or in-laws for a time. Demand for housing triggered a tremendous construction boom, the evidence of which can be seen in most Canadian cities. Most of these new homes were built beyond the existing built-up or urban area, which explains the terms "suburban" and "**suburbia**."

Entire neighbourhoods were constructed quickly using a few basic floor plans for five- or six-room single-family bungalows and "storey-and-a-half" houses. Some suburbs reflected the latest principles of good urban planning, with curved streets to slow down traffic, and land set aside for central parks and schools. Others grew helter-skelter, with little provision for adequate services. For example, in the Toronto area there was so little co-ordination of police services between the city and its suburbs that, from 1949 to 1952, police could not catch the well-armed Boyd Gang, who fearlessly robbed at least 10 banks there.

Key Concepts

suburbia

infant mortality rate

nuclear family

national debt

authoritarian education

progressive education

Boomers' upbringing compared to previous generations'

* About four out of five front-end boomers were delivered in the hospital, compared to only one out of five of their parents. For late boomers, the ratio of hospital-born babies increased to nine out of ten. Medically assisted delivery helped to lower Canada's **infant mortality rate**.

* Baby formula and small prepared bottles of baby food often replaced the breast-feeding and mashed "adult food" of the previous generation. These commercial foods for babies and toddlers were advertised as the modern way to bring up happy, healthy children.

* Family Allowance benefits introduced across Canada in 1944 by the federal government provided families with a monthly "baby bonus" to help feed and clothe each child. This allowance helped to nurture the healthiest generation of children Canada had known.

* Some parents consulted books written by child-care specialists, such as American pediatrician Dr. Benjamin Spock, for advice on raising their children, instead of relying on the advice of relatives and friends as their own parents had done. The baby boom generation was often raised more permissively than their parents had been.

* Popular television programs, such as *Leave it to Beaver*, presented a stereotypical view of the happy, suburban, father-led family of the 1950s. While these programs did reflect the lifestyles of some middle-class families, they helped to shape the roles played by fathers, mothers, and children in many other homes.

GROUNDBREAKERS
DR. BENJAMIN SPOCK, 1903-1998

Dr. Spock was a leading member of the Behaviourist school of thought in psychology, praised by many as the most influential child-care expert of the century, but condemned by others as "the father of permissiveness." His best-known book, *Common Sense Book of Baby and Child Care* (1946), and its sequels, sold 50 million copies in 25 different languages. In this book, Spock urged parents to trust themselves, and not to constantly worry about spoiling their children. His critics claim that this advice backfired and created a self-centred generation. In fact, in the early 1970s, US Vice President Spiro Agnew accused Dr. Spock of corrupting the youth of America!

Figure 5.9 Dr. Benjamin Spock

Dr. Spock's basic philosophy was to "respect children because they're human beings who deserve respect—they'll grow up to be better people." His books advised parents to let children develop and grow at their own pace, rather than according to the strict schedules and rules advocated by an earlier psychologist, Dr. John B. Watson. Today, most of Spock's advice seems perfectly reasonable; for example, babies should be fed when they're hungry, and they should not be toilet trained until they are toddlers, when they are developed enough to control their bodily functions. Children should be kissed and hugged by their parents. He believed that this sort of parental behaviour would nurture well-adjusted adults.

Later editions of his books emphasized that children must also respect their parents, and should not be allowed to be unco-operative and impolite. But, according to his critics, the damage had already been done. In his own defence, Dr. Spock claimed that it was the shift in societal values, not his advice, that was responsible for any disrespect for elders and authority evident among some of the baby boomers and youth of today.

Questions

1. How was Dr. Spock's advice different from that of earlier psychologist John B. Watson?

2. Why have some critics opposed Dr. Spock's views? What is your opinion on the issue?

For some Canadians, owning a suburban home completed the security triangle, which they sought by early marriage and a growing family. Each suburban home was built with a driveway because the suburbs were at, or even beyond, the edge of the city, making the car a necessity for most families. This soon led to the development of the familiar features of suburban car-culture: fast-food restaurants, shopping plazas, and the now-obsolete drive-in movie theatres.

Since the suburbs contained so many young families, certain social patterns usually developed within them. After their work was done, women often met at one another's homes for coffee while their kids were at school and their husbands were at work. Some evenings there were adult card parties or bowling, and on the weekends there were organized sports for the kids. Such social organizations as Brownies and Guides were as popular for girls as Cubs and Scouts were for boys. Each weekend, 60 per cent of all Canadians attended religious services, and on Sunday, many frequently engaged in family visits or social activities, since provincial laws forbade shopping and most other commercial activity.

A Child-Centred Universe

While many enjoyed the stability of suburban culture, others were critical. The words of a popular folk song written by American social activist Malvina Reynolds summarizes the distaste some had for suburban life. The song goes on to describe the sameness of the people who lived in these little boxes.

Little Boxes

Little boxes on the hillside,
Little boxes made of ticky-tacky
Little boxes on the hillside,
Little boxes all the same.
There's a green one and a pink one
And a blue one and a yellow one,
And they're all made out of ticky-tacky,
And they all look just the same.

Source: Reynolds, Malvina. 1962.

Figure 5.10 Post-war housing suburb. In your opinion what would be some of the advantages and disadvantages of growing up in such a community?

Two age groups did dominate the post-war suburb: children under 15, and young adults aged 25 to 44. In the 1961 Census of Canada, nearly half the population of some suburbs comprised children under 15 years of age, and in only a few suburbs was the over-55 population greater than 10 per cent. There weren't many teenagers yet, and grandparents lived somewhere else; generally, only the **nuclear family** of two parents and young children lived together. Author Doug Owram describes the suburbs as an environment completely focused on children.

> *What is most important is that the baby boomers lived in a world of children.... Their parents had moved into the suburbs in large part for the sake of the kids. There, as the baby boomers moved from the toddler years to childhood, they discovered a vast peer group. The absence of generational continuity only sharpened this sense of a child-centered universe.*
> *(Owram, 1996, pp. 82–83)*

Baby Boom Fashion and Fun

Figure 5.11 Surfing Culture (1960s)

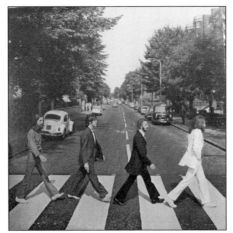

Figure 5.12 The Beatles (1964)

Figure 5.13 "Love Ins" (1960s)

Figure 5.14 Roller Discos (1970s)

Figure 5.15 Led Zeppelin (1970s)

Figure 5.16 Movie Ad Saturday Night Fever (1970s)

1. From what you see on this page, would you rather have grown up in the '60s or the '70s? Explain.
2. Are any of these music groups or fashions still around today? If so, how can you explain their popularity? If not, why do think they disappeared?
3. What differences do you detect between these items and their general equivalents today?

The Baby Boom Goes to School

It is fortunate that the Canadian economy was growing rapidly at the same time as its population, because the baby boom put great pressure on public institutions. New hospitals were built, or the delivery rooms and nursery wards of existing hospitals expanded to keep pace with the exploding population. During the Great Depression of the 1930s and World War II, very few new schools had been built. But by 1952 and 1953, the first wave of the early boomers had arrived at school and the number of students increased every year. A boom in elementary-school construction began, followed by new secondary-school projects in the late 1950s and early 1960s.

Then, by the mid- to late 1960s, universities were bursting at the seams. Ontario responded in three ways: by enlarging existing universities; by constructing new ones, such as Trent, York, and Brock; and by developing a province-wide system of community colleges. All levels of government borrowed heavily for these building projects. Today, Canadians are left with a sizeable **national debt**, which began to grow in the era after the war. The cost of borrowing to educate the baby boom generation is a part of that debt.

Not all the early boomers had the advantage of new schools; in fact, many endured very crowded older buildings, and, in some cases, a split school day with two different sets of students using the same schoolrooms. But most of the baby boom generation was educated quite differently than their parents and grandparents had been. Earlier generations had usually learned under a teacher-centred **authoritarian education**, in which they were expected to master a standard school program that was strongly focused on the "3 Rs": reading, writing, and arithmetic. Students were seen as empty vessels to be filled, all the while following a fairly strict code of behaviour.

However, by the 1950s, most Canadian schools outside of Quebec were applying the **progressive education** ideas of American philosopher and educator John Dewey, whose basic principles are still applied today. The new schooling was more child-centred, and teacher training emphasized that students were naturally eager to learn. The important thing was to develop lessons and activities that would keep them interested. Baby boomers were the first large group of students to experience an education system which, like the family of the day, focused on them.

Pause and Reflect

1. What effects did each of the following have on the upbringing of many baby boomers?
   a) television
   b) Dr. Spock
   c) government in Canada
   d) the education system

2. Make a chart to summarize the best and the worst aspects of suburbia in the 1950s and 1960s.

3. How did the education of the baby boomers differ from that of previous generations?

4. Explain the following quote from this section: "…the baby boomers lived in a world of children…a child-centered universe."

Section 5.4   Baby Boomers Transform Society

Key Concepts

counterculture

political activism

Just Society

sexual revolution

the Pill

materialism

economic inflation

recession

The 1960s Counterculture

By the mid- to late 1960s, the front wave of this demographic group had reached their late-teenage years and had become not only very visible, but also highly vocal. To many, their manners were considered rude and their music too loud. Some people thought that their suburban parents had turned them into spoiled brats. Others believed that their Benjamin Spock–John Dewey upbringing had made the boomers into a self-centred crowd of long-haired rebels. Adults often worried about the attitude of a generation that didn't seem to follow the rules, or care much about people older than themselves. Certain popular songs of the day expressed this attitude quite clearly:

My Generation

I.   *People try to put us down*
     Just because we get around.
     Things they do look awful cold.
     Hope I die before I get old.
     This is my generation.
     This is my generation, baby.

II. *Why don't you all fade away*
     And don't try and dig what we all say.
     I'm not tryin' to cause a big sensation,
     Talkin' about my generation.
     This is my generation.
     This is my generation, baby.

Words and music by Peter Townsend. © 1965 (Renewed) Fabulous Music Ltd. London, England.

You weren't alive in the 1960s, but you probably have some images of it in your mind. People often think of hippies, drugs, The Beatles, Vietnam, "sit-in" demonstrations, peace symbols, and other pictures of this colourful era between 1964 and 1972. Half the people of Canada were not yet legally adults,

and they were strongly influenced by television and the music industry. They were fully aware of events in the United States; for example, television showed the magical world of San Francisco's Haight-Ashbury hippie district, while radio delivered its music: Jim Morrison and the Doors, the Grateful Dead, and Joni Mitchell. In 1969, half a million people gathered in upstate New York to be part of Woodstock, a rock concert immortalized in a movie that millions of other baby boomers flocked to see.

Much of the music of the era focused on protest and rebellion against authority in general, and the Vietnam war in particular. Freer attitudes toward sex and drugs were also important themes. The media projected images of a new **counterculture**, in which many young people expressed values and behaviours that conflicted with society's norms. Members of this counterculture revelled in the shock value of pushing personal freedoms well beyond societal boundaries.

The *appearance* of a counterculture exaggerated the actual extent of the real thing. While some Canadian baby boomers did travel to Haight-Ashbury, Woodstock, and to the large anti-Vietnam war protests, most simply adopted the look and the sound of the times. There were campus demonstrations and "sit-ins" at some Canadian universities, and small communities of hippies in major cities. Sexual promiscuity and the use of illegal drugs certainly did increase. But it would be wrong to directly link more than a minority of young Canadians with this lifestyle. The following quote from an early Canadian boomer suggests that some were adventurous, but still rather conventional, in spite of their clothing, long hair, and musical tastes:

A lot of Canadian kids went to Montreal

that summer of 1967 to see Expo—the world's fair. It was Canada's 100ᵗʰ birthday party and it seemed like the whole country was celebrating. I went by train with three of my friends. We felt "free," enjoying the city, the Exposition, and the lower drinking age in Quebec. We met some girls there from Toronto and stayed in the city until we ran out of money. So we sold our return tickets and hitch-hiked home. That's one thing I remember when I think about the '60s.

Some young Canadians actively participated in more positive aspects of the counter-culture by working to change society through **political activism**. Besides student anti-war and anti-nuclear protests, activism focused on environmental issues and on the rights of women and Aboriginal people. For example, in 1968, 23-year-old Harold Cardinal was elected to lead the Indian Association of Alberta, a position he held for almost a decade. Cardinal initiated many programs to affirm Aboriginal culture, traditions, and religion, and he wrote two important books that attacked the policies of the Canadian government. At the same time, thousands of young people volunteered for low-paid service with the ambitious federal-government-sponsored project, the Company of Young Canadians (CYC). Established in 1966, the CYC aimed to develop social and economic programs in poor neighbourhoods and communities across the country. It gave idealistic young people in the late 1960s a chance to work for change. Equally popular was CUSO, Canadian University Students Overseas, a program of volunteer international service that was active in many developing nations.

FILM SOCIETY

Title: American Graffiti (1973)
Rating: PG
Director: George Lucas

This film has become a video classic that illustrates adolescence in the later period of the baby boom. Lighthearted entertainment with an excellent rock 'n' roll soundtrack, *American Graffiti* is set in the California "car-culture" of the early 1960s. The cast includes Ron Howard, Richard Dreyfuss, and Harrison Ford.

Figure 5.17 As justice minister, Trudeau had showed that he favoured reform by introducing changes to old laws concerning divorce, abortion, and homosexuality. As prime minister, he promoted what he called the **"Just Society,"** in which individual freedoms were very important.

Skill Builder:
Recognizing Bias in Sources of Information

An important part of senior-level research requires that you recognize any bias that might be present in the information sources that you have located. This feature will provide you with examples and a template to help you to spot bias in your sources. First, let's clarify the meaning of the term.

The *Canadian Oxford Dictionary* defines **bias** simply as "a predisposition or prejudice" toward or against something or someone. Bias develops from the personal and societal backgrounds of the people who provide information. Opinions are shaped by many different factors such as family and friends, education and social status, and culture and religion. People's backgrounds act as the filters through which they see the world around them. Their opinions are biased when they contain inaccurate and limited views of individuals and groups, or of situations and events.

Information containing bias can distort the focus of your research and change the direction your essay or report takes. The use of one or more biased sources to support your hypothesis can weaken your entire work and make the rest of its findings suspect. Therefore, it is very important to be able to identify any bias present in the sources you use.

Step One: Consider the background
1. When was the information created? Consider whether the opinions or point of view are still current, or whether they have become outdated.
2. Is this a first-hand account? Consider whether the author is closely connected to the situation or is simply repeating second-hand knowledge.
3. Who is the intended audience? Consider whether the information presented is intended to shape a certain opinion or behaviour in the audience.

Step Two: Assess the information
4. Are emotionally charged words and phrases used? Consider whether such vocabulary presents a positive or negative opinion about people or events.
5. Are facts used to support opinions? Consider whether the author is expressing opinions not supported by facts that can be proven true.
6. Are important facts left out? Consider whether the author has oversimplified an issue by presenting only one side when there could be many.

Step Three: Find supporting evidence
7. Who is the source of the information? Try to find out more about the author's background and qualifications to provide information about this topic.
8. Are the author's opinions carefully documented? Consider whether sources of proof have been cited to support the author's point of view.
9. Are the author's views different from those of other sources? If so, try to determine which author or information source is the most reliable and credible.

Practise It!
1. Make a list of the negative opinions expressed about young people in the passage below.
2. Which of these opinions uses emotionally charged words?
3. Suggest which groups in society may have felt this way about youth. Explain your reasoning.
4. Are the opinions supported by facts? What supporting negative information have you learned about young people in the 1960s in this section of the chapter?
5. Are important facts left out? What positive information have you learned about young people in the 1960s from this section of the chapter?

"By the mid- to late 1960s, the front wave of this demographic group had reached their late-teenage years and had become not only very visible, but also highly vocal. To many, their manners were considered rude and their music too loud. Some people thought that their suburban parents had turned them into spoiled brats. Others believed that their Benjamin Spock–John Dewey upbringing had made the boomers into a self-centred crowd of long-haired rebels. Adults often worried about the attitude of a generation that didn't seem to follow the rules, or care much about those older than themselves."
(From page 156.)

The Sexual Revolution

The 1960s brought with it the **sexual revolution**, a time during which behaviour and morals in North America began to change quite dramatically. For example, graph 5.18 of children born to all unmarried mothers, at that time called "illegitimate births," shows a sharp rise throughout the decade. This could be interpreted in two different ways: either more couples were living together instead of becoming legally married, or more people were engaging in premarital sex. The answer is probably a combination of both explanations. Figure 5.19 indicates a steady rise in Canadian marriage rates from the mid-1960s onward, representing the weddings of the front-end boomers. But a comparison of the two graphs indicates that births outside of marriage were increasing at a faster rate. Canadians were influenced by the growing emphasis on personal and sexual freedom that was an important part of the baby boom era.

Technology played an important part in the sexual revolution through the development of the birth control pill ("**the Pill**"), which was made widely available at a relatively low price, through doctor's prescription. Although contraceptive devices had long been available at drugstore counters without a prescription, the birth control pill was very successful after its introduction in 1961. In fact, it is part of the reason for the collapse of the baby boom.

Although there was a surge in the number of front-end boomers either marrying or living together between 1965 and 1975, the overall birth rate sagged sharply during these years. For one thing, female boomers were the best-educated Canadian women up to that time, and more and more young women chose to continue their careers after marriage. In addition, the birth control pill was the most popular means used by front-end boomers to delay child-bearing so that women could work outside the home. Young married women, baby boomers aged 15 to 24 in 1971, were having far fewer children than married women the same age had had 10 years earlier. The baby boom was over. The next generation, called the echo boom, wouldn't appear on demographic graphs until about 1980, when a great number of baby boomers began to have their own families.

Percentage of Live Births Termed "Illegitimate," Canada, 1945–1973

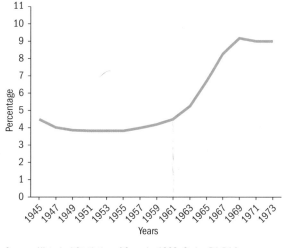

Source: *Historical Statistics of Canada*, 1983, Series B1-B14.

Figure 5.18 Identify the period called the "Sexual Revolution."

Marriage Rate Per 1000 Population Canada, 1945–1973

Source: *Historical Statistics of Canada*, 1983, Series B75-81.

Figure 5.19 Identify the point on the graph that represents the leading edge of the baby boomers reaching the age of marriage.

Pause and Reflect

1. What is a counterculture? How important were the media in spreading the 1960s counterculture? Give examples.

2. Explain this line from the chapter: "The *appearance* of a counterculture exaggerated the actual extent of the real thing."

3. Draw two important conclusions from Figure 5.18. Relate them to the "sexual revolution" of the late 1960s and early 1970s.

4. Brainstorm a list of factors that caused the collapse of the baby boom. Then, use your own judgment to rank them in order downward from the most important. Explain reasons for your two top rankings.

Section 5.5   The Echo Boom (1980–1995)

Key Concepts

echo boom

Generation Y

millennium kids

Generation Z

"six-pocket" phenomenon

reality television

The Echo Effect

The baby boom generation has had a great social and economic impact on the second half of the twentieth century. But their biggest effect of all will probably be the generation that follows them—their children. There were so many baby boomers born between 1946 and 1966 that they created a demographic echo that will remain long after the baby boom is gone. The so-called **echo boom** can be explained using the analogy of waves in water. Imagine that you are canoeing along a river with a steep, rocky shore. A passing powerboat will rock you with small waves stirred up by its motor—waves that will shake you once again as they bounce off the shoreline and move back across the river. The second set of waves is an echo of the first, but is a separate force to be reckoned with by you, the canoeist. In the same way, the echo boom reflects the original baby boom, but has become a separate social and economic influence in its own right.

Recent population pyramids are a useful way to identify the development of the echo boom in Canada. The pyramid in Figure 5.20 shows more width in the 10- to 19-year-old cohorts [2001] than in the 0- to 9-year-olds at the base. These teenagers are the echo boom, that is, the offspring of the baby boomers, born between about 1980 and 1995. The tapering in of this population pyramid at the base shows that the echo (sometimes called **Generation Y**) has come to an end. This cohort at the base (the **millennium kids**, or **Generation Z**) will be a smaller demographic group because there are fewer of their Twentysomething parents (from the baby bust era) than there were baby boomers. In this way, each generation can leave an echo of itself in the demographic record.

Regional Differences in the Echo Boom

Because of variations in birth rates and migration patterns, not every Canadian province or territory has a population pyramid the same as Ontario's. Figure 5.21 shows that the echo boom is strong in the northern territories and Saskatchewan, reflecting the high birth rates of areas with large Aboriginal populations. Popular migration destinations such as Ontario and the West have also experienced the echo boom. But most Atlantic provinces haven't, because they have not attracted many young immigrants. Furthermore, many young people have left the region for jobs in the provinces with strong economic growth. As a result, their population pyramids don't show the distinctive bulges of boom and echo seen elsewhere.

These differences are very important to demographers, because they show that some regions will have to prepare for the needs of the echo kids, while others won't. For example, areas with large Aboriginal populations must provide more services for children and adolescents because Aboriginal family sizes now rival those of Canada's original baby boom. Therefore, the need for improved housing, education, recreation, health, and other family services is proportionally greater in these communities than elsewhere. In October 2001, Matthew Coon-Come, National Chief of the Assembly of First Nations, asked the House of Commons Finance Committee for $4.2 billion over five years for construction and social pro-

grams in Aboriginal communities. He told the committee, "First Nations...want to deal with bread-and-butter issues of health, education,

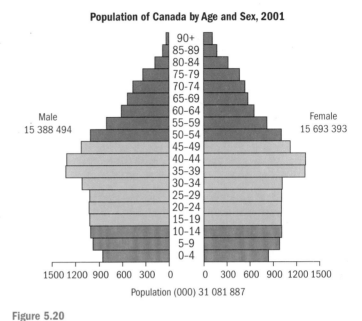

Figure 5.20

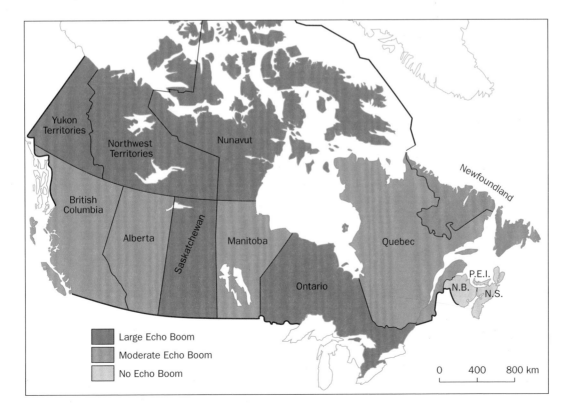

Figure 5.21 This map shows where in Canada the Echo Boom has its greatest presence. Explain why the Maritime provinces are shown as having "No Echo Boom."

eradicating poverty, land claims and treaty rights" (*Sarnia Observer*, 2001, p. B10). High Aboriginal birth rates across Canada necessitate more funding to improve the present lives and future prospects of echo kids in Aboriginal communities.

Meanwhile, Ontario projections call for about 80 000 extra university students by 2010, a problem accelerated by the "double cohort," beginning in September 2002. For the first time, two graduating classes (Grade 12 and OAC—Ontario Academic Credits) will be eligible to enter university together. But, even with the double cohort aside, the echo boom requires that every university in the province lay plans now for the near future. The Atlantic region faces a different type of problem. Demographers wonder if there will be enough young people in these provinces to take over labour, business, and professional fields as the baby boomers reach retirement age.

You may be wondering why your generation, the echo boom, is not as large as your parents' generation on the 2001 population pyramid. The answer is simple. The average number of children born to each Canadian woman dropped from about 3.5 in 1960 down to 1.5 in 1980. For a generation to replace itself, each couple must have at least two children. Your grandparents' generation was more than replacing itself, but your parents' generation was not. The rise of two-income families and the availability of the Pill saw to that. However, your generation is still large in number (almost 7 million, a bit short of one-quarter of Canada's population) because of the sheer size of the baby boom itself.

Impact of the Echo Kids

Although you are not yet full-time wage earners, your generation, the echo boom, has already had important effects upon Canadian society. Since your group is large, it put a strain on both the elementary and secondary school systems. Some of you benefited from this by attending new schools built to accommodate your numbers; however, many echo kids have had to make do with portable classrooms and overcrowded conditions instead. Your post-secondary impact will be the same, as colleges and universities brace themselves for your arrival. But you can expect this further education to be of tremendous benefit to you, because you will step into the jobs and careers that the front-end baby boomers are leaving. For example, half of the teachers in Ontario will retire over the next 10 years, and the situation is similar in many other professional careers across Canada. You will not have to "wait your turn" behind the leading edge of the baby boom, as both Generation X and the Twentysomethings had to do.

Already, your generation has had a strong impact upon the Canadian economy because, as a group, you have buying power. Large numbers of secondary-school students work at part-time jobs during the school year, averaging about 10 hours per week, although some work many more. And, as demographer David Foot explains, others get spending money from their parents and grandparents, usually more than their parents received when they were young:

> When the boomers were young, they had to compete for their parents' money with two or three siblings because, at the peak of the boom, the average Canadian woman was producing four children. The boomers themselves, however, produced only 1.7 children per family; that means that two-income boomer households have more money to lavish on each.
>
> …What some marketers call the **"six-pocket"** phenomenon—kids getting cash from two parents and four grandparents—explains why many echo boomers can afford to spend $50 for a Nike sweatshirt when a similar garment without the trademark can be had for only $15.

The brand name is increasingly important. Echo kids have been saturated in television since birth and, as a result, they are the most brand-conscious cohort in the history of the planet. (Foot, 1998)

Of course, Foot is writing in very general terms, because not all echo kids have jobs or parents and grandparents who can afford to give them spending money. Nor do all echo kids want to spend $50 on name brand sweatshirts. But, overall, some market analysts believe that the economic impact of the echo kids will be as large as that of the original baby boom because, on average, they have more money to spend. A good indicator is the strong shift of radio and television programming to youth markets just as programs shaped themselves around the baby boomers in the past. Youth market stations attract advertisers for a wide range of goods and services, including electronics, music and video products, live entertainment, convenience foods, clothing, and other fashion services. A strong dimension in youth programming and marketing is the focus on "experience"; examples include **reality television** (such as the hit program *Survivor*) and extreme sports, from mountain biking to paintball games. One popular slogan of the new millennium sums up this view of the world: "If you aren't living on the edge, then you're taking up too much space."

It is unfair to talk about the impact of your generation solely in economic terms. For example, some young Canadians have already shown themselves to be very concerned with community and global issues. Many thousands of elementary and secondary school students across Canada participate enthusiastically each year in raising money for cancer research through the Terry Fox Run. Others actively join environmental clubs to clean up local streams and trails or purchase hectares of tropical rain forest to protect it from destruction. One Ontario

freethechildren.com

This site describes Free the Children as "an international network of children helping children through representation, leadership and action." Explore the history and purpose of this organization on this site and go to the "You Can Help" page to find out if you might be interested in getting involved in this cause.

If the Web address does not connect you with the site, do a Web search using "free the children" as a search string.

WEB LINK

echo kid, Craig Kielburger, organized a "Free the Children" group at his school to draw attention to the issue of child labour in developing nations. His efforts were supported by labour unions and other concerned groups. In 1996 he travelled to India and Pakistan where he organized a press conference with child labourers to urge Prime Minister Jean Chrétien to raise the issue in his economic trade talks with Asian leaders. "Free the Children" has added its voice to other national and international organizations, making an impact on an important human rights issue.

Talking About Your Generation

Refer back to the article at the beginning of this chapter. In it, student Darrell Tan states that Generation Y is the victim of negative stereotypes. "There is hardly a young person today who has completely escaped the stereotype of the 'obnoxious teenager'—the word 'youth' seems forever linked with suspicion and disrespect," he writes. Some people believe that the media sensationalize stories about incidents of youth crime, resulting in an inaccurate picture of today's teenagers. However, there are other people who believe that picture is accurate—and worrisome, as a result. The following Competing Perspectives feature explores this issue.

COMPETING
PERSPECTIVES

Is Generation Y out of control?

Each generation of adults seems to characterize the upcoming generation of youths as more rebellious in comparison to themselves at that age. Is the echo generation of Canada actually more criminally inclined than the previous generation, or are young people today being unjustly cast as "out of control" when viewed through the lens of the media's camera?

The first article in this feature uses statistics to show that the crime rate of young Canadians has risen sharply, and is a "very big concern" to some as a result. The second article claims that while the youth crime rate may have increased, it is not at a crisis level and does not connote a generation of wayward youths.

Yes: Violent crime up 7.5% in Greater Toronto: Young people have highest rate, Statscan says
By Elaine Carey, Demographics Reporter

Greater Toronto's violent crime rate has risen dramatically for the first time in seven years and a leading criminologist blames the Harris government.

"It seems to me that we would have an increase in violence because we have policies designed that way," said Anthony Doob, a criminology professor at the University of Toronto.

Violent crime in Toronto rose by 7.5 per cent last year..., Statistics Canada said in its annual report on crime yesterday. But property crimes, including theft, break and enter and fraud, fell by 6.8 per cent.

Young people aged 15 to 24 have the highest crime rate of any group. Across Canada, violent youth offences rose by 7 per cent after falling for eight years. They included an 18 per cent rise in sexual assaults, a 7 per cent increase in assaults and a 2 per cent rise in robberies. Doob said cuts to welfare and other social programs means problem kids get less help, which has an effect on violent crime.

"What we know about crime is that all these things, particularly for kids who are at risk, are things which in the past have helped reduce crime and now they're no longer there," he said. "Why should we be surprised?"

The increases are consistent with numbers gathered by Toronto police.

"Overall crime took a little bit of a dive, but the concern for us, obviously, is that violent crime is up," Staff Inspector Bruce Smollet said yesterday. "Especially in an area…like youth crime. It's a very big concern."

Doob said Ontario's response to kids who are in trouble at schools is all wrong. "You kick them out, you punish them, rather than trying to make the kids' experience in school more positive so they don't act out," he said. "Schools are being told 'get rid of the kid, make the kid somebody else's problem, have the kid charged.'

"The question is, do you try to keep them in the one institution where you have the opportunity to do something positive or do you say 'get out of here.' Well, we have a tendency now to say 'get out of here.'

"Teachers have less time to work with individual students who are beginning to have problems or to spend time on things like extracurricular activities that kids enjoy," he said.

"All these things make school a less positive experience for kids and we know that's going to relate to the amount of crime the kids who are at risk are doing," he said. "It's not mysterious."

Source: Carey, Elaine. 2001. "Young people have highest rate, Statscan says." *The Toronto Star.* 20 July 2001.

COMPETING PERSPECTIVES

No: A Brief from the John Howard Society of Canada

"The empirical and statistical evidence on the youth crime rate to date shows that youth crime generally is not increasing and, although violent youth crime may be increasing, it has not reached a level that should alarm us (Doob et al., 1995). However, there is, as Grossberg (1992: 284) suggests, an "affective [emotional] epidemic" throughout North America. Regardless of the empirical evidence, it is clear that "youth gone wild" is a popularly recognized and increasingly forceful area of social concern....

"A 1993 poll reported that 64% of Canadians felt that the "behaviour" of young people had "become worse" compared to a similar poll in 1990 which reported only 47% of Canadians indicating such an opinion (General Social Survey, 1993). In addition, one in three Canadians believe that the rate of violence in Canada is the same as or worse than that of the United States (Abraham, 1993). These misconceptions have been promoted through more and more media attention drawn to those rare cases of violent youth behaviour in Canada and the United States as a form of "public education." The reality of the youth crime picture is, however, quite different. When one looks at the homicide rate, persons under the age of 18 years accounted for 6% of all persons accused of homicide in 1992–93 which is down from 9% for the previous year. In comparing youth homicide rates between 1972 and 1993, there is no discernible trend in the number of persons charged between the ages of 12 to 17 years. The numbers range from a high of 68 in 1975 to a low of 35 in 1987 (Silverman, 1990; Meloff and Silverman, 1992; Siverman and Kennedy, 1993)....

"Why has there been such an affective [emotional] response of fear, terror and panic among the general public to youth crime in recent years? A number of explanations are plausible... It may be that the current "youth crisis" is more a reflection of the uncertainty that all Canadians feel regarding social and economic stability and is merely reflected in the policies and practices surrounding children and youth who have always been seen as a potential threat to the social order. Gilbert (1986) suggests that there was no actual rise in youth crime during the 1950s when there was an equally alarming public response to youth as that which is being experienced today....The paranoia experienced in the present day "youth crisis" has been seen at other points in history wherein the category of youth becomes seen as a problem.

Source: John Howard Society. Brief on Young Offender Policy. [Online]. Available <http://www.johnhoward.ca/document/brief/Jhsdoc3.htm> November 1995.

Questions

1. Read the "Yes" position. Make a list of evidence in this section that suggests that "Youth is out of control." Summarize the different causes that experts suggest are responsible for the problem.

2. Read the "No" position. Make a list of evidence in this section that suggests that "Youth is *not* out of control." Summarize the different reasons that experts give to explain the apparent situation.

3. Is Generation Y out of control? Explain your point of view on this question in writing, in a poster, or with a cartoon.

4. What connections do these articles suggest exist between youth crime rates, the economy, and public social policy?

Figure 5.22 What, in your opinion, are some of the dominant values and interests of your generation?

As a member of the echo boom, how would you describe your generation with regard to its beliefs, values, and interests? To answer this question you would likely rely on your personal experiences, social environment, and personal beliefs, as well as the beliefs of your friends. As a result, your description may vary greatly from that of other teens across the country. When sociologists address this question, they rely on research to inform their answers.

The following case study illustrates how two Canadian social science researchers approached this question.

Practitioners of Social-Demographic Research

Reginald Bibby and Donald Posterski are two Canadians who have specialized in social research about young people. Bibby is a sociologist at University of Lethbridge (Alberta), while Posterski is Vice-President of Youth Programs at World Vision Canada. Between 1975 and 1992, Professor Bibby conducted four national surveys of Canadian adults, and, with Posterski, three more of youth. The information that these two researchers have gathered and published profiles major attitudes and values of a generation of Canadian teenagers. In this case study, they describe the purpose and methods used in their popular book, *Teen Trends: A Nation in Motion*.

Purpose

"*Teen Trends* represents an effort to provide Canadians with a clear picture of where young people are headed, along with sound thoughts on how we might respond to what is taking place…. Committed as we are to good scholarship and good communication, we have tried for balance. For those readers looking for theory, the book is grounded in classic sociology's assertion that the key to understanding individuals is understanding the social environments from which they come. Accordingly, we view Canadian young people as products of an ever-changing Canadian culture.

Just as Canada is a country under construction, young people are in the process of building their lives out of the materials our society is giving them.

Methodology

"Our method has been to engage in conversations with teenagers through a series of national surveys. In 1984, in an attempt to address the problem of limited information on youth, we carried out what we believe was the first comprehensive national survey of young people in Canada…. In 1992, we completed another large-scale survey of youth, involving almost 4000 high school students across the country….

"The 1992 national youth survey was entitled Project Teen Canada 92. Funded by the Lilly Foundation, it was conducted over approximately a four-month period, from November 1991 to mid-March of 1992….

Sample Size

"As in 1984, a sample of 3600 teenagers was pursued, a figure that, if representatively selected, makes it possible to generalize to the overall high school adolescent population (about 1.5 million) with a high level of accuracy (within about three percentage points, either way, 19 times out of 20). A sample of that size also increases the accuracy of analysis involving various aggregates—such as region, community size, gender and race.

Sampling Frame

"Once again, since our interest was in the segment of young people on the verge of becoming adults, the sample was restricted to Canadians 15 to 19 years old in grades 10 to 12 across Canada, including CEGEPs in Quebec...."

Sampling Procedures

"In pursuing the sample size of 3600 high school students, we again randomly selected high school classrooms rather than individual students because of the significant administrative advantages and minimal negative consequences for a random sample. The design involved choosing one classroom in each school selected. Based on an average class size of perhaps 25 students, this meant that some 150 schools needed to participate. On the basis of a projected response rate of about 75 per cent—based on our

1984 experience—the sample was comprised of approximately 200 schools.

"The schools were chosen using **multi-stage stratified** and **cluster sampling procedures**. The country was first stratified according to the five major regions, with each region then stratified according to community size (100 000 and over, 99 000 to 10 000, less than 10 000). Each community size was in turn stratified according to school system (public, separate, private).... Finally, one school in each of these communities was chosen randomly....

The Response

"Questionnaires were returned from 180 of the 193 designated classrooms—a return rate of 93 per cent. ...A total of 4190 questionnaires were received, with 226 of these discarded, primarily because they had been filled out by students younger than 15 or older than 19. The number of usable questionnaires totalled 3 964. The 1984 total was 3530."

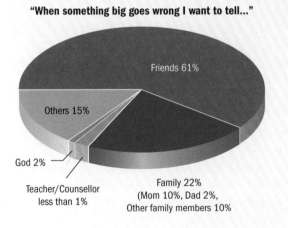

"When something big goes wrong I want to tell..."

Friends 61%

Others 15%

God 2%

Teacher/Counsellor less than 1%

Family 22% (Mom 10%, Dad 2%, Other family members 10%)

Figure 5.23 This pie graph shows who Canadian youths want to share their problems with. Who would you choose to tell?

Source: Bibby, Reginald W. and Donald C. Posterski. 1992, 2000. *Teen Trends: A Nation in Motion* (abridged paperback edition). Toronto. Stoddart.

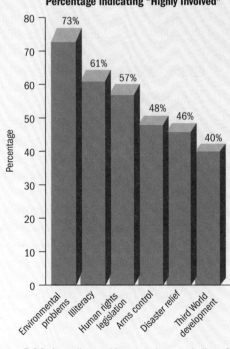

Percentage indicating "Highly Involved"

- Environmental problems 73%
- Illiteracy 61%
- Human rights legislation 57%
- Arms control 48%
- Disaster relief 46%
- Third World development 40%

Figure 5.24 According to this research, teens believe Canada should help solve the world's problems. Do you agree?

CASE STUDY

Sample Results from the Survey

One interesting piece of information to come out of the study revolved around the psychological impact that the baby boom generation had on their children. From the teens' responses it appears that many young people agree with and respect the values and attitudes of their parents on some contentious issues such as drugs, sex and discipline.

Asked to rate their sources of enjoyment, teens predictably put their friends (94 per cent), music (90 per cent), and their own room (75 per cent) at the top of their lists. But Mom places a respectable fourth (71 per cent) while Dad finishes seventh (62 per cent).... Fully 91 per cent cite the way they were brought up as their main influence, while 71 per cent agree with the statement "I want a home like the one I grew up in." And despite the popular image of teens as rebellious and resentful of adult authority, 56 per cent of the respondents concur with the premise that "discipline in most homes today is not strict enough." (Bergman, 2001)

Questions

1. The authors describe their work as "grounded in classic sociology." Find this section of the case study, and explain what they mean. Identify four different professions that might find *Teen Trends* useful.

2. In your own words, list any four strictly controlled research procedures that Bibby and Posterski applied to their youth surveys. Why were they so careful with their research methods?

3. In your own words, explain what the sample results from the survey suggest about your generation. Do you agree?

4. What psychological impact does the study suggest baby boomer parents have on their children?

Pause and Reflect

1. Why are the job prospects for your generation actually very good?

2. Give two examples of the ways in which the echo kids are already influencing each of the economy and the society of Canada.

3. Create a "Fashion and Fun" collage (like the one on page 154) as it relates to you and other teens of your generation.

4. If you could change when you were born, would you prefer to be a part of the early baby boom, Gen-X, or Generation Z, instead of your own group? Explain your thoughts.

Section 5.6   Impact of the Aging Boomers

The Dependency Load

The baby boom generation and their children, the echo boom, have both benefited by growing up in periods of economic prosperity. Both generations have found themselves at the centre of society, the boomers in nuclear, suburban families, and the echo kids as offspring of "Me Generation" yuppies. Of course, these descriptions are broad generalizations, demographic stereotypes, but they do apply to many members of the two most favoured generations in Canada's history. Today, many front-end baby boomers are preparing for retirement, and the echo kids will fill their places in the workforce. By the year 2020 most baby boomers will either be retired or very close to it. The echo kids and the Twentysomethings of today will dominate Canadian jobs, professions, and business. Even so, some people wonder if they will be able to support the large mass of aging boomers who will increasingly rely upon them.

To help answer such questions, demographers have developed the concept of **dependency load**. This is a measure of the portion of the national population that is dependent, that is, not actively employed. The age cohorts of the population pyramid can be used, with dependents generally identified as children and youth aged 0 to 14 years, and seniors aged 65 or older. Countries with a broad-based pyramid (as found in many parts of Africa and Asia) have a high dependency load. So do Japan and several countries in Europe, which have had two generations of low birth rates and many seniors.

High dependency loads make it very difficult for the working population to meet the needs of children and seniors. When the proportion of income earners in a population is low, governments must either levy high taxes or borrow heavily to provide essential social, educational and medical services. For example, in 1961, during the peak of the baby boom, the **dependency ratio** in Canada was 87 dependents for every 100 persons of working age. The great majority of dependents were children and youth, and, as you have seen, governments spent heavily to build schools and recreational facilities for this demographic group. By 2001, the ratio had fallen to 58 per 100 working-age people. However, during the next three decades, the dependency load will climb again, but this time to supply medical and social services for a large seniors population—the aging boomers. Not only will there be more seniors in the future, but, also, they will have a greater **life expectancy** than today—an average of three extra years, reaching 78.5 years for men and 84.0 for women.

The Boomers as Seniors

A first glance at Figure 5.25 suggests that Canada will face difficult years during the early twenty-first century as more and more baby boomers become seniors and the dependency load increases. Health care and social services for the elderly can be very expensive because the needs of an aging population are great. However, there are good reasons to expect that Canada can cope with these changes. Many front-end baby boomers are already well prepared for their fast-approaching retirement. They have been depositing as much as 10 per cent of their income into company or union **pension funds** for years, with further amounts deposited by employers or government. For example, the cash value of a skilled industri-

Key Concepts

dependency load

dependency ratio

life expectancy

pension fund

retirement savings plan

ecotourism

Seniors in Canada, 1931–2031

Year	Approximate Population Aged 65+	Proportion of Total Population
1931	0.6 million	6 per cent
1941	0.8 million	7 per cent
1951	1.1	8
1961	1.4	8
1971	1.7	8
1981	2.4	10
1991	3.2	12
2001 projection	3.9	13
2011 "	4.9	14
2021 "	6.6	18
2031 "	8.3	22

Source: Norland, J.A. 1991. *Profile of Canada's Seniors.* Statistics Canada and Prentice Hall Canada, 1991, p. 6.

Figure 5.25 Outline reasons why Canada's senior population is expected to rise so sharply in the early twenty-first century.

al worker's retirement pension could range from $350 000 to more than $500 000 after 30 years of service.

About a third of Canadian taxpayers also contribute to Registered Retirement Savings Plans (RRSPs), encouraged by tax incentives from the federal government. Ottawa is eager to see fewer people dependent upon government pensions in the future, because these funds cannot support a generation expected to live 15 to 25 years or more after they retire. Many middle-class and upper-middle-class baby boomers can also expect to receive inheritances from their aging parents, some of whom accumulated wealth in property and investments during the prosperous 1980s. However, since about one-fifth of Canadian families live in relative poverty, many baby boomers have not been able to prepare financially for the future.

Two other factors suggest that the impact of aging baby boomers need not be negative. Canada has seen increasing emphasis on fitness and healthier lifestyles for the past 30 years; many boomers enjoy good health and look forward to embarking upon "second careers" after they retire. They will be able to either fill or develop part-time jobs in the huge service sector of the economy. For the next two or three generations, many baby boomers will actively contribute to the national economy by working, paying taxes, and investing. At the same time, remember that the echo boom is large—about 70 per cent as big as the original boom. Combined with the Twentysomethings, there should be plenty of people in the full-time labour force to keep the dependency ratio well below 1961 levels. Therefore, many baby boomers will be able to support themselves in old age through their own pensions, **retirement savings plans**, and inheritances. Others can expect that a basic government pension plan, funded by the Twentysomethings and the echo kids, will remain available to those without other resources to rely upon.

As the baby boomers age, they continue to influence the economy in important ways. For example, in the 1990s the major development in the automobile market was the SUV, the Sport Utility Vehicle. As the echo kids grew up, suburban boomers often replaced their boxy minivans with muscular, four-wheel-drive vehicles that could climb mountains, but usually just went to the mall. Slick advertising encouraged the aging boomers to project a young, outdoorsy image.

Are All the Aging Baby Boomers the Same?

Michael Adams is one of Canada's leading market researchers. He has applied a social values tracking system developed in France to identify four different subgroups among Canadians aged 30 to 49 in 1997. He establishes a field of values bounded by two pairs of opposites—traditional versus modern, and individual versus group. Then, he uses responses to public opinion polls to place people into four categories based on their combination of values: traditional individual, modern individual, traditional social, and modern social.

In Figure 5.26, the position of the four groups on the field reflects the strength of a particular value. For example the Connected Enthusiasts are highly social in their outlook. Among the Disengaged Darwinists, women tend to be more social, while men are more individual. Thus, the two figures stand apart from one another. The name of this subgroup is based on the late-nineteenth-century Social Darwinists, who believed that society should follow the rule of nature, "Survival of the fittest."

Four Social Groups Among the Boomers

Boomer Subgroup	Number	Prime Motivators	Key Values
Disengaged Darwinists (traditional, individual)	41%	Financial independence, Stability and security	fear, nostalgia for the past
Autonomous Rebels (modern, individual)	25%	Personal independence Self-fulfillment	freedom and individuality, suspicion of authority and traditional institutions
Anxious Communitarians (traditional, social)	20 %	Traditional communities and Institutions, Social Status	family and community, fear and duty, need for respect
Connected Enthusiasts (modern, social)	14%	Traditional and new communities, Experience-seeking	family and community, hedonism and instant gratification

Source: Adams, Michael. 1997. -Sex in the Snow: Canadian Social Values at the End of the Millennium. Toronto. Penguin.

Figure 5.26 Why do you think the "Disengaged Darwinists" make up the largest portion of the baby boomers?

Questions:

1. Summarize the methods Michael Adams uses to classify people into demographic subgroups.
2. Think of some baby boomers you know. Try classifying them into Adams's four subgroups, using the diagram and the chart. What are the difficulties of classifying people this way? What are the advantages of this method?

Entrepreneurs can expect a boom in travel, as young retired boomers indulge in fantasy vacations. Social researcher Michael Adams has identified two large subgroups, totalling 39 per cent of the baby boomers, who could be attracted to travel adventures. The group he calls the "Autonomous Rebels" seek self-fulfillment, while the "Connected Enthusiasts" value experience and gratification. **Ecotourism**, a type of travel based on the enjoyment of nature, should particularly benefit, with group package tours to places as far away as Antarctica available. Caribbean and Alaskan cruises, and historical trips to Europe, Egypt, and the Holy Land will likely become even more popular than they already are. Other "soft" outdoor recreational activities, such as golf, cycling, walking, and even birdwatching, will gain in popularity as the boomers age.

Demographer David Foot identifies one important broad trend that will affect the marketplace as Canadian boomers grow older. As a group, they will value quality over price. Retailers and restaurateurs should prepare themselves to offer high-quality goods and services in settings that enhance the shopping or dining experience. The present era has seen the growth of the "big box stores"—Canadian Tire, Wal-Mart, Home Depot—and fast-food chains, which profit from sales volume. Foot believes that the near future will witness the revival of smaller "Main Street" shopping districts, with specialty shops full of quality merchandise. After all, many baby boomers will have a large amount of disposable income and plenty of time as they become seniors. And, life has taught them that they deserve only the best.

Pause and Reflect

1. How are the concepts "dependency load" and "dependency ratio" similar? How do they differ?

2. Do you feel that the aging baby boomers will become a burden for your generation in the future? Explain your answer.

3. Why will the baby boom generation have a strong economic impact as they age? Give three examples.

4. Use Figure 5.26 to predict which aging baby boomer segments would likely be most interested in the following activities, then explain your choices:
   a) golf course membership
   b) historical society membership
   c) gourmet cooking and wine-making clubs
   d) individual hobby pursuits such as wood carving

5. Brainstorm a chart to compare the pros and cons of having a large population of seniors in Canada. If you asked an older adult to make a similar list, how might the results differ? Why?

Chapter Activities

Show Your Knowledge

1. What sorts of problems would Canada have if the country had no demographers and had not bothered to collect census data over the years?

2. Answer these three related "cause" questions: Why did the baby boom begin? What helped it to continue for two decades? Why did it end?

3. Explain the meanings of these chapter terms from psychology and sociology, then give an example for each one: "nuclear family," "counterculture," "materialism," "self-fulfillment."

4. Explain the meanings of these demographic terms and give an example of each: "dependency load," "life expectancy," "cohort," "birth rate," "infant mortality rate."

5. Explain how both Benjamin Spock and John Dewey were important in shaping the outlook of the baby boomer generation.

Practise Your Thinking

6. Study the population pyramids data in Figure 5.8. Compare the pyramid for 1941 to the pyramid for 1956, and explain reasons for the differences you see.

7. Brainstorm a list of the positive and the negative effects that the sexual revolution of the 1960s has had up to the present time.

8. Do you think that it is important for echo kids to get involved with international issues such as Free the Children? Why, or why not?

9. Construct two web charts in which you trace out the social, political, and economic impacts of the baby boomers up to about 1980, and after 1980.

10. In your opinion, will the social and economic impacts of your generation be less than, as great as, or greater than those of the baby boomers? Explain your reasoning.

Communicate Your Ideas

11. Imagine that you are either a returning World War II veteran or a newly arrived British war bride. Write a realistic one-page diary entry describing the mixed emotions you feel in coming to Canada.

12. Work with a partner to develop an 8- to 10-point survey to learn about the viewpoints and values of the echo kids generation. Then, administer the survey to at least 10 students, half of them girls and half boys. Do the two genders differ in their views and values?

13. Develop a large summary chart, along with a concise set of teaching notes, for a short talk you would give about *either* the social and economic impacts of the baby boom generation or the differences between the baby boom generation and the echo kids.

14. Use catalogues and magazines to create a poster illustrating the childhood of the millennium kids (born after 1995).

Apply Your Knowledge

15. Interview a member of Generation X whom you know. Find out whether or not his or her life experiences closely compare to those described in the text on pages 145–146. You'll need to prepare some questions in advance.

16. Show the "Baby Boom: Fun and Fashion" layout (page 154) to people you know who are 40 to 55 years of age. Which of the items shown can they personally relate to? What other items do they think should have been included in the layout?

17. Is John Dewey's "progressive education" progressive enough for you? If not, design a curriculum that you would find more interesting and valuable than the one that you are taking this year. Show your timetable for the week.

18. Suppose that you are an entrepreneur. Outline plans for a new business or investment you could start in your community to cater to the aging baby boomers. It could either be set in the present time or 10 to 20 years from now.

19. Visit the following Web site, which predicts the population pyramids of Canada and most other countries each year up to 2050. Compare the years 2025 to Canada's 1996 [or 2001] pyramid, looking for the baby boomers, echo kids, and millennium kids. How do the two population pyramids differ?

   Go to the United States Census Bureau home page at <www.census.gov>. Click on "Projections" and then on "International Demographic Data" to go to "Population Pyramids."

CHAPTER 6

TRENDS RELATED TO FERTILITY AND FECUNDITY

INTRODUCTION

Very few aspects of life are more important than fertility and fecundity. In this chapter you will learn that, while fertility issues are important on a personal level, they also have profound implications for our local communities and the larger society. For example, as family size decreases and fertility rates decline, it becomes more and more expensive for taxpayers to pay for the social programs that keep societies functional.

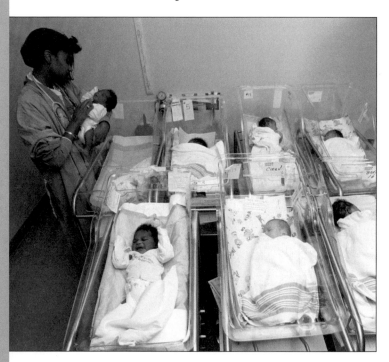

Canadian women are actually having fewer and fewer babies. How long do you think this trend will continue? Why?

On a personal level, from the time we are preteens and begin to mature physically, we have to grapple with feelings regarding sexuality and relationships. When we mature and become sexually active, we have to make important decisions regarding birth control and family planning. The decision of whether or not to become a parent can be very difficult, especially with the added pressures and expectations society places on couples to produce children. For some people, the choice of whether or not to have children is taken away when they find out that they, or their partner, is infertile. This, too, proves to be a traumatic experience for many couples. Some infertile couples choose to remain child-free, but for those who want a family, adoption and reproductive technologies are sometimes the only options.

Further, people's decision to have or not have children affects fertility rates, which, in turn, have an impact on our local communities. For example, as birth rates decline, our society ages and a greater burden is placed on our pension and health care systems. Declining birth rates also have an impact on immigration rates, as increased immigration is the only way that population rates can remain stable.

Focusing on the Issues

I happily choose to be childless

By Lesly Mayhue

At a recent extended family dinner, the topic of conversation turned to the fact that my partner and I have not blessed my parents with a grandchild. I coyly told them, "I already have a family."

"The cats don't count," my mother scowled.

Before I had a chance to tell her to stop knocking my beloved kitties, everyone else started firing their two cents at my head. "You'll change your mind"; "You'll regret it someday"; "Who'll look after you when you're old?"

The pressure to reproduce is everywhere, especially for women. A friend about the same age as I am (28) has been trying for years to get her tubes tied and cannot find a doctor who will do it (one even told her she couldn't believe my friend would deny herself the joy of motherhood). Though sympathetic organizations, like Child-free By Choice www.childfree.net) are growing in number and supporting the decision not to procreate, it's still a hard sell. If you tell most people that you are happy being child-free, they perceive you as selfish. Or secretly miserable.

At some point during our little round-table discussion, an uncle chimed in and told me that I may think I am fulfilled, but only having a child would really enrich my life. No one disagreed with him. So, am I to believe that my numerous hobbies, extensive volunteer work, staying out late, and budding career are just frivolous diversions?

How many women have felt needlessly inadequate because they couldn't produce offspring? I also wonder how many people out there are raising families when they really have no business doing so. It's disturbing that so many people breed because they are lonely or bored. Or because they simply cannot think of anything else to do. So much for parenthood being inherently noble.

Raising your own brood can be a great thing, and I have immense respect for those who do it well. But there are so many other legitimate paths that deserve serious deliberation. It is not anyone's duty to reproduce.

If I get the urge to hold something cute, tiny and cuddly, I'll scoop up one of the cats. If someday I should regret my decision (and who goes through life without remorse?) I will deal with it. The alternative is to have kids I don't want "just in case." And that is a hell of a lot more selfish than not having them.

Source: Mayhue, Lesly. 2001. "I happily choose to be childless." *The Toronto Star.* 27 August 2001.

THINK ABOUT IT

1. What are some of the reasons the author gives for not wanting children? What are the reasons her relatives give as to why she should have children?

2. Do you feel there is pressure or expectation on couples in Canada to have children? Discuss.

3. Do you want children someday? Why or why not?

■ Learning Expectations

By the end of this chapter, you will be able to

- demonstrate an understanding of the relationship between fecundity and culture (for example, age at marriage, average number of children per family)

- explain the psychological impact of the choice of whether or not to have children

- evaluate the social impact of current birth patterns on Canadian communities

Section 6.1   Setting the Stage: World Population Trends

Key Concepts

developed world

developing world

fertility

fecundity

fertility rate

replacement level

infertile

estrogen

Changes in fertility have a profound effect on our society. An increasing birth rate can result in overpopulation, starvation, and a drain on dwindling water supplies and other resources. Over the past 150 years or so it certainly looked as though overpopulation was going to become a crisis. After all, although it took thousands of years for the population of the planet to reach the one billion mark in the 1830s, it took only 100 years to add the second billion. The third billion took only 30 years, and a mere 12.5 years was all that was needed for the population of the world to leap from four to five billion (Cleland, 2001, p. 9).

Surprisingly, though, demographers and policy-makers are now grappling with the fact that population rates are falling. Not only are women having fewer children, the population itself is aging. This trend is occurring in both the developed and developing world. (The **developed world** is defined by the United Nations as North America, Europe, Japan, Australia, and New Zealand. In general, these are industrialized, wealthy countries. The term "industrialized countries," is often used interchangeably with the term "developed countries.") The falling birth rate in the developed world is problematic because there are fewer and fewer people to pay for the increasing pension and health care needs of the aging population. As well, the shift to an older population will likely slow economic growth over the next 50 years.

Adding to this complicated picture is the situation in the **developing world**. Defined as all other countries not listed above, developing countries are non-industrialized and are less wealthy than developed nations. Ninety-five per cent of all the world's population growth today is happening in the developing world, where about half of the population is under the age of 15. These young people have

little health care and education (Williams, 2001). Even in the developing world, women are having fewer children as contraception becomes more widely available and women begin to assume positions of greater responsibility in the economy.

In this chapter you will frequently read the words "fertility" and "fecundity." **Fertility** refers to *actual* reproduction, whereas **fecundity** denotes the ability to reproduce. A woman who is bearing children is fertile; a woman is considered fecund if she is capable of bearing live offspring (Bongaarts and Potter, 2001, p. 121). **Fertility rates**, the actual number of children had by women, can be affected by physical and environmental factors as well as social and cultural factors.

Trends in Developed and Developing Nations

You may have been surprised to read that fertility rates on a global scale are on the decline. At the heart of this decline is the fact that the developed world's population is shrinking. In fact, of the developed nations, only the United States is replacing itself through high immigration and fertility. Japan and many European countries will have to allow huge numbers of immigrants across their borders just to keep their population constant. In fact, in Germany, Italy, and Sweden, deaths now outnumber births. Specifically, in Sweden, the fertility rate over the past 10 years has declined from 2.1 children per woman to 1.5 (Taylor and Taylor, 2001, p. 3). In Britain, women will have an average of 1.7 children each, compared to 2.4 children 30 years ago. And according to the Office of National Statistics, this rate is expected to fall to 1.66 in the future (Appleyard, 2001, p. 6). In Canada, the average fertility rate is expected to drop from 1.54 to 1.48 births per woman in the next five years. Across the country, only the Northwest Territories and Nunavut show birth rates above the **replacement level**—the number of births required to maintain a stable population (Owens, 2001, p. A5).

The developing world is undergoing a reproductive revolution of its own. Throughout such countries, women of vastly different backgrounds are having fewer children. Birth rates have declined by one-third since the mid-1960s: women formerly had six children on average, but today they have four (Robey, Rutstein, and Morris, 2001, p. 227).

Although fertility rates are dropping globally, there is still a tremendous difference in the quality of life of those living in developed nations and those in the developing nations. In the following case study, Nobel laureate and University of Chicago professor Gary S. Becker argues that wealthy nations should open their doors to those from poor nations to help eliminate economic inequality in the world. Do you agree that those of us lucky enough to be born in a wealthy nation have an obligation to those not as fortunate?

Is there an obligation on the part of the "Haves" toward those who "Have" much less?

While world population has doubled during the past several decades to more than 6 billion persons, birth rates in many countries have fallen to unprecedented low levels. The result is a demographic divide between nations with high and low rates of population growth that will have enormous economic and political significance.

Virtually all high-income countries, and a few poorer ones, especially China and Russia, have fertility rates that are too low to fully replace their populations. The average is only a little above one child per woman during her lifetime in Spain, Italy, Russia, and several other nations. Even in the US, which has the highest fertility rate among rich nations, women give birth to only about two children in their lifetime.

The picture is different in most very poor nations, including all of Africa and most of South and Central America, since their much higher birth rates are causing their populations to grow rapidly. This difference in population growth between rich and poor nations will widen further the gap in per capita incomes between developed and other nations. Indeed, faster population growth in less developed regions contributed to the considerable widening of world income inequality during the past couple of decades.

An efficient remedy for this population divide would be for many men and women in countries with low incomes and growing populations to move to those with high incomes and stable or declining populations.

The recent estimates from the UN show that developed regions absorbed about 20 million immigrants from poorer nations during the last decade of the twentieth century. This global shift contributed about half the growth in the populations of richer nations, although Japan has refused to accept many immigrants, despite the prospects in that country of a rapidly falling and aging population. Immigration to Western Europe was especially important and accounted for more than 70 per cent of its population growth during the past decade. The US absorbed almost as many immigrants as did Europe, but immigration contributed a smaller part of its growth, since birth rates in the US are higher than in Europe. In addition, many persons entered both the US and Europe illegally, so that the total contribution of immigration to population growth in both regions was even larger than official figures indicate.

Still greater emigration from poorer to richer nations would help alleviate the continuing inequality among the world economies created by the higher population growth of the less developed world. But rich nations are reluctant to open their borders any wider to immigrants because many powerful interests and most politicians oppose large-scale immigration. Trade unions fear that competition from immigrant labour will result in lower wages for their members. Many taxpayers believe that the welfare state attracts immigrants who mainly seek government benefits and contribute little to production. Other groups worry about the effect of immigration from Third World countries on the racial and ethnic mix of their populations.

Many of these arguments could be countered if host nations gave greater priority to younger and more skilled immigrants who work hard and who contribute much more in taxes than they receive in benefits. However, even skilled immigrants are not readily welcomed, as seen from the political difficulties in expanding the H-1B American visa program, which gives temporary visas to high-tech personnel.

These obstacles ensure that legal immigration will not solve the conflicts that arise from different rates of population growth. The problems would be greatly reduced if poorer nations promoted economic growth by encouraging entrepreneurship and making greater investments in human and physical capital. Birth rates invariably fall rapidly when countries have faster economic growth and expanding education, especially the education of women.

Unless immigration and population policies change, conflict between the economic haves and have-nots will inevitably increase as growing numbers of young men and women from the underdeveloped world try to gain access to the opportunities in rich nations.

Adapted from: Becker, Gary S. 2001. "How Rich Nations Can Defuse the Population Bomb." *Business Week.* 28 May 2001.

Questions

1. What is per capita income? Explain how the fertility rate of a country can affect its per capita income.

2. In two columns, generate a list of arguments *in support of* and *against* the idea that wealthy nations should accept more immigrants from poor nations.

3. Conduct additional research to find out how many immigrants (not refugees) Canada accepted over the past couple of years. The Web sites for Statistics Canada and the Citizenship and Immigration Department of the Government of Canada will be useful. When you locate the information, analyze the data to address the following questions:

   a) How many came from developing nations and how many from developed nations?

   b) What were the ages of the immigrants?

4. Use the information you organized in Question 3 to update the arguments you created in Question 2. Be prepared to defend your arguments.

But why has there been such a change in fertility rates around the world? As with most social trends, a variety of factors have combined to produce the change. These factors can be explored in two broad categories: physical and environmental factors, and socio-cultural factors. The link between social and cultural factors and fecundity will be explored in Section 6.2 of this chapter.

Physical and Environmental Factors and Fertility

A couple is considered to be **infertile** when they have been trying to conceive for over one year without success. In Canada it is estimated that as many as one in five couples is infertile (Infertility Awareness Association of Canada, 2001). There appears to be a host of physical and environmental factors linked to increased infertility. One of these is the rapid spread of sexually transmitted diseases (STDs). In particular, the STD chlamydia, which is a symptomless condition, often results in the blockage of the female's fallopian tubes.

Another factor linked to the increase in infertility is a decline in sperm counts in men living in developed countries. Sperm counts appear to be about half of what they were just 60 years ago, and some studies indicate that the rates are continuing to decline by as much as 2 per cent per year (Hughes, 2000). Although research in this area is still considered inconclusive, the drop in sperm counts has been linked to high levels of **estrogen**, the female sex hormone, in water supplies. These high levels of estrogen are believed to be due to small amounts of women's oral contraceptives finding their way into the water system. As well, by-products of the chemicals found in food packaging and plastics mimic the action of the female sex hormone, thereby raising the level of estrogen in men and decreasing sperm counts.

There is also a growing trend for women to delay motherhood until after they get their careers established. As a result, many women are having their first babies in their thirties rather than in their twenties. In fact, more than a third of all babies born in Canada today are born to women in their thirties. This social change has led to a decrease in the birth rate because a woman's fertility declines rather considerably as she ages, as you will see in the case study that follows. As well, late motherhood also leaves women with fewer reproductive years in which to produce other children, so the trend of delayed motherhood is resulting in lower fertility rates.

Figure 6.1 Growing numbers of Canadian women are waiting to establish their careers before deciding to have children. What effects do you think this trend may have on the workforce in Canada?

Delaying Childbirth May Not Be Such a Good Idea

You've seen the pictures of fortyish celebrities proudly holding new babies. You've read about high-tech fertility miracles. Maybe you've heard the statistics on mature moms: the number of Canadian women giving birth after age 39 has more than doubled since 1985. So if you work out, don't smoke and look younger than your 40 years, you should be able to have a baby too, right? Think again. Despite the hype, medicine—even the most expensive high technology—can't necessarily deliver a baby.

At any age, getting pregnant is never guaranteed. Even if you time intercourse for your fertile days, healthy women under 35 have a 20 per cent chance each month of conceiving a healthy baby. Five years later, your chances plummet to 5 per cent. "Women have been duped into thinking you can delay," said Dr. Ruth Fretts, a Canadian obstetrician who teaches at Harvard Medical School. "Age matters."

It's mainly because of the eggs. You have 300 000 when you are born, but your stock declines throughout life. More important, the quality of the eggs declines in your late thirties, which significantly increases the risk of chromosomal abnormalities such as Downs syndrome. Older eggs don't function as well every step of the way—from fertilization to implantation—which explains why 40-plus women miscarry nearly three times more frequently than women who are 10 years younger.

Another less serious roadblock is the quality of the uterine lining, says Dr. Arthur Leader, Chief of Reproductive Medicine at the University of Ottawa. As you approach menopause, you produce less of the hormone progesterone, so the lining of the uterus may not thicken enough to permit the fertilized egg to grow. Fortunately, progesterone levels can be topped up, either by injection or vaginal suppositories.

Even the most sophisticated treatments can't turn back the clock for aging eggs. Fertility drugs, for instance, might help regulate a woman's ovulation if her problems don't relate to menopause. But many reproductive specialists doubt the utility or ethics of using fertility drugs to pump out more 40-year-old eggs of poor quality. These treatments can cause side effects ranging from pelvic discomfort to double vision or hyper-stimulation of the ovaries, which can result in metabolic problems or even internal bleeding. Fertility drugs might also increase the risk of ovarian cancer.

Reproductive technology is getting closer to helping overcome the aging-egg factor by experimenting with some yet-unproven techniques. Drilling holes in shells of in vitro embryos—since older eggs can have thicker shells—may help them "hatch" once they are implanted in the womb. Some IVF clinics now grow embryos in laboratory cultures for five days instead of two in order to weed out the ones that would have otherwise died. In the US, futuristic techniques such as injecting older eggs with cytoplasm or gel from younger eggs have produced a couple of babies.

Still, age is relative. Some women's biological clocks wind down more slowly than others', suggests a 1998 study co-authored by Dr. Fretts. Among women who lived to age 100, a stunning 20 per cent had given birth in their forties. And that was long before test-tube babies.

Adapted from: Scott, Sarah. 1998. "Baby Time Any Time?: Old Age is Not the Time to Have Babies." *Chatelaine*, Vol. 71. 9 January 1998.

Questions
1. Identify and explain the main reasons women's fertility declines with age.
2. Discuss the success of reproductive technologies in overcoming these age-related factors
3. What are some of the side effects of reproductive technology on women's health?

Pause and Reflect

1. With specific examples, explain how fertility rates are changing in the developed world.

2. Discuss some of the physical and environmental factors linked to infertility in both males and females.

3. What is the physical impact of delayed motherhood?

4. When you think of your own future, what factors would you want to be in place in your life before you become a parent? If you do not want to have children of your own, what factors do you think others should have in place before becoming parents?

Section 6.2   The Relationship Between Fecundity and Culture

As mentioned earlier, fecundity denotes the ability to reproduce. Although the number of children a woman has can be affected by a host of physical and environmental factors, the desire to have children, the number of children an individual wants, the way women give birth, and beliefs about child rearing are all the result of social and cultural factors.

When discussing cultural or social factors we must be careful not to generalize research findings or jump to conclusions. Just as individual cultures vary greatly from one another, individuals *within* a culture vary greatly from one another. That being said, there are a number of cultural and social factors that do have an impact on fecundity.

Fertility and Cultural Norms

In order to understand the causes of fertility variation from culture to culture, demographers John Bongaarts and Robert G. Potter study the **proximate determinants** of fertility. Proximate determinants are the biological and behavioural factors through which social, economic, and environmental variables affect fertility. If a proximate determinant—such as contraceptive use—changes, then fertility necessarily changes also. In their

article "Fertility, Biology, and Behaviour: An Analysis of the Proximate Determinants" (2001), development specialists John Bongaarts and Robert Potter compare the cultural norms of developed societies, developing societies, and the Hutterites (members of an Anabaptist sect in the northern United States and Canada).

What they found is that, in contemporary Western populations, women bear an average of two children during their reproductive years. Marriage generally occurs when a couple are in their early twenties, and their first child follows two years later. The second child is spaced to occur approximately two to three years after the first. Contraception is used to delay the second conception, and surgery is used to avoid further births.

The fertility rates of many developing societies in Africa, Asia, and Latin America have also been dropping, but not as dramatically. Families remain larger in these countries, with the average woman giving birth to seven babies. Marriage usually takes place when a woman is in her teens, and the first child arrives about three years thereafter. Subsequent births are generally spaced about three years apart and continue until the woman enters menopause. The longer birth

Key Concepts

proximate determinant

prolactin

ovulation

weaning

menarche

plagiarism

barrenness

Figure 6.2 Explain why Hutterite families are larger than most others on average.

interval is the result of more prolonged and frequent breast-feeding than in Western populations. (The connection between breast-feeding and fecundity is discussed under the next heading.)

The Hutterites have the highest fertility rate of any population with reliable records. Hutterites live in small self-contained communities in which strict social and religious control exists over most aspects of daily life. Women in this culture bear an average of nine children. Although marriage occurs when women are in their early twenties, a strict ban on contraceptive use and a shorter period of breast-feeding results in a birth interval of about two years.

The work of Bongaarts and Potter concludes that cultural norms are affected by age of first menstruation, age at marriage, frequency of intercourse, length of breast-feeding, use and effectiveness of contraception, and onset of permanent sterility.

Links Between Breast-feeding and Fecundity

In many countries in the developed world, individuals are expected to be autonomous and independent, and this ideal extends to mothers and their babies. In the United States and Canada, for example, babies are expected to sleep in their own cribs, spend a considerable amount of time playing alone, and are often breast-fed for only a few months. Most women in the United States get only six to eight weeks maternity leave, so mothers return to work when their infants are quite young and usually stop breast-feeding at that time. This is unfortunate because many studies show that infants benefit greatly from breast milk. It is the only food that is perfectly matched to the nutritional needs of infants; it immunizes infants against many diseases, it results in improved digestion and optimal growth of the infant's body systems, and it reduces the risk of infants' developing allergies (Whitaker, 1999, p. 52).

The Public Health Branch of Health Canada reports that over 70 per cent of Canadian women initiate breast-feeding, but about 40 per cent stop by the time their babies are three months old. Although a variety of factors have an impact on a woman's choice to breastfeed, in general, breast-feeding rates are higher among older mothers and those with higher education and income levels. One of the most common reasons cited by Canadian women for quitting breast-feeding was that they had to return to work. Women used to receive six months maternity leave, but in January 2001 that was extended to 12 months. Perhaps this change will result in an increase in the number of women who breast-feed and in the length of time that babies are breast-fed.

Although it is undeniable that breast-feeding is good for babies, how does the prevalence of breast-feeding affect fecundity? When breast-feeding is done "on demand"—which means the baby is fed whenever it is hungry, even if that is every hour or so—and no supplementary food is given to the infant, nursing has a contraceptive effect on the woman. Breast-feeding results in the release of

prolactin—a pituitary hormone that regulates the production of progesterone—and inhibits **ovulation** (the monthly release of an egg or eggs). In many developing-world cultures where breast-feeding is done on demand and complete **weaning**—meaning the removal of breast milk from a young child's diet—does not occur until between two-and-a-half and four years of age, births are often spaced four or five years apart (Whitaker, 1999, p. 53).

In contrast, in countries like the United States that have low breast-feeding rates, births often happen in quick succession. The United States government launched a campaign in the year 2000 to increase the rates of breast-feeding in that country. The campaign, entitled Healthy People 2000, aims at getting 75 per cent of women to breast-feed for at least the first three months of their babies' lives. In Canada, the Canadian Paediatric Society, Dieticians of Canada, and Health Canada recommend exclusive breast-feeding for the first four months of life (the World Health Organization recommends the first six months) and continued breast-feeding with complementary foods for up to two years of age and beyond.

🌀 Age of Menarche and Marriage

The age at which a woman experiences **menarche**, her first menstrual period, and her age upon marriage are other cultural factors that affect fecundity.

Menarche and Fecundity

You may be surprised to learn that the age of menarche is influenced by culture rather than being simply a biological occurrence. But it is. In foraging (pre-industrial) societies, women have much less protein in their diets and tend to eat more low-calorie proteins than do Westerners. Their low-calorie diet is made up exclusively of wild plant parts (roots, seeds, stalks, leaves, nuts and fruits) and game or fish

and does not include dairy products or processed grains. In addition, they travel 10 kilometres or more on foot every day and routinely carry heavy loads, often 15 to 20 kilograms (Whitaker, 1999, p. 53). This lifestyle results in menarche occurring between 16 and 18 years of age, and a first child within three or four years of that.

Because the women in these societies tend to breast-feed on demand, subsequent children are born every four or five years. This cycle repeats itself between four and six times until the woman reaches menopause, at around the age of 45. As a result, a woman in this type of culture experiences about 150 ovulations in her lifetime (Whitaker, 1999, p. 53).

In contrast, women in developed countries eat a diet high in fat, protein, and calories. They also experience very little physical stress from exercise or exposure to the elements. Over the centuries this has lowered the age of menarche to 12 or 13 and has delayed menopause until the age of 50 to 55. Significantly, the birth of a woman's first child is delayed, on average, to 13 or 14 years after menarche. The average number of births is reduced to two or three, and these births often occur in quick succession. Because Western women do not have a long period of infertility associated with breast-feeding, the average woman will ovulate around 450 times over her lifetime, which is 300 times more than the average woman in developing societies.

Age at Marriage

Since most people do not begin families until after marriage, the age at which couples marry can have an important impact on the number of children they have. For example, a woman who marries at age 18, will have more fertile years during which to produce children than a woman who marries at 32. Therefore, if the average age at which women marry increases in a particular country, the fertility rate for that country may decrease.

Figure 6.3 A young Kalahari San woman gathers food for her family. Female members of hunting gathering societies tend to reach menarche at a later age than North American females, due in part to their diet.

In a study published in the *Asia-Pacific Population Journal* in 1998, researchers M. Nurul Islam and Ashrraf U. Ahmed noted that age at marriage varies in Asian countries and has a direct impact on fertility rates. In South Asia, the age at marriage for females increased from under 15 years in the early part of the century to well over 15 years or even approaching age 20 by the 1980s. The female age at marriage in India increased by nearly five years over this period, from 13.2 to 18.1 years. Pakistan experienced an even greater jump, from 13.3 to 19.7 years, during the period 1921–1981. Sri Lanka started out with a much later female age at marriage, 18.1 years in 1901; nevertheless, the age at marriage increased to 24.2 years in 1981 and 25.5 in 1993. While the age at which females marry has been increasing, the fertility rate for all of South Asia has been decreasing. It dropped from 5.4 in the 1970s to 3.3 by the end of the 1990s.

 **Government Intervention in Fertility**

Those who study anthropology have found that cultural norms related to fertility are not only shaped and nurtured by parents and family, they are also moulded by government policies and programs. Governments can pursue policies to increase populations as well as decrease populations. For example, in Russia, politicians are currently so worried about the low birth rate that they are debating banning abortions and imposing a childlessness tax as ways to increase the country's population (Karush, 2001). In contrast, in 1979 the Chinese government imposed a one-couple, one-child policy in an attempt to reduce the country's population growth. The program has been so successful that in the early 1990s the government was able to modify it to allow couples in most rural regions to have two children, or to have a second child if their first was a daughter (Sun, 1993).

Here at home, the provincial government in Quebec launched a program in 1988 to encourage people to have children. The program provided a cash bonus to couples for each child born. The more children a couple had, the greater the bonus. For example, couples received $500 for a first child and $8000 for a third child. This policy did not increase the Francophone population and was quietly withdrawn in 1997 (Baker, 2001, p. 278.)

Skill Builder:
Using Sources Ethically

The foundation of all good writing is research. The better your research, the better your final product will be. As you conduct your research, however, and write your report, essay, or presentation, it is crucial that you properly acknowledge your sources.

Quite simply, acknowledging your sources means telling the reader or your audience where you found your information. You must do this for all of the material you use in your final product, *not* just for information that you directly quote. Some students worry that they will reference too many sources in their work and that this will make it look like they have not done any of their own work. Except for an original poem or piece of fiction, *all* work that you produce will be based on information you have read, watched, or listened to that was written by someone else. It is, therefore, a *good* thing to have many references or citations in your own finished product because that is the only way you can get credit for all the hard work you put into your research.

If you do not accurately acknowledge the sources you have used, you are committing **plagiarism**, which means you are claiming someone else's work as your own. This is a very serious transgression that can result in your receiving a grade of zero on your project, a failure in the course or, at university, sometimes suspension from a program.

Step One: Accurately record source information
As you conduct your research, get in the habit of recording the source information of all materials you download, photocopy, or make notes from: even if you do not know if you will end up using the information. This will save you a lot of time and hassle later, because it is very difficult to retrace your steps and locate source information at a later time.

Source information you should record includes the following:
- the author's name
- the date of the work
- the title of the article or work
- the title of the journal, newspaper, magazine, or book in which the work was published
- the name of the publishing company and the city of publication
- the page number where you found the information
- the book editor's name, if the item is a chapter in a book

Step Two: Cite the work in the body of your essay or report
Once you have gathered all of your information and have begun to write your final product, you must make sure that you properly *cite* or acknowledge your sources *as you use them*. You cannot just list your sources at the end of your report in a bibliography or reference list (although you must do that too!). In the body of your paper, whenever you refer to a study, fact, or piece of information that is not common knowledge, you must acknowledge your source. And you must do this whether it is a direct quote or not.

To acknowledge a source, place the author's last name, the date of the publication, and the page number in parentheses. Or, if you use the author's name in your sentence or example, then you only need to include the date and page number in parentheses. See the examples below.

Example 1
In a review reported in *Canadian Social Trends* magazine, Alain Belanger reported that in Canada, compared with other industrialized nations, voluntary sterilization for contraceptive purposes is remarkably widespread (1998, p. 16).
[This tells the reader that the author's name is Alain Belanger, the article was written in 1998, and the information was found on page 16.]

Example 2
"Among the poor in rural Bangladesh, women's lives are severely restricted by their social and economic dependence on men. Many cannot avail themselves of family planning, health, and other services unless these services are brought to their homes" (Schuler & Hashemi, 1995, p. 258).
[This tells the reader that there are two authors, the work was published in 1995, and the quotation was taken from page 258.]

Step Three: Create a reference list or bibliography
After you have completed your product, you need to prepare a bibliography (also called a Reference List or Works Cited Page), which lists *in alphabetical order* all of the sources you used in your project. Although there are various ways to set up a reference list, many social sciences use APA (American Psychological Association)

format. Although the specific rules for creating a refer-ence list are too detailed to list here, you can find com-plete instructions in the *Publication Manual of the American Psychological Association*, or visit a universi-ty Web site that posts the guidelines online, like the one for California State University at <www.calstatela.edu/-library/guides/3apa.htm>. Below are the two in-text citations featured in Step 2 written in proper APA bibli-ographic format.

Belanger, Alain. (1998). Trends in contraceptive sterilization. *Canadian Social Trends*, Autumn 1998, 16–19.

Schuler, S.R., & Hashemi, S.M. (1995). Family planning outreach and credit programs in rural Bangladesh. In A. Podolefsky & P.J. Brown (Eds.), *Applying anthro-pology: An introductory reader*. (pp. 36–42). Toronto: Mayfield Publishing Company.

Practise It!

1. Locate five sources dealing with fertility or fecundi-ty. For each, write the correct in-text citation needed if you used the source in your final product. Then create a five-item reference list using proper APA style format.

2. Take a look at the online style guides of the American Anthropological Association <www-.aaanet.org/pubs/style_guide.htm> and the American Sociological Association <www.cal-statela.edu/library/bi/rsalina/asa.styleguide.html> and determine how they differ from the APA guide-lines. Rewrite the two example entries above in these formats.

3. Why do you think these three social sciences have dif-ferent guidelines for published papers and written sub-missions? Why don't they all use the same format?

Government-funded family-planning programs have also had a major impact on fertility rates. In Canada, government-funded programs have been established to reduce the rate of teen pregnancy in the country, and these programs have proven effective. The teen pregnancy rate in Canada has dropped from 54 per 1000 women aged 15 to 19 in 1974, to 47 per 1000 in 1995. Sex education programs in Canadian schools, strong public health departments, and easier access to con-traceptives have all been cited as reasons for the dropping rate (Schaefer, 1999). By con-trast, the teen pregnancy rate in the United States—a country that does not have manda-tory sex education programs in schools—is more than double the Canadian rate.

An example of a successful government intervention program in a developing nation can be found in Bangladesh. In Bangladesh, which has one of the world's poorest popula-tions and very low levels of female employ-ment and literacy, fertility has fallen by 40 per cent since the late 1970s (Cleland, 2000, p. 18). Part of the program involved "incessant" birth-control messages using all available media, a network of clinics, and outreach workers. The objective was to transform con-traceptives from something looked upon with distrust and disapproval to something regard-ed as normal and part of everyday life. Also, since Bangladesh is an Islamic country where *purdah*—a requirement for women to remain secluded, out of view of men or strangers—still confines many women to their own

Figure 6.5 Have you ever read any of the government sponsored advertisements to combat teenage pregnancy? How effective do you feel these messages are?

homes, a group of literate, married women were recruited, trained, and sent back to their villages to deliver contraceptive advice and supplies to the doorsteps of their neighbours.

Demographer John Cleland stresses that government-sponsored family-planning programs need to be delivered very carefully so that they are able to generate the desired results. Poorly implemented programs create additional problems to the ones they attempt to solve. In most of Central and South America, for example, the push toward lower fertility initially expressed itself in very high rates of illegal abortion. The horrendous health consequences of poorly performed abortions motivated governments to start providing proper family-planning services.

 ## Marriage and Family Trends in Different Cultures

So far in this section we have learned that social and cultural factors such as attitudes toward breast-feeding, the age of menarche, and government policies can have an impact on fertility rates. But culture can affect fertility rates in other ways as well. Some of these are

Figure 6.6 An elephant is used as a billboard to publicize birth control in India in the 1970s. Women were encouraged to limit their families to two or three children.

overt, or open, and some are covert, or implied. The following case studies explore marriage and family trends in different cultures. As you read the cases, ask yourself what factors are at play and how they might influence the fertility rates in the places profiled.

Culture and Fertility in China, Hong Kong, and Israel

Feature Country: China

"No white gown for Li Rong on her wedding day. No veil either. A husband was there, but Li wasn't planning on connubial bliss. When Li, 35…, decided to get married, she hustled down to the registry office with her fiance, signed her name and promptly went back to living alone. 'Of course I love my husband,' she said. 'But we had a mutual agreement. Freedom was the priority.'

"Across this rapidly modernizing metropolis of 12.6 million people, links to Chinese traditions are being sundered…Many of Beijing's 'walking married,' especially women, were raised as single children; and as adults, they say they don't want to be 'crowded' by

living with their husbands. 'I don't care what it is called,' Li said. 'It's just important to be free.'

"Then why get married in the first place? 'You have to consider your parents' feelings,' she said. 'I wanted to make my parents happy. Secondly, the most important thing is to get a house.' Chinese state institutions and companies still control many of Beijing's apartments and offer them only to married couples. 'So, you get married to get a house,' Li said…Walking marriages appear linked to a desire by many women in Beijing not to have children. A recent poll in the city found that 15.6 per cent of people do not want even the single child that Chinese law permits couples who live in cities. Walking marriages and the choice of childlessness are 'disassociated from Chinese traditional culture and…absolutely non-Chinese,' said Li Yinhe, a research fellow at the Institute of Social Studies of the Chinese Academy of Social Science.

"…Zhen Zhen makes her living following Western trends. As an associate professor of design at China's only fashion school…Zhen has embraced the idea of a walking marriage. 'I've been married 12 years…In the first year, we lived together. But then…I found that living together in an apartment with my husband was like a prison. So…I wanted to escape.'

"'So now,' she said, 'my husband has a home, and I have a home. We need some time to ourselves. If we lived together, we would have no privacy.' Zehn and her husband meet on weekends, and, she said, 'we call each other very often.' Li Yinhe, the research fellow, says she doubts walking marriages will have much impact on the structure of the population and other parts of the society."

Adapted from: Gargan, Edward A. 2001. "Just Married—but Living Separate Lives." *The Los Angeles Times.* 27 April 2001.

Feature City: Hong Kong

In the year 2000, the Year of the Dragon, the number of babies born in Hong Kong exceeded the projected number of births by 3000. Researchers Dr. Paul Yip Siu-fai and Joseph Lee Man-kong from the University of Hong Kong explain that in Chinese culture the Dragon is the symbol of divinity and good fortune. It is believed that children born in the Year of the Dragon will be bright, smart and sensitive. As a result, couples have a strong desire to give birth in such a year, hoping to bring their children good fortune. Hong Kong has the lowest fertility rate in the world, setting a record of 0.974 in 1999 (Moy, 2001).

Feature Country: Israel

In Israeli culture, parenthood is an extremely important goal. So much so that **barrenness**, or the inability to have children, is seen as tragic, and marriages can be dissolved after 10 years of childlessness. In her book, *Reproducing Jews: A Cultural Account of Assisted Conception in Israel,* Susan Martha Kahn describes how Israelis are willing to go to great lengths to avoid the stigma and suffering that childlessness brings. To foster this aspect of the culture, the government subsidizes fertility treatments for all of its citizens, regardless of marital status. As a result, there are more fertility clinics per capita in Israel than in any other country in the world.

The use of reproductive technologies to produce a child is considered legitimate by society and is sanctioned by rabbinical authorities for three reasons: the technology helps fulfill the commandment to be fruitful and multiply, alleviates the suffering of the couple, and helps keep the marriage together (averting the obligation to divorce after 10 childless years.) As well, reproductive technologies are accepted because there is no adultery or lust involved and because issues of paternity are simplified in Israeli culture since any child born to a Jewish mother is always considered a fully-fledged Jew. Therefore, even if a child is created through the use of sperm donated by a non-Jew, the baby is still considered to be fully Jewish and is automatically eligible to be an Israeli citizen.

But the origins of maternity can become complicated by ovum-related technologies. What determines a Jewish mother—producing the eggs or carrying the child in the womb? The rabbis are still considering the issues. Novel views have developed: Rabbi Ezra Bick suggests an "agricultural" model in which conception occurs when men "sow the seeds in women's fertile soil"; in this view, the gestational mother is the true mother. Naturally, the issues become even more confused when it comes to surrogacy, but, again society relies on the concept that Jewish babies are born only from Jewish wombs.

Adapted from: Youval, M. 2000. "Love & marriage, but where's the baby carriage?" *Jerusalem Post*, 1 December 2000.

Questions

1. Why do "walking" marriages appeal to some Chinese?
2. What larger cultural changes does this type of marriage reflect?
3. Does a form of "walking" marriage exist in Canadian culture? Explain.
4. a) Does the example of the babies born in the Year of the Dragon in Hong Kong address an overt or covert influence in the culture? Explain.
   b) Think of a similar phenomenon in Canada and share it with the class.
5. Explain the link between fecundity and culture in Israeli society.
6. How have rabbis embraced the use of reproductive technologies?

Pause and Reflect

1. How do cultural norms affect fertility rates?

2. Why do fewer women breast-feed in developed societies than in developing societies? What impact does this have on fecundity?

3. Provide examples of government policies around the world designed to increase or decrease family size.

4. With a classmate, design a plan to increase the breast-feeding rate in Canada. For example, a Sears store in Kitchener, Ontario, has a breast-feeding lounge set up with couches, rocking chairs, and change tables in a quiet area. Include at least five suggestions in your plan. Be prepared to discuss your ideas with the class.

5. In what ways do you think Canada is less kid-friendly than Israel?

Section 6.3   Involuntary and Voluntary Childlessness

"Children are the cloth of the body. Without children, you are naked." This is an African saying that commonly means that a man's wealth is measured, in part, by the number of children he has, and a woman's value to her husband is determined by her ability to bear children. Among many of the peoples of Ghana, a marriage without children is seen as incomplete. As a result, family members, especially in-laws, start to instigate a break or divorce when a marriage has not produced children after a certain number of years. As we learned on page 188, for Israelis, a marriage that remains childless for 10 years is

Key Concepts

involuntary childlessness

reproductive technology

in vitro fertilization

Key Concepts

intrauterine
insemination

superovulation

IVF and GIFT

AID

surrogate

voluntary
childlessness

seen as grounds for divorce. Although both of these examples may seem harsh, many societies regard children as an important component of a complete marriage. For this reason, childless couples are often subject to pity, suspicion, and sometimes overt hostility.

Psychological Impact of Involuntary Childlessness

Involuntary childlessness occurs when a couple or individual wants to have children and cannot. This state is generally the result of one of two factors: the first is not having a mate with whom to produce a family, and the second is infertility. As mentioned earlier, somewhere between 10 and 20 per cent of couples in the developed world are not able to have children. In 40–50% of these cases, the infertility is the result of a physical problem (such as hormonal imbalance, pelvic infection, or a reproductive abnormality) on the part of the woman. About 40–50 per cent of the cases are due to a physical problem (such as low sperm count, hormone deficiency, or impotence) on the part of the man. And, in about 10 to 20 per cent of cases, the infertility is the result of contributing factors by both partners, or no cause can be identified (Resolve, 2002).

Individuals and couples who find that they are not able to conceive a child, although they want one, are often emotionally devastated. Undergoing a reproductive treatment causes additional stress and is a major event. In fact, each step of treatment results in an increased stress level and new uncertainties between the couple because the doctors cannot predict whether the treatment will be successful.

In 1999, German sociologist Corinna Onnen-Isemann conducted 52 interviews with women and men in Germany who had undergone one or several treatments for infertility. She found that the burden of undergoing reproductive treatments can be divided into three categories. The first category concerns the physical effects of the medical treatment itself, such as side effects from fertility drugs. These range from hot flashes, blurred vision, and irritability to an increased risk of all reproductive cancers.

The second category addresses the objective burdens of the treatment, such as the major expenditure of time and the organization required. This is because couples must perform the reproductive act or have reproductive treatment at a specific date each month and must also organize the rest of their lives around these dates. Onnen-Isemann found that in many cases working women had to use all of their holidays for one year for one reproductive treatment.

The third category deals with the subjective psychological strain that patients are exposed to. The emotional relationship between the partners is tested as feelings of guilt or blame arise each month. As well, all spontaneity is removed from the relationship as the couple steps through each stage of treatment each month. And finally, treatment often results in personal interests being given up entirely, which leads to further stress, anxiety, and depression.

Although the decision of whether or not to have a child can be very stressful, psychologists report that involuntary childlessness—where that decision does not exist—is one of the most emotionally traumatic situations a couple may experience. Even though couples may have friends who have experienced infertility and are aware that it is a common disorder, the news is almost always unexpected. Infertile couples progress through a number of emotions similar to the stages involved in grieving a death. After the initial shock of a diagnosis of infertility, most couples experience feelings of guilt, sadness, loss of control, anger, and isolation.

Guilt is a particular problem if one of the partners is found to be physically "responsible" for the infertility. Such people feel that they have let their partners down and are responsible for their unhappiness. They may also feel that they have let their parents down; this is particularly true of those who come from large families that place great importance on having children.

Couples who want children experience feelings of sadness and depression once they discover they are infertile. For those who have experienced miscarriage, infertility represents the loss of fulfilling a dream and the loss of a relationship that they might have had with a child. Couples mourn for what could have been, and this type of sadness can be especially hard to deal with. The nature of infertility is such that couples may never know definitely whether they are able to conceive, and they may never identify what is causing the problem; as a result, they have nothing on which to focus their grief. There is the persistent hope that "this will be the time," which can leave their emotions painfully suspended, creating a continual hoping-against-hope attitude. Couples may have even more difficulty dealing with these losses because friends and family often underestimate the emotional impact of infertility.

Another psychological impact of infertility is the feeling that the couple has lost control of their lives. Many couples plan their lives so that they will be able to begin a family at the most favourable time. They likely practised birth control for years and waited until their careers were well established before trying to have a baby. Not being able to have a baby is often the first time couples experience failure against forces that are beyond their control, no matter how hard they try. During fertility treatment, couples often put other parts of their lives on hold. This might include postponing moving to a new home, continuing their education, changing jobs, or establishing new relationships. The more they give up, the less in control they feel.

Other predominant emotions are anger and isolation. Anger arises from having to

Figure 6.7 It has been estimated that one in five couples in Canada will not be able to produce children. How might you react if your doctor informed you that you were infertile?

confront a great deal of stress and many losses, including the loss of control. It is not unusual for infertile couples to resent pregnant women and friends and family who do not seem to understand the emotional tension associated with infertility. Often the anger is directed toward doctors—this being one of the reasons why so many infertile patients change doctors so frequently. This anger often results in isolation, as infertile couples pull away from those who make insensitive remarks, such as "just relax and you'll get pregnant." These remarks are not based on fact and can cause a great deal of pain. It is not unusual for relationships to change if friends and family are unable to understand and empathize with the feelings of the couple. When someone dies, the death brings family and friends together to grieve the loss, which helps in healing. In contrast, infertility is a very private form of grief—you grieve alone without social support because the loss is hidden.

Overcoming Infertility

When faced with a diagnosis of infertility, some couples decide to accept their child-free state and move on with their lives. Although this can be a very hard decision to make, a life without children can be satisfying, with more disposable income, more freedom, and a strong bond between the partners in the marriage. For couples who decide to pursue their dream of becoming parents, adoption is one alternative.

Domestic adoption—adoption within the country—is a good option for couples who do not feel it is necessary to adopt an infant. According to the Adoption Council of Canada, there are approximately 20 000 Canadian children in need of families, but only about 1200 are adopted each year. Many of these children are considered to have too much baggage: having a brother or sister also up for adoption; having a special need; or simply being "too old." Since many couples desire an infant, and very few infants are available in Canada, about 2000 children are adopted internationally each year, often at a cost of up to $35 000 (Rankin, 2001).

Advances in technology have certainly made it possible for some couples to over-come their infertility and become parents. These **reproductive technologies** help improve a couple's chances of conceiving and carrying a child to term through medical manipulation of the woman's reproductive cycle or the male's sperm quality or count. The success rates of these technologies are still rather low, but for couples with almost no chance of conceiving and carrying a child to term on their own, they offer hope.

Unfortunately, these technologies are expensive and the procedures are not covered by government health plans or private health insurance in most countries. In Canada, for example, **in vitro fertilization** (IVF) procedures are not covered by the country's health care insurance unless both of the woman's fallopian tubes are blocked. Otherwise, couples have to pay for the procedure themselves. Each cycle of IVF costs between $6000 and $10 000. As a result, reproductive technologies are creating a two-tier system of health care in this country: affluent couples can come up with the money for the procedure, while couples on the lower end of the income scale may not be able to.

Focus on Reproductive Technologies

The following are some of the more common reproductive technologies available to couples trying to conceive. In some cases, single women can access these technologies as well. For example, single women can be artificially inseminated in a clinic with donor sperm.

- **Intrauterine insemination (IUI)**
  This procedure assists conception by increasing the chances that the man's sperm and the woman's egg(s) actually meet. The woman is given fertility drugs to cause her to produce more than one egg per cycle (**superovulation**). When the woman ovulates, which is determined by daily ultrasounds and blood work, she is inseminated with a selection of the man's "best" sperm. The man produces a semen sample in the clinic's laboratory, where the

Figure 6.8 Some people oppose reproductive technologies on moral grounds since they feel scientists are "playing God" by interfering. What is your opinion on this?

healthiest, strongest sperm are removed from the seminal fluid. The sperm are then injected directly into the uterus through a small catheter. In this way, the sperm have a far greater chance of meeting and fertilizing an egg, as they do not have to swim up through the woman's vagina.

- **IVF (In vitro fertilization) and GIFT (Gamete intrafallopian transfer)**
  IVF is the assisted reproduction technique in which fertilization occurs *in vitro* (which literally translates as "in glass"). The man's sperm and the woman's egg are combined in a laboratory dish, and after fertilization the resulting embryo is then transferred to the woman's uterus. Initially, IVF was used only when the woman had blocked, damaged, or absent fallopian tubes (tubal factor infertility), but today, IVF is used to circumvent infertility caused by practically any problem, such as unexplained infertility and male factor infertility.

  GIFT is similar to IVF except that during GIFT the sperm and eggs are mixed and injected into one or both fallopian tubes. After the gametes (reproductive cells) have been transferred, fertilization can take place in the fallopian tube as it does in natural, unassisted reproduction. Once fertilized, the embryo travels to the uterus by natural processes.

- **AID (Artificial Insemination by Donor)**
  IUI, IVF, and GIFT can all be conducted with sperm from the woman's mate or, if the mate's sperm is of poor quality, extremely low in numbers, or carries a genetic problem, the procedures can be conducted with sperm from a donor. The donors are men between the ages of 20 and 40 who are healthy and have no family history of illness. They provide a sperm sample for testing. The semen is analyzed and is accepted only if it has a high sperm count and good motility. Donor sperm is frozen with a cryoprotectant medium (a chemical that prevents the sperm from being damaged even at very low temperatures) and is loaded into plastic straws. These are uniquely coded and sealed and then placed in steel tubs of liquid nitrogen where they are frozen to minus 196 degrees Celsius. One day later, one straw is removed and thawed to see how the sperm survived the cold. Only samples that contain at least 25–40 million actively mobile sperm are accepted. The sperm are then kept in cold storage for three months, which is the amount of time it takes for the HIV virus to be detected.

- **Surrogate Mothers**
  The word **surrogate** means "substitute or replacement," and a surrogate mother is one who lends her uterus to another couple so that they can have a baby. In the West, where fewer and fewer babies are available for adoption, surrogacy is gaining popularity despite controversial legal and ethical hassles (see case study p. 196).

  The most common reason a woman needs a surrogate is that she has no uterus. This may be the result of a birth defect (Mullerian agenesis), or because it had to be removed surgically for life-saving reasons in an operation called a hysterectomy. Other women who may wish to explore surrogacy include those who have had multiple miscarriages, or who have failed repeated IVF attempts for unexplained reasons.

  There are two main kinds of surrogacy. In the first case, the surrogate mother provides the egg. In this case, the surrogate is inseminated artificially by the man's sperm, which results in her having a genetic relationship to the baby. In the second case, and more commonly, the infertile woman provides the egg, which is then either transferred to the surrogate's uterus by GIFT or IVF with the man's sperm. The surrogate mother, who has no genetic relationship to the baby, then acts as an incubator for the next nine months.

COMPETING
PERSPECTIVES

Countries Differ on Rules Governing Reproductive Technologies

In May 2001, then Health Minister Allan Rock presented his recommendations for legislating reproductive technologies to a House of Commons health committee to study. The committee members agreed with Rock on most issues, including placing a ban on payment to egg and sperm donors, and refusing such donors anonymity from any resulting children.

The United States, on the other hand, has no such legislation and the purchasing of eggs and sperm still takes place in that country. As well, children resulting from such donated genetic material have no legal right to know the identity of their biological parents.

Health Committee Supports Ban on Payment for Sperm, Egg Donations
By Maureen McTeer

Santa has come early for Health Minister Allan Rock. In response to his request, the standing committee on health has released a report that offers an excellent blueprint for the long-awaited law to regulate fertility clinics and research on human embryos.

Urging immediate action, committee members from all five political parties in the House of Commons generally support sweeping changes to the status quo. Mr. Rock has yet to set a date to table his bill. But it's clear that, if adopted, the standing committee's far-reaching recommendations will take Canada down a very different path than our U.S. neighbour's.

First, the committee recommends five basic principles as the backbone of a new law: respect for human individuality, dignity and integrity; caution; refusal to treat humans as commodities or objects of commerce; informed choice; accountability and transparency. That would mean, for instance, that payments for sperm, ova or surrogate mothers would end.

The committee's priority is the health and well-being of children. Children born using reproductive technologies and practices—artificial insemination, in vitro fertilization—would be able to know the person whose donation gave them life. Provincial laws would be changed to ensure that donors are not financially or otherwise responsible for such children, but they would have to agree to their identity being known to the child.

Second, the committee rejected Mr. Rock's proposal to run the show from his office and department. In a sign of respect for Parliament's role, the committee proposed that a "semi-independent" regulatory body, with a broad mandate, be established outside the Health Department. The board's nine members, at least half of whom would be women, would be appointed by the Prime Minister after consultation with provinces, stakeholders and the health committee. To ensure its independence, this all-important board must be funded publicly and not by private companies or institutions.

Maureen McTeer is a medical-law specialist and a former member of the Royal Commission on New Reproductive Technologies.

Source: McTeer, Maureen. 2001. "Health Committee Supports Ban on Payment for Sperm, Egg Donations." *The Globe and Mail.* 14 December 2001.

COMPETING PERSPECTIVES

The Quest for a Beautiful Baby

Wendy, an all-American girl...[with] all the requisites—blonde hair, green eyes, model figure and a personality that bubbles like a geyser, is an egg donor. [She] is one of 5,000 American women—and a growing number of Britons—who this year will donate their genetic material to infertile couples, making anything from $5,000 (£ 3,500) to $50,000 per donation.

No longer satisfied by renovating their own bodies to meet the preternatural standards of American beauty, wealthy and infertile American parents are now custom-building their children like luxury cars. Which puts girls with archetypal all-American looks in a very lucrative position. ...

...Welcome to the fertility of the 21st century... It all boils down to supply and capital. If you have the cash and can find a suitable donor, in nine months, parenthood can be all yours. Women in the US are bombarding fertility clinics with applications to donate, while British women are likewise contacting US agencies with offers of healthy eggs bearing DNA stamped with the Union Jack. Some are no doubt motivated by altruism, others are facing up to the reality of university fees.

...Of course, there are ethical questions: is it right to pay vulnerable young girls to part with their genetic material? Will they regret it later? So while the American Society for Reproductive Medicine recommends that women be paid no more than $5,000 for their eggs, there are desperate and demanding parents across the US waving huge sums of money in front of women, the kind who for five grand may not have been takers.

"Intelligent, Athletic Egg Donor needed for loving family," read the half-page advertisement published in newspapers at Ivy League universities, including Yale and Stanford. "$50,000, to an egg donor with an SAT score of at least 1,400 [the equivalent of straight As], athletic ability and a height of at least 5ft 10in." Two hundred women, most of them students, responded.

"I think it's disgraceful," says Shelley Smith, director of The Egg Donation Program in Los Angeles, who won't accept donors under the age of 21, because she thinks women of 18 or 19 are too young to comprehend the ramifications of their actions. "This is America; we are a consumer-oriented culture. First we wanted a car with bells and whistles, now we want a baby with bells and whistles. I get a set of parents who come to me and demand a designer baby—certain height, college scores, athletic ability, musical talent ... I always ask, why are you doing this?"

Excerpts from: Krum, Sharon. 2001. "American Beauty: Here is Lauren Bush, this year's model." First published in *The Independent*. 17 June 2001.

Questions

1. Make an organizer in which you outline the pros and cons of paying egg and sperm donors and surrogate mothers.

2. Why have Canadian politicians proposed legislation to ban such payments? Do you support such a ban? Why or why not?

3. How will a ban on sperm and egg donation, as well as a ban on anonymity for donors, affect the use of reproductive technologies in Canada?

Although some couples view surrogacy as a solution to infertility, other people see it as a source of ethical dilemmas. For example, as we have seen in the Competing Perspectives feature on the previous pages, our government is proposing to ban payment to surrogates. As well, in the United States at least, this technology has raised some legal questions.

In 1985, a landmark case involving custody of a nine-month-old infant was heard in a New Jersey courtroom. "Baby M" was born to her surrogate mother, Mary Beth Whitehead, under contract to William and Elizabeth Stern. After handing over the child to the Sterns, Whitehead regretted her decision to give up the child and began a battle to regain custody. As you read the following story, consider the ethical issues raised by this case, and whether these issues are still relevant today.

CASE STUDY

The "Baby M" Case

"In the crowded courtroom in Hackensack, N.J., listeners heard repeated last week the now familiar outlines of the story. William Stern, 40, a biochemist, and his wife Elizabeth, 41, a paediatrician, contracted with Whitehead early in 1985 for her to conceive a child through artificial insemination and carry it on their behalf. The three were brought together through the Infertility Center of New York, a for-profit Manhattan agency. The Sterns chose Whitehead, now 29, after reviewing and rejecting the applications of 300 women. Some drank. Some smoked cigarettes or marijuana. Some just did not look the part. The Sterns wanted a candidate 'who might have looked like us,' said Elizabeth Stern.

"Mary Beth Whitehead seemed perfect. A housewife with two school-age children by her husband Richard, she had wanted to become a surrogate mother to help a childless couple. She claimed to want no more children of her own. After she met the Sterns for the first time at a New Jersey restaurant, the three became friends, trading phone calls back and forth. Whitehead signed a contract, promising among other things that she would not 'form or attempt to form a parent-child relationship' with the resulting infant. The Sterns promised to pay her $10,000, plus medical expenses. They paid the center $10,000. But during delivery, Whitehead told the court last week, she decided she could not go through with it. 'Something took over,' she said. 'I think it was just being a mother.'

"Whitehead, who did not accept her fee or sign over custody, took the child home with her. Three days later the Sterns collected the baby from the Whitehead home, but next morning Whitehead came by to beg for the infant's temporary return. After a two-hour encounter that both sides say was punctuated by emotional outbursts, the Sterns reluctantly agreed. 'We thought she was suicidal,' William Stern said. Two weeks later, when the Sterns came to her home, Whitehead told them she would not give up the child.

"The following month, after obtaining a court order that required the infant to be handed over to them, the Sterns returned, accompanied by five policemen. In the confusion, Richard Whitehead slipped away with the child through a bedroom window. The Whiteheads then fled with the baby to Florida, where they were tracked down by a private detective hired by the Sterns. Authorities took the infant and returned her to New Jersey. Last September, Judge Sorkow gave temporary custody to the Sterns, but he allowed Mary Beth Whitehead to spend two hours twice a week with Baby M. on the neutral turf of a local children's home.

"In deciding the case, New Jersey Superior Court Judge Harvey Sorkow becomes the first judge in the U.S. asked to enforce a surrogate agreement. He could treat the case mainly as a contract dispute, rule that the contract is valid and award the child to the Sterns.

Or he could opt to treat it basically as a custody battle; then the best interests of the child would be the guiding principle.

"If a society legitimates surrogacy, what has it done? Has it imperiled its most venerable notions of kinship and the bond between mother and child? Has it opened the way to a dismal baby industry, in which well-to-do couples rent out the wombs of less affluent women, sometimes just to spare themselves the inconvenience of pregnancy? Yet if surrogacy is prohibited, has a promising way for childless couples to have families been denied them? And what if the truest answer to those questions is also the most problematical—yes to all the above?"

Adapted from: Lacayo, Richard. 1987. "ETHICS: Whose Child Is This? Baby M. and the agonizing dilemma of surrogate motherhood." *Time*, 19 January 1987.

Questions

1. Describe how the Sterns would have felt when they learned that Whitehead had left the hospital with "their" baby. Describe how Whitehead would have felt when she realized she had made a mistake in agreeing to be a surrogate. How do we decide whose feelings are paramount?

2. Most child custody cases are resolved according to what the judge decides is in the best interests of the child. What is best for the child in this case? Make sure you enumerate your reasons.

3. As of January 2002, there was no law regulating surrogacy in Canada. Some Canadian surrogates post ads for their services on the Internet, and, in most cases, their babies end up in the United States. Canadian surrogates are popular because they are less expensive than their American counterparts. Canadian women receive about $20 000 (Cdn) for their services, and any other expenses they incur are paid for by the buyers. American women charge $20 000 US. The federal government is planning to introduce legislation in 2002 to ban advertising of surrogates and any payment to them. Do you agree with this proposal? Why? What other legislation, if any, do you think is necessary?

Voluntary Childlessness

Voluntary childlessness refers to couples or individuals who freely choose to remain childless. Some have always known they wanted to live a life without children; for others, voluntary childlessness of a temporary nature sometimes evolves into involuntary childlessness of a permanent state. For example, many women delay child-bearing until they have their careers established only to find that at a later age they are unable to conceive or carry a pregnancy to term.

Stereotypes of Those Who Choose Childlessness

There is a wide range of reasons why couples or individuals choose to remain childless, but there is much controversy surrounding the interpretation of these reasons. This is because people who choose to remain childless are often stereotyped. At the very least, most childless couples have had to deal with unwanted sympathy from others who assume their childlessness is not by choice. As well, childless couples are often attacked for being selfish. Certain social scientists have even been known to stereotype childless women. For example, in her work with Australian women in 1994, social demographer Fran Baum categorized women who were voluntarily childless as one of the following:

- "Hedonists"—women who choose to remain childless to preserve their standard of living and who are unwilling to invest either their time or money in raising children.
- "Emotional"—women who do not have an emotional draw toward babies or children.
- "Idealistic"—women who do not want to bring a child into a world they feel is unsuitable.
- "Practical"—women who have a practical reason for being childless, such as not wanting to pass on a genetic defect to their child.

In contrast, in her book *Reconceiving Women: Separating Motherhood from Female Identity*, clinical psychologist Mardy S. Ireland concluded that most women who made the decision not to have children did so not because they did not want a relationship with children, but because they did not want to be the primary caregivers of children. Ireland's book was based on interviews with more than 100 married, childless women from a number of cultures. Other research supports this view. For example, a 1998 study by Fiona McAllister and Lynda Clarke of the Family Policy Studies Centre in London, England, found little evidence to suggest that a child-free lifestyle resulted from "alternative" values or self-centredness. Those interviewed took a thoughtful and responsible view of family responsibilities. Many played an important part in extended family net-

works—supporting brothers and sisters who did have children, or caring for older parents. Yet the respondents had, variously, concluded that it would be undesirable, difficult, or impossible to make parenthood part of their own lives. Many of the respondents echoed the feelings of Faith Mann, 30, who said: "I've… always felt very strongly that unless you're willing to give time to a child, you shouldn't have a child."

Despite this reality, women, in particular, have to deal with cultural attitudes that imply that they are somehow abnormal or "less of a woman" if they do not have children. This seems to be because motherhood is such a primary feature of our cultural construct of women. It is considered "natural" for women to want to be mothers, and few would question a mother who chose to stay home full-time to raise her child or children. But fatherhood is considered to be only one of several roles that a man plays. Men are still largely defined by their occupation, not their parental status.

Feminists Gayle Letherby and Catherine Williams (1999) note that even the label "childless" implies a negative state, as opposed to the term "child-free." In an article by Irene Middleman Thomas (1995), Eva Lopez Clayton recalls being horrified when she overheard two co-workers compare her to a "barren cow" because she did not have children. Lopez Clayton says that she decided early in her life to remain childless, primarily because she wanted to dedicate herself to her career. Ironically, she believes being childless has worked against her in her career because she has had to work shifts for women with sick children and has generally been misunderstood for her choice. She says, "I always felt like I had to try harder, even to be more feminine. People think you're not normal if you don't have kids."

It is true, however, that the pressures and conflicts faced by women who choose not to have children are sometimes similarly faced by men. Vancouver resident Jerry Steinberg, who decided early in life to remain child-free, experienced great difficulty trying to find a doctor who would perform a vasectomy on him.

I had to visit three doctors before I finally found one who was willing to give me a vasectomy. The first told me that I was too young (34) to have one, and to come back in 10 years. The second wouldn't perform a vasectomy on someone who wasn't married. The third said, "But you don't have any children yet. Come back after you've had some kids." I replied, "By then it'll be too late!" The fourth interrogated me for more than 15 minutes. I asked him if he would have had so many questions if, instead of wanting a vasectomy, I had announced that I planned to have 10 kids. He paused a while, and then answered, "No, probably not." I retorted, "Who am I hurting by having none?" After much reflection, he finally said, "You're absolutely right. How's three weeks from next Wednesday?" I had my vasectomy on Valentine's Day, no less! (Steinberg, 2002)

Due in part to the lack of social support available to child-free people, Steinberg decided to start his own "child-free" social club. The Canadian-based club, called No Kidding!, was begun in 1984 and now boasts over 70 chapters around the world.

Figure 6.9 Clubs like No Kidding! have been established to provide an accepting environment for people who choose a child-free lifestyle.

www.nokidding.net

This is the Internet Web site for No Kidding!, a social club for child-free people. The site contains testimonials from people around the world who have grappled with the decision of whether or not to have children.

If the Web address does not connect you with the site, do a Web search using "no kidding" as a search string.

WEB LINK

Pause and Reflect

1. Summarize the psychological impact of involuntary childlessness.

2. Conduct an Internet search of government Web sites to find out which reproductive technologies are available to Canadians.

3. Are reproductive technologies an option for all infertile people? Explain your answer.

4. What unique psychological challenges do couples who are voluntarily childless have to face?

5. Discuss the differences in the way society looks at men and women who decide to be childless.

Section 6.4 Impact of Current Birth Patterns in Canada

Key Concepts

disposable income

Canada Pension Plan (CPP)

Like other developed countries in the world, Canada has a declining fertility rate. Statistics Canada predicts that within 25 years deaths will outnumber births in this country and population growth will come only from immigration. The average fertility rate in Canada is expected to drop from 1.54 to 1.48 births per woman in the next five years and hover around that level until 2025, according to the projections. Across the country, only the Northwest Territories and Nunavut show birth rates above the replacement level. Nunavut's birth rate is expected to be the highest in the country in 2025, at 2.27 per woman, but this is still a drop from its current level of about three births per woman (Owens, 2001).

The declining birth rate is going to have an impact on every aspect of our society. Currently, for every Canadian senior there are four working taxpayers, but by the year 2030, as our population ages and retires, there will be one senior for every two workers. (*The Toronto Star*, 2000, p. A12). This means that the average worker will have to pay twice as much to support the cost of public programs that support the elderly. Benefits to the elderly already cost the federal government 22 cents out of every program dollar. Consider the pressures that will develop when that figure rises to 44 cents of every dollar.

The Impact on the Economy

In 2000, the United States Department of Commerce released a report analyzing the impact of the aging population in British Columbia. The Department of Commerce completed this report to provide insight into emerging markets for American manufacturers. A quick look at their report, however, sheds some light on the positive and negative changes that may occur along with a declining fertility rate and an aging population.

The report noted that the first impact on the general economy will be an increase in jobs available to young workers. As approximately 25 per cent of the workforce retires, it is expected that labour shortages will occur. In a 1998 report entitled "Making Career Sense of Labour Information," statisticians note that even with an increase in immigration to offset the declining birth rate in Canada, there will not be enough young workers to meet demand as we move into the twenty-first century. Today's high-school students and groups that have formerly met resistance entering the labour market (Aboriginal people, people with disabilities, visible minorities, and women) may find themselves in demand if they have the right qualifications. The industries most likely to face labour shortages are education, health care, utilities, government, and forestry.

Figure 6.10 The lower birth rate means that as older employees retire, there may be a shortage of workers available to replace them.

Another impact of the rapidly aging population is that there will be great demand for retirement and nursing homes. In fact, the president of CPL Long Term Care, based in Toronto, expects that there will be a demand for 1000 to 1500 *new* nursing-home beds a year in Canada for the next 15 to 20 years. This will provide new construction jobs and work in related sectors, but we should anticipate a "housing crunch" as we wait for these beds to be made available.

A third impact of current birth patterns in Canada is that companies providing services such as financial planning and long-term investment will experience growth. A large portion of the aging population is affluent and has **disposable income** to spend and invest. In addition, as members of this group also have more leisure time, and money, the travel and tourism industries should experience growth as well, the American report said.

Impact on the Canadian Pension Plan

Another significant impact of smaller family size is changes to the **Canada Pension Plan (CPP)**. In 1997 the federal government made a significant change to the CPP—this is the federal earnings-related social insurance program that provides a measure of protection against loss of income due to retirement, disability, and death. The maximum CPP contribution from an employee will be raised to $1635 a year by 2003 (Pape, 1997). The maximum contribution used to be just under $945, so the change results in an increase of almost 75 per cent in seven years. If you have an employer, the amount you pay to CPP is matched by them. If you are self-employed you must pay the entire amount yourself—almost $3300 a year.

The changes to this program will have an adverse impact on younger Canadians. In fact, the younger you are, the more these changes are going to cost you, because you will be paying the higher premiums your entire working life. Older Canadians get a bargain because they won't have to pay the higher premiums even though they will be able to receive full benefits from the plan. Nonetheless, the government claims that the changes are necessary.

The Situation in Aboriginal Communities

Although the birth rate in Aboriginal communities is higher than in the non-Aboriginal population, birth rates are declining in these communities as well. The Department of Aboriginal and Northern Affairs in Manitoba reports that fertility rates among First Nations women declined from 5.7 births in 1970, to 4.1 in 1975, to 3.4 in 1980, to 3.2 in 1985, to 2.7 in 1990 and 2.55 in 1995.

The fertility rate for Status Indians remains 50 per cent higher than for the general population (1.8 births per woman), and the decline in the fertility rate has been more than offset by increases in the numbers of women in their young child-bearing years. This has not resulted in a demographic bulge, but in a birth rate (births per 1000 population per year) that has stabilized at almost twice that of the non-Aboriginal population. The large numbers of young children, aging into their reproductive years, guarantees that Aboriginal birth rates will remain extremely high in Manitoba for several decades to come, regardless of declining fertility rates.

The myth that there is a "mini baby boom" occurring in Aboriginal communities seems to be the result of the fact that the three Prairie provinces have the highest fertility rates for First Nations women in the country. This, combined with a generally younger age profile for this group, means that birth rates in the Prairies for Status Indians will remain well over the national average, and that the percentage of Aboriginal people in the Prairie provinces—as compared to the rest of the country—will increase.

On the other hand, the increase in the total Aboriginal population will be slowed by the lower birth rate among the Metis, who are also concentrated in the Prairie provinces.

The Impact on Health Care

One problem that all Canadians are going to have to face, regardless of where they live, is the increased strain on our health care system. Provincial governments are already feeling the impact of the declining birth rate. The largest portion of their budget goes to health care, and the elderly consume a disproportionate share of every health care dollar. Additional funds will be needed for hospital beds and for the provision of long-term care.

The average age for those entering long-term care facilities is 85, and the number of people over 85 is expected to quadruple by the year 2028 (Mandel, 2001, p. SR12). In Ontario alone, the number of people with Alzheimer's disease, which is one of the key reasons for placement in a long-term care facility, is expected to triple to 300 000. This, in turn, will lead to a greater shortage of long-term care beds as the facilities that provide such beds are already trying to cope with funding problems.

Some Canadians, however, do not believe that an increase in the proportion of elderly people will necessarily lead to a health care crisis. A group called the Good Samaritan Commission, which was organized by the Coalition of Physicians for Social Justice, makes this point in the following case study.

Figure 6.11 Experts estimate the number of long-term care facilities for the elderly will have to increase dramatically to house the aging baby boomers. What impact do you think this situation will have on the younger generations?

Declining Birth Rates and the Aging Population

Scare tactics citing stories of impending catastrophe caused by the aging population are not a sensible basis for deciding public policy, the Good Samaritan Commission argues.

The Coalition of Physicians for Social Justice, organizers of the Good Samaritan Commission, set up its own inquiry into Quebec's health care system because it believed the government's own commission—the Clair Commission—while claiming to be independent, was biased toward privatization from the outset.

The Good Samaritan Commission's investigation into problems of delivery of health services under medicare discovered a number of unfounded assumptions concerning the needs of the elderly.

According to the coalition report, many projections that argue that aging and sickness go hand in hand are based on outdated statistics on rates of illness among the elderly and a lack of understanding of the real causes of the increased cost of looking after the elderly. Dr. Norman Kalant, professor of medicine at the Jewish General Hospital, said that most European countries are already dealing with populations as old now as Canada's will be in 10 or 15 years' time. These countries do not spend more on health care than Canada does, he said, and yet they provide care that is just as good.

In Britain, for example, 17 per cent of the population is more than 65 years old, compared with Canada's present 12.5 per cent. "Where is the impending catastrophe?" asked Dr. Kalant. "The problem is the misconception that the elderly now have as many illnesses as the elderly did two or three decades ago. That simply is not true any more. The population's health has since improved for socio-economic reasons."

The major problem in explaining the high cost of care of the elderly is that physicians tend to over-treat and over-investigate even when they know there is nothing much that they can do, said Dr. Kalant. "We believe this problem should be handled by re-educat-ing physicians on appropriate treatment of the elderly," he said.

At the December conference of the Good Samaritan Commission, guest speaker Dr. Michael Rachlis, a Toronto physician, told delegates that proper management of at-risk groups was the key to improving health outcomes and cost-effectiveness within medicare, rather than assuming the problems were unavoidable because they were due to the aging population. "Aging is not automatically expensive," Dr. Rachlis stressed. "It's sickness that costs money."

He pointed out that 70 to 80 per cent of Canadians with hypertension were receiving proper drug therapy. "Uncontrolled high blood pressure leads to high rates of strokes, kidney damage and heart attacks," he said.

Proper community support for heart attack patients to ensure they are taking the right medications would also cut the rate of heart attacks, and better prescribing practices could reduce mortality as well as cut unnecessary costs, Dr. Rachlis added. "Many patients are prescribed overly expensive medications costing $3 a day instead of older, just-as-effective medications costing three cents a day," he said.

The Good Samaritan report recommended that drug costs should be controlled by shortening the length of patent protection, securing better bulk purchasing deals and reference-based pricing, and training physicians in prescribing practices.

The report also denounced the recommendation of the Clair Commission that partnerships be struck between the public and private sectors. Such arrangements lead to conflicts of interest, compromise clinical research, and result in higher costs for patients. "Costs for diagnostic tests can be 12 to 13 times higher in private laboratories than in hospital laboratories," said Dr. Kalant.

Adapted from: Benady, Susannah. 2001. "Being old doesn't cost more money—being sick does." *Medical Post*, 27 February 2001.

Questions

1. What stereotypes about aging and health does this article refute?
2. What proof is provided in the article to support these assertions?
3. What cost-cutting measures are suggested by the Good Samaritan Commission?
4. Discuss other perspectives about aging and health care costs with which you are familiar.

Pause and Reflect

1. What financial impact will the declining birth rate have on individual taxpayers?
2. Why will changes to the CPP disadvantage younger Canadians?
3. In what ways are Aboriginal and non-Aboriginal communities experiencing the decline in fertility rates similarly and dissimilarly?
4. What are the economic benefits of an aging population?
5. What advantages and challenges will you face as you grow up in an era of declining birth rates?

▶ ▶ ▶ ## Chapter Activities

Show Your Knowledge

1. Why are fertility rates dropping in both developed and developing nations?
2. Explain why the Hutterites currently have the highest fertility rate on record.
3. Explain the procedure used in each of the following reproductive technologies: IUI, IVF, GIFT and AID.
4. What are the only areas of Canada that show birth rates above the replacement level? Why is this so?

Practise Your Thinking

5. If delaying child-bearing results in reduced fertility for women, yet women want to establish careers before becoming mothers, in what ways can developed nations end the current rise in infertility?
6. With a partner, conduct an informal investigation about Canada's cultural attitudes toward breast-feeding. Do this by counting the number of ads and pictures of formula or babies being bottle-fed versus babies being breast-fed. You may want to use such magazines as *Today's Parent* or *Homemaker* for this investigation.
7. Identify another life event that has a psychological impact similar to that of involuntary childlessness. Explain the similarities between the event you have selected and involuntary childlessness.
8. What pressures, subtle or otherwise, exist in our culture that encourage child-bearing and can therefore make those who choose childlessness feel strange or awkward?
9. Why are fertility rates tracked by demographers? What impact do these rates have on society?

Communicate Your Ideas

10. Write a short report that further explores the impact of environmental factors on lowered fertility. When conducting your research, you might include a search for information under the topics of "pesticide use," "antibiotics and steroids in food and water supplies," and "plastic by-products."

11. Reread the section on government policies that encourage larger families on pages 184 to 187 and the case study about Israel on page 188. With a partner, brainstorm a list of steps Canada could take to increase the birth rate in this country. Present your suggestions to your classmates.

12. Currently, treatment for infertility is not covered by medicare. Many people believe this is unfair because infertility is a medical problem. Others think this policy is fair because children are a luxury, not a right. Prepare a statement that explains your point of view.

13. Write a diary entry in which a person is debating with himself or herself the decision of whether or not to become a parent.

14. Reproductive technologies allow doctors to "play God." Write a statement that supports or refutes this belief.

Apply Your Knowledge

15. Conduct research on the number of immigrants and refugees that have been accepted into your city (or the largest major centre near you) over the past five years. Are the numbers higher or lower than you expected? What countries did the new Canadians come from? What types of skills or experience did they possess?

16. Some countries have higher birth rates than Canada because in some cultures it is seen as very important that couples give to birth male children. Explore the reasons why this preference might exist in one of the following: China, India, Pakistan, Indonesia, Afghanistan, or Latin communities in the United States.

17. Explore the Canadian government's position on surrogacy by visiting the Health Canada Web site at <www.hc-sc.gc.ca>. Prepare a short report that includes the government's position as well as your feelings on the matter, and present it to your class.

18. Prepare a short report for your municipal government outlining the changes your area may experience as a result of the aging population.

19. Conduct a short survey to determine whether or not adolescents in your school are aware of steps they can take to protect their reproductive health and future fertility.

CHAPTER 7

TRENDS RELATED TO THE LIFE CYCLE

INTRODUCTION

The term "**life cycle**" refers to the different stages that an individual may pass through from birth to death. The first stages are infancy and childhood, followed by adolescence, young adulthood, marriage, parenthood, mid-life, and finally old age. These stages vary from culture to culture and from person to person. As well, our individual experiences at each stage are shaped by our gender, family background, income level, ethnicity, and events occurring in the larger society.

This chapter will explore a few of the major stages of the human life cycle from the differing perspectives of anthropologists, sociologists, and psychologists.

Anthropology is the focus of the first section, which explores how the concept of adolescence has changed throughout history, and compares adolescence in industrial and pre-industrial societies. The second section of the chapter looks at factors that influence contemporary youth culture, including psychological factors, socialization, and other influences such as television.

The third section of this chapter explores another major stage in the human life cycle—parenthood.

And the last section explores the psychological and social challenges faced by families and our society as more and more adults move into the final stage of the life cycle—old age.

■ Learning Expectations

By the end of this chapter, you will be able to

- demonstrate an understanding of the influence that anthropological, psychological, and sociological factors have on youth culture
- evaluate the influence of education, career choice, and medical advances on decisions about child-bearing
- assess the social implications of an aging population for families and communities, and formulate strategies for responding to this shift in demographics

Focusing on the Issues

Rave: Dancing the Night Away

It was early on a Sunday morning in September 1999 that the darker side of the rave culture suddenly was exposed to the light in Nova Scotia. Just outside Halifax, the largest rave in Atlantic Canada's history was in high gear. It was three in the morning, and 3000 people…were dancing through the night to loud techno and industrial music. A feeling of euphoria filled the room, and the rave drug Ecstasy took its effect on many of the patrons.

But something went wrong. Jaimie Britten, a 23-year-old from Port Hawkesbury, Nova Scotia, started to go into convulsions and passed out. His friends were able to remove him from the rave party inside, and paramedics were called, but it was too late. Britten died in the parking lot of Exhibition Park from an overdose of Ecstasy.

Unfortunately, this was not an isolated incident. In Ontario alone, nine deaths during 1999 have been attributed to Ecstasy—which creates a euphoric feeling and a sense of peace and love.

Raves, all-night dance parties that have become increasingly prevalent in Canada during the last few years, have had an association with drugs since their inception. As DJ Chris Sheppard, who was responsible for the first rave held in Toronto in 1988, points out, "Rave for me has always been a celebration of love, a large gathering of people. That's always been the meaning [of a rave—young people] gathered together to celebrate life, love, energy, and compassion.…"

Mass participatory events in the adolescent subculture are nothing new. The rave as a psychological and sociological phenomenon—some might even call it a spiritual response—may be fraught with meaning, something that the ravers seem to be searching for or even experiencing, depending on whether you believe the sensations they are experiencing are real or illusory. Or, it may have

Raves are popular among Canadian youths. What other trends help define the current teen culture?

more mundane significance. Human rituals have always been part of social organization. Ritual dancing has been around since the beginning of human civilization.

Is the rave the most recent manifestation of age-old themes of the search for an "ecstatic" heightened sense of reality in a world in which reality seems banal or threatening; a revolt against contemporary mores and restrictions; a rite of passage in which the self merges with the collective? Or is it a quasi-industry where a buck is to be made? Or is it simply a helluva good party, with all the fun and risks that go with that?

Source: "Raves: Dancing the Night Away." CBC News in Review. March 2000.

THINK ABOUT IT

1. Why do you think raves are so popular among North American teens? What purpose do they serve?

2. What role do music, clothes, and dance play in defining teen culture? Describe some of the different teen subcultures that exist in your school.

3. Reread the last paragraph of this article. How would you describe a rave? Why?

Section 7.1   Adolescence: How We See and Celebrate This Stage of the Life Cycle

Key Concepts

adolescence

Young Offenders Act

menarche

initiation ritual

On 27 March 1995, an article appeared in the *Alberta Report* (now the *Western Report*) describing a teenage party that went awry and ended in tragedy. The story concerned an Edmonton high-school student named Edna Pinckney, who invited about 25 friends over for a party when her parents were vacationing in Hong Kong. At about 2 A.M. a fire broke out in a second-floor bedroom where 15-year-old Grant Cunningham lay passed out on the floor. The smoke and flames engulfed him before his intoxicated pals could drag him to safety. The subsequent investigation revealed that the blaze had been deliberately set.

Not surprisingly, the author of the article, Peter Verburg, described how the incident led to renewed concerns about the ease with which young people obtain alcohol. One of the politicians in the area, Little Bow MLA Barry McFarland, tabled a bill to raise the drinking age in the province from 18 to 19. He pointed out that raising the drinking age would make young people wait longer for the legal authority to imbibe. As a result, he believed teen drunkenness and its associated ills would be fewer and less devastating.

Others, however, disagree that raising the drinking age reduces the number of house-wrecking parties, impaired-driving accidents, and other alcohol-related crimes. Barry Baldwin, professor of classics at the University of Calgary, is one of these people. He argues that the problem is not that kids drink, but that they have not been taught how to drink responsibly. "Look at the Europeans. There, kids have a glass of wine at the parental table." They learn how to handle alcohol at a young age. "If alcohol consumption becomes a part of the normal socialization process, teens will have an easier time handling liquor and abiding by the rules." University of Alberta history professor Ronald Hamowy agrees. "As it is now, the legal drinking age…is viewed as the cut-off at which they [can] get legally bombed for the first time. This becomes their rite of passage into adulthood."

In addition to the debate over the drinking age, the Pinckney house party also resulted in a debate over the problem of reckless teens in general. Verburg wrote that the community was in shock over the "sheer brainlessness of the teens." He included a quotation from Thomas Fleming, the editor of *Chronicles*, a North American cultural analysis magazine, which said that every generation of youth seems to get worse than the last, and that as a society we need to accept that

Figure 7.1 In many European countries, such as Italy, youths are socialized to handle alcohol at a younger age than Canadians. Do you think our government should change the legal drinking age? Explain your answer.

our "social planning has been wrong and that our society is deeply disordered." But is this true? As a society, do we prolong the maturation of young people far too long, cultivating irresponsibility and rebellion?

Adolescence as a Period of Transition

Although sexual maturation gives males and females the ability to produce children, many societies do not consider its onset to mean the complete transformation of a child into an adult. In their book *Humanity* (1991), anthropologists James Peoples and Garrick Bailey explain that, while a 13-year-old boy may be able to father a child, "he still usually lacks the strength and stamina, as well as the mastery of technical and social skills needed to assume the full economic and social responsibilities required of a husband and parent."

Sexual maturation, therefore, is often considered the physiological cue that begins the transformation of a child into an adult. The transition period between these two stages of the life cycle is called **adolescence**, and its duration depends on the social-cultural characteristics of a particular society.

Adolescence has not always been legally and politically recognized as a separate social category in industrialized societies. Some social scientists, such as Michael Boyes, professor of developmental psychology at the University of Calgary, go further by claiming that adolescence itself didn't exist in industrialized societies until the late 1890s, when it was invented for economic reasons (Verburg, 1995, p. 30). He explains that the labour force had to shrink as technological innovations rendered jobs previously filled by teens obsolete. These teens could not find other work, and, as a result, ended up on the streets, sometimes getting into trouble. Social workers and missionaries became concerned about inner-city youth and opened "settlement houses" to keep street kids from becoming criminals. In cases where

adolescents did break the law, the delinquents were sent to "juvenile" homes, where attempts to reform them were made. It was at this point, according to historian Joseph Kett, that the government's role as a surrogate parent was created.

In Canada, this thinking yielded the Juvenile Delinquents Act in 1908. Teens under 16 were handed punishments that were supposed to correct bad behaviour. Author Peter Verburg argues that sentences were chosen to fit the offender, not the crime. The Juvenile Delinquents Act remained in place until 1984, when it was repealed and replaced by the controversial **Young Offenders Act**, which delayed adult justice for youths until they turned 18 based on the belief that they could possibly be rehabilitated up to this age. In effect, both pieces of legislation entrenched adolescence as a life cycle stage *separate* from childhood and adulthood.

During this same period, social scientists began to study the unique characteristics of adolescents. In 1904, American psychologist G. Stanley Hall published a two-volume work titled *Adolescence*. He defined the teen years as a distinct stage in life that begins at puberty and is marked by inner turmoil. According to Joseph Kett (1977), this view was used "to justify the establishment of adult-sponsored institutions that segregated young people from casual contact with adults." Starting in the first decade of the twentieth century, youth were sequestered in their own institutions: first high school, then college. There, they were to develop the social skills expected of adults, which all previous generations had learned simply by being around adults. New laws soon prohibited child labour and made longer schooling mandatory.

The notion that youths mature best in the accompaniment of their elders was dismissed as primitive in the twentieth century. According to *Dancing in the Dark*, a 1991 book on popular teen culture written by six professors from Calvin College in Grand Rapids, Michigan, "The new ideology of adolescence made possible a new youth community with a powerful influence that could surpass any outside influence on its members' lives." Adult concerns—about religion and vocation, for example—were not welcome in the new community. Instead, the Calvin scholars argued, the new guardians grew to develop their own cultural priorities.

Adolescence in Pre-industrial Societies

As noted earlier, the duration of adolescence varies from society to society. For many Canadians, adolescence can last from 12 years of age to the end of the teen years. In some hunting and gathering societies, adolescence is often a relatively short period, if it exists at all. For example, one of the San peoples, the !Kung (the "!" represents a click in their spoken language), who inhabit the vast Kalahari Desert of Africa, consider a female a woman once she has reached **menarche**, her first menstruation cycle, and has passed through a short coming-

of-age ceremony. Likewise, San males are considered men after they kill their first buck and participate in a coming-of-age ritual that lasts only a few days (Liptak, 1994).

Generally, children in societies with a short period of adolescence, or none at all, are required to mature quickly so that they can take over the roles of their parents. The sooner each member of the society accepts adult responsibilities, the better for the entire group. Similarly, in some agricultural societies the entire group needs to work in the fields to survive. Here, too, the needs of the society are best served by a relatively short adolescence.

Both industrialized and pre-industrial societies commonly hold coming-of-age ceremonies to mark the passage of children to adulthood. In Canadian societies, such ceremonies can include "sweet-sixteen" birthday parties, graduation from high school and university, engagement parties, and marriage ceremonies, as well as legal milestones such as obtaining a driver's license or the right to vote and drink alcohol. In many pre-industrial societies, these ceremonies, or **initiation rituals**, are often elaborate and mean as much to the community as they do to the individual. The ceremonies help to ensure that the group will survive as its traditions are passed on. Also, as initiates usually go through the same rituals their parents and grandparents did at the same age, a link is formed with the past and between family and community.

In her book on coming-of-age rituals in pre-industrial societies, Karen Liptak identifies a number of common threads that exist in many of these ceremonies:

1. *Symbolic death and rebirth.*

    In most of the ceremonies recorded by anthropologists, the initiate dies as a child and is reborn as an adult. Many symbols are incorporated into the ceremonies to support this theme; for example, the initiate may be formally presented to the community as if he or she were a person the others had not known before.

Figure 7.2 Members of the Maasi Moran tribe in Kenya cover each other's heads with ochre having been shaved as part of their initiation into manhood.

2. *Isolation of the initiate.*

   Many communities believe the initiate is particularly vulnerable to harm as he or she moves from being a child to an adult. Isolation is a way to protect the initiate from danger; as well, it gives the community time to adjust to the initiate's new identity.

3. *Physical changes.*

   Tattoos, scars, or piercings are permanent physical changes that mark an individual as having progressed through a coming-of-age ceremony. These visible signs are often more important for boys than for girls, as menarche is a concrete event that lets a girl know she has become a woman.

4. *Cleansing.*

   Many initiates are ritually cleansed as they enter or leave seclusion. This helps them prepare for receiving a new identity.

5. *Tests of endurance, bravery, or competence.*

   Of greater importance with boys than girls, successful passage of these tests indicates that the initiate is ready for the challenges and responsibilities of adulthood.

6. *Teaching and learning.*

   Most coming-of-age ceremonies involve youngsters being taught by their elders. Some of the lessons are secrets finally revealed to the adolescent, while others simply involve information that adolescents need to know to function as adults. The lessons often help the initiates to establish a kinship with their instructors; if they go through group initiation, the ties are with their peers as well.

7. *Community and sharing of food.*

   Coming-of-age rituals, at least parts of them, are usually witnessed by other members of the community. The ceremonies help the entire society adjust to the initiates' transition from childhood to adulthood. The most common form of community participation is eating together.

Liminality and Becoming a Soldier

CASE STUDY

The late anthropologist Victor Turner pioneered the modern study of rites of passage. In his study of initiation rites among the Ndembu of Zambia, Turner noted that the rites have three phases: separation, liminality, and incorporation. These phases correspond to the basic nature of rites of passage: individuals who go through them are separated from their former statuses in society, go through a transition ("liminal") period during which they are "betwixt and between" normal statuses and social categories, and finally are reincorporated into society as new people with new rights and obligations.

These phases are seen clearly in common cultural themes and behaviors involved in male initiation rituals among numerous peoples. Often the boys are forcibly removed from their homes, a frequent practice being to separate them from the company of women (especially their mothers, who sometimes are expected to mourn as if their sons had died) so they can become real men. The boys are often secluded during the rituals and subjected to tests of their ability to endure pain without crying out. They may have to fast or go without drink for days. Nearly always, some painful operations are performed on their genitals; they may be circumcised or have their penises mutilated in other ways. Scarification of face and body is common, for it is a visible symbol that a male has gone through the proceedings and is entitled to the privileges of manhood. Although sometimes the proceedings last for years, the initiates may have to refrain from eating certain foods or from coming into contact with females or female things, for the period of transition into manhood is regarded as a dangerous time.

A simple social structure characterizes the liminal period: the initiates are equal in status and utterly subordinate to the control of the men who are in charge of the proceedings. Typically, the boys are stripped of all possessions, their faces or bodies are painted in an identical way, they are dressed alike, and their heads are shaven, all to make them look alike and to emphasize their common identity.

[Developed societies] also have rites of passage that serve similar functions: births, graduations, marriages, and deaths are generally marked by some kind of public ceremony signifying the social transitions involved. Baptisms, betrothals, promotions, installations of new public officials, birthdays, and many other ceremonial gatherings also are rites of passage.

But one of our most interesting rites of passage—because of its similarity to the initiation rituals discussed earlier—is entering military service. Many of the behaviors involved in entering the military are reminiscent of puberty rites. Basic training is a liminal period—recruits have been separated from civilian life but have not acquired the secret knowledge and skills needed to become a soldier. Recruits are stripped of possessions, their hair is cut, they are issued identical uniforms, they are secluded from most contact with the outside, they all have identical (low) rank that requires complete subordination to sergeants and superior officers, they must undergo arduous trials and perform daring physical feats (such as getting up before sunrise), and they live in a common barracks where they have identical sleeping and eating facilities. In the military, too, the aim is to grind down a boy so that he can be rebuilt into a man (as the Marines used to say). Masculine qualities of courage, toughness, dedication, discipline, and determination are supposed to be instilled. When the recruit has successfully completed his training, he is incorporated into a new group, the military, and acquires a new status (rank and job).

We should not carry the analogy too far—recruits are not operated on (but note that voluntary tattooing used to be fairly common), nor is it necessary for a boy to enter the military to be a real man (although many men who were not in the military are looked down upon by many of those who were). Still, the similarities are striking enough for us once again to see our common humanity with preindustrial peoples. Their behaviors and beliefs may seem strange to us, but often we engage in similar activities that only seem perfectly natural because we are used to them.

Source: Peoples, James and Garrick Bailey. 1991. *Humanity*. St. Paul. West Publishing Company.

Figure 7.3 A new army recruit performs push-ups in his barracks in Halifax.

Questions

1. Based on this case study, record at least five values that societies try to instill in young males, for example, that it is shameful for boys to cry. In what ways do these values both benefit and hurt individual men and the society at large?

2. Some men, like Marc Brzustowski, co-leader of an Ontario group that organizes a march against male violence, argues that we must *redefine* the concept of masculinity in a less aggressive, less destructive form. How might we do that?

3. In what ways does this case study refute the idea that gender differences are innate?

Pause and Reflect

1. Explain why some people believe that raising the legal drinking age will not reduce irresponsible drinking on the part of teenagers. Do you agree? Why?

2. Is adolescence an arbitrary construct in industrialized societies such as Canada? Explain your answer.

3. According to the social scientists in this section, what economic, legal, and social factors led to the creation of adolescence in industrialized societies?

4. On a personal level, record five values/beliefs/needs that connect you with your friends.

Section 7.2   Factors That Influence Youth Culture

Although our concept of adolescence has changed over time, and the nature of adolescence varies from culture to culture, there is no doubt that in the majority of cultures, adolescence is a major stage in the life cycle. The importance of this life cycle stage can be measured by the fact that an entire youth culture has developed. This means that teenagers tend to have their own unique tastes in clothing, music, and symbols, as well as their own language, concerns, and behaviours. Of course, teens are individuals and have individual tastes, therefore there is no single youth culture that is common to all. The experience of adolescence is affected by ethnicity, gender, and socio-economic status, and many other factors. That being said, some psychologists believe that most youths proceed through a series of developmental changes where the primary influences on their lives shift away from parents and toward their friends.

Psychological Factors and Developmental Trends

A major factor that leads to the existence of youth cultures in many developed countries is the fact that adolescents pull away from their parents to establish their own identities.

This process is a **developmental trend** in that it is a "normal" life-cycle process through which adolescents journey—although, there are great variations in the way individuals begin to define themselves as separate and in the speed with which this occurs. One explanation of how this process works was identified by noted psychologist Erik Erikson. He believed that humans have to resolve different conflicts as they progress through each stage of development in the life cycle. At the adolescent stage, teens must try to figure out who they are, in a conflict he called an **identity crisis**.

Erikson argued that in order to establish a sense of identity, teens must engage in exploration. They must try out new ways of thinking and behaving. Erikson would describe the many "phases" that teens go through as their attempts at exploration. They explore by trying new styles of appearance, new ideas, new groups of friends, new styles of music, etc. Only after exploring a variety of options do teens commit to an identity.

According to Erikson, there are two potential outcomes to the identity search process: **identity achievement** or **identity diffusion**. The identity-achieved person is one who has come to a firm sense of self after engaging in a long search full of exploration.

Key Concepts

developmental trend

identity crisis

identity achievement

identity diffusion

separation-individuation process

socialization

gender identity

socialization agent

GROUNDBREAKERS

ERIK ERIKSON (1902–1994)

One of the most influential psychologists of the early twentieth century, Erik Erikson was born in Germany in 1902. He was an artist and a teacher in the late 1920s when he met Anna Freud, an Austrian psychoanalyst and daughter of the famous Sigmund. At this point, Erikson began to study child development at the Vienna Psychoanalytic Institute. In 1933 he immigrated to the United States where he studied groups of Aboriginal children to learn about the influence of society and culture on child development. From this work, he developed a number of theories, the most famous being his psychosocial theory of development.

Figure 7.4 Erik Erikson

Erikson's theory consists of eight stages of development. Each stage is characterized by a different conflict that must be resolved by the individual. He believed that people respond to each conflict in either an adaptive or maladaptive way. Furthermore, he stated that only when each crisis is successfully resolved and a change in personality has taken place is the person ready to move on to the next stage of development. The eight stages are as follows:

1. Oral-Sensory Stage: Birth to 12–18 months
The basic conflict at this stage is trust versus mistrust. The infant must form a loving, trusting relationship with the one who feeds him/her, or else a sense of mistrust will develop in the baby.

2. Muscular-Anal Stage: 18 months to 3 years
The conflict here is autonomy versus shame/doubt. At this stage the child learns toilet training. If it is successfully handled, the child will learn control rather than develop feelings of shame and doubt about his or her abilities.

3. Locomotor Stage: 3 to 6 years
The conflict at this stage is initiative versus guilt. If the child successfully gains independence, he or she will continue to take more initiative. If the child is unsuccessful, he or she may be left with feelings of guilt.

4. Latency Stage: 6 to 12 years
In this stage, the child has to resolve conflicting feelings of industry versus inferiority while dealing with school. If the child is able to handle the demands of school and learn new skills, this conflict will be positively resolved. If not, the child may end up with a sense of inferiority, failure, and incompetence.

5. Adolescence: 12 to 18 years
The major conflict at this stage is identity versus role confusion. As teenagers deal with relationships with their peers, they must achieve a personal sense of identity.

6. Young Adulthood: 18 to 25 years
The major conflict here is intimacy versus isolation. Erikson believed that people at this stage need to develop intimate relationships or else suffer feelings of isolation.

7. Adulthood: 25 to 65 years
At this stage, the conflict involves generativity versus stagnation. Although he did not believe everyone had to have their own children, Erikson believed each adult must find some way to satisfy and support the next generation or else they would suffer in a life that was not actively progressing toward something meaningful.

8. Maturity: 65 years to death
Erikson believed that during the final stage of life each person must resolve a conflict of ego integrity versus despair. This involves reflection on, and acceptance of, one's life. If this conflict is positively resolved, the person feels fulfilled.

Questions

1. Are you able to place yourself in one of Erikson's stages? That is, does the information seem to be an accurate reflection of where you are at in your life? Explain.

2. Why do you think developmental stage theories like Erikson's are sometimes criticized by other psychologists? What are the strengths of these types of theories?

3. One weakness of Erikson's theory is that he did not believe that a person could move to the next stage without successfully resolving the conflict at the previous stage. For example, unless a person's sense of identity was determined by the end of adolescence, the person could not move on to develop an intimate relationship. Explain how this is a weakness and identify and explain two other specific weaknesses of his theory.

He or she tends to have high self-esteem, is socially skilled, and does well in life. At the opposite end of the spectrum is the identity-diffused person. This person has not been able to achieve a sense of identity. Erikson argued that the person who is identity diffused is likely to have low self-esteem, have trouble making friends, and will be much less successful than the identity-achieved person.

Because Erikson's stages build upon one another, the person who is identity diffused, or who has not successfully resolved the identity crisis, will have difficulty resolving the conflicts to come later in life. For example, such a person, may have great difficulty regarding intimacy in young adulthood—how can people find someone to share their lives with if they do not yet know themselves?

In 1967, psychologist Peter Blos introduced the term **separation-individuation process** to explain how teens gradually pull away from their parents and become independent. He believed this developmental stage to be very significant because it involves the restructuring of teens' entire network of significant others. At the start of adolescence, parents occupy the central position in their child's personal network, but gradually friends, and later, a partner, become increasingly important and take the place of the parents as the most important reference persons.

In 1995, Dutch psychologists Maja Dekovic and Wim Meeus decided to explore the concepts established by these pioneers to examine how identity develops for adolescents of this generation. In their study of nearly 3000 youths between the ages of 12 and 24 they found that, as adolescence proceeds, both males and females begin to think more about relationships outside their immediate families and derive their identities from these external relationships to an increasing degree. School identity also develops with time, but it seems to peak at about 15 years of age, as does occupational identity (the strong sense of what one is going to do later in life). A gender difference exists as well, with girls having a stronger relational identity throughout adolescence than boys have. However, for both males and females over the age of 21, relational identity is more important than school or occupational identity. The study by Dekovic and Meeus confirmed that, during adolescence, peers replace parents as the most important reference persons.

The work of Dekovic and Meeus is supported by large-scale studies here in Canada conducted by sociologist Reginald Bibby, of the University of Lethbridge, and Donald Posterski, Vice-President of National Programs at World Vision Canada. Bibby and Posterski surveyed approximately 3500 teenagers in 1984 and 1992. The pair learned that teenagers consistently report that the most important personal relationships in their lives are with their friends. A full 93 per cent cite friends as their greatest source of enjoyment, while relationships with their parents fall considerably behind: 67 per cent report also having enjoyable relationships with their mothers, while 60 per cent report the same with their fathers.

On another measure of relationship importance, Bibby and Posterski found that 61 per cent of teens reported wanting to tell a friend when something big goes wrong in their lives. By comparison, only 22 per cent wanted to tell a member of their family the same thing. When asked who they want to tell when something great happens, again, friends come first at 47 per cent, with family being mentioned by only 15 per cent of adolescents. So it does appear that, during this stage of the life cycle, teens are definitely pulling away from their parents and identifying more closely with their peers.

Skill Builder:
Developing a Thesis

In Chapter 1, you learned how to develop a hypothesis. Your own hypothesis (or hypotheses if you had more than one) has guided you in your research up to this point. Now it is time to stop, take stock of the information you have been able to gather, and determine what you will *specifically* argue in your project. That argument will be your **thesis**. A strong thesis statement is a necessary part of any project you write or present.

For most major assignments you complete at school, you will arrange your work to demonstrate that you were able to *prove* your thesis. That is, if you selected a hypothesis that turned out to be well supported by the research you located, then you will turn that hypothesis into your thesis. In the pure sciences, and in an *original* social science study, researchers often disprove all, or part of, their thesis. That is because the results of their survey or study turned out differently than they expected. But if you are writing a research paper or essay, you need to focus on proving your thesis.

Step One: Check your hypothesis against your research findings
At this point in your project, you need to stop and assess your overall results. Review your hypothesis to remind yourself what you thought you were going to argue or what you expected to find in the research. Then, look critically at all of the articles, statements, and facts you have located and ask yourself whether you have enough proof to support that hypothesis. Do not be afraid to admit you have not found what you expected. That does not mean you have to start over. It simply means you have to take your findings into account when you craft your thesis.

Step Two: Craft your thesis
You want to keep your thesis clear and simple so that your audience can easily understand your argument. Try to keep it to one sentence. The best way to write your thesis is to jot down your original hypothesis and then modify it to suit your actual findings. If you have more than one hypothesis, choose the one your research material seems to support most strongly. Below, you will find a couple of example topics and hypotheses generated from the material in this chapter. A sample thesis has been crafted for each topic.

Example 1
Topic/Research Question: Why does peer pressure have a negative effect on some teenagers?

Hypotheses:
a) Because some teenagers have low self-esteem.
b) Because some teenagers come from dysfunctional families.
c) Because some teenagers have not developed mentally as quickly as others.

During your research you discover that the majority of the published information in the area of teens and peer pressure supports Hypothesis A. You will therefore turn Hypothesis A into your thesis.

Suggested Thesis: All teens experience peer pressure, but it seems that only teens with low self-esteem are negatively influenced by this pressure.

Example 2
Topic/Research Question: Why is adolescence a developmental stage characterized by anxiety and depression?

Hypotheses:
a) Because teens undergo great hormonal changes and rapid physical development.
b) Because teens are not mature enough to regulate their moods.
c) Because Western culture does not treat teens like adults.

Your research determines that while both A and B have some merit, you have found more information to support Hypothesis C. So, you craft a thesis based on this hypothesis.

Suggested Thesis: In the West, most teens experience emotional upheaval and engage in rebellious behaviour because society delays giving them the full rights and responsibilities of adulthood.

Step Three: Organize your project based on your thesis
Once you have written your thesis, you should then use it to sort through your research findings. Begin by setting aside any information that does not *directly* support your thesis. This may be material that deals more specifically with one of your other hypotheses. Do not panic if you seem to be getting rid of a lot of material. A research report that includes unrelated material will not

earn you as good a mark as a report that is shorter and properly focused.

Take the material that is left and organize it into separate categories. These categories will make up the different sections of your report. Although there are different ways of ordering the sections, in the social sciences, most often the *strongest* material is located at the beginning of the report. Then, additional proof may follow.

Example
Thesis: All teens experience peer pressure, but it seems that only teens with low self-esteem are negatively influenced by this pressure.

Section 1: Research studies that explore the link between low self-esteem and criminal behaviour.

Section 2: Findings that show that low self-esteem can lead to self-destructive behaviours.

Section 3: A review of the literature that explores the personality characteristics of high-achieving teens.

Step Four: Take stock and complete your research
At this point in your project, now that you have organized your research into sections that best support your thesis, you may find that you have a few "holes" in your information. This is the time to do some final research to fill those holes so that there are no gaps in your argument. This should not take you nearly as long to complete as your original research, so do not despair!

Practise It!
1. With a partner, review one of the four sections of this chapter.
   a) Generate five possible research topics/questions that could be explored from this material.
   b) Generate three possible hypotheses for each research topic.
   c) Conclude the exercise by crafting a specific thesis for each of the topics.

Socialization Within the Home

Socialization refers to the process by which children are shaped into responsible members of society. This involves acquiring the norms and values of their culture, learning to control their impulses, and developing their self-concept. In a child's early years, the family is the primary agent of socialization.

One of the outcomes of the socialization process is the development of the child's self-concept. And one aspect of self-concept of fundamental importance is **gender identity**—one's concept of maleness or femaleness. Gender identity is of great importance because it is a central organizing principle in a male's and female's self-image and in the construction of his or her social world.

Research demonstrates that gender socialization is perpetuated in both overt and covert ways within families. In his review of the literature surrounding adolescent gender socialization, John F. Peters (1994), a sociologist from Wilfrid Laurier University, reported

that there is a tendency in North American culture for parents to be more protective of female children than of male children, and more permissive toward male children than female children. As a result, girls may be socialized toward dependence, and boys toward independence. Dr. Peters demonstrated this gender socialization in his own study of Canadian youth when he found that male teens were shown favouritism with respect to family car usage, and that curfews were stricter for daughters.

Another way that gender identity is taught within some Canadian homes is through parental expectations and demands regarding household chores. Parents tend to assign their children gender-appropriate chores and family roles—even those parents who consider themselves to be "enlightened." Peters found that parents are afraid their children will be misfits in society if they are not trained to function in a gender-appropriate manner. In Peters' study, almost all parents made their daughters responsible for doing

Figure 7.5 Are chores divvied up according to gender in your home? For example, do the female members of the family do the indoor jobs such as ironing and do the males usually do outdoor chores such as taking out the trash?

chores *inside* the home, while sons were expected to complete chores *outside* the home. Interestingly, these findings were consistent whether the mother in the household worked for wages outside the home or performed unwaged work within the home.

These studies seem to provide evidence that gender identity is a function of nurture; that is, that gender identity is *learned*. After all, if parents have different expectations of their children based on each child's gender, and if they treat children differently because of gender, it stands to follow that they are shaping the gender-specific behaviour of their children. Thus, behaviour that may seem to be "naturally" female or "naturally" male may indeed be the result of nurture. This would be in keeping with the work of anthropologist Victor Turner that you learned about on pages 211 to 212 in this chapter. The information in the case study below, however, seems to contradict these assumptions.

As you read the following article, ask yourself whether this child's gender identity was innate or whether it was created and shaped by the child's parents.

His Name Is Aurora

Even before her son turned two, Sherry Lipscomb noticed that he wasn't like other boys. When she took him shopping, he would go gaga at sparkly dresses. He would toss his baby blanket around his head like a wig and prance on the balls of his feet. Around age 3, he announced one day that when he married his friend Emily, they would both wear red wedding gowns at the ceremony. Yet, says Mom, her child "was still a little boy to me at the time."

Not so anymore. After struggling with their six-year-old's nonconforming gender behavior for years, Sherry and Paul Lipscomb decided a few months ago to treat their little one like a girl, at least at home. In kindergarten last year, he was Zachary, but after school, she was Aurora—Rori for short—a name the Lipscombs say their child chose in honor of the princess in Sleeping Beauty. Over the summer, when the child asked to have pierced ears and announced to neighbors, "I'm a girl," the Lipscombs came to believe that it was wrong not to "let Aurora express her gender in public," as Paul says. So with the help of a Cleveland, Ohio, support group for transgendered people, they hired an attorney to seek a legal name change for their child. And last month they informed the school principal that it was Rori who would be enrolling, not Zach.

The Lipscombs' unusual decision has dumbfounded Westerville, Ohio, a homogeneous Columbus suburb. After the Lipscombs met with the principal, an anonymous tipster contacted the Franklin County Children's Services agency, which swiftly asked a court to remove the minor from the home. A magistrate granted the agency temporary custody, citing "reasonable grounds to believe that the child is suffering from illness…and is not receiving proper care."

Thus a complicated family dynamic became a legal struggle. And a public event—the Lipscombs insisted on turning their child over to social workers before cameras at a local TV-news station. (The parents say the media scrutiny will keep the children's services office in check.) Gender PAC, a Washington-based group that lobbies for equality for transgendered people, has also helped publicize the case. Transgender activists around the world have contacted the county children's agency in protest. A growing media circus greets each court development. Last week the child's case was stalled while everyone argued for days over whether cameras should be in the courtroom.

But underneath the layers of tabloid story lines and political opportunities lies a family that's struggling through a gray time. The children's services department had actually first encountered the Lipscombs in February, when the parents voluntarily began working with the agency to get help with a host of family problems: Paul and Sherry both have bipolar disorder; they have fought in the past, sometimes violently; Paul struggles with memories of being beaten as a child; Sherry told *TIME* she has never allowed her husband to be home alone with her child overnight. ("They are both too hotheaded," she explained.) She said she has occasionally become overwhelmed by the many physical and psychological needs of her child, who has been found to have Asperger's syndrome (which is related to autism), bipolar illness and obsessive-compulsive disorder, in addition to gender-identity disorder. And although he hadn't come out in public until an interview with *TIME*, Paul now says he believes he too has gender-identity disorder and that he intends to make the transition from male to female. For now, Sherry is supporting Paul as he writes this new chapter in his life. But both say their main focus is regaining custody of their child, who is living with a foster family.

In short, you might safely say the Lipscombs aren't the Cleavers. But the county, perhaps recognizing that it's not a crime for a family to be dysfunctional, never saw reason to break up the Lipscombs—until the parents began to refer to their youngster as a girl in public. Since then, some county officials have treated the Lipscombs, including the troubled child, as pariahs. Claims and counterclaims abound. The Lipscombs say the child told them the foster parents won't use the name Aurora and hid the dresses they bought for Aurora; they've also allegedly belittled the vegetarian diet Paul and Sherry follow. County officials do call the child Zachary but say the youth has access to the dresses and doesn't want them. Both sides have alleged that the other hasn't provided proper medication for the child.

What's best for this youngster? Unfortunately, few experts study children with persistent gender variance, and the ones who do are in disagreement about what to do about it, if anything. "I think it's just the way they are born," says Catherine Tuerk, a mental-health nurse who runs a Washington support group for parents of kids who are gender-atypical. Her group has nine families at the moment, and Tuerk encourages them to support their children's unconventional gender expression "in a world where they will be stigmatized."

Some child psychologists, on the other hand, believe that children who express discomfort with their birth gender probably have larger problems. "There's a lot of pain in many of these families, and part of the

CASE STUDY

way the child has dealt with the pain is to have this fantasy solution," says Ken Zucker, a psychologist who runs the Child and Adolescent Gender Identity Clinic in Toronto. Zucker also encourages children and parents to recognize that boys and girls don't have to maintain rigid gender roles to remain boys and girls. Zucker says that widening his young patients' conception of gender may save them the difficulty of pursuing sex-reassignment surgery later in life.

Other rogue therapists mistreat gender-variant children by trying to force them to conform to gender rules. They use blunt behavior-modification techniques such as rewarding tomboys for wearing frilly dresses or punishing effeminate boys for playing with a Barbie. "Many of those kids become runaways, and they are damaged for life," says Gender PAC's Riki Anne Wilchins.

Amid all the problems, the Lipscomb child apparently has loving parents. But whether Aurora remains Aurora, or returns to Zachary—or decides on another identity—the kid is destined to conduct this search with armies of lawyers battling nearby.

Abridged from: Westerville, John Cloud. 2000. "Behavior: His Name Is Aurora. When a boy is raised as a girl, an Ohio suburb is suddenly in the throes of transgender politics." *Time.* 25 September 2000.

Questions

1. Record evidence to demonstrate that the gender identity of this child was both innate (with him from birth) and learned (shaped by his parents and other external forces).
2. Why has the government intervened in this case? What are the potential advantages and disadvantages of the state's becoming involved in the lives of this family?
3. Outline the differing explanations provided by child psychologists for "gender variance."
4. What do you believe should happen in this case? Explain your answer fully.

Other Socialization Factors: The Role of Television

Although the family is seen as the primary **socialization agent**, over time, peers, neighbours, school, and the media have an important impact on youth culture. Much has been written about the significant effects of the media, particularly television, on youth. Consider for a minute the fact that the average Canadian child watches 23 hours of television a week (Canadian Paediatric Society, 2002). This means that by high school graduation the average teen will have spent *more* time watching television than he or she spent in the classroom.

But why is this a problem? After all, adults watch a great deal of television as well. Some social scientists believe that children and adolescents are going through a developmental stage in which they are more easily influenced than adults. As a result, exposure to violence, inappropriate sexuality, and offensive language are more convincing and have a greater impact on youths.

Figure 7.6 Sarah Jessica Parker, star of *Sex and the City*, portrays one of a group of thirty-something friends whose various relationships and sexual exploits are the focus of the show. Do you believe that shows such as this have an effect, either positive or negative, on the values and/or behaviours of Canadian teens?

As well, the Canadian Paediatric Society (CPS) believes that frequent television watching is a problem because it takes away from other activities, namely, reading and school work. Studies have shown that even one to two hours of television daily has a significant negative effect on academic performance, especially reading.

As you have probably noticed, there is increased concern about television violence after real-life violent episodes in our society such as the horrendous shooting rampages that occurred in Littleton, Colorado, and Taber, Alberta, in 1999. In each of these incidents, several students were killed by their fellow classmates. Post-shooting analysis involves condemnation of violence on television and in video games, a lack of positive role models, the breakdown of the nuclear family, lack of parental supervision in two-income households, and concern over the general decline in moral values in Western society.

COMPETING
PERSPECTIVES

Does Television Influence Teen Sexuality?

Because the average Canadian teenager watches 23 hours of television a week, many people are concerned about the influence television may be having on teens' attitudes toward sex, or on actual sexual behaviour.

The Web site of the Canadian Paediatric Society notes that the average teenager views more than 14 000 sexual references annually. Adult sexual behaviour is presented in a way that portrays these actions as risk-free, frequent, and with minimal discussion of sexually transmitted diseases and unwanted pregnancy. But does this information actually *change* teenage attitudes and behaviour? Read the following two excerpts and decide for yourself.

What a Difference a Decade Makes: A Comparison of Prime Time Sex, Language, and Violence in 1989 and 1999

"Television images are tremendously influential, especially among impressionable youth. Teens, with their disposable income, and searching to find acceptance and develop an identity outside their own families, are especially susceptible to media influence, making them one of the most targeted television advertising demographics of the late 1990s.

"Professional organizations like the American Academy of Pediatrics have drawn links between television's depictions of sexuality and real-life behaviors. A 1995 poll of children 10 to 16 years of age showed that children recognize that 'what they see on television encourages them to take part in sexual activity too soon, to show disrespect for their parents, [and] to lie and to engage in aggressive behavior.' More than two-thirds said they are influenced by television; 77 percent said TV shows too much sex before marriage and 62 percent said sex on television and in movies influences their peers to have sexual relations when they are too young. Two-thirds also cited certain programs featuring dysfunctional families as encouraging disrespect toward parents."

In their own review of prime-time television programs, the Parents Television Council of America (PTC) found that the overall number of sexual references per hour during prime time went up by over 300 per cent. The PTC kept track of both visual acts and verbal content. The Council found that they had to develop six new subcategories in their 1999 analysis: references to oral sex, pornography, masturbation, "kinky" practices, homosexuality, and genitalia. Material in the sexual subcategories was more than seven times as frequent in 1999 as it was in 1989. The most dramatic increase was in homosexual references, which were more than 24 times as common. And though on a lesser scale, instances where sex was mixed with violence or was graphically depicted went up significantly in percentage terms.

Adapted from: The Parents Television Council of America. 2002. [Online]. Available <www.parentstv.org/publications/reports/Decadestudy/decadestudy.html>

COMPETING PERSPECTIVES

Not So Hot to Trot

Maclean's reporter Susan McClelland sat down with 11 students from Toronto's Oakwood Collegiate Institute to listen to their views on sex. McClelland found that although this generation of teenagers has been raised in a highly sexualized culture it does not mean that they are all "sex obsessed." In fact as Reginald Bibby reports in his book *Canada's Teens: Today, Yesterday, and Tomorrow,* only about half of the country's youth engage in sex—pretty much the same percentage as two decades ago.

"'Parents think we are all doing it,' says 16-year-old Yota Lambrakos. Franky Isovski, 17, interrupts: 'No. Every parent thinks everyone else's kid is having sex, but their own.' The other young people nod their heads in agreement. 'But, it's just not true,' continues Yota. 'Not all teens are having sex. The general perception that a lot of adults have about teens is that they can't form their own opinions, make their own decisions, or if they make their own decisions, they're not informed. We definitely do make wise decisions, including whether to have or not have sex.'"

"Alexander McKay, research co-ordinator at the Toronto-based Sex Information and Education Council of Canada, agrees that fewer kids are sexually active than popular culture would have us believe. 'We have a propensity,' he says, 'to ring alarm bells about adolescent sexuality when we shouldn't be.'"

Some of the teenagers who talked to *Maclean's* stated that they were simply too busy to become sexually active. "Stephen Rahey, a 15-year-old Grade 10 student in Halifax, maintains an A average, takes karate classes, and has a wide circle of friends. 'There are lots of parties, people to hang out with and things to do other than school work, so it's hard to stay on top of my studies,' says Stephen. 'This is a priority for me. Anyways, sex isn't some great race to the finish line.'"

Although the same number of teens are having sex today as was the case 20 years ago, teenagers today are much more tolerant and open about sexuality. Eighty-two per cent of teens believe in heterosexual sex before marriage if people love each other, 54 per cent of teens approve of same-sex relationships, and 75 per cent believe homosexuals are entitled to the same rights as anyone else.

Adapted from: McClelland, Susan. 2001. "Not So Hot to Trot." *Maclean's.* 9 April 2001.

Questions

1. How do you account for the different opinions expressed in these two excerpts?

2. Do you feel television has a negative or positive influence on teenagers' sexual behaviour, or do you believe it has no influence? Discuss.

3. What could be done to decrease the amount of sex and sexual references on television?

Figure 7.7 Marilyn Manson is a controversial shock rocker whose lyrics some believe influenced the two teenaged gunmen in the Columbine massacre in the United States.

But does television violence truly have a negative effect on attitudes and behaviour? Many studies argue that it does not; after all, most adolescents are exposed to television violence, but very few ever act in a violent manner. On the other hand, the statistics are disturbing. The average child sees 12 000 violent acts on television annually, including many depictions of murder and rape. As well, more than 1000 studies confirm that exposure to television violence does increase aggressive behaviour, especially in males 15 to 17 years old (Canadian Paediatric Society, 2000).

Again, the good news is that the majority of youths are, in fact, productive and positive people. The following case study shows that many of today's teens do not have the same feelings of rebellion and angst as past generations. Indeed, the author suggests that the old stereotypes adults like to apply to teenagers simply no longer fit.

CASE STUDY

The Values of Youth Today

A new generation is rising. The Millennial Generation. Starting next year, half of all college students will be Millennials. They're a social and cultural tsunami, no less than boomers were 40 years ago, but their wave is heading in a very different direction.

If producers want evidence, they should consider this: The cutting edge of new pop music consumers is age 13 to 15, while the cutting edge of new moviegoers is age 17 to 19. That's a four-year time gap. Four years ago, sales of older and edgier styles—grunge, death metal, alternative, gangsta rap—suddenly plummeted. A year later, the new phenoms were the upbeat and synthetic "boy band" and "cover girl" sound, from 'N Sync to Britney Spears. Many music-makers dismissed the rising "O-town" trend, but a few invested in it. Guess which ones are prospering now?

Hollywood, wake up and smell the double mocha latte. Today's teens aren't Gen-X. They're not like you.

Not even close. And the kids coming along behind them, now in middle school, are even less like you.

Millennials are the grown-up kids of "Barney" (not "Sesame Street"), of soccer moms (not latchkeys), of "Have you hugged your child today?" bumper stickers (not "We're spending our children's inheritance"), of "Where do you want to go today?" ads (not "This is your brain on drugs"). They like action-packed adventure in which good triumphs over evil (Harry Potter books) and are less likely to go for feelings and healings (Judy Blume books).

Today's Millennial teens experienced a very different kind of upbringing than Xers. They've been protected, treasured, prodded to achieve. Whole new genres of books, cartoons, movies, museums and school curricula have been created for them. Movies, too. When they were small, back in the mid-1980s, filmmakers began shunning the evil-kid genre so popular through the Gen-X childhood (from "Rosemary's Baby" to "The Exorcist" to "The Omen" to "Bugsy Malone"—it's a very long list) and replacing them with sweet-child movies ("Parenthood," "Baby Boom," "Three Men and a Baby," "Angels in the Outfield"—also a very long list).

Crotch-jokers beware: This new generation is more modest than most people think. Fully two-thirds of high-achieving high school students say that explicit sexual programming on TV is offensive to some degree. Go to a health club, a beach club, anywhere people of different ages change clothes. Who do you see changing quickly in the corner? Teens. Who prances around naked? Fifty-year-olds. Back in the 1960s, teenagers revelled in nudity: Fifty-year-olds did not.

So what kinds of movies are winning with Millennial teens and middle-schoolers? Action-oriented movies with bushels of slapstick fun and uplifting finales ("The Emperor's New Groove," "Shrek") or with heroic, positive depictions of young people ("Spy Kids," "Pearl Harbor"). Just look at the biggest teen money-makers expected later this year—from "Lara Croft: Tomb Raider" and "Atlantis: The Lost Empire" to "Harry Potter" and sequels to "The Matrix." Plenty of laughs and gasps, but hardly an embarrassed snicker in the bunch.

Millennials love scripted jokes and staged pratfalls, not free-form wit and sarcastic commentary. They're "George of the Jungle," not "Ghostbusters." In their own theater projects, they go for big productions, elaborate sets, synchronized choreography, tight harmonies—exactly the opposite of where boomers were going at that age, back in the '60s.

Millennials like stories that are about something important, something epic. Stories about real people doing things, not phoney people hyping things. Introspection is dispensable, and violence or stereotypes are acceptable to move the action along. But like the viewers of "Dawson's Creek," with its SAT-prep vocabulary, Millennials gravitate to producers who respect their intelligence. Any adult skeptical of their prodigious appetite for left-brained complexity is hereby required to challenge a 4th grader to a Pokemon contest. "Dumb and Dumber" is out. Smart and Smarter is a better bet.

Every year, Millennials get another year older. Now they've filled the high school ranks and are flooding into college, where they will soon emerge as the major movie market. Films they dislike will flop. Hard.

It won't be long before some producer and director achieve fame and fortune by making the next generation-defining movie—which will be for Millennials what "The Graduate" was for boomers and "Breakfast Club" was for Xers. What will this movie be like? Here's one easy bet: It will be something fresh and creative, something that captures this rising generation.

Source: Howe, Neil. 2001. "Youth Culture: Teens Shun Gross-out Movie Genre." *The Los Angeles Times.* 15 July 2001.

Questions

1. According to this article, how does the youth culture of the Millennial Generation contrast with stereotypes of teens from past generations?

2. What reasons does the author suggest are responsible for this change in youth culture? Do you agree with the author? Why or why not?

3. Do you think that external forces such as advertisements, films, and music influence teen culture, or that teens influence the development of new music and the types of movies that are made? Explain your answer.

4. What does this article seem to imply with regard to the issue raised in Question 3? Give evidence from the article to support your answer.

Pause and Reflect

1. How does the relationship between adolescents, parents, and peers evolve during the teen years?

2. Explain why the family is considered to be the primary socialization agent of children.

3. How do parents have an impact on their child's gender identity? With reference to your own family, give examples of the ways males and females were socialized into gender roles. Discuss what effect you feel this has had on your life.

4. Apply Erik Erikson's theory of adolescent development to your own life. Have you achieved a personal sense of identity? Explain your answer.

5. With a partner or in a small group, draft an opinion piece that addresses your feelings about, and offers guidelines for, adolescents' exposure to television.

Section 7.3   Parenthood: Changes in This Stage of the Life Cycle

Key Concepts

religiosity

Each new stage of the life cycle is profound. As we just discussed, adolescence brings about a host of changes, and industrialized societies provide a lot of time for each individual to sort out the type of adult he or she will become. This includes making decisions about education, career, relationships, and parenthood—the subject of this section.

There is no doubt about it; becoming a parent is a huge change. For most women, this change occurs even during pregnancy as they anticipate their future child and dream about the baby growing inside them. The physical acts of birth and nursing result in a strong attachment between mother and infant and a period of intense interdependence. For men, the transition to "father" occurs more slowly, usually following the birth of the baby and continuing to develop as the infant becomes older and is less dependent on the mother.

Ask any new parents how they feel and, after they finish talking about how tired they are, they may also share that they had no idea they could love a child as much as they love their new son or daughter. These powerful feelings provide the adrenaline to get through those sleepless early months and the

many challenges and obstacles that come over the following years (See Case Study, page 227). And although the joys and challenges of parenthood remain the same from generation to generation, the nature of parenthood itself does not. Each generation has new beliefs about nutrition, different expectations about appropriate and inappropriate behaviour, and new ideas about child rearing. Economic and social factors also combine to change the nature of parenthood from one period of time to the next.

Factors That Influence Decisions About Parenthood

In 1998, Dave Dupuis wrote a report on a survey that examined factors that influence people's plans to have children. The report, published in *Canadian Social Trends* magazine, indicated that marital status, family values, and religious beliefs and practices all have an impact on a person's decisions of when to have children and how many to have. First of all, marriage leads people to want children. Despite the increase in common-law unions in Canada, nearly two-thirds of live births still occur within

Parenthood—The Most Difficult Transition of the Life Cycle?

You may be surprised to learn that couples report a significant drop in marital satisfaction with the arrival of their first child. Researchers have found that marital satisfaction does not return to previous high levels until the child (or children) leave the family home for school or employment (Olsen and McCubbin, 1983). Before we have children, we tend to believe that having a child strengthens a relationship and helps the couple to establish an even closer bond. While that is true, the following excerpt, from a chapter written by Nina Howe and William M. Bukowski (2001), outlines the reasons why this life cycle transition is so difficult.

"The transition to parenthood has sometimes been characterized as a time of crisis, but more recently, as a period of developmental change accompanied by stress. Solly and Miller (1980) identified four types of stresses associated with this period. First, physical problems associated with a loss of sleep, the extra work of looking after an infant and assuming a new role (particularly for mothers)…Second, strains in the marital relationship that occur as a result of changes in the sexual relationship, for example, lack of interest in sex because of tiredness. Third, the emo-tional stress of feeling overwhelmed, responsible for a new life, the recognition that parenthood is a life-long commitment, and doubt concerning their ability to be good parents. Finally, there are opportunity costs and restrictions such as the limits on social life, spontaneous decisions such as going to the movies, and perhaps a reduced income and opportunities for career advancement for the caregiving parent…

"There are individual differences in how couples adjust to the transition to parenthood, but adjustment is easier when fathers are more closely involved, especially in caregiving (Levy-Shiff, 1994). The contribution of the infant, specifically temperament, can affect the level of stress in the transition…Realistic and practical expectations regarding the new child appear to facilitate an easier transition (Cowan and Cowan, 1995). Finally, the quality of emotional and practical support in the marital relationship is important in influencing the ease of transition, especially for women (Coltrane, 1990; Hackel and Ruble, 1992)."

Source: Howe, Nina and William M. Bukowski. 2001. "What are Children and How Do They Become Adults?: Child Rearing and Socialization." In M. Baker. (Ed.) *Families: Changing Trends in Canada. 4th Edition.* Toronto. McGraw-Hill Ryerson.

Questions

1. In what ways might the transition to parenthood be considered a time of crisis?
2. What factors might help to reduce the stress associated with this stage of the life cycle?
3. What social and economic factors might exacerbate the stress associated with the transition to parenthood?
4. Why do you think there is a difference between our expectations of parenthood and the reality of parenthood?

marriage. Furthermore, the birth rate among married women is nearly double that of women who spent their entire reproductive life in a common-law relationship.

The second factor that influences decisions about parenthood, according to the survey, is family values. Parents transfer attitudes and behaviour related to child-bearing

Figure 7.8 As more and more women invest increasing amounts of time and money in attaining their university education, their desire to give up a career to raise a family diminishes.

to their children, so young adults who have many siblings tend to want more children than young adults with few siblings. It is interesting to note, however, that one aspect of family history that does not appear to have an impact on child-bearing attitudes is parental divorce. One might expect that children of divorced couples would have negative attitudes toward family and a reduced desire to have their own children. But Dupuis found that the impact of parental divorce dissipates over time, having no effect on the intentions of people in their thirties to have children, and affecting people in their twenties only if the split had occurred when the child was more than 15 years old.

Dupuis's survey also found that **religiosity** plays a large role in family size. Religiosity refers to a person's religious affiliation and his or her attendance at religious services. Young adults who report having no religion tend to have the smallest average number of children (1.76). Non-Christians—for example, Eastern Orthodox, Jewish, and Muslim—have a much

higher number of children (2.48). And people in their thirties who attend religious services every week tend to have at least 0.5 per cent more children than those who never attend religious services. Dupuis believes that people who attend religious services regularly plan on having larger families because they tend to view marriage and family as very important to their happiness.

In Dupuis's report, the factor that had the greatest impact on decisions about parenthood was education level. In general, the more education women have, the fewer children they bear. This is particularly true of women in their thirties with a university degree. Although increased opportunities are available to women with advanced education, women remain the primary caregivers of children and have to interrupt their employment for childbirth and childcare. The costs associated with interruptions to their careers tend to constrain and delay child-bearing. It is interesting to note that the opposite relationship exists for men; men with more

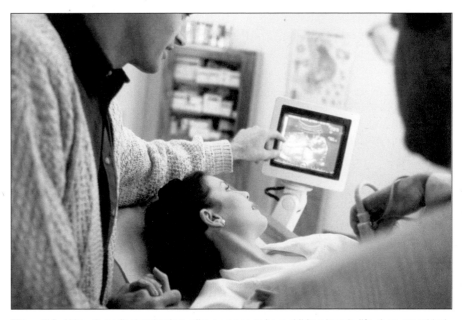

Figure 7.9 Although medical technology allows women to have children later in life, there are ethical concerns with this practice. For example, some people point out that elderly parents have a greater chance than younger parents of dying before their child is independent enough to care for itself. What is your opinion of this concern? What other possible concerns can you think of?

education tend to father more children. Dupuis states that this finding probably reflects the fact that university-educated men more often have well-paid, stable employment and are better able to afford more children. As well, having children has a much smaller impact on men's careers.

Trends Associated with Parenthood

Social and economic factors can have an impact on decisions about parenthood. For example, fertility declined and childlessness rose during the Great Depression of the 1930s—a time when many people were unemployed and therefore in no financial position to get married and have children. Likewise, widespread availability of birth control in the late 1960s allowed women more control over their fertility, and birth rates fell as a result. And as you have already learned, because so many women today pursue post-secondary education and choose to

have careers, a full one-third of all babies are born to women in their thirties—which once would have been considered middle-aged.

In the book *Families: Changing Trends in Canada* (2001), sociologist Susannah J. Wilson notes that two contradictory trends now seem to be affecting child-bearing decisions. The first is the trend for women to postpone child-bearing until later in life, despite the fact that this significantly reduces the likelihood that they will become parents. The second trend is the relationship between parenthood and spousal and family commitment. That is, people who expressed doubt about the stability of their relationships were much more likely to remain childless. And all studies indicate that the desire for children is greater for married than unmarried adults.

As mentioned in Chapter 6, as a woman's education level increases, *in general*, the number of children she has decreases. This variable is very closely linked to the particular career a woman chooses. Understandably, if a woman spends a considerable amount of time pursuing her education so that she can qualify for a particular career, she will be unlikely to want to give up that career for motherhood. Likewise, some professions (such as law and international journalism, for example) can be extremely demanding on a person's time or may require a lot of travel and time spent away from home. Women in such professions may believe that it would be especially difficult for them to raise children. This belief may influence them to forgo motherhood.

Sylvia Ann Hewlett, an economist and president of the National Parenting Association in the United States, and Cornel West, a professor of philosophy and religion at Harvard University, conducted a study of women who chose childlessness in their twenties and thirties. Of the women surveyed, 24 per cent did not want to have children because they did not want to give up their careers. The 1995 General Social Survey conducted in Canada, with nearly 11 000 respondents, indicated that declining fertility rates are directly related to women's rising level of education and increasing labour market participation (Belanger & Oikawa, 1999). The researchers noted that the greater a woman's economic independence, the higher the costs of motherhood through loss of income, daycare costs, and setbacks or delays in career advancement.

The Effect of Medical Advances on the Age of Parents

Another trend associated with parenthood today concerns reproductive technologies that have helped to extend the fertility period, and fertility options, for women. These developments are largely available only to women in industrialized nations. The ability to buy the eggs of a younger woman for fertilization and implantation into an older woman has extended the fertility period, as has the ability to freeze fertilized embryos for future implantation. As a result, births to women in their forties are no longer unusual. The reproductive technologies discussed in Chapter 6—such as artificial insemination by donor and the use of surrogates (see page 193) allows previously infertile married women, single women, and lesbian women to conceive. It also allows women to postpone child-bearing until after their careers have been fully established.

Margrit Eichler, a sociologist at the University of Toronto, notes that the new reproductive and genetic technologies are fundamentally reshaping families because "they contradict fundamental assumptions, including that a child's parents should be alive at the moment of conception and that families have clearly identifiable generational lines" (1996).

Pause and Reflect

1. How do men and women experience the transition to parenthood differently?

2. What impact does divorce have on a child's decision to become a parent when he or she becomes an adult?

3. Why does family size increase along with a person's religiosity?

4. Do you think men spend as much time considering how they will balance their career and parenthood as women do? Explain your answer.

5. In what ways are reproductive and genetic technologies fundamentally reshaping families?

Section 7.4   Aging: The Impact on Caregivers, Housing, and Health Care

Over the next several decades, countries in the developed world will experience an unprecedented growth in the number of their elderly and an unprecedented decline in the number of their youth. The timing and magnitude of this demographic transformation have already been determined. Next century's elderly have already been born and can be counted—and their cost to retirement benefit systems can be projected…Unlike with other challenges…the costs of global aging will be far beyond the means of even the world's wealthiest nations— unless retirement benefits are radically reformed. Failure to do so, to prepare early and boldly enough, will spark economic crises that will dwarf the recent meltdowns in Asia and Russia.

How we confront global aging will have vast economic consequences costing quadrillions of dollars over the 21st century. Indeed, it will greatly influence how we manage, and can afford to manage, the other major challenges that will face us in the future.

For this and other reasons, global aging will become not just the transcendent economic issue of the 21st century, but the transcendent political issue as well. It will dominate and daunt the public-policy agendas of developed countries and force the renegotiation of their social contracts. It will also reshape foreign policy strategies and the geopolitical order…(Peterson, 2002, p. 247)

This quotation is taken from the introduction of a chapter on global aging. The author, Peter Peterson, sees the issue as a *crisis* because he believes this demographic shift is going to place an unprecedented economic burden on working-age people as they try to pay for health care, medicine, pension plans,

and other retirement benefit programs for the elderly. While some social scientists do not agree that we are heading for an economic crisis (for reasons discussed in Chapter 5, pages 169 to 170), the fact remains that Canada's population will undergo considerable aging as it moves into the twenty-first century, and this demographic shift will have social impacts on Canadians.

According to Statistics Canada, by 2016 Canada's population will rise to 37 million from 29 million, and half of those people will be over 40, while 16 per cent will be over the age of 74. That is up from the current 12 per cent, and that proportion will increase to almost one-quarter by 2041. Over the same period, the number of people under 15 will shrink to 19 per cent from the current 25 per cent (Statistics Canada, 2002).

This section of the chapter will focus on the sociological implications of aging, as well as some of the economic impacts. Specifically, we will explore the impact of aging on caregivers, options for independent living, and the shift to a focus on preventative health.

Role of the Caregiver

According to the Caregiver Network of Ontario—a resource centre created to help caregivers of the elderly and ill—over the next 10 years about 47 million baby boomers in North America will find themselves facing the role of caregiver to a parent, relative, or elderly friend (Statistics Canada, 2001). This does not include the countless thousands of seniors who will be caring for a chronically ill spouse. The unpaid help given by friends, neighbours, and family is known as **informal support**, while the term **formal support** refers to the doctors, nurses, and social workers involved in

Key Concepts

informal support

formal support

developmental stake

caregiver burden

quasi-widowhood

sheltered housing

granny flat

wellness clinics

Figure 7.10 Most elderly Canadians rely on their spouse for care and support.

caring for the elderly. We will focus on the pressures facing those who provide the elderly with informal support.

Adult children provide much of the support needed by their elderly parents, although researchers have found that daughters provide more care to parents than do sons (Aronson, 1990, p. 234). This is likely a reflection of the fact that women in North American culture are seen as more nurturing than men and play a greater caregiving role within their own families. Nonetheless, both male and female caregivers report feeling strongly that children should give emotional, physical, and financial support to their parents.

Interestingly, one of the stresses associated with the caregiving relationship is that adult children and their elderly parents see the amount of support provided by the children differently. Specifically, older people feel they receive less support than their children say they give (Bond and Harvey, 1991, p. 33). Psychologists refer to this difference as the

developmental stake (Bengtson and Kuypers, 1971, p. 249). Older people have a greater stake in the relationship and may de-emphasize the amount of support they receive in order not to see themselves as a burden on their children. This difference in perception can result in tension if the adult children do not feel that the parents appreciate how much they do for them.

The other area of informal support for the elderly is provided by spouses. In fact, most older Canadians report that their spouse is their main source of support, even when the spouse is old and frail (McDaniel, 1994, p. 49). Some estimates place the percentage of elderly persons relying exclusively on their spouses for care at 75 per cent—this can mean an average of 75 hours a week of caregiving work (Novak, 1997, p. 275). Even in late old age, when people have serious disabilities, married people have half the institutionalization rate of unmarried older people (Novak, 1997, p. 275).

Caregiver Burden

Not surprisingly, providing care to a physically disabled or cognitively impaired older person can lead to **caregiver burden**. This refers to problems and stress due to caregiving. Some research suggests that spouses of those receiving care suffer a greater burden from caregiving than do adult children, particularly when they see their partner decline mentally and physically (Hadjistavropoulos et al., 1994, p. 312). Spouses may have health problems themselves that make caregiving difficult, and they may also have fewer financial and social resources to call on than a middle-aged caregiver would.

Although taking care of an elderly relative or spouse can be rewarding, it can also be very stressful and, at times, depressing. Researchers note that these stresses are likely to increase in the future because of ongoing changes facing the family, for example, more women in the workforce, smaller modern homes, greater

Take the following quiz and learn more about the burden facing caregivers today. Answer "true" or "false" to each of the following:

Caregiver Quiz

1. Most Canadian families maintain frequent contact with and are very supportive of their older relatives.
2. At least 10 per cent of the aged are living in long-term care facilities.
3. Research links employee care for elderly relatives with productivity losses due to increased absences, stress, and extra time on the telephone for family needs.
4. Fifty per cent of Ontario families match the traditional nuclear family with father as sole breadwinner and mother at home.
5. Helping elderly relatives with one task each day, such as bathing or dressing, can require up to nine hours from the caregiver each week.
6. There are hidden "job opportunity" costs when providing eldercare while working.
7. There are fewer men involved in caregiving than women.
8. Women today spend 17 years caring for their children and 18 years helping an elderly parent.
9. A person is no longer a caregiver when their relative moves to a long-term care facility.
10. Family conflicts are reduced when care for an elderly relative is required.

Answers

1. True: 80% of families stay in touch. There is a strong informal support system in Canada.
2. False: 6–8%
3. True
4. False: 16%
5. True
6. True: Job opportunity costs include financial losses, vacation time lost, sick days lost, social opportunities lost (people go home instead of going out), job advances lost (cannot relocate, take training courses).
7. True: 3.5 women for every man are involved in caregiving, but this is gradually changing.
8. True: according to the Ontario Women's Directorate
9. False: Caregiving never ceases; the move results in a new role to which one must adapt.
10. False: Family conflicts increase with the amount of eldercare that must be provided.

numbers of 18- to 25-year-olds at home, and greater geographic mobility.

The caregiver burden does not end after a spouse enters an institution. Caregivers with institutionalized spouses still have to deal with the strain of long visits and travel to and from the institution. As well, caregivers often feel they are unable to get on with their lives and are lonely. Drs. C. Rosenthal and P. Dawson, faculty members at the University of Ottawa Institute of Palliative Care, conducted a 1991 study of 40 wives who had placed their husbands in nursing homes. They found that the women were in a state of

quasi-widowhood. This refers to the fact that the women felt relief after their spouses were placed in institutions, but they also felt failure, anger, guilt, sadness, depression, and grief. Eventually, most of the women accepted the loss of their spouse as a friend and companion and restructured their lives outside of the institution.

Independent Living Arrangements for the Elderly

As our population ages, one issue of paramount importance will be housing arrangements for the elderly. Since less than 5 per cent of the elderly live in long-term care facilities, and in Ontario alone there are over 100 000 people on the waiting list for beds, it is important that Canadians understand the needs of the elderly and make appropriate plans.

For healthy, able-bodied seniors, living alone in the family home is usually the most preferred living arrangement. The family home provides comfort and security and allows older people to feel, and be, more independent. This kind of living arrangement, however, not only requires good health, but also knowledge of home repairs and enough income to pay for food, heat, and taxes. Since these resources are not available to many elderly persons, alternative living arrangements such as moving into an apartment, living with older children, or living in some type of **sheltered housing**—where help with meals and cleaning is provided—need to be explored.

One of the most pronounced trends in living arrangements in the past several decades in Canada has been the increase in the proportion of older people, particularly women, who live alone. This corresponds to a drop in the proportion of older people who live with other family members (Novak, 1997, p. 211). Researchers suggest that the fact that people have fewer children may play a role in the shift to more elderly people living alone, but it is more likely that the values of independence and autonomy prevalent in our society have had a greater impact on this trend. In a 1992 study of 75 older women on Prince Edward Island, social researchers found that the women reported that it was their desire for independence that resulted in their living alone (Hamilton and Brehaut, 1992, p. 19). Furthermore, a 1994 study conducted in British Columbia found that older women who lived alone enjoyed their freedom (Doyle). In fact, a full 88 per cent of the women said that living alone allowed them to do what they wanted, when they wanted.

Nonetheless, the requirement for suitable living arrangements continues to be one of the greatest obstacles facing the elderly and their families. In his book *Aging & Society: A Canadian Perspective* (1997), Mark Novak reports that housing ranked as the "second-highest unmet need for women aged 65 to 79, the third-highest unmet need for women aged 80 to 84, and the fourth- or fifth-highest unmet need for women aged 85 and over." (Novak, 1997, p. 210). Novak explains that housing declines as an unmet need with age in part because more very old people, compared with younger old people, live in institutions.

Granny Flats

As our society ages, residential planners are starting to explore new ideas in housing. **Granny flats** (also called garden suites) are one of these options. A granny flat consists of a portable modular cottage, which is placed onto the son or daughter's property. The flat is then connected to the electricity, sewer, water, and telephone services of the house. When the older person dies or moves to an institution, the granny flat is dismantled and taken off the property.

Canada has very restrictive zoning laws, which currently limit the ability of the elderly and their children to pursue this option. As well, residents seem reluctant to allow the construction of granny flats on properties neighbouring their own. However, granny flats are very popular in Australia, some European countries, and some parts of the United States, so it may be that these concerns are unwarranted. Canadians seem to prefer the option of in-law apartments, which provide for the accommodation of an elderly person within the adult child's home. Few people have homes large enough to accommodate such an arrangement, however.

⬤ Embracing the Health Promotion Model

As Canadians, we highly value our system of medicare, which provides medical treatment regardless of a person's ability to pay. In fact, our health care system is one of the defining features of the Canadian identity. However, most of us are well aware of the warning signs that seem to indicate that our health care system is in trouble. Costs keep rising, there is a shortage of doctors and nurses, waiting times in hospital emergency departments continue to lengthen, and periodically someone dies because an ambulance was not able to take a patient to the nearest available hospital.

As our society ages, more pressure will be put on our health care system. While it is unclear that greater numbers of older people actually result in increased health care costs (see the case study titled "Declining Birth Rates and the Aging Population" in Chapter 6, page 203), it does appear that the elderly consume a higher proportion of pharmaceutical drugs—either because of true need or because cultural norms result in doctors being more willing to prescribe medication to the elderly. It is also evident that the elderly use hospitals for longer periods of time than do younger people, and that some require the services of special care homes. However, many researchers point out that there are

Figure 7.11 The number of older Canadians, particularly women, who live on their own has been increasing. Why is this the trend?

problems with Canada's current health care system itself that account for the increased costs, and that it is time for Canada to switch to a new model of health care.

Three models of health care are currently in use in Canada, although the model that we rely on most heavily is the medical model. This model focuses on the *treatment* of diseases and injuries. It favours surgery, drug therapy, and rehabilitation provided in a physician's office, hospital, or other health care institution. Physicians control both the organization of health care and the work of other health care professionals. This is a very expensive way to deliver health care.

The social model of health care is growing in importance as more older people need continuing or long-term care, but it still occupies only a small part of our entire system. The social model incorporates personal and family counselling, home care, and adult daycare programs as *part* of the health care system. The doctor works as part of a team that includes a variety of other professionals, and care takes place within the community as opposed to in an institution. The focus of this model of health care is to keep the elderly in their own homes, which makes it less expensive than the traditional medical model.

The health promotion model focuses on *prevention* of disease through lifestyle change, increased knowledge about healthy behaviour, and environmental improvement. Programs that promote fitness and try to decrease the amount that people smoke and drink follow this model, as do workplace safety regulations, seatbelt legislation, and pollution control measures. The Canadian government has only begun to use this model, but it is the only method that may actually save the health care system by keeping people healthier longer.

Clinics that focus on disease prevention and health promotion are known as **wellness clinics**. These clinics encourage people to take responsibility for improving or maintaining a healthy lifestyle. In 1987, Well Women's Clinics were begun in Shelburne County, Nova Scotia. Services offered at the clinics included breast exams, pap smears, vaccines, and blood glucose and blood pressure checks. Health education brochures on depression, heart health, eating disorders, and abuse issues were made available. As well, presentations on menopause, stress reduction, and sexually transmitted diseases were introduced. The success of the Well Women's Clinics prompted the introduction of Well Men's and Teens' Wellness Clinics. In the future, it is hoped that the use of wellness clinics will expand across Canada as a way to promote health and decrease reliance on our overburdened and expensive health care system.

University of Toronto demographer David Foot is an expert on the social and economic implications of Canada's aging population. In the following case study, Foot predicts the health care issues he believes Canada, and Toronto in particular, will face in the coming years, and he proposes some solutions to deal with these issues.

Demographer David Foot on Health Care for the Future

The most remarkable thing about Canada's health care system at the end of the 1990s is that it is perceived to be in crisis and underfunded at a time when Canada still has a relatively young and healthy population. Our population is younger than that of the western European countries, most of which, on a per capita basis, spend less on health care than we do.

The boomers make up about a third of Toronto's population, and most of them haven't gotten sick yet; their health won't start to deteriorate for another decade. The need for health care services increases sharply among those over 60 and doubles after the age of 70. Even by 2021, less than half the boomers will be seniors, so they won't have hit the health care system in full force yet.

When they do, however, they are going to put major pressure on hospitals and home care services.

During the 1990s, the Ontario government has reduced reliance on hospitals, which are the most expensive part of the health care system. Some hospitals have been closed, and patient stays have been reduced. To take up the slack, an increasing amount of health care is being delivered in the home. Home care will continue to grow and develop over the next decade. But a home care system, no matter how efficient, is not much use to someone who has just suffered a stroke.

When large numbers of boomers start having strokes and heart attacks, in the second decade of the new century, hospitals will take on new importance. Existing ones will be expanded and new ones will have to be built. Because a lot of semi-retired people will be living in nearby semi-rural areas, the focus will be on hospitals located on major traffic arteries on the outskirts of the GTA. These hospitals will be accessible both to the expanding ex-urban population and the 6.4 million GTA residents.

Governments prefer to ignore demographics if they can, but even before 2021 the significance for the health care system of the aging boomers will be too great to ignore….The provincial government, regardless of which party is in power, will have no choice but to undertake major restructuring. The key to reform is integration of all aspects of health care—hospitals, home care, drugs, doctors and other health care workers—under one budget.

Integration is crucial because separate budgets for different aspects of health care are the reason the current system is so inflexible and expensive. For example, an expensive drug might be able to keep a patient out of hospital, saving the overall health care system huge sums. But there is no budget in the existing system to pay for the drug, so the patient winds up in hospital instead. An integrated organization would have every incentive to opt for the drug because doing so would be best for the patient and would save money as well.

Experience in other countries indicates that integrated systems are most successful when they cover about 100,000 people. The health care organization would get a fixed amount per year for each patient, based on the patient's age, gender, and health status. Known as "rostering" or "capitation," this system gives doctors and other staff an incentive to keep patients healthy through such means as counselling on fitness and nutrition, and it gives them a disincentive to encourage unnecessary visits or to perform unnecessary procedures.

Source: Foot, David. "The Toronto That Will Be." *Toronto Life.* Jan 2000.

Questions

1. What impact does David Foot believe the aging baby boom generation will have on health care in communities such as Toronto?
2. What solutions does he propose to deal with these issues?
3. Do you agree with his predictions and solutions? Explain why or why not.

Putting a New Face on Aging

The elderly population today is not the same population that existed in the past. This group survived two world wars and a depression to get to retirement. As a result, they are a hardy lot, although poverty—particularly among widows—can be a problem. The "blessed ones" are currently between the ages of 49 to 65. They generally have access to money, and because they have been a successful cohort, they still view the future as "limitless." As a result, they bring a new attitude toward aging.

Health and Welfare Canada reports that more than any other group, people over the age of 55 say they exercise daily and eat less fat and fried food than they did in the past. Compared with younger people, they also skip breakfast less often, smoke less, drink less, and use fewer illicit drugs. They also reported higher levels of seatbelt use and lower levels of drinking and driving.

As the population ages, the marketplace has responded to this growing consumer group. Dozens of seniors magazines are now produced, most of them focused on health and fitness, reducing the signs of aging, travel, and leisure activities. And these leisure activities—snowboarding, rock climbing, and mountain biking—might not be what you would traditionally imagine seniors

Figure 7.12 Why do you think sports such as snow boarding and mountain biking are becoming more popular with elderly Canadians these days?

doing. As well, across the country, fitness clubs are starting to advertise sessions specifically designed for seniors, and the recent boom in gardening has been propelled by the aging population.

An article in the London paper *The Independent* notes that most purchasers of new Harley Davidson motorcycles and Fender Stratocaster guitars are middle-aged professionals, and that each year some 50 000 businesses are started by people over 50. The seniors of today, and those in their fifties who will be the next generation of seniors, are actually redefining what it means to age.

Redefining Aging

The number of people reaching the increasingly mythic retirement age of 65 [in America] has zoomed from about seven and a half million in the 1930s to 34 million today. By the turn of the century, that figure will be 61.4 million. If the boomers' luck holds out, they will be spared what amounts to the psychological torture of uselessness and burdensomeness that every graying generation this century has faced before them. For there is an attitude shift in the wind. In an irony that boomers will no doubt appreciate, a revolution in attitude about age is coming largely from a corner of the population that has traditionally been content to enjoy the status quo—a cultural elite whose median age is surely over 65.

A small but growing gaggle of experts (themselves mostly elders)—a diverse lot of gerontologists, physicians, psychologists, sociologists, anthropologists, philosophers, ethicists, cultural observers, and spiritual leaders—are the vanguard of a movement to change the way society looks at and deals with growing old. They seek to have us stop viewing old age as a problem—as an incurable disease, if you will—to be "solved" by spending billions of dollars on plastic surgery in an attempt to mask visible signs of aging, other billions on medical research to extend the life span itself, and billions more on nursing and retirement homes as a way to isolate those who fail at the quest to deny aging.

Separately and together, this cultural elite is exploring ways to move us and our social institutions toward a new concept of aging, one they call "conscious aging." They want us to be aware of and accept what aging actually is—a notice that life has not only a beginning and a middle, but an end—and to eliminate the denial that now prevents us from anticipating, fruitfully using, and even appreciating what are lost to euphemism as "the golden years."

"Conscious aging is a new way of looking at and experiencing aging that moves beyond our cultural obsession with youth toward a respect and need for the wisdom of age," explains Stephan Rechtschaffen, M.D., a holistic physician who directs the Omega

Institute, a kind of New Age think-tank that is a driving force in this attitude shift. He would have us:

- Recognize and accept the aging process and all that goes with it as a reality, a natural part of the life cycle; it happens to us all. The goal is to change the prevailing view of aging as something to be feared and the aged as worthless.
- Reverse our societal attitude of aging as an affliction, and instead of spending billions on walling off the aging, spend more to improve the quality of life among the aged.

A series of studies by psychologists Ellen Langer, Ph.D. of Harvard and University of Pennsylvania President Judith Rodin, Ph.D. (then at Yale) suggests how we grow to revile our aging selves. Influenced by the fairy tales we hear as children, and what we see on television and hear in everyday life, we develop negative stereotypes about aging by the time we are six years old, the same age we develop negative stereotypes about race and sex. These stereotypes persist as we grow up, completely unaware that we even acquired them or granted them our unconditional acceptance. With our understanding of the subject forever frozen, we grow into old age assuming the stereotypes to be true. And we live down to them.

If there is a single myth about aging that most symbolizes our dread, it is the assumption that our memory will inevitably decline in old age. In a stunning new study, psychologist Langer has demonstrated that it is our own psychology—the near-universal expectation of memory loss—that actually brings that fate upon us. The lesson to be learned is an extraordinary one: Fear of aging is the single most powerful agent creating exactly what we fear.

Still, we continue to mythologize and denigrate aging because we devalue death itself. "We refuse even to admit that we die of old age," says Sherwin Nuland, a retired Yale surgeon, whose book embodies the proposition that death is a normal stage in the life cycle. This refusal is perpetuated by the medical profession and the law. "I cannot write 'Old Age' on a death certificate even though people over 70 die because they're over 70," he says. He deplores the prevailing view of aging as a disease that can be cured and the biomedical search for a fountain of youth....

So long as we lock ourselves into an obsession with the youth culture, we can only develop age rage and dehumanize ourselves, says writer Betty Friedan. Those who give up their denial of age, who age consciously, "grow and become aware of new capacities they develop while aging.... [They] become more authentically themselves."

Source: Daniel, Jere. 1994. "Learning to love (gulp!) growing old." *Psychology Today*. Vol. 27. 9 January 1994.

Questions

1. According to the article, what attitude shift is occurring with respect to aging?
2. Why do some of the experts cited believe this attitude shift is important?
3. What do we stand to lose if we do not change our attitude toward aging?
4. What potential benefits might arise from this attitude shift?

Pause and Reflect

1. Why is global aging being referred to as the "transcendent" economic and political issue of the twenty-first century?

2. What are the main areas of formal and informal support available to the elderly?

3. What impact does taking care of an elderly person have on the caregiver?

4. What has been the major trend in living arrangements for the elderly in the past 20 years?

5. What are the main differences between the medical model of health care and the health promotion model?

6. How do today's seniors differ from seniors of the past? Describe three impacts that you think these differences will have on Canadian families and/or communities.

▶ ▶ ▶ ## Chapter Activities

Show Your Knowledge

1. Why do some anthropologists believe that the extended adolescent period in the West results in problematic behaviour on the part of youth?

2. Identify the reasons why Sherry and Paul Lipscomb (in the Case Study on page 219) decided to let their child declare himself to be female.

3. How does the parenthood experience differ for men and women?

4. Explain the major changes that will occur in Canada's population by the year 2016.

5. What tension exists in the caregiving relationship between elderly parents and their adult children? Discuss fully.

Practise Your Thinking Skills

6. Brainstorm reasons why a couple may decide to wait longer to have children than their parents and grandparents did.

7. List and explain four factors that may influence a couple's decision regarding how many children to have.

8. Explain how and why the fertility period of women in industrialized nations has been extended.

9. How might *formal support* measures for the aged in our society be improved? Include at least five suggestions.

10. Explain the impact that a major life-cycle stage like adolescence has on all members of the family. Consider the impact on siblings, parents, grandparents and the adolescents themselves.

11. How and why does our gender identity affect the way we see ourselves and the way others see us?

Communicate Your Ideas

12. Choose one side of the following argument and create a one-paragraph personal opinion piece on the following: Drinking age laws do not control the drinking patterns and behaviour of youth.

13. Create a time capsule or collage that represents the values of the Millennial Generation.

14. Write two corresponding journal entries related to the admission of an elderly person to a nursing home. One should be from the perspective of the elderly person and the other from the perspective of the adult child admitting his or her mother or father to the home.

15. Design a brief lesson that encourages or aims to influence students to reflect upon the importance of reducing the number of children women have. Include a variety of facts and information and at least two teaching strategies that you believe will have an impact.

16. Research Federal Health Minister Allan Rock's May 2001 policy announcement on surrogacy and reproductive technologies. Select one aspect of the report to review, and prepare a short class presentation that addresses the facts and controversies associated with the aspect chosen.

Apply Your Knowledge

17. Working with a partner or small group, identify five products that you believe are marketed specifically to adolescents. What phrases, gimmicks, or subliminal messages are used to get the attention (and money) of teens. Locate copies of advertisements for the products you selected and use these in your report to the class.

18. Interview 10 teenagers from your school, asking what factor(s) has the most important influence on the way they live their lives. Once you have finished recording the answers, organize them in a chart under the headings Anthropological Factors, Psychological Factors, and Sociological Factors. Which type of factor seems to be the most common influence on the teens you spoke with?

19. Identify five Web sites that target a service to the elderly or that have the elderly as their primary demographic market. Summarize the contents of each Web site in a short report. Make sure you include the URL of each Web site.

20. In a group of three or four, design an ideal home for a senior. This can be a single-family home, an apartment, an in-law suite, a granny flat, a retirement community, or a nursing home. Draw a floor plan of the home and point out any special features you think it should have.

21. Compare the living arrangements, programs, facilities and services provided by a private nursing home and a public nursing home in your area. Prepare a report of your findings, including your recommendation about which of the two facilities is the preferred option.

SUMMATIVE PROJECT

STAGE TWO: PROCESSING AND INTERPRETING YOUR RESEARCH

■ Your Assignment

The second phase in the completion of this project involves using the skills you learned in Chapters 5, 6, and 7 to evaluate your sources for bias, make sure you are using your sources ethically, and develop a specific thesis for your project. This phase gives you the chance to ensure that you are using quality research materials and that you have a thesis that is manageable.

■ The Three Steps

In Unit 2 you were introduced to three skills and given an opportunity to practise them. Now you are going to put each of those skills into action by approaching them as a series of steps.

1. *Evaluating sources for bias*—Because information containing bias can distort the focus of your research and change the direction your essay or report takes, it is very important to be able to identify any bias present in the sources you use. This step is important no matter if you are writing a research paper or conducting a survey or participant observation.

Review the Skill Builder on page 158 and follow the steps to assess the sources you have accumulated thus far for your project. You may find that some of your sources are unacceptable and must be replaced through additional research. Or, you may come to the conclusion that you need additional sources in order to balance the views in the materials you already have.

The work you submit for assessment must include the following:
- a list of five of your strongest sources (make sure the five sources include different types of reference materials, e.g., journal articles, newspaper articles, books, encyclopaedias, or Internet Web pages, etc.).
- a paragraph for each source that answers the following questions: What is the background of your sources (i.e. when was it created, is it a first-hand account, who is the intended audience)? Does the information contain any emotionally charged words and phrases, or is it factual and reasoned? Give examples. Are sufficient facts used to support any opinions offered, and have any important facts have been left out? Explain. What is each author's background and qualifications? Have the author's opinions been carefully documented, and if the author's views are different from those of other sources, why this is so?

2. *Using sources ethically*—After you have evaluated your sources for bias, ensure that you are using your sources ethically. To do this, check that all information used in your project that is taken from another source is cited properly. No matter what type of project you are complet-

ing, proper citation will require you to know the author's name; the date of the work; the title of the article or work; the journal, newspaper, magazine, or book name in which the work was published; the name of the publishing company and the city of publication; and the page number where you found the information. Review the Skill Builder on page 185 for more detail on this process.

Remember that there are some stylistic differences when you are completing a psychology, sociology, or anthropology project. Make sure you double check with your instructor to ensure you are adhering to the appropriate guideline.

The work you submit for assessment must include the following:
- five of your best sources to date in proper bibliographic format. Make sure you identify whether you are reporting your information in APA, ASA, or AAA format.

3. *Narrowing Your Focus/Developing a Thesis*—The final skill in this unit requires you to narrow the focus of your research and develop a specific thesis. In order to do this, you have to evaluate your hypothesis in light of your research findings. You may want to review the Skill Builder on page 216 before you begin. If you determine you have enough proof to support your original hypothesis, craft your thesis accordingly. If not, you may have to amend your working thesis. Remember to keep your thesis clear and simple; your audience must be able to understand your argument.

You will use your thesis to help organize your project. Do this by separating your findings into separate sections and placing the information that most strongly supports your thesis at the beginning of your research paper, or survey or observation Introduction. Make sure you weed out any information that does not clearly support your argument.

The work you submit for assessment must include the following:
- a clear, concise thesis statement
- an organized outline of your project, which fits research into specific sections. You should include enough information in your outline that your teacher can tell whether or not your thesis can be properly "proven."

■ Taking Your Project Through Stage Two

What you do at this stage of your project will differ slightly depending on whether you are completing a research paper, survey, or field observation, instructions for each are outlined below. Remember that you will be submitting written evidence of your mastery of this stage of the project. Make sure you follow the instructions carefully.

The Research Paper

At the conclusion of this stage of the summative project you will be handing in two items to be marked: i) your research notes, and ii) a rough outline of your paper.

i) Refer to page 366 of the Skills Appendix for specific information about creating research notes. It is important for you to know now, however, that you will be handing in all of your research notes to your teacher, as opposed to just the information you think will support your research proposal. This will allow your teacher to see the depth and breadth of your research to date. Remember that you must include full source information with all of your research notes.

ii) You will use your research notes to generate a detailed outline of your paper a couple of pages in length. This outline will actually help you assess where you are going and how much more research you need to do. At the top of the first page, state your thesis, then group your research notes according to topic and jot your findings under specific topic headings in the order they will appear in your finished paper. Wherever it is necessary, break the topic headings down into sub-topics and fill in the points you indent to make under each. This will allow your teacher to see whether or not your paper is starting to take shape.

The Survey

At the conclusion of this stage of the summative project you will be handing in two items to be marked: i) your research notes, and ii) a list of your survey questions.

i) Refer to page 366 of the Skills Appendix for specific information about creating research notes. Your research notes will demonstrate that you have located and read related, published material on the topic of your survey.

ii) Your choice of questions for your survey is very important. You will want to include at least 20 questions, avoiding leading questions and other biases. Review page 373 of the Skills Appendix for specific information about creating a survey. Make sure you include the questions in what you consider to be finished form so that your teacher can check spelling and grammar before you type up the final survey. As well, indicate how many people you intend to survey: their ages, genders, or any other relevant information you will be using to analyze your data.

Finally, administer the survey according to the parameters you set for it. The data you acquire through your survey will be analysed and presented in the third stage of the Summative Project.

Field Observation

At the conclusion of this stage of the summative project you will be handing in two items to be marked: i) your research notes, and ii) the raw data you have collected for field research.

i) Refer to page 366 of the Skills Appendix for specific information about creating research notes. The research notes you compile will demonstrate that you have located and read other field research conducted on your topic.

ii) You will also be submitting the raw data collected during your field research. Review the skill "Designing a Field Observation" on page 379 of the Skills Appendix. As the skill explains, you must create record sheets before beginning your field research. Your raw data will be recorded on these sheets. Make sure you hand in all record sheets, even those that you do not think you will use in your final report. Again, your instructor needs to see that you attempted a detailed field observation, even if some aspects of your research went awry.

Conduct the field observation according to the parameters you set for it, and accurately record the data you obtain on the record sheets.

■ Communicating What You Learned

Your teacher may ask you to share with the class some aspect of the work you completed during this stage of the project. If so, choose from one of the two suggestions below.

Visual Organizer

Create an organizer in which you list the sources you've found to date. Categorize your sources as *useful* or *not useful* depending on how unbiased and reliable the information is and how qualified the author is. For each source you will need to give a reason(s) to explain why you have categorized each source. Conclude by choosing your best and worst source for a class organizer on sources.

Mind Map

Review "Using a Mind Map to Narrow a Research Focus" on page 369 of the Skills Appendix. Create your own mind map to show how your research or data collection has helped you to narrow your inquiry from your original hypothesis to your specific thesis. You may present your mind map on the board, on chart paper, through a computer projection device or other medium.

■ Meeting the Criteria

In order to demonstrate that you have successfully completed the second stage of your project, must meet the following criteria

The Three Steps:
- a list of five of your strongest sources
- a paragraph for each source explaining its usefulness and qualities
- five of your best sources to date in proper bibliographic format.
- a clear, concise thesis statement
- an organized outline of your project

Taking Your project Through Stage Two:
- proper research notes
- one of either a) research paper outline b) a list of survey questions, and completed surveys, or c) raw data collected for field research

Organizer	Mind Map
• include a title	• include a title
• categorize an appropriate number of sources (this number may be dictated by your teacher)	• make sure the connections between points on the map are reasonable
• give sound reasoning for each categorization, using brief examples	• pay careful attention to overall presentation of the map so that it is neat, clear, and easy for your audience to follow
• pay careful attention to grammar, spelling and overall neatness	

UNIT 3

SOCIAL CHALLENGES

Focus Questions

1. What are the most pressing social challenges of today, particularly in the areas of health care, prejudice and discrimination, and globalization?

2. What underlying forces have caused these problems?

3. What actions can we take individually, as a community, and as a nation to meet these social challenges?

Our world presents us with social challenges that we must confront as we make our way into the future. To undertake these challenges, we first need to understand the related issues and recognize the forces that shape them. Many of Canada's Aboriginal peoples, for example, live in substandard conditions of poverty and ill-health. Average life expectancies are much shorter than those of the rest of the Canadian population—a serious discrepancy in one of the world's wealthiest countries. The forces causing these problems are complex. However, many social researchers believe that long-standing prejudice and discrimination faced by indigenous people, both here and around the world, play a large part in their social and economic situations.

In the picture above, the Blizzard Hockey team cheers after winning the Manitoba Junior Hockey Championships for the third year in a row in 2001. This Opaskwayak Cree Nation team includes non-Aboriginal players too. They draw enthusiastic fans from both the Aboriginal community and The Pas, a nearby town long troubled by cultural conflict. Bringing together native and non-native players and fans has built a bridge in a divided community. Our challenge is to find equally innovative ways to meet the social challenges we face.

■ Unit Learning Goals

Overall Expectations

- appraise the differences and similarities in the approaches taken by anthropology, psychology, and sociology to the study of social challenges pertaining to health, social injustice, and global concerns
- demonstrate an understanding of the social forces that shape such challenges

Skill Expectations

- communicate the results of their inquiries effectively
- define and correctly use the terminology of anthropology, psychology, and sociology
- compare explanations of human behaviour drawn from anthropology, psychology, and sociology, and evaluate the strengths and weaknesses of each approach
- effectively communicate the results of their inquiries, using a variety of methods and forms
- explain conclusions made as a result of an inquiry, using appropriate structure, argument, and documentation

Unit Contents

CHAPTER 8

HEALTH AND WELLNESS CHALLENGES

INTRODUCTION

People's health and well-being are affected by a multitude of factors. How we live our lives and how we cope with stress affect our ability to remain happy and healthy. The conditions within our society affect our access to high-quality health care. As the values of society shift, so do the approaches to various ethical issues related to health care.

In this chapter, we will investigate the factors that affect health and well-being, with particular emphasis on the situation in Canada.

Nova Scotia nurses on strike in June 2001. Note the pun on the name of the Nova Scotia premier, John Hamm. Striking health care workers are just one sign of a weakened Canadian health care system.

■ Learning Expectations

By the end of this chapter, you will be able to

- analyze, from the perspectives of the social sciences, social practices that lead to health-impairing behaviours
- discuss cultural, psychological, and sociological barriers to health care access
- demonstrate an understanding of the ethical issues relating to health care provision
- evaluate the impact of changing social mores on the well-being of Canadians

Focusing on the Issues

Why Canada's nurses are so angry
By Andre Picard

Nurses are among Canada's sickest workers because they toil in abysmal conditions, a new report says.

A poor work environment can be blamed, at least in part, for the ever-worsening nursing shortage, say the researchers who conducted the study. They warn that the situation is getting so bad that it is undermining the quality of patient care.

"The Canadian health-care system is facing a nursing shortage that threatens patient care," wrote Andrea Baumann, co-director of the Nursing Effectiveness, Utilization and Outcomes Research Unit at McMaster University in Hamilton, [Ontario].

"While caring for the sick and dying has always been demanding, many of the problems facing nurses today seem to arise from work environments that have grown increasingly difficult through the cutbacks and upheavals of the 1990s."

The study, commissioned by the Canadian Health Services Research Foundation, is a summary of existing research. It says

- 8.5 per cent of nurses call in sick every day, one of the highest rates of absenteeism of any profession;
- Nurses suffer more and costlier job-related injuries than traditional high-risk professions such as fire-fighting and police work;
- Nurses are facing increasing violence and abuse on the job;
- Growing workloads are adding to stress and illness rates among nurses, which may harm patients;
- Unless changes are made, the situation will grow worse, exacerbating [worsening] the nursing shortage.

Canada needs another 20 000 nurses, and the shortfall could reach 113 000 within a decade, the Canadian Nurses Association says.

"Canada's nursing shortage is at least in part due to a work environment that burns out the experienced and discourages new recruits," the researchers wrote. "But that environment can be changed."

The 30-page report, entitled *Commitment and Care: The Benefits of a Healthy Workplace for Nurses, Their Patients and the System*, makes 48 recommendations for improving the work environment.

They range from long-term financing commitments so nurses have some job security to parking spots close to the hospital for the safety of nurses on night shifts.

The researchers also recommended that the working conditions of nurses be monitored and made an integral part of hospital accreditations, that all institutions have chief nursing officers, and that the widespread [and recent] practice of casualization (hiring nurses as casual workers, rather than providing permanent full- or part-time work) be abandoned....

Dr. Baumann said that, while the timing is just a coincidence, the report could address some of the issues raised by nurses who are staging job actions in British Columbia, Nova Scotia, and Ontario.

Source: Picard, Andre. 2001. "Why Canada's nurses are so angry." *The Globe and Mail.* 20 June 2001.

THINK ABOUT IT

1. What difficulties do Canadian nurses face in their work?

2. What suggestions could you offer to make Canadian nurses' work experience less frustrating?

3. US recruiters are busy snapping up Canadian nurses to staff American hospitals. Their main draw is their rate for fully experienced nurses: about $60 (Cdn) per hour compared with Ontario's $31 per hour. How does this factor play into the Ontario government's goal of providing quality care for all Ontario residents at a reasonable cost?

4. Knowing the challenges faced by the health care system, would you feel confident about the care you would receive should you be admitted to hospital today? Support your answer with reasons.

Section 8.1   Health-Impairing Behaviours

Key Concepts

domestic-scale culture

morbidity

social practice

medical intervention model

health-promotion perspective

clinical psychology

peer pressure

curfew

peer group

Social scientists consider individual and collective health to be significant factors contributing to human well-being. They have therefore devoted much effort to exploring these aspects of our lives. As you might imagine, the three disciplines that form the focus of this book adopt different approaches to the subject.

Anthropologists have tended to focus on two aspects of human health. Much has been written about health considerations in **domestic-scale cultures**, or small kinship-based societies in which production and distribution of goods is organized on a household basis. In such tribal cultures, populations are typically very healthy. For example, James Neel (1970), after eight years of research among the peoples of the Amazon, concluded that they were "in excellent physical condition." Factors that frequently contribute to general good health in domestic-scale cultures include a high-

fibre, low-fat diet; low population density; active lifestyle; and isolation from viruses from the outside world (Bodley, 2000, p. 144). Overall good health is achieved because these people are able to avoid **morbidity**—illness or physical harm. In many ways, this situation is the opposite of mainstream Western medical practices, which achieve overall good health by developing technologically sophisticated cures for diseases.

The second major area of interest to anthropologists is the status of health among the people of modern industrialized societies. They observe that declining social cohesion and growing stress, both of which are typical of these cultures, lead to an increase in the incidence of disease. Illustrating this connection were studies such as a longitudinal study conducted between 1960 and 1990 in an isolated Pennsylvania village of about 1500 people of Italian origin. The anthropologists concluded that villagers remained noticeably free from heart attacks as long as their family and clan structure remained strong. If and when the social cohesion began to erode—and the family-centred values and ethnic identification weakened as a consequence—the rate of heart attacks rose to the national average (Bodley, 2000, p. 356). Anthropologists note that as the gap between rich and poor rises, as it has in most Western industrialized countries since the early 1990s, social cohesion breaks down and morbidity increases.

In contrast to anthropologists, sociologists examine the ways in which social structure, allocation of resources, and **social practices** (the activities and behaviours of people in groups) affect overall health. In Canada today, for example, too many people lead physically inactive lives, getting little or no cardiovascular exercise. A steady intake of fast food—a diet common among young people

Figure 8.1 How do our eating habits affect our society's level of morbidity?

who lead busy lives—leaves people with insufficient fibre and vitamins and too much fat. Tobacco use and alcohol consumption can also be major detriments to individual health. Sociologists ask, What can society do about the situation? Will allocating more money to health care have a significant impact? A 1991 study of the Canadian health care system concluded that the answer is no, because lifestyle—not inadequate health care or human biological factors—is the main contributor to premature death. The main results are shown in Figure 8.2.

Other sociological studies have concluded that we need to shift away from the **medical intervention model**, which assumes that we need not worry about our health because doctors will be able to cure us if we fall ill. This should be replaced by the **health-promotion perspective**, which assumes that we must adopt healthy lifestyles to reduce the likelihood of our becoming sick. A Winnipeg study underlined the limitations of the medical intervention model by observing that between 15 and 30 per cent of all medical services provided resulted in no measurable benefit to the patient (Chappell, 1995, Ch. 11, pp. 2–3). Sociologists believe that shifting public attitudes toward acceptance of the health-promotion perspective, and persuading people to change their lifestyles accordingly, will involve the efforts of many major social institutions. The roles of the family, schools, religious institutions, employers, and governments will be crucial.

The branch of psychology that focuses on health and wellness issues is called **clinical psychology**. Clinical psychologists hold many of the assumptions of psychology generally, believing that individual factors relating to the patient, rather than larger societal factors, can best explain why people become ill. Because clinical psychologists frequently practise their profession in association with hospitals and mental institutions, they constitute a significant aspect of the health care

Causes of Premature Deaths, Canada, 1985–1990

Factor	% of Premature Deaths
Unhealthy lifestyles	50
Environmental factors	20
Human biological factors	20
Inadequate health care	10

Source: USGAO, 1991.

Figure 8.2 According to the data in this chart, how much control do you have over the possibility of dying young?

delivery system. Together with their research colleagues, many of whom work at universities, they have built up a vast body of work on the subject of health and wellness.

The balance of this section will examine the issues surrounding three social practices and their impact on health. These issues are as follows: (1) Formula feeding versus breast-feeding of infants in developing countries; (2) Isolation and depression among the elderly; and (3) Smoking among teenagers. You will be encouraged to investigate one of these issues further.

Issue 1: Formula Feeding Versus Breast-Feeding

How we raise and teach our children is a highly significant aspect of human culture. By transmitting cultural values to our young, we ensure the stability and endurance of our society. Anthropologists therefore include child-rearing practices as an important component of their inquiry.

Domestic-scale cultures typically nurture their infants by breast-feeding. Mother's milk is an ideal food. It is easy to digest and provides all necessary nutrients as well as antibodies that help ward off disease and the development of allergies. Scientists, including anthropologists, are largely agreed that

Figure 8.3 A nursing mother, unless she expresses her milk, cannot leave her baby for a long period of time. Why might families appreciate the flexibility of bottle feeding? With one-year of parental leave, is flexibility as important as it once was?

the best food for babies in the first 12 months of their lives is their mothers' milk. In addition, strong evidence suggests that babies and mothers benefit psychologically from the breast-feeding experience (*Psychology Today*, 1996, p. 15). Nonetheless, infant-formula feeding became a popular alternative in Western industrial nations.

The first breast-milk substitute was developed and sold by Henri Nestlé, a Swiss chemist working in Germany, in 1865. At that time, mothers in every culture in the world nursed their children. The only way for companies to make money in the area of infant nutrition was to convince mothers that an alternative to breast milk was better for their babies. The companies have been remarkably successful. The sale of infant formula has become an important worldwide industry and the Nestlé Company, based in Geneva, is the leading supplier of the product. It is estimated that only 44 per cent of babies in developing countries, and an even lower percentage in developed countries, are exclusively breast-fed (Barrington-Ward, 1998, p. 64).

Baby-formula companies worked hard in the twentieth century to develop their markets around the world. Their task, at first, was a difficult one because the cultural practice of breast-feeding was well entrenched in both developed and developing countries. Companies promoted their product as a healthy substitute for mother's milk, especially in societies where mothers were likely to be undernourished.

Studies have shown, however, that formula-fed babies experience higher levels of asthma, allergies, eczema, diabetes, colitis, and childhood cancers than do breast-fed babies (Barrington-Ward, 1998, p. 66). The problem becomes more acute in developing nations. Nestlé and other companies regularly supply free infant formula to maternity hospitals in the developing world. Babies who are fed with bottles, however, are much less likely to learn how to breast-feed. Women who cannot establish breast-feeding must then purchase infant formula after leaving the hospital—an expense that will take up as much as 50 per cent of a family's income. Not surprisingly, many babies are not provided with enough formula. In addition, formula is often mixed with unclean water, so that more babies develop conditions such as diarrhea. James Grant, executive officer of the United Nations International Children's Fund (UNICEF), has stated that, every day, 3000 to 4000 infants die because they are denied access to breast milk.

In 1981, UNICEF and the World Health Organization (WHO) developed a code of practice for the worldwide sale of infant formula, and this code was adopted by the World Health Assembly (WHA) in 1981 (Bar-Yam, 1995, p. 56). The Infant Formula Action Coalition (INFACT) launched an international boycott on all Nestlé products, claiming that the company was not adhering to the UNICEF/WHO code.

Support for the boycott has not been universal. Many mothers, particularly in Western countries, argue that formula feeding is a safe and flexible method of nourishing babies. The following letter to the editor to the *Globe and Mail* is a typical reflection of this view.

> *I have two sons in their 30s. One has a PhD in political science, is executive director of the internationally respected Gendercide Watch and holds a teaching post at a research institute in Mexico City. The other is a successful lawyer in Vancouver who is about to begin a master's degree at Harvard Law School. Each has published numerous articles and books. Neither was breast-fed. What else did I do wrong?*
>
> —Jo Jones (2001, A14)

Is formula feeding, especially in developing countries, a modern and scientifically proven way to ensure that babies receive all the nutrients they need for healthy development, particularly when mothers themselves are not in robust health? This is the position taken by the formula manufacturers, who argue that many babies will simply die from malnutrition if the industry is restricted. Or is formula feeding an expensive, unnecessary, and potentially health-impairing behaviour, as INFACT and other critics contend? Further research may help you make this decision for yourself.

Issue 2: Elderly and Alone

Clinical psychologists largely accept that variables of personality allow us to predict the likelihood that a person will become ill. Individuals with neuroses, for example, are likely to react more negatively to stress than non-neurotic people. Extreme stress can lead to depression, and neurotic individuals are more likely to experience depression and require clinical treatment for it (Brown and Seigel, 1988).

Depression among the elderly is comparatively common. In one psychological report, almost 20 per cent of non-institutionalized elderly people displayed significant depressive symptoms, although only 3 per cent could be diagnosed with major depression (Pollock and Reynolds, 2000, p. 3). Between 10 and 20 per cent of widows and widowers experience significant depression in the first year after their spouse's death. As many as half the elderly in long-term care suffer from depression at some time. These reports are based on American studies, but their findings would largely apply to Canada as well.

Depression among elderly people, especially those living in institutions, is frequently caused by their perception that they have lost control over their own environment (Rodin and Langer, 1977). This loss of control tends to lead to a lowering of self-esteem. Institutional workers tend to regard residents with low self-esteem as less competent, and so take over more responsibilities for them. This leads to a cycle that repeats itself over and over again (Rodin and Langer 1980). In extreme cases, elderly people's belief that they have lost control over their own environment can lead to psychological withdrawal, mental illness, or physical deterioration (Langer and Rodin, 1976). Psychologists have concluded that removing from elders control of their own environment to a greater degree than their medical condition makes necessary is a health-impairing behaviour that can have severe consequences.

With people living longer, the number of elderly people in society is rising. In Canadian society, elders tend to live on their own, or in institutions when they can no longer care for themselves. A few elders live with their extended families, but this practice is not common. Many elders can successfully perform all the functions of everyday independent life, although some require a certain amount of support to do so. For many years this support has been provided by visiting nurses, social workers, housecleaning services, agency volunteers, friends, and relatives.

Selected Health Consequences for Elderly With Housecleaning Services and Elderly Without Housecleaning Services After Three Years, British Columbia, 1997		
Item	**With Housecleaning Services**	**Without Housecleaning Services**
Year 3 medical costs	$7 808	$11 903
In long-term care by year 3	7 %	17 %
Dead by end of year 3	15 %	22 %
Source: Picard, 2001, p. A1.		

Figure 8.4 In British Columbia, in 1994, cuts were made to services for elders who needed home support. In some jurisdictions, housecleaning services were eliminated; in others they were continued. In what ways might housecleaning services, or lack thereof, affect medical costs? The situation after three years can be seen in this table.

A significant reduction in spending on social support services in the late 1990s dramatically reduced the ability of many elderly people to live independently. Denied the support they needed to live independently, many elders' mental health deteriorated. Predictably, their physical health deteriorated as well, for example, with injuries they sustained while doing housework. The Canadian Health Economics Research Association released a study in May 2001 that illustrates the link between access to social support and elders' mental and physical health. It found that those who were denied such support required $4000 more a year on health services and were more than twice as likely to end up in costly nursing homes (Picard, 2001, p. A1). Costs have clearly shifted from support services to medical services, as can be seen in Figure 8.4.

What is the best solution for dealing with isolation and depression among the elderly? Should elders be encouraged and supported as they try to maintain their independence? Or should they be encouraged to seek institutional care, where they will have the company of others? At what point does living alone become a health-impairing behaviour for an elder? Who should decide when this point has been reached? Further research may help you make these decisions for yourself.

 Issue 3: Teenaged Smokers

Another health-impairing behaviour is smoking. Why do people start smoking in the first place? It has been widely known since the US Surgeon General's 1964 Report on Smoking and Health, and the Canadian Department of Health and Welfare's 1974 report entitled *A New Perspective on the Health of Canadians*, that smoking is addictive and harmful. Yet people continue to take up smoking, often in their early teen years.

Sociologists believe that social factors create pressures, particularly on young people, that make them receptive to smoking. They demonstrate the role of **peer pressure** (influence from the members of our peer groups) as a major factor. They cite the pressure, particularly on females, to be thin, which leads some people to use tobacco as an appetite suppressant. Indeed, young females constitute the fastest-growing category of smokers in the entire population, leading to the conclusion that the desire to be thin may be a significant factor in this issue.

Knowing that smoking is detrimental to human health, governments have adopted various strategies for changing this behaviour. For example, the federal government has enacted laws restricting who may buy

Percentage of Smokers in the Population, Canada, 1998–1999

	12 years and over	12–14 years	15–19 years	20–44 years	45–64 years	65 years and over
Both sexes	23	3	22	28	23	11
Males	24	X	19	30	25	13
Females	21	X	25	26	22	10

X: Data not available, not applicable, or confidential

Source: Statistics Canada. 2001. Catalogue no. 82M009XCB.

Figure 8.5 Compare the percentage of male and female smokers in the 15- to 19-year-old category. Why might these figures alarm sociologists?

tobacco products and where they may smoke them. Tobacco taxes have been increased, and the ability of tobacco companies to advertise and promote their products reduced. By changing these social practices, the government hopes to discourage smoking, which health professionals regard as the avoidable human behaviour most destructive to human health.

How should society deal with teenage smoking and the health-impairing consequences that result from it? Are stricter laws and penalties on the sale to and possession by teens the answer? Do anti-tobacco programs need to be specifically targeted toward either females or males, or will the same ones work for both genders? Further research may help you make these decisions for yourself.

Figure 8.6 Ottawa teenagers on a puff break in Rideau Centre. Sociologists note that movies may affect our habits when they glamorize smoking, making the habit seem sophisticated. Would the desire to look cool influence whether or not you start smoking?

COMPETING
PERSPECTIVES

Why Do Girls Smoke?

Physicians, politicians, parents, and many young people are concerned about the high rates of smoking among teenagers, particularly teenaged girls. What encourages this destructive behaviour, and what, if anything, can we do about it?

Up in Smoke: Why teen girls don't quit
By Mimi Frost and Susan Baxter

Behind the mall, on the butt-strewn steps that serve as the smoking lounge for the bargain outlets and busy food courts, four girls arrange themselves in a nearly closed circle. Jen, who has a model's figure and red ringlets that take at least 45 minutes out of her morning, sits in the centre, surrounded by friends who gather like ladies-in-waiting, laughing at her jokes, adding quips to her pronouncements. In unison, they reach for their cigarettes and commune in a cloud of nicotine....

...Smoking for two years, the 15-year-old [Jen] wears a short top, flaunting a landscape of skin and her boyfriend's key around her neck. Loaded with confidence, she probably started smoking to rebel. Her three friends may represent the other type of girl smokers, who puff to blend in. Unlike their willowy leader, they fear gaining weight if they quit, and say smoking instead of eating lunch saves money....

Sitting in a neighbourhood doughnut shop, a flimsy aluminum ashtray before her, 14-year-old Terra has been smoking for three years. A basketball and soccer player, Terra wears a black T-shirt and leather jacket. Her brown hair has been lightened a few shades. In Grade 5, she and her friends used to light butts her parents left in ashtrays: "We all thought it was cool, and if we did it we were older and more mature...we would talk like we were grown-ups and have coffee." For many kids, cigarettes serve as a rite of passage, one deep drag into the grown-up world. Vancouver pediatrician Roger Tonkin, head of the division of adolescent health at the University of British Columbia's department of pediatrics, says, "In the absence of clear social customs, young people in western society use alcohol and cigarettes as a sign of growing up." Just like Terra, girls typically take up smoking between the ages of 11 and 13. According to Dr. Michele Bloch, of the American Medical Women's Association, they want to feel adult faster than boys [do]. And the earlier they start, the more likely they are to get addicted.

Besides experiencing bad feelings about her body, Terra is starting to notice a difference between how boys and girls are treated....

Psychologist Carol Gilligan has written that girls Terra's age withdraw as they start to perceive women's still-unequal place in the world. This realization could be another factor in making girls more vulnerable to smoking, says Lorraine Greaves, a London, Ont., sociologist who studies women and smoking....

"Looking at it as simply a health problem won't work," says...Greaves, author of *Smoke Screen: Women's Smoking and Social Control.* Greaves says we need to understand the issues behind girls' smoking—such as body image, inequality, and social needs—and address them as well. As more and more girls smoke, Health Canada has finally responded by creating an initiative on women and tobacco. This year [1996], it unveils three special programs developed especially for girls—which teach media literacy, promote sport, and teach coping skills.

Source: Frost, Mimi and Susan Baxter. 1996. "Up in Smoke: Why teen girls don't quit." *Chatelaine*, vol. 69, no. 7. July 1996.

COMPETING PERSPECTIVES

Health authorities couldn't make smoking more attractive to teens even if they tried.
By Mariette Ulrich

…My dad and grandfather smoked. I watched with fascination as they rolled their own. I tried rolling them too. I also remember hating the smell of smoke and, along with my siblings, bugging Dad to quit. Our perseverance paid off: by [the] time I was in third grade, he'd kicked the habit.

As a preteen I thought smoking was cool, and even spent $1.75 on a pack of cigarettes. My friends and I crouched in the caragana bushes at the far end of the track behind the high school and we smoked the whole pack. This began and ended my career as a smoker.

The question is "Why?" The odds were against my emerging unscathed from my smoke-filled upbringing, my consumption of candy cigarettes, [and] my exposure to tobacco ads on billboards and in magazines. In those days, smoking was even associated with the Women's Movement…I gazed impassively at those Virginia Slims "babies" that had come such a long way, and had no inclination to go with them. In university I attended ballets and symphonies sponsored by DuMaurier, and felt no compulsion to dash out and buy tobacco.

I simply chose not to smoke. Based on instinct and on what I'd heard in health class, I knew it could make me sick. I didn't need the government to intervene.…

Kids know smoking isn't good for them, but some do it anyway. I'm fairly certain that Joe Camel or the local jazz festival has virtually nothing to do with it.…

I suspect they think smoking is cool because it's one of the few forbidden adult things left in the world. We give them loads of spending money and don't pester them with chores. We let them take in the most depraved movies, music and TV shows. We give them free contraception and abortion. But let them light up a cigarette in public and it makes the national news.

The ridiculous part is what the government is doing to get them to stop. Like prohibiting tobacco company sponsorship of arts, cultural and sporting events (which are mostly attended by adults). Like printing big scary words on cigarette packages, which no one heeds; or putting bigger, scarier pictures of cancer victims on packages, which will be so gross one comedy troupe has suggested kids will think they're funny and start collecting them.…

Here's a novel idea: hand out cigarettes…freely…, teach kids to smoke safely and offer to let them do it in our own homes (at least that way, we know where they are). They might just lose interest in smoking overnight.

If that fails, let's print a picture of Jean Chrétien on cigarette packages, with this message: WARNING: WHEN YOU SMOKE YOU ARE SUPPORTING THE FEDERAL GOVERNMENT.

If that doesn't turn Canadians off smoking, nothing will.

Source: Ulrich, Mariette. 2000. "Health authorities couldn't make smoking more attractive to teens even if they tried." *Alberta Report*, vol. 27, no. 13. 6 November 2000.

Questions
1. List the social practices that encourage teenagers to smoke, according to each writer.
2. List the social practices that can be introduced to discourage teenagers from smoking.
3. On what major points do the two writers agree? On what major points do they disagree?
4. What factors, in your opinion, need to be incorporated into successful anti-smoking campaigns?

CASE STUDY

Curfews

Many parents struggle to keep their teenaged children from engaging in behaviours that would be detrimental to their health and general well-being. For example, from experience they know that the social practice of staying out late can lead to trouble. As you learned in Chapter 1, sociologists believe that every role in society carries with it certain values. When it comes to staying out late, the values of teenagers and their families often conflict.

Many families opt for a simple solution by maintaining a **curfew**. This social practice sets strict limits on the time one should be home. Teenagers may feel pressured on the one hand from their parents to follow the rules, and on the other hand from their **peer group** to stay out and have fun. (Your peer group has the same age, status, and interests that you do.) Who is right? Consider the following suggested strategies for making curfews work, not from social scientists but from parents who have struggled with this issue. Keep in mind that someday you may be the parent of a teenager!

Curfew Tips for Parents

- Do set an appropriate curfew. You can always add or restrict this time when they have something special to do or you need them at home earlier.
- Do not allow them to just walk out the door and say "I'll see you at such and such a time." They still should tell you where they are going and call in if their plans change.
- Do allow some leeway on special occasions such as proms.
- Do not allow them to call half an hour before they are to be in to ask if they can sleep over at a friend's. This is generally a red flag saying "something is up."
- Do set a reasonable time for all involved. If you would like to get some sleep before midnight on a Friday evening, then set the time for 11 p.m.
- Do not get sucked into what "everyone else is allowed to do."
- [When I was young,] if I missed my curfew for some frivolous reason ("Oh, I forgot the time!" or "We just got caught up in stuff." Or the ever-popular "But Mom, my friends get to stay out later than that.") then one of two things happened. I was put on restriction (no dating, no phone calls) or, since my parents knew exactly where I was, they'd come and get me. I'd rather have them beat me than come and get me! (It never came to that either!) How mortified I would be. So I did it all the time with my own kids...even the boys!

Source: "Tips on Curfews," *Parenting of Adolescents Newsletter*, [online] <parentingteens.about.com/parenting/parentingteens/library/weekly/aa111699.htm>

Questions

1. Brainstorm a list of health-impairing behaviours staying out late could encourage. Are curfews generally a good idea for teenagers? Explain your opinion.
2. Make a three-column chart listing each suggested strategy in the first column. In the second column explain the reasoning behind each suggestion. In the third, indicate whether or not you agree with each recommended strategy, and give a reason.
3. In a small group, develop your own list of Curfew Tips for Parents designed to make curfews work without impairing your social life.

Pause and Reflect

1. Why are some groups opposed to the sale of baby formula, particularly in developing countries? How do formula manufacturers counter this argument? Present your ideas in the form of a chart. If and when you have a child, would you like it to be breast-fed? Explain.

2. What are some of the signs that an elder is depressed? What are some of the causes?

3. Why do so many teenaged girls smoke? Suggest a strategy that you think would help teenaged girls quit smoking. Why do you think your strategy could work?

4. What factors pressure students to smoke? In your school environment, how are student smokers regarded by other smokers? By non-smoking students? By non-smoking teachers?

5. Under Ontario provincial law, it is an offence for anyone to smoke on any property owned by a publicly funded school board. Do you think that this is a good law? Why or why not?

Section 8.2   Barriers to Health Care

Cost

Sociologists examining health care have a special interest in how the system is structured. How much does it cost? Who has access to it? Does it meet the collective needs of society? These are the types of questions they consider.

Health care costs in Canada are rising as the population ages and as new techniques—which are usually expensive—become available. The case study on the next page deals with the issue of whether society should ration health care by denying treatments to people who are unlikely to benefit from them. This illustrates a barrier in the provision of medical care that is becoming more and more influential: the cost barrier.

The cost of delivering health care in Canada has been increasing steadily. In 1960, it consumed 5.5 per cent of Gross Domestic Product (GDP), a figure that rose to 7.4 per cent by 1980, and to 9.4 per cent by 1990 (Boase, 1996, p. 2). In 2000, the figure was 9.1 per cent. The demand for medical services is increasing steadily in Canada, and the costs to governments of providing it are clearly rising. People of all stripes, including politicians, taxpayers, health care providers, and recipients of health care, are showing a heightened interest in discussing what services should, and should not, be paid for by the health system.

To contain costs, a variety of tests and procedures, once paid for by provincial health care plans, have already been "delisted"—or made ineligible for free coverage. Eligibility for certain services, such as home health care, has been severely curtailed. Other services require that patients pay a user fee. In Nova Scotia, for example, routine removal of ear wax has been delisted, so patients must pay for the service themselves. In Ontario, PSA tests—for detecting prostate enlargement in men—carries a $20 fee. In both British Columbia and Ontario, vaccinations for travel outside Canada are no longer covered.

The story of Alice C., in the case study on the next page, took place in a British hospital.

Key Concepts

health literacy

architectural barrier

attitude barrier

knowledge barrier

two-tier system

The dilemma faced by the granddaughter of Alice C. and the physician on emergency duty is an extreme one because it deals with a troubling ethical issue involving life and death. Nonetheless, this study raises issues that are pertinent in Canada. Should we use public funds to pay for medical procedures for elderly people whose chances of successful recovery are slight?

Can We Afford Medical Care for Alice C.?
By Norman G. Levinsky

Three minutes after she reached the emergency room, Alice C. (name changed for confidentiality) stopped breathing. The 88-year-old woman had been talking to the doctor, word by laboured word, separated by gasps for breath. She had told him that she had been well until the previous evening, when she had begun to feel short of breath. By morning, her breathlessness had become so severe that she had overcome her repugnance for medical care and allowed her granddaughter to drive her to the hospital.

The physician in the emergency room had never seen Alice before. Her granddaughter did not know whether she wanted to be resuscitated. In the absence of any advance directives, the doctor—although he believed the elderly woman was "as good as dead"—opted for vigorous treatment. Within minutes, a tube had been positioned in Alice's airway and attached to a ventilator. She was transferred to the medical intensive-care unit for further treatment.

The next morning I was making rounds with the residents assigned to the intensive-care unit. "Do you think," one resident asked me, "that it is appropriate to give such expensive treatment to an 88-year-old woman who is probably going to die anyway?"

Three unstated ideas underlie the resident's question. First, that so much of our national wealth is consumed by the cost of health care that it is appropriate to withhold potentially beneficial care to save money. Second, that such rationing should be based on age. Third, that much of the expenditure on medical care of elderly people is wasted on aggressive care of old people who are dying.

During the past 20 years, [and] for the first time, age-based rationing of health care has been proposed publicly in the USA by prominent politicians and policymakers....

These public figures were stating explicitly support for the viewpoint implicit in the medical resident's question. The opinions of philosophers and ethicists usually do not greatly influence public policy. But in this case, several ethical analyses supporting age-based rationing of health care...have provided ethical cover for policymakers who want to reduce national health care expenditures for the elderly.

Source: Levinsky, Norman G. 1998. "Can we afford medical care for Alice C.?" *Lancet*, vol. 352, no. 9143. 5 December 1998.

Questions

1. What ethical arguments could be made for and against rationing health care to the elderly?
2. Who do you think should have decided whether Alice C. would receive treatment, assuming she could not make the decision for herself? The emergency-room doctor? Her family? Medical ethicists? Religious figures? Administrators of the government health plan? Explain.

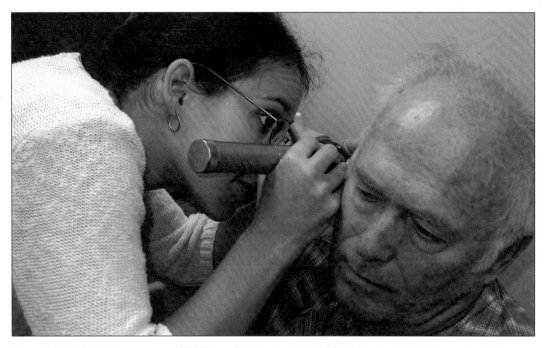

Figure 8.7 Beginning in the summer of 2001, any Ontario resident being fitted for a hearing aid by an audiologist had to pay for the service out of his or her own pocket. Hearing tests not supervised by physicians were also delisted. How do these steps raise health barriers?

 Health Literacy

Medical practitioners believe that their patients are more likely to experience good outcomes from medical procedures when they participate in a culture of **health literacy**. This means that they must have sufficient reading and comprehension skills to be able to understand what doctors tell them about diagnosis and treatment, and they need to be able to follow complicated medication regimes to bring them back to health. Lack of health literacy is a significant barrier to accessing health care.

Alejandro Jadad is a member of University of Toronto's Program in eHealth Innovation, which develops software for providing medical information. He believes that part of the problem is that many patients do not understand the medical terminology that doctors use, and that doctors do not fully comprehend their patients' lack of under-

standing (Pirsi, 2000, p. 1828). The stigma attached to low reading literacy extends to low health literacy. Fear of appearing unintelligent frequently prevents patients from either seeking medical advice or following the treatment plan. Further, a culture that accords doctors a great deal of respect discourages people from questioning a doctor's advice or suggesting that he or she may have missed an important factor.

A related factor in health literacy is the cultural insensitivity built into clinical language and literature. Particularly problematic are diagrams in medical literature, which can be too explicit for some cultures. In addition, diagrams or photographs rarely show members of minority groups. A US study showed that only 54 per cent of breast cancer documents and 40 per cent of prostate cancer information could be regarded as culturally sensitive to African-Americans (Pirsi, 2000, p. 1828). Discussions about treatments for reproductive disorders and sexually transmitted diseases can pose particular difficulties for some cultural groups. Insensitive medical practitioners might discuss or provide literature on a topic that people of particular cultures consider inappropriate for open discussion. Conflicts such as these can hinder the health literacy of patients and cause a significant barrier to access.

An Anthropologist Studies the Ties Between Social Factors and Emotional Well-Being

Anthropologist Parin Dossa, in her studies of the experiences of immigrant Iranian women in Vancouver, British Columbia, concludes that structural factors of exclusion and racism are partly to blame for the barriers these women face in achieving mental health. (For a description of Parin Dossa's study, see the Skills and Methods feature on page 10.) As Dossa says, "…the biomedical model of care…does not address structural and social issues, not to mention the fact that it is an 'illness' rather than a wellness model." When an immigrant woman says, for example, "I live with pain everyday," the DSM-IV (Diagnostic Statistical Manual) mapping of mental health would render this woman into a patient in need of therapy.

Dossa suggests that a better approach would be to investigate the experiences of immigrant women who have a broad appreciation of emotional well-being. For

Figure 8.8 Anthropologist Parin Dossa participated in this ESL class as part of the initial research for her study.

example, the participant group Dossa studied rejected the label "mental illness," preferring *Salamat-e Ruh*, an Iranian term conveying a lack of well-being. *Salamat* means "peace" and *Ruh* is translated as "soul." In the following excerpt from her study, Dossa illustrates how she gained insight from one participant's story.

Reading the Stories of Immigrant Iranian Women
By Parin Dossa

Stories/narratives have the potential to effect social change provided they form part of the larger political, social, historical, cultural, and literary landscapes of societies. The possibility of the Iranian/immigrant women becoming part of the Canadian landscape is remote as their structural and social exclusion is intense. Yet their stories must be heard if we want to write a different kind of Canadian history: a history where women from different cultural and linguistic backgrounds have an active presence. As Trinh (1989) has expressed it: "It will take a long time, but the story must be told," (119). It is in this spirit that I present stories from the group session on emotional well-being....

Simin's Narrative:

Simin is a mother of four children three of whom live in the United States, and one resides in Germany. This situation is painful for her as, in her words, "I am all alone with my husband." But she did not plan it this way. The sole reason why she left Iran was, "There is nothing left in Iran for me. My children came to Canada and so I joined them." Her children went where the jobs were—a step they were compelled to take as there was no work for them in Canada despite the fact that they are all professionals. Simin said that it was a long and difficult process for her to get landed immigrant status and she did not want to go through the same

cycle to join her children in yet another foreign country. This is because, as Thobani (2000) has shown, women's applications are processed through the family class of dependency compared with the independent class allocated to men. Women's secondary status translates into a slower and more arduous process; hence Simin's reluctance to go through this process a second time.

A second factor at work is the market economic model. Rooted in colonial capitalism, this model shortchanges racialized minorities, people in the non-western world, and, most severely, the women (Harrison 1997, Tinker 1997). Hierarchical structuring of labour compounds this situation: the market economic model requires the labour of younger and educated individuals; aging women, especially racialized women, fall by the wayside (Dossa 1999). Simin explained that her separation from the children would not be so painful if she was gainfully occupied. She desires the opportunity to learn English and work in her area of expertise, [as] a hairdresser, and beyond that [as] an advocate of women's rights. But none of these are within her reach and it is this void— "when I get up in the morning, I have nothing to look forward to"—that she identifies as the source of disruption of *Salamat-e Ruh*. It is at this juncture that she tells her story of what work meant to her in Iran and how lack of meaningful work is undermining her sense of well-being.

To being with, Simin presents herself as a very active woman.

I was the executive director of a hairdressing salon and beauty salon. I was called upon to act as an examiner of hairdressing graduates. As the director of [a] women's association, I sat in the parliament. My work made it necessary for me to travel. I was very, very busy. I have a lot of

CASE STUDY

pictures of myself. My sister, she stayed at home and cooked ghormeh sabji [Iranian delicacy].

I very much regret that I do not know English. I could have continued to work as a hairdresser. I can tell what color of hair would be suitable for each person and what style would suit her best.

Now I feel [like] nobody. My life is useless. I feel tired.

At this point, we may make one observation: Simin gives a relatively longer account of her life accomplishments compared with her "symptoms" of a disrupted state of well-being. This is because Simin's interest in telling her story is to emphasize one point: the importance of being meaningfully occupied....

In Canada, "there is nothing for me to do," she explained. It is at this fundamental level—the non-existence of opportunities to set and reach goals—that she grounds her state of *Salamat-e Ruh.*

Bibliography

Dossa, P. 1999. (Re)imagining Aging Lives: Ethnographic Narratives of Muslim Women in Diaspora. *Journal of Cross-Cultural Gerontology* 14:245-272.

Harrison, F. 1997. The Gendered Politics and Violence of Structural Adjustment. In *Situated Lives: Gender and Culture in Everyday Life,* L. Lamphere et al. Ed. New York: Routledge, 451-468.

Thobani, S. 2000. Sponsoring Immigrant Women's Inequalities. *Canadian Woman Studies:* 19(3):11-17.

Tinker, I. 1997. *Street Foods: Urban Food and Employment in Developing Countries.* Oxford: Oxford University Press.

Trinh T.M. 1989. *Woman Native Other.* Bloomington: Indiana University Press.

Source: Dossa, Parin. "Narrative Mediation of Conventional and New Paradigms of 'Mental Health': Reading the Stories of Immigrant Iranian Women." November 2001. (Forthcoming in the *Medical Anthropology Quarterly: International Journal for the Analysis of Health.*)

Questions

1. Paraphrase Simin's narrative. Describe her general frame of mind. What would you say are the primary causes of Simin's feelings?
2. What does Dossa mean when she says there is little chance that Iranian-immigrant women will become part of the "Canadian landscape"? What reason does she give to support this statement?
3. What is the anthropologist's goal in presenting the stories of immigrant Iranian women?
4. The participants in Dossa's study rejected the label of "mental illness," used by medical practitioners, and the form of treatment the Canadian medical system appeared to offer (that is, the quick fix of anti-depressants). How might this be a barrier to health care? On the other hand, as Dossa pointed out, the medical system does not recognize the larger social realities faced by immigrant women. How might this also be a barrier to health care?

Facilities for People with Disabilities

People with disabilities routinely experience structural and cultural barriers to health care access that are normally not encountered by the rest of the population. Dr. Margaret Nosek, director of the Center for Research on Women with Disabilities (CROWD) at Baylor College, in Texas, says, "Women with disabilities face architectural, attitude, and knowledge barriers" ("Women with disabilities," 1999, p. 14.) She refers to **architectural barriers**, or structural problems. For example, women with physical disabilities have difficulty getting onto regular examination tables, while mammograms are very difficult for women who cannot stand up. Specialized equipment is needed to treat such people.

Then there are the cultural barriers. According to Dr. Nosek, the common misconception that women with physical disabilities have no sexual or reproductive health needs constitutes an **attitude barrier**. Physicians who share this misconception may skip pelvic examinations, thereby failing to detect diseases until they manifest themselves with obvious symptoms.

The biggest barrier to full medical treatment of people with disabilities, Dr. Nosek believes, is both structural and cultural. The **knowledge barrier** is a lack of knowledge about how a disability affects normal health needs. Little research has been done, for example, on how being confined to a wheelchair affects the heart, or on how pregnancy affects women with spinal cord disorders. The lack of research in these areas means that medical students learn little about these matters, creating a systemic barrier to adequate health care for the people with disabilities.

 ## Income

Sociologists interpret income distribution as a structural factor. People who have significantly lower incomes than others in society

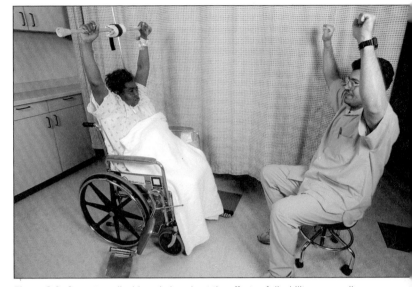

Figure 8.9 Current medical knowledge about the effects of disability on overall health is limited. In what ways might that knowledge deficiency prove to be a health barrier?

www.hc-sc.gc.ca

This is Health Canada Online, a great site for finding out about health issues related to First Nations and Inuit communities as well as other groups such as seniors, immigrants, and people with disabilities. You can find out about special initiatives undertaken to help these people overcome health barriers. At the home page, follow these links: English > Just For You. Then click on the name of whatever group you're investigating.

If the Web address does not connect you with the site, search the Web using the search string "Health Canada."

tend to benefit less from society's resources such as education and health care services. Lack of income represents a significant barrier to health care.

According to a 1991 study by the Canadian Institute for Advanced Research, it is not the absolute wealth of individuals that is the determinant, but their relative wealth. People in the top quintile are healthier than those in the second quintile, even though the latter have adequate incomes to sustain good health. The study concluded that the more money a person earns in the 12 years before retirement, the longer that person is likely to live. People with incomes in the bottom 5 per cent in the years before retirement are twice as likely to die before age 70 than those with incomes in the top 5 per cent. All told, people with high incomes experience 12 additional years of good health than do people with low incomes (Canadian Institute for Advanced Research, 1991).

These figures may be even further exaggerated in the United States, where no universal government health programs exist (other than those for the elderly) and an estimated 15 per cent of the population is unable to afford health insurance of any kind (Boase, 1996, p. 7). A racial factor is also involved in the American example, because a disproportionate number of low-income families are African-American. Nonetheless, even among Americans 65 years of age and over (and therefore covered by Medicare), low-income and minority people face additional barriers to care. The Health Care Financing Administration concluded in 1995 that race and socio-economic status were barriers to accessing important medical services ("Medicare doesn't...," 1995, p. 14). Recent statistics in Canada confirm a race bias in Canadian society.

From the foregoing, we can conclude that even in a country like Canada, which offers universal government-funded health care, income distribution is a structural factor that has an influence on people's health. In the United States, without Canada's broad-based scheme, unequal income distribution has an even greater effect on the population's overall health.

Two-Tier System

Under an ideal one-tier health care system, all citizens of a country enjoy equal access to free health care. Since the 1960s, all Canadians have been covered by a universal standard of health care supplied by the provincial and territorial governments and co-funded by the federal government. Although health is a provincial jurisdiction, the federal government contributes funds to provinces to pay for health care, and thereby has some power to ensure a universal standard of care across the country. Under the federal Canada Health Act (1984), physicians are not currently allowed to charge extra fees to patients for services delivered under provincial health plans. Hospitals are not allowed to charge user fees for use of public facilities. The taxation system pays for the health services of all Canadians. The US version of health care, in contrast, is a **two-tier system**. Only the elderly and the very poor have access to public health coverage. Those who can afford to do so purchase their own health care coverage, or their employers purchase it for them. Between the well-off and the poor is a middle-income group that does not have any health care coverage whatsoever.

As the Canadian population ages and new, expensive medical technologies develop, the financial pressures on the Canadian health care system are bound to increase. In Ontario, for example, spending on health consumed 44 per cent of the provincial government's program spending in 2001–02. The costs of removing some of the barriers to access discussed earlier in this section might prove even more expensive. As a result, there has been increasing discussion among the provinces about the possibility of introducing a two-tier system. Under such a system, Canadians who chose to do so would be permitted to purchase additional medical services, in public or private facilities, beyond those provided to everyone else by the government health care plan. In the United Kingdom, a two-tier system has operated for decades, and some Canadians believe that this approach represents a future direction for Canada.

Many Canadians believe that a two-tier system would constitute a significant access barrier. They point, hypothetically, to a low-income individual who might have to wait three months for a magnetic resonance imaging (MRI) scan, while a high-income individual might be able to purchase the service in a public hospital within 24 hours. Those who support the introduction of some private health care argue that allowing patients to purchase services privately would reduce overall public health care costs in addition to providing a new revenue stream for underfunded facilities.

Canadians tend to feel very strongly about the issue of publicly versus privately funded health care. Consider the following opinions:

- "Since they chopped music programs at the school, I'm paying for private lessons for my kids and if I could get [medical] test results faster, I'd be willing to pay for them." (Bob Smye, 45, financial consultant, Halifax, Nova Scotia.)
- "It would be a horror show in the making. [Our current health care system] is one of the things that made Canada great." (Al Yarr, 66, retired university physical education instructor) (Wickens et al., 2000, p. 26)

Would a two-tier system constitute another barrier to health care access? Or is it a sensible way of reducing public health costs

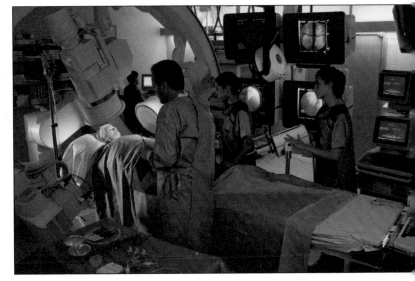

Figure 8.10 Medical personel prepare a patient for an MRI scan to help determine the extent of an illness and appropriate treatment. In what way might two-tier health care, in which patients may purchase immediate diagnosis and treatment, constitute a health barrier for some Canadians?

and allowing individuals to purchase medical services? This issue is likely to spark more public discussion as governments struggle to contain their health costs as the population ages. Unfortunately, issues concerning the structure of the health care system are so complex that they may draw attention away from other barriers.

Pause and Reflect

1. What are some of the cultural issues that contribute to low health literacy? Propose solutions for three problems related to health literacy.

2. Describe the three categories of barriers facing people with disabilities. In chart format, rate these barriers from least to most problematic for patients, from simplest to most complex, and from least to most expensive to solve.

3. List the various access barriers to health care in Canada. Summarize each in one sentence. Which category of access barrier do you think is the most significant in Canada? Why?

4. In Chapter 3, you learned that, in Canada, certain groups are more likely than others to live in poverty. From what you have read in this section, how will poverty affect these groups' access to health care, both now and in the future?

5. In your own words, identify the major characteristics of (a) a one-tier and (b) a two-tier system of health care delivery. Which do you think makes most sense in Canadian society? Why?

Section 8.3   Ethical Health Care Provision

Key Concepts

ethical issue

oncologist

cloning

embryo

ethicist

informed consent

Nuremberg Code

stem cell

in vitro fertilization

All medical practitioners, from time to time, face **ethical issues**, dilemmas involving important moral principles. Wrestling with ethical issues involves trying to determine which of a number of courses of action is most appropriate. You have already read about one ethical issue earlier in this chapter: should we provide extensive and expensive treatments to seriously ill elderly people who will likely die anyway? Other ethical issues abound in medicine.

This section of the chapter will examine the ethical issues surrounding three aspects of modern medicine: (1) the blood supply, (2) organ harvesting, and (3) medical research.

Issue 1: The Blood Supply

For most of the twentieth century, the Canadian Red Cross (CRC) was the agency

Blood products and their uses

Blood Product	Recipients
Red blood cells	• accident victims • surgical patients • people with anemia
Platelets	• leukemia patients • cancer patients
Plasma	• patients suffering from burns or shock
Cryoprecipitate	• people with hemophilia • people with other blood disorders

Source: Canadian Blood Services Web site. [Online]. Available <http://www.bloodservices.ca> 13 January 2002.

Figure 8.11 Many patients receive blood or blood products as a crucial step in their treatment, as you can see in this table. Why should we be concerned about the safety of these products?

responsible for collecting, storing, and distributing blood products. Its operations were largely admired until the mid-1980s, when more than 1200 Canadians contracted human immunodeficiency virus (HIV) from blood or blood products supplied by the agency. This infection can lead to acquired immune deficiency syndrome (AIDS), which is terminal. In addition, some blood recipients were infected with hepatitis C, an infection which, if left untreated, can destroy the liver, causing death.

Why hadn't the CRC been able to ensure the safety of the blood supply? Many of the problems related to the simplicity of the CRC's donor-screening procedures. The CRC had inadvertently allowed people who did not know they were infected to continue as donors, thereby infecting the people who received their blood. It should be noted that the CRC was a registered charitable organization and was therefore subject to restrictions on the amount it could spend on administrative operations, as opposed to on helping the needy. Conducting more comprehensive screenings would have drastically increased the CRC's administrative costs. In addition, the dangers posed by HIV were not fully understood at this time.

What was the solution? The CRC was unwilling to continue in the role of blood provider when it became obvious that greater government oversight was to be implemented (Kondro, 1996b, p. 816). A new agency had to be created to take over the CRC's role in the Canadian blood supply system. Should it be a private, for-profit agency? Should it be an arm of the federal or provincial governments? Or should it be an independent agency, created by, and responsible to, governments?

The prospect of a for-profit company controlling such a vital component of the medical system was not seriously pursued, as it was felt to be contrary to the general principles of the Canadian medical system. One has to consider, though, whether it is truly unethical for a private company to profit from providing a vital medical product. Pharmaceutical companies, for example, certainly make a profit this way.

Similarly, there was little serious consideration of the possibility of a direct government takeover of the service. Perhaps fears of government bureaucracy, whether well-founded or not, were enough to scare the medical community away from this sort of solution. One has to consider, though, whether it is truly unethical for governments to be the providers of the blood supply. They already fund around 72 per cent of all spending on health care in the nation (Boase, 1996, p. 2), so why should they be excluded from providing this service?

In the end, a new agency, funded by the federal and provincial governments but independent of them, took over the blood supply functions of the CRC. On 1 September 1998, Canadian Blood Services (CBS) assumed control of the CRC's blood assets, including 17 regional transfusion centres, a national laboratory, and a distribution network.

Was an independent but government-funded agency the best ethical choice available for assuring a reliable blood supply? Was it a more ethical solution than the other choices available? Further research may help you make these decisions for yourself.

 ## Issue 2: Organ Harvesting

Perhaps you are familiar with the consent form that accompanies drivers' licences. In Ontario, these forms are part of the Multiple Organ Retrieval and Exchange (MORE) program. If you sign the consent card, you authorize doctors to harvest any tissues or

Figure 8.12 Blood donations are now handled by the independent but government-funded Canadian Blood Services. Why is it so important that the organization that handles blood donations be accountable to the public yet independent of government?

organs, or those specified by you, upon your death. In practice, however, your wishes may not be followed. Most doctors will not harvest organs—despite a signed donor card—if the family objects to the procedure. In 1999, only 617 transplant procedures were carried out in Ontario, at a time when 1720 Ontarians were waiting for organs. About 100 of those people died (Priest, 2000, p. A1).

The Issues

We must consider two issues here: one practical and the other ethical. The practical issue relates to grieving family members and how we define death. The organs most likely to be used in transplants would come from relatively young, healthy people who die suddenly, usually because of an accident. Many young accident victims have intact bodies even though their brains have ceased functioning. (Doctors normally use the absence of brainwaves as evidence of death.) Family members of such an accident victim are usually not prepared to cope with the sudden loss of this

Figure 8.13 Multi-transplant survivor Noah Kasper at home in Victoria, B.C., in December 2001. Many others awaiting organ donations will die or suffer for years waiting for a match. How can we fix this situation?

person whom they love. They are usually not willing or able to make rational decisions about harvesting their loved one's organs, especially if the person's heart is still beating. We are not a species that gives up hope easily.

Dr. John Yun, a British Columbia **oncologist**, a doctor who treats cancer patients, says, "If you ask why people are reluctant to donate organs, they will tell you that intuitively they feel if Mom's heart is still beating and she's still breathing, she's still alive" (Parker, 2001, p. 17).

Finding a New System

The ethical issue affecting the ability of doctors to harvest organs deals with who owns the organs in question. As a living person, we clearly own all the organs and tissues in our bodies, but as a brain-dead accident victim, is

this still the case? Spain's 1979 organ donation law is regarded by many as the way to go. It operates on the principle of presumed consent and that, after death, organs and tissues do not belong to any one person. Unless there is evidence that a person specifically resisted organ donation, Spain's donation law requires doctors to pass details on to the Spanish central registry for organ donation and make arrangements for harvesting (Parker, 2001, p. 17). A registry such as this drastically raises the numbers of available organs because only people strongly opposed to organ donation—such as people whose religious beliefs condemn it—would go to the trouble of ensuring that their beliefs are well known.

In August 2000, a 77-page report on organ donation was delivered to the Ontario government, and new legislation adopting the report's major recommendations was expected by early 2002. A new agency, the Trillium Gift of Life (TGL), is to be created to co-ordinate and oversee all donations. Once in place, the law would require all Ontario doctors to assume that all suitable organs are available for transplant, and to report the availability of organs to TGL. Hospitals would be required to maintain trained counsellors to deal with families and assist them in their grieving.

We should consider what the situation might be like under the new system. Is it, for example, ethical to forcibly take the kidneys from a brain-dead child whose parents are strongly opposed to this action? Whose interests are paramount: those of the family of the accident victim or those of the recipient?

In many countries without this system, the demand for organ donations exceeds the supply. This fact has led some jurisdictions to believe that incentives are necessary. In 1999, Pennsylvania passed a law providing for payment of $300 toward the funeral expenses of organ donors (Krauthammer, 1999, p. 100). Is this ethical? Read about one opinion on this question in the case study on the following page.

Yes, let's pay for organs
By Charles Krauthammer

...[T]he real objection to the Pennsylvania program is this: it crosses a fateful ethical line regarding human beings and their parts. Until now we have upheld the principle that one must not pay for human organs because doing so turns the human body—and human life—into a commodity. Violating this principle, it is said, puts us on the slippery slope to establishing a market for body parts. Auto parts, yes. Body parts, no. Start by paying people for their dead parents' kidneys, and soon we'll be paying people for the spare kidneys of the living.

Well, what's wrong with that? the libertarians ask. [Libertarians advocate absolute freedom of expression and action.] Why should a destitute person not be allowed to give away a kidney that he may never need so he can live a better life? Why can't a struggling mother give a kidney so her kids can go to college?

The answer is that little thing called human dignity. According to the libertarians' markets-for-everything logic, a poor mother ought equally to be allowed to sell herself into slavery—or any other kind of degradation—to send her kids through college. Our society, however, draws a line and says no. We have a free society, but freedom stops at the point where you violate the integrity of the self (which is why prostitution is illegal [in the United States]).

We cannot allow live kidneys to be sold at market. It would produce a society in which the lower orders are literally cut up to serve as spare parts for the upper. No decent society can permit that.

But kidneys from the dead are another matter entirely. There is a distinction between strip-mining a live person and strip-mining a dead one. To be crude about it, whereas a person is not a commodity, a dead body can be. Yes, it is treated with respect (which is why humans bury their dead). But it is not inviolable. It does not warrant the same reverence as that accorded a living soul.

The Pennsylvania program is not justified, it is too timid. It seeks clean hands by paying third parties—the funeral homes—rather than giving cash directly to the relatives. Why not pay the sum directly? And why not pay $3000 instead of $300? That might even address the rich/poor concern: after all $3000 is real money, even for bankers and lawyers.

Source: Krauthammer, Charles. 1999. "Yes, let's pay for organs." *Time*, vol. 153, no. 19. 17 May 1999.

Questions
1. What justification does the writer give for his opinion that society should pay for organs from the dead but not the living?
2. Do you agree or disagree with the opinion expressed in the above extract that relatives should be paid for the organs of their loved ones? Explain.

Issue 3: Medical Research

American scientists at a private company have stunned the world's medical community by cloning [reproducing asexually] a human embryo for the first time, a move they say holds hope of ridding our species of illness and pain.

Massachusetts-based Advanced Cell Technology, Inc. said it had created the clones in order to produce a store of lifesaving embryonic stem cells, not cloned humans. At present, though, few rules prohibit other scientists from using the technique as they wish. (Mitchell, 2001, p. A1)

Media currently contain many reports about developments like the one described, holding out hope that previously incurable conditions may be treated and reversed. Most people would agree that the ability to reverse spinal cord damage, Alzheimer's, Parkinson's disease, cancer, and a host of other illnesses, would be of enormous benefit to humanity.

Yet there are many ethical dilemmas associated with this research. Much debate has arisen within the medical profession, for example, about whether scientists and doctors have the right to manipulate human cells in this way, no matter how beneficial the potential outcome. Is it ethical to clone **embryos**—fertilized human eggs—for research and medical treatments? Should scientists develop techniques that could be used unethically by others? For example, although ACT Inc. has stated it will not clone humans, nothing is stopping other scientists from using ACT's research to do so. Medical **ethicists**, people who research and write about which medical techniques should be morally permissible, believe that it is important not to let the promise of amazing cures override our responsibility to ensure that our techniques are humane and ethical. So far, stem cell research is a largely unregulated field in Canada, but the federal government announced in December 2001 that it intended to introduce appropriate legislation in 2002 (McCarthy, 2001, p. A15).

Nuremberg Code

Although medical ethics have always been important, when evidence of Nazi experiments on inmates of concentration camps became public at the end of World War II, interest and concern about this matter was heightened. Between December 1946 and August 1947, 23 Nazi doctors and medical researchers were tried in Nuremberg, Germany, for performing cruel and inhumane experiments on prisoners. An estimated 100 000 people died horrible deaths in the concentration camps, as doctors researched such things as how long people could survive while immersed in cold water, how long they could survive while drinking only sea water, and at what point the lungs burst because of atmospheric pressures (Moreno, 1997, p. 32). These experiments were conducted supposedly to assist in developing better survival procedures for Nazi pilots whose planes were shot down. Such experiments were clearly unethical, primarily because the experiments required that the subjects be killed, but also because they were inhumane and were conducted without the **informed consent** of their subjects. Informed consent means that the subject of a medical procedure or experiment must be able to understand the risks involved and to give permission for it to proceed, knowing these risks.

When the three-judge panel delivered its verdict at Nuremberg, it decided to do more than simply punish the guilty. (Seven people were executed, and eight were sentenced to long prison terms.) The panel created what is now known as the **Nuremberg Code**, an ethical guideline for researchers. "The voluntary consent of the human subject is absolutely essential. This means that the person involved should...be so situated as to be able to exercise free power of choice, without the element of force, deceit, duress, over-reaching, or any other ulterior form of constraint or coercion" (Moreno, 1997, p. 33). Although the Code had no legal authority, it was a powerful statement to future courts dealing with similar cases.

It would be nice to imagine that only obviously warped regimes such as that of the Nazis ever conducted unethical experiments. This is not the case. It has become clear, for example, that between the 1930s and the early 1970s the US Public Health Service engaged in a longitudinal study of more than 400 African-American men in Macon

County, Alabama, who were suffering from syphilis. The subjects were not told that they had the disease; nor were they offered any kind of treatment, even after the introduction of penicillin as an excellent treatment in 1943 (Moreno, 1997, p. 34).

In another example—this one Canadian—medical personnel connected with Montreal's McGill University administered LSD and electroconvulsive treatment (ECT) on 23 female prisoners at the Kingston Prison for Women in the 1960s. Not only were the prisoners not informed of the possible effects of these treatments, a recent report has concluded that the treatments were not administered for the benefit of the patients, but to render them easy to handle.

Such experiments are no longer permissible in Canada. The law and established medical ethics now require that physicians obtain informed consent from patients before testing or treating them.

Figure 8.14 A medical administrator speaks with an inmate test subject at a Pennsylvanian prison in 1966. By 1969 85 per cent of new drugs were tested on inmates. How can we prevent such unethical research from taking place again?

Stem Cell Research

Perhaps the most controversial aspect of current medical research relates to the use of **stem cells**. These are cells from which stem all the "branches" of an organism. This means that they have the potential to become any tissue or structure of an organism (Kavanaugh, 2000, p. 24). Researchers hope that stem cells can eventually be used to cure diseases such as diabetes or Parkinson's disease by growing new cells to replace damaged ones. For example, stem cells might one day be used to grow new hearts, or they might be injected into damaged spinal cords so that paraplegics might one day walk again.

Stem cell research is particularly controversial because it opens up the debate about what constitutes a live human. For although stem cells can be found in umbilical cords and in the bone marrow of adults, fresh stem cells—those found in embryos—are more potent. In the case of stem cell research, the embryos used are a few hours old and consist of a few hundred cells. Embryos for research can come from several sources. They can be cloned, as we have seen. More commonly, at this point, they are extra embryos created during **in vitro fertilization**.

In vitro fertilization of human eggs has become a relatively common procedure since it was successfully pioneered in the 1980s. As a treatment for infertility, eggs and sperm are donated by the potential parents and fertilized in a petri dish. Because in vitro fertilization can be difficult, it is normal to harvest and fertilize a number of eggs. Any embryos not required for implantation in the mother's womb are normally destroyed or stored. Stem cell researchers have asked why they should not use stem cells from these "surplus" embryos in an attempt to develop cures for diseases.

Is it ethical to harvest stem cells from these embryos for experimentation, a process that destroys the embryo? The answer depends partly on our definition of human

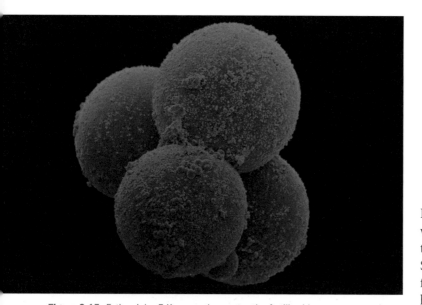

Figure 8.15 Father John F. Kavanaugh equates the fertilized human egg, as shown above, with a convicted murderer awaiting execution. What is your opinion about this comparison?

life. Many religious and political leaders have spoken out against this practice. They regard it as unethical to create human life and later destroy it, no matter how beneficial the eventual results might be. Other leaders, including the staunch American anti-abortion activist Senator Orrin Hatch, disagree. Their opinions tend to favour the potential benefits of the research, research that could improve and lengthen human lives.

Father John F. Kavanaugh, S.J., disagrees with this point of view. He argues by equating fertilized human eggs with human beings:

> ...Rather than destroy [embryos] or throw them into the garbage, why not use them for therapeutic miracles?
>
> These questions seem eminently reasonable, I suppose. But, depending on just what these embryos are, such questions are also profoundly disturbing. The point at issue here is perhaps more easily seen if we first consider another group of living beings who are destined to be "thrown away," namely criminals who have been con-

demned to death. If they are going to die anyway, why not put their bodies to some use—harvesting their hearts and lungs, collecting their corneas, liberating their livers, maybe even using their hair or skin? Perhaps we could experiment on them (administering the appropriate painkillers, of course) to help us understand the nature of various diseases.
>
> (Kavanaugh, 2000, p. 24)

Kavanaugh goes on to say that most people would be opposed to this because it denies the criminal the status of a human being. Similarly, he argues, extracting stem cells from surplus embryos denies the embryos human status and, for this reason, the procedure is unethical.

Alta Charo, a professor of law and medical ethics at the University of Wisconsin—where scientists first isolated stem cells from human embryos—takes a different point of view. In this excerpt, she addresses the issue of creating embryos specifically for the purpose of harvesting their stem cells.

> [Charo] said there could be scientific or therapeutic benefits from using stem cells from embryos that are "so-called made to order," and if this was the case, the interests of patients who might be helped by the research takes precedence over the interests of the embryos.
>
> "We must consider the interests of the patients as paramount, because the patients are sentient, they're aware, they're currently suffering," Charo said. "And I think that has to take precedence over the preservation of early forms of life that cannot be self-aware, cannot suffer, cannot be disappointed."
>
> (Zabarenko, 2001)

The debate is likely to continue. In August 2001, US president George W. Bush, normally regarded as conservative on questions of human life, published an order preventing the use of federal funds for research involving stem cells harvested from the 100 000 embryos frozen in laboratories across the United States. Nor could federal funds be used for harvesting stem cells from embryos left over after in vitro fertilization. However, the order does permit the use of existing stem cell lines taken from embryos that had already been destroyed when the order was issued. Such stem cell lines can be extended indefinitely. Many commentators saw this as an attempt to satisfy concerned parties on both sides of the issue, and many felt that Bush had successfully walked a fine ethical line on the issue ("Bush position…," 2001, p. 1).

Pause and Reflect

1. Outline the events that led Canada to create a new, independent but government-funded agency to ensure a reliable blood supply.

2. What definition of "death" do medical practitioners normally use when deciding whether human organs or tissues can be harvested? What problems arise from this definition?

3. Two values that many people hold are a belief in the value of life and a belief that the dignity of the person should be respected. How might these two values conflict in a consideration of the ethical issues related to organ donation?

4. What is the Nuremberg Code? What circumstances led to its creation?

5. Make a list of the ethical issues surrounding the issue of stem cell research. For each issue, outline two opinions based on two different perspectives.

Section 8.4   Changing Social Mores in Canada

Social cohesion is normally maintained by an elaborate system of behaviours. Sociologists classify these behaviours into a number of categories. They call customs and conventional behaviours **folkways**. These are the behaviours that a typical member of society would usually practise. If you violated a folkway—for example, if you were to go into a steak restaurant and asked to eat your dessert before your main course—you might be considered eccentric but still acceptable to society. In contrast, sociologists define **social mores** as the behaviours regarded as essential to the welfare and survival of the group. For example, behaving in a non-violent manner is considered part of Canadian social mores. If you act violently, you are not considered eccentric; you are regarded as harmful.

Social mores change over time. New experiences, rising or falling expectations, shifts in the political or economic climate, and a variety of other factors change people's attitudes and practices. It should come as no surprise to observe that Canadian folkways and social mores have both changed significantly over the last couple of generations. This section of the chapter will look at four areas in which Canadian social mores have changed, and at how these changes affect our well-being.

Key Concepts

folkway

social mores

work-related stress

burnout

 Tolerance for Violence

Many academics and social commentators are dismayed to observe a growing tolerance for depictions of violence in the media. Psychologists, in particular, worry that much media programming designed for young people provides them with poor role models. Children's exposure to media violence starts with the Saturday morning cartoons, the highlight of the week for many children. The Media Awareness Network (2001), a Canadian organization that tries to assist parents in moulding healthy television-watching habits in their children, reports the following:

- A study from Heritage Canada (a department of the federal government) found that by the time most Canadian children are 12 years old they have seen up to 12 000 violent deaths on television.
- A Canadian study at Laval University showed that children's television programs actually contained 68 per cent more violent scenes than did programs for adults.

Defenders of such programming often state that children recognize that cartoon and other media violence is fake, and that it does not cause them to act violently. Psychologists point out, however, that violence is a learned behaviour, and that early and continued exposure to it can condition children and adults to act in violent ways.

Particular concern is often directed at movies and music created for the teenage market. If young people are fed a constant diet of conflict and violence in the media material aimed at them, the argument runs, they must eventually internalize the message. This is the argument put forward by many experts attempting to explain recent examples of extreme teenage violence, such as the high school shootings in W.R. Myers High School in Taber, Alberta, and the massacre in Columbine High School in Colorado, USA. Richard Aquila, director of the American Studies Program at Ball State University in Indiana, has extensively examined the impact of media violence on people. He muses in *USA Today Magazine* about the level of violence we now find acceptable:

> *"I would compare it to raising the volume on a radio. At first it seems loud, but you get used to it. Then you turn up the music a little more and then more. We are just a few decibels from full volume right now. I am sure there are things out there that can shock people, but I couldn't say what it would be."*
>
> *("Music and movies…," 1997, p. 1)*

Figure 8.16 James Gandolfini conducts a little business in his role as a mobster in the television series *The Sopranos*. Richard Aquila believes that the insatiable desire of big entertainment businesses for increased short-term profits, regardless of the effect on their customers, has ratcheted up the willingness of media outlets to include violent content. How do violent scenes affect you?

Organized religion and the family are now less able to counter the messages of the media, and groups like Marilyn Manson have flourished. This band has reportedly experimented with a variety of drugs, the occult world, and devil worship. In spite of this, or perhaps because of it, the band regularly plays to sold-out houses of devoted fans ("Music and movies...," 1997, p. 2). Inevitably, American media influences have spilled over into Canada, and there is growing concern that they have contributed to a desensitization to, and tolerance for, violence in this country.

Many psychologists believe that desensitization to violence has a negative effect on society as a whole, by creating a climate of fear. Four out of five Canadian women feel that television contributes to violence in society, and over 35 per cent of Canadian women say that, for this reason, they avoid shows featuring violent themes (Health Canada, 2001). MediaWatch, a Canadian organization that lobbies governments and the industry on media matters, concluded that there is a paradox regarding media violence.

> Watching television may lead to the development of attitudes that portray the world as a more dangerous place than it actually is because violence is more salient and frequent on television than it is in most real-life experiences. In fact, it seems that paradoxically television may both desensitize individuals to violence and sensitize them to it. Perhaps perceiving oneself as more vulnerable to violence also serves to legitimize violent actions as a defence.
>
> (MediaWatch, 1994)

Whether media violence increases real-life violence, as many psychologists claim, or merely makes the population overly fearful of its likelihood, it effectively diminishes the well-being of Canadians. This problem is unlikely to go away, at least in the short term.

Attitudes Toward "Recreational" Drugs

A second aspect of changing mores can be seen in society's attitudes toward the use of non-medicinal drugs. Reports like those in the following *Newsweek* article are common in the media.

Kate returns to the runway

She's back, after a few weeks recuperating at a London rehab clinic, where she checked herself in last November upon admitting to "too much partying." Supermodel Kate Moss pranced down the catwalk for the first time during Fashion Week in Milan. Moss, who sported brown hair (replacing her pinkish dye job) and revealing frocks by Donatella Versace, looked healthy and fit, her days as the poster girl for the forlorn-waif look seemingly behind her. According to the British tabs, her overpartying had to do with drinking and recreational drug use, and she's been attending Narcotics Anonymous meetings since her stay at the clinic. She spent Christmas with her family in West Sussex and reportedly flew to Morocco with ex-boyfriend Tarka Cordell, a wealthy British songwriter. She celebrated her 25th birthday over the weekend—presumably with ginger ale.

(Seligmann, 1999, p. 45)

The above report is interesting for the slightly humorous way in which it reports what is a tragic story. A young and successful woman has developed a drug problem. Yet the tragedy is downplayed, and the report is presented as just another story about one of the rich and famous. One has to ask, however, if Moss's fans who read this lighthearted article about her drug use would be more likely to experiment with drugs themselves.

Not all members of society believe that conventional social mores have resulted in

Figure 8.17 Actor Robert Downey Jr. sits in court before pleading no contest to possessing cocaine in 2001. Celebrities must sometimes struggle with their substance abuse problems in public. How might increased acceptance of substance abuse among celebrities influence the public?

good social practice. For example, a growing tolerance for reformed drug laws can be found in academic literature. The authors of *Illegal Leisure*, a book based on a sociological longitudinal British study of 800 young people, conclude that current drug policies are based on three misconceptions (Parker, et al., 1998). These are as follows:

- drug use usually leads to criminal behaviour
- drug use usually leads to addiction
- most adolescents are pressured to use drugs

The authors argue that current anti-drug policies need to be reconsidered in light of these findings. At the same time, some police officers appear to be frustrated with the current laws. In September 2001, for example, Julian Fantino, Chief of the Toronto Police Service, stated at a press conference his belief that simple possession of marijuana should result in only a small fine and no criminal record.

Arguments among academics, politicians, and police about how to deal with changing attitudes toward recreational drug use are likely to continue. Perhaps this should not surprise us. Sociologists see society as an ever-changing organism, of which attitudes to drug use are only one aspect.

 Work-Related Stress

In the 1990s, a number of factors came together to change the way Canadians view the workplace. A growing perception emerged that government had become too big and costly, and that its role in the economy should be reduced. Pension plans and other large financial investors began to invest only in the most efficient and promising of companies. The pressures of globalization, about which you will read more in Chapter 10, forced Canadian companies to reduce production costs or go out of business. The growing perception that the Canadian economy should be privatized, efficient, and globalized had a significant impact on the workplace. Employees were expected to do more with less. Departments were merged, perks reduced, and benefits cut back.

Generally, social mores have shifted so that employees now expect to work harder and to put in more hours than they did even 20 years ago. All this leads to a level of **work-related stress** (distress caused by work pressures) that is seriously threatening many Canadians' health and well-being.

In 1998, Priority Management Systems, a company based in Vancouver, conducted a survey about conflicting pressures between work and family, and the stress that they caused. Among its findings were the data in Figure 8.17.

What causes work stress? Studies have found that it is most prevalent where mental pressure is persistent and the sense of personal control low (Weiss, 1994, p. 3). Because many employed people have little control over major

Percentage of Respondents Agreeing with Statements About Work Stress, British Columbia, 1998

Statement	Agree
I work more than my workplace's normal workweek.	91%
I believe I will put in these, or longer, hours in the next decade.	54%
I took two weeks' vacation or less in the last year.	41%
To produce measurable results, I face more pressure than I did five years ago.	87%
I feel stress regularly	82%

Source: Leidl, David. 1998. "Some things never change: another stress survey says...we're all feeling more stressed." *BC Business.* Vol. 26. No. 11. November 1998.

Figure 8.18 Considering that you will probably participate in the Canadian workforce for upwards of four decades, how do the data in this table relate to you? Which figures surprised you most, and why?

aspects of their work lives, stress will be unavoidable. Their only option is to develop coping strategies to deal with the ensuing problems. To make matters worse, workers today have little time to spend with their families and resolve household problems.

Unless people facing ongoing high levels of work stress develop successful coping strategies, they are likely to develop a serious condition known as **burnout**. Burnout may be defined as "a syndrome of emotional exhaustion, depersonalization, and reduced personal accomplishment that can occur among individuals who do people work of some kind" (Rowe, 2000, p. 215).

Treatments for work stress are frequently short-term, involving rest, counselling, and drug therapy. The sources of stress are long-term, however, because of the attitude of employers, who expect more from their employees than they did in the past. Further, burnout sufferers frequently lack the skills to change their own contributing behaviours (Rowe, 2000, p. 216). Some studies have found that burnout sufferers who participate in systematic follow-up "refresher" sessions, at 5, 11, and 17 months after the crisis, showed consistent decreases in burnout over

a 30-month period (Rowe, 2000, p. 215). These people learned to cope with the increased demands of the modern workplace.

Whatever the contributing factors, stress and burnout are major symptoms of the changing mores in society. People expect to work longer hours, and under more demanding conditions, than was the case as recently as a decade ago. People get sick more often and pay the psychological cost of devoting less time and energy to their families than their parents did. The impact on the well-being of the sufferers and their families—and the financial cost for health care services—are of great concern for the future.

Aboriginal Health Initiatives

When considering health matters related to Aboriginal people, many specific cultural factors come into play. At root exists a fundamental difference between Canada's existing health care system and Aboriginal attitudes toward healing. The existing system is based on a Western worldview, which sees the human body as a machine and illness as a breakdown in the machine. In this worldview, the role of medical personnel is to repair the

Figure 8.19 Clare McNab, Kikawinaw (Cree for mother) of the Okimaw Ohci Healing Lodge in Maple Creek, Saskatchewan, talks about the spiritual healing aspects of Okimaw Ohci. In the background is the spiritual lodge where morning circle is held.

For many years, social mores in Canadian society were such that the government delivered Western health care equally to all Canadians, including Aboriginal people. Social mores have changed in this regard because anthropologists have demonstrated that it is necessary to respect cultural differences among the population when designing effective health programs. Aboriginal people in Canada require culturally sensitive methods of dealing with health issues in their communities. The Assembly of First Nations, the umbrella organization of non-Inuit Aboriginal peoples' organizations, notes that one of the priorities for Aboriginal health care must be "development and implementation of holistic approaches" (Assembly of First Nations, 2001a, p. 2).

The case study on the following page illustrates how a holistic approach helped one Aboriginal woman.

Although major differences exist between the worldviews of mainstream and Aboriginal approaches to health care, the Assembly of First Nations recognizes that both have a role to play in treating Aboriginal people. In the First Nations and Inuit Regional Health Surveys, conducted in 1997, more than 85 percent of respondents indicated that a return to traditional ways would be a good method of promoting Aboriginal wellness. "This does not mean that everyone wants traditional health care *instead* of the usual 'Western' type: people may want both kinds of care" (Assembly of First Nations, 2001a, p. 2).

Health Canada is the federal department that regulates health care matters. It recognizes that programs are more likely to be successful in Aboriginal communities if they take into account the importance of traditional healing approaches. Health Canada is currently working with Aboriginal organizations to develop such programs on a number of fronts.

machine. In First Nations and Inuit traditions, however, the human body is not regarded as a machine that can be fixed independently of a person's spirit. According to this worldview, all parts of a patient's life must be healed. Aboriginal medicine views healing as a process of restoring balance in the patient's life. This healing worldview emphasizes the physical, emotional, social, and spiritual aspects of healing, and it promotes the patient's personal role in the healing process (Assembly of First Nations, 2001b, p.1).

Healing

Margaret Lavalée admits she knew better.

A health-care worker herself, she was a smoker and obese when diagnosed with...diabetes five years ago. Now 61, she's turned her life and health around, and speaks publicly to her Aboriginal communities to urge that others do the same.

"I quit smoking and I started to do exercise," recounts Lavalée, who with her husband runs Red Willow Lodge, a native teaching centre an hour east of Winnipeg....

Lavalée also uses traditional healing methods such as sweat lodges, participation in Sun dances with their accompanying fasts and vision quests.

Virtually unknown among Canada's Aboriginal peoples 50 years ago, diabetes threatens to engulf 27 per cent of that population within 20 years. The current epidemic is generally attributed to the cultural change from an active lifestyle to a sedentary one, an increasing obesity and what may be a Native tendency to store fat....

Saskatoon-based Aboriginal producer Doug Cuthand is working on a 13-part television series... *The Sweetness of Life: A Diabetes Story.* Due for broadcast on APTN, the Aboriginal network, the shows will also become teaching tools on video....

Poignantly, the title refers to a Native elder's observation that diabetes came to his people when they lost "the sweetness of life," that is, access to their traditional ways....

Source: Canadian Diabetes Association. "Aboriginal strategy aims to help those at risk." 2001. *Globe and Mail* (supplement), 1 November 2001. p. D3.

Questions

1. What can we learn from Margaret Lavalée's personal experiences as an Aboriginal person with diabetes?

Pause and Reflect

1. In what ways do the media contribute to Canadians' desensitization to violence?

2. Describe the approach *Newsweek* took to Kate Moss's brush with drug addiction in the extract on page 277. How does the article reflect social mores? How might reports like this influence teenagers considering engaging in risky behaviour?

3. How do the findings of the book *Illegal Leisure*, and the opinions of Toronto Police Chief Julian Fantino, illustrate that society's mores toward recreational drug use are changing? Speculate on how this shift may affect drug use in future.

4. In the first column of a three-column chart, list three factors that lead to work-related stress and burnout. In the second column, list strategies individuals can use to better cope with their stress. In the third column, describe ways that society could attempt to change the factors themselves to decrease work-related stress.

5. What is the difference in outlook between Canada's existing health care system and Aboriginal attitudes toward healing? What do you think mainstream medicine can learn from Aboriginal attitudes toward healing? How might society as a whole benefit?

Skill Builder:
Maintaining Intellectual Objectivity

Many of the assignments you undertake in Grade 12 require that you take a position on an issue or question. Sometimes the issue is one on which you have a strong opinion, while at other times you may feel fairly neutral. Whatever the situation, your goal should be to prevent your personal thoughts and biases from influencing your work. This is **intellectual objectivity**, which requires that you research a number of sides on an issue before presenting your conclusion. It is not enough to present research supporting only one opinion.

Step One: Utilize a variety of sources

You will see that the Competing Perspectives feature in this chapter (on page 256) deals with teenaged female smokers. There are various views about why teenaged girls start smoking. Some people believe that teenaged girls think smoking makes them seem attractive and sophisticated. Others suggest that many use it as a way of reducing appetite and remaining slim. Still others believe that smoking is simply an act of rebellion—part of a stage that most young people go through—and that advertising the health risks of smoking to young people may be counterproductive. Perhaps you have an opinion on this subject. Whether you do or not, if you were to research this topic, you would have to try to find a variety of sources so that you would uncover different points of view and thereby maintain intellectual objectivity.

The two sources used in the Competing Perspectives feature provide different viewpoints. The first, *Chatelaine* <www.chatelaine.com>, is a secular (non-religious) liberal magazine designed to appeal to women who believe that they should play an important role outside the home, at work, and in the community. The second, *Alberta Report* <report.ca>, is a conservative magazine targeted to a readership that believes that women's role within the family is their primary one, and that religious values are a necessary component of society.

Within newspapers, you are likely to find differences in editorial opinion. If you were a Toronto resident, you might read *The Toronto Star* <www.thestar.com> (a liberal daily), The Toronto Sun <www.fyi-toronto.com/torsun.shtml> (a populist daily), *The Globe & Mail* <www.globeandmail.ca> (a conservative national paper), or *The National Post* <www.nationalpost.com> (an even more conservative national paper). Finding editorials from these four newspapers on a common topic is likely to provide you with a cross-section of opinion on the subject.

On social issues, particularly those relating to women and the family, REAL Women of Canada (Realistic, Equal, Active for Life) <www.realwomenca.com> will provide a more conservative commentary than the more liberal Women's Legal Education and Action Fund <www.leaf.ca>.

Although you may not know the bias of a source as you read it, it is important to obtain a number of sources to increase the chances of finding variations in opinion. Be sure to reject sources you cannot trust. For guidance in detecting untrustworthy sources, see the Skill Builder feature in Chapter 5 on page 158.

Step Two: Represent your sources in your findings

If you feel that a source is valuable enough to include in your bibliography, at least one reference to it should normally be included in your submitted materials. If your bibliography contains many works that you do not refer to in your text, the reader may draw the conclusion that your bibliography is "padded." It is therefore important to check that every bibliographical entry is referenced somewhere in your text.

Step Three: Frame different viewpoints

When writing up your findings, it is critical to demonstrate that you know which sources are complementary and which ones are contradictory. Sources that complement each other should be presented with links such as: "X presents a similar view by observing…," or "X agrees with this interpretation in the following quote…." When a source provides a contradictory argument, you should be explicit: "X disputes this opinion by writing…," or "X is of a contrary opinion, as the following quote demonstrates…."

When you organize your text, and frame it with links as suggested, you can then legitimately draw your own conclusions. If your research and findings are too narrow, however, your readers are less likely to pay attention to your findings.

Practise It!

Consider the following pair of quotes from this chapter. Do you think they are complementary or contradictory? (a) After looking at them yourself, work with a partner to explain what your conclusions are and why you have arrived at them. (b) What links would you provide in your text, to connect these quotes? (c) What conclusion of your own would you draw, after presenting the quotes and linking text? (d) Now, as a pair, go back to the chapter and select two quotes on another issue. Repeat (a), (b), and (c).

- Studies have shown, however, that formula-fed babies experience higher levels of asthma, allergies, eczema, diabetes, colitis, and childhood cancers than do breast-fed babies. The problem becomes more acute in developing nations.... James Grant, executive officer of the United Nations Children's Fund (UNICEF), has stated that, every day, 3000 to 4000 infants die because they are denied access to breast milk.

- "I have two sons in their 30s. One has a PhD in political science, is executive director of the internationally respected Gendercide Watch and holds a teaching post at a research institute in Mexico City. The other is a successful lawyer in Vancouver who is about to begin a master's degree at Harvard Law School. Each has published numerous articles and books. Neither was breast-fed. What else did I do wrong?"

Chapter Activities

Show Your Knowledge

1. Pick two social practices examined in this chapter, and explain how they lead to health-impairing behaviours.

2. What access barriers to health care are described in this chapter? Rank these barriers in order of significance. Explain why you ordered the barriers as you did.

3. What are some of the ethical issues surrounding (a) the blood supply system in Canada, (b) organ harvesting and donation, and (c) medical research and treatment on live human patients?

4. What are some of the causes and results of (a) desensitization to violence, (b) recreational drug use, and (c) work-related stress and burnout?

Practise Your Thinking

5. Pick one of the health-impairing behaviours described in Section 8.1. What are the factors that encourage the behaviour? Imagine that you were hired to develop a program to raise public awareness of an issue of your choice. What sorts of things would you build into your program?

6. To what extent is society responsible for removing access barriers, and to what extent is the individual responsible for trying to overcome them? Discuss this issue in your class.

7. Pick one of the ethical issues described in Section 8.3. What are the arguments presented by the two sides on this issue? What is your position on the issue? Discuss this issue in your class.

8. Working in a small group, pick one of the changing mores that affect health and well-being, as described in Section 8.4. Brainstorm what could be done by (a) governments, (b) schools, (c) employers, and (d) individuals and families to alleviate its impact on well-being. Develop an action plan for decreasing the impact in Canadian society.

Communicate Your Ideas

9. Pick one of the health-impairing issues described in Section 8.1. Do further research on the issue. Write a letter to the editor, summarizing the nature of the issue and what you think society should do about it. Read your letter aloud in class. Discuss with your classmates the various letters, and then vote on which one should be sent to the local paper.

10. Choose an access barrier that interests you. Do some research, both in your community and online, to find out what programs and services are available to help individuals overcome this barrier. Create a pamphlet designed to give people guidance on how to overcome this barrier. Your pamphlet should be on 8-by-11-inch paper, folded in half to give four sides. It should contain pictures and text to (a) identify the barrier, (b) explain where to find out more about it, (c) demonstrate how it limits access, and (d) identify and explain programs, services, or resources that can assist in overcoming the barrier. Show your pamphlet to your classmates, and compare the information that you found and the suggestions you made.

11. Pick one of the ethical issues described in Section 8.3. Imagine that you are to be a witness at a Royal Commission to determine which ethical principles should influence policy on this issue, and to provide guidelines. Prepare a position paper, complete with your opinions and the reasons for them, and recommendations you would make to the commission about what it should put into its report. Meet with others who wrote about this issue, and debate your conclusions.

12. Pick one of the aspects of changing mores and public well-being described in Section 8.4. Create a poster that shows your ideas about the causes and solutions of the problem. As a class, display your posters, and discuss the ideas that they raise.

Apply Your Knowledge

13. Work in a group of four. For a country other than Canada, find out about (a) how the elderly are treated, (b) how people with disabilities are accommodated, (c) how the health care system operates, and (d) how young people are regarded and treated. Overall, would you say the country you are studying is more likely or less likely to promote social health and well-being than Canada is? Explain your reasons.

14. Organize your class into pairs to research health care in countries around the world. One half are A pairs; the other half are B pairs. Each A pair will examine an industrialized country. Each B pair will examine a non-industrialized country. Use such statistics as per cent GDP per capita, absolute spending per capita, per cent public versus private spending, and so on to identify how the health care system in each country operates. How do Canada's health care indicators (examples: life expectancy, infant mortality) compare with those of the other industrialized countries? How do the industrialized countries' indicators compare with those of the developing nations? What conclusions can you draw from the class findings?

15. Try to identify additional ethical issues relating to health care provision. (These could be related to the issues described in this chapter, or entirely different ones.) Choose one of interest to you. What is the issue? What are the positions and reasons for the positions of the various parties involved in the issue? What are your conclusions about the issue, and the reasons for them? Why do you consider the issue to be ethically important?

16. Organize a survey to see whether or not one of the social mores in your community is changing. You could ask people what they thought about your chosen issue five years ago, and what they think about it now. If their opinions have changed, you could ask what factors encouraged this change, and what factors discouraged it. You could ask whether they have become more conservative or more liberal in their opinions. After collating your results, speculate on what effects the changes you observed—both positive or negative—might have on public health and well-being in the coming years. Subjects you might consider include

    • protection of the environment
    • smoking restrictions in public places
    • legal rights for same-sex couples
    • providing increased public access for people with disabilities
    • pornography

CHAPTER 9

PREJUDICE AND DISCRIMINATION

INTRODUCTION

Issues of prejudice and discrimination are serious social challenges for every Canadian. As our society becomes more diverse, we must be aware of the subtle connections between stereotyping, prejudice, discrimination, racism, and hate crimes. They can combine to diminish people's sense of worth and to block their full participation in society. Many social scientists have analyzed prejudice and discrimination. They offer us valuable insights that can help us understand and deal with these volatile feelings and actions.

There are four major sections in this chapter. The first section introduces many important concepts about the topic, using examples drawn mainly from Canadian society. The second section discusses the research and insights of several psychologists, sociologists, and anthropologists regarding the concept of race. Particular attention is paid to how children develop their concepts of other peoples. The third section focuses on the problem of hatred toward groups in society, and how it is dealt with by both international and Canadian law. The chapter ends on a positive note. The last section examines "paradigm shifts"—research and practical applications to reduce prejudice and discriminatory practices.

■ Learning Expectations

By the end of this chapter, you will be able to

- explain the relationship between prejudice and discrimination, and assess the impact of both on ideas of self-worth
- assess the role of stereotyping as a barrier to full participation in society
- analyze patterns of hate crimes and differentiate ways in which social scientists (for example, John Ogbu, Gordon Allport, George Dei, Beverly Tatum, Stuart Hall) would attempt to understand racism

Focusing on the Issues

Guilty plea entered in cross burning

Moncton, N.B. (CP) – A young man has pleaded guilty to a charge of promoting hatred after a cross was found burning on the front lawn of a black family a month ago.

James Hanley, 18, of Moncton, N.B., entered the plea in provincial court Friday morning. He will be sentenced September 26.

A passerby in Moncton's affluent Kingswood Park neighbourhood saw the metre-high cross ablaze on the front lawn of a black family's home in the early morning hours of July 14.

The family has lived in the area since 1992.

The RCMP initially treated the crime as property mischief connected to a number of acts of vandalism in the neighbourhood.

But as details surfaced, many Moncton residents and multicultural groups responded with outrage to the incident.

After days of deliberation, New Brunswick Justice Minister Brad Green decided last month to charge Hanley under Canada's hate crime laws.

Source: "Guilty plea entered in cross burning." *The Sarnia Observer.* 25 August 2001.

The Criminal Code of Canada considers the act of burning a cross in public a symbol of racial hatred. Those charged in Canada with committing a hate crime will face trial and possibly jail time.

THINK ABOUT IT

1. Why should James Hanley have been charged with a hate crime offence for his actions? Explain your views.

2. Outline reasons that might explain why residents and multicultural groups were outraged with the original property mischief charge.

3. Do you think that prejudice and racial hatred are feelings that a person is born with, or are they learned behaviours? Explain your opinion.

Section 9.1   Identifying Prejudice and Discrimination

Key Concepts

racism

discrimination

prejudice

stereotype

anti-Semitism

perception

the image

paradigm

systemic racism

systemic sexism

standardized IQ
test

genocide

What's in a Word or Symbol?

There is a big difference between being charged with a hate crime and being charged with property mischief. In James Hanley's case, discussed in the chapter opener, the difference was a small burning cross, a symbol for so much more. You've probably heard of the Ku Klux Klan, a secret society of white supremacists who burned crosses as a part of their ritual lynchings of African-Americans in the southern United States. Section 319 of the Criminal Code of Canada considers public cross-burning a statement of racial hatred. Hanley, who had previously been suspended for bringing hate literature to high school, was sentenced to four months in jail, followed by two years' probation and racial sensitivity training. During sentencing, Judge Sylvio Savoie stated, "This crime offends the very fabric of our Canadian society."

Racism is negative behaviour based on an incorrect assumption that one race is inherently superior to others. This is just one form of **discrimination**—unfair actions directed against people based on their race, gender, ethnicity, nationality, language, faith, or sexual orientation. Accusing people with these words, and others like them, can quickly bring on powerful emotions. Yet, people often toss these terms around without really understanding what they mean. See if you can spot which students are mistaken in their accusations.

- One girl says that she has been *discriminated* against because another girl doesn't like her.
- A white boy accuses someone who calls him names of being a *racist*.
- Another student claims that the teacher is *prejudiced* in favour of the athletes in the class.

Let's look at the ways in which all three students misused these words. The first case isn't about discrimination at all. For one thing, there is only the mention of feelings of

Figure 9.1 Flow Chart of Definitions. Give an example for each definition.

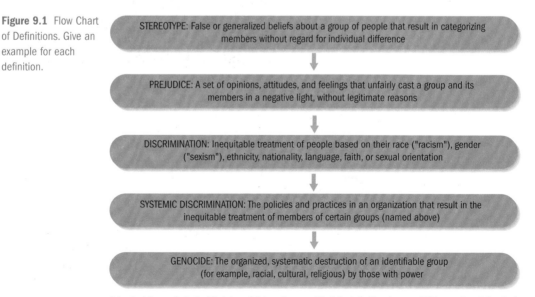

STEREOTYPE: False or generalized beliefs about a group of people that result in categorizing members without regard for individual difference

PREJUDICE: A set of opinions, attitudes, and feelings that unfairly cast a group and its members in a negative light, without legitimate reasons

DISCRIMINATION: Inequitable treatment of people based on their race ("racism"), gender ("sexism"), ethnicity, nationality, language, faith, or sexual orientation

SYSTEMIC DISCRIMINATION: The policies and practices in an organization that result in the inequitable treatment of members of certain groups (named above)

GENOCIDE: The organized, systematic destruction of an identifiable group (for example, racial, cultural, religious) by those with power

Adapted from: Ontario Ministry of Education and Training. *Antiracism and Ethnocultural Equity in School Boards: Guidelines for Policy Development and Implementation.* 1993.

dislike and nothing about how the other girl acted on those feelings. The situation gives no sense that the girl who is complaining is being mistreated because she is a member of a particular group in society. In the next case, the use of name-calling is certainly not acceptable. But, the white boy is wrong to use the powerful accusation of racism, since he is a member of the dominant culture in Canada. The student in the third example should have used the term "bias" instead of "prejudice." While both words can describe judgments about a group in society, **prejudice** is normally used for negative situations. Perhaps the teacher really has a bias in favour of the athletes, but the student needs to present some evidence to prove it.

Prejudice, Discrimination, and Power

Issues of prejudice and discrimination involve people who are outside the mainstream of society or outside positions of power and authority. Disadvantage can be based on several factors or combinations of them, including religious affiliation, age, sex or sexual preference, race and ethnicity, and physical or mental characteristics. Figure 9.1 shows the steps that disadvantage can pass through as attitudes toward a group harden.

As we take in information, it is easy for us to form beliefs about particular groups in society. Once we apply these beliefs to individual members of a group, the beliefs are called **stereotypes**. For example, we can categorize individuals as "babes," "gays," "jocks," or "nerds," then make positive or negative judgments about them as members of these groups. Reinforcement of stereotypes comes from many sources, including news and entertainment media, jokes and put-downs, and the powerful influence of friends and family.

Prejudice emerges when stereotypes are negative or inaccurate in nature or when a person fails to change them in the face of contrary evidence. Only when those who hold the stereotype have some power or authority can prejudice go to the next level, discrimination. At this point, prejudices are acted upon to mistreat or deny rights to a member or members of what psychologist Gordon Allport called an "out-group." The biggest kid in the fourth grade can make life miserable for the boy with a speech impediment. A business manager can routinely assign jobs to people from his own ethnic group at the expense of other experienced candidates.

In 1948, social scientist S.L. Wax worked with the Canadian Jewish Congress to conduct a simple experiment to demonstrate the depth of individual discrimination in Canada. He responded to about 100 advertisements for summer resorts in Ontario, and requested room reservations for exactly the same dates. Wax sent two identical sets of letters, one signed "Mr. Greenberg," and the other signed "Mr. Lockwood." Both sets of letters were sent out at the same time. Nearly all the resorts contacted Mr. Lockwood and offered him accommodations, while about half responded to Mr. Greenberg, and only about a third of all the resorts offered him a room.

Commenting on the study, psychologist Gordon W. Allport reported that the business people identified the name Greenberg as Jewish and about two-thirds of them rejected him as an "undesirable" paying guest. This particular kind of discrimination is called **anti-Semitism**. Later, the same experiment was repeated using holiday resorts across Canada, but with the names "Mr. Smith" and "Mr. Little Bear" substituted for Lockwood and Greenberg. The results were even more negative. While Smith was offered a room at almost every resort, only 20 per cent offered Little Bear accommodation, suggesting a high level of individual discrimination directed toward Aboriginal people. This sort of behaviour is called racism (Sioux Lookout (Ontario) Anti-Racism Committee, 2002).

 Understanding Prejudice and Discrimination

A key idea in understanding prejudice and discrimination came from British economist and philosopher Kenneth E. Boulding. He wanted a broad way to understand human actions and choices in different aspects of life, and, in 1956, published *The Image: Knowledge in Life and Society*. In it, he outlined a view of **perception**, in which incoming information is shaped and changed by the personal background and experiences of individuals. Boulding used the phrase **"the image"** to describe how people do not perceive things exactly as they exist in the real world. Instead, they respond to an *image* of reality, and this image can differ from person to person.

While Boulding's work did not focus on prejudice or discrimination, it is easy to grasp the implications. People use their background and experiences to form images of others. If the image of a certain group in society is negative, we call it a negative stereo-type, or if the negative feelings are strong, a prejudice. Then, if someone acts upon this prejudice, it becomes discrimination.

In 1989, American psychologist Joel Barker expanded Boulding's ideas to include the concept of **paradigm**. This is what he called the set of rules and conditions stored in the brain that a person uses to interpret and understand sensory experience. A paradigm acts like the filter through which information is processed by the brain to create an image. For example, the approach of a stranger can be seen by one person as a possible threat, while someone else may see it as just another passerby. The difference is based upon the sets of rules and conditions—the paradigms—that two people use to evaluate the same thing. Social scientists believe that it is possible to change the set of rules and conditions by which people judge situations. They call this a paradigm shift—a concept that will be explored further in Section 9.4 of this chapter.

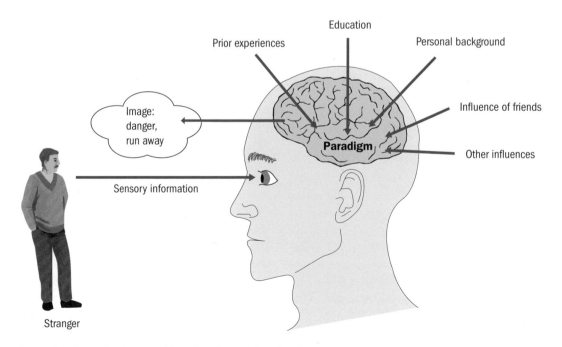

Figure 9.2 Perception: Image and Paradigm. Kenneth Boulding discussed the image, while Joel Barker described the paradigm used to form the image.

The Problem of Systemic Discrimination

Prejudice and discrimination can be part of a whole system, that is, systemic. In this case, a large corporation, a public organization, or even a whole country discriminates against members of an identifiable group. This is not just a case of a few well-placed individuals blocking human rights or career advancement. **Systemic racism or sexism** means that inequality is a part of the operation of the whole company, organization, or government. The philosophy and laws that prevented Quebec women from voting in provincial elections until 1940 demonstrated systemic sexism. The harsh apartheid laws and practices used until 1991 to separate the races in South Africa is an example of systemic racism.

Systemic discrimination has a long history in Canada's official policies. For example, in the late nineteenth century, Canada's immigration regulations blatantly favoured white Europeans over any other racial groups.

Severe restrictions were imposed against blacks and against Chinese, Japanese, Sikh, and other Asian immigrants. In 1939, Canadian officials (and those of other countries) refused landing to the *St. Louis*, a ship carrying 907 Jewish refugees from Europe. The ship was forced to return to Europe, where many of the refugees eventually died in Nazi concentration camps.

The rights of citizenship have been denied to groups living in this country. For example, despite years of political agitation, Canadian women were not eligible to vote before Nellie McClung led a breakthrough in Manitoba in 1915. Nor were women fully identified under the law as "persons" until the famous Persons Case of 1929. Meanwhile, Aboriginal people living on reserves did not obtain the right to vote in federal elections until 1962. A recent employment study shows that significant barriers still block the full participation of Aboriginal people and other groups in Canadian society.

Aboriginal People Face Systemic Racism in Canadian Workforce

Toronto, January 9, 2001– Good jobs and promotions elude many visible minorities and Aboriginal people who believe that subtle forms of racism prevail in the workplace, according to a new study released today. The study…is based on recent quantitative statistics and focus group discussions with visible minorities and Aboriginal people in cities across Canada.

[Among other things] the study reveals that:

- Aboriginal people, visible minorities, and immigrants to Canada have more difficulty than others in finding employment in all regions of Canada.
- Compared to white Canadians, visible minorities and Aboriginal people with university education are less likely to hold managerial and professional jobs…
- Foreign-born visible minorities and Aboriginal people are over-represented in the bottom 20 per cent and are under-represented in the top 20 per cent of income earners.
- Higher education yields fewer payoffs for minorities and Aboriginal people in terms of employment and income. Given the same level of education, white Canadians (both foreign-born and Canadian-born) are three times as likely as Aboriginal people and about twice as likely as foreign-born visible minorities to be in the top 20 per cent of income earners.

"Clearly the talents of Aboriginal peoples and visible minorities are being under-utilized or wasted as a result of systemic discrimination. This is not good for the productivity of the Canadian economy and the cohesion of our society," says Dr. Jean Kunz, senior research associate at the Canadian Council on Social Development (CCSD).

CASE STUDY

...Racism is a "hidden thing" in the workplace, and "subtle discrimination" includes being passed over for promotion and senior positions often held mainly by white Canadians. A disturbing revelation in the study is that even with post-secondary education, job opportunities may still be out of reach for Aboriginal peoples, and that Aboriginal youth lagged far behind in rates of university completion compared to all other groups.

"This report should be required reading for employers in both the public and private sectors," says the Honourable Lincoln Alexander, chair of the Canadian Race Relations Foundation. "The results demonstrate that we need to make greater efforts to eliminate systemic discrimination in Canada."

Source: Canadian Race Relations Foundation. 2002. " 'Hidden discrimination' and 'polite racism' prevents Aboriginal peoples and visible minorities from gaining access to jobs, study finds." [Online]. Available <http://www.crr.ca/EN/MediaCentre/News Releases/eMedCen_NewsRe20010110.htm . 6 February 2002.>

Questions

1. Rank the degree of "employment disadvantage" faced by the three groups named in the study. Explain your ranking.
2. Give two reasons why all employers should read this report.

IQ Testing: Systemic Discrimination?

You have probably taken standardized academic tests in Math and English, and may even have taken an IQ test. **Standardized IQ (Intelligence Quotient) tests** were first developed in 1905 by two French psychologists, Alfred Binet and Theodore Simon, then brought to the US about a decade later by Lewis M. Terman of Stanford University. Later revisions of these IQ tests were called Stanford-Binet tests. These tests have been used widely in education ever since, sometimes with negative results for students outside "mainstream" white society. For example, in 1926, psychologist N.D.M. Hirsch used Stanford-Binet tests to compare the intelligence of children from three different groups in society. The average scores were a bit higher for white children. At that time, intelligence tests were thought to be entirely unbiased measures of intellectual ability—measures that had proven that whites were smarter. Today we know that both these claims are untrue.

IQ tests are built upon a body of vocabulary and knowledge familiar to "mainstream" culture, and as a result they are not very solid measures of the capabilities of anyone outside this group. Canadian educational psychologist Ronald Samuda has criticized the longstanding practice of using standardized intelligence tests on students from different racial backgrounds. He says the tests "are essentially culturally loaded and the students who get the best results will naturally be those who have imbibed the values, skills and motivational patterns from their middle-class homes and neighbourhood environment" (Samuda, 1986, p. 50).

Samuda points out that culturally loaded IQ tests have been used to label and place students from minority races and cultures into

www.queendom.com/tests/iq/index.html

Use the free sections of this commercial Web site to try a variety of IQ tests. If the Web address does not connect you with the site, do a Web search using the search string "+queendom +IQ tests." This should produce a list of hits containing the correct address.

Try the sample questions below to see how important good English reading skills are in understanding how to answer the classical IQ questions.

Classical IQ Test Sample Items

1. If you rearrange the letters UGNAIA, you would have the name of a

    a) River   b) Planet   c) City   d) Animal   e) Plant   f) I don't know

2. Emily is four years old. Her big sister Amy is three times as old as Emily. How old will Amy be when she is twice as old as Emily?

    a) 14   b) 16   c) 18   d) 20   e) 22   f) I don't know

Source: Classic IQ Test. [Online]. Available <http://www.queendom.com/cgi-bin/tests/transfer.cgi>
6 February 2002.

Culture-Fair Test Sample Items

1. What number should replace the question mark?   2, 4, 8, 14, 22, 32, ? 44

2. Which image continues the sequence and replaces the question mark?

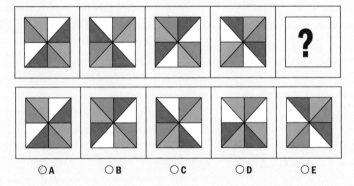

○A   ○B   ○C   ○D   ○E

Source: Culture-Fair IQ-Test. [Online]. Available <http://hem.passagen.se/dpref/iq/> 6 February, 2001.

Figure 9.3 How does the culture-fair test try to solve the problem of too much reading in the classical IQ test?

special classes or lower-level programs in Canadian schools. In recent years, Canadian school systems have struggled to replace the "classic" Stanford-Binet-originated IQ tests with a new breed of "culture-fair" intelligence tests. Meanwhile, a great deal of damage has probably unknowingly been done to students from non-white backgrounds over the years.

 **Genocide**

Genocide, the deliberate policy of those in power to eliminate a group of people, is the ultimate form of discrimination. Adolf Hitler's deadly gas chambers during World War II aimed to wipe out European Jews and anyone else he deemed unfit to live in Nazi-dominated Europe. More recently, Bosnian Serbs undertook two brutal campaigns of torture, rape, and murder, which they called "ethnic cleansing," in an effort to eliminate Muslims and other ethnic groups from the region. At present, the former president of that country is coming to trial before the United Nations International Court of Justice under the charge of genocide. This topic will be discussed further in Section 9.3 of this chapter, which deals with hate crimes.

Recently, Matthew Coon Come, Chief of the Assembly of First Nations, accused the Canadian government of systemic racism directed against Aboriginal people. He claimed that the Aboriginal people of Canada "are faced with the threat of extinction as a result of government laws and actions." Some people reacted strongly against the accusation of potential genocide, while others supported it.

CASE STUDY

Do Aboriginal People in Canada Face Genocide?

The Accusation: Natives face "systemic" racism, says AFN chief

Ottawa (CP) – Assembly of First Nations Chief Matthew Coon Come took a swipe at Canadian politicians and news media Sunday before leaving for a high-profile international anti-racism conference, saying Canada is a society of "two realities" that discriminates against Aboriginal people.

"There is the reality of a highly developed, just society that the world knows, and then there is the harsh and deadly reality which Aboriginal peoples endure," Coon Come said during a brief news conference in Ottawa.

The social and economic conditions endured by Aboriginal people in Canada are clear evidence of the "discrimination and systemic racism" directed at them, he said.

He accused some media outlets of taking "a racist slant" against Aboriginal people, a viewpoint that is then reflected by politicians.

Coon Come said racism contributes to the higher unemployment, lower life expectancy rates and greater rates of disease and suicide suffered by Aboriginal people in Canada.

If Aboriginal people in a country as wealthy and developed as Canada "are faced with the threat of extinction as a result of government laws and actions," Coon Come said, Aboriginal peoples in other countries have little hope.

Source: "Natives Face 'Systemic' Racism Says AFN Chief." *The Sarnia Observer.* 27 August 2001.

Editorial Response: Scalding Words

No Canadian can be proud of this country's treatment of its Aboriginal people....

Matthew Coon Come, National Chief of the Assembly of First Nations, had every right to reveal Canada's ugly little secret to the world, at the anti-racism conference taking place in Durban [South Africa] this week.

But his contention that Aboriginal people are wilfully oppressed by the Canadian government was, to say the least, an exaggeration....

Last month in Halifax, Coon Come accused Ottawa of "implementing policies of assimilation and extinguishment through infliction of conditions of social despair."

These are irresponsible words. Not only do they scald, they alienate fair-minded Canadians. This cannot be what Coon Come wants.

Source: Editorials and Letters. *The Toronto Star.* 2 September 2001

Letter to the Editor: Get Over the "R" Word

Both your editorial writer and federal [Indian Affairs] minister Bob Nault chastised Matthew Coon Come for using the "r" word. To say he has poisoned the atmosphere of dialogue about the situation of Canada's First Nations sounds utterly pathetic and self-serving when set against continuing conditions of degradation, disease and neglect...

Coon Come's words are surely better seen as a call for action—real deeds and honest, effective policies to counteract centuries of inaction, dithering or outright hostility to recognize the rights and needs of his people.

It's high time for Canadians to stop being miffed about his language and begin to seriously listen to his message.

Source: Editorials and Letters. *The Toronto Star.* 5 September 2001.

Questions

1. What is meant by "systemic racism"? What evidence does Matthew Coon Come use to support his view that systemic racism affects Aboriginal people in Canada?
2. Compare how the situation is viewed in the *Toronto Star* editorial and by the reader in the "letter to the editor." Explain the difference in their opinions.
3. Do Canada's Aboriginal people face genocide? What further information might be useful to help you clarify your own opinion on this issue?

Prejudice, Discrimination, and Self-Esteem

What does it feel like to experience prejudice and discrimination? How does it affect one's feelings of "worth"? Some students will know and understand this first-hand. Others probably never will. In 1959, a white Texan named John Howard Griffin conducted an unusual experiment to experience prejudice himself.

Griffin used dark pigment and tanning lamps to temporarily change his skin to a deep ebony colour. Then, he arranged with an African-American magazine to publish a series of stories about his day-to-day encounters with prejudice as a black man travelling across the southern US in search of work. His life changed overnight as he experienced what blacks had known all along—that people are treated very differently, based solely on skin colour. He was denied access to washrooms, restaurants, accommodation, and jobs, and he was threatened with violence.

Griffin's greatest impact came when his published journal, *Black Like Me*, reached audiences across the United States and Canada. It helped rally white support behind the emerging American civil rights move-

ment of the 1960s and continues to be used in many classrooms today as basic reading about the impact of prejudice. When you read the excerpt from *Black Like Me* (on page 296), you will see how profoundly the experience affected Griffin's self-esteem.

John Howard Griffin's rush to remove his skin colour shows clearly that the comments and actions of others deeply affect how people feel about themselves. Psychologists know that young children tend to judge their own sense of worth as others value them. Negative messages directed toward children who live outside "mainstream" white society can hurt their self-esteem. It can even lead them to deny their own racial or cultural identity—as researchers in Brantford, Ontario, learned. Their study compared the attitudes of white and Aboriginal children, aged five to nine years. It found that both groups of children expressed positive images of whites, and negative images of Aboriginal people in pictures that they drew. In fact, the Aboriginal children had such poor self-images that they generally tried to deny their Native identity to the researchers altogether (Bain and Colyer, 2001, p. 54). Prejudice and discrimination do have a great impact on self-esteem.

Black Like Me

by John Howard Griffin

I went to the bus stop and boarded a bus for Atlanta [Georgia] via Auburn, Alabama. The trip was without incident until we changed buses at Auburn. As always, we Negroes sat at the rear. Four of us occupied the back bench. A large, middle-aged Negro woman sat in front of us to the left, a young Negro man occupied the seat in front of us to the right.

At one of the stops, two white women boarded and could find no place to sit. No gallant Southern white man (or youth) rose to offer them a place to sit in the "white section."

The bus driver called back and asked the young Negro man and the middle-aged Negro woman to sit together so the white women could have one of the seats. Both ignored the request. We felt the tensions mount as whites turned to stare at us.

A redheaded white man in a sports shirt stood up, faced the rear and called to the Negro, "Don't you hear the driver? Move out, man."

…I was the last to leave the bus. An elderly white man, bald and square of build, dressed in worn blue work clothes, peered intently at me. Then he crimped his face as though I were odious, and snorted, "Phew!" His small blue eyes shone with repugnance, a look of such unreasoning contempt for my skin that it filled me with despair.

It was a little thing, but piled on all the other little things it broke something in me. Suddenly I had had enough. Suddenly I could stomach no more of this degradation—not of myself but of all men who were black like me. Abruptly I turned and walked away. The large bus station was crowded with humanity. In the men's room, I entered one of the cubicles and locked the door.

I took out the cleansing cream and rubbed it on my hands and face to remove the stain. I then removed my shirt and undershirt, rubbed my skin almost raw, and looked into my hand mirror. I could pass for white again….

Source: Griffin, John Howard. 1960. *Black Like Me*. New York. Houghton Mifflin Co.

Pause and Reflect

1. Explain the differences between the meanings of the words in each of these pairs:
   a) stereotype and prejudice
   b) prejudice and discrimination
   c) discrimination and systemic discrimination

2. What is perception? How are the ideas of Kenneth Boulding and Joel Barker about perception connected to one another?

3. Why are standardized IQ tests often criticized? Is their use in schools systemic discrimination? Explain your opinion.

4. One reader said this about John Howard Griffin in an Internet review of his book. What do you think she meant by it?

   "Fortunately for him, when the experiment was over, he could stop taking the pigment pills and laying under the sunlamp and turn white again. …No matter where I go, or what I do, I will be black forever. And it's not going to be erased."

Section 9.2   The Psychology of Race

Is Race Relevant?

The idea of **race** is often at the centre of issues surrounding prejudice and discrimination. It is a vague concept usually associated with physical characteristics, particularly skin colour, facial features, and hair texture. In the past, people spoke of five major races, inaccurately identified by the colours white, yellow, red, brown, and black. Parallel scientific and geographic names were also used for the five races: Caucasian, Oriental, Native Indian, Indo-Pakistani, and Negroid.

Today, we realize that humans are not biologically divided into racial subgroups. Scientists have found no significant genetic differences between peoples that justify any division into races. The idea of race comes from history and culture, not from science. Today, experts regard race as "an out-of-date and useless concept from the viewpoint of understanding biological diversity" (Podolefsky and Brown, 2001, p. 207). The prestigious American Anthropological Association identifies race as an entirely learned concept, part of our **cultural behaviour**. (See page 298.)

Early Explanations of Prejudice

Social scientists also believe that, like race, prejudice is learned, not innate. More than half a century ago, psychologists Gordon W. Allport and Theodor Adorno used questionnaires and interviews to measure the strength of individual prejudice. Then, analysis of background information suggested possible reasons for these feelings; for example, Allport found a rough correlation between higher education and what he called "tolerance," or the acceptance of differences between peoples. He noted that, to a certain extent, the more educated one's parents, the more tolerant—that is, the less prejudiced—one's views.

In a separate study just a few years later, psychologist Theodor Adorno identified characteristics of the opposite to the tolerant personality, the "**authoritarian personality**." Such people are quick to judge things as either right or wrong, good or bad. There is little room for any judgment that falls in-between. Adorno concluded that this personality has a low tolerance for what he called **ambiguity**. This is something that can be interpreted or understood in more than one way. For example, such people strongly favour "their own kind" of ethnicity and culture over others, an attitude that social scientists term **ethnocentrism**. Adorno found the authoritarian personality more prejudicial and concluded that this personality was formed during childhood, the result of bigoted parenting

Key Concepts

race

cultural behaviour

authoritarian personality

ambiguity

ethnocentrism

classical conditioning

reference group

group norms

cognition

subordinate cultures

Ebonics

Education	More Tolerant Half [of study group]	Less Tolerant Half
Both parents college graduates	60.3%	39.7%
One parent college graduate	53.0%	47.0%
Neither parent college graduate	41.2%	58.8%

Source: Allport, Gordon M. 1954. *The Nature of Prejudice*. Don Mills. Addison-Wesley. Citing G.W. and B.M. Kramer. "Some Roots of Prejudice." *Journal of Psychology*, 22, 1946.

Figure 9.4 Percentage Distribution of Prejudice Scores as a Function of Parental Education

Official Statement on "Race": American Anthropological Association

In the United States both scholars and the general public have been conditioned to viewing human races as natural and separate divisions within the human species based on visible physical differences. With the vast expansion of scientific knowledge in this century, however, it has become clear that human populations are not unambiguous, clearly demarcated, biologically distinct groups.

Evidence from the analysis of genetics (e.g., DNA) indicates that most physical variation, about 94 per cent, lies within so-called racial groups. Conventional geographic "racial" groupings differ from one another only in about 6 per cent of their genes. This means that there is greater variation within "racial" groups than between them.

Historical research has shown that the idea of "race" has always carried more meanings than mere physical differences; indeed, physical variations in the human species have no meaning except the social ones that humans put on them. Today scholars in many fields argue that "race" as it is understood in the United States of America was a social mechanism invented during the 18th century to refer to those populations brought together in colonial America: the English and other European settlers, the conquered Indian peoples, and those peoples of Africa brought in to provide slave labor.

Proponents of slavery in particular during the 19th century used "race" to justify the retention of slavery. The ideology magnified the differences among Europeans, Africans, and Indians, established a rigid hierarchy of socially exclusive categories underscored and bolstered unequal rank and status differences, and provided the rationalization that the inequality was natural or God-given. The different physical traits of African-Americans and Indians became markers or symbols of their status differences.

As they were constructing US society, leaders among European-Americans fabricated the cultural/behavioral characteristics associated with each "race," linking superior traits with Europeans and negative and inferior ones to blacks and Indians. Numerous arbitrary and fictitious beliefs about the different peoples were institutionalized and deeply embedded in American thought. Ultimately "race" as an ideology about human differences was subsequently spread to other areas of the world. It became a strategy for dividing, ranking, and controlling colonized people used by colonial powers everywhere.

At the end of the 20th century, we now understand that human cultural behavior is learned, conditioned into infants beginning at birth, and always subject to modification. No human is born with a built-in culture or language. Our temperaments, dispositions, and personalities, regardless of genetic propensities, are developed within sets of meanings and values that we call "culture." Studies of infant and early childhood learning and behavior attest to the reality of our cultures in forming who we are. ..

Source: American Anthropological Association. "Statement on 'Race.'" 1996-2002.

Questions

1. Why does the American Anthropological Association believe that race is not a valid construct?
2. Briefly summarize their explanation of the way in which the idea of "race" developed.
3. How was genetic evidence used to help deny the validity of the concept of race?

Adorno described the parents as cold and aloof, and more likely to discipline their children harshly. Thus, both Allport and Adorno believed that the children's first teachers, the parents, are very important agents in the learning of prejudice.

According to modern-day psychologist Stuart Hall, we know a lot about the effects of racial prejudice in the world but need to learn more about how people acquire these beliefs. Hall acknowledges that people often do respond to the visible signs of racial difference, and he asks why these signs have so much psychological impact. The next subsection will examine the views of contemporary social scientists on the psychology of race. Three experts, Frances Aboud, Beverley Tatum, and John Ogbu, will identify how we learn racial concepts and how these ideas affect people in our society.

Figure 9.5 Children often can acquire their personalities and their prejudices from their parents.

GROUNDBREAKERS
GORDON W. ALLPORT, 1897–1967

In 1954, Gordon W. Allport completed *The Nature of Prejudice*, a landmark book that has helped shape much of our thinking about prejudice since then. More than half a million copies of the book had already been sold when the twenty-fifth anniversary edition was released in 1979. *The Nature of Prejudice* reviewed research done in the first half of the twentieth century, and developed insights that reflected Allport's view of personality development.

Allport researched and taught psychology at Harvard University in the United States from 1930 until his death. He published many articles and books during his long career, all with the underlying theme that human personality grows and develops very gradually. Allport opposed the then-popular view that a person is little more than a set of physical drives, responding to external stimuli through conditioned (trained) responses. This idea

Figure 9.6 Gordon W. Allport

was based on the work of Ivan Pavlov, who had conducted experiments with dogs in which he trained them to drool in anticipation of food by ringing a bell or flashing a light before he actually fed the animals. This type of stimulus-response training is called **classical conditioning**. Instead, Allport expressed a more optimistic view of human nature: that a person is shaped more by striving from within, than by outside environmental forces.

Some Important Ideas from *The Nature of Prejudice*

A. In-groups and Group Norms

By age five, children realize that they belong to certain groups and can develop strong in-group loyalties. There are psychological "rewards" for membership in these groups, including a feeling of belonging and a sense of identity. People particularly value membership in what Allport called reference groups, those with whom they have close social connections, such as family and friends. They readily adopt group norms—the attitudes, beliefs, and behaviours of the reference group—as the price of belonging.

B. Out-groups and Prejudice

Out-groups are any groups that are seen either as a direct threat or as being in direct contrast to the reference groups with which people have identified. In-group members learn to direct their frustrations and hostilities toward out-group members. This is called the group norms theory of prejudice. Present-day researcher Marilyn Brewer writes that Allport never claimed that out-group hate is necessary to develop in-group loyalties. Research and experiments both show that group identification is independent of negative attitudes toward out-groups. Therefore, not every in-group develops prejudices toward out-groups (Brewer, 1999).

C. Children and Prejudice

Children can learn prejudice in two ways: either by adopting it or by developing it. In the first case, children simply take on attitudes and stereotypes that they notice in the family or the surrounding cultural environment. Words and gestures and their associated beliefs and feelings are transmitted. Children can also develop a prejudiced nature based on the way in which they are raised by their parents. For example, children whose training focuses on strict obedience learn that power and authority, not trust and tolerance, dominate human relationships. Allport believed that this lays the groundwork for the development of prejudices at some point in life.

Questions

1. How was Allport's view of people different from the view developed from Pavlov's work?

2. Summarize the group norms theory of prejudice. Does prejudice develop from in-group loyalty? Explain.

3. According to Allport, how do children develop prejudice? Compare this to Theodor Adorno's views.

Figure 9.7 Through extensive observation and testing, child development psychologists have learned a great deal about the typical growth stages of children.

Linking Prejudice to Child Development

Frances Aboud focuses on the processes by which children first learn race awareness, then either reject or form racial prejudices. She calls it the social-cognitive theory of prejudice. As a professor of psychology at McGill University in Montreal, she brought early research about prejudice in children up to date by evaluating many different social and psychological factors affecting them.

Like Gordon Allport, Aboud believes that children become aware of different ethnic groups at about four to five years of age. She also agrees with him that parents and the surrounding society have an important influence on what a child learns. However, she goes beyond these external factors and concentrates on the capabilities of the growing child. Aboud believes we must understand children's views of people in terms of thinking or **cognition**, which allows them to distinguish between "self" and "others."

Development Stages Affecting Children Aged 4 to 12 Years

Stage	Age Group	Typical Characteristics
1. Jean Piaget (1896-1980), Cognitive Development Stages		
Pre-operational	2-7 years	They rely on perceptions of how things seem to be. For example, young children see themselves as right, and other children as wrong.
Concrete operational	7-11 years	They develop internal rules to guide what they see. For example, they understand how others feel if it is tied to some concrete experience of their own.
Formal operational	11 years +	They think abstractly and can see other points of view. For example, they can understand how someone feels without having actually experienced the feeling.
2. Lawrence Kohlberg (1927–1987), Moral Development Stages (in males)		
Pre-moral level	before age 7	They are not capable of moral reasoning.
Pre-conventional level	7–10 years	They act mostly out of self-interest and obey rules only to avoid punishment. For example: "What's in it for me?" and "It's OK because I didn't get caught."
Conventional level	10–16 years	They recognize that needs of others can be more important than their own needs. For example, "I'm doing this because I promised them that I would."

Figure 9.8 According to the developmental stages outlined here, at what age do you think it would be most appropriate to begin a child's education in multiculturalism? Explain your reasoning.

Aboud builds her theory on the human development stages identified by other twentieth-century psychologists, such as Jean Piaget and Lawrence Kohlberg.

Aboud's theory of prejudice is based on two overlapping development sequences. From Piaget come the stages of change in cognition that affect functioning as children grow older, and from Kohlberg and others comes the shift in children's attention away from themselves. At about age four, when children are most attentive to self-concerns, they also become aware of ethnic differences. Their early ethnic concepts, taken in from parents and the media, often reflect in-group membership and out-group stereotypes. Aboud's research found prejudices in many white children aged four to seven, and to a lesser extent in minority-group children. However, their ideas are incomplete and often confused because of the limits of cognition at this age.

Striking changes occur after age seven due to the child's rapidly developing mental capabilities. Children's attention starts to shift away from self and toward other groups around them. Aboud found that prejudices can begin to decrease with children's growing ability to handle information and look beyond themselves. She believes that after age seven, children are cognitively capable of being less prejudiced, making it an ideal time for exposure to education programs that will help them form more positive images of other groups.

Finally, as children reach 10 to 12 years of age, their skills and reasoning allow them to identify individuals more clearly, with less emphasis on group characteristics. In short, they are more capable of seeing individuals, without using group labels. However, Aboud makes it clear that even though children do have maturing abilities, they will still develop and hold on to prejudices if they are bombarded with negative images of other groups.

The social-cognitive theory of prejudice improves upon earlier theories that place great emphasis on the role of parents in the emergence of the intolerant authoritarian personality. Frances Aboud acknowledges the initial role of parents, but ties her ideas closely to the child-development studies of other prominent psychologists. The strength of her theory lies in its recognition that children constantly change their views of others as they grow. This makes it possible for schools to create learning activities that encourage tolerance. One criticism of the social-cognitive theory applies to all developmental stage frameworks: there is a great deal of variation in the maturation rates of children, and they therefore pass through stages at different ages.

Affirming Racial Identity

Psychologist Beverley Tatum believes that it is important for people to engage in conversation about race, even though it can seem to be an awkward subject. Although race is not a biological trait, Tatum says that we all have a racial identity, which we must strive to affirm. This means that for our personal sense of well-being, we all must recognize who we are and be comfortable with ourselves. Tatum explains how members of racial minorities (she discusses African-Americans, Hispanics, Asians, Aboriginal people, and those of mixed racial background) can develop constructive racial identities. First, they must be able to recognize and reject negative stereotypes held about them in the broader society. Then, they need to learn how to act in certain situations so that they do not become passive victims. For example, members of minority groups must be able to deal effectively with unequal treatment when they encounter it.

Beverley Tatum sets a task for whites too. She believes that they enjoy subtle "rewards" and advantages in society based on their visible identity. They must become aware of this and recognize that privilege rather than merit has been responsible for injustices, past and present.

American educator Peggy McIntosh sheds new light on the subject of racial power

Figure 9.9 Peggy McIntosh suggested that, as a member of the racial majority culture in her workplace, she carries an invisible knapsack full of subtle privileges that she was taught to take for granted.

Unpacking Peggy McIntosh's Invisible "White Privilege Knapsack"
(Examples from list of 46)

- I can, if I wish, arrange to be in the company of people of my race most of the time.   *least noticable*

- I can go shopping alone most of the time pretty well assured that I will not be followed or harassed.   *4*

- I can turn on the television or open to the front page of the paper and see people of my race widely represented.   *5*

- When I am told about our national heritage or about "civilization," I am shown that people of my colour made it what it is....   *6 non-white morale*

- I am never asked to speak for all the people of my racial group....   *3*

- I can criticize our government and talk about how much I fear its policies and behaviours without being seen as a cultural outsider.   *2. prevalent problem.*

Source: McIntosh, Peggy. 1988. "White Privilege: Unpacking the Invisible Knapsack." In Aaron Podolefsky and Peter J. Brown. *Applying Anthropology: An Introductory Reader.* 2001. Toronto. Mayfield Publishing.

relations. She suggests that people of Anglo-European descent, like her, carry an invisible, weightless knapsack of skin-colour privileges that the bearer takes for granted. After comparing herself with African-American women in her workplace at Wellesley College, MA, she made an autobiographical list of 46 daily ways in which she experiences unearned advantage because of her skin colour.

 ## Subordinate Cultures

Psychologist John Ogbu looks at the impact of race from the opposite side of white privilege. He focuses on **subordinate cultures**—his term for American minorities such as immigrants, African-Americans, and other racial groups. He uses the word "subordinate" because he believes that minority groups are at a disadvantage in society, required to follow the norms of the white majority culture. For example, Dr. Ogbu has researched the reasons why African-American students are often found in the non-academic streams of American schools. One important factor he identifies is that many African-American children come from an oral culture—that is, one that puts more focus on speaking and hearing than on reading and writing. They often find school difficult because it rewards reading and writing much more highly.

John Ogbu is known for his work on the relationship between language and identity among African-Americans. Linguists are social scientists who study language, and they have recently termed the informal language of some blacks **Ebonics**. This new word is a combination of the words "ebony" and "phonics" and literally means "black sounds." Ebonics is spoken by some blacks, especially in informal conversation. Ebonics first developed on Southern plantations during the era of slavery, then was carried north as African-Americans sought urban jobs in the late nineteenth and the twentieth centuries. It is an important part of the social identity of some blacks.

Many linguists and educators, including Ogbu, favour using Ebonics to help bridge the gap to better use of standard English for formal situations. They recognize that inner-city students will be less likely to advance in the mainstream society without learning how to speak and write standard English. Evidence suggests that standard English can be more easily mastered by building upon the differ-ences between it and the student's home language. For example, a Chicago study showed a 59 per cent reduction in the use of Ebonics in the writing of inner-city students who learned by this method. Meanwhile, a control group taught by conventional methods actually showed a small increase in the use of Ebonics in their writing.

How Well Can You Understand Ebonics?

Match the Ebonics phrase on the left with the scrambled standard English translations on the right.

1. She runnin.

2. She be runnin.

3. She be steady runnin.

4. She bin runnin.

5. She *bin* runnin.

A) She is usually running in an intense, sustained way.

B) She has been running.

C) She is running.

D) She's been running a long time and still is at it.

E) She is usually running.

Source: Based upon Rickford, John R. 2001. "Suite for Ebony and Phonics." In Aaron Podolefsky and Peter J. Brown. *Applying Anthropology: An Introductory Reader.* Toronto. Mayfield Publishing.

[Answers: 1-C; 2-E; 3-A; 4-B; 5-D]

Pause and Reflect

1. According to the early studies of Allport and Adorno, which children would be more likely to be prejudiced? To what extent do you agree with these notions? Explain.

2. How are the terms "stereotype," "group norms," and "out-groups" connected in the group norms theory of prejudice?

3. Why does Frances Aboud believe that many children actually become less prejudiced as they grow older? In what circumstances does this not happen?

4. What does Peggy McIntosh mean by "skin-colour privilege"? What is your impression of this idea? Explain.

5. In your own words, explain John Ogbu's term "subordinate culture," using an example. Why does he believe that Ebonics can improve school success for inner-city African-American students?

Section 9.3   Analyzing Hate Crimes

What Causes Hate?

It was one more of those terrible clashes that characterize the ongoing religious conflict between Catholic and Protestant extremists in Northern Ireland. In September of 2001, television showed disturbing scenes of terrified elementary-school girls, some only four years old, passing by mobs of shouting and cursing adults to get into their school. Some of these people were throwing things at them, and one girl saw her mother get struck in the face by a bottle. The little girls' "crime" was their religion. That was enough to cause complete strangers to hate them. One parent compared the ugly scene to the school integration battles in the United States, saying, "This looks like Alabama in the '60s." Another man was as shaken as the crying children: "The abuse I heard was unbelievable. It was one of the most savage experiences of my life."

Fortunately, world reaction to these scenes was so negative that after a few days, the mob stopped harassing the women and children as they walked to and from the school ("Belfast children…," 2001, p. A5).

Most people find it difficult to understand the level of **hatred** directed by adults at these children. It may be even harder to figure out why a Montreal man gunned down 14 female engineering students at the Ecole Polytechnique in 1989, or why white Texans dragged a black man to his death behind their pickup truck in 1998. It is as incomprehensible as the "gay-bashing" incident, which left a young man beaten and tied to a country fence post to die in the Wyoming winter, and as bizarre as the plan to destroy a few hundred students at Columbine High School in Colorado by two of their peers. More recently, the September 2001 terrorist attacks on the World Trade Center and the Pentagon, which killed close to 3000 people, seem almost unbelievable. Why do people carry such intense hate?

Psychologists, and even philosophers, have struggled to explain the cause of hatred. For example, the ancient Greek philosopher Aristotle observed the differences between anger and actual hatred. He said that anger is usually felt toward individuals, while hatred may be directed at whole classes of people. After an angry outburst, a person often feels sorry for his or her words and actions, but hatred is more deep-rooted. Aristotle pointed out that there is seldom repentance for acts of hatred because a person really aims to negate the object of his or her intense feelings.

Four Characteristics of Hate Crimes

1. The hatred is intense and impersonal
Hatred of this type is not the same as strong anger directed at an individual with whom

Key Concepts

hatred

scapegoat

white supremacist

Holocaust

crimes against humanity

Universal Declaration of Human Rights

war crimes

Holocaust denier

hate group

Figure 9.10 A mother leads her daughter to school in Belfast, Sept. 2001. What caused this mob of grownups to harass young children on their way to school?

there was previous conflict or rivalry. To psychologist Gordon Allport, anger is an emotion, while hatred is a sentiment, "an enduring organization of aggressive impulses toward a person or toward a class of persons…. composed of habitual bitter feeling and accusatory thought…." (Allport, 1979, p. 91).

Hatred is not part of what police and lawyers call "crimes of passion," for these are characterized by intense personal anger directed at a someone well-known to the perpetrator. The Belfast mob didn't know anything about the schoolgirls except their religion. Mark Lepine ordered all the men out of the room before he turned his gun on the women. James Byrd was dragged to his death because of the colour of his skin. Matthew Sheppard had just met his killers at a bar, where they had deliberately gone to pick a homosexual victim. At Columbine High School, Eric Harris and Dylan Klebold mostly shot at people wearing sports hats and team shirts as revenge on "jocks" who wouldn't accept "losers" like them. And, the hijack terrorists were simply intent on killing the enemy—any American. In all of these cases, intense hatred was directed at unknown people, who represented, or even seemed to represent, the perpetrator's out-group.

2. The hatred is based on prejudice and power

You have already learned how stereotypes can harden into feelings of prejudice. Discriminatory actions can follow, but only when the perpetrators have some power of authority or physical advantage over the intended victim or victims. Often, but certainly not always, the power of those who hate comes from strength of numbers, weapons, and surprise. For example, a threatening crowd of youths and adult men used rocks and bottles against women and little girls in Belfast. Mark Lepine used surprise at Montreal Polytechnique by bursting into the school heavily armed. Three men forcibly tied a black hitchhiker to a truck bumper, while two men, intent on "gay-bashing," picked up one victim smaller in stature than themselves. The high-school killers used an arsenal of guns and pipe bombs to terrorize several hundred students, while the hijackers relied on knives and bold surprise to fly commercial airplanes into selected targets. The perpetrators in all these cases acted from positions of power to lash out at the objects of their hatred.

3. The hatred is directed at scapegoats for other frustrations

Allport suggests that frustration and the difficulties of life may be found at the centre of intense hatred toward out-groups:

> Because of severe frustration, it is easy to fuse one's recurring anger into rationalized [reasoned out] hatreds. In order to avoid hurt and achieve at least an island of security, it is safer to exclude than to include…. By taking a negative view of great groups of mankind, we somehow make life simpler. For example, if I reject all foreigners as a category, I don't have to bother with them—except to keep them out of my country.
>
> (Allport, 1979, p. 93)

Out-groups selected as targets for this displaced frustration and hostility are called **scapegoats**. They are easily identifiable minority groups on which those with power can lay blame and against which they can act out their aggressions. For example, in the late nineteenth century, hundreds of blacks were hanged each year in the southern US, often as a part of cross-burning rituals organized by Ku Klux Klan **white supremacists**. Sometimes these illegal lynchings were conducted by mobs of poor white farmers, one rung above the victim on the social ladder, for no reason other than to "keep the blacks in their place." Their aim was to create terror and submission among members of the hated scapegoats whom they attacked. The perpetrator of the 1989 Montreal Massacre left a suicide note claiming that he killed the female engineering students because they were "feminists." Sadly, he felt that women had to be kept in their place, too.

4. Genocide is an expression of national hatred

The greatest excesses of hatred directed against minority scapegoats are those that have been carried out by order as national policy. Many considered the anti-Semitic opinions of Adolf Hitler the pathetic ravings of a frustrated man when he first wrote *Mein Kampf* (which means "My Struggle"). In this book, Hitler blamed the Jews for the failures of his own life and for the problems of Germany. When he become the *führer*, Hitler ordered a series of laws and actions to first isolate, and later eliminate, Jews from Germany and Europe. They were systematically denied basic human rights and subjected to acts of terror by police and the military. Finally, they were rounded up and forcibly moved to specially built extermination camps. By 1945, Hitler and the Nazis were responsible for the deaths of more than 6 million European Jews.

The **Holocaust** is the worst case of racial-cultural genocide the world has known in terms of the number of lives lost. But there have been other twentieth-century examples in which great numbers of people have been exterminated as a group simply because of their race, culture, religion, or nationality. For example, Armenians hold Turkey responsible for the lives of 1.5 million people, banished to almost certain death in the desert in 1915. Turkey had waged deadly campaigns against these Christians a generation earlier, and took advantage of the chaos of World War I to try to eliminate them. In 1994, extremist members of the ethnic Hutu majority in the African nation of Rwanda savagely murdered about 800 000 minority Tutsi people, and any sympathizers, in just a few weeks of unrestrained violence. Four years later, the United Nations International

Figure 9.11 This photo shows Nazi leader, Adolf Hitler, during World War Two. Why is it against the law in Canada and other countries to display the Nazi flag in public?

Court of Justice found Hutu leaders guilty of genocide and **crimes against humanity** for their role in the slaughter.

Hate Crimes and International Law

After World War II, the international community agreed that such events as the Holocaust must never happen again. In 1948, the newly formed United Nations declared its **Universal Declaration of Human Rights**. Much of it was written by little-known Canadian lawyer John Humphrey. This was the first international statement outlining the rights and freedoms of people globally. It states that every person has the right to life, freedom, and security. No one must be treated in a cruel, degrading, or inhuman way. In 1998, 98 countries set up the United Nations

Genocide in Bosnia and Croatia

Slobodan Milosevic to face genocide charges

The Hague [Netherlands] (AP) – The chief prosecutor of the Yugoslav war crimes tribunal said today she will file charges of genocide against former president Slobodan Milosevic for massacres in Bosnia.

The prosecutor, Carla Del Ponte, said she expected to file new indictments against Milosevic on Oct. 1 for crimes committed in Bosnia and Croatia in the early 1990s. Those indictments would be combined with charges for crimes against humanity in Kosovo in 1999, and would likely go to trial in the autumn of 2002.

She said the mass graves of Kosovo Albanians recently discovered in Serbia were not enough to charge the former leader with genocide in Kosovo. Investigators revealed at least four common burial sites across Serbia— graves that contain the tangled remains of at least 800 victims of a brutal 1998–99 crackdown on ethnic Albanians in Kosovo.

Del Ponte had previously said she was investigating Milosevic for genocide, but it was the first time she confirmed that the most serious war crimes charge would be included in at least one indictment.

Dozens of Serb police and army officers have been indicted for the persecution of Muslims and Croats during the Balkan wars in the early 1990s, ended by the Dayton peace accord in 1995 that Milosevic signed.

Figure 9.12 Thousands of ethnic Albanians were forced to flee Kosovo in terror as the Serbian forces attacked.

Only one, Radislav Krstic, has been convicted of genocide. He was sentenced earlier this month to 46 years imprisonment.

The prosecution was building a case accusing Milosevic of ultimate responsibility for war crimes in Bosnia and Croatia, since he stood at the top of the chain of command.

In previous trials, senior officers were convicted of war crimes committed by subordinates, even if it could not be proved they had issued orders to commit those crimes. Those cases established the law holding commanders responsible if they knew of the atrocities and failed to prevent them....

Source: "Slobodan Milosevic to face genocide charges." *The Sarnia Observer.* 30 August 2001.

Questions
1. Summarize the two charges that Milosevic is going to be charged with.
   a) Which of these two is the most serious in international law?
   b) What principle is the international court following in charging him with these crimes?
2. Prove that hatred is central to this case. How would psychologists explain the degree of hatred directed at Albanian Muslims in Kosovo [a region of Serbia]?

International Criminal Court to investigate and prosecute individuals guilty of **war crimes**, crimes against humanity, and genocide. These are the most extreme crimes of hatred and are defined as follows.

- *war crimes:* murder, torture, and hostage-taking of civilian nationals, and/or wide-scale destruction of their property
- *crimes against humanity:* murder, torture, enslavement, and deportation of innocent civilian nationals
- *genocide:* deliberate mass murder of any national, ethnic, racial or religious group

Hate Crimes and Canadian Law

Hate crimes do occur in Canada—one example is the New Brunswick cross-burning incident described at the beginning of this chapter. After the terrorist attacks on the World Trade Center and the Pentagon, there were several random attacks on Muslims and their property in Canada. Other religious minorities, such as Sikhs and Hindus, were sometimes mistaken for Muslims and harassed too. In recent years, neo-Nazi "skinheads" have been convicted of violent acts against racial minorities and the desecration of Jewish synagogues. "**Holocaust deniers**," such as Alberta teacher Jim Keegstra and German national Ernst Zundel, have preached that this event, thoroughly documented by the Nazis themselves, is a hoax created by the Jews to discredit Germany. Keegstra was convicted and Zundel was deported.

Our Charter of Rights and Freedoms outlines the personal right to life, liberty, and security of each Canadian. However, Section 1 of the Charter states that there are "justifiable limits" to our personal freedoms beyond which they threaten the right to security of others. For the greater good of society, Canadians are *not* free to say whatever they want about other individuals and groups.

In 1985, the Criminal Code of Canada was revised to reflect the guarantees of the Charter. Sections 318 and 319 of the Criminal Code define laws and punishment relating to genocide and hatred against "identifiable groups," such as those distinguished by colour, race, religion or ethnic origin. It is against the law to communicate hateful comments by any means, including the Internet. However, it is extremely difficult to control Web site content, especially if the site originates outside Canada. Today, the Internet gives organized **hate groups** and individuals better opportunities than ever before to spread their twisted messages.

FILM SOCIETY

Title: Swing Kids (1993)
Rating: PG-13 (some violence and profanity)

This is an entertaining, youth-oriented movie with a serious underlying theme of anti-Semitism. Three young German friends drawn to American pop music on the eve of World War II try to avoid being conscripted into Hitler Youth. One does join, while the other two rebel against it, one friend taking his own life to escape. The film demonstrates in-groups, out-groups, and scapegoats. The rewards of membership in Hitler Youth contrast with the persecution of scapegoats: Jews, people with disabilities, and resistors who speak out against Nazism.

COMPETING
PERSPECTIVES

Does the Heritage Front organization promote hatred in Canada?

The Heritage Front is an "underground" Canadian organization focused on race. Supporters describe themselves as "militantly pro-white" and strongly opposed to multiculturalism and immigration. The first article, representing the "no" argument, is their mission statement, as seen on the organization's Web site.

In the second article, representing the "yes" side, a former Heritage Front member describes her experiences with the organization. Examine this information carefully, against the background of Canadian law (see page 312), to decide whether or not this group promotes hate.

No: The Heritage Front Web site

We are concerned Canadians. While we are strong numerically, our voice and right to representation has been (and continues to be) compromised to a welter of special interest and minority lobby concerns. Without guarantees—without a cap on immigration—we realize that it is only a matter of time before we find ourselves a minority in our own nation. Strong numbers are not enough when we are subject to a relentless campaign to demean and denigrate our heritage, traditions, culture, values and historic contributions.

"The Heritage Front is an organization that was created to support Euro-Canadians. Discrimination against traditional Euro-Canadian values is common in Canada and we are seeking to change that. Our membership comes from all walks of life, and is open to men and women who are supportive of equal rights for Euro-Canadians and special privileges for none. The Heritage Front has been in public existence for over 10 years and is Canada's largest Racialist Organization. The Heritage Front's mandate is to preserve our heritage—in a militantly pro-White, militantly positive sense. We are proud of who we are, our history and accomplishments.

* * * *

...If you don't think that our opponents have a "plan" that they are holding to, you had better think again. Is it just co-incidence when they forcefully curtail freedom of speech and ram more multiculturalism and immigration down out throats? Is it just "increasing public safety" when they proceed to enact the most repressive gun laws in the western world? If they really give a damn about public safety, wouldn't they start by rounding up and turfing out some of the criminal scum that has made it into Canada and also immediately halt the flow of such undesirables? If they actually cared about public safety, why do they provide encouragement for some of the most questionable elements on the face of the planet to come here?

...As far as recruitment goes... we will continue our policy of no recruiting as it has always existed. We are interested only in those Euro-Canadians that have reached the same conclusions as we have, of their own accord. In most cases this results from the individual's observations not corresponding to what is being presented by the system-controlled media.

The notion that we go out and try to influence people, such as students, is sheer rubbish and our opponents know it. The same goes for the distribution of literature, which we won't do. If anyone on their own goes out and distributes any type of "racist" or anti-semitic material that clearly violates Canadian "Hate" laws, they will have to bear the repercussions. No such act is sanctioned or encouraged by the HF leadership.

Source: Gordon, Frank (Ed.). 2002. Heritage Front Web site. [Online]. Available <http:// www.freedomsite.org/ hf/hf_report_jan97.html>. January 2002.

COMPETING PERSPECTIVES

Yes: "Elizabeth Moore: Her Story, In Her Own Words"

...Five years ago, when I was in grade 12, I met a guy named Hans. Hans was different from other people I knew. He was German-born, for one, and a couple of years older than the rest of the class. I helped him with his assignments because he still had trouble with English grammar, and he, in turn, slowly introduced me to National Socialism. Eventually, he gave me a couple of flyers about the Heritage Front. He told me that they were "the white man's answer to multiculturalism." The flyers said they were a group of ordinary men and women concerned about the future of Canada, and persecuted by the Human Rights Commission for speaking out.

...They worked on empowering me, by telling me that I was better than my family, friends and teachers because I was racially aware....They constantly told racist jokes and made racist remarks in order to saturate my conversations with racist rhetoric.

They introduced me to Holocaust denial literature, which came from 3 sources: Ernst Zundel, The Institute for Historical Review in America, and other Front members. For example, Gerry Lincoln gave me and my boyfriend access to videos in his extensive collection such as *The Eternal Jew* and *Triumph of the Will*. Holocaust denial is important to the movement because if a person is willing to believe that one of the worst mass human rights abuses in the history of the Western world was a hoax, dreamed up by the victims themselves, that person is willing to believe just about anything the movement's leaders tell them.

I quickly got hooked on the euphoria of hatred, the empowerment, and the sense of belonging, which I never had before. My attachment to the group grew so strong that I was always willing to do more, regardless of the potential costs, monetary or otherwise. By the time I was ready to leave the group, I was "staff reporter" for *Up Front* [their magazine], I ran a telephone hateline, and I was a media spokesperson. I put up flyers, made speeches, attended demos, infiltrated left wing organizations and public meetings, including one when Bernie Farber, the National Director of Community Relations for the Canadian Jewish Congress, came to Queen's.

I basically lived the "Aryan Life," in which every action was seen as a contribution to the betterment of the race. This Aryan Life affected not only my political actions, but also my taste in music, clothing, TV and movies, to name a few. When I was ready to leave the group, my boyfriend, 90% of my friends, all my thoughts, my hopes and dreams for the future, were wrapped up in the Heritage Front....

Source: Farber, Bernie. 1997. *From Marches to Modems: A Report on Organized Hate in Metropolitan Toronto.* "The Recruits: Elizabeth Moore." Canadian Jewish Congress. Toronto.

Questions

1. Summarize the position of the Heritage Front in a paragraph. Use your own words.

   a) What is the purpose of the information posted on their Web site?

   b) Identify points the organization's Web site makes to show that they do not promote hate, especially among young people.

2. Summarize Elizabeth Moore's present point of view about the Heritage Front in a paragraph.

   a) What purpose do you think she is trying to serve by printing her personal story?

   b) Identify points that she makes to show that the Heritage Front promotes hate, especially among young people.

Criminal Code of Canada, Chapter C-46, Revised Statutes of Canada, 1985:

Section 319

(1) Every person who, by communicating statements in any public place incites hatred against any identifiable group where such incitement is likely to lead to a breach of the peace is guilty of

(a) an indictable offence and is liable to imprisonment of a term not exceeding two years; or

(b) an offence punishable on summary conviction.

(2) Every one who, by communicating statements other than in private conversation, wilfully promotes hatred against any identifiable group is guilty of

(a) an indictable offence and is liable to imprisonment of a term not exceeding two years; or

(b) an offence punishable on summary conviction....

(7) In this section, "communicating" includes communicating by telephone, broadcasting, or other audible or visible means; "identifiable group" has the same meaning as in Section 318; "public place" includes any place to which the public have access as of right or by invitation, express or implied; "statements" includes words spoken or recorded electronically or electromagnetically or otherwise, and gestures, signs or other visible representations.

Pause and Reflect

1. Summarize the major differences between anger and hatred. What reasons for hatred are suggested in this section?

2. Gather information about the Montreal Massacre from this section. Then, write a bold news headline and a short news article, with personal commentary linking it to hatred.

3. What is genocide? Make a chart to compare any three examples from this section.

4. Carefully examine Section 319 of the Criminal Code of Canada above. Where does it say that burning a cross or painting a swastika can be an act of hatred against a group? What is the maximum penalty, if convicted?

5. Is there any information in the two Competing Perspectives readings that could be used either to prove or disprove the statement, "The Heritage Front organization promotes hatred in Canada."

6. *Either:* Imagine that you are a lawyer hired to defend the Heritage Front against charges laid under Section 319 of the Criminal Code of Canada. Try to prove that they operate within the limits of the law and the Charter of Rights and Freedoms.

   Or: Imagine that you are prosecuting the Heritage Front under Section 319, using the testimony of Elizabeth Moore as a key part of your case. Try to prove that they have violated the law and the Charter of Rights and Freedoms.

Section 9.4   Paradigm Shift: "Unlearning" Prejudice

Can Prejudice Be "Unlearned"?

People are not born with prejudice—they learn it. Social scientists have long been interested in whether or not people can "unlearn" prejudice, too. The 1954 Robber's Cave study, led by researchers M. Sherif and L.J. Harvey, is the classic experiment that tested this question. Two groups of 11-year-old, middle-class white boys went to summer camp at Robber's Cave State Park in Oklahoma. The two groups were kept isolated from each other as the boys enjoyed a week of typical recreational activities, named their groups, and printed the name on their shirts and caps. Then, the researchers suddenly brought the two groups together for a series of competitive athletic events. Almost immediately, the boys disliked members of the other groups, whom they had never seen previously. As the two groups competed for prizes, they became very antagonistic toward one another off the field, engaging in food fights, cabin break-ins, vandalism, and theft.

In the second part of the Robber's Cave experiment, the researchers tested whether they could get the boys to unlearn the prejudice and ill-will that had been created. In the following weeks, they created a series of emergency situations around the camp, then assigned inter-group teams to solve them. In one case, mixed teams were organized to search for a big leak that seemed to have cut off the camp's water supply. In another, boys from the two teams were needed to get a truck carrying campers out of the mud, where it had become stuck. By the end of the experiment, the boys from the two teams had formed many inter-group friendships, and peace prevailed. Group identification and intense competition had created prejudice,

while **inter-group co-operation** had largely eliminated it (Sternberg, 1994, p. 546).

Though the Robber's Cave study is considered a classic, you probably noticed an important weakness—it deals only with the experience of one type of group: white, middle-class boys. It is quite possible that other groups may have responded differently to the camp situation that the researchers created. For example, Carol Gilligan's studies of women found that they do not see moral issues the same way men do. Women tend to focus more on caring and compassion and are often more concerned about human welfare and interpersonal relationships than men are. They may not have reverted to such overt displays of aggression as the boys in the study did. However, the most important part

Key Concepts

inter-group
co-operation

paradigm shift

desegregate

equal status
social contact

Jigsaw learning

multiculturalism

anti-racism

institutional
barriers

culture-fair
testing

Figure 9.13 The Robber's Cave experiment tested whether it would be possible for boys to unlearn prejudice. Do you believe it possible?

of the study is the second half—unlearning prejudice. To use the terms of Joel Barker and Kenneth Boulding (see page 290), co-operative activities led to a **paradigm shift**, which allowed the boys to form new images of their former enemies.

 **Equal Status Social Contact**

One result of the American Civil Rights Movement was the Supreme Court decision to **desegregate** schools, ruling that separate facilities violated equality. When Austin, Texas, schools were desegregated in 1971, white, African-American, and Hispanic students there were put together for the first time. Old suspicions, fears, and distrust soon resulted in hostility and classroom problems.

Social psychologist Elliot Aronson was asked to identify ways to ease the tensions, and he quickly saw parallels between these classrooms and the Robber's Cave experiment. He observed that the classrooms were competitive environments in which students were struggling with one another for limited "rewards," such as a chance to gain recognition by answering questions, or receiving praise from the teacher. Aronson decided that learning would need to be restructured in a more co-operative way, based on mixed teams made up of different races, like the boys at the summer camp. His solution also followed important conditions for reducing prejudice, which had been outlined by Gordon Allport in *The Nature of Prejudice*:

> *To be maximally effective, contact and acquaintance programs should lead to a sense of equality in social status, should occur in ordinary purposeful pursuits, avoid artificiality, and if possible, enjoy the sanction [support] of the community in which they occur. The deeper and more genuine the association, the greater the effect…. the gain is greater if those members regard themselves as part of a team.*
>
> *(Allport, 1979, p. 489)*

GROUNDBREAKERS

ELLIOT ARONSON (B. 1932)

Elliot Aronson has distinguished himself as a writer, teacher, and researcher, winning the American Psychological Association's highest awards in all three categories. He is a social psychologist, interested in human social behaviour (and misbehaviour) individuals use in relating to others around them. His best-known book, *The Social Animal*, has been reprinted numerous times since 1972 and translated into 14 languages. He is currently a professor at Stanford University in California.

Probably the most important aspect of Aronson's work is his strong interest in improving society by changing people's negative attitudes and behaviours. He has done a great deal of research on reducing prejudice and promoting more positive relations between people through **equal status social**

Figure 9.14 Elliot Aronson

contact on shared tasks. An important body of his work has dealt with schools, where he has developed classroom strategies to help students unlearn prejudice.

Most recently, Aronson addressed the problem of hatred and violence in schools. His book *Nobody Left to Hate: Teaching Compassion After Columbine* offers suggestions built on the social contact model to help reduce the interpersonal tensions that sometimes lead to shootings, such as the massacre at Columbine High School in Littleton, Colorado, in 1999. He argues that if teachers can create a classroom atmosphere in which there are no outsiders or "losers," then there will be nobody left to hate. This represents a broader application of co-operative learning than originally intended when it aimed to reduce interracial prejudice.

Elliot Aronson named the system of teaching and learning he developed **Jigsaw learning** because each member of the team becomes an "expert" on a different piece of a topic. Each group of students must co-operate as a team in order to learn the whole topic. Examine the flow chart below to see if your teachers have used this popular method of instruction in your schools.

In order to examine the impacts of his system, Aronson compared desegregated classes using Jigsaw methods and traditional instruction. After only eight weeks, his research team observed marked improvements both in learning and in co-operation between students from different backgrounds. Equal status social contact seemed to have been effective. Psychologist Robert Slavin, of Johns Hopkins University in Maryland, expanded Aronson's work to include new variations on Jigsaw learning, such as Teams-Games-Tournaments (TGT). This method combines co-operation and competition by having students demonstrate their team's mastery of learned material by competing against other teams in academic tournaments. His research confirmed the same sort of positive results in prejudice reduction that Elliot Aronson had observed.

Despite the support of researchers and most teacher training centres, Jigsaw and other co-operative learning methods see fairly limited use. The main criticism comes from parents who do not like a regular routine of group work situations in which students must assist one another. They believe that their children are "held back" in their own progress as a result of having to spend too much time helping others. Some parents feel that their children would benefit more from the help of the teacher rather than from the well-intentioned but less-informed efforts of other students. To be effective in reducing prejudice, co-operative learning strategies require frequent use and skilful management by the teacher. Most teachers have been trained to use these techniques and recognize their value; however, they generally regard them as one more teaching tool by which to add variety in the classroom.

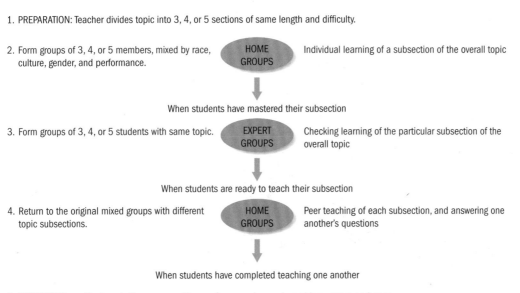

1. PREPARATION: Teacher divides topic into 3, 4, or 5 sections of same length and difficulty.

2. Form groups of 3, 4, or 5 members, mixed by race, culture, gender, and performance.   HOME GROUPS   Individual learning of a subsection of the overall topic

When students have mastered their subsection

3. Form groups of 3, 4, or 5 students with same topic.   EXPERT GROUPS   Checking learning of the particular subsection of the overall topic

When students are ready to teach their subsection

4. Return to the original mixed groups with different topic subsections.   HOME GROUPS   Peer teaching of each subsection, and answering one another's questions

When students have completed teaching one another

5. EVALUATION: use the learning in a measurable way, for example, a quiz, problem, report, and so on.

Figure 9.15 Jigsaw Co-operative Learning Strategy. Why is the Expert Group phase considered such an important part of the Jigsaw process? How does it also reinforce the equal status social contact theory of reducing prejudice?

Skill Builder:
Using Visuals to Show Information

Social scientists must be skilled at working with visuals to represent and present data. Selecting and using graphs and charts, maps, and photographs effectively for a report or presentation is very important. This can make the difference between an interesting and organized report and one that makes little sense to the readers or listeners. Complementary visuals can structure information in a way that communicates it clearly to others.

Step One: Use Charts and Graphs

If you have accumulated statistical information, enter your number table into a computer spreadsheet program. This will make it easy for you to select and produce an appropriate graph to illustrate your findings.

- Bar Graph: Useful for comparing information about different topics or different places at one point in time. If the information is complex and detailed, either a multiple bar graph or a compound bar graph may be the solution.

- Line Graph: Useful for comparing change over a period of time, for one topic or one place. If the information is complex and detailed, either a multiple line graph or a compound line graph may be the solution. For example, a simple line graph could be used to show immigration to Canada between 1960 and 2000; however, if this information were broken down into different continents of origin, then either a multiple- or a compound-line graph would be required.

- Pie Graph: Useful for showing the percentage that parts of a topic make up when compared to the whole. In a pie graph, the information must add up to 100 per cent. To compare more than one time period or place, you can make several pie graphs.

Origin of Urban Population

Birthplace	Toronto* Population	Vancouver* Population
Canada	60.2%	66.5%
Europe	16.2%	10.1%
Asia	14.5%	18.7%
Caribbean and Bermuda	3.5%	0.3%
Central and South America	2.8%	0.9%
Other	2.8%	3.5%

*These figures refer to the Toronto and Vancouver Census Metropolitan Areas.

Source: Statistics Canada

Figure 9.16 Explain why this information could not be illustrated by using a simple bar graph.

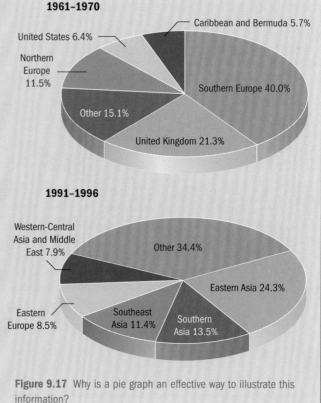

Origins of Immigrants to Canada

1961–1970

Caribbean and Bermuda 5.7%
United States 6.4%
Northern Europe 11.5%
Other 15.1%
Southern Europe 40.0%
United Kingdom 21.3%

1991–1996

Western-Central Asia and Middle East 7.9%
Other 34.4%
Eastern Asia 24.3%
Eastern Europe 8.5%
Southeast Asia 11.4%
Southern Asia 13.5%

Figure 9.17 Why is a pie graph an effective way to illustrate this information?

- Scatter Graph: Useful for showing whether or not two different factors (variables) are related to each other. For example, a scatter graph could identify if there is any relationship between a student's place of birth and his/her success in school in Canada.

Step Two: Use Maps

If you have gathered information from different locations, interesting maps can illustrate place-to-place variations. Statistics Canada gathers detailed census information from small areas across Canada called census tracts. This information would allow you to compare the ethnic composition of different neighbourhoods within a city, region, or province. For example, a map could be produced to show the distribution of people, by place of birth, within Metropolitan Toronto or Metropolitan Vancouver.

Step Three: Use Photographs

Pictures can make your report much more appealing to your intended audience, especially if you follow these guidelines from the Canadian Press Style Guide in making your selections. Always prepare a caption to concisely identify and explain each photograph that you use.

- Is the photograph new or unusual in some way?
- Is it connected with some current event or topic of interest?
- Does it show action to catch the reader's attention?
- Does it show people and appeal to emotion?
- Does it relate to an important person, event, or place?
- Does it wrap up a story or give an overall view of it?

(Buckley, 1995, p. 330)

Practise It!

1. Examine Figure 9.16. Identify two different graph techniques that could be used to illustrate this information. Explain your choices.
2. Examine Figure 9.17. List important conclusions about Canadian society that can be drawn from these pie graphs.
3. Examine Figure 9.18. Which aspects of the Canadian Press Style Guide does this photograph meet? How does it connect to the other information illustrated in this section?
4. Explain how each of these visuals could be useful to support the theme of the following section of the textbook: "From Multiculturalism to Anti-Racism."

Figure 9.18 This photo shows a recent citizenship court in Ottawa. The children sitting in front of the judge have just become Canadians.

From Multiculturalism to Anti-Racism

Canada and the United States are mainly nations of immigrants. Through most of the twentieth century, about one-fifth of Canada's people were born somewhere else, and that ratio continues today.

In the 1970s, the government of Canada developed a policy of **multiculturalism**, which encouraged people to preserve their ancestral cultures while living under Canadian laws and institutions. Many schools responded by promoting multicultural projects and events designed to promote pride and understanding in the diverse heritages of Canadians. Students shared traditional foods, flags, costumes, histories, music, and dance in colourful festivals. Such activities might help to reduce prejudice between people, depending upon how they are organized and presented. In *The Nature of Prejudice*, Gordon Allport points out research indicating that prejudice reduction can result from intercultural programs that use either active participation or shared experience. Developing acquaintances with members of other cultures is most preferred, but the use of films, novels, and drama can be effective if they let the student vicariously "walk a mile in another person's shoes."

There are limitations to multicultural education in that this approach is often mostly informational and does not discuss the issues and misunderstandings that divide people. Allport tells us that "Mere information... does not necessarily alter either attitude or action. What is more, its gains, according to available research, seem slighter than those of other educational methods employed" (p. 486).

Figure 9.19 Have you ever taken part in a multicultural festival or project at school? In your opinion, how effective is learning about other cultures in reducing prejudice?

Psychologist Frances Aboud has taken an approach that goes beyond mere information and strongly promotes intercultural discussion programs for children aged 7 to 12 years. This is the time when their developing cognitive skills allow them to fine-tune their perceptions of other groups and individuals. In fact, Aboud worked with a group called Alternatives to Racism and the University of British Columbia to develop a Grade 5 unit called "More Than Meets the Eye." It focused student discussion on three subtopics: "Understanding Yourself," "Understanding Others," and "Understanding Differences." Other researchers found that similar programs were successful both in reducing prejudice and in creating stronger attachments between minority students.

In the 1980s some educators in Britain, the US, and Canada began to use the term "anti-racist education", which carries multiculturalism a step farther. **Anti-racism** aims not only to reduce prejudice, but also to eliminate **institutional barriers** to equality between different peoples. For example, in Section 9.1 of this chapter, Ronald Samuda was critical of standard IQ tests, which he believes are weighted in favour of the majority culture. Anti-racist educators press to have these tests eliminated, or at least replaced by **culture-fair testing**, which measures capability without relying upon language skills and a middle-class background.

They also look closely at the books and materials that students are using in the classroom, some of which could contribute to racism and ethnic prejudice. For example, the central character of Shakespeare's play *The Merchant of Venice* is Shylock, a Jewish moneylender. A strong anti-Semitic theme runs through this play, which, until recent years, was frequently studied in Grade 9 or 10 English classes. Anti-racist educators recognize the potential reinforcement of stereo-

www.crr.ca/rt/

The Canadian Race Relations Foundation's aim is to "foster racial harmony and cross-cultural understanding and help to eliminate racism." The foundation, which operates at arm's length from the government, sponsors initiatives against racism. This Web site describes the projects they have sponsored since 1998. Read through the list and choose a project you feel would be especially effective in helping the foundation reach its goal.

If the Web address does not connect you with the site, do a search using "Canadian Race Relations Foundation" as a search string.

WEB LINK

types, which can develop into feelings of prejudice and acts of discrimination that can, and do, result from this book choice.

Anti-racism aims to create paradigm shifts both in the majority culture, and in what John Ogbu termed "subordinate cultures." For this purpose, psychologist Beverly Tatum (see pages 296 to 297) organized an anti-racist education demonstration project in the Northampton, Massachusetts, school district. It was a three-part initiative directed to teachers, students, and their parents. Teachers participated in an anti-racist education professional development course, while students were involved in an after-school cultural identity group project. Parents were engaged in workshops designed to increase their ability to think about and discuss issues of racism.

Many Ontario school boards, particularly in large urban centres, have been actively involved in anti-racist education projects since the 1980s. Sociologist George Dei, from the Ontario Institute for Studies in Education at the University of Toronto, has conducted important research into the development of such initiatives. In one series of investigations, Dr. Dei attempted to examine the problem of minority students' disengagement and dropping out of the school system.

He felt that an inclusive curriculum—for example, one that offered Afrocentric knowledge—would help to solve this problem. In the following case study, Dr. Dei outlines the methodology he used to examine the experiences of minority students in Ontario and thereby gain some insight into the meaning of "inclusive curriculum."

CASE STUDY

Listening to the Voices of Students

As part of a series of investigations into the nature of an inclusive curriculum, in 1992 a group of graduate students in the Ontario Institute for Studies in Education and I examined some experiences of Black/African-Canadian students in the Ontario public school system. The researchers solicited individual and group responses from 150 Black students from four Toronto high schools. Students were selected randomly to provide a representation of male and female students from general- and advanced-level programs, and to include Grade 10 and 12 students. The Grade 10 students selected were those considered at "high risk" of dropping out of school, as indicated by such criteria as below-average marks, poor attendance, and inadequate accumulation of credits (Waterhouse, 1990; Ziegler, 1989). The Grade 12 students were selected to provide information on their reasons for staying in school, and their attitudes toward the school system. The researchers also interviewed two dozen students, as well as 21 actual "dropouts" and youth designated "at risk" of dropping out, randomly chosen from other Toronto schools.

During interviews, the researchers asked such questions as "What do you like/dislike about school?," "Why do you think some students drop out?," and "Why do others stay on to complete their education?" Students were asked how the dynamics of social difference (race or ethnicity, class, and gender) affected their schooling experiences, and what changes they desired in the school system. The themes emerging from these interviews centred on race, identity, and representation (Dei, Holmes, Mazzuca, McIsaac, & Campbell, 1995).

Three primary concerns were expressed in the students' narratives about school experiences: differential treatment according to race, the absence of Black teachers, and the absence of Black and African-Canadian history in the classroom. These concerns arose even in response to seemingly unrelated questions or descriptions. Students described encounters with authority and power structures they perceived not to work in their interest. They also discussed difficulties in constructing personal and group cultural identities in a school environment that did not adequately highlight their cultural presence, heritage, and history. They also talked of attempts to excel in the face of unflattering teacher expectations. Although students were interestingly split in terms of a desire for intensified parental involvement in schooling, many acknowledged their parents' assistance and sacrifices on their behalf. A number of students said they persevered because they wanted to be like their parent(s) (and noted the absence of role models in the school environment).

In subsequent phases of the project, in part to cross-reference some of the students' narratives, the researchers talked to 41 teachers (including some administrators and guidance counsellors), 59 non-Black students, and 55 Black/African Canadian parents. School staff and non-Black students were selected from the four schools that were the focus of the research project. Interviews with Black parents and community workers solicited concerns about, and solutions to, the problems of public schooling in Canada. Interesting parallels, convergences, and divergences arose between Black/African-Canadian parents' and teachers' narrative discourses and those of the youth. In sum, the project gathered a wide range of voices.

The sample of students, however, was not statistically representative. The narratives should be read as interpretations from the standpoint of the informants and not from the standpoint of statistical significance. Nevertheless, the "random" selection of informants to cross-reference the students' narratives mitigated some of the effects of self-selection. The evidence from this research seeks not to answer how it is "representative of" the school experiences of all Black youth, but rather *to represent* those experiences. It seeks to display a multiplicity of voices as it leaves open the possibility for other voices to be heard. It is both a narration of social realities and a challenge to other researchers. There is no mistaking the final message: in school, Black youth experience exclusions and racism on many levels.

A few student voices in the study highlight the three interrelated concerns of differential treatment according to race, the absence of Black teachers, and the inadequacy of school curricular content…. For example, Michael, a 19-year-old, general-level student, came to Canada from Jamaica nearly nine years ago. His frustrations and the emotions with which he speaks about the de-privileging of Black peoples' history and contributions to society throughout his public schooling cannot be missed by listeners.

I only know about Canadian history, which is White history. I did not learn anything about Black people. And then, probably in the last two years, I would say we have improved in our geography, but we don't really learn about the cultural background. We just learn about…not even the people, but just the city or the country. Basics, nothing deep. Is it tough? I mean, I would like to know more about my history, yes. A lot more. I think I need to know a lot more than I know.

(15/11/92)

Source: Dei, George. 1996. "The Role of Afrocentricity in the Inclusive Curriculum in Canadian Schools." *Canadian Journal of Education*, Vol. 21, Spring 1996.

Questions

1. In your own words, explain the meaning of an "inclusive curriculum." Compare this to Michael's school experiences.
2. Identify three important aspects of the research techniques applied by this study. Explain why each is important.
3. Summarize three key findings of the study. Suggest ways in which schools could be more "inclusive" of students from different racial or cultural backgrounds.

Pause and Reflect

1. In the Robber's Cave experiment:
   a) What conditions were responsible for causing out-group hostility?
   b) What conditions were responsible for ending out-group hostility?
2. How did Elliot Aronson reorganize classrooms to create a "paradigm shift"? Why isn't this successful method more widely used?
3. What is multiculturalism? Why do multicultural festivals and similar events usually have only a limited effect in reducing prejudice?
4. How are anti-racism programs different from multicultural programs? Outline three examples of "anti-racist education" activities.

▶ ▶ ▶ **Chapter Activities**

Show Your Knowledge

1. Identify one important idea for which each of these psychologists is known:

   a) Frances Aboud   b) Beverly Tatum   c) Theodor Adorno   d) John Ogbu

2. Summarize three important general characteristics of hate crimes. Then, show how one particular example from this chapter demonstrates each of these characteristics.

3. Psychologists Gordon Allport and Elliot Aronson are profiled in this chapter. For each one, explain why their contribution to our knowledge of prejudice is so important.

4. Use a flow chart and an example to trace the development of systemic racism, beginning with stereotypes. Then, trace development of homophobia through the same steps.

5. What part does each of the following play in attempts to control hate and hate crimes?

   a) Universal Declaration of Human Rights   b) International Criminal Court

   c) Charter of Rights and Freedoms   d) Criminal Code of Canada, Section 319

Practise Your Thinking

6. Compare two theories of prejudice: the group norms theory and the social-cognitive theory. How are they similar? How are they different?

7. Examine the questions used on a standardized IQ test to see if you can find examples that are not acceptable according to Ronald Samuda (page 293).

8. What sorts of people are attracted to hate groups? Brainstorm a list of the types of people who might be most open to, or vulnerable to, the messages of hate. Then, compare your list to the work of psychologists Theodor Adorno and Gordon Allport, discussed in this chapter.

9. Do you think that young people are more accepting than their parents and grandparents toward others who are different from themselves? Or is there no difference? Discuss your views in a small group, and report on your conclusions.

10. Work with a partner of the opposite sex to brainstorm a list of ways in which your school could improve the relationship between "in-groups" and "out-groups" within the school.

Communicate Your Ideas

11. Work as a group to gather news items about prejudice and discrimination from newspapers and magazines. Develop a bulletin board display, and discuss items as they are added to it.

12. Obtain current statistics on the ethnic origins of Canadians. Prepare graphs to compare the 10 largest groups by population. Discuss whether or not this information is reflected in your own community. If not, suggest reasons for this.

13. Conduct a survey of ethnic origins in your classroom to compare to the Canadian statistics used in Question 12. Students identify their ethnic origin on one side of the family, tracing back to the origin outside Canada (except for Aboriginal people). Prepare a graph similar to the one in Question 12. How do the two graphs compare?

14. Read the book *Black Like Me* by John Howard Griffin. Prepare a report about your impressions of the book and its impact on you. Make a brief presentation to the class.

15. Design an attractive poster based on the theme "Paradigm Shift: Unlearning Prejudice." Remember, the prejudice need not be based on race or culture.

Apply Your Knowledge

16. Prepare a set of questions that you could ask an Aboriginal person about his or her life in Canada. Perhaps the teacher can arrange to have an Aboriginal person visit the class to give his or her views on a current Aboriginal issue, and answer your questions.

17. Investigate the policies of an organization, such as your school or local government, from the following perspectives:

    a) Are any barriers in place that seem unfair to groups within the organization?

    b) Are any programs or policies in place that aim to create equality or improve relations between groups within the organization?

18. Design a plan of action that would make your school (or some club or organization to which you belong) more "inclusive" of people from other races and cultures.

19. Find out how the Ontario Human Rights Commission operates. Outline examples of specific cases in which the Commission acted to protect the rights of people discriminated against on the basis of race or culture, sex, and disability.

20. Use print and electronic sources to research and report upon a specific case of genocide. Try to identify reasons for the intense hatred behind this case.

CHAPTER 10

GLOBALIZATION AND THE SOCIAL SCIENCES

INTRODUCTION

One of the few things we really know for sure in the twenty-first century is that nothing stays the same. The phenomenon of social change surrounds us, altering our everyday reality whether we like it or not. The social changes of recent decades, in particular, have drastically changed how we see ourselves. How do we fit into this changing world? How do we define our communities? Where do our responsibilities lie?

Perhaps the most overpowering force of social change in the early twenty-first century is **globalization**. Regional, national, and continental organizations are all coming under growing pressure to integrate the entire world into one economic system. The inadvertent result has been the erosion of local cultures under the onslaught of economic pressure and Western culture. National governments are quickly giving away their powers in the hopes of bettering their nations' economic position. How do the economic benefits of globalization measure up? Whom does globalization benefit? Who is hurt by it? What forces operate to support it? How does Canada fit into this process? This chapter will look at how social scientists have tried to answer these questions. You will be challenged to take a position on the issues.

In November 2001, Canadians staged major street demonstrations to express their opposition to the General Agreement on Trade in Services (GATS) and other globalization initiatives. Nothing since the protests against the Vietnam War had drawn so many protestors into the streets all over the West. Why do you think the issue of globalization inspires so much anger?

Focusing on the Issues

Where Is My Society?
By Martin Albrow

You get up in the morning, turn on the TV, and watch a mob burn down a temple in India. You snatch a croissant and coffee and are about to leave the apartment when your landlord, who comes from Pakistan, calls and asks if you wouldn't mind buying some Basmati rice [grown in India and Pakistan] on your way home after class. You're unable to run the errand because you've arranged to go to a meeting of the Worldwide Fund for Nature, so you ask a friend to get the rice. He comes back with American rice because he is against the exploitation of child labour in India. You have a fierce argument with him because you can't afford to offend your landlord, since the rent is low and you are saving to go on vacation in Europe this summer. But the argument ruins your plans anyway, because you were going to travel with that very friend, who speaks good French. You regret this turn of events because you very much wanted to see your cousins in France. You telephone your uncle [in France], who reminds you that he has already bought you a plane ticket, because it is cheaper to do so from there. It's all a mess, and you finish up on your own in a [café] drinking a [Pepsi] and listening to a cool local reggae band.

Source: Albrow, Martin. 1995. "Globalization." In Robert J. Brym, ed., *New Society: Sociology for the 21st Century*. Toronto. Harcourt Brace Canada.

THINK ABOUT IT

1. Referring to the above piece, list the different ways that globalization has touched this day in the life of an ordinary Canadian. List three ways that it has influenced *your* life in the past few days. For example, consider the products you use, the television programs you watch, and the foods you eat.

2. Although this piece was written by a Canadian, it mentions only one American influence. Create another story with your class. Each person takes a turn adding one sentence to the story of a Canadian student's life, each sentence incorporating an international influence. What proportion of the influences were American?

3. All the influences mentioned in the story are harmless. Identify some potentially harmful influences of globalization on everyday Canadian life.

■ Learning Expectations

By the end of this chapter, you will be able to

- Demonstrate an understanding of the anthropological significance of the relationships among globalization, tribalism, and transnationalism for Canadians

- Analyze, from a Canadian perspective, the social structures that support, and those that weaken, global inequalities

- Evaluate, from a psychological perspective, the role of perception in Canadians' understanding of themselves, their families, and their local and global communities

Section 10.1   How Anthropologists Interpret Globalization

Key Concepts

tribe, tribalism

nation, nationalism

cultural evolutionism

sphere of influence

transnational, transnationalism

financialization

free market forces

deterritorialization

cash crop

modernization theory

dependency theory

world-system theory

neo-Marxian theory

globalization theory

paradigm shift

How does globalization affect culture? Primarily, globalization is an economic force. By selling products and services around the world, we rapidly increase the process of diffusion you read about in Chapter 2. Because the United States has a huge number of very large companies with the economic means to market their goods to many countries, globalization results in a massive diffusion of American culture all around the world. At one time, for example, North American companies made cars largely for North America. Then, in the 1950s, various automobile manufacturers assembled some specific models for sale in North America, others for sale in Europe, and still others for Asia. In the 2000s, automobiles look much the same all over the world. Today, popular music groups tour the world, performing their music, usually in English, on every continent. American films and magazines are exported everywhere. Clothes with familiar American brand names are in demand in virtually every country. You can get a Big Mac or a Pizza Hut slice anywhere from Beijing to Brandon, Manitoba. You can find people drinking Coca Cola in a market in Belize or in the Kalahari Desert.

What is the result of this diffusion of largely American culture? The big danger is how overwhelming American culture can be. Diversity of culture has always made the world a richer place, as various peoples can share the accomplishments of their distinctive cultures. Our differences allow us to learn from each other. The cultures of some peoples can become sidetracked from their normal course of development, however, because of the undue influence of American culture. For example, it can force English on non-English-speaking peoples, reducing the use of distinct languages. At its worst, through trashy movies and television shows such as

Baywatch, it introduces sleazy values, like consumerism and easy sex, into traditional cultures. (Islamic nations are particularly resentful of this.) The deterioration of unique cultures and the loss of languages worry anthropologists greatly. To better understand the anthropological point of view, we must first look at the background.

Studying Cultures

As you have already learned in Chapters 1 and 2, anthropologists have spent many years producing ethnographic studies detailing the cultures and values of peoples around the world. Much emphasis was placed on tribal organization and culture.

The word "**tribe**" is sometimes used colloquially in a disparaging sense, to imply that a group of people lacks civilization or dignity. Anthropologists reject this usage of the term. To an anthropologist, the word "tribe" simply indicates a human organization ruled by an uncentralized form of government. A **nation**, or state, on the other hand, is a human organization ruled by a centralized form of government. The major differences are summarized in the organizer in Figure 10.1.

Many anthropologists in the early twentieth century believed in **cultural evolutionism**, the principle that all human societies and cultures develop in a regular series of predictable stages. Franz Boas (1858–1941) challenged this principle after extensively studying the Aboriginal cultures of North America. When tribal societies reach a certain size, they tend to evolve into chiefdoms, and eventually into states. However, they follow one of a number of routes to accomplish this transition. While anthropologists agreed that there were significant similarities among tribal and national cultures, it was obvious that

Selected Characteristics of Human Organization in Tribal and National Structures

Factor	Tribal Structure	National Structure
Subsistence method	Small-scale agriculture and live-stock cultivation	Intensive agriculture and industry
Leadership	Charismatic individual with little formal power but some influence and authority	Formalized leadership with supporting institutions
Method of social integration	Kinship, voluntary associations	Loyalty to the state overrides all kin or class loyalties
Economic structure	Sharing and exchange (barter)	Formalized taxes, monetary values, and trading patterns
Social stratification	Egalitarian	Classes and ranks
Property ownership	Communal, by kinship or by clan	Private and state ownership; little communal ownership
Law and enforcement	Little formalized law; right to punish belongs to kin or clan	Formal laws and punishments controlled by the state
Religion	Shamans interpret divine laws among their regular duties	Religious figures interpret divine laws and support the state

Source: Based on Lewellen, 1983, pp. 20–21, as described in Schultz and Lavenda, 1998, pp. 68–69.

Figure 10.1 Examine this table to determine if Canadian society's characteristics fit a national structure.

the path from tribal culture to national culture varied significantly around the globe. This reality was underlined in the period after World War II, when the European nations' colonial empires, especially in Africa and Asia, were broken up, and the newly independent nations were challenged with the task of recovering after centuries of exploitation. They took a variety of paths as they attempted to convert their cultures from a tribal structure to a national structure. India, for example, became a democratic state allied with the West, while Tanzania became a one-party communist society based on the model of the former Soviet Union. Because these nations evolved in their own way, each country retained its distinctive character.

 ## A New and Powerful Force

Whereas **tribalism** and **nationalism** had occupied much of anthropologists' attention for the better part of a century, in the late twentieth century anthropologists were forced to acknowledge that powerful forces were coming together to make it increasingly difficult for cultures to remain isolated from the rest of the world. Western industrial countries looked everywhere for sources of cheap raw materials, drawing developing countries into their **sphere of influence** (the area over which a society has economic and cultural influence). Communications technology improved so that sporting events or coverage of wars could be beamed live from virtually any part of the world to another.

International organizations like the United Nations High Commission for Refugees (UNHCR), or charities such as Médecins Sans Frontières and Free the Children, were able to provide humanitarian aid anywhere in the world at short notice. Such organizations became known as **transnational**, meaning that they saw their role as international or global, trying to assist wherever needed. **Transnationalism** implies that organizations, be they charitable organizations or businesses, operate freely in a number of nations.

The transnational organizations advocating globalization belong to three groups: large manufacturing corporations, banks, and international government organizations. The large manufacturing corporations include companies such as Nike, Mattel, and Sony. These companies produce their goods in a variety of countries, usually those that offer the best tax incentives and the lowest wages. The companies then sell their goods to markets all over the world, though usually to industrialized countries, whose citizens have plenty of disposable income.

The international banks tend to have increasingly anonymous-sounding names such as RBC (formerly the Royal Bank of Canada) and HSBC (formerly the Hong Kong and Shanghai Banking Corporation). These corporations sell their financial services throughout the world. **Financialization** has emerged as a major global influence. Financialization is the increasing flow of money, as opposed to goods and services, between nations. The effect of this process has been to concentrate increasing wealth in the hands of financial elites, and to take it away from ordinary citizens, particularly in developing and non-industrial countries.

The international government organizations include the United Nations (UN), the World Trade Organization (WTO), the World Bank, and the International Monetary Fund (IMF). The United Nations, to which over 160 nations belong, was founded in 1945 and is based in New York City. It strives to maintain international peace and security, and facilitates international co-operation in economic, social, cultural, and humanitarian matters. The World Trade Organization (formerly the General Agreement on Tariffs and Trade) is a specialized agency of the United Nations whose role is to reduce restrictions on international trade. Its critics believe that it plays a key role in allowing the exploitation of developing countries by advocating that the role of government in society be reduced.

The World Bank, whose official name is the International Bank for Reconstruction and Development, was formed in 1945 and is headquartered in Washington, DC. Its role is to provide loans and technical assistance to developing countries as they expand their economies. Because the World Bank controls these funds, it holds a great amount of power in influencing the domestic policies of nations in need of this money. The International Monetary Fund, also founded in 1945 and based in Washington, tries to maintain orderly exchange rates among the

Figure 10.2 Thai workers assemble Reebok athletic shoes at a plant in Ayathaya, Thailand. At the heart of globalization is the desire of multinational companies to produce products such as these in developing nations for sale in the developed world. In many cases the goods are produced by subcontractors. Who benefits in this arrangement, and how?

world's currencies in an attempt to secure steady expansion of world trade. These four organizations play key roles in promoting globalization.

Globalization has occurred via two processes. First, culture has become increasingly international in nature, as the Western industrial and capitalist countries, particularly the United States, have come to have greater dominance over most other nations around the globe. The second process associated with globalization has been the increasing concentration of wealth within financial elites, particularly in these developed countries. The response of modern anthropologists has been to pay closer attention to globalization's cultural impact on societies, and its effects on poor—often marginalized—people, particularly those in Africa and Asia.

Supporters of globalization believe that it allows developing countries to make the transition to development. They point to the international financial assistance available from organizations like the World Bank to nations that decide to reposition their economies within global trade patterns. The governments of such nations, they point out, want the foreign investment of multinationals building plants in their countries and employing people. Multinationals also generate tax dollars for the host nation, which can be used to build the infrastructure of the country. Living standards in such nations should rise.

Social scientists are divided on the accuracy of claims that globalization will significantly benefit developing nations, and many case studies have cast doubt on the issue. The situation in Costa Rica is a good example of what can happen to an economy and culture rooted in raw materials production when **free market forces** become the norm. That means that the government exerts little control over business activities, and allows the economy to regulate itself. Marc Edelman, an American anthropologist, studied the effect of globalization on the peasants in Costa Rica. Although not all the results described in the case study on the next page can be attributed to the free market forces typical of globalization, they have certainly made the situation in Costa Rica considerably worse than it was.

The Cultural Cost

Until the fairly recent past, it could be assumed that particular cultures were rooted in different regions of the world and that they would display significant differences. Globalization has tended to internationalize culture, which explains why we are exposed to so many international influences in our everyday lives. Anthropologists have begun to write about a homogenization, or blending, of peoples and culture. The mass migration of peoples around the world, a result of the development of cheap air travel from the 1970s on, has led anthropologists to talk of the **deterritorialization** of cultures. This means that distinct cultures are no longer firmly attached, in relative isolation, to specific regions of the world. Anthropologists note that many cultures can be overwhelmed by the culture of Westernized, capitalist, principally English-speaking nations.

The ability of globalization to devastate cultures should not be underestimated. American products and values become the norm in a community, a change that usually comes at the expense of a local culture's character and stability. Young Inuit, for example, learn early to value the lifestyles and products that they see on television programs made in the south. Instead of living self-contained, independent lives in tune with their traditional culture, many of these young people become uninterested in their culture, losing their sense of identity in the process.

The Opposition

The government of Quebec's efforts to strengthen the use of French as the language of

Globalization and the Peasants in Costa Rica

Costa Rica is an independent republic in Central America with a population of approximately 3.5 million. From the sixteenth century until 1821, it was a colony of Spain, and Spanish is the official language of the nation, although a number of Aboriginal languages are spoken as well. Agriculture is an important component of the economy, accounting for about 17 per cent of Gross Domestic Product (GDP) and 70 per cent of exports. The main agricultural products are coffee, beef, bananas, and sugar, all of which are **cash crops**, that is, crops grown specifically for sale, not consumption.

Costa Rica is a poor nation. GDP per capita—the value of all goods and services produced per year divided by the total population—is approximately $3800, compared with Canada's figure of just over $32 300. In addition to the low GDP per capita figure, Costa Rica's overall wealth is divided even more unevenly than Canada's, with the result that the urban workers and many of the agricultural labourers live a precarious existence. Wage rates are low, and prices for sugar, coffee, and other exported products on the international market can fluctuate rapidly, making earnings for agricultural workers unpredictable.

In *Peasants Against Globalization* (1999), American anthropologist Marc Edelman divides the story into a number of stages. In stage 1, from independence in 1821 until the late 1970s, Costa Rica expanded social welfare programs, and the state intervened in economic affairs to protect workers.

In stage 2, from the early 1980s to the early 1990s, social welfare programs experienced a gradual but steady erosion. International financial organizations, including the IMF and World Bank, are prepared to invest money in developing countries only if they can be assured that wage rates and taxes will remain low. Transnationals prefer to set up their assembly-line operations in low-wage, low-tax countries because it keeps their production costs down. Costa Rica acted to make itself fit the necessary pattern for entry into the global market. It chose the route taken by many

developing countries attempting to keep taxes and wages low: it cut back on its social programs.

Without solid social welfare programs, however, Costa Rican workers became more desperate to find employment no matter how low the wages. If the state was not prepared to help them, they reasoned, they should confront and fight it. They became radicalized by their own desperation. One of the most dramatic events of this period was the spectacular strike of sugar workers in Guanacaste Province in 1988 in which the state and the international financial organizations successfully worked together to defeat the strikers.

In stage 3, from the early 1990s onward, the agricultural workers changed their focus. If they could not win by confrontation, then perhaps negotiation would work better. They continued to try to negotiate with employers for improved conditions, so far with very limited success.

It is interesting that, in stage 3, Costa Rican workers chose a different path from the one chosen by frustrated protest movements in some other countries. Sometimes such groups go underground. Independence movements in many former colonial countries followed this path. Perhaps Costa Rica was different because it is a small nation, is already independent, and has a history—if not a present—of strong social welfare programs.

In many ways the Costa Rican experience is typical of that of resource-based economies in a globalized world. Industrialized countries want developing countries to produce cash crops in raw or partially processed form for transportation overseas. The greatest profit can be made in the manufacturing and distribution parts of the process. When these parts of the process take place in the industrialized countries, the profit is not shared with the workers who harvest the crop in the first place. As Marc Edelman's study shows, policies designed in the West to benefit Western-owned international businesses frequently damage the lifestyles of workers in developing countries.

Questions

1. Make a list of the characteristics of Costa Rica.
2. What factors caused the living standards of agricultural workers to fall from the early 1980s onward?
3. What appears to be Marc Edelman's overall opinion about the effects of globalization on Costa Rica? What reasons might supporters of globalization use to show why economic reforms were necessary there?
4. In what ways is Costa Rica typical of what can happen to resource-based economies in a globalized world?
5. Costa Rica has a higher GDP per capita than other Central American countries. Do some research to compare Costa Rica's economy with those of these countries.

business and everyday life is a clear example of a government attempting to ward off the overwhelming influence of North American, English-speaking culture. Other peoples, including Aboriginal groups such as the Kayapo people in the Amazonian rain forest, are also attempting to preserve their cultures in the face of globalization.

The Amazonian rain forest has been seriously depleted in recent years as loggers have clear-cut tracts of land under licence from the government of Brazil and other national governments in the region. In the 1990s, the Brazilian government decided to build a hydroelectric dam on the Xingu River in Brazil. This development, which was to be financed by a $10.5 billion loan from the World Bank, would have devastated the habitat and cultures of the Aboriginal people of the Amazon, flooding the lands of the Kayapo people. Paulinho Paiakan, the leader of the Kayapo, brought 28 Aboriginal groups together to fight the decision to build the dam. Paiakan travelled to Europe to publicize their cause. British rock musician Sting took up their cause, holding benefit concerts to raise funds for the Amazonian Aboriginal people's attempt to resist globalization and protect their way of life. The World Bank loan

Figure 10.3 Many individuals in developed countries try to take a stand against the harsher effects of globalization through their purchasing decisions. By buying Fair Trade coffee, like that shown here, they can be sure that their money is going to an independent coffee grower who is being paid a fair price. Would you pay a little more to be sure an independent farmer could stay in business?

was cancelled and the Brazilian government was forced to delay its plans to build the dam.

Various groups in central and South America have tried to resist the negative impacts of globalization. In Argentina and Brazil, for example, Roman Catholic charities have tried to encourage multinationals to contribute to the relief of small-scale farmers displaced from the land by the development of large agri-businesses. In Panama, peasant farmers who made a meagre living by the cultivation of rice and the small-scale sale of sugar cane tried unsuccessfully to maintain their independence from large capitalist producers. Unable to compete, however, the peasants were forced off the land they rented and into factory jobs, working for the multinationals. Generally, peasant cultures have been unable to withstand the economic competition that globalization has introduced (Gledhill, 1994, p. 198).

What will happen to society in an increasingly globalized world? Sociologists have suggested three major possibilities. The first is that independent nations will become overwhelmed by global forces and unable to regulate their societies, leading ultimately to their destruction. A second possibility is that human cultures and societies will become more alike, and new forms of world government will replace existing national ones. A third possibility is that national societies, cultures, and governments will remain intact, but will adopt an increasingly global focus in order to do so (Brym, 1995, Ch. 15, p. 21).

Anthropological Theories About Globalization

The Costa Rican case study that you read on page 330 illustrates what can happen when global capitalist forces enjoy free reign in a small, raw-materials-producing country. This process, repeated in countries around the world, has caused much anguish among the poor of these nations and has alarmed many anthropologists. Capitalism—which serves as the backbone of globalization—implies that the only things worth having are those that can be assigned a monetary value and sold. Since capitalism is centred in Western nations, this means that globalization is generally explained in terms of the economic relationship between the developed, capitalist, Western countries, and the rest of the world. Anthropologists have developed a number of theories to explain this relationship.

1. **Modernization theory** owes its roots to the work of Herbert Spencer (1820–1903), who regarded the colonial relationship between the West and what he termed the more "backward" regions of the world as beneficial for these regions, because they could learn capitalist and entrepreneurial skills from the experience. The Spencerites judged how modern a nation was by how like the West it had become. This theory, which displays the biases prevalent in the

FILM SOCIETY

Title: Medicine Man
Rating: PG-13
Director: John McTiernan

In this film, the Amazonian rain forest is under pressure from developers, who are displacing indigenous plants and Aboriginal people. Sean Connery plays a research scientist who produces a cure for cancer in the Brazilian rain forest but cannot repeat the process . Lorraine Bracco plays a character who controls the funds for Connery's research grant and is pressuring him for results. Although the story is fictional, this film highlights the fact that most medicines are developed from species found only in the natural environment. The conflict between local needs and outside pressures is clearly defined.

nineteenth century, has now been largely discarded by anthropologists.

2. **Dependency theory** explains the lack of economic development in many developing countries as stemming directly from the same colonial relationship that Spencer trumpeted. Unlike Spencerites, dependency theorists believe that this relationship was largely destructive for the colonies, as their economies and cultures were distorted and exploited to meet the needs of the colonial power. For example, many countries eliminated small farms in favour of large holdings that were more efficient at growing and harvesting cash crops for sale overseas. This transition left many peasant farmers without their traditional holdings. Hawaii experienced this development in the nineteenth century as American corporations took over large tracts of land to grow sugar cane and pineapples.

3. **World-system theory** is largely the outgrowth of the work of sociologist Immanuel Wallerstein (see Chapter 2, page 62). Wallerstein argues that the basic relationship between the West and the rest of the world was established in colonial times. While it is theoretically possible for an individual nation to move from an exploited to a dominant position—or the other way around—examples of such movement have been comparatively rare. Canada, for example, once dominated by Britain, is now an independent nation.

4. **Neo-Marxian theory** suggests that many nations outside the West consciously rejected pure capitalism. Because capitalism places humans in direct competition with one another, Neo-Marxian theorists view it as a negative force. Nations that rejected capitalism tried to develop their own organizational structures in which indigenous systems of production were joined with commercial ideas from the West. As a result, such nations are only partially transformed, and do not fully participate in the realm of international finance and trade. Cuba is an example of such a country.

5. **Globalization theory** has been the major focus of this section of the chapter. According to globalization theory, Western transnational corporations have gained control of global trade and development, and continue to grow in influence. Because these corporations are generally owned by shareholders in the West, profits tend to flow from developing countries to developed countries. As a direct result of this situation, wealth is concentrated in the West, and living standards for most of the world's population are desperately low.

No matter to which of the above theories you subscribe, all seem to arrive at the same place. A few Western nations enjoy high living standards, although even these nations have a sizable population of poor people. In all the rest of the world, however, a vast proportion of the population lacks many of the amenities that even the poor in developed countries take for granted. It will surely be one of the challenges of the future to ensure that the disparity between developed and developing countries is addressed.

Shifting Values

Whatever the causes of the vast disparities of wealth in the globalized world, it will take a huge shift in values before people will turn their thoughts, sense of purpose, and money to the task of addressing world poverty. Vaclav Havel, the former president of the Czech Republic has written,

We often hear about the need to restructure the economies of the developing or poorer countries. But I deem it even more important

that we should begin to think also about another restructuring—a restructuring of the entire system of values which forms the basis of our civilization today. …Given this state of affairs, we have only one possibility: to search, inside ourselves as well as the world around us, for new sources of a sense of responsibility for the world.

(Vaclav Havel quoted in Camdessus, 2001, p.6)

In a provocative article, from which the above quotation is derived, former director of the International Monetary Fund Michel Camdessus calls for the adoption of three key values. Should we adopt them, he believes, we will then be empowered to address many of the issues raised by globalization. He states that we should accept

- the responsibility of each country—large or small—for the world at large
- the responsibility of the world community to institute an ethically rooted new development paradigm
- the responsibility of all agents in society, not just governments, to play their part in the direction the world takes (Camdessus, 2001, pp. 6–7)

Camdessus writes that Catholic social doctrine teaches that each person has a duty and a responsibility to bring about a general prosperity. Such sentiment is not confined to Catholic, or even Christian, teaching. All the world's major religions emphasize the human duty to work for the common good. Most anthropologists who have documented the harmful effects of globalization on various peoples outside the West contend that little improvement can be expected until Western culture begins to value the common good more than profit.

Figure 10.4 These young Canadians enjoy a lifestyle intimately tied to global trade. The Canadian economy benefits enormously by exporting resources, goods, and services to other developed countries, and by importing goods produced cheaply in developing countries. What role do you play in globalization? What values does this role reflect?

Backing Up Canadian Values

The Canadian federal government has taken a stern approach to the country's economic affairs, trimming federal government spending in order to eliminate the deficit and keep spending in line. Many social programs have suffered cutbacks under this regime, including Canada's foreign aid spending. Does this approach reflect Canadian values? On the one hand, many Canadians support fiscal responsibility. On the other hand, they also reject the idea that Canada cannot fulfill its responsibilities to the poor. Here is one person's opinion on the matter of foreign aid in a letter to the editor of the *Toronto Star*.

Shameful Statistics

It must be getting more and more embarrassing for Finance Minister Paul Martin to host international meetings like the G-20, being held this weekend in Ottawa.

The economic downturn and fallout from Sept. 11 have hit poor countries the hardest, and will increase misery around the world. According to the World Bank, 10 million more people will fall below $1 per day in income next year, and tens of thousands more children will die.

With this backdrop of extreme need, Canada is in the awkward position of providing less foreign aid than ever before—0.25 per cent of GNP. Canada's aid to the world's poor has fallen more than any other country's in the last decade.

We now rank 17th of 22 developed countries, down from 6th place in 1995.

When Martin meets with the G-20 group of the world's largest countries—a group he helped create to address global poverty and other issues—he will know that Canada is doing far less than it could.

When he sits down beside colleagues like Gordon Brown, Chancellor of the Exchequer in the U.K., he will know that Britain increased aid by 35 per cent last year, responding to the desperate global need. Martin will know that Canada should do more, and could do more, but will in fact do very little, even in his next budget.

At a certain point, Canada will no longer be able to ride on an international reputation for fairness and generosity earned long ago. How long before Martin's personal reputation follows Canada's into decline?

—Blaise Salmon, Ottawa

Source: *The Toronto Star*. 2001. [Online] Available <http://www.thestar.com> Article Number: 1005865300835. 19 November 2001

Questions

1. What criticisms does Blaise Salmon make against Canada's efforts to combat global poverty?
2. What changes, if any, would you make to Canada's approach to global development? Why?
3. Do individual Canadians' values have to change before the Canadian government will take more action to address global poverty? Why or why not?

Pause and Reflect

1. What are the main features of transnationalism and deterritorialization?

2. How does financialization affect the concentration of wealth in the world?

3. Explain how globalization is tending to homogenize cultures. What is the value in preserving independent cultures?

4. What values do Vaclav Havel and Michel Camdessus believe must be adopted if we are to reduce the negative effects of globalization? How likely is it that we will make this value shift? Explain.

5. What steps could you as an individual take in your lifetime to ensure that the effects of globalization are positive? How likely are you to do these things? Explain.

Section 10.2 Sociology, Globalization, and Inequality

Key Concepts

convergence

global village

relativization

modernity

disembedding

paradigm shift

deskilling

liberation theology

social development index (SDI)

per capita real gross domestic product (PCRGDP)

micro-level

macro-level

Globalization is a comparatively new field of study for sociology. Early sociological considerations of the topic reflected the Western bias prevalent in the society of most sociologists. In the early part of the twentieth century, for example, when structural-functionalism was in its heyday, sociologists generally assumed that any society that was "modern" would be industrial and capitalist in nature. Countries that wanted to "progress" would have to become like the rich Western nations, and those that did not would remain "backward." According to these early sociologists and the bias they brought to their investigations, there appeared to be only one path to modernity.

In the 1950s, social scientists developed the concept of **convergence**. If all or most countries became capitalist and industrial, then many of the differences that existed among these countries would be gradually eliminated. The rest of the world would become more like the West (Kerr et al., 1960). To a certain extent, this is exactly what has happened. The sociologists and economists were mistaken in one fundamental respect, however. They assumed, in the 1960s, that the shift toward capitalism would benefit every-

one. Today, sociologists and others are far less certain that this rosy prediction reflects the current reality.

Thinking Globally

It was University of Toronto's Marshall McLuhan (1911–1980) who invented the term **global village** (1962), inspiring much academic study on the concept that the world is a single community, connected by its telecommunications network. McLuhan realized that the revolution in transportation and communications that was underway in the 1960s made it possible for a person to receive speech and images from all over the world. With the coming of the Internet, we have seen McLuhan's predictions become a reality for more and more people, particularly in developed countries such as Canada where, in 2000, 53 per cent of the population over the age of 15 enjoyed Internet access in their home or work environment (Statistics Canada, 2001).

Sociologists have interpreted globalization to include "all those processes that link what were once isolated, independent human activities to a global frame of reference, thereby changing their very nature" (Albrow, 1995, Ch. 15, p. 4). Because of transportation capabilities and the relatively new phenomenon of selling on the Internet, even small entrepreneurs can manufacture products to sell, not simply in a local market, but anywhere. Even in remote mountain villages, residents are hooked up to the world via television. This is good in the sense that television has the power to inform and entertain, but it can be damaging when local cultures are undermined by foreign programming.

One of the positive features of this shift in frame of reference, as sociologists point out, is an increased overall awareness of global values, such as a clean environment. Instead of taking a narrow perspective that considers only consequences to the local community, many Canadians are now more aware that damaging the environment in our own backyard harms the world environment. Pollution crosses borders. In another example, many Canadians have realized that cutting down the Amazonian rain forest does not affect just the Aboriginal people who live there, but all humanity as well—the rain forest produces about 30 per cent of the world's oxygen, which is vital for human survival. Some critics of globalization see the environmental movement in a negative light, as a creation of developed countries who have already become rich by destroying their own forests and now wish to prevent the developing countries of the South from doing the same.

Sociological Theories of Globalization

Although globalization is a comparatively new field of study for sociologists, and others, a number of different interpretations of globalization's origins have emerged.

1. **Richard Robertson** (1992) sees globalization as a process at least 2000 years old. He traces the history of institutions of social order that have long operated at a transnational level, such as the major religions. Buddhism, for example, spread far from its birthplace in India to become a major religion in other countries. Robertson also believes that respect for the environment, which is closely related to global thinking, has traditionally been a central human value, although humans temporarily lost sight of it during the era of unrestricted industrial expansion (approximately 1820–1960). Robertson also describes what he calls **relativization**, the relationship between self and society. As the world system changes, the outlooks of both our society and ourselves change as well. Robertson's theories explain, for example, how societies that are strongly racist and exclusionist at one period of their history can become more inclusive. South Africa is one such example.

2. **Anthony Giddens** (1991) believes that the roots of globalization do not lie in our distant history; he sees globalization, rather, as stemming directly from **modernity**—the modern age. He believes that the development of modern communications technologies unleashed globalization at a rate enormously faster than anyone in, for example, 1950 could have anticipated. Central to Giddens's approach is the concept of **disembedding**. This term describes the process by which people put their faith in abstract, largely anonymous, systems such as financial institutions, airline companies, and Web browsers. These systems have broken down many of the limits to our mobility and our thinking.

3. **Martin Albrow** (1995) proposes another view that is gaining some currency: that globalization is an even more recent phenomenon than the invention of the commercial jet engine and satellite television. He suggests that it was not until the end of

the Cold War, with the collapse of Soviet communism in 1990 and the concentration of global capital that took place in the decade that followed, that globalization became the force that it is today.

The issue that separates these schools of thought is how they identify key developments that set the globalization movement in progress. Was it the development of armies, 2000 to 3000 years ago, that could go out and conquer distant lands? Was it the development of technology such as the telephone and radio, 70 to 100 years ago, that could provide live links between people on opposite sides of the globe? Or was it the fundamental realignment that took place in the early 1990s, with the collapse of the Soviet Union and the emergence of the USA as the world's only superpower? Some see globalization as merely a modern extension of colonialism. Others believe that it did not begin until formal colonial-

ism was largely finished. These issues continue to be hotly debated.

The remainder of this section will examine three aspects of globalization. You will read about new technologies and globalization, poverty and globalization, and literacy and globalization. In each of these sections, you will see how various factors or developments have driven globalization, and how various social structures have directly or indirectly affected global inequalities.

New Technologies Supporting Globalization

Sociologists, like other social scientists, see technological developments as crucial in the globalization of the world. Many regard technological changes as constituting a **paradigm shift** (or a fundamental change in approach), to the point where they entirely transform the interrelationships of different parts of the world (Prabhu, 1999, p. 2). You can see this in the ways that Canada relates to the rest of the world. Instead of functioning primarily as an exporter of raw goods to a few nations, Canada has developed its manufacturing and communication technology to the point where it now also exports a wide variety of manufactured goods and knowledge services to many countries. Further, the Internet has transformed how Canadians connect with other global citizens.

Critics of globalization have charged that, within the globalized world, new technologies have increased inequalities of income. According to this view, countries that lack the infrastructure for informational technology become poorer, as they are limited to growing and harvesting raw materials for processing elsewhere, or to basic assembly-line production of consumer items for sale in developed countries. Since wage rates are considerably lower in such countries, many manufacturing plants in Europe and North America have been shut down, and

Figure 10.5 A replica of the Nonsuch, the eight-gun ketch that sailed into Hudson Bay from England in 1688, marking the beginning of the Canadian fur trade. Some theorists contend that globalization is not so young, but is just a new form of colonization. After all, colonization is a form of control by one country over foreign lands for the purpose of controlling natural resources. In what ways might this comparison be legitimate or not?

production has shifted to countries such as Mexico, India, and the Philippines. Canadian workers, of course, lose their jobs as a result. And although the recipient countries welcome the extra employment, many find that they must keep wages and taxes very low in order to keep the transnationals from packing up and moving production to yet another country. In more than one case, a transnational clothing or toy manufacturer has exploited workers by engaging subcontractors that employ children, pay low wages, expect exceedingly long hours, or provide unsafe working conditions.

Knowledge-based industries, by definition, require access to sophisticated informational technologies, and these remain largely the preserve of developed countries such as Canada, the United States, Singapore, and Germany. Even in Canada, communities outside major centres are not currently capable of supporting broadband (fast) Internet connections. In poorer regions of the world, most people cannot afford the technology—that is, a computer—even if the infrastructure were in place. To make matters even worse for developing countries, the Internet is largely dominated by English. Non-English-speaking entrepreneurs are immediately competing at a distinct disadvantage. Globalization, the critics charge, is further contributing to the division between rich and poor countries.

Has information technology contributed to further inequalities of income in Canada? Some earlier studies concluded that incomes were in fact becoming polarized in developed countries, depending on whether or not employees required informational technology access or skills to do their jobs (Myles, 1988). Various studies in Canada have shown that the earnings gap between low- and high-paying jobs has widened (or "polarized") since the 1960s, although the reasons for this have not been fully explained. In the United States, Robert B. Reich concluded that technological change and globalization were significant components in wage polarization (Reich, 1991).

Some sociologists, however, charge that the links among globalization, new technologies, **deskilling** (making skilled workers obsolete), and earnings polarization have not been fully demonstrated. Simply because all these trends exist at the same time does not, in itself, mean that one causes the others. A recent Canadian sociological study compared computer use at work, and linked this variable with job skills required and wages paid (Hughes and Lowe, 2000). It concluded that the links were tenuous, at best, and that variables such as gender and education levels were likely to have just as much influence as computer use on earnings polarization.

One area in which there can be little doubt as to the influence of new medical technologies in facilitating a form of global trade and increasing the inequalities between the rich and the poor is the gruesome international trade in human body parts (HBP). If you're prepared to learn about some truly horrifying practices, read the case study on the next page.

---

sunsite.berkeley.edu/biotech/ organswatch/?uniq=5832

The above address will take you to the site of Organs Watch, a project maintained by the University of California, Berkeley Campus. It contains much information about the worldwide trade in HBP, particularly about issues of organ stealing. If you have difficulty locating the site, try going to Berkeley's home page at <www.berkeley.edu>. Then connect through the following links to reach the specific page: Academics > Academic Departments and Programs > Anthropology > Organs watch project (under Research Links).

WEB LINK

The New Trade in Human Body Parts (HBP)
By Trevor Harrison

Until recently, human organ transplantation remained a relatively minor and uncertain medical procedure…. Since the early 1980s, however, both the number and variety of organ transplants have increased enormously. While transplant surgery offers undeniable benefits to suffering recipients, the emergence of a commercial market for organs has been greeted with concern by governments and professional organizations alike…. These concerns are heightened by reports that, in some instances, especially in the underdeveloped world, human body parts are being sourced coercively from the young, the poor, the illiterate, the captive, and the infirm…. Frequently, the "consumers" of these organ "products" come from countries other than those in which the organs were obtained….

In the world of globalized capitalism, all objects lose distinction. They stand apart merely on the basis of their relative equivalence, each with a price, or rather an exchange value…. Thus, wombs are rented; sperm is sold; and, finally, human organs, "harvested."…

The development of specialized and precise surgical techniques—necessitated by the fact that the organ must afterwards remain functional in order to retain its use, hence its exchange value—was fairly quickly mastered…. Likewise, means of preservation were soon developed, progressing from simple hypothermia, to whole organ storage (in the 1950s), to the later development of various flushing solutions. Today, with extended preservation times, and with "the possible exception of the heart, cadaveric organs can now be stored long enough to permit relatively unhurried transportation."…

Today, kidney transplants both in Israel and India sell for between US$10 000 and $30 000, with very little of this—in India, perhaps $500 to $2000—going to the "donor."… In Argentina, meanwhile, private cornea transplants cost $7000, liver transplants more than $80 000—most of this being "pure" profit insofar as the organs are often "sourced" from people — either dead or living—without recompense…. With so much money at stake, it was not long before a number of private European and American entrepreneurs emerged who viewed organ transplantations as a "potentially lucrative area to exploit."…

Initially, there were few laws regulating the extraction and sale of organs. In those countries where the unregulated market particularly thrived—South and Central America, Russia—the state had either collapsed and/or was simply corrupt. Corruption and laxity also infused customs controls, allowing for easy transport of the organs. In the end, the HBP business soon attracted a number of unscrupulous entrepreneurs, doctors, and various "middle men."…

In August, 1994, Human Rights Watch–Asia released a report on the organ transplant business in the People's Republic of China…. Based in large part on government documents, medical journal articles, and statements by doctors and other persons, the report concluded that executed prisoners are the main source for organs. Executions are scheduled according to transplant needs. Hospitals and prospective recipients are notified prior to executions that a particular organ, usually a kidney, will be available. A prisoner's consent is rarely sought, or is coerced in the last few hours before death. In some cases, kidneys are removed from prisoners the night before execution. In other cases, executions are deliberately botched in order to keep the host body alive longer. The manner in which the execution is conducted also depends upon the organ required. For example, if corneas are required, the prisoner will be shot in the heart; if kidneys are required, the rifle shot is to the base of the skull.

According to the Human Rights Watch report, kidneys and corneas are the main organs of transplant in the People's Republic. In 1992, between 1400 and 1700 kidneys from executed prisoners were used in transplant operations....

The arguments put forward by proponents of commercial markets to regulate the trade in HBP follow classical liberal economic premises. There are two classes of arguments: first, libertarian arguments "in support of the use of incentives and markets"; and, second, utilitarian arguments.... The former argument is buttressed by...claims that individuals have proprietorial rights over their own bodies which enable them to decide whether to alienate not merely their labour, but also their body, including its individual parts.... The latter argument is supported by claims that payments actually lead to increased donations. Both arguments underlie a specifically capitalist conception of the human body-as-commodity....

Outright prohibition of organ sales, in any case, has not restricted the trade in HBP; indeed, prohibition has tended to foster the trade, even as it has shaped the trade's emergence along traditional world economic lines. The case of Japan is instructive in this regard. While Japan has long had laws that prohibit live donations, the chief result of these [has] been the stimulation of organ markets on Japan's periphery....

Figure 10.6 In Latin America and other countries, homeless adults and children have been murdered for their organs, which command exorbitant prices. How has the supply and demand of international trade facilitated this situation?

This example suggests the complexity and difficulty of regulating the HBP trade—indeed, many forms of trade in the late twentieth century.

Source: Harrison, Trevor. 1999. "Globalization and the trade in human body parts." *Canadian Review of Sociology and Anthropology*, Vol. 36, Issue 1. February 1999.

Questions

1. Some of the features of globalization are (i) the spread of new technologies, (ii) the harvesting of resources in developing countries for the benefit of the developed countries, and (iii) emphasis on private profit. To what extent is the trade in HBP a good example of globalization?

2. What factors led to an increase in our ability to supply human body parts for an international market?

3. In a chart, compare the arguments in favour of international trade in human body parts with those opposed. Keep in mind the issues of individual rights, human dignity, the profit motive, human health, and global inequities.

4. What is your opinion of China's involvement in the HBP trade? Give your reasons in detail.

5. What ethical principles would you put in place to guide the HBP trade? Remember that the current demand far outstrips the supply.

 Globalization and Poverty

Various organized religions have been accused of contributing to generalized poverty by supporting governments that favour the rich. Nonetheless, many religious figures, particularly in the developing world, have long been concerned about generalized poverty. In Latin America, for example, they found the situation extremely demoralizing, as there seemed to be no end in sight. In response, they developed **liberation theology**, which combines spirituality with political activism to obtain better conditions for the poor. Gustavo Guttierez, one of liberation theology's founders, concluded that extensive poverty was caused by structural factors such as a lack of free education, little investment at home by financial elites (leading to a lack of jobs), emphasis of the private profit motive over the general welfare of the community, and governments committed to serving the needs of the wealthy. Liberation theology's followers also believed that poverty could not be alleviated unless the economic and political structures were changed. Guttierez wrote:

I discovered three things. I discovered that poverty was a destructive thing, something to be fought against and destroyed, and not merely something that was the object of our charity. Secondly, I discovered that poverty was not accidental. The fact that these people are poor and not rich is not just a matter of chance, but the result of a structure. Thirdly I discovered that poor people were a social class. When I discovered that poverty was something to be fought against, that poverty was structural, that poor people were a class (and could organize), it became crystal clear that in order to serve the poor, one had to move into political action.

(Quoted in: Prabhu, 1999, p. 3)

Guttierez's conclusions are interesting from a sociological viewpoint. Sociologists would be likely to agree that, if poverty in Latin America is a structural phenomenon, no solution is possible until the structure is changed. Many sociologists have concluded, with regret, that the power of transnationals—a fundamental component of the world's social structure—is so great that structural change to alleviate poverty is unlikely for the foreseeable future.

One of the results of the growth of transnational corporations has been a transfer of power to them, and away from sovereign governments. By the early 1990s, if you identified the largest 100 economic entities in the world, you would have found that only 53 were national governments. The remaining 47 were transnational corporations

Figure 10.7 In the film *Romero*, Raul Julia portrays the El Salvadoran archbishop Oscar Arnulfo Romero, who identified the causes of the suffering of the El Salvadoran people as greed, capitalism, the doctrine of national security, and indifference. He was assassinated, probably by a right-wing death squad, because of his political activism. How would events like this serve to both discourage and encourage others to fight poverty?

(Laxer, 1995, p. 297). Laxer charges that these transnationals have such economic weight that they can threaten national governments if and when they raise issues such as poverty.

> *The implicit threat is: Bring in strict anti-pollution regulations, promise public auto insurance or higher minimum wages, and we the corporation will move out. You the wage earners and citizens who voted for such policies will be left hurting. Not us: we are mobile and responsible to shareholders, not communities. Global corporate-citizenship rights enhance the transnationals' ability to use blackmail to discipline democracies.*
>
> *(Laxer, 1995, p. 299)*

Laxer, in short, is strongly opposed to globalization as currently practised, because he believes that it gives the transnationals undue dominance over the economic and social development of sovereign nations. In the Competing Perspectives feature on page 344, you will find two views about the World Bank and its culpability in regard to world poverty.

Globalization and Literacy

Another issue relating to globalization that is of interest to sociologists is whether or not there is any causal link between social development and economic growth. In other words, what happens if a nation tries to institute social policies to benefit the majority of the population, such as free post-secondary education? Would a measure like this raise the level of well-being of the general population? Will the population's increased literacy skills attract more international businesses that want an educated workforce? Or will the added costs of these social programs drive the transnationals to seek other countries in which to do business, thereby reducing the economic development of the nation?

Sociologists involved in this type of research work closely with economists, using the data that they have compiled about social development and economic growth. They use a seven-point index, called a **social development index (SDI)**, to measure each country's level of social development. The index includes such items as the adult literacy rate as a percentage of the population over the age of 15, life expectancy at birth, and teacher/pupil ratio in primary education. This figure is then compared with **per capita real gross domestic product (PCRGDP)** in each country, to see what, if any, relationships exist. The PCRGDP is a measure of the amount of goods and services, adjusted for inflation, produced on average by every member of the population.

One study by economist Krishna Mazumdar assembled figures from over 90 countries. In order to make the sample as representative as possible, examples were chosen from three categories, based on their PCRGDP. The high-income group (HIG) consisted of 20 countries, such as Canada, the Netherlands, and the United States. The middle-income group (MIG) was made up of 40 nations, including Brazil, Cameroon, Iran, and Turkey. The low-income group (LIG) of 32 countries contained Bangladesh, Ghana, Malaysia, and Nicaragua.

The results suggest that the relationship between the social development index and national wealth is complex and depends on the type of country being studied. The researcher came to the conclusions shown in Figure 10.8 on page 346.

The overall conclusion of Mazumdar's study was that no uniform causal relationship exists between economic growth and social development. It cannot be assumed that economic expansion will automatically increase adult literacy or any other component of the social development index.

In contrast to the approach taken in the study described above, some writers have concluded that social development results from influences at the **micro-level** (or small

COMPETING
PERSPECTIVES

On the World Bank

Is the World Bank just a tool of the transnationals, which want to increase profits at all cost? Or is it an independent organization bent on improving the chances of developing countries to participate in the world economy? The articles below contain different opinions on the subject of the World Bank and its increasing global role. The first piece is written by The Council of Canadians—which calls itself "Canada's pre-eminent citizens' watchdog organization"—and is posted on their Web site. The second article presents the views of James Wolfensohn, president of the World Bank.

The IMF and the World Bank
By The Council of Canadians

- The International Monetary Fund (IMF) and the World Bank were established in 1944 at the historic conference of 44 nations at Bretton Woods, N.H. Their mandate was to help with post-war reconstruction by fostering international cooperation in financial and economic development. Although originally based on progressive liberal principles, both institutions by the 1970s had fallen under G-7 (predominantly U.S.) influence. They have since become the "enforcers" of free trade, unfettered financial mobility, and other market-driven neoliberal policies, particularly in the Third World. With devastating results.
- Most developing countries sooner or later feel the need to apply to the IMF or the World Bank for loans. Such loans are given only on condition that the recipients agree to implement severe structural adjustment programs (SAPs). These SAPs force indebted countries to adopt a wide range of "free market" policies, including cuts in social pro-

grams, the privatization of public agencies and services, switching agriculture from domestic to export crops, and of course dropping all restrictions on foreign investment and ownership.
- The IMF/World Bank SAPs have increased poverty levels around the world. In the two regions most affected by these programs—Latin America and Africa—per capita income has stagnated, and in many countries has fallen sharply. Governments have been obliged to cut health, education, and other social spending and divert the money to their debt repayments. The SAPs have also further widened the gap between rich and poor in the developing world.
- The IMF and World Bank have driven post-communist Russia into a deep economic depression. Before they imposed their SAPs on that country, 2 million Russians were living in poverty. That number has now soared to 60 million— a peacetime slump of unprecedented scale. The recent financial

crisis in Asia was also created and worsened by the IMF, whose introduction of speculative finance caused the problem, and whose SAPs then triggered a surge in layoffs, bankruptcies, and poverty…
- Women tend to be disproportionately hurt by IMF/World Bank programs. Social spending cuts force women to provide social assistance to those deprived of government help. Higher levels of stress within families harmed by SAPs has led to increases in violence against women. The IMF/World Bank emphasis on growing crops for export has pushed women farmers away from growing food for family consumption, and left them poorer in the process. The high interest rates often dictated by SAPs have also made credit less accessible for small women-owned enterprises.

Source: The Council of Canadians. 2002. "The IMF and the World Bank." [Online]. Available <http://www.canadians.org/> 23 January 2002.

COMPETING PERSPECTIVES

World Bank President Refutes Protesters' Claims
By Heather Scoffield

OTTAWA—World Bank president James Wolfensohn is taking on the protesters who brought downtown Ottawa traffic to a standstill this weekend, saying his international institution is doing more for the world's poor than it gets credit for.

In an interview with The Globe and Mail, Mr. Wolfensohn said he's been hearing the same arguments for years, and while the World Bank has listened—and changed—the protesters haven't.

"There's a need for us to change in the bank, but there's also a need for civil society to give us credit for the ways we do change," he said....

[Commentators have] acknowledged that the World Bank has made progress in shifting its lending from large and often destructive infrastructure programs to social programs, but said that trend is overwhelmed by its embrace of the free-trade, privatization agenda [which involves selling public institutions].

Mr. Wolfensohn defended [the World Bank's] approach, saying free trade—if it means fewer trade barriers against poor countries' goods and lower subsidies for European and U.S. farmers—will help developing countries compete and prosper. Privatization is never advocated at the expense of public social services, he added.

He said that more than ever the rich are primed to take concrete action against poverty because the terrorist attacks of Sept. 11 shocked the rich into a deep reflection about how they work with the poor.

"We saw the two worlds coming together. All of a sudden, we found Afghanistan in Wall Street, we found Afghanistan in the Pentagon," he said in the interview. "It's my hope…we can advance the agenda, so that developed and developing countries, rich and poor countries, can work all together."

Terrorism thrives on poverty, he said, and the fight against terrorism is necessarily a fight for better health, education and environmental conditions for the poor.

He wants developed countries to double their aid for developing countries. At the same time, he wants the developing countries to clean up corruption within their governments and stabilize their regimes so that when the money arrives, it will be put to good use.

Britain's Chancellor of the Exchequer, Gordon Brown, speaking on behalf of the IMF, said rich and poor countries are ready to strike a "new deal."

"The real issue is not whether you are for or against globalization, because globalization is moving forward. The real issue is whether you are for or against social justice on a global scale. And I believe there is an increasing recognition that we have to work together to make the world and the global economy a better place for the world's poor."

Source: Scoffield, Heather. 2001. "World Bank President Refutes Protestors' Claims." *Globe & Mail.* 19 November 2001.

Questions

1. a) What is The Council of Canadians? It suggests that the World Bank works in the interest of industrialized countries. What arguments does this organization use to support its claim?

   b) Who is James Wolfensohn? What arguments does he use in favour of free trade and its effect on developing countries?

2. What biases are contained in each person's or organization's view?

3. Of the different opinions you have read about in these extracts, which one comes closest to your own view on global development? Explain.

Comparing SDI and PCRDP by Income Group

Low-Income Countries	Middle-Income Countries	High-Income Countries	Implications
As world PCRGDP rises, so does world SDI.			This suggests that economic growth permits greater spending on social development.
In MIC and LIC countries, rises in SDI lead to rises in PCRGDP.			This suggests that, up to a certain level, there is a causal relationship between social development and economic growth.
		In HIC countries, rises and falls in PCRGDP do not necessarily lead to rises and falls in SDI.	This suggests that, once a minimum level of economic growth has been reached, further economic growth and social development move independently of each other.
In LIC countries, SDI is low.			This suggests that where there is low social development—low literacy, life expectancy, and infant survival rates—there is also underdeveloped infrastructure and low labour productivity, which translates into low economic growth. This creates a vicious circle for such nations, as it is extremely difficult to increase social development or obtain economic growth.

Source: Adapted from Mazumdar, 1996, p. 372.

Figure 10.8 The relationship between social development (SDI) and national wealth (PCRGDP) is complex. What major advantage do high-income group countries enjoy over low-income group countries?

scale), such as the family, rather than at the **macro-level** (or large scale) of the state. They believe that the household and the assumptions it makes about factors such as religion, education, literacy, and gender are crucial to understanding a country's social structure. This in turn influences the level of its social development index. According to this view, because women play a significant role in the private sphere of the family, it is necessary to understand their role in social contexts to appreciate a nation's ability to increase its SDI.

Diane Singerman and Homa Hoodfar's (1999) edited collection of essays examines the role of women in Cairo, Egypt, in this light. The collection contains an essay by K.R. Kamphoefner, about low-income women and literacy. Kamphoefner concludes that a woman's decision to learn to read and write depends on her occupation. She will likely reject a government-sponsored literacy program unless she can see that she might be able to use her new-found skill in her job. This reinforces the observation that the success or failure of all social movements depends on a multitude of personal and family decisions. The policy of a national government to extend, or to restrict, female literacy will succeed or fail largely on how well it addresses the needs of individuals and groups.

Pause and Reflect

1. In a three-column point-form chart, compare the three general theories of globalization's origins (Robertson, Giddens, Albrow) described at the beginning of this section. Assess them from your perspective, citing reasons.

2. Give one example of a way that a technological development has increased global inequality.

3. Read the quotation from Gustavo Guttierez in the section about globalization and poverty. If he is correct in his observations, what do societies need to do to eliminate or reduce poverty?

4. What conclusions did Mazumdar's 1996 study reach about the relationship between social development and economic growth?

5. Assume you work for a government in a developing country. Choose one social structure, such as technology, capitalism, education system, labour law, or welfare organization, that has increased global inequality. Develop a government policy to alter your chosen social structure, thereby increasing the living standard in your country. Include your goals, implementation steps, costs, and benefits.

Section 10.3   Our Perceptions of the Community: Psychology and Globalization

A Canadian living and teaching in South Korea was upset and offended when she read a letter in the *Korea Herald* that was critical of Canadians sporting the maple leaf and of Canada itself. To express her feelings, she responded with a letter to the editor of the same newspaper. Here is an excerpt from that letter.

To sport a Canadian flag is in itself an expression of cultural diversity, prosperity, and goodwill to all. Our country is not a 'patriotic force to be reckoned with.' We don't have an army to conquer the world. We are a cultural mosaic, a society that embraces equality and the betterment of the planet through peacekeeping, policies that ensure a high standard of living, and the importance of human rights.... I had no idea that our flag could be an offensive symbol for anyone; this is not my experience. My flag is a welcome mat, a notice that my door is always open.

— Kara Kilfoil (10 July 2001)

Do you agree with Kara Kilfoil's assessment of what the Canadian flag represents and what it means to be Canadian? What points would you add or change? Why is it that Canadians cannot agree on what it means to be Canadian?

If you do believe we have a unique **national identity**, then you probably believe that we have a unique culture, composed of values, beliefs, and programs, that sets us apart from other nations. You and your classmates may identify as Canadian such values as tolerance and acceptance, government provision of universal health care and education, strict gun control, multiculturalism, and respect for the natural environment. Indeed, a survey conducted for the Canadian Heritage Department in 2001 found that the one aspect of Canadian life that makes us feel most attached to our country is our natural surroundings. Seventy-six per cent of respondents mentioned the natural environment as a top priority (Kappler, 2001, p. 14).

Key Concepts

national identity

perception

constancy

unconscious inference

selective attention

cocktail-party phenomenon

Rorschach card

hallucination

misperception

perceptual set

memory modification

post-event information

forgetting curve

Until the terrorist attacks on America on 11 September 2001, our definition of ourselves also included a significant amount of anti-American sentiment. As you will read later, the attacks on New York City and Washington made many Canadians feel much closer to their neighbours to the south. Some Canadians are no longer inclined to have their national identity dependent on the ridicule or criticism of others.

Many Canadians would disagree with the very idea that a single set of ideas can define Canada. They argue that despite the common threads listed above, a single national Canadian identity does not exist. They would point to the many different groups of Canadians, such as Quebec separatists, the Inuit, urban professionals, and Hutterite farmers, all Canadians with quite disparate views and cultural characteristics. The existence of these individual cultures may preclude the possibility of a truly national culture.

Figure 10.9 Most Canadians identify the natural environment as a defining aspect of the Canadian identity. Not everyone agrees. What factors might affect what we consider to be typically Canadian?

At the other extreme, many Canadians feel that Canadian culture doesn't exist because it's really just a subset of North American culture. They point to the fact that our airwaves are dominated by American television programs; that we are exposed to the same music, books, and advertising; and that we drive the same cars, wear the same brand name clothing, and play the same sports. These Canadians would argue further that we might as well establish a common North American currency because the economy of the United States and Canada is so closely linked anyway.

Why is there such disagreement over our national identity? Politicians might credit people's different political views. Anthropologists might examine the formative influence of the communities where we grew up. Psychologists would argue that **perception** plays a major role in how we see ourselves as a nation. Perception refers to the process by which our brain tries to make sense of incoming messages. Psychologists would say that Canadians have different views about themselves, their families, their local communities, and their countries because of the different ways that we interpret the onslaught of information we encounter in our daily lives. Before we explore the issue of national identity further, we should first find out what psychologists have found out about perception and how it influences our thought processes.

Understanding the Role of Perception

How does perception work? Our brains are constantly being bombarded with messages through all our senses. To get through a day, we simply cannot focus on all this information thoroughly. For example, to pay attention to every single sound that it is possible for us to hear would be such an engulfing exercise that we wouldn't be able to function on any other level. To help us, our brains create shortcuts to try to solve the mystery of incoming stimuli and the events we are experiencing. In its broadest sense, then, perception refers to those processes that give coherence and unity to sensory input. It includes an assessment of physical stimulus as well as the actual experience caused by the stimulus.

The study of perception begins with recognition of the fact that what we perceive is not uniquely determined by the physical stimulation we experience. Instead, what we perceive is determined by a host of factors. One of these factors is **constancy**. This refers to the fact that our perceptual world tends to remain the same despite drastic alterations in sensory input. For example, we perceive the front cover of a book as a rectangle whether we see it straight on or from an angle.

The German social scientist Hermann von Helmholtz coined the term "**unconscious inference**" for the phenomenon of constancy, arguing that we make these judgments (for example, that the front of the book is a rectangle) based on a limited amount of evidence or data, and that we make these judgments without awareness. In other words, we are not even aware that we are making these perceptual adjustments.

Another factor that influences perception is **selective attention**, or the ability to focus on certain physical stimuli and exclude others. As we noted above, we would be unable to function if we paid attention to all physical stimuli that we encounter. Instead, we tend to focus on stimuli that seem significant. When we pay attention to one stimulus, however, we tend to inhibit, or suppress, the processing of others. Psychologist C. Cherry coined the term **cocktail-party phenomenon** to characterize the ability to attend selectively to a single person's speech in the midst of the competing speech of many others.

Motivation and emotions also influence perception. Classic perception experiments conducted about the role of motivation involved showing patients ambiguous stimuli such as pictures on **Rorschach cards**.

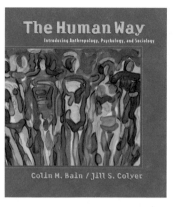
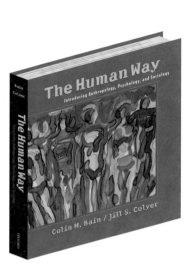

Figure 10.10 When we look at one book from different angles, the retinal image (what our eyes see) changes. Unconscious inference tells us that the book covers shown above are both rectangular, even though the retinal image of the book cover on the right is a parallelogram (a quadrilateral image with opposite sides parallel). Think of another example of unconscious inference.

Figure 10.11 When you try to communicate with a friend in a crowded environment, you screen out other sounds as you attempt to concentrate on what your friend is saying. In what situations might you experience the cocktail-party phenomenon?

(Rorschach cards are a standard set of ink blots on cards. By asking a patient to say what the ink blots look like, psychologists are able to learn more about the patient's personality.) For the perception experiments, the cards were shown to people who hadn't eaten and were hungry. These patients tended to perceive food objects in the ink blots. In another experiment, children were asked about the size of coins. Children from low-income families tended to overestimate the size of coins more than did children from middle-income families. Similarly, strong emotional feelings can distort perceptions rather dramatically, even to the extent that they lead to **hallucinations**. These "perceptions" of things that do not exist can be produced by a variety of causes including drugs, lack of sleep, sensory deprivation, emotional stress, and psychosis (severe mental derangement). In effect, motivation and emotions can both result in **misperceptions**, or errors in judgment.

Another factor that influences perception and can result in perceptual errors is a phenomenon known as **perceptual set**. Each person has his or her own perceptual set, or set of assumptions about the world. These include everything from our assumptions about the physical world (for example, that a rock will be heavy) to our assumptions about our society (for example, that when we say "How are you?" people will usually say "Fine.") A person who has a fixed perceptual set interprets new or contrary information in a way that makes it fit with his or her existing beliefs. For example, imagine that a visitor to Canada believes that Canadians tend to be meek and mild. Imagine that this person then has an encounter with a Canadian who is quite aggressive. It is possible that the person would dismiss the new information on the grounds the Canadian was "having a bad day" rather than change his or her established set of beliefs.

Because perception is such a complex process, there is great variation in how each individual sees a particular event or situation,

and there is great variation among the errors in perception made by individuals. (See the case study on page 351.) In addition, perception has an impact on our behaviour as well as on our beliefs, thus affecting how we see and treat others.

Globalization and Our Sense of Ourselves

As we have seen in the previous section, we form our understanding of the world via perception. We "gather" data and interpret this input to create our perceptual set. Thus we form our own views of the world and world issues, as well as of Canada's place within the global community. Let's look at some Canadians' opinions about globalization and how it is affecting Canada.

A national poll taken by Ekos Research Associates (an Ottawa-based research firm) in June of 2001 indicates that many Canadians are becoming more accepting of globalization and free trade. In an article for the *Halifax Daily News*, Diane Francis explained that a majority of the polled Canadians felt positive about globalization and North American integration. Fifty-five per cent of Canadians stated that integration with the United States was having a positive impact on Canada's economic well-being, and 60 per cent stated that globalization was a positive force. As well, nearly one in every two Canadians polled expected to be part of a North American union within 10 years.

Despite this apparent acceptance of globalization, Canadians also strongly believe in maintaining their own sovereignty. This tendency is revealed by the fact that a full 75 per cent of the polled Canadians felt that maintaining our own currency is essential to Canada's economic sovereignty and national identity. Furthermore, although the polled Canadians believe that free trade has had a positive economic impact on the country, the majority stated that they believe it has had a

Problems with Eyewitness Testimony

One area in which mistakes of perception are particularly serious is in the courtroom: faulty eyewitness testimonies lead to wrongful conviction in a staggering number of criminal trials. Researchers in the United States have found that mistaken eyewitness identification is responsible for 80 per cent of wrongful convictions (Napp, 2000, p. 10). Psychologist Maryanne Garry reports that many of these people were found guilty of serious crimes and were serving multiple life sentences. This is not just an American problem.

In one famous Canadian case, Steven Truscott, in 1959, was convicted of the rape and murder of 12-year-old Lynne Harper when he was only 14. In 2002 he came forward to have his name cleared, and his case came under review. He has always maintained he is innocent of the crime. Although Truscott's conviction appears to be the result of a faulty police investigation, the eyewitness testimony of one witness—10-year-old Philip Burns—was definitely a contributing factor. Burns could not remember seeing the suspect and victim on the road at the time of the murder. The police argued that therefore the two must not have been on the road. In fact, however, Burns also failed to remember seeing other people on the road who definitely had been on the road and had seen him. Instead of questioning the witness's perception, the police used his testimony to help convict Truscott of rape and murder. Visit the Web site of *The Fifth Estate* at <www.cbc.ca/fifth> to review the complete transcript of Philip Burns' testimony and the Truscott case.

Professor Alvin Esau, director of the University of Manitoba's Legal Research Institute <www.umanitoba.ca/Law/Courses/esau> and a visiting professor at the University of Victoria, notes that eyewitness errors can occur in any of three separate processes. First, errors can occur in the perception of the event itself. In this case, exposure time, lighting, stress, or prior personal or cultural expectations can all interfere with a person's perception of an event.

Second, errors can occur in the retention of the event. Retention can be affected by **memory**

Figure 10.12 Steven Truscott was nearly hanged after his conviction in 1959, but his sentence was changed to life in prison. As it turns out, a faulty eyewitness testimony may have been partly responsible for his conviction. Why do juries tend to believe eyewitness testimony is accurate?

modification, **post-event information** and the "**forgetting curve**." Memory modification is the process whereby humans alter their memories to fit any number of internal or external variables. Post-event information can alter retention of the event by causing us to question our own memories. And the "forgetting curve" applies to the concept that specific details of events can blur or fade with time.

A number of factors may also affect our retrieval of the event. One such factor is whether or not a person is given recall or recognition questions. In recall questioning, no specific information about the event under question is given to the person trying to retrieve the event. In recognition questioning, information about the event is provided to the person being questioned. An open-ended question such as "What specific details can you recall from the night in question?" would be an example of a recall question, whereas, a recognition question might be, "Was the accused wearing a blue jacket or a red jacket on the night in question?"

Questions

1. Identify three reasons eyewitness testimony at criminal trials is not always accurate.

2. Review the factors affecting perception in this section of the textbook. Which of those factors do you believe contribute to problems with eyewitness testimony? Explain your answer fully.

negative effect on Canada's environment, social programs, and culture.

Forming Our Views

How do we gain these particular views? Like all of us, the polled Canadians read newspapers and books, listen to the radio, watch television, and talk with friends and family. Using this information, we form our views or revise them to fit what we see as a new reality. For example, many Canadian teachers' opinions about Canada and its place in the world have shifted, as we can see in the developments at a summer conference held for teachers at the University of Alberta in July 2001. The conference focused on the fact that "old concepts about Canada, largely based on ethnic nationalism, won't help young people negotiate a world increasingly defined by globalism" (Chambers, 2001, p. B4). As such, University of British Columbia scholar John Willinsky believes that schools should find new ways to convey the idea of Canada as a nation based on the civil and political arrangements of the people who live here, not on old concepts of nationhood based on two founding races and "patronizing" ideas about multiculturalism that do not reflect our current reality.

Willinsky believes that "the nation we take for granted is in question," citing the external forces of globalization and internal forces such as the determination of Aboriginal people to assert their rights and the changing composition of Canadian society. Rather than try to reinforce "nostalgic" ideas about the country, the schools should be doing what they can to reflect the new realities. That means teaching students to grasp critically the changing ideas of what Canada is. He believes that the idea of two founding races or cultures served to exclude too many Canadians. More than half the students in Vancouver's schools speak a first language that is neither English nor French, and the city has two Chinese-language daily newspapers as well as two English-language papers. Willinsky believes that Canada's young people will fare better in the world—and so will Canada—if students learn to

Figure 10.13 Education plays a role in how we see ourselves because teachers can expose us to eye-opening information, different views, and engaging possibilities. Why is it important that the information being presented in classrooms be up to date and accurate?

define the nation by its political and civil arrangements (Chambers, 2001, p. B4).

As teachers begin bringing into the classroom a new view of Canadians and our role in the world, and as texts and other media used in the classroom begin to reflect these new realities, young Canadians' views of themselves, their families, their communities, and their world will shift in turn.

Mistaken Views

It is important to remember that not all our views are necessarily "true." As you saw in the case study on page 351, what we perceive may in fact be erroneous because of one reason or another. By extension, we must acknowledge that our understandings of ourselves, our families, our communities, and our world may be inaccurate. Many Canadians, for example, are proud of our role as a major participant in peacekeeping missions around the world. They cite the fact that Canada has participated in virtually every peacekeeping mission since the inception of the force. Canada's participation numbers, however, are generally quite small. For example, in early 2002, Canada's 314 peacekeeping troops represented less than 1 per cent of the 47 778-member international peacekeeping force. We can perhaps keep in mind Canada's 1619 men and women in Bosnia (not, technically, a peacekeeping mission), and the 2500 Canadian soldiers participating in the War on Terrorism in January 2002. These soldiers are not peacekeepers, however. What other views do Canadians hold about themselves and their relationship to the world that might not be accurate? Only when we recognize that who we are has changed—or was never true in the first place—can we make changes to our perceptual set.

Canada's Uneasy Relationship with Our American Neighbours

What aspects of our Canadian identity will change in the future? Some experts speculate

that a major area of change will involve our crucial relationship with the Americans. Let us first look at one facet of this relationship and how it has changed as a result of one unexpected, shocking event.

For many years, a defining aspect of the Canadian identity has been a tendency to poke fun at our neighbours to the south. Molson's award-winning "I Am Canadian" beer ads dripped with anti-American sentiment. The farcical television series *This Hour Has 22 Minutes* (produced by Salter Street Film in association with the CBC) featured a regular segment entitled "Talking to Americans." In this recurring skit, comic Rick Mercer interviewed Americans about "current events" in Canada, thereby encouraging them to make fools of themselves. Notable episodes included Americans congratulating Canada on hooking up to the electrical grid, signing a petition to stop the seal hunt in Saskatchewan, and commenting on Canada's recent move to legalize insulin.

It has always been easy for Canadians to criticize Americans for their lack of knowledge about our country. Most Americans don't know much about Canada. And why should they? The Americans have a stronger economy, a stronger voice in the world community, an entertainment industry that dominates the world, and a culture that is definable and identifiable by most everyone who lives within and outside the country. Seeing Americans reveal their weakness has in some ways been a unifying force for Canadians. In our perception of ourselves as the underdog, it's been comforting to know they're not perfect. After all, it's fun to watch the popular kid trip up...right?

Perhaps it was at one time, but a great sea change has taken place in Canada's perception of itself in relation to its southern neighbour when the United States suffered the biggest terrorist attack in its history on 11 September 2001. Many Canadians felt outrage that someone—anyone—would dare to attack civilian Americans as they went about

Figure 10.14 Canadian comedian Rick Mercer gained fame and notoriety for giving Americans a chance to make a mistake on his interview segment "Talking to Americans." Why might Canadians enjoy seeing Americans make fools of themselves? What does this have to do with how we see ourselves in relation to Americans?

their daily lives. Some Canadians mourned because they lost loved ones in the attacks. Others mourned because they had American or Canadian friends who died. Most Canadians mourned simply because so many people—who suddenly seemed so much like us—died such horrible, violent deaths.

For most Canadians, the attacks on September 11 made the Americans seem more vulnerable and human than we had previously considered them to be. In response, Canadians have raised money for the victims of the attacks. School children have donated teddy bears and other toys to children who lost family in the attacks. Countless numbers of Canadians have volunteered at the site of the attacks, or at home, to try to help in some small way. Many Canadians flew American flags to show their support for their neighbours. Only time will tell whether or not the events of September 11 will result in a lasting closer bond with the Americans. Nonetheless, many Canadians feel closer to their American neighbours, and we'll probably be less likely to laugh at the next anti-American joke.

Whether or not we joke about Americans may seem a bit trivial when considering the larger question of Canada's place in the world. Yet this factor plays into the larger issue of Canada's relationship with the United States. Several experts, including *Toronto Star* columnist Richard Gwyn, believe this relationship is just beginning a dramatic transformation. In the article in the case study on the next page, Gwyn argues that the Canada–United States relationship will be the defining national issue of the first decade of this century. He believes that the fallout of September 11 is just starting to be felt in Canada, and that public debate on the Canada–US relationship is needed. What form will this relationship take? Will it be reflective of a Canadian identity of which you'll be proud? Only with the involvement of ordinary Canadians in issues like this will we have a realistic hope of evolving our view of ourselves into a Canada we want to be. Would you like to participate? Read on and get a taste of what we're in for.

Canada–U.S. Relationship is Defining National Issue
By Richard Gwyn

Throughout the decade of the 1980s, our defining national issue was continental free trade. We staged a coast to coast debate about it that was fierce and feisty and well informed.

On the "Yes" side were the Conservatives led by then prime minister Brian Mulroney. On the opposition side were the Liberals, then led by John Turner. An important subsidiary role on the "No" side was performed by the New Democrats. During the middle years of the 1990s (as well as earlier, from the mid-1970s until well into the 1980s), our defining national issue was Quebec's future within Confederation.

Fast forward to today. Beyond the least doubt, our defining national issue for the present—and for at least the first decade of this century—is the Canada-U.S. relationship.

The nature of that relationship has been changed radically by the events of September 11. In one way or another, and despite official denials, we're going to end up with some form of a "common security perimeter." At the same time, the issue of "dollarization"—a common continental currency, the greenback, of course—has been thrust onto the public agenda by the continued erosion of the loonie, down to an all-time low of below 62 cents.

The effect of developments like this—one is as yet only potential—will be to erode our sovereignty by forcing us to treat some of the U.S. national interests as synonymous with our own national interests.

The impending "convergence" in visa systems is a good example. U.S. standards of deciding who should be allowed to enter that country will become effectively Canada's standards for determining who should enter this country—or, at least, will do this for the small number of individuals (tourists, business [people], students, refugee claimants) who might be terrorists and who, once in Canada, could threaten U.S. security by slipping across the border.

Another factor in play that may be more influential in reshaping the Canada–U.S. relationship is that post-September 11, Canadians have had to come to terms with a kind of in-your-face dependence of this country on the U.S. We've had to accept that U.S. security interests are, largely, our national security interests—this because keeping the Canada–U.S. border open is so essential to our economic health.

We've had to accept that militarily we are inconsequential and so—unlike Britain to at least some degree—cannot influence U.S. foreign policy at its most vital points. And we've had to accept the seemingly irreversible weakness of our currency.

Our cross-border bargaining capacity has probably never been weaker in our history—this, as is especially disheartening, even though in many respects our national condition is stronger today than it has been in a long time (no budget deficits, an end to separatism threats, at least for the time being).

We need a national debate to plot out how best to reorient ourselves to our changed circumstances. We need, that is to say, to apply to this challenge the same kind of intelligence and passion that we once mustered up to deal with free trade and with the possibility of Quebec [separation]....

[Politicians are not taking up the debate.] That debate, though, has to happen. It's going to happen instead, therefore, in the only way that remains for it to happen—by starting entirely outside our political system and then by forcing its way inside, with the politicians scrambling to catch up. Watch for that debate to start somehow and for the politicians to start to scramble.

Abridged from: Gwyn, Richard. 2001. "Ottawa fails to lead border debate." *The Toronto Star*. 28 November 2001.

Questions

1. Why does Gwyn believe Canadian sovereignty is being quietly eroded? What examples does he provide?
2. How does globalization affect the Canadian-American relationship?
3. According to Gwyn, in what ways have the events of September 11 highlighted Canada's dependence on America?
4. Why does Gwyn think a national debate is needed on this issue? Do you? Why or why not?
5. In what ways might the outcome of this debate affect Canadians' views of themselves and their relationship with the world?

Pause and Reflect

1. What qualities do Canadians use to describe their country, according to the text? What would you add to the list?
2. List and explain all the factors that influence perception. What factors influence perception in a way that can result in misperceptions?
3. According to the research cited in the text, how do Canadians feel about globalization? Do you agree with these views? Explain.
4. The chapter material indicates that Canada's role in international peacekeeping may not be as grand as our national mythology would have us believe. Make a list of other aspects of our "Canadian-ness" that may also be overrated, or possibly untrue (for example, our famous "niceness"). Be prepared to defend your choices in class.
5. Make two lists that describe what you believe will be the short- and long-term effects the September 11 attacks on the US will have on Canada. In what ways will these changes affect your personal opinion of your country?

Skill Builder:
Validating Your Conclusions

In the course of any research project, the time will come when you have to validate your conclusions. This process allows you to ensure that the evidence you have presented does in fact support the conclusions you have drawn.

Step One: Select key material
Imagine that this chapter represents your project and that you now wish to draw the following conclusions.

List of Conclusions
- Explanations of the forces causing globalization are fairly consistent across the social science disciplines.
- Arguments about whether or not globalization is beneficial tend to vary depending on whether your focus is the developed or the developing world.
- The relationship between economic growth and social development is relatively consistent throughout the world.

Your first step is to review your project (in this case, the chapter) for the purpose of selecting key material related to your conclusions.

For practice, go through this chapter and identify material related to the above conclusions. Choose two brief selections related to each conclusion.

Step Two: Assess your key material
Imagine that you have identified the following extracts from this chapter as key pieces of material relating to the conclusions listed above.

List of Key Material
a) International financial organizations, including the IMF and World Bank, are prepared to invest money in developing countries only if they can be assured that wage rates and taxes will remain low. Transnationals prefer to set up their assembly-line operations in low-wage, low-tax countries because it keeps their production costs down. Costa Rica acted to make itself fit the necessary pattern for entry into the global market. It chose the route taken by many developing countries attempting to keep taxes and wages low: it cut back on its social programs. (Page 330.)
b) Whereas tribalism and nationalism had occupied much of anthropologists' attention for the better part of a century, in the late twentieth century anthropologists were forced to acknowledge that powerful forces were coming together to make it increasingly difficult for cultures to remain isolated from the rest of the world. Western industrial countries looked everywhere for sources of cheap raw materials, drawing developing countries into their **sphere of influence** (the area over which a society has economic and cultural influence). Communications technology improved so that sporting events or coverage of wars could be beamed live from virtually any part of the world to another. International organizations like the United Nations High Commissioner for Refugees (UNHCR), or charities such as Médecins Sans Frontières and Free the Children were able to provide humanitarian aid anywhere in the world at short notice. Such organizations became known as **transnational**, meaning that they saw their role as international or global, trying to assist wherever needed. **Transnationalism** implies that organizations, be they charitable organizations or businesses, operate freely in a number of nations. (Page 328.)
c) Sociologists have interpreted globalization to include "all those processes that link what were once iso-

lated, independent human activities to a global frame of reference, thereby changing their very nature" (Albrow, 1995, Ch. 15, p. 4). Because of transportation capabilities and the relatively new phenomenon of selling on the Internet, even small entrepreneurs can manufacture products to sell, not simply in a local market, but anywhere. Even in remote mountain villages, residents are hooked up to the world via television. This is good in the sense that television has the power to inform and entertain, but it can be damaging when local cultures are undermined by foreign programming. (Page 336.)
d) The overall conclusion of Mazumdar's study was that no uniform causal relationship exists between economic growth and social development. It cannot be assumed that economic expansion will automatically increase adult literacy or any other component of the social development index. (Page 336.)
e) Knowledge-based industries, by definition, require access to sophisticated informational technologies, and these remain largely the preserve of developed countries such as Canada, the United States, Singapore, and Germany. Even in Canada, communities outside major centres are not currently capable of supporting broadband (fast) Internet connections. In poorer regions of the world, most people cannot afford the technology—that is, a computer—even if the infrastructure were in place. To make matters even worse for developing countries, the Internet is largely dominated by English. Non-English-speaking entrepreneurs are immediately competing at a distinct disadvantage. Globalization, the critics charge, is further contributing to the division between rich and poor countries. (Page 339.)
f) [Some writers] believe that the household and the assumptions it makes about factors such as religion, education, literacy, and gender are crucial to understanding a country's social structure. This in turn influences the level of its social development index. According to this view, because women play a significant role in the private sphere of the family, it is necessary to understand their role in social contexts to appreciate a nation's ability to increase its SDI. (Page 343.)

Compare the two lists above. Which items from the list of key material go with which item in the list of conclusions?

During your comparison, you will have seen that key materials items (b) and (c) are related to conclusion 1; items (a) and (e) are related to conclusion 2; and (d) and (f) are related to conclusion 3. You will also have noticed that conclusions 1 and 2 are consistent with the key materials items that go with them. You may have noticed a problem, however, with conclusion 3. Key materials items (d) and (f) do not support conclusion 3; they offer no proof of its validity.

Step Three: Modify your conclusions
Assuming that you have an inconsistency, you have a choice. You can review your project to find other pieces of key material that will support your conclusion, or you can modify your conclusion to fit the evidence. Before you make a decision on this matter, consider what is wrong. Have you chosen a conclusion that is incorrect? Have you chosen one that cannot be supported with the evidence in your project? Have you simply made a poor selection of key material? Now find additional evidence to support conclusion 3, or modify it as necessary.

Practise It!
Pick one of the two following conclusions that could be drawn from this chapter.

a) Globalization has been of more benefit to the developed nations than to the developing nations.
b) Being part of the globalized world offers developing nations their best chance of raising their economic and social-development levels.

Following the steps above, go through the chapter, identifying key pieces of information related to this conclusion. Then assess your conclusion based on the key material you collected, and modify the conclusion or select other key material as necessary.

Conclusion
It is important that your conclusions have as much impact as possible, for they are probably the last thing that your reader will encounter. One way of giving them impact is to keep them short but meaty—they should pack a punch. Back up your conclusions by summarizing key material that has already been presented.

▶ ▶ ▶ Chapter Activities

Show Your Knowledge

1. In your own words, describe the key differences between a tribal and a national form of organization. How are they both different from transnationalism?

2. How did globalization negatively affect the Costa Rican agricultural workers described in the case study on page 330? How was their experience typical, and how was it different from other similar experiences?

3. Does it appear that sociologists tend to believe that the effects of globalization have been generally beneficial or generally harmful? Support your answer by selecting three quotations from this chapter. Document these quotations properly.

4. In what ways is perception a complex process? How can this complexity cause people to make errors in what they perceive?

Practise Your Thinking

5. What are the main beliefs of (a) modernization theory, (b) dependency theory, (c) world-system theory, (d) neo-Marxian theory, and (e) globalization theory? Which one do you think best explains the globalized world?

6. Krishna Mazumdar's studies suggest that the link between social development and economic expansion depends on which of three types of country is being studied (LIC, MIC, HIC).

   (a) Summarize their findings about the link for each type of country.
   (b) Based on what you observe in Canada (an HIC), would you agree with his findings? Why, or why not?

7. Speculate on why a developing country might want or need more government control of its economic sectors. Consider the issues of foreign ownership, the proportion of the population with low incomes, the need for government revenue, the size and expertise of the economic elite, and the ability of the nation to attract foreign investment.

8. University of Manitoba's Dr. Todd Mondor states, "I often study how the perception of a specific sound may be enhanced or compromised depending on the context in which it is presented." If you were listening to some music for the first time, what are some factors that could (a) enhance, and (b) compromise your perception of it?

9. Read the material about the national poll taken by Ekos Research Associates in June of 2001 (page 350) What factors are likely to make (a) 55 per cent of Canadians believe that integration with the United States was having a positive impact on Canada's economic well-being and (b) 60 per cent state that globalization is a positive force? Do you agree with these majority views? Why or why not?

Communicate Your Ideas

10. Do some research into the struggle of Aboriginal people in Canada to retain their cultures and resist the pressures of globalization and transnationalism. Compare your findings with the description in this chapter of the efforts of Paulinho Paiakan, leader of the Kayapo people, to resist the economic pressures of development. As a class, discuss how successful the Aboriginal people in this country have been in this struggle, and the reasons for their success or failure. (A good place to start is the Assembly of First Nations' Web page. Visit its search page at <afn.ca/search.htm>. Put "globalization" and other related terms used in this chapter in the search box, and see what you come up with.

11. Work with a partner. Visit Berkeley University's Organ Watch site at <sunsite.berkeley.edu/biotech/organswatch/?uniq=5832>.

   What parts of the world seem to be the current "hotspots?" Does the trade seem to be growing or declining? Browse through the site to ensure that you are familiar with its contents. With your partner, draw up a list of ethical principles that you think should govern the exchange of HBP. (Should for-profit trade be permitted? Should private organizations be allowed to participate? How much government involvement and regulation should there be?) Then, in small groups, develop a list of guidelines to govern how the exchange of HBP could take place in a way that prevents the exploitation of donors.

12. Visit the Web site of the One World Foundation at <www.oneworld.org/ni/index4.html>. Among other things, this site contains access to the *New Internationalist* magazine, which investigates various topics under the theme of "one world." Enter "globalization" into the search screen for access to hundreds of articles on this topic. (Try also entering the British spelling, "globalisation.") Select an article of interest to you at this site (or at another related site) and briefly report its contents to your class. What additional aspects of globalization, not covered in this chapter, has the class been able to find? What conclusions about globalization have you been able to come to from your research?

13. Organize a class debate on the following statement: "Globalization is inevitable and beneficial. Canadians have a duty to promote it now." Whatever side of the debate you are on, be sure to include social science evidence to support your position.

14. Conduct a straw poll among friends and family, formulated to find out what your community's views are about the Canada–US relationship. As a class, create about three questions about the issue, for example, "Did the September 11 attacks on the United States cause you to feel closer to Americans?" and "Should Canada adopt the US dollar?" Be sure to ask yes-no questions. For the poll, each student can ask the questions of three friends or family. Compile all your answers as a class and discuss your results.

Apply Your Knowledge

15. Eric Wolf wrote: "The guiding fiction of [capitalist] society—one of the key tenets of its ideology —is that land, labor, and wealth are commodities, that is, goods produced, not for use, but for sale" (1969, p. 277). What does Wolf's statement mean? Do some research into land development pressures in Canada today—for example in the Oak Ridges Moraine north of Toronto, or in the area around Banff National Park. Examine Wolf's argument critically. Is it correct? Speculate on why or why not?

16. Organize this activity as a class. Select a developed country and a developing country. Find out information about such things as life expectancy, adult literacy, physicians/1000 population, urban population as a percentage of the total, percentage of school-aged population in education. (These are all indicators of SDI.) What is the per capita gross real domestic product (PCGRDP) for each country? Do the class's findings agree overall with the conclusion of Mazumdar's 1996 study? What conclusions can you reach from this exercise?

17. Identify ways—both positive and negative—in which globalization is likely to have an impact on your life. What can you do to prepare for these impacts (a) in the next five years? (b) over the course of your lifetime?

18. How do you think globalization will affect the lives of people living in developing countries? Do you, or does Canada, as an industrialized nation, have a responsibility for the changes to these people's lives? Explain. If these changes will be negative, what can you do to prepare for these impacts (a) in the next five years? (b) over the course of your lifetime?

SUMMATIVE PROJECT

STAGE THREE: CREATING A FINISHED PROJECT

■ Your Assignment

The third and final phase in this summative project requires you to use three important skills that you learned and practiced in Chapters 8, 9, and 10 to produce a finalized report. These skills demonstrated how to maintain intellectual objectivity, use visual representations to display information, and validate the conclusions that are reached. By applying these skills, you can ensure that the product of your research will be accurate and clear to those who examine your findings.

■ The Three Steps

In Unit 3 you learned and practiced three skills. At this stage, you will apply them in an organized series of steps.

1. *Maintaining intellectual objectivity*—In scholarly research, you must prevent your personal views from shaping your findings. Review the Skill Builder on page 282 to ensure that you demonstrate objectivity by incorporating the research of authorities who both agree and disagree with the conclusions you express.

The work that you submit for assessment must include the following evidence of objectivity. Your teacher may require that it be either handed in separately, or incorporated into the marking scheme of your summative project.
   - At least one good example to demonstrate that you have incorporated the work of authorities who present different viewpoints concerning the topic you have chosen. Summarize each of their viewpoints in a separate paragraph, and include source documentation for each one, done in correct format.
   - At least one good example to demonstrate that you have incorporated the work of authorities who confirm one another's viewpoint on some aspect of your topic. Summarize their supporting opinions in one paragraph, and include source documentation for both authors, done in correct format.

2. *Using visual representations to show information*—By creating visuals to illustrate numerical data, you may be able to identify trends and patterns that weren't as apparent when you gathered the information through research, survey, or field observation. Review the Skill Builder on page 316 to ensure that you take advantage of visuals to reinforce your findings properly.

The work that you submit for assessment must include the following visual aspects. Your teacher may require either that it be handed in separately, or incorporated into the marking scheme of your summative project.
   - At least one significant chart or graph that you have either constructed by hand on graph paper, or by using a computer spreadsheet program.
   - At least one map, diagram, or photograph that you have either drawn, produced using a computer program, or photographed yourself.

- The visuals must be concisely explained. Compose a clear title for each visual, which fully identifies the topic, then write a caption that states an important observation or conclusion that can be drawn from the visual.
- Each visual must be fully documented. Identify the information source from which either the visual or the information used to construct it originated. For survey or field observation, record the date(s), location(s) and the subject(s), where appropriate.

3.   Validating your conclusions—It is important that your research, survey, or field observation present conclusions about the topic you set out to investigate. Review the Skill Builder on page 356 to ensure these conclusions are supported by a body of evidence that you have gathered.

The work that you submit for assessment must include the following aspects of validation. Your teacher may require either that it be handed in separately, or incorporated into the marking scheme of your summative project.

- A list of at least three conclusions that you have drawn as a result of your research, survey, or field observation.
- For each conclusion, write a paragraph that outlines the supporting evidence that validates it. You may refer to professional researchers, or to trends observed in your own surveys and field observations. Include source documentation for any authors cited, done in correct format.

■ Taking Your Project Through Stage Three

How you complete your final product will vary, depending upon whether you are preparing a research paper, survey, or field observation. Separate instructions for each type of project are outlined below. (Don't forget to refer to the Skills Appendix, "Using Inclusive Language in Social Science Research," page 371, as you prepare your final report.)

The Research Paper

This stage marks the conclusion of your summative project assignment. You will be handing in three items to be marked: i) a formal essay, ii) visual representations to complement the essay, and iii) bibliographical references.

i) *Formal essay*—Refer to "Structuring Your Research Paper," on page 383 of the Skills Appendix for detailed information about the essay format. Since the formal essay does not use topic subheadings, it is very important to craft an excellent opening paragraph to guide the reader. It must clearly identify the topic or issue and your thesis, in addition to presenting a "blueprint" that identifies the sequence of subtopics your essay will progress through.

ii) *Visual representations to complement the essay*—Your teacher may suggest that you put all your visuals at the end of your formal essay, in order to maintain the flow of ideas without interruption. If so, arrange your visuals in numbered sequence, and refer to each one by number in the body of your essay. For example: "Early research identified a strong link between education and prejudice. (See Figure 1, Appendix)."

iii) *References to sources used in your essay*—No matter what type of project you are completing, proper citation requires you to list the following information for sources used: author(s); title of the article or work; city and date of publication; name of the publisher; and page(s) from which the information came. For more details on citing sources within your essay and bibliography see skill feature "Using Sources Ethically," on pages 185-186.

The Survey:

This stage marks the conclusion of your summative project assignment. You will be handing in three items to be marked: i) a final survey report, which includes a section or appendices that detail your survey procedures, ii) visual representations to complement the report, and iii) references to sources used in your survey report.

i) *Final survey report*—Refer to the Skills Appendix, "Structuring Your Survey/Field Observation Report," page 386, for detailed information before you begin. It is essential that your final report include full details of your survey procedures, including the following: a copy of the survey questions; the location(s) and date(s) of the survey(s); the size of the survey sample; and other such details. This will help convince those who examine your project that the results are valid and reliable. Two good sources for assistance are "Presenting Survey Results," located on page 375 of the Skills Appendix, and the detailed Case Study excerpt from the survey report, Teen Trends: A Nation in Motion (Bibby and Posterski), on page 166.

ii) *Visual representations to complement the report*—Refer to the Skills Appendix, "Interpreting Statistics," page 367, to help you to apply simple statistical and graphic techniques to identify characteristics and patterns in numerical data gathered in your survey. Visuals can be entered in your final report in two different ways. For maximum impact, place them in the body of the report, as you would see pictures, graphs, and maps placed in a textbook. Your teacher may suggest that you put all your visuals at the end of your report. If so, arrange them in numbered sequence, and refer to each one by number in the body of your report.

iii) *References to sources used in your survey report*—No matter what type of project you are completing, proper citation requires you to list the following information for sources used: author(s); title of the article or work; city and date of publication; name of the publisher; and page(s) from which the information came.

Field Observation:

This stage marks the conclusion of your summative project assignment. You will be handing in three items to be marked: i) a final field observation report, which includes a section or appendices that detail your procedures, ii) visual representations to complement the field observation report, and iii) references to sources used in your field observation report.

i) *Final field observation report*—Refer to "Structuring Your Survey/Field Observation Report," on page 386 of the Skills Appendix, for detailed information before you start to write. A good example of an outline of field observation procedures is anthropologist Parin Dosa's "Study of Muslim Women" on pages 10-11.

ii) *Visual representations to complement the field observation report*—Refer to the Skills Appendix, "Interpreting Statistics," page 367, to help you to apply simple statistical and graphic techniques to identify characteristics and patterns in numerical data gathered from field observation. Visuals can be entered in your final report in two different ways. For maximum impact, place them right in the flow of the report, as you would see pictures, graphs and maps placed in a textbook. Your teacher may suggest that you put all your visuals at the end of your report. If so, arrange them in numbered sequence, and refer to each one by number in the body of your report.

iii) *References to sources used in your field observation report*—No matter which type of project you are completing, proper citation requires you to list the following information for sources used: author(s); title of the article or work; city and date of publication; name of the publisher; and page(s) from which the information came.

■ Communicating What You Have Learned

Your teacher may ask you to inform the class about the major conclusions you have reached as a result of working through your summative project. If so, choose one of the two formats that follow.

Creating a Bulletin Board Display

This display could take the form of either a light cardboard poster, or a free-standing, heavy cardboard or foam-board panel. Use colourful display paper as a backdrop to highlight point-form notes, visual representations, and sample survey or field observation sheets used in the project. Draw viewers to your display with a large, bold title across the top of your poster or panel, and direct them through it by using smaller, subheadings to identify particular aspects of your work. Whether you researched a formal essay, or conducted a survey or field observation, your display could be used to highlight the criteria described in the "Three Steps" section of this Summative Project.

Making a Web Site

Refer to the Skills Appendix, "Making a Web Page to Present Your Findings", page 389. This approach is particularly recommended for students with advanced computer skills. Whether you researched a formal essay, or conducted a survey or field observation, your Web site could be used to highlight the criteria described in the "Three Steps" section of this project outline.

If you do not have access to a computer, but you are still interested in this type of presentation, lay out the Web site on several sheets of paper, indicating where "hot links" and special features are located.

■ Meeting the Criteria

In order to demonstrate that you have successfully completed the third and final stage of your project, you must meet the following criteria:

The Three Steps:
- At least one good example of authorities who present different viewpoints
- At least one good example of authorities who confirm one another's viewpoint
- One or more significant charts or graphs—documented and captioned
- One or more maps, diagrams, or photographs—documented and captioned
- A list of at least three conclusions, with a summary of supporting evidence

Taking Your Project Through Stage Three:
- a formal research paper or final survey/ field observation report
- visual representations of your findings
- organized references to sources which you have used

Presenting Your Findings

Bulletin Board Display
- include a bold title and smaller subtitles
- use captioned visual representations
- include point-form notes
- highlight your conclusions
- include sample survey and observation pages

Web Site
- Include your finding and any other information a visitor may find interesting
- Organize the information logically so that the links are easy to follow
- take advantage of special features such as chat rooms to draw in and kept visitors at your site longer
- include photographs and graphs, if at all possible

Skills Appendix

Introduction

When we begin learning about a particular topic or issue we have not studied before, we can sometimes feel overwhelmed by the amount of information and the various connections between different aspects of the topic. One way to help our brains process and simplify this information is to arrange it in an organizer. This technique is also helpful when we attempt to present a topic or issue to someone else. Three different types of organizers are presented: the Cause and Effect Chart, the Future Wheel and the Lesson Log.

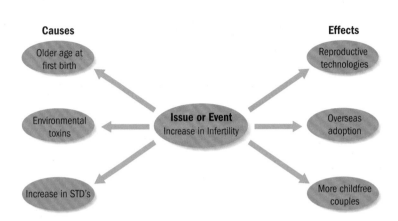

Figure 11.1 This is an example of a Case-and-event chart based on the topic of an "Increase in Infertility."

Example One: Cause and Effect Chart

One way to simplify an issue or event is to create a cause and effect chart (see Figure 11.1). This type of organizer requires you to categorize the information you have learned and encourages you to make connections between different ideas related to the issue or event. The following example is taken from material in Chapter 6 and deals with the issue of infertility.

Example Two: Future Wheel

Organizing information into a future wheel can help you to make connections between ideas, see how events have a domino effect, and force you to think about the long-term impacts of social events and issues. The following example, in Figure 11.2, is taken from material in Chapter 6 and deals with declining populations.

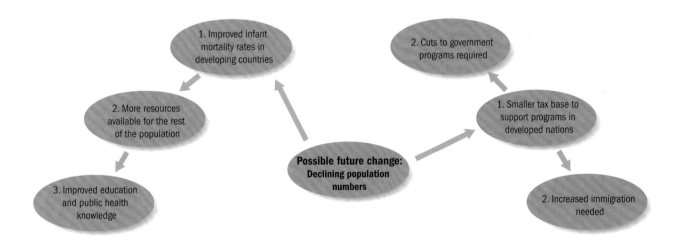

Figure 11.2 An example of a Future Wheel

Example Three: Lesson Log

One of the best ways to improve your understanding of material is to review your notes once or twice a week and turn the most challenging lessons into "lesson logs." Or you can use this as a way to prepare for tests. This is a much more useful process than simply rewriting or rereading your notes because it forces you to actively engage with the material. Organizing the material into lesson logs will improve your understanding and your recall of the information. The example in Figure 11.3 is taken from Chapter 10, Section 10.3.

Practise It!

1. Now it is your turn to create one example of each of the three organizers. You may select information from any section of the text to complete your organizers, but make sure each one deals with *different* information. (That is, all three shouldn't deal with the baby boom.)

Key points

- global-ization has affected Canadians

- many Canadians see it (via free trade) as a positive force, but many are also fearful that we will lose our own sovereignty

- while many citizens believe globalization has had a positive economic impact, they also feel it has had a negative impact on our environment, social programs, and culture

Connections This is like...

the way in which many Canadians felt about their country during World War I.

the way in which many Canadians view American mass media.

Questions:

What else do we need to know to fully assess the impact of globalization?

How has globalization affected citizens in less wealthy nations?

Do Americans have the same ambivalent feelings toward globalization? If not, why?

Figure 11.3 This Lesson Log was made using the topic of globalization and Canada.

Taking Research Notes

Introduction

Learning how to take research notes properly is an important skill. Not only will it save you time in the long run, it will also reduce frustration when it comes to writing a research paper or survey or field study report. Poorly taken notes can often be impossible to understand and you simply won't have time to go back and check your sources again for clarification. The following skill builder, generated from a University of Toronto writing support Web site <www.utoronto.ca/writing/notes.html>, will help you avoid some of the pitfalls of poor research note-taking skills.

Step One: Reviewing Your Hypothesis

Review your hypothesis or thesis before you start your research. Ask yourself what subtopics you would expect to find in your reading and write them down on a list. This will help you to read with purpose in mind and you will be able to sort out relevant information from that which is extraneous. The following example illustrates this step.

Tentative thesis: Gender identity in humans is not innate, it is created.

Expected sub-topics:
1. Treatment of babies (colour and type of clothing, language used to describe them, tone of voice and type of communication, selection of toys ...)
2. Socialization into gender appropriate behaviours (acceptance for girls to cry, greater acceptance of rough play for boys, types of chores expected of children...)
3. Expectations and treatment during adolescence (the encouragement of girls to babysit, the engagement of boys in car culture, different curfews for boys and girls...)

Step Two: Organizing Your Notes

Every time you consult a different source, begin organizing your notes by writing down the publication information at the top of a new sheet of paper or file card. On that same paper, record any important information from the source you feel may be useful, even if you decide to take only a line or two. Make sure you write the page number beside every piece of information you record. As well, you can save time and hassle later by developing a working reference list or bibliography as you go. This will also force you to make sure you have properly recorded all of the source information.

Leave extra space on the sheet for comments of your own, such as questions, reactions, and cross-references to ideas in other sources. Your research notes and these comments will provide you with the bulk of the first draft of your paper, report, or presentation.

Step Three: Understanding Your Sources

Your research notes will be more useful to you if you record only main ideas rather than detailed information. Instead of writing down copious notes, invest your research time in understanding the points and perspectives being put forward by the source. On your note cards or note sheets record only ideas that are relevant to your focus on the topic. Copy out exact words only when the ideas are memorably phrased or surprisingly expressed. Such expressions make good direct quotations to use in your own paper or report.

Practise It!

1. Below are five theses generated from the material in Chapters 6 and 7. Select one of the these (or generate your own) and create a list of potential sub-topics to guide a person in their research note-taking. To do this, consider the thesis, re-read relevant sections in the chapter that address the statement, and then generate the sub-topics.

    Theses for consideration:

1. Raves are a way for teenagers to express their dismay with mainstream society and are no more radical than sock hops of the 1950s.
2. Despite the desire of teenagers to spend time with their peers, youths mature best in the accompaniment of their elders.
3. The desire for a "perfect" baby today is an extension of the rampant materialism and commercialism of our larger culture.
4. Children born to older mothers enjoy more advantages than those children born to teenaged moms.
5. Old age could be a stage of the life cycle we all look forward to if we change our attitudes and the negative stereotypes associated with it.

Intrepreting Statistics

Introduction

Social scientists often collect and analyze statistical data in their work. This information may be gathered from interviews, surveys and observations, or found in scientific journals or government census reports. While it may be true that numbers never lie, it is also true that they can be manipulated to tell many different stories. Understanding how to organize and interpret statistics correctly is very important to social science research.

Step One: Interpreting Statistical Results

Numbers can be made to support many different perspectives, depending upon the method used to interpret them. Consider the example of test marks received by members of a school class. One group of friends compared their scores and found that they nearly all had marks below 60 per cent. They concluded that it had been a hard test, maybe even unfair. Of course, they would need to see how the whole class scored in order to make an accurate judgement about the test.

Figure 11.4 shows the results for the 25 class members who wrote the test, arranged from highest to lowest.

The Class Test Scores (in %)				
A+ 97	82	74	66	56
93	B 77	73	64	53
A 87	76	72	63	F 41
86	74	70	60	30
83	74	C 68	D 57	22

Figure 11.4 Based on these results, do you think it was a fair test or not?

In order to decide whether or not the test was too hard, there are five different ways to interpret these statistics. These same five methods can be applied to a wide range of social science research information.

1. Mean

This term refers to the average of a sum of numbers in a series. It measures the central tendency based on all the numbers; therefore, extreme numbers at either end of the series can have an effect on the mean. The total of all the test scores was 1698, and with 25 students in the class, the mean score was 67.92 per cent—almost 68 per cent. Many students felt that this was a low mark.

2. Mode

This is the number which occurs most frequently in a series. Mode can be useful to give a quick indication of the most common tendency in the distribution of numbers. The teacher spotted a group of three 74s among the test scores, and observed that 74 per cent was the test mode—a perfectly acceptable test level, more than 6 per cent above the mean score.

3. Median

This refers to the middle number within an ordered sequence of numbers. Median scores can be the best measure of "normal" because they are not affected by extreme numbers at either end of the series. If there are 25 students in a class, the median mark is the score of the 13th ranked student. However, if there is an even number of students, for example 24, the median is halfway between the scores of 12th and 13th ranked student. The median score on the test was 72 per cent.

4. Variance and Range

The variance measures the difference between the mean and each number in the set of numbers. For example, the highest mark on the test, 97 per cent, has a variance of +29.08 above the median, while the lowest mark, 22 per cent, has a variance of −45.92 below the median. Together, the range of test variances (the difference between 97 and 22) is 75.

Step Two: Graphing Results

In addition to calculations, graphic representations of statistics can be completed. A frequency distribution graph shows the overall pattern of the number data. It can be drawn either as a line or a bar graph. However, if a line is used, the mean, median and mode can also be positioned on the graph. This graph shows how frequently a particular number or category of numbers occurred in the sample of data collected. For example, the test scores in Figure 11.4 could be graphed in groups from left to right, as A+ (2), A (4), B (8), C (5), D

(3), and F (3). They could also be graphed in declining order by 10s, as shown in Figure 11.5.

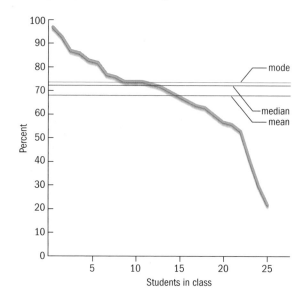

Figure 11.5 Social scientists would call this a "normal distribution" skewed (pulled) a bit to one side. Would you consider this distribution of marks normal or unusual? Explain.

Step Three: Using Other Statistical Measures

You should be familiar with the following statistical principles as you design or interpret social science research:

Correlation and Prediction

Correlation graphs show whether or not a relationship exists between two factors, and if so, whether that relationship is positive or negative. A positive correlation means that an increase in one factor causes an increase in the other. For example, you can usually predict that the longer a person studies, the higher their test mark will be. Studies also indicate that the more hours a student spends at a part-time job per week, the lower their test marks tend to be. This is an example of a negative correlation—as one factor increases, the other decreases.

Reliability

Reliability indicates the degree to which the same observations could be expected if the experiment or survey was conducted again using the same method. For example, public opinion polls often end with this sort of statement: "The results are accurate to within plus or minus 3 percentage points, 9 times out of 10."

The larger the size of the sample, the greater the reliability of the results.

Statistical Significance

Statistical significance is the degree to which a result deviates from a hypothesis for reasons other than errors in sampling. In other words, the difference between results is too great to have happened by chance. To be statistically significant, differences between the experimental group and the control group cannot have been coincidental. For example, surveys showed that students who had been taught using Elliot Aronson's "Jigsaw" technique (page 315, Chapter 9) demonstrated significantly less prejudicial views than others taught using traditional methods.

Validity

Validity demonstrates how well a survey or experiment measures what it is supposed to be measuring. Valid research uses carefully controlled conditions that are fully outlined in the social scientist's final report. For example, on page 166 in Chapter 5, *Teen Trends* authors, Reginald Bibby and Donald Posterski, provide a detailed description of the sampling methods used in their cross-Canada surveys of the attitudes of young people.

Practise It!

1. Plot the statistics in Figure 11.6 on a conventional timeline graph. What pattern do you observe? Identify the period of the Baby Boom on the graph.
2. Plot a frequency distribution graph for these numbers, using the following five categories: 28–30, 25–27, 22–24, 18–21, and 15–17. Describe the distribution pattern of the numbers (i.e., normal distribution or skewed?) Why does this graph not look like the first one you drew?
3. Calculate the mean and median birth rates for this 30-year period. Mark these two points on your frequency distribution graph. Identify the most extreme variances and the range.
4. Explain why identifying mode for these statistics would be meaningless?
5. Suggest another set of statistics that you could compare to birth rate to obtain a good degree of correlation. Explain your choice.

Canada, Birth Rates per 1000, 1945-1974

1974	15.4	1968	17.6	1962	25.3	1956	28.0	1950	27.1
1973	15.5	1967	18.2	1961	26.1	1955	28.2	1949	27.3
1972	15.9	1966	19.4	1960	26.8	1954	28.5	1948	27.3
1971	16.8	1965	21.3	1959	27.4	1953	28.1	1947	28.9
1970	17.5	1964	23.5	1958	27.5	1952	27.9	1946	27.2
1969	17.6	1963	24.6	1957	28.2	1951	27.2	1945	24.3

Figure 11.6

Mind Mapping

Introduction

A mind map is a method of note-taking that some educators feel closely resembles the categorizing functions of the brain. Since the brain builds on existing knowledge through associations and relationships, a mind map is an excellent skill for students to master. A good mind map allows a person to remember and retrieve information based on associations and relationships through the use of words and pictures.

Step One: Identifying the Central Idea

A mind map begins with a central idea. The central idea is written or drawn at the centre of an unlined sheet of paper. Next, it is important to look for associations that relate to the central idea. The associations should be written or drawn quickly, without pausing to reflect, edit, or dwell on them. This is very similar to the process of brainstorming.

Step Two: Linking Ideas

Using one of the key themes in Chapter 3, we will create a mind map around the central idea of "Poverty and Affluence." Remember, a good mind map allows a person to retrieve information that they have stored under a certain heading. For instance, under "gender gap" they may have recorded the fact that women tend to earn less than men or under "quintile" they may have stored the fact that, between 1920 and 1970, the gap between the richest and poorest quintile narrowed (see Figure 11.7).

Step Three: Applying Emphasis

Finally, it is important to leave plenty of space on the sheet of paper so that additional information or new branches of information can be added to your map. A completed mind map looks like a web of ideas. It combines words and pictures that draw attention to the central idea. Often people use bold arrows, colours and highlight markers to emphasize their points.

Practice It!

1. Pick a section of your text and make a mind map. Section headings are good representations of central ideas. A corresponding mind map based on a section heading is a good place to start.

Key points to remember:
- Put the idea in the centre of the page
- Write and/or draw your ideas quickly
- Use capital letters for key words and ideas
- Draw pictures that help you associate with the central idea
- Leave plenty of space to add new information

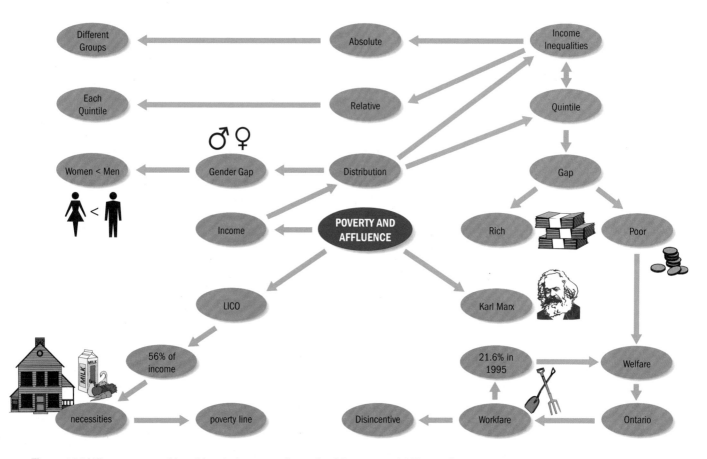

Figure 11.7 What can you add to this mind map on the topic of Poverty and Affluence?

Using Inclusive Language
in Social Science Research

Introduction

Twenty-first century social science research places emphasis on the use of inclusive language. Inclusive language has become the norm in social science for two reasons. First, social scientists realize the importance of recognizing the broad similarities among all people, and of avoiding the exclusion of particular groups unless there is a specific academic reason for doing so. When specific groups are excluded from a study, they and all included groups should be specifically identified. Second, social scientists wish to avoid using stereotypes, especially negative ones, in describing humans and their behaviour.

The use of inclusive language reflects the author's state of mind. A social scientist is expected to use language and methods of study that exclude people only when it is relevant to the subject at hand. (For example, a scientist should exclude men from a study about whether or not a particular drug alleviates morning sickness during pregnancy!) All conclusions must be value-free and clearly demonstrated by the research findings.

Step One: Identifying Problematic Areas

You might think that using inclusive language means avoiding the use of terms like "spokesman" or "stewardess." While it is true that "spokesperson" and "flight attendant" work as non-gender-specific terms, using inclusive language means much more than this.

The American Psychological Association (APA) identifies three major areas that require particular attention. To adhere to APA guidelines in their documentation of their studies, social scientists must remove bias in the language they use to describe

- disabilities
- sexuality
- race and ethnicity

Your first step, then, is to spot any language relating to the above three areas.

Step Two: Recognize Why Certain Language May Be Problematic

Your second step is to examine the language relating to these areas and identify any problems. To do so, you need to know what to look for. The following extracts from the APA outline the principles involved in language use the three areas identified.

1. Disabilities

The guiding principle for non-handicapping language is to maintain *the integrity of individuals as whole human beings* by avoiding language that (a) implies that a person as whole is disabled (e.g., *disabled person*), (b) equates persons with their condition (e.g., *epileptics*), (c) has superfluous negative overtones (e.g., *stroke victim*), or (d) is regarded as a slur (e.g., *cripple*).

Guidelines for Non-Handicapping Language in APA Journals, [Online] Available at http://www.apastyle.org/disabilities.html 30 January 2002

2. Sexuality

Problems occur in language concerning lesbians, gay men, and bisexual persons when language is too vague or concepts are poorly defined.... First, language may be ambiguous in reference, so that the reader is not clear about its meaning or its inclusion and exclusion criteria. Second, "homosexuality" has been associated in the past with deviance, mental illness, and criminal behavior, and these negative stereotypes may be perpetuated by biased language.

Avoiding Heterosexual Bias in Language, [Online] Available at http://www.apastyle.org/sexuality.html 30 January 2002

3. Race and Ethnicity

The problems of racial/ethnic designation are twofold: Authors must determine **when** to report these descriptions and **how** to refer to ethnic minority samples or other special interest groups. Researchers must determine the extent to which their investigation should report real or potential racial/ethnic variation. When such variation exists, racial/ethnic factors should be reported in theoretical and empirical aspects of the research.... When racial/ethnic variables are unimportant to the investigation, authors should state the basis for this assumption....

Authors are encouraged to write in accordance with the principles of cultural relativism, that is, perceiving, understanding, and writing about individuals **in their own terms**. Thus, indigenous self-desig-nations are as important as designations by others, although authors must be cognizant of the fact that members of different groups may disagree about their appropriate group designation and that these designations may change over time.

Guidelines for Avoiding Racial/Ethnic Bias in Language, [Online] Available at http://www.apastyle. org/race.html 5 February 2002

Step Three: Use Inclusive Vocabulary and Style

The final step is to replace problematic terms with more acceptable language. Thirty years ago, your high school's rules might have said something like the following:

- "A student who has been absent should always bring a note of explanation from his parents."

This statement is regarded as biased language today. Not all students are male, and not all live with both parents. Instead the wording might be changed to read as follows:

- "A student who has been absent should always bring a note of explanation from his or her parent or guardian."

Inclusive language can sometimes be a little more awkward to use (e.g., "his or her"), but the goal of inclu-siveness supercedes the goal of easy reading. (In some cases, the awkwardness can be overcome by rewriting the sentence, for example, in the plural.)

The list in Figure 11.8 identifies some unacceptable terms, terms that you might use to replace these unac-ceptable terms, and the reasons.

Visit the three Web sites listed earlier in this feature, to learn more fully about inclusive and non-biased lan-guage.

Practise It!

1. Following the three steps outlined above, transform the following statements into inclusive and preferred language, giving your reasons for each revision.
   1. Homosexuals have a sexual preference for people of the same sex.
   2. AIDS victims have a shorter life expectancy than non-infected people.
   3. Ordinary diagnostic medical technology is not designed to examine disabled people.
   4. When a mother has many children to care for, her husband may have to increase his normal house-hold responsibilities.
   5. This typically gorgeous Chinese-Canadian woman will find it easy to find a professional modelling job.

Unacceptable and Preferred Terminology

Unacceptable	Preferred	Reason
Disabled person	Person (who has) a disability	Put person first, not the disability.
Stroke victim	Individual who had a stroke	Use emotionally neutral language.
Sexual preference	Sexual orientation	Sexuality is a biological function, not a social choice.
Subjects were asked about their homosexuality	Subjects were asked about the experience of being a gay man or a lesbian	"Homosexuality" is considered a slur because of previous usage.
One hundred aboriginal people were sampled.	One hundred Aboriginal people (50 Cree, 25 Mohawk, and 25 Inuit) were sampled.	People should be fully described when possible, and identified by the names they use to identify themselves.
The artistic Afro-Canadian...	The Afro Canadian...	Using "artistic" this way might suggest that it is an unusual quality for such a person. Avoid hyphens in designating race/ethnicity.

Figure 11.8

Creating a Survey

Introduction
To develop sound plans that address the needs of society, organizations first need to know about the trends in people's opinions and behaviours. One of the most effective tools for gathering up-to-date data about a population is the survey. Governments use surveys to find out about citizens' opinions on various issues. This information helps the government design legislation that reflects citizen's wishes. Commercial organizations use surveys to find out about consumers' buying habits, information that helps companies make products or provide services that people want to buy. Advocacy groups also gather information through surveys to bolster their efforts to effect social change.

Specifically, a **survey** is a set of questions designed by social scientists to generate specific information in a usable format. Surveys may be conducted on a wide range of people, to represent all members of society. Alternatively, particular groups within society may be investigated. Researchers design questions carefully, giving respondents a choice of answers. Let's take an example. Suppose you wanted to design a survey to find out the following as it applies to high school students: What is the relationship between academic performance and hours spent working at a part-time job?

Surveys are vital to understanding people at any given moment. They provide a snapshot of the respondents' beliefs and behaviours in a fairly cost-effective manner. That's why we get asked to participate in so many surveys—through the mail, over the phone, even at the mall. Which car would you be most likely to buy? Which political party would make the most effective government? Should the criminal justice system for young offenders be changed? How much of your total income do you spend on recreation and entertainment? These are typical of the sorts of questions you will be asked in the many times you will likely participate in surveys during your lifetime.

Step One: Formulate a hypothesis
The first thing you must do is to formulate a hypothesis based on the question you want answered. The hypothesis must be specific. Your survey should be designed to either support/prove your hypothesis, or reject/disprove it.

Sample hypothesis: Students who work more than 16 hours a week have lower academic performance than students who work fewer than 16 hours a week.

For more on developing a hypothesis, see the Skill Development feature on page 65.

Step Two: Develop your questions
Now you can develop a series of questions that you will ask people to answer, for the purpose of proving or disproving your hypothesis.
Sample questions (round 1):
1. Do you have a part-time job?
2. How many hours a week do you work?
3. What is your level of academic performance?
Adjust your questions in a second round if they are not specific enough. Do this by imagining the possible responses. For example, Question 2 might be hard to answer if the hours vary. It could be adjusted to
Sample Question 2 (round 2):
2. "How many hours a week do you work on average?"
    or "How many hours did you work last week?"
Question 3 also might be hard to answer. It could be adjusted to
Sample Question 3 (round 2):
3. "What was your overall average last semester?"

Step Three: Create multiple-choice answers for your questions
If you allow respondents to write in their own answers, you might not get usable results. For example, some respondents might answer Question 3 with a letter grade, while others might answer with a percentage. To eliminate this problem, you can create multiple-choice answers. Multiple-choice questions have two advantages: (1) they set objective limits for the respondents' answers to your questions, and (2) they are easy to score. By giving respondents a series of choices, you make the job of interpreting the results much easier.
Sample multiple-choice answers for Question 3:
a) lower than 50 per cent
b) 50–59 per cent
c) 60–69 per cent
d) 70–79 per cent
e) higher than 79 per cent

Step Four: Add distracter questions

Add **distracter questions**, which are questions designed to obscure the true purpose of the survey. Without these distractions, the purpose of the survey may be obvious. If respondents were to know the purpose of the survey, they might not answer as objectively as pos-sible. For example, someone who wants to keep their part-time job even though they have low grades, may be tempted to represent their marks as higher than they really are. In the sample survey in Figure 11.9, six of the nine questions are distracters.

Personal Survey

1. How many rooms are there in your home, count-ing all bathrooms and bedrooms?
   (a) fewer than 5
   (b) 5–6
   (c) 6–7
   (d) more than 7
2. Do you have a part-time job?
   (a) yes
   (b) no
3. If you answered "yes" to Question 2, are you required to wear a uniform in your job?
   (a) yes
   (b) no
4. What is your favourite subject area in school?
   (a) languages
   (b) arts
   (c) social science
   (d) math/science
   (e) technology
   (f) other
5. How many CDs do you own?
   (a) fewer than 10
   (b) 10–20
   (c) 21–30
   (d) more than 30
6. If you answered "yes" to Question 2, how many hours on average do you work in a typical week?
   (a) fewer than 5
   (b) 5–12
   (c) 13–15
   (d) 16–20
   (e) more than 20

7. How do you feel about the following statement? "The depiction of violence in the media increases violent behaviour among teenagers."
   (a) strongly agree
   (b) agree
   (c) neutral or unsure
   (d) disagree
   (e) strongly disagree
8. What was your average percentage in all the courses you took last term?
   (a) lower than 50 per cent
   (b) 50–59 per cent
   (c) 60–69 per cent
   (d) 70–79 per cent
   (e) higher than 79
9. How many people do you regard as your really close friends?
   (a) fewer than 2
   (b) 2–4
   (c) 5–7
   (d) more than 7

Figure 11.9

Practise It!

1. Explain the role and importance of each of the following in creating survey questions:
   a) specific information
   b) a format that is usable
   c) a choice of answers
   d) distracter questions

2. Following Steps Two and Three, rewrite each of the following questions, together with possible answers, so that they would provide specific information in a usable format:
   a) What do you like to do outdoors?
   b) Do you think that the legal system is too soft on young criminals?
   c) How important are good friends?
   d) Is it important for a happily married couple to have similar interests?
   e) Are looks more important than intelligence when choosing a mate?

3. With a partner, pick one of the following hypotheses:
   • A link exists between the way teenagers dress and the type of music they like.
   • High-school students who like to read a lot do better in languages and the social sciences than those who do not.
   • Teenagers who watch a lot of television or movies are likely to have fewer friends than those who watch less.

   Imagine that you are doing a survey to prove or disprove the hypothesis you have chosen.
   a) Following Steps Two to Four, create eight survey questions, together with possible answers, that meet all the necessary criteria described above. Three questions should help you prove or disprove your chosen hypothesis. The remaining five should be distracter questions.
   b) Compare your survey questions with those of another pair of students (working on the same or a different hypothesis). What changes would you make to the two sets of questions and answers?

   What have you learned about surveys from this exercise?

■ ■ ■ Interpreting and Presenting Survey Results ■ ■ ■

Introduction

Collecting the raw data of a survey is but one step social scientists take in finding the answers to the questions they ask. Next they must tally the results, organize them into tabular form, and finally present them in a visual format that clearly communicates their significance.

Step One: Tally your results

Having accumulated a mass of raw material, researchers must tally the information, possibly converting them to percentages so they can better identify patterns, similarities, and differences within it.

Step Two: Organize your survey results in tables

Your next task is to organize and present your data in a way that provides maximum clarity and impact. On page 376 is a table showing the results of an Environics survey done for the Canadian Teachers' Federation. The survey asked adults if they would support the use of advertising to students in schools, as a way of raising money to buy audio-visual equipment. It employed the following questions. (Only people who chose 1(b) were asked Question 2.)

1. Which one of these two statements most closely represents your point of view?
   a) Advertising has no place in schools.
   b) Advertising in schools is perfectly acceptable if it allows the school to receive cash, services, or equipment in exchange.
2. Would you agree or disagree with allowing advertising in schools if it meant requiring students to watch video or computerized commercial advertising on TV or computers as part of their instructional day?

You can see the results tallied in the tables (Figures 11.10 and 11.11).

Responses to Question 1 (percentage)

Opinion	Canada	Atlantic	Quebec	Ontario	Man.	Sask.	Alberta	BC
Advertising has no place in schools	70	75	61	75	71	79	74	67
Advertising in schools is perfectly acceptable	29	23	38	24	28	20	25	32
Don't know	1	2	1	2	1	1	1	1

Figure 11.10

Responses to Question 2 (percentage of subgroup that answered 1(b))

Opinion	Canada	Atlantic	Quebec	Ontario	Man.	Sask.	Alberta	BC
Disagree	71	62	80	64	58	66	63	78
Agree	28	38	19	35	42	34	35	22
Don't know	1	nil	nil	1	nil	nil	2	nil

Source for both tables: Environics Research Group. 1999. *Canadians Say No to Advertising in Schools*. Canadian Teachers' Federation.

Figure 11.11

Step Three: Present Your Results

Format 1: Create a bar graph

The bar graph in Figure 11.12 is a simple representation of the data shown in the tables above. Note how the two bars are displayed side by side, in response to two slightly different questions.

Format 2: Create a circle graph

Circle graphs, like bar graphs, are good at displaying absolute information. This means that they effectively represent simple, measurable numbers (for example, number of respondents in a category, percentage of respondents in a category).

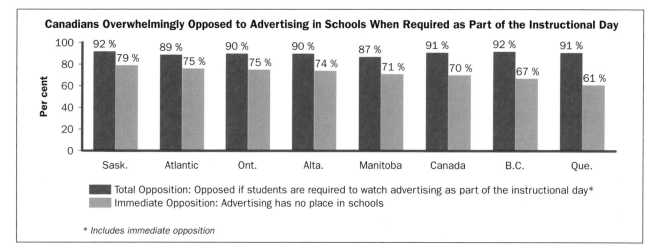

Figure 11.12 Bar graph showing opposition to advertising in schools

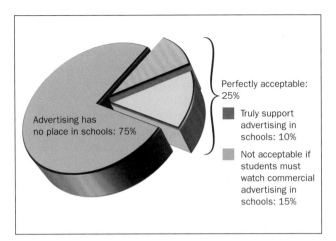

Figure 11.13 Circle graph showing opposition to advertising in schools in Ontario

From its 1999 survey about in-school advertising, Environics learned that, in Ontario, 75 per cent of the sample said that advertising has no place in schools, while 15 per cent say advertising is not acceptable if students must watch commercial advertising during the instructional day. Most of the remaining 10 per cent truly support advertising in schools (with a small remainder answering that they don't know). A circle graph visually shows how large a proportion of the total each of these opinions represents—it gives an immediate graphic sense of how heavy the majority opinion is (see Figure 11.13).

Format 3: Create a Scattergraph

Scatter graphs show how two sets of results relate to each other. They are used when the hypothesis the survey was designed to test states how one variable correlates with a second variable. (In a negative correlation, an increase in one variable coincides with a decrease in the other variable. In a positive correlation, an increase in one variable coincides with an increase in the other variable.)

Recall the survey that we talked about in the Create a Survey Skill Building feature on page 373. Suppose you designed the survey to ask specific hours of work and specific percentage grades and obtained the results in the table in Figure 11.14.

The scattergraph in Figure 11.15 plots these results. The x-axis represents the hours worked, and the y-axis represents the average percentage. A single dot is plotted on the graph for each student, showing both variables.

Practise It!

1. Imagine that you had conducted a survey in which you investigated parents' attitudes towards their children's Internet computer use, and compared these with actual use by young people. Suppose your hypothesis was:
   - There is a significant discrepancy between what parents believe is happening with young people's Internet computer use, and what the young people themselves report is happening.

Hours worked at a part-time job vs. average grade (percentage)

Student	Hours worked	Average percentage	Student	Hours worked	Average percentage
A	0	73	K	18	72
B	0	84	L	24	68
C	18	72	M	12	84
D	6	68	N	0	73
E	0	77	O	22	78
F	8	86	P	14	81
G	4	72	Q	0	88
H	0	58	R	14	78
I	20	60	S	23	72
J	16	72	T	28	70

Figure 11.14

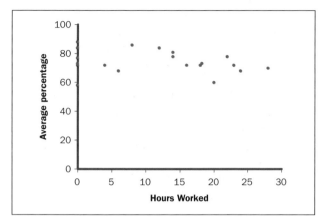

Figure 11.15 Scattergraph showing hours worked at a part-time job vs. average grade (percentage)

In 2000, Environics Research Group, an opinion survey company based in Toronto, surveyed 1080 Canadian families about children's Internet use. In 2001, it similarly surveyed 5682 students. The data could be used to prove or disprove the thesis above.

The surveys discovered that parents ranked "after-school studies" as most common Internet use by their children, while students ranked this use at number 8 (behind such things as downloading music, e-mailing, downloading games, surfing, chat rooms, etc.). Further, 71 per cent of parents believed that their families fully talk about appropriate Internet use, while only 30 per cent of students believed this. Finally, 90 per cent of parents thought that their families had rules for talking to strangers in chat rooms, while only 18 per cent of students thought this. (Source: Cole. 2002. "Frontier: Net Smut")

The *Globe and Mail* report from which these figures are drawn went on to report statistics gathered by the Media Awareness Network, an Ottawa-based, not-for-profit agency. The report stated that 30 per cent of 9 to 10 year olds say they visit adults-only chat rooms. The percentage increases to 58 per cent for 11 to 12 year olds, 70 per cent for 13 to 14 year olds, and 72 per cent for 15 to 17 year olds.

Step 1, the tallying of the results, has already been done for you. Your next task, Step 2, is to organize your results into a table. Copy the chart in Figure 11.16 into your notebook, and fill it out using the information given above.

2. a) Create a bar graph comparing the results of the Environics 2000 family survey and the 2001 students survey.

   b) Create a bar graph of the findings of the Media Awareness Watch survey about young people's use of adult Internet chat rooms.

Results of Environics surveys of parents (2000) and students (2001) about students' internet use

Topic	2000 Family Survey	2001 Student Survey
Families that talk about appropriate Internet use "a great deal or a fair bit?"		
Families that have rules about talking to strangers in chat rooms		
Ranking of "after-school studies" as most common Internet use		

Figure 11.16

Percentage of respondents surveyed by Media Awareness Network, who visit adults-only private chat rooms, Canada, 2001.

Age Group	9 to 10 years	11 to 12 years	13 to 14 years	15 to 17 years
Percentage of respondents				

Figure 11.17

c) What pattern do you see in the bar graph? What conclusions can you come to?

d) Why do bar graphs represent these findings well?

3. The Media Awareness survey reported that 53 per cent of young Internet users had been sent pornographic junk mail, and that 78 per cent of these recipients did not tell their parents. These figures can be represented by bar graphs, but circle graphs are another dramatic way of representing this information.

a) Create two circle graphs to show the percentage of students who had received pornographic junk mail and the percentage of these who had told their parents.

b) Because the second figure is a percentage of the first figure, the number of people represented in

each one is different. Why are circle graphs a good way to represent this information?

c) What pattern do you see in the circle graphs? What conclusions can you come to?

4. a) Using the information contained in Figure 3.11, on page 84, create a scattergraph of all the LICO settings. Ensure that your dots for each of the three community types is of a different colour.

b) Do the LICO settings appear to follow a consistent pattern? Explain.

c) Why are scattergraphs a good method for representing this type of information?

■ ■ ■   Designing a Field Observation   ■ ■ ■

Introduction

Field observation is one of the methods social scientists use to gather data about people's behaviour in groups. In field observation, the investigator observes one or more subjects in their own environment. Like surveys, field observations are conducted to prove or disprove specific hypotheses about people's behaviour. It is critical that field observations respect their subjects' right to privacy. Therefore, they are conducted in public places where subjects do not engage in private actions.

Let's take an example. Suppose you wanted to answer the following question as it applies to high school students: How does gender influence how comfortable students are with each other in group interactions?

Step One: Formulate your hypothesis

First, formulate a hypothesis based on the question you want answered. As with surveys, the hypothesis must be specific. It should identify the key target groups you need to observe at the same time that it identifies the prediction you need to prove or disprove. In this case, you might formulate a hypothesis like the one below.

Three or four all-female teenagers in a group are more comfortable with each other than the same number of all-male or mixed-gender teenagers.

For more on developing a hypothesis, see the Skill Development feature on page 65.

Step Two: Identify specific and measurable behaviours to record

Unless the behaviours are specific and measurable, you will not be able to observe and record them accurately. In the case of the above hypothesis, you might decide that a number of "comfort indicators" are observable and measurable. These might include

- the degree to which subjects sit or stand close to each other
- the degree to which subjects' facial expressions are mostly friendly
- the degree to which subjects' physical contact is mostly friendly
- the degree to which subjects speak in low voices instead of shouting

After you have identified the specific factors you want to record, you should decide on a time limit for your observation. Within this time limit, you will observe and record relevant aspects of your subjects' distance from each other, facial expressions, physical contact, and voices.

Step Three: Design a record sheet for your observations

Your record sheet should allow you to measure by check marks or simple numbers exactly how often the specific behaviour occurs during the time limit. The sample pages in Figure 11.18 show a possible design for such a

Field Observation Sheet

Observer(s): _____   Timer: _____

_____

Location: _____

Time: _____ a.m./p.m.

Length of observation: _____ minutes

Group details: all-female/all male/mixed-gender

(Note: Each group must consist of 3 or 4 teenagers.)

Distance of group members from one another:

Less than 30 cm	30–60 cm	60 cm – 1 m	More than 1 m

Observable Behaviours:

Facial Expression	friendly	passive	aggressive
Touch	friendly	warning	aggressive
Voice	whisper	talk	shout

Other Observations: _____

_____

_____

_____

Figure 11.18

record sheet. Try to fit the complete sheet onto one piece of paper. Note that you fill out one sheet for each group.

You can indicate which group you are observing by circling one of the options listed in a row separated by slashes (in this case all-female, all-male, or mixed gender).

The "Distance" section is designed so that you can put a check mark in the box corresponding to the targets' position at the beginning of the observation. Each time the distance changes during the observation because a subject moves, add an additional check mark in the appropriate box.

The "Observable Behaviours" section is designed so that you can add a check mark each time you observe a particular behaviour.

In the "Other Observations" section, you can record any additional information that might affect behaviour. For example, if the observation occurs outside, weather conditions might be a factor and should be recorded.

Step Four: Conduct your observations

Follow these three guidelines:

Choose locations that allow you to observe discreetly (without being too obvious).

Do not discuss your observations.

Try to make the same number of observations for each target group. For example, if you observe 25 all-female groups, observe 25 all-male and 25 mixed-gender groups.

Step Five: Obtain your subjects' informed consent

Inform your subjects that you have observed and recorded their behaviours. This step is taken for ethical reasons. Obtaining the informed consent of subjects before including them in any findings is a strict requirement of social science research. In this case, you must tell each person observed when, where, and how the observation took place. You must tell them the purpose of the observation. You must guarantee that you will not identify them to anyone other than your partners in the observation. If any individual does not consent, the entire observation for that subject group must be discarded.

Practise It!

1. a) Following Step One, formulate a hypothesis that you think could be proved by field observation within a high school setting.

   b) Write out your hypothesis, making sure that it is measurable. Also make sure that your hypothesis identifies the key target group(s) you need to observe.

2. a) Following Step Two, identify when, where, and how you would conduct your observation.

   b) Identify the measurable behaviours on which you would focus.

   c) How would you ensure that your observation was both discreet yet close enough to record behaviours?

3. a) Following Step 3, design a Field Observation Sheet similar to the one shown on page 380.

   b) Ask a partner to evaluate whether or not your worksheet is likely to be easy to use and will produce useful, measurable results. Make modifications as necessary.

4. Devise a method—perhaps with a form subjects can sign—for obtaining the informed consent of all the subjects of your observation.

5. Following Step 4 and 5, conduct your observations and obtain your subjects' informed consent.

Interpreting and Reporting Field Observation Results

Introduction

In the Designing a Field Observation Skill Building feature (on page 379), you learned how to design and conduct a field observation. The next stage that the social scientist encounters is to interpret and report the results. Interpreting involves examining the data from observation sheets for completeness and consistency. Reporting involves organizing the data into categories, scoring data, and drawing conclusions.

Let us return to the sample field observation in the previous Skill Builder. Recall that the goal was to observe teenagers for the purpose of determining their comfort levels with each other. Let us assume the observation is now complete.

Step One: Examine all Field Observation Sheets for Completeness

It is important for the reliability of your observations that you include in your results only observation sheets that are complete. Discard any sheets that lack crucial information. If some sheets are almost but not completely filled in, use your own judgement about whether to keep or discard them. Let us return to the sample sheets developed on page 380 for an example.

Suppose you have 25 fully complete sheets for the all-female group observations and the same number for the all-male groups. You have only 20 fully complete sheets of mixed-gender group observations. In five of your incomplete mixed-gender group sheets, you missed some facial expressions because one of the subjects was facing away from you. You may choose to use the other data from these five sheets so that you have an equal number of mixed-gender, all-female, and all-male sheets for most of your results. When you report the results for facial expression, however, you must clarify that you are using different totals for mixed-gender groups than for the other groups. This is usually done by including on tables and figures an annotation such as "n=20." This tells the reader that the number of groups observed and summarized in a graph was 20.

Step Two: Compare all the completed Field Observation Sheets

Check that the data are consistent with one another. When you find inconsistencies, you should either discard the inconsistent data or identify the cause of the inconsistencies as an intervening variable. Here are two examples of inconsistencies and how to deal with them:

Inconsistency #1: You observed students on a Tuesday and a Thursday. A tragic road accident killed three students on Wednesday afternoon. On Thursday, the students were dealing with their grief. Thursday's data are very different from Tuesday's data.

Solution: Discard all observations from that week and begin again the following week.

Inconsistency #2: You observed students outside in a smoking area, and the weather conditions on two observation days were different. The data from the second day, which was rainy, differ somewhat from the data from the first day, which was sunny.

Solution: Note the weather conditions as an intervening variable. In Step 5, you will deal with this variable in detail.

Step Three: Total the number of observations

Add up the total number of observations. Use a tally sheet like the one shown in Figure 11.19. You may want to discard sheets to make your totals in each subgroup match.

Tally sheet

	Total number of groups observed
Subgroup 1: All female	28
Subgroup 2: All male	25
Subgroup 3: Mixed gender	25

Figure 11.19

An example of a scoring sheet is shown in Figure 11.20.

Write as many preliminary summary statements as you can. Here are some examples of statements that could be made from the scoring sheet shown on this page.
- All-female groups had the highest number of check marks for standing or sitting extremely close to one another (less than 30 cm).
- All-male groups had the highest number of check marks for standing 60 cm or more from one another.

Scoring Sheet

	All-female groups of 3 or 4 (# of checkmarks)	**All-male** groups of 3 or 4 (# of checkmarks)	**Mixed-gender** groups of 3 or 4 (# of checkmarks)
Distance			
less than 30 cm	31	21	26
30–60 cm	45	45	26
60 cm – 1 m	8	45	27
more than 1 m	9	19	14
Facial Expression			
friendly	15	6	10
passive	13	25	19
aggressive	6	6	0
Touch			
friendly	12	1	8
warning	0	0	1
aggressive	0	8	4
Voice			
whisper	14	2	1
talk	15	15	20
shout	9	15	4

Figure 11.20

- All-female groups had the highest number of friendly facial expressions.
- All-female groups had the highest number of friendly touches.
- All-female groups had the highest number of whispered conversations.

c) Look back at any intervening variables you noted in Step 3. If you suspected in Step 3 that an intervening variable affected the data, you may wish to score the data a second time. For example, suppose that you identified weather conditions as an intervening variable. To check if it affected results, divide each set of sheets into two piles. One pile is observations taken on the sunny day and the other is for observations taken on the rainy day. Redesign your recording sheet so that each column is divided into two subcolumns, showing checkmarks on either sunny days or rainy days. After completing this revised scoring sheet, revise or add to your summary statements if necessary.

Step Five: Decide whether your original hypothesis is correct or incorrect

Depending on your decision, you should do one of the following.

- If you conclude that your hypothesis is correct, explain how the numbers support the hypothesis.
- If you conclude that your hypothesis is incorrect, come up with another statement that accurately reflects the data.
- If you conclude that your hypothesis is partially correct, explain which part of the hypothesis is correct and which part is incorrect.
- If you have difficulties coming to any conclusion at all, describe what further research you would need to do to reach a conclusion. If your problem is that you have too much information to process, revise the hypothesis into a more specific or limited statement. Use only the information relevant to the revised hypothesis to draw conclusions.

Step Six: Present your findings in a written report or a visual display

Include your completed Field Observation Sheets with your report. Ensure that there are absolutely no marks, numbers, or descriptions on the sheets that could identify any of the subjects. Decide whether bar graphs, circle graphs, or scattergraphs are the best methods of representation. (See the Skill Building feature "Presenting Survey Results," on page 375.) Make and include graphs to represent your findings.

Practise It!

If you did not conduct a field observation, create a simulation, as follows. Make 30 copies of the Field Observation Sheet that you created for Step 3 of the Skill Building feature "Designing a Field Observation," page 379. Exchange your sheets with another student. Fill in each other's sheets with random check marks as if you had conducted an observation. Return the 30 sheets to their designer. Now you will have "raw data," which you can work with to practise interpreting and representing results.

Using your returned sheets (either simulated sheets or sheets recording the data from a real observation), complete Steps 1 to 5. For Step 5, use your hypothesis from Step 1 in the Skill Building feature "Designing a Field Observation" on page 379.

Which kind(s) of graph would you use to represent your results? Explain your choice.

Following Step 6, create a report, complete with visuals, to communicate the results of your field observation.

Structuring Your Social Science Research Paper

Academic research papers are highly structured pieces of work, which place many specific requirements on authors. By standardizing the ways in which authors present their research findings, social scientists hope that readers will be more able to compare different papers on the same and related topics.

The *Publication Manual of the American Psychological Association*, described in the previous skill development feature Structuring Your Social Science Report (p. 386), is designed to present the structure and style required for reports about experiments, surveys, or observations. The principles contained in it can, however, be applied to social science research papers. This skill development feature shows you how to do this. Your completed research paper will contain the following components.

- Title page
- Abstract
- Introduction
- Evidence (main body)
- Conclusion
- Implications
- References
- Appendix (optional)
- Author note

Because this skill development feature builds on what has been presented in the previous skill development feature, you must be familiar with its contents before you can follow this one. If you have not done so already, carefully read Structuring Your Social Science Report, noting the three steps that are described. The first two components in Step 1, and all components in Step 3 are also required components for a research paper, so you should pay particular attention to them.

Steps 1 to 3 will concentrate on adapting the Introduction, Method, Results, and Discussion of a report into the Introduction, Evidence, Conclusion, and Implications of a research paper.

Step One: Create your introduction

One of the most critical components of a research paper is an effective introduction. As the name implies, this component introduces the reader to your topic by focusing attention on what you intend to do in the paper. After reading the introduction, the reader should know (a) what your paper will examine, and (b) what it will try to prove.

Step Two: Present your evidence (main body)

Having explained to the reader what you are trying to do in your paper, now you must do it by presenting the evidence you have discovered that pertain to your thesis. Some of the evidence available may be contradictory, but you must be intellectually honest by presenting evidence that both supports and challenges your thesis. You must not merely select the information that supports it and ignore the evidence that does not. (Review the skill development feature Maintaining Intellectual Objectivity, on page 282, if necessary.)

This component will undoubtedly be the longest component of your paper, probably taking up between 60 and 70 per cent of the total (see Figure 11.23).

Step Three: Develop your conclusion and implications

By this point in your research paper, you will have introduced all the new evidence that you will present. In the balance of the paper, you will review what you have already presented, evaluate its meaning, and assess its implications for further study (see Figure 11.24).

Step Four: Complete additional components

After stages 1 to 3 are finished, you should create a title page and write an abstract to appear at the beginning of your paper. In addition, you should document your references and write an appendix (optional) and author note to appear at the end.

Component	Purpose	Guidelines
Introduction	Focuses the reader' attention on what you intend to accomplish in the research paper	• Do not label. • Discuss related background information to provide context for the paper. • Develop key questions that arise regarding the topic. • Identify problems (from your list of key questions) that the paper will try to address. • Define the scope of the investigation, by identifying subheadings if necessary. • Present the thesis of your paper—what it is you are trying to prove or demonstrate. • Explain how your paper will contribute to a greater understanding of the subject area.

Figure 11.22 Introduction for a social science research paper

Component	Purpose	Guidelines
Evidence (main body)	Demonstrates that you have undertaken varied research and assembled it into a logical argument	• Divide the main body into labelled sections. • Summarize evidence from major sources. • Identify major sources from which evidence comes. • Identify different arguments, interpretations, or schools of thought relating to the subject. • Use direct quotes and paraphrases (fully acknowledged by citations) from major sources to demonstrate your understanding of what is crucial material. • Create tables or figures that summarize statistical evidence clearly and economically. • Suggest factors that you consider to be relevant when examining the validity of each argument, interpretation, or school of thought.

Figure 11.23 The main body of a social science research paper

Component	Purpose	Guidelines
Conclusion	Summarizes evidence presented in the main body, and establishes whether or not your thesis is correct.	• Briefly review major pieces of evidence presented in the main body. • Identify the key pieces of evidence that support or oppose your thesis. • Suggest whether the weight of the evidence supports or contradicts your thesis. • Suggest how your thesis needs to be modified—if it does. • Suggest reasons why your thesis is incorrect—if it is.
Implications	Identifies the significance of the paper's conclusions. Broadens the focus of the paper to suggest other factors that could be considered in the future.	• Identify how the paper's conclusions relate to the social science discipline it represents. • Identify other factors that might be considered if further studies on the subject were to be undertaken, and the possible impact of those factors on your conclusions. • Identify any other factors that you think may give the subject of the paper and its conclusions a broader scope for society as a whole.

Figure 11.24 Conclusions and Implications for a social science research paper

Practise It!

Imagine that you had just completed the research relating to one of the following Competing Perspectives features in this book.

- Hate literature on the Internet (Chapter 9, page 310)
- Welfare cuts (Chapter 3, page 88)
- The influence of sexual content on television (Chapter 7, page 222)
- The influence of the World Bank on the developing world (chapter 10, page 344)

Imagine that you were writing this up as a research paper. Create the following items for it, ensuring that they comply with the APA *Style Manual*. Some items,

such as the Evidence, may have to appear in a shorter version than they would in an actual research paper. Feel free to expand on what you find in this text about your chosen topic. (For example, you may have to make up an author and author note.) The point of this exercise is to practice the skill of writing a research paper according to APA style.

- Title page
- Abstract
- Introduction
- Evidence (main body)
- Conclusions
- Author note

Structuring Your Social Science Report

Introduction

Whenever you create a report about an experiment, a survey, or a field observation that you have conducted, certain conventions of style apply to it. This does not mean only that your writing style must conform to the conventions of good language and expression. Style describes all the conventions associated with report writing, including the structure of the report, use of academic language, presentation of bibliographic information (as you learned about in the Skill Development feature Using Sources Ethically on page 185), plus all necessary components that must be included.

All style guidelines are an attempt to standardize methods of investigation and reporting so that readers may more easily compare the findings of a number of studies on the same and related topics. Because all reports include a section called "Methods," for example, readers can easily find and compare the methods used by scientists conducting related studies.

The American Psychological Association (APA) has published clear guidelines for adhering to acceptable academic style in social science reports. These guidelines are followed by social scientists throughout the academic world. The remainder of this feature is based on information contained in the APA guidelines. For greater detail see the following reference:

The Publication Manual of the American Psychological Association, 5th ed., 2001 (Washington, DC: American Psychological Association).

You can find style guidelines specific to anthropology and sociology published by the American Anthropological Association (http://www.aaanet.org/pubs/style_guide.htm) and the American Sociological Association (http://www.asanet.org/pubs/style.html) by going to these Web sites or visiting a well-stocked library. These guidelines deal with matters of style that are specific to those disciplines.

To structure your research report according to accepted APA style, follow the three steps outlined in Figure 11.25, to create introductory sections, the main body, and concluding sections. Incorporate all the mandatory components in the order given, creating each according to the guidance provided.

Component	Purpose	Guidance
Title page	Summarizes the main idea of the report	• Give author's name. • Give author's academic institution. • Give full title. • Provide running head (abbreviated title of 50 characters maximum, which is placed at the top of each page in the report)
Abstract	Allows potential readers to decide if report is relevant to their studies, through this brief but comprehensive summary	• Be accurate. • Create a self-contained paraphrase. Do not use specific quotes from the report. • Place most important information first. • Do not exceed 120 words.
Introduction	Identifies the problem and the research strategy of the report	• Do not label. • Discuss related background readings. • State hypothesis. • Identify variables. • Develop rationale for hypothesis and variables.

Figure 11.25 Introductory sections of a social science report

Step One: Create the introductory sections
See Figure 11.25 on the previous page.

Step Two: Create the main body of your report
See Figure 11.26 below.

Step Three: Create your concluding sections
See Figure 11.27 below.

In practice, the appendix and author note are not likely to apply to work completed at the secondary education level. You should be aware of their existence, however,

Component	Purpose	Guidance
Method	Describes in detail how the experiment or observation was conducted	• Divide into labelled sections (e.g., subjects/ participants, materials, procedure) • Describe what you did and how you did it in detail, so that reader could, if desired, reproduce the experiment or observation.
Results	Summarizes the data obtained and the method of analysis	• Provide tables and figures to display results clearly and economically. • Provide statistics to help reader understand your analysis, and possibly to arrive at alternative explanations.
Discussion	Evaluates and interprets results and their impact on your hypothesis	• Clearly state whether results support or contradict your hypothesis, either partially or fully. • Identify the conclusions you have come to as a result of your research. • Note and explain any similarities between your results and those of others (as described in related readings in your introduction). • Comment on the degree of importance of your findings.

Figure 11.26 The main body of a social science report

Component	Purpose	Guidance
References	Provides comprehensive summary of all works cited in the previous components	• Provide in alphabetical order all relevant details for print sources. [Author(s). Date. "Article title." Magazine/Book Title. Place: Publisher.] • Provide all relevant details for electronic sources. [Title. [Online]. Available at http://reference. Date of retrieval.] • Be concise but not exhaustive. Do not add references not cited in the manuscript.
Appendix	Provides additional material.	• Include only material about specific matters that are so detailed that they might distract from the body of the manuscript. • Include an appendix only if it is necessary. This element is not a requirement.
Author note	Links the reader more fully with the author.	• Provide university department or organization of author. • Identify sources of financial support. • Disclose whether or not this report is part of a larger study.

Figure 11.27 Concluding sections of a social science report

because you may be required to assess or provide these components at the post-secondary level.

Practise It!

Imagine you had just completed one of the research studies presented in the Skills and Methods features that appear in Chapter 1 of this book, as listed below.

- A Study of Muslim Women, by Parin Dossa (page 10)
- A Study of Game Theory, by Robert West (page 17)
- A Study of Equity in Education, by George Dei (page 24)

For a better understanding of these studies, you may wish to read the related extract or article in the case studies beginning on pages 262, 113, and 320 respectively.

Imagine that you were the researcher of your chosen study, and you're ready to write it up as a report. Create seven components of the report, as listed below. Ensure that your components comply with the structure and guidelines recommended in the APA *Style Manual*, as summarized in the three steps outlined above. Feel free to expand on what you find in this text about your chosen research study. (For example, you may have to make up a few bibliographic notes or financial sources.) The point of this exercise is to practice the skill of writing reports according to APA style. Some items, such as the Method, may have to appear in a shorter version than they would in an actual report.

- Title page
- Abstract
- Introduction
- Method
- Results
- Bibliography (sample citations only)
- Author note

Plotting and Interpreting a Population Pyramid

Introduction

A population pyramid shows important demographic information at one point in time. The information used to make the pyramids in this book was gathered using the Census of Canada. Between 1851 and 1951, census information was collected every 10 years; however, since 1956, there has been a shorter census taken half way between the major Canadian census dates.

Information from the 1931 Census of Canada can be graphed to show you the baby boom that occurred after World War I. Born in the 1920s, these were the parents of the post-World War II boomers. Some of the younger people on the graph you construct in this practice exercise may be your grandparents or great-grandparents.

Step One: Begin with the Axis

Begin drawing a population pyramid by forming two axes in the form of an inverted letter "T". Label age cohorts upwards on the vertical axis in 5-year intervals. (You may want to use the other pyramids in Chapter 5, page 150, as a guide.) Then, establish two scales across the horizontal axis of the graph, one for males on the left, and the other for females on the right.

Step Two: Graphing the data

The overall pyramid should be approximately square, that is, as wide as it is tall. When you have set the scales, construct separate horizontal bars for males and females, working upward from the bottom scales. Complete the population pyramid by adding a title and labels, as shown on the examples on page 150.

Practise It!

1. Construct a population pyramid for Canada (in 1931) using the data in Figure 11.28.
2. Which population cohort is the largest? Between which years were the members of this cohort born? Explain why this cohort is large.
3. During the period from 1914 to 1920, 60 000 Canadians (mostly young males) were killed in World War I and about 40 000 more (all ages, male and female) died during the post-war influenza epidemic. How are these events shown in the 1931 population pyramid?

Canada, Population by Age and Sex, 1931

Population (000)	5 375	5 002	10 377		
Age Cohorts	Male	Female	Age Cohorts	Male	Female
under 5	543	531	40-44	346	298
5-9	573	560	45-49	322	264
10-14	543	531	50-54	268	221
15-19	526	514	55-59	199	168
20-24	464	448	60-64	157	138
25-29	410	376	65-69	121	110
30-34	368	341	70 and over	174	171
35-39	358	329			

Figure 11.28

Making a Web Page to Present Your Findings

Introduction
You may be asked to present the findings of your Summative Project directly to your class. With today's technology, however, it is possible to present your work to a much larger audience. You could use the Internet to create your own Web page, accessible to anyone in the world with the right technology. If you decide to try this method of presentation, there are a number of steps to go through.

Step One: Decide which Web site hosting service to use
There are two basic types of Web site hosting services to choose from: commercial and free-to-user. Commercial operations normally allow you a free introductory membership period, after which time you will owe a per-month payment. Commercial sites designed for small businesses, with more sophisticated features, are usually much more expensive than personal sites. Free-to-user Web-hosting services, on the other hand, do not charge you to create or maintain your Web site. Instead, they sell advertising space—over which you will have no control—on all sites in their server. Most keep all of the advertising revenue for themselves.

When choosing a site, make sure you understand what is being offered to you and how much free space on the host's Web server can will receive (12 Mb to 50 Mb is the normal range.) The more space you get, the more features you can include on your site.

Step Two: Protecting Your Privacy
Before you begin to create a Web site, you must make sure that no information available to login users identifies you. You do not know who may try to contact you directly, and for what purposes, if you provide private information.

Step Three: Decide the purpose of your Web site
Do you want to present a simple summary of your findings on your site? If you do this, you will probably not keep many visitors for long. Research shows that people tend to navigate a site more completely, and stay longer, if there are a number of features to engage their attention.

Do you want to provide visitors with an opportunity to give you feedback, and even communicate with you? Do you want visitors to see your site as standing alone, or do you want them to see it as part of a larger system, by providing them with links to other sites?

Feature	Advantages
Creative background	Initially engages visitors and encourages them to stay.
Photographs and visuals	Engages visitors. Gives them a quick idea of the things they may find in the site.
Web poll (Visitors are given a question and then vote their answer. You publish the results.)	Engages visitors. Makes them feel they have input into the site.
Chat room (Visitors post messages that all other visitors can read.)	Allows visitors to respond to you and to others about what they see on the Web site. Gives visitors a greater sense of belonging.
Links to other sections on the page or to a later page.	Allows visitors to navigate site quickly, looking only at the information that interests them.
Hot links to other Web sites	Shows visitors that you have done the background work on the topic you have presented. This feature will encourage visitors to return to your page later to look for more links.

Figure 11.29

Clearly define the purpose of your site before you start to design it.

Step Four: Deciding What Features to Use on Your Site

Here is a list in Figure 11.29 of features commonly available for Web site builders to consider using.

Step Five: Use the web hosting service's software to create your Web site

Depending on which Web-hosting service you choose, there will be different types of software available. Fortunately, most of these hosting sites are user-friendly, and you should be able to follow the prompts. You will be asked to consider such things as:

- What style you want to use (clean/simple, artistic/creative, historical, etc.)
- Where to place your navigation area (top, side, etc.)
- What pages to include (basic, links, message centre, visuals, newsletter, etc.)

If you are inexperienced at using these applications, start by creating a single page. Test access to the site by logging on to the URL as a visitor. If there are problems, log back on to the hosting service's page and follow the troubleshooting procedures. Once you have the first page working, you can add more pages to your site.

Give the site's address to a number of people. Have them access and navigate it and then give you an assessment of its user-friendliness, interest value, and academic level. Make adjustments as necessary. Your classmates may have expertise that you can use. Check to see if anyone in your group or class has made a Web page, and tap into their knowledge and experience.

When your Web site is operational, check back regularly. If you allow visitors to leave messages about the site, don't neglect to check what they say. Update the site as necessary.

Practise It!

1. Take an in-depth look at three of your favorite Web sites. List and describe their features. Make a chart for each site in which you point out what aspects you really liked about it, and what, in your opinion, could use improvement. Make sure you give reasons for your criticisms.
2. Using several plain sheets of paper, design and colour them as if you were creating an actual Web site. Indicate the types of features you would use, and paste in any photographs and diagrams you would like to appear.

abiotic change change in our habitat brought on by non-living factors such as weather and climate

absolute income inequality the amount of money earned by different groups in society

acculturation prolonged contact between two cultures, during which time they interchange symbols, beliefs, and customs

accumulation the belief that social change results from the growth of human knowledge from generation to generation

actors the term used by social scientists for people who become active participants in given situations

adolescence the transition period between childhood and adulthood

advocacy research research that assumes that the researcher will retain complete control over the research, and then become an advocate for the group being studied

alienation a feeling that one does not share in the major values and goals of society

alternative environmental paradigm a belief that society must place a higher importance on non-material values, encourage stronger communities built on better personal relationships, and act with a greater respect for nature

ambiguity a term used by psychologist Theodor Adorno to describe situations that can be interpreted in more than one way

anarchists people who try to destroy the society in which they live through armed struggle, hoping to build a purer society on the ruins of the old one

anomie Durkheim's term to describe the condition of the industrial workers who seemed to be without any roots or norms as they struggled daily to survive

anthropology the social science discipline that examines the development of the human species and human cultures throughout the world

anti-racism education policies which aim to reduce prejudice and to eliminate barriers that stand in the way of equality between different peoples

anti-Semitism particular forms of individual or systemic discrimination directed against Jews

anti-social personality disorder category of mental disorder, characterized by a habitual pattern of rule-breaking and harming others

architectural barriers physical barriers built into health facilities that, for example, make it difficult for disabled people to climb onto examination tables

artificial insemination by donor (AID) when a woman's egg is fertilized by the previously frozen sperm of a donor

assimilationist the outdated view that racial and ethnic minorities would gradually be absorbed into the culture of the majority, through public institutions like schools

attitude barrier unwarranted assumptions made by health professionals such as, for example, that all disabled women have no sexual or reproductive needs. These impair the quality of health care delivery.

attitudes what people think and believe

authoritarian education a fairly strict teacher-centred form of education, strongly focused on student mastery of traditional subject matter

authoritarian personality a term used by psychologist Theodor Adorno to describe intolerant people who are quick to judge things as either right or wrong, good or bad

baby boom a demographic phase marked by an increase in the birth rate of a country, and a corresponding population increase

baby bust the period of declining birth rates between 1966-1979, immediately after the post-World War II baby boom

bargaining for reality the struggle for power by groups and organizations who try to convince others that their view of the situation is the correct one

barrenness the inability to have children

behaviour measurable actions, thoughts, or feelings displayed by humans

behaviour modification theories of psychologists attempting to determine the methods that can successfully change or modify problem human behaviour

binary opposites Bronislaw Malinowski's principle that humans tend to see things in terms of two forces that are opposite to each other, such as night and day, good and evil, female and male

biotic change change in our habitat brought on by living factors such as vegetation and animal populations

birth rate the average number of births per thousand people (both sexes, all ages) in a country during a particular year

burnout emotional exhaustion, depersonalization, and reduced personal accomplishment caused largely by work-related stress

Canada Pension Plan federal earnings-related social insurance program, which provides income upon retirement, disability, or death

capitalism, capitalist an economic system dependent on private investment and profit-making

caregiver burden problems and stress due to caregiving

cash crops crops grown specifically for sale, not consumption

charisma, charismatic Weber's term to describe a leader characterized by large vision, magnetic style, having strong popular support and aspects of extraordinary, superhuman, and supernatural character

classical conditioning a term used to refer to the stimulus-response training pioneered by Russian psychologist Ivan Pavlov

clinical psychology is the branch of the discipline that develops programs for treating individuals suffering from mental illnesses and behavioural disorders

clinical psychology the branch of psychology that focuses on health and wellness issues

clone (to) to create a living mammal, including humans, though asexual reproduction

cocktail-party phenomenon term coined by psychologist C. Cherry to characterize the ability to attend selectively to a single person's speech in the midst of the competing speech of many others

cognition the act of knowing or learning something

cognitive consistency the desire to avoid attitudes that conflict with each other, which generally results in the ability live more satisfying lives

cognitive dissonance theory the theory that people try to avoid conflicts between what they think and what they do

cohort the term which refers to a population age group, such as children less than five years old

computer communication technology use of computer technology for the purposes of sending and receiving information (ie. e-mail, electronic banking, etc.)

confederates people who are members of an experimental team although not everyone in the experiment may know it

conscious the term used by psychologists for the part of our mind of which we are aware

conspicuous consumption publicly demonstrating excessive wealth by purchasing luxury items

constancy our perceptual world tends to remain the same despite information which is contrary to our beliefs

convergence the belief, popular in the 1950s, that all or most countries would become capitalist and industrial, so eliminating many of the differences that existed among these countries

core Wallerstein's term for rich countries at the centre of international trade

counterculture a large group of people in society who express values and behaviours that conflict with society's norms

crimes against humanity identified by the United Nations as the murder, torture, enslavement, or deportation of innocent civilian nationals

cultural behaviour human behaviour which is learned as a member of a society, rather than being innate or in-born

cultural evolution the belief that cultures evolve in common patterns, moving from hunter-gathering cultures to industrialized states in predictable stages

cultural evolutionism the principle, now disproved, that all human societies and cultures develop in a regular series of predictable stages

cultural lag the view that, while some members of society adapt to technological innovation, others lag behind the new discovery

culture-fair testing pencil and paper intelligence tests which measure capability without relying on language skills and middle-class background

cultures the ways of living of a group of people, including their traditions, inventions, and conventions

curfew a requirement that one be home by a certain time

demography the study of human populations

dependency load a measure of the portion of the national population that is not actively employed. Frequently, this includes children, youth, and seniors.

dependency ratio a numerical comparison that identifies the average number of dependents in a country for every one hundred adults of working age

dependency theory explains the lack of economic development in many developing countries as stemming directly from the treatment they received under colonialism

desegregate a term referring to the integration of students from different racial backgrounds in American schools, as required by the U. S. Supreme Court

deskilling making skilled workers obsolete, and replacing them with mechanized processes

determinism the belief that the types of technology and economic methods that are adopted always determine the type of society that develops

determinist a person who believes that a specific factor will determine the entire outcome of the social change that takes place

deterritorialization the observation that distinct cultures are no longer firmly attached, in relative isolation, to specific regions of the world

developed countries the roughly 30 industrialized nations of the world

developed world countries that are industrialized, modern, and wealthy—specifically countries in North America, Europe, Japan, Australia, and New Zealand

developing countries the roughly 180 nations that have little or no industry, where most of the population depends on agriculture for their livelihood

developing world countries that are non-industrialized and where citizens practice more traditional lifestyles

developmental stake the difference between the amount of support older people feel they receive from their children, and the amount of help their children report giving

developmental trend any life cycle process through which individuals journey

deviance any behaviour that is different from the societal norm

diffusion of innovations the sociological theory that social change is caused by the emergence of innovations in society

diffusion the spread of ideas, methods, symbols and tools from one culture to another

directed change acculturation through dominance of one culture over another, forcing the defeated to change aspects of its culture, or its entire culture

discipline an individual branch of study within the social sciences, such as anthropology

discourses the set of topics and the way of describing them that is used by a group of people with a common interest

discovery finding something that was previously unknown to a culture

discrimination inequitable treatment of people based on their race, gender, nationality, language, faith, or sexual orientation

disembedding a term describing the process by which people put their faith in abstract, largely anonymous systems, such as financial institutions, airline companies, and web browsers

disincentive anything that discourages people from doing

disposable income income that does not need to be applied to the necessities of life; it can be spent on luxuries such as travel and hobbies

domestication the taming of plants and animals in order to control their availability for human use

domestic-scale cultures small kinship-based societies in which production and distribution of goods is organized on a household basis

dominant paradigm a belief that humans have a duty to create material wealth to make this and future generations richer, and a right to dominate, change, or even corrupt the natural world in order to do so

draft plough a sturdy, animal driven device used to till land to prepare farm land

dysfunctional unable to perform an intended purpose and having a destructive effect

ebonics a term coined by linguists by combining the words "ebony" and "phonics", literally meaning "black sounds". Ebonics is spoken by some blacks in informal conversation.

echo boom the demographic phase in which a population increase is created as people born during the post-World War II baby boom have their own children

ecotourism a type of travel based upon the enjoyment of nature

ego Freud's term for the part of the unconscious mind that referees between the id and the superego

élite groups skilled and educated people with access to development funds, and who are in a position of influence

embryos fertilized human eggs

enculturation the process by which members of a culture learn and internalize shared ideas, values, and beliefs

endogenous coming from within the society being studied

equal pay for work of equal value an employment system in which job classifications must be compared for the skills they require, the responsibilities they involve, their working conditions, and the effort required. All jobs scoring equally according to these categories must be paid at the same rates

equal status social contact relations between members of different "reference groups" (Gordon Allport) marked by social equality

estrogen the female sex hormone

ethical issues situations where there are important moral principles to consider, and competing arguments over the most appropriate course of action

ethicists people who research and write about which medical techniques should be morally permissible

ethnocentrism the learned belief held by people who feel that their cultural group is superior to other cultural groups

ethnography the scientific study of human races and cultures

everyday forms of peasant resistance Scott's term to describe such things as desertion, sabotage, theft, and slow working, for the purpose of undermining the power of landowners

exogenous foreign; coming from a society other than the one being studied

experimental psychology is the branch of psychology that sets up experiments to see how individuals act in particular situations; deals with measuring and explaining human behaviour

extensive horticulture the use of a large area of land for farming as farmers move to new plots once old ones have been exhausted

extroverts Jung's term for people who use their psychological power to draw close to other people, and rely on them for much of their sense of well being

fecundity denotes the ability to reproduce. Once a girl reaches menarche, she is fecund.

fertility rates the actual number of children had by women

fertility refers to actual reproduction. A woman is fertile if she has born, or is bearing, offspring

fictive kinship the practice of acknowledging as kin people who are not biologically related

field observation a method by which social scientists observe one or more subjects in their own environment, for the purpose of gathering data about their behaviour in groups

financialization the increasing flow of money, as opposed to goods and services, between nations

flood irrigation diverting rivers so that water flows through an artificial ditch onto farmers' fields

folkways behaviours that a typical member of society would usually practice, but are not particularly significant

forgetting curve the blurring of specific details of events over time

formal support refers to help provided by doctors, nurses, and other professionals involved in caring for the elderly

free market forces a system in which government exerts little control over business activities, and allows the economy to regulate itself

functional repercussion the logical and predictable outcome of a given situation

future shock disorientation brought on by technological advancement, creating a sense that the future has arrived prematurely

gender identity one's concept of maleness or femaleness

Generation X a term used for people born between 1946 and 1966, during the post-World War II baby boom

Generation Y a term used for the group born between 1980 and 1995, most of them the children of parents born during the post-World War II baby boom

Generation Z a term used for children born after the mid-1990s, some of them the off-spring of so-called Twentysomethings demographic group

genetically modified (GM) foods foods produced, in whole or in part, by genetic engineering or biotechnology

genocide the most extreme form of systemic discrimination, by which deliberate attempts are made by authorities at mass murder of any national, ethnic, racial, or religious group

global village McLuhan's principle that the world is a single community, connected by its telecommunications network

globalization the coming together of regional, national, and continental organizations to integrate the entire world into one economic system

globalization theory a theory that suggests that Western transnational corporations have gained control of global trade and development, and continue to grow in power and influence

granny flats a portable modular cottage that is placed on to a son or daughter's property to provide housing for an elderly person, usually a parent

gross domestic product (GDP) per capita the total wealth produced by a country's economy divided by total population

group norms the attitudes, beliefs, and behaviours that people learn from social groups with whom they have close social contact

hallucinations a perceptual "error" that results in a person believing they see, hear, or feel something which is not there

hate group a term referring to organizations whose purpose is to create hatred toward target groups, usually racial or cultural minorities

hatred a very strong dislike, directed either at individuals or members of a group of people

health literacy the principle that people must have sufficient reading and comprehension skills to be able to understand what doctors tell them about diagnosis and treatment, and the ability to follow complicated medication regimes to bring them back to health

health-promotion perspective the approach of health issues which assumes that we must adopt healthy lifestyles to reduce our likelihood of becoming sick

hierarchy a ranking of authority and power

high technologies sophisticated communication devices, like computers, used by social scientists to conduct research

Holocaust denier a neo-Nazi or racial supremacist who preaches that the Holocaust is a hoax, fabricated by the Jews themselves, in order to discredit Germany

Holocaust the genocidal murder of at least six million European Jews planned, organized, and fully documented by Adolf Hitler and the Nazis

horticulture the domestication of plants

hunter-gatherer people who travel across a given territory collecting plants and hunting animals; also called foragers

hunting-gathering obtaining food by hunting wild animals, and gathering fruit and wild vegetables

hyperculture refers to the staggering rate of change in modern technological societies

id Freud's term for the part of the unconscious mind that encourages us to seek physical (sexual, nutritional, etc.) satisfaction

identity achievement one of the possible outcomes of the identity crisis. The identity-achieved person is one who has a firm sense of self.

identity crisis a term coined by psychologist Erik Erikson to explain the central conflict of the adolescent stage of development

identity diffusion one of the possible outcomes of the identity crisis. A person with identity diffusion has not been able to achieve a sense of identity

ideology a structured philosophy against which all actions and events are judged

immigration the migration of people from one country to another, with the intention of taking up permanent residence

in vitro fertilization (IVF) assisted reproduction technique where fertilization occurs in a laboratory dish when sperm and egg are introduced to one another

in vitro fertilization a treatment for infertility in which human eggs and sperm are donated by the potential parents and fertilized in a laboratory dish

inclusiveness the belief that that all law-abiding people, regardless of their particular background or circumstances, should be able to play a constructive role in the life of the nation

income inequalities the gap between what the rich and the poor earn in a society

incorporation acculturation through free borrowing of ideas and symbols from one culture to another

infant mortality rate the average number of infants less than one year of age, who die for each 1000 children born

infertile the inability to conceive a child. The term is usually applied to a couple (or individual) who has been trying to conceive for over one year without success.

infomated household homes with at least five information technologies (computer, fax machine, pager, cell phone, etc)

informal support unpaid help given by friends, neighbours, and family in caring for the elderly

informational influence a psychology term to describe the human desire to accept that the information another, admired person tells us is valid

informed consent the subject of an experiment or medical procedure must be able to understand the risks involved and to give permission for it to proceed, knowing these risks

initiation rituals elaborate ceremonies that mark the passage of children to adulthood

institutional barriers practices within public organizations and private corporations that stand in the way of equal opportunity for people from all different backgrounds

institutions established laws, practices, and customs within a society

institutions those organizations within society that act to mould us into individuals

intensive horticulture use of technologies, like irrigation and fertilizers, to allow farmers to concentrate farming in a smaller area

interaction contact with other cultures

intergroup cooperation refers to cooperative activity between members of different "reference groups" (Gordon Allport)—the social groups with whom people have close contact

intrauterine insemination (IUI) assisted reproduction technique that introduces the strongest of a man's sperm directly into the woman's uterus via a catheter

introverts Jung's term for people who use their psychological power to look inward, becoming emotionally self-sufficient

intuition believing something to be true because a person's emotions and logic support it

invention new products, ideas, and social patterns that affect the way people live

involuntary childlessness occurs when a couple or individual wants to have children and cannot

irrigation the practice of supplying water to plants that would otherwise not receive any due to lack of rain or proximity to an adequate natural water source

jigsaw learning a teaching-learning technique intended to help students unlearn prejudice, developed by American psychologist Elliot Aronson

just society the term used by Prime Minister Pierre Trudeau in the 1970s to refer to a Canadian society in which individual freedoms are very important

kinship a family relationship based on what a culture considers to be a family

knowledge barrier a lack of knowledge about how a disability affects normal health needs

liberation theology Christian teachings which combine spirituality with political activism to obtain better conditions for the poor

life cycle the different stages that an individual may pass through from birth to death

life expectancy the average number of years which a person can expect to live. It is calculated separately for males and females, and is a strong indicator of living standards in a country or among a group of people.

longitudinal studies studies in which a group of people is tracked over a long period of time, sometimes even incorporating the group's children into the study as they come along

low-income cut-off line (LICO) a complex statistical measure by Statistics Canada, commonly known as "the poverty line"

Luddite member of society who vehemently opposes new technology and does everything he/she can to halt its progress

lumpenproletariat Marx's term for unemployed people

macro-level focussing on large-scale examination, such as the state

mass culture when a large proportion of the population participates in cultural activities

materialism a way of life with personal or societal values preoccupied with obtaining material possessions

materialism the belief that technological and economic factors are the most important ones in moulding a society

matrilineal a method of tracing and organizing families though the mother's line

medical intervention model the approach to health issues which assumes that we need not worry about our health because doctors will be able to cure us if we fall ill

memory modification the process whereby humans alter their memories to fit any number of internal or external variables

menarche a woman's first menstrual period

micro-level focussing on small-scale examination, such as the family

millennium kids a term used for children born after the mid-1990s, some of them the offspring of the so-called Twentysomethings demographic group

modernity the notion that all social change is inevitable and of benefit because it leads to an improved society

modernization theory Spencer's idea, now disproved, that "backward" regions of the world benefited from colonialism because it made them more "modern"

modernizing elites Eisenstadt's term for groups of people who create significant social change and influence the direction in which it goes

morbidity illness or physical harm

multiculturalism a policy developed by the government of Canada, which encouraged people to preserve their ancestral cultures while living under Canadian laws and institutions

nation (also known as a **state**) an anthropology term for a human organization ruled by a centralized form of government

national debt money borrowed by a country to finance government spending. The debt to be repaid includes the accumulated interest on these loans.

national identity a country's unique values, beliefs, and programs that sets it apart from other nations

natural decrease in demography, a negative population balance where a country's death rate exceeds its birth rate

natural increase in demography, a positive population balance where a country's birth rate exceeds its death rate

negative reinforcement punishment of people who do something of which society disapproves

neomarxian theory a theory, based on Marx's original observations, that sees globalization as a negative force, because capitalism places humans in direct competition with one another

net migration in demography, the rate at which a country's population is increasing or decreasing when four factors are considered: birth rate, death rate, immigration, and emigration

neurosis (plural, **neuroses**) a category of mental disorder in which the patient has feelings of high levels of anxiety or tension in managing our daily lives

neurotic abnormal, usually connected with anxiety or obsessiveness

nomadic moving from region to region

normative influence a psychology term to describe the pressure to conform to the positive expectations of others

norms customary types of behaviour; specific rules that outline what is considered to be standard behaviour for a role

nuclear family a family group consisting only of a mother and father living with their children

Nuremberg Code an ethical guideline, established after World War II, outlining rules and procedures for future experiments carried out on humans

oncologist a doctor who is a specialist in the treatment of cancer patients

operant conditioning the psychological theory that learning can be programmed by whatever consequence follows a particular behaviour

ovulation the monthly release of an egg in a woman's reproductive cycle

paradigm shift a dramatic shift in the set of rules and conditions stored in the brain to interpret and understand sensory experience

paradigm shift or a fundamental change in approach

paradigm the set of rules and conditions stored in the brain, and used to interpret and understand sensory experience

paranoia a category of mental disorder in which the patient suffers from irrational thoughts of persecution or foreboding

participant-observation a method of study in which anthropologists live with their subjects for a long time, participate as a group or community member, and record their observations

participation rates the percentage of the population, or a group within it, 16–64 years of age, available for paid work who are actively employed in the paid economy at any given time

participatory research research in which the subject group participates in deciding what the goals and methods of the study should be, and how the findings should be used

pastoralism the domestication of animals; pastoralists are also called herders

patriarchy a place historically designed for the convenience of men, and structured according to rules that men find comfortable; a term used by feminist sociologists to describe a society in which men dominate most institutions and use this position to oppress women

patrilineal a method of tracing and organizing families through the father's line

pecuniary emulation clearly demonstrating one's monetary worth

peer group a group of people with the same age, status, and interests

peer pressure the influence from the members of our peer groups that encourages us to behave in prescribed ways

pension fund a type of group savings plan by which people save money to draw out almost like a pay cheque after they retire

per capita real gross domestic product (PCRGDP) a measure of the amount of goods and services, adjusted for inflation, produced on average by every member of the population

perception in psychology, the process by which objects, people, events, and other aspects of our surroundings become known to us

perception the process by which our brain tries to make sense of incoming messages

perceptual set each person has their own assumptions about the world. A person with a fixed perceptual set interprets new or contrary information in a way that makes it fit with his or her existing beliefs.

periphery Wallerstein's term for poor countries, far from the centre of international trade

Plagiarism claiming someone else's work as your own, usually in written form

pluralism the belief that there should be widespread acceptance of differences in culture, religion, values, and lifestyle within a society

pluralistic societies societies in which minorities maintain their cultural traditions

political activism movements for political change that focus on public activities such as marches, demonstrations, "media events", and petitions

population pyramid a type of multiple bar graph used to show the proportions of males and females of different ages in the population of a country

positive reinforcement rewarding of people who display what society considers good behaviour

post-event information this can alter our retention of an event by causing us to question our own memories

prejudice a set of opinions, attitudes and feelings that unfairly cast a group and its members in a negative light without legitimate reasons

private sphere the parts of our lives that are generally private

production the methods by which people extract a resource from our habitat and then exploit that resource

progressive education a more child-centered form of education, based upon the assumption that students are eager to learn material presented in an interesting way

prolactin pituitary hormone that regulates the production of progesterone levels

proletariat Marx's term to describe working people

proximate determinants the biological and behavioural factors through which social, economic, and environmental variables affect fertility

psychology the social science discipline that examines people's feelings, thoughts, and personality development

psychosis (plural: **psychoses**) a category of mental disorder in which the patient has lost touch with the real world, and may suffer from delusions or hallucinations

public policy questions social questions of such significance that politicians and social agencies are obliged to take part in public discussions about possible solutions

quasi-widowhood the term used to describe the state of a woman whose spouse has been institutionalized

quintile one-fifth of the population

race a culturally-learned concept which attempts to categorize people on the basis of physical characteristics, particularly skin colour, facial features, and hair texture. It has no biological basis.

racism negative attitudes and accompanying behaviour based on the assumption that one race is inherently superior to another

reality television a new style of television format developed in the late 1990s, focused on active situations involving the experiences of real people

recidivism rate the percentage of criminal offenders later convicted for further offences

reductionist believing that a single factor causes social change

reference group term used by American psychologist Gordon Allport referring to social groups with whom we have close contact, such as family and friends

rehabilitation the re-education and resocializion of inmates so that they grow to accept society's values and norms

relative income inequality comparing the percentage of total income that each population quintile enjoys

relativization Robertson's belief that the relationship between self and society is vital to our identity. As the world system changes, the outlooks of both our society and ourselves change as well.

religiosity a person's religious affiliation and his or her attendance at religious services

replacement level a population term referring to the number of births required to maintain a stable population

reproductive technologies medical manipulation of a woman's reproductive cycle or a man's sperm quality or count designed to result in conception

retirement savings plan a type of individual savings plan by which people save money for retirement, encouraged by a tax break from the Canadian government

retribution forceful punishment of criminals in the belief that this will reduce the crime rate.

role a particular set of behaviours that we must follow in order to be recognized as an actor

role conflict the conflict that occurs when individuals try to play two roles that are in conflict

Rorschach cards a standard set of ink blots on cards. By asking a patient to say what the ink blots look like, psychologists are able to learn more about the patient's personality

schizophrenia a complex mental disorder that leads to feelings of distress and social isolation

school of thought a certain way of interpreting a discipline's subject matter that has gained widespread credibility

selective attention the ability to focus on certain physical stimuli and exclude others

self-actualization Maslow's term for the final stage of human needs, in which a person integrates the self, making the personality whole

semi-periphery Wallerstein's term for medium wealth countries that are between the centre and the edges of international trade

separation-individuation process term introduced by psychologist Peter Blos to explain how teens gradually pull away from their parents and become independent

sexual revolution a time during the late 1960s and early 1970s when sexual behaviour and morals in North America and Europe changed dramatically

sheltered housing housing where meals and cleaning help is provided

singularity a belief that everyone in society should act and think the same way

six-pocket phenomenon a term used by marketing people in reference to Generation Y, a demographic group receiving spending money from two working parents and four grandparents

social change changes in the way society is organized, and the beliefs and practices of the people who live in it

social change theory theories that examine the factors that contribute to the change in the structure of society

social development index (SDI) a seven-point index that measures each country's level of social development

social mores the behaviours regarded as essential to the welfare and survival of the group

social practices the activities and behaviours of people in groups

social sciences those subjects that use research and analysis to explain human behaviour

socialization agent a group or institution which has a significant impact on the values and beliefs of a culture. Primary socialization agents include the family, peers, and the media.

socialization the process by which children are shaped into responsible members of society

sociology the social science discipline that looks at the development and structure of human society and how it works

sphere of influence the area over which a society has economic and cultural influence

standardized I.Q. test pencil and paper tests purported to be unbiased measures of a person's natural intelligence

state (also known as a **nation**) an anthropology term for a human organization ruled by a centralized form of government

status the term used to describe our position in an institution

stem cells cells from which stem all the "branches" of an organism. This means that they have the potential to become any tissue or structure of an organism.

stereotype false or generalized beliefs about a group of people that result in categorizing members without regard for individual difference

stimulus-response effect the principle that if the subject is correctly stimulated it will give the appropriate response

subjective validity social psychologists' term for the virtually universal belief that our attitudes are right and proper

subordinate cultures a term used by psychologist John Ogbu referring to American minority groups, such as immigrants, African-Americans, and other racial groups

suburbia new residential areas built beyond the existing built-up area of a city

superego Freud's term for the part of the unconscious mind that encourages us to do the moral thing

superovulation when a woman produces more than one egg per cycle, usually as the result of fertility drugs

surrogate literally meaning "replacement," in this text a surrogate mother is one who lends her uterus to another couple so that they can have a baby

survey a set of questions designed by social scientists to generate specific information in a usable format

systemic discrimination describes a system that favours one or some groups over others in terms of hiring, benefits, promotions, and pay increases

systemic racism discrimination based on a sense of racial superiority is part of the philosophy and practices of a company, institution, or a whole society

systemic sexism discrimination based on a sense of male superiority is part of the philosophy and practices of a company, institution, or a whole society

technological determinism the view that social change is initiated by technology and not necessarily by the individual

technology the creation of tools or objects that extend both our natural abilities, and later our social environment

technosis an overblown attachment to or dependency on technology

technostress a reliance on technology that results in tremendous anxiety when the technology is not functioning properly

tension and adaptation the structural functionalists' belief that social change results from a process of tension between one aspect of society and the rest

textual discourse communication through symbols such as written words, movie roles, paintings, and photographs, as opposed to face-to-face communication

the image Kenneth Boulding's term to describe how people do not perceive things exactly as they exist in the real world. Instead, they see an image, or a mental picture, shaped by their own experiences and characteristics.

the Pill oral birth control contraceptives first developed during the 1960s

traditional worldview the view that society should adhere to old practices, particularly those of charity and consideration for the poor

transnational having international or global influence

transnationalism the principle that organizations, be they charitable organizations or businesses, should operate freely in a number of nations

tribe an anthropology term used to describe a human organization ruled by an decentralized form of government

twentysomethings a term referring to the relatively small group of people born between 1966 and 1979, during the so-called baby bust

two-tier system a health delivery system in which those who can afford to pay are able to enjoy better health care than those who cannot

unconscious inference term coined by German social scientist Hermann von Helmholtz for the phenomenon of constancy

unconscious the term used by psychologists for the part of our mind of which we are not aware

Universal Declaration of Human Rights the 1948 United Nations statement, largely written by Canadian John Humphrey, which outlines the rights and freedoms of people around the world

value-free free of the bias of the author

values the beliefs of a group that provide standards for members' behaviour

variable a factor that has an influence on the outcome of an experiment or study

voluntary childlessness couples or individuals who freely choose to remain childless

war bride a term for the European wives of Canadian soldiers who came to Canada with their husbands after World War II

war crimes identified by the United Nations as the murder, torture, and hostage-taking of civilian nationals, and/or the widescale destruction of their property

weaning the removal of breast milk from an infant or young child's diet

wellness clinics clinics which focus on disease prevention

white supremacist racist individuals or organizations who believe that people of white or European ancestry are inherently superior to other races

work-related stress distress caused by work pressures

world-system theory Wallerstein's theory that the basic relationship between the developed and developing countries was established in colonial times, and that this relationship is a small one

Young Offenders Act the act that deals with criminals between the ages of 13 and 18

youthquake a media term used during the late 1960s and early 1970s to describe the culture of protest which emerged among adolescent and young adult baby boomers

BIBLIOGRAPHY

Chapter 1

Bain, Colin, and Jill Colyer. 2001. *The Human Way: Introducing Anthropology, Psychology, and Sociology.* Toronto. Oxford University Press Canada.

Boyd, Monica. 1992. "Gender, Visible Minority Status, and Immigrant Earnings Inequality: Reassessing an Employment Equity Premise." In V. Satzewich, ed. *Deconstructing a Nation: Immigration, Multiculturalism, and Racism in Canada.* Halifax, NS. Fernwood.

Cernetig, Miro. 2001. "American Dream shows its dark side." *The Globe and Mail.* 17 September 2001.

Darley, J.M., and B. Latane. 1968. "Bystander Intervention in Emergencies: Diffusion of Responsibility." *Journal of Personality and Social Psychology.* 8.

Durkheim, Emile. [1895] 1964. *The Rules of the Sociological Method.* New York. The Free Press.

Gordon, Milton. 1964. *Assimilation in American Life.* New York. Oxford University Press.

Harris, Marvin. 1968. *The Rise of Anthropological Theory.* New York. Thomas Y. Crowell.

Knox, Paul. 2001. "What does he want?" *The Globe and Mail.* 19 September 2001.

Li, Peter. 1988. *Ethnic Inequality in a Class Society.* Toronto. Wall and Thompson.

Megyery, Kathy, ed. 1991. *Ethnic Cultural Groups and Visible Minorities in Canadian Politics: The Question of Access.* Royal Commission on Electoral Reform and Party Financing. Ottawa. Dundurn Press.

Nolte, Dorothy Law. 1972. *Children Learn What They Live.* New York. Workman Publishing Company, Inc.

Park, Robert. 1950. *Race and Culture.* Glencoe, IL. Free Press.

Parsons, Talcott, and Edward Shils, eds. 1952. *Toward a General Theory of Action.* Cambridge, MA. Harvard University Press.

Scheper-Hughes, Nancy. 1992. *Death Without Weeping: The Violence of Everyday Life in Brazil.* Berkeley. University of California Press.

Talking Point. 2001. BBC News Online. [Online]. Available <http://newsvote. bbc.co.uk/hi/english/talking_point/newsid_1550000/1 550327.stm>. 2 November 2001.

Chapter 2

Alcock, J.E., D.W. Carment, and S.W. Sadava. 1988. *A Textbook of Social Psychology.* Scarborough, ON. Prentice-Hall Canada, Inc.

Bibby, Reginald. 1990. *Mosaic Madness: The Poverty and Potential of Life in Canada.* Toronto. Stoddart.

Bischoff, Angela, and Tooker Gomberg. 2002. "Ten Commandments for Changing the World." [Online]. Available <http://www.greenspiration.org/Article/ TenCommandments.html>. 23 January 2002.

Bratton, Angela R. 2001. *A Look at Sherry Ortner's Contributions to Anthropology.* [Online]. Available <http://wwwindiana.edu/~wanthro/ortner.htm>. 15 June 2001.

Brym, Robert J., ed. 1995. *New Society: Sociology for the 21st Century.* Toronto. Harcourt Brace & Company Canada.

Fertig, Gary. 1996. "Investigating the Process of Cultural Change from an Anthropological Perspective." *Social Studies.* 87 (4).

Festinger, Leon, and James M. Carlsmith. 1959. "Cognitive Consequences of Forced Compliance." *Journal of Abnormal and Social Psychology.* 58.

Frideres, James. 1988. *Native Peoples in Canada: Contemporary Conflicts.* Scarborough, ON. Prentice-Hall Canada.

Hendley, Nate. 2000. "The shine is off boot camps." Eye. 20 January 2000. [Online]. Available <http://www.eye.net/eye/issue/issue_01.20.00/news/bootcamp.html>. 27 October 2001.

Hoff, Bert H. 1995. "An Interview with Marion Woodman." *M.E.N. Magazine*. November 1995. [Online]. Available <http://vix.com/menmag/woodiv/htm>. 15 June 2001.

Lee, Richard B, and Irven DeVore. 1968. *Man the Hunter*. Chicago. Aldine Publishing Co.

Maslow, Abraham. [1954] 1970. *Motivation and Personality*. New York. Harper & Row.

———. 1962. *Toward a Psychology of Being*. Princeton, NJ. Van Nostrand.

McCormack, Thelma. 1975. "Toward a Nonsexist Perspective on Social and Political Change." In Marcia Millman and Rosabeth Moss Kanter, eds. *Feminist Perspectives on Social Life and Social Science*. Garden City, NY. Anchor Books.

———. 1991. *Politics and the Hidden Injuries of Gender: Feminism and the Making of the Welfare State*. CRAIW Paper 28. Ottawa. Canadian Institute for the Advancement of Women.

———. 1994. "Codes, Ratings, and Rights." *Institute for Social Research Newsletter*. 9 (1) Toronto. York University.

Meloff, William, and David Pierce, eds. 1994. *An Introduction to Sociology*. Scarborough, ON. Nelson Canada.

Ministry of Correctional Services. 2001. "Ontario's First Young Offender Boot Camp a Success." [Online]. Available <http://www.corrections.mcs.gov.on.ca/english/cservices/PT_nr.html>. 12 October 2001.

Oliver, Chad. 1981. *The Discovery of Humanity: An Introduction to Anthropology*. New York. Harper & Row.

Prochaska, James, John C. Norcross, and Carlo C. DiClemente. 1995. *Changing for Good*. New York. Avon Books.

Rachman, S.J., and R.J. Hodgson. 1980. *Obsessions and Compulsions*. Englewood Cliffs, NJ. Prentice-Hall.

Skinner, B.F. 1938. *The Behavior of Organisms: An Experimental Analysis*. New York. Appleton-Century-Crofts.

Smith, Dorothy. 1990. *Texts, Facts, and Femininity*. New York. Routledge.

Wallerstein, Immanuel. 1974. *The Modern World-System*. New York. Academic Press.

Chapter 3

Alverson, Hoyt. 1978. *Mind In the Heart of Darkness*. New Haven, CT. Yale University Press.

Bailey, Sue. 1999. "Programs vary wildly between provinces." Canadian Press. 3 March 1999. [Online]. Available <http://www.st-matthew.on.ca/bulletin/hap/welfrpt.htm>. 29 October 2001.

Brym, Robert J. 1995. *New Society: Sociology for the 21st Century*. Toronto. Harcourt Brace Canada.

Canadian Council on Social Development. 1996. Percentage Distribution of Total Income of Families by Quintiles, 1974, 1984 and 1994 in Canada. Cat. 13-207, 1996. [Online]. Available <http://www.ccsd.ca/fs_quifa.html>. 27 July 2001.

———. 2001. *Canadian Low-Income Cut-Offs*, 1999. [Online]. Available <http://www.ccsd.ca/factsheets/fs_lic99.htm>. 1 November 2001.

"Causes of Social Change." 2001. [Online]. Available <http://www.usi.edu/libarts/socio/chapter/socialchange/causes.html>. 14 June 2001.

City of Toronto. 2001. *Social Services Policy*. [Online]. Available <http://www.city.toronto.on.ca/socialservices/Policy/BasicNeeds.htm>. 28 July 2001.

Cotgrove, S.E. 1982. *Catastrophe or Cornucopia: The Environment, Politics, and the Future*. Chichester, UK. John Wiley & Sons.

Cox, Kevin. 2001. "Public meeting over tar ponds turns violent." *The Globe and Mail*. 2 August 2001.

Curley, Bob. 1995. "Massive welfare cuts invite more drug problems." *Alcoholism and Drug Abuse Weekly*. 7 (20).

Deutsch, M., and H.B. Gerrard. 1955. "A study of normative and informational social influences upon individual social judgment." *Journal of Abnormal and Social Psychology*. 51.

Edelson, Max. 1992. "Where to find the hot issues of 2020." *American Demographics*. 14 (9).

Eisenstadt, S.N. 1973. *Building States and Nations*. Beverly Hills. Sage Publications.

"Further tests confirm high arsenic levels." 2001. *The Globe and Mail*. 27 July 2001.

Hondagneu-Sotelo, Pierrette. 1993. "Why advocacy research? Reflections on research and activism with immigrant women." *American Sociologist*. 24 (1).

Jobsearch Canada. 1999. "Back Pay for Federal Employees: Five BILLION tax dollars at work." [Online]. Available <http://jobsearchcanada.about.com/library/weekly/aa1 02399.htm>. 28 July 2001.

Liu, Melinda, and Lijia Macleod. 1998. "A taste for the good life." *Newsweek*. 14 December 1998.

Manstead, Anthony S.R., and Miles Hewstone, eds. 1995. *The Blackwell Encyclopedia of Social Psychology*. Oxford, UK. Blackwell.

Mathabane, Mark. 1994. *African Women: Three Generations*. New York. HarperCollins Publishers.

Milgram, S. 1992. *The Individual in a Social World: Essays and Experiments*. Edited by J. Sabatini and M. Silver. 2nd ed. New York. McGraw-Hill.

Ministry of Community and Social Services. 2001. "Harris government celebrates 600 000 people moving off welfare." [Online]. Available <http://www.gov.on.ca/ CSS/page/news/oct2601.html>. 29 October 2001.

Prager, Carol A.L. 1988. "Poverty in North America: Losing Ground?" *Canadian Public Policy*. 14.

PSAC [Public Service Alliance of Canada]. 2000. *Analysis of Employment Equity in the Public Sector, 1999–2000*. [Online]. Available <http://www.psac.com./H&S&E/ EmploymentEquity/EE_PSAC_Analysis-e.htm>. 27 July 2001.

Rosen, Lawrence. 1984. *Bargaining for Reality: The Constructions of Social Relations in a Muslim Community*. Chicago. University of Chicago Press.

Scott, James C. 1985. *Weapons of the Weak*. New Haven, CT. Yale University Press.

Sierra Club of Canada. 1999. "Nightmare on Frederick Street." [Online]. Available <http://www.sierraclub. ca/stp/stp-factsheet.html>. 28 July 2001.

Sillars, Les. 1994. "Homeless by choice or necessity?" *Alberta Report*. 5 September 1994.

"Social change very slow in Qatar, a small Islamic country." 1997. *The New York Times*. 20 July 1997.

Statistics Canada. 1999. *Participation Rates and Unemployment by Age and Sex, Canada and Selected Countries*. [Online]. Available <http://statcan.ca/english/Pdgb/People/Labour/labor23a.htm>. 28 July 2001.

———. 1999. "Survey of Labour and Income Dynamics: The wage gap between men and women." *The Daily: Monday, December 20, 1999*. [Online]. Available <http://www.statcan.ca/Daily/English/991220/d991220 a.htm>. 28 July 2001.

———. 2000. *People With Low Income After Tax, 1994-98*. Cat. 75-202-XIE. [Online]. Available <http://www.stat-can.ca/english/Pgdb/People/Families/famil19a.htm>. 27 July 2001.

———. 2001. *Highlights: Family Income After Tax, 1998*, Cat. 75-202-XIE. [Online]. Available <http://www.stat-can.ca./english/Pgdb/People/Families/famil05a.htm>. 25 October 2001.

Suzuki, David. 1994. "The buzz saw of 'progress' hits Sarawak." *The Toronto Star*. 17 March 1994.

U.S. Census Bureau. 1999. "Income by race, 1997–1999." [Online]. Available <http://census.gov/hhes/income/ income99/99tableb.htm>. 15 November 2001.

Chapter 4

Aboriginal Multi-Media Society. Web site. Available <www.ammsa.com>. 7 March 2002.

Aboriginal Youth Network. Web site. Available <www.ayn.ca>. 7 March 2002.

Avis, Andrew. 1995. "Public Spaces on the Information Highway: The Role of Community Networks." Thesis, University of Calgary. 1995.

Becklake, John, and Sue Becklake. 1991. *Food and Farming*. Toronto. Gloucester Press.

Benedetti, Paul, and Nancy DeHart, eds. 1996. *Forward Through the Rearview Mirror: Reflections on and by Marshall McLuhan*. Toronto. Prentice Hall.

Bertman, Stephen. 1998. "Hyperculture: The Human Cost of Speed." *The Futurist*. 1 December 1998.

Blaine, Sean. 1999. "The Genetics Revolution." *Patient Care: The Practical Journal of Primary Care Physicians*. 10.

Blakemore, Douglas. 1998. "The Role of Technology in Social Change." Abstract, Graduate School of America.

Buckley, Richard, ed. 1997. *Understanding Global Issues: The Future of Farming*. Cheltenham. Understanding Global Issues Ltd.

Caplan, Arthur L., Glenn McGee, and David Magnus. 1999. "What is Immoral About Eugenics?" *British Medical Journal*. 13 November 1999.

Chadwick, Keith. 2000. "European Controversy Continues Over Canadian GM Canola Seeds." *Chemical Reporter*, 12 June 2000.

Crowley, David. 1994. "Doing Things Electronically." *Canadian Journal of Communication* 19 (1). [Online]. Available <http://cjc-online.ca>. 8 March 2002.

Dickinson, Paul, and Jonathan Ellison. 1999. *Getting Connected and Staying Unplugged: The Growing Use of Computer Communications Services*. Ottawa. Statistics Canada / Ministry of Industry.

Dobel, Reinald. 1999. "Power and Powerlessness in the Global Village: Stepping into the 'Information Society' as a 'Revolution from Above.'" *Electronic Journal of Sociology*. [Online]. Available <http://www.sociology. org/content/vol004.003/globvlg2.html>. 7 March 2002.

English-Lueck, J.A. 1998. "Technology and Social Change: The Effects on Family and Community." Consortium of Social Science Associations Congressional Seminar, June 1998.

Fields, Scott. 1996. "High-Tech Hazards." *Environmental Health Perspectives*. July 1996.

Glenday, Dan, and Ann Duffy, eds. 2001. *Canadian Society: Meeting the Challenges of the Twenty-First Century*. Toronto. Oxford University Press.

Grace, Eric. 1998. "Better Health Through Gene Therapy." *Futurist*. January-February 1998.

Henslin, James M., and Adie Nelson. 1996. *Sociology: A Down-to-Earth Approach*. Toronto. Allyn and Bacon Canada.

Kanner, Allen D. 1998. "Technological Wisdom." *ReVision*. 22 March 1998.

Ling, Richard. 1996. "Cyber McCarthyism: Witch Hunt in the Living Room." *Electronic Journal of Sociology*. [Online]. Available <http://www.sociology.org/content/vol002.001/ling.html>. 7 March 2002.

Mansfield, Neil. 1982. *Introductory Sociology*. Toronto. Collier Macmillan Canada, Inc.

Marchand, Philip. 1989. *The Medium and the Messenger*. New York. Ticknor and Fields.

McLuhan, Marshall. 1963. *Understanding Media: The Extensions of Man*. New York. Signet Books.

Moland, John Jr. 1996. "Social Change, Social Inequality, and Intergroup Tensions." *Social Forces*. 1 December 1996.

Mumford, Lewis. 1952. *Art and Technics*. New York. Columbia University Press.

Nestle, Marion. 1998. "Food Biotechnology: Labeling Will Benefit Industry as well as Consumers." *Nutrition Today*. 1 January 1998.

Ogburn, William. 1955. *Technology and the Changing Family*. New York. Houghton Mifflin.

Perrolle, Judith A. 1987. *Computers and Social Change*. Belmont, CA. Wadsworth Publishing Company. (New material 1996, 1998, 1998 by Judith A. Perrolle.) [Online]. Available . <http://www.ccs.neu.edu/home/ perrolle/book/>. 7 March 2002.

Podolefsky, Aaron, and Peter Brown, eds. 2001. *Applying Anthropology: An Introductory Reader*. 6th ed. Toronto: Mayfield Publishing Company.

Postman, Neil. 1985. *Amusing Ourselves to Death*. New York. Viking Press.

Postman, Neil. 1992. *Technopoly*. New York. Alfred A. Knopf.

Rifkin, Jeremy. 1995. *The End of Work*. New York. Jeremy P. Tarcher/Putnam Inc.

Rifkin, Jeremy. 1998. *Biotech Century*. New York. Jeremy P. Tarcher/Putnam Inc.

Rosen, Larry, and Michelle Weil. 1997. *Technostress: Coping With Technology @Work @Home @Play*. New York. Wiley.

Rosen, Larry, and Michelle Weil. 1998. "Multitasking Madness." *Context Magazine*. September 1998.

Rosen, Larry and Michelle Weil. 2002. "Technostress: Coping With Technology @Work @Home @Play." Web site. Available <www.technostress.com>. 7 March 2002.

Rothman, Stanley. 1997. "The Media and Personality and Identity." *International Journal of Peace*. December 1, 1997.

Sainte-Marie, Buffy. 1997. "Cyberskins: Live and Interactive." [Online]. Available <http://members tripod.com/~fasters/ati128.html>. 7 March 2002.

Schlein, Lisa. 2001. "Canada Calls For International Ban on Human Cloning." Canadian Press. 16 May 2001.

Schniederman, Ben. 1990. "Human Values and the Future of Technology: A Declaration of Empowerment." [Online]. Available <http://www.lanl.gov/SFC/95/bios/ papers/shneiderman.html>. 7 March 2002.

Ward, Darell E. 1993. "Gene Therapy: The Splice of Life." *USA Today Magazine*. January 1993.

Young, Kimberly, Molly Pistner, James O'Mara, and Jennifer Buchanan. 1999. "Cyber-Disorders: The Mental Health Concern for the New Millennium." Paper presented at 107th APA convention, 20 August 1999. [Online]. Available <http://netaddiction.com/ articles/cyberdisorders.htm>. 7 March 2002.

Chapter 5

Adams, Michael. 1997. *Sex in the Snow: Canadian Social Values at the End of the Millennium.* Toronto. Viking, Penguin Books.

Aliphat, Susan, et al. 1996. *Decades: Forces of Change.* Toronto. Prentice Hall Canada.

Bibby, Reginald, and Donald Posterski. [1992] 2000. *Teen Trends: A Nation in Motion.* Abridged paperback ed. Toronto. Stoddart.

Cranny, Michael, and Garvin Moles. 2001. *Counterpoints: Exploring Canadian Issues.* Toronto. Prentice Hall Canada.

Foot, David K. 1996. *Demographic Trends in Canada, 1996-2006: Implications for the Public and Private Sectors.* Ottawa. Industry Canada, Micro-economic Policy Branch.

Foot, David K., and Daniel Stoffman. 1996. *Boom, Bust and Echo: How to Profit from the Coming Demographic Shift.* Toronto. Macfarlane, Walter and Ross.

Leacy, F.H., ed. 1983. *Historical Statistics of Canada.* 2nd ed. Ottawa. Statistics Canada, Ministry of Supply and Services.

Marsh, James, ed. 1985. *The Canadian Encyclopedia.* Three volumes. Edmonton. Hurtig Publishers.

Martin, Brendan. 1998. "Douglas Coupland's Generation X: Tales for an Accelerated Culture: an alternative voice." [Online]. Available <http://www.qub.ac.uk/english/imperial/canada/coupland.htm>. 8 March 2002.

Norland, J.A. 1991. *Profile of Canada's Seniors.* Toronto. Prentice Hall and Statistics Canada.

O'Malley, Martin, Owen Wood, and Amy Foulkes. 2002. "The Pill and Us." CBC News Online. [Online]. Available <http://cbc.ca/news/indepth/background/birthcontrol_pill.html>. 8 March 2002.

Owram, Douglas. 1996. *Born at the Right Time: A History of the Baby Boom Generation.* Toronto. University of Toronto Press.

"Coon Come asks for $4.2 billion for social programs." 2001. *Sarnia Observer.* October 2001.

Statistics Canada. 2002. *Population Pyramids.* [Online]. Available <http://www.statcan.ca/english/kits/animat/pyone.htm>. 8 March 2002.

Verbeek, Lynne. 1994. "Dr. Spock's Last Interview." *Parent's Press.* [Online]. Available <http://www.parentspress.com/drspock.html>. 8 March 2002.

World Book Encyclopedia. 1989. Toronto: World Book Inc.

Chapter 6

Appleyard, Bryan. 2001. "Sorry, Baby, But Our Lifestyle Comes First." *Sunday Times (London).* 27 May 2001.

Baker, M. 2001. *Families: Changing Trends in Canada.* 4th ed. Toronto. McGraw-Hill Ryerson.

Baum, F. 1994. "Choosing Not to Have Children." *Australian Demographic Statistics.* 2 (3).

Becker, Gary S. 2001. "How Rich Nations Can Defuse the Population Bomb." *Business Week.* 28 May 2001.

Benady, Susannah. 2001. "Being old doesn't cost more money—being sick does." *Medical Post.* 27 February 2001.

Bongaarts, John, and Robert G. Potter. 2001. "Fertility, Biology, and Behaviour: An Analysis of the Proximate Determinants." In Frank Trovato, ed. *Population and Society: Essential Readings.* Toronto. Oxford University Press.

British Broadcasting Corporation. 2000. "Russia's Gene Pool Under Threat if Children Not Saved, says Deputy Duma." BBC Monitoring Former Soviet Union. 28 May 2000.

Chu, Johanna, and Avard, John W. 2000. "Canada: Impact of Aging Population." U.S. Department of Congress: National Trade Data Bank. 3 November 2000. [Online]. Available <www.tradeport.org/ts/countries/canada/mrr/mark0219.html>. 8 March 2002.

Cleland, John. 2001. "Population Growth in the Twenty-First Century: Cause for Crisis or Celebration?" In Frank Trovato, ed. *Population and Society: Essential Readings.* Toronto. Oxford University Press, 2001.

Dupuis, Dave. 1998. "What Influences People's Plans to Have Children?" *Canadian Social Trends.* Spring 1998.

Editorial. 2000. "Fiscal Tug-of-War Between Generations." *The Toronto Star.* 30 January 2000.

Gargan, Edward A. 2001. "Just Married—but Living Separate Lives." *The Los Angeles Times.* 27 April 2001.

Hughes, Mary. 2000. "Britain's Falling Birth-Rate." *Banner of Truth,* 29 May 2000, [Online]. Available <www.banneroftruth.co.uk>. December 2001.

Infertility Awareness Association of Canada. Web site. Available <www.iaac.ca/main.htm>. 8 March 2002.

Ireland, Mardy S. 1993. *Reconceiving Women: Separating Motherhood from Female Identity*. New York. Guilford Publications.

Islam, Nurul M., and Ashrraf U Ahmed. 1998. "Age at First Marriage and Its Determinants in Bangladesh." *Asia-Pacific Population Journal*. 13 (2).

Karush, Sarah. 2001. "Russia Looking For Ways to Stop Population Decline." *Amarillo Globe News,* 29 April 2001. [Online.] Available <www.amarillonet.com/stories/042901/usn_russialook.shtml>. 8 March 2002.

Krum, Sharon. 2001. "American Beauty: Here is Lauren Bush, this year's model. Americans want her looks, her figure, even her brains. But most of all, they want her eggs." *The Independent*. 17 June 2001.

Lacayo, Richard. 1987. "ETHICS: Whose Child Is This? Baby M. and the agonizing dilemma of surrogate motherhood. *Time*. 19 January 1987.

Letherby, Gayle, and Williams, Catharine. 1999. "Non-Motherhood: Ambivalent Autobiographies." *Feminist Studies*. Fall 1999.

"Making Career Sense of Labour Information." 1998. [Online]. Available </workinfonet.bc.ca/lmisi/making/chapter2/IMPACT2.HTM>. November 2001.

Malpani, Aniruddha, and Anjali Malpani. 2001. "How to Have a Baby: Overcoming Infertility." [Online]. Available <fertilethoughts.net/malpani/new/main.htm>. November 2001.

Mandel, Michele. 2001 "How to Stop the Care Crisis From Getting Worse." *The Toronto Sun*. 10 June 2001.

McAllister, Fiona, and Clarke, Lynda. 1998. *Choosing Childlessness*. London. Family Policy Studies Centre.

Middleman Thomas, Irene. 1995. "Childless By Choice: Why Some Latinas Are Saying No to Motherhood." *Hispanic*. 31 May 1995.

Moy, Patsy. 2001. "Dragon Brings Baby Boom: 3,000 More Born as Birthrate Rises for the First Time in Six Years." *South China Morning Post*. 26 February 2001.

Onnen-Isemann, Corinna. 2000. "Involuntary Childless Marriages and the Effects of Reproductive Technology: The Case of Germany." *Forum: Qualitative Social Research [On-line Journal]*. January 2000. [Online]. Available <http://qualitative-research.net/fqs>. November 2001.

Owens, Anne Marie. 2001. "More deaths than births expected within 25 years: Declining fertility rate: Immigration only way to ensure population will grow." *National Post*. 13 March 2001.

Pape, Gordon. 1997. "What the Proposed Changes to the Canada Pension Plan Mean to Individuals." CBC Radio. 4 March 1997.

Province of Manitoba, Department of Aboriginal and Northern Affairs. 1998. "Aboriginal People in Manitoba 2000." [Online]. Available <www.gov.mb.ca/ana/apm2000/l/m.html>. November 2001.

Rankin, Jim. 2001. "Nobody's Children." *The Toronto Star*. September 29, 2001.

Resolve: The National Infertility Association. Web site. Available <http://resolve.org>. 8 March 2002.

Schaefer, Anne. C. (Anny) 1999. "Teenage Pregnancy in Canada and the Provinces, 1974 to 1998." [Online]. Available <www.bctf.bc.ca/Research Reports/99sd01/report.html>. November 2001.

Scott, Sarah. 1998. "Baby Time Any Time? (Old Age is Not the Time to Have Babies.)" *Chatelaine*. 9 January 1998.

Steinberg, Jerry. 2001. No Kidding! Web site (home page). Available <www.nokidding.net/>. 8 March 2002.

Sun, Lena H. 1993. "China Lowers Birthrate to Levels in West." *World Tibet Network News*. 22 April 1993. [Online]. Available <www.tibet.ca/wtnnews.htm>. 8 March 2002.

Taylor, Laurie, and Matthew Taylor. 2001. "People: Why Don't We Have Kids Any More?" *The Observer (London)*. 3 June 2001.

Whitaker, Elizabeth D. 1999. "Ancient Bodies, Modern Customs, and Our Health." In Aaron Podolefsky and Peter J. Brown, eds. *Applying Anthropology: An Introductory Reader*. 5th ed. Toronto. Mayfield Publishing Company.

Williams, Juan. 2001. "Analysis: Contributing factors to the rate of world population growth." *Talk of the Nation* (US National Public Radio). 12 March 2001.

Youval, M. 2000. "Love & marriage, but where's the baby carriage?" *Jerusalem Post*. 1 December 2000.

Chapter 7

Argetsinger, Amy. 2001. "College Sticker Shock x 5; Maryland Quints Go From Adorable To Unaffordable In 18 Quick Years." *The Washington Post*. 22 May 2001.

Aronson, Jane. 1990. "Women's Perspectives on Informal Care of the Elderly: Public Ideology and Personal Experience of Giving and Receiving Care." *Aging and Society.* 10.

Belanger, A., and Oikawa, Cathy. 1999. "Who Has a Third Child?" *Canadian Social Trends.* Summer 1999.

Bengston, Vern L., and Kuypers, Joseph A. 1971. "Generational Differences and the Developmental Stake." *International Journal of Aging and Human Development.* 2.

Bennett, Oliver. 2001. "The kids are all wrong: the baby boomers are pushing 50 and they're not going to be pushed around." *The Independent.* 9 April 2001.

Bibby, Reginald, and Donald Posterski. 2000. *Teen Trends: A Nation in Motion.* Toronto. Stoddart Publishing.

Blos, Peter. 1967. "The Second Individuation Process of Adolescence." *Psychoanalytic Study of the Child.* 23.

Bond, J.B., Jr., and C.D.H. Harvey. 1991. "Ethnicity and Intergenerational Perceptions of Family Solidarity." *International Journal of Aging and Human Development.* 33.

Doyle, V. 1994. "Choice, Control, and the Right to Age in Place." In G. Gutman and A.V. Wister, eds. *Progressive Accommodation for Seniors: Interfacing Shelter and Services.* Vancouver, BC. Gerontology Research Centre.

Eichler, M. 1996. "The Impact of New Reproductive and Genetic Technologies on Families." In Maureen Baker, ed. *Families: Changing Trends in Canada.* 3rd ed. Toronto. McGraw-Hill Ryerson.

Hadjistavropoulos, T., S. Taylor, H. Tuokko, and B.L. Beattie. 1994. "Neuropsychological Deficits, Caregivers' Perception of Deficits and Caregiver Burden." *The Journal of the American Geriatrics Society.* 42.

Hall, G. Stanley. 1904. *Adolescence: Its Psychology and Its Relations to Physiology, Anthropology, Sociology, Sex, Crime, Religion and Education.* New York. Appleton & Company.

Hamilton, K., and T. Brehaut. 1992. *Older Women: A Study of the Housing and Support Service Needs of Older "Single" Women.* A report for the Canada Mortgage and Housing Corporation. Charlottetown. Renaissance Communications.

Howe, Neil. 2001. "Youth Culture: Teens Shun Gross-out Movie Genre." *The Los Angeles Times.* 15 July 2001.

Howe, Nina, and William M. Bukowski. 2001. "What Are Children and How Do They Become Adults?: Child Rearing and Socialization." In M. Baker, ed. *Families: Changing Trends in Canada.* 4th ed. Toronto. McGraw-Hill Ryerson.

Jere, Daniel. 1994. "Learning to love (gulp!) growing old." *Psychology Today.* 27 (1).

Kett, Joseph. 1977. *Rites of Passage: Adolescence in America 1790 to the Present.* New York. Basic Books.

Liptak, Karen. 1994. *Coming-of-Age: Traditions and Rituals Around the World.* Brookfield, CT. The Millbrook Press.

McClelland, Susan. 2001. "Not So Hot to Trot." *Maclean's.* 9 April 2001.

McDaniel, S.A. 1994. *Family and Friends.* Statistics Canada Cat. No. 11-612E, No. 9. Ottawa. Minister of Industry, Science and Technology.

Meeus, Wim, and Maja Dekovic. 1995. "Identity Development, Parental and Peer Support in Adolescence: Results of a National Dutch Survey." *Adolescence.* 30

Novak, Mark. 1997. *Aging & Society: A Canadian Perspective.* 3rd ed. Toronto. ITP Nelson Publishing Company.

Olsen, David H., and Hamilton McCubbin. 1983. *Families: What Makes Them Work?* Beverly Hills. Sage Publications.

O'Reilly, Elaine, and Diane Alfred. 1998. "The Impact of Demographics on Employment." 1998. In Elaine O'Reilly and Diane Alfred. *Making Career Sense of Labour Market Information.* Government of British Columbia, Department of Education. [Online]. Available <http://workinfonet.bc.ca/lmisi/Making/Mcstoc.htm>. 18 September 2001.

Parents Television Council. 2002. "What a Difference a Decade Makes: A Comparison of Prime Time Sex, Language, and Violence in 1989 and '99." [Online]. Available <www.parentstv.org/publications/reports/Decadestudy/decadestudy.html>. 8 March 2002.

Peters, John F. 1994. "Gender socialization of adolescents in the home: research and discussion." *Adolescence.* 29.

Peterson, Peter G. 2002. "Grey Dawn: The Global Aging Crisis." In F. Trovato, ed. *Population And Society: Essential Readings.* Toronto. Oxford University Press.

Rosenthal, C., and Dawson, P. 1991. "Wives of Institutionalized Husbands." *Journal of Aging and Health.* 3.

Schultze, Quentin J. 1991. *Dancing in the Dark: Youth, Popular Culture, and the Electronic Media.* Grand Rapids, MI. W.B. Eerdmans Publishing Company.

Shaw, Randy. 2000. "The Argument in Favor: Legalizing Granny Flats Will Ease the Housing Crunch for a City in Crisis." *San Francisco Chronicle.* 30 July 2000.

Verburg, Peter. 1995. "The age of exile." *Alberta Report / Western Report.* 27 March 1995.

Westerville, John Cloud. 2000. "Behaviour: His Name is Aurora. When a Boy is Raised a Girl, an Ohio Suburb is Suddenly in the Throes of Transgendered Politics." *Time.* 25 September 2000.

Wilson, Bud. 2000. "The Argument Against: Foes say they'll lower home values and crowd neighborhoods." *San Francisco Chronicle.* 30 July 2000.

Wilson, Susannah J. 2001. "Intimacy and Commitment in Family Formation." In Maureen Baker, ed. *Families: Changing Trends in Canada.* 4th ed. Toronto. McGraw-Hill Ryerson.

Chapter 8

"Aboriginal strategy aims to help those at risk." 2001. *The Globe and Mail.* 1 November 2001.

Alcohol Research Foundation. 2000. "Tips on Curfews." [Online]. Available <http://www.arf. org/isd/infopak/youth.html>. 20 May 2000.

Assembly of First Nations. 2001a. "First Nations Health Priorities." [Online]. Available <http://afn.ca/pro-grams/health%20secretariat/first%5Fnations%5Fhealth%5Fpriorities.htm>. 7 December 2001.

————. 2001b. "The Search for Wellness." [Online]. Available <http://afn.ca/programs/health%20secretari-at/search%5Ffor%5Fwellness.htm>. 7 December 2001.

Bar-Yam, Naomi Bromberg. 1995. "The Nestlé boycott." *Mothering.* Winter 1995.

Barrington-Ward, Simon. 1998. "Putting babies before business." *Mothering.* May/June 1998.

Boase, Joan Price. 1996. "Health care reform or health care rationing? A comparative study." *Canadian-American Public Policy.* 26 (26).

Bodley, John H. 2000. *Cultural Anthropology: Tribes, States, and the Global System.* 3rd ed. Mountain View, CA. Mayfield Publishing Company.

Brown, J.D., and J.M. Siegel. 1988. "Attributions for negative life events and depression: The role of perceived con-trol." *Journal of Personality and Social Psychology.* 54.

"Bush position on stem cells welcomed." 2001. [Online]. Available <http://news.bbc.co.uk. /hi/english/sci/tech/newswid_1484000/1484529.stm>. 10 September 2001.

Canadian Blood Services. Web site. Available <http://www.bloodservices.ca>. 13 January 2002.

Canadian Diabetes Association. 2001. "Aboriginal strategy aims to help those at risk." *The Globe and Mail.* (Supplement). 1 November 2001.

Canadian Institute for Advanced Research (CIAR). 1991. *Determinants of Health.* CIAR Publication No. 5. Toronto. CIAR.

Chappell, Neena L. 1995. "Health and Health Care." In Robert J. Brym, ed. *New Society: Sociology for the 21st Century.* Toronto. Harcourt Brace & Company.

Dossa, Parin. 2001. "Narrative Mediation of Conventional and New Paradigms of 'Mental Health': Reading the Stories of Immigrant Iranian Women." November 2001. Forthcoming, in *The Medical Anthropology Quarterly: An International Journal for the Analysis of Health.*

Flynn, Gillian. 1995. "Recreational drug use may not be the biggest threat." *Personnel Journal.* 754 (5).

Frost, Mimi, and Susan Baxter. 1996. "Up in Smoke: Why teen girls don't quit." *Chatelaine.* July 1996.

Health Canada. 2001. "The Effects of Media Violence on Children." [Online]. Available <http://www.hc-sc.gc.ca/hppb/familyviolence/media_violence/eng-lish/>. 12 December 2001.

Jones, Jo. 2001. "Breast-beating." *The Globe and Mail.* 23 August 2001.

Kavanaugh, John F. 2000. "Stem cell secrets." *America.* 182 (20).

Kondro, Wayne. 1996a. "Canadians propose overhaul of research-ethics guidelines." *Lancet.* 347 (9011).

————. 1996b "Canada unveils plans for new blood authority." *Lancet.* 348 (9030).

Krauthammer, Charles. 1999. "Yes, let's pay for organs." *Time.* 17 May 1999.

Langer, Ellen, and Judith Rodin. 1976. "The effects of choice and enhanced personal responsibility for the aged: A field experiment in an institutional setting." *Journal of Personality and Social Psychology.* 34.

Leidl, David. 1998. "Some things never change: another stress survey says…we're all feeling more stressed." *BC Business.* 26 (11).

Levinsky, Norman G. 1998. "Can we afford medical care for Alice C.?" *Lancet.* 352 (9143).

McCarthy, Shawn. 2001. "MPs ask Rock to tighten rules on cloning." *The Globe and Mail.* 13 December 2001.

Media Awareness Network. 2001. "Media Violence and You." [Online]. Available <http://www.media-aware-ness.ca/eng/med/home/resource/cctapamp.htm>. 12 December 2001.

MediaWatch. 1994. "The Relationship Between Television Watching and Fearfulness." 1994. [Online]. Available <http://www.hc-sc.gc.ca/hppb/familyviolence/media_violence/english/fearfulness.htm>. 13 December 2001.

"Medicare doesn't erase all barriers to care, HCFA studies indicate." *Nation's Health.* 25 (11).

Mitchell, Alanna. 2001. "Scientists clone human embryo." *The Globe and Mail.* 26 November 2001.

Moreno, Jonathan D. 1997. "The dilemmas of experimenting on people." 1997. *Technology Review.* 100 (5).

"Music and movies are desensitizing us." 1997. *USA Today Magazine.* December 1997.

Neel, James V. 1970. "Lessons from a 'Primitive' People." *Science.* 170.

"Off the chest." 1996. *Psychology Today.* 29 (1).

Parker, Howard, Judith Aldridge, and Fiona Measham. 1998. *Illegal Leisure: The Normalization of Adolescent Recreational Drug Use.* London. Routledge.

Parker, Shafer. 2000. "Wanted dead or alive: Ontario's new organ donation law points toward presumed consent." *Report Magazine* (national edition, special insert). 14 August 2000.

Picard, Andre. 2001. "Cutting frills to seniors care costs thousands, report says." *The Globe and Mail.* 26 May 2001.

———. 2001. "Why Canada's nurses are so angry." *The Globe and Mail.* 20 June 2001.

Pirsi, Angela. 2000. "Low health literacy prevents equal access to care." *Lancet.* 356 (9244).

Pollock, Bruce G., and Charles F. Reynolds III. 2000. "Depression late in life." *Harvard Mental Health Letter.* 17 (3).

Priest, Lisa. 2000. "Grieving families to face organ-donation pitch: Ontario plans to change transplant rules." *The Globe and Mail.* 13 July 2000.

Rodin, Judith, and Ellen Langer. 1977. "Long-term effects of a control-relevant interaction with the institutionalized aged." *Journal of Personality and Social Psychology.* 35.

———. 1980. "Aging labels: The decline of social control and the fall of self-esteem." *Journal of Social Issues.* 36.

Rowe, Michelle. 2000. "Skills training in the long-term management of stress and occupational burnout." *Current Psychology.* 19 (3).

Save Medicare.com [Online]. Available <http://www.savemedicare.com/n20no00a.htm>. 11 December 2001.

Seligman, Jean. 1999. "Kate returns to the runway." *Newsweek.* 25 January 1999.

Statistics Canada. 2001. *Percentage of Smokers in the Population.* Catalogue no. 82M009XCB. [Online]. Available <http://www.statcan.ca/english/Pgdb/People/Health/health07a.htm>. 31 August 2001.

"Texas, California pitch top pay, unique lifestyles: Canadians popular among U.S. recruiters." 2001. *The Globe and Mail.* 11 June 2001.

"Tips on Curfews," *Parenting of Adolescents Newsletter.* [Online]. Available <http://parentingteens.about.com/parenting/parentingteens/library/weekly/aa111699.htm>. 15 May 2000.

Ulrich, Mariette. 2000. "Health authorities couldn't make smoking more attractive to teens even if they tried." *Alberta Report.* 6 November 2000.

USGAO [United States General Accounting Office]. 1991. *Canadian Health Insurance: Lessons for the United States.* Gaithersburg, MD.

Weiss, W.H. 1994. "Coping with work stress." *Supervision.* 55 (4).

Wickens, Barbara, John Demont, Brenda Branswell, Susan McClelland, Brian Bergman, and Ken Macqueen. 2000. "Divisions over health care." *Maclean's.* 13 November 2000.

Wilcox, Melynda Dovel. 1999. "Coming: A 12-step plan for computer addicts?" Kiplinger's *Personal Finance Magazine.* September 1999.

"Women with disabilities face healthcare barriers." 1999. *New York Amsterdam News.* 29 April 1999.

Wood, Chris. 2001. "Dealing with tech rage." *Maclean's.* 19 March 2001.

Zabarenko, Deborah. 2001. "Made-to-order stem cells spark ethics debate." [Online]. Available <http://www.ignonsandiego.com/news/science/20010711-1507-health-stemc.html>. 11 July 2001.

Chapter 9

Aboud, Francis. 1988. *Children and Prejudice*. Montreal. McGill University.

Allport, Gordon W. 1954. *The Nature of Prejudice*. Don Mills. Addison Wesley.

———. 1979. "The Nature of Hatred." Reprinted in Robert M. Baird and Stuart E. Rosenbaum, eds. *Hatred, Bigotry and Prejudice: Definitions, Causes and Solutions*. Amherst, NY. Prometheus Books. 1999.

American Anthropological Association. 1997. "Official Statement on 'Race.'" *Anthropology Newsletter*. 38 (6).

Bain, Colin. 1994. *Canadian Society: A Changing Tapestry*. Toronto. Oxford University Press Canada.

Bain, Colin, and Jill Colyer. 2001. *The Human Way*. Toronto. Oxford University Press.

Baird, Robert M., and Stuart E. Rosenbaum, eds. 1999. *Hatred, Bigotry and Prejudice: Definitions, Causes and Solutions*. Amherst, NY. Prometheus Books.

Barker, Joel. 1989. *The Business of Paradigms*. Bainsville, MN. Chart House Learning.

"Belfast Children Return to School in Crossfire of Sectarian Hatred." 2001. *The Sarnia Observer*. 4 September 2001.

Boulding, Kenneth E. 1956. *The Image: Knowledge in Life and Society*. Ann Arbour, MI. University of Michigan Press.

Brewer, Marilyn B. 1999. "The Psychology of Prejudice: Ingroup Love or Outgroup Hate?" *Journal of Social Issues*. Fall 1999.

Buckley, Peter. 1995. *Canadian Press Style Book*. Toronto: The Canadian Press.

Canadian Race Relations Foundation. 2002. "'Hidden discrimination' and 'polite racism' prevents Aboriginal peoples and visible minorities from gaining access to jobs, study finds." [Online]. Available <http://www.crr.ca/EN/MediaCentre/NewsReleases/eMedCen_NewsRe20010110.htm>. 6 February 2002.

"Classic IQ Test." [Online]. Available <http://www.queendom.com/cgi-bin/tests/transfer.cgi>. 6 February 2002.

Criminal Code of Canada (Section 319). [Online]. Available <http://totse.com/en/politics/political_documents/sec319.html>. February 2002.

Editorials and Letters. 2001. *The Toronto Star*. 2 September 2001.

Farber, Bernie. 1997. *From Marches to Modems: A Report on Organized Hate in Metropolitan Toronto*. Toronto. Canadian Council of Christians and Jews.

Gordon, Frank, ed. 2002. Heritage Front Web site. Available <http://www.freedomsite.org/hf/hf_report_jan97.html>. January 2002.

Griffin, John Howard. [1959] 1997. *Black Like Me*. 35th ed. New York. NAL Paperbacks.

"Guilty Plea Entered in Cross Burning." 2001. *The Sarnia Observer*. 25 August 2001.

Jigsaw Classroom. Web site. Available <http://www.jigsaw.org/>. 6 February 2002.

Kehoe, John W. 1984. *A Handbook for Enhancing the Multicultural Climate of the School*. Vancouver. University of British Columbia.

McIntosh, Peggy. 2001. "White Privilege: Unpacking the Invisible Knapsack." In Aaron Podolefsky and Peter J. Brown. *Applying Anthropology: An Introductory Reader*. Toronto. Mayfield Publishing.

Media Education Foundation. 2002. Review of *Stuart Hall: Race, the Floating Signifier*. [Online]. Available <http://www.mediaed.org/catalog/race/hallrace.html>. 8 March 2002.

"Natives Face 'Systemic' Racism Says AFN Chief". 2001. *The Sarnia Observer*. 27 August, 2001.

Ogbu, John. 1999. "Ebonics, Proper English and Identity in a Black-American Speech Community." American Educational Research Journal. 36 (2). [Online]. Available <http://www.aera.net/pubs/aerj/abs/aerj3622.htm>. 8 March 2002.

Podolefsky, Aaron, and Peter J. Brown. *Applying Anthropology: An Introductory Reader*. Toronto. Mayfield Publishing. 2001.

"Professional Profile: Elliot Aronson." 2001. [Online]. Available <http://aronson.socialpsychology.org/>. February 2002.

Rickford, John R. 1997. "Suite for Ebony and Phonics." *Discover*. December 1997.

Samuda, Ronald J. 1986. "The Role of Psychometry in Multicultural Education: Implications and Consequences." In Ronald J. Samuda and Shiu L. Kong, eds. *Multicultural Education: Programmes and Methods*. Kingston, ON. Intercultural Social Sciences Publications.

"Slobodan Milosevic to Face Genocide Charges." 2001. *The Sarnia Observer.* 30 August 2001.

Sternberg, Robert J. 1994. *In Search of the Human Mind.* Toronto. Harcourt Brace.

Teachers.Net. 1999. "Author Chat: Dr. Beverly Tatum." [Online]. Available <http://teachers.net/archive/tatum111099.html>. 8 March 2002.

World Book Encyclopedia. 1989. Toronto. World Book Inc.

Chapter 10

Albrow, Martin. 1995. "Globalization." In Robert J. Brym, ed. *New Society: Sociology for the 21ˢᵗ Century.* Toronto. Harcourt Brace Canada.

Camdessus, Michel. 2001. "Church Social Teaching and Globalization." *America.* 185 (11).

Chambers, Allan. 2001. "Old 'ethnic' idea of Canada ignores global issues – prof." *Edmonton Journal.* 14 July 2001.

Council of Canadians. 2001. "The IMF and the World Bank." [Online]. Available <http://www.canadians.org/>. 1 December 2001.

Edelman, Marc. 1999. *Peasants Against Globalization: Rural Social Movements in Costa Rica.* Stanford, CA. Stanford University Press.

Francis, Diane. 2001. "Sell all but our sovereignty: We accept free trade to a point." *The Halifax Daily News.* 1 July 2001.

Giddens, Anthony. 1991. *Modernity and Identity: Self and Society in the late Modern Age.* Cambridge, UK. Polity.

Gledhill, John. 1994. *Power and Its Disguises.* London. Pluto Press.

Gwyn, Richard. 2001. "Ottawa fails to lead border debate." *The Toronto Star.* 28 November 2001.

Harrison, Trevor. 1999. "Globalization and the trade in human body parts." *Canadian Review of Sociology and Anthropology.* 36 (1).

Hughes, Karen D., and Lowe, Graham S. 2000. "Surveying the 'post-industrial' landscape: Information technologies and labour market polarization." *Canadian Review of Sociology and Anthropology.* 37 (1).

Kappler, Brian. 2001. "Think forests, not culture: Canadian identity lies more in nature than in government programs." *The Halifax Daily News.* 8 June 2001.

Kerr, C., J.T. Dunlop, F.H. Harbison, and C.A. Myers. 1960. *Industrialism and Industrial Man.* Cambridge, MA. Harvard University Press.

Kilfoil, Kara. 2001. "The Maple Leaf: A symbol of goodwill." *Korea Herald.* 10 July 2001.

Laxer, Gordon. 1995. "Social solidarity, democracy and global capitalism." *Canadian Review of Sociology and Anthropology.* 32 (3).

Lewellen, Ted. 1983. *Political Anthropology.* South Hadley, MA. Bergin and Garvey.

Mazumdar, Krishna. 1996. "An analysis of causal flow between social development and economic growth: The social development index." *American Journal of Economics and Sociology.* 55 (3).

McLuhan, Marshall. 1962. *The Gutenberg Galaxy.* Toronto. University of Toronto Press.

Mitchell, Alanna. 2001. "Scientists Clone Human Embryo." *The Globe and Mail.* 26 November 2001.

Myles, J. 1988. "The expanding middle: Some Canadian evidence on the deskilling debate." *Canadian Review of Sociology and Anthropology.* 25 (3).

Napp, Bernie. 2000. "Eyewitness evidence often wrong – research." *The Evening Post* (Wellington, NZ). 10 September 2000.

Prabhu, Joseph. 1999. "Globalization and the emerging world order." *ReVision.* 22 (2).

Reich, R. 1991. *The Work of Nations: Preparing Ourselves for 21st Century Capitalism.* New York. Random House.

Robertson, Roland. 1992. *Globalization: Social Theory and Global Culture.* Newbury Park, CA. Sage.

Salmon, Blaise. 2001. "Shameful statistics." *The Toronto Star.* [Online]. Available <http://www.thestar.com>. Article Number: 1005865300835. 19 November 2001.

Schultz, Emily, and Robert Lavenda. 1998. *Cultural Anthropology: A Perspective on the Human Condition.* Mountain View, CA. Mayfield Publishing Company.

Scoffield, Heather. 2001. "World Bank president refutes protesters' claims." *The Globe and Mail.* 19 November 2001.

Statistics Canada. 2001. *Changing our ways: Why and how Canadians use the Internet.* [Online]. Available <http://www.statcan.ca/english/IPS/Data/56F0006XIE.htm>. 10 January 2002.

Winland, Daphne N. 1998. "'Our home and native land'? Canadian ethnic scholarship and the challenge of transnationalism." *Canadian Review of Sociology and Anthropology.* 35 (4).

Wolf, Eric. 1969. *Peasant Wars of the Twentieth Century.* New York. Harper & Row.

INDEX

CREDITS

Text Credits

Every possible effort has been made to trace the original source of text material contained in this book. Where the attempt has been unsuccessful, the publisher would be pleased to hear from the copyright holders to rectify any omissions.

3 Excerpted from the book *Children Learn What They Live* © 1998 by Dorothy Law Nolte and Rachel Harris. The poem 'Children Learn What They Live' © Dorothy Law Nolte. Used by permission of Workman Publishing Co., Inc., New York. All Rights Reserved. 39 Adapted from 'Ten Commandments for Changing the World' by Angela Bischoff and Tooker Gomberg, from http://www.greenspiration.org. Reprinted by permission. 57 Excerpts from 'The shine is off boot camps' by Nate Hendley from http://www.eye.net/eye/issue/issue_01.20.00/news/boot-camp.html, 20 January 2000. Reprinted by permission of Eye Weekly. 89 Excerpts from 'Homeless by choice or necessity?' by Les Sillars from *Alberta Report*, Vol. 21, no. 38, September 1994, pp. 16-17. Reprinted by permission of Report Newsmagazine. 70 Excerpts from 'A taste for the good life' by Melinda Liu and Lijia Macleod from *Newsweek*, 14 December 1998. © 1998 Newsweek, Inc. All rights reserved. Reprinted by permission. 69 Copyright © 1997 The New York Times Company. 88 Excerpts from 'Massive welfare cuts invite more drug problems' by Bob Curley from *Alcohol and Drug Abuse Weekly*, Vol. 7, no. 20, 15 May 1995. Reprinted by permission of Manisses Communications Group, Inc. 1-800-333-7771 www.manisses.com 75 Reprinted by permission of Transaction Publishers. Excerpts from 'Why advocacy research? Reflections on research and activism with immigrant women' by Pierrette Hondagneu-Sorelo from *The American Sociologist*, Vol. 24, Issue 1, Spring 1993. Copyright © 1993 by Transaction Publishers. 84 Chart: Canadian Low-Income Cut-Offs, 1999 from http://www.ccsd.ca/factsheets/ fs_lic99.htm, used with the permission of the Canadian Council on Social Development. 132 Norman Borlaug: excerpts from 'Biotechnology will save the poorest' from http://biotechknowledge.com Third World Network 133 Dr Mae-Wan Ho: Excerpts from 'Say No to GMO' from http://www.twnside.org.sg/ title/mwho2-cn.htm Third World Network. 128 Excerpts from 'Creating a New Rural Economy in Honduras' from http://www.acdi-cida.gc.ca ©Canadian International Development Agency 113 Reprinted from *Journal of Cognitive Systems Research*, Vol. 1, Robert L. West and Christian Lebiere, 'Simple games as dynamic, coupled systems: randomness and other emergent properties'. Copyright © 2001. Reprinted with permission from Elsevier Science. Excerpts from 'CyberSkins: Live and Interactive' from www.cradleboard.org. © Buffy Sainte-Marie 1996. Reprinted by 115 Excerpt from *The Infinite Bonds of Family* by Cynthia Toronto: University of Toronto Press, 1999), pp. 80-1. mission of University of Toronto Press. 116 Excerpts by Martin Regg Cohn from *The Toronto Star*, 8 July permission - The Toronto Star Syndicate. 231

Peter G. Peterson: Four-paragraph excerpt from 'Grey Dawn: The Global Aging Crisis' from *Foreign Affairs*, 78 (1), January/February 1999, p. 42 110 'The Social Transformation of Society' and 'The Cultural Lag Theory' adapted from *Sociology: A Down-to-Earth Approach*, Canadian Edition, by James M. Henslin and Adie Nelson (Toronto: Allyn & Bacon Canada, 1996), pp. 146 and 637-8. Reprinted with permission by Pearson Education Canada Inc. 143 Darrell Tan: excerpts from 'Today's Youth Do More than Echo the Past' from *The Toronto Star*, 1 May 1995, p. A17 164 Excerpts from 'Violent Crime up 7.5% in Greater Toronto' by Elaine Carey, *The Toronto Star*, 20 July 2001. Reprinted with permission - The Toronto Star Syndicate. 165 Excerpts from 'Young Offender's Act, Phase II Review, November 1995' Rights Holder: The John Howard Society of Canada 148, 153 Excerpt from *Born at the Right Time* by Doug Owram (Toronto: University of Toronto Press, 1996), pp. 82-3. Reprinted by permission of University of Toronto Press. 159 'Births per Woman in Canada' graph was created by David Nowell, Sheridan College, Oakville, Ontario, based on data from StatsCanada, *Time* Magazine, and his own estimates. Reprinted from http://www.sheridanc.on.ca/~nowell/ markstuf/fecund/birthbyyr.htm by permission. 145-46 Excerpt from *Boom, Bust and Echo 2000: Profiting from the Demographic Shift in the New Millennium* by David K. Foot with Daniel Stoffman. © 1996 by David K. Foot. Reprinted by permission of Stoddart Publishing Co. Limited. 148 Table: Birth rates and births in Canada, 1921-71 from *Historical Statistics of Canada*, 2nd Edition, F.H. Leacy, ed., (Ottawa: Statistics Canada, 1983). 149 Table: Immigration to Canada, 1945-1960 from *Historical Statistics of Canada*, 2nd Edition, F.H. Leacy, ed., (Ottawa: Statistics Canada, 1983) 150 Graphs: Population by Age and Sex, Canada: 1941, 1956, 1971" from *Historical Statistics of Canada*, 2nd Edition, F.H. Leacy, ed., (Ottawa: Statistics Canada, 1983) 153 From the song 'Little Boxes'. Words and music by Malvina Reynolds. © Copyright 1962 Schroder Music Co. (ASCAP) Renewed 1990. Used by permission. All rights reserved. 156 MY GENERATION. Words and Music by Peter Townshend. © Copyright 1965 (Renewed) Fabulous Music Ltd., London, England. TRO - Devon Music, Inc., New York, controls all publication rights for the U.S.A. and Canada. Used by Permission. 159 Tables: 'Marriage Rate per 1000 Population, Canada, 1945-73' and 'Percentage of Live Birth Termed Illegitimate, Canada, 1945-73' from *Historical Statistics of Canada*, 2nd Edition, (Ottawa: Statistics Canada, 1983) 170 Table: Seniors in Canada, 1931-2031 from *Profile of Canada's Seniors*, J.A. Norland, (Statistics Canada and Prentice Hall Canada, 1991), p. 6 166-67 Adapted excerpts from *Teen Trends: A Nation in Motion*, Abridged Edition, Reginald W. Bibby and Donald C. Posterski, (Toronto: Stoddart, 2000), pp. vii, 3, 195-6 203 Adaptation of 'Being old doesn't cost more money—being sick does' by Susannah Benady from *The Medical Post*, 27 February 2001. Reprinted by permission of The Medical Post. 177 Gary S. Becker: 'How Rich Nations Can Defuse the Population Bomb' (with deletions as indicated) from *Business Week*, 28 May 2001 180 Sarah Scott: first five paragraphs from 'Baby time any

the World Bank' by Ed Finn from http://www.canadians.org. Reprinted by permission of The Council of Canadians. 341 Excerpt from 'World Bank President Refutes Protesters' Claims' by Heather Scoffield from *The Globe and Mail*, 19 November 2001, reprinted with permission from The Globe and Mail. 343 Kara Kilfoil: Excerpt from a letter to the Editor: 'The Maple Leaf: A symbol of goodwill' from *The Korea Herald*, 10 July 2001. 351 Excerpts from 'Ottawa fails to lead border debate' by Richard Gwyn, *The Toronto Star*, 28 November 2001. Reprinted with permission - The Toronto Star. 353 Three excerpts from the APA web site guidelines for use of language, from http://www.apastyle.org/disabilities.html,http:www.apastyle.org/sexuality.html,and http://www.apastyle.org/race.html.

Photo Credits

t=top; b=bottom; c=centre; l=left; r=right
CP=CP Picture Archive   NAC=National Archives of Canada

2 I. Devore/Anthro-Photo File; 4 Tom Hanson/CP; 5 © Liss Steve/CORBIS SYGMA/MAGMA; 7 © Reuters NewMedia Inc/CORBIS/MAGMA; 8 AP Photo/Pat Sullivan/CP; 10 Courtesy of Professor Parin Dossa; 13 © Color Day Production/Getty Images/The Image Bank; 16 Toronto Star/Boris Spremo/CP; 17 Courtesy of Dr. Robert L. West; 20 © Zigy Kaluzny/Getty Images/Stone; 21 Al Harvey/The Slide Farm; 22 Victor Last/Geographical Visual Aids; 25 Courtesy of Professor George Dei; 28 Kobal Collection; 29 Frank Gunn/CP; 36 Frank Gunn/CP; 37 tl Aaron Harris/CP, bl Tom & Dee Ann McCarthy/Firstlight.ca; 37 r AP Photo/John Moore/CP; 38 AP Photo/Mary Lederhandler/CP; 40 Aaron Harris/CP; 42 CORBIS RF/MAGMA; 43 Courtesy of Oxfam Canada and Gee, Jeffery & Partners; 45 © The Mariners' Museum/CORBIS/MAGMA; 49 R. Katz/Anthro-Photo File; 50 NA-3482-8/Glenbow Archives, Alberta, Canada; 51 Courtesy of Professor Sherry Ortner/Photograph by Dan Fry; 52 Everett Collection/MAGMA; 54 © Bettmann/CORBIS/MAGMA; 55 © Bettmann/CORBIS/MAGMA; 60 Edmonton Sun/Christine Vanzella/CP; 63 Courtesy of Thelma McCormack; 64 © Bettmann/CORBIS/MAGMA; 68 AP Photo/Don Ryan/CP; 70 AP Photo/Chien-min Chung/CP; 71 Doug Ball/CP; 72 Toronto Star/Boris Spremo/CP; 75 © FK PHOTO/Corbis/Magma Photo; 78 Dick Hemingway; 80 AP Photo/John Moore/CP; 81 Frank Gunn/CP; 86 Al Harvey/The Slide Farm; 91 Dick Hemingway; 92 Al Harvey/The Slide Farm; 95 Andrew Vaughan/CP; 103 Kobal Collection; 104 © Bettmann/CORBIS/MAGMA; 107 © Bettmann/CORBIS/MAGMA; 111 Kobal Collection; 112 Dick Hemingway; 115 Lake County Museum/CORBIS/MAGMA; 116 Savita Kirloskar/REUTERS; 119 Tom & Dee Ann McCarthy/Firstlight.ca; 126 Courtesy of the artist, Lewis Parker; 127 © Keren Su/CORBIS/MAGMA; 128 CIDA Photo: Brian Atkinson; 130 © Maiman Rick/CORBIS SYGMA/MAGMA; 140 Inc..Lambert 03RLAM Archive Holdings/Getty Images/The Image Bank; 141 **Top Left** © Roger Ressmeyer/CORBIS/MAGMA; 141 **Bottom Left** Mark Tuschman/Firstlight.ca; 141 **Right** Owen Franken/CORBIS/MAGMA; 142 Paul Barton/Firstlight.ca; 145 Illustration by Paul Rivoche, From *Generation X: Tales for an Accelerated Culture* by Douglas Coupland, Copyright © 1991, St. Marin's Press, New York; 148 DesRivieres; 149 George Hunter/National Film Board of Canada/NAC/PA-123476; 152 Getty Images/Archive Photos; 153 York University Archives/Toronto Telegram Collection B117/F844/#1123; 154 tl AP Photo/CP, tc Dick Hemingway, tr © Bettmann/CORBIS/MAGMA, bl © Roger Ressmeyer/CORBIS/MAGMA, bc © Neal Preston/CORBIS/MAGMA, br Everett Collection/MAGMA; 157 t Kobal Collection, b Ottawa Le Droit/CP Picture Archive; 166 B&D Productions/Firstlight.ca; 174 Richard Nowitz/Valan Photos; 179 Owen Franken/CORBIS/MAGMA; 182 © Kevin Fleming/CORBIS/MAGMA; 184 M. Shostak/Anthro-Photo File; 186 Dick Hemingway; 187 © Hulton-Deutsch Collection/CORBIS/MAGMA; 191 LWA/Dann Tardif/Firstlight.ca; 192 LWA/Stephen Welstead/Firstlight.ca; 199 Courtesy of Todd Kneib; 200 Al Harvey/The Slide Farm; 202 Jeff Greenberg/Valan Photos; 207 Scott Houston/Corbis Sygma/MAGMA; 208 © V.C.L./Getty Images/FPG International; 210 A. Arbib/Anthro-Photo File; 212 Andrew Vaughan/CP; 214 © Ted Streshinsky/CORBIS/MAGMA; 218 Donna Disario/Firstlight.ca; 221 Kobal Collection; 224 Kevin Frayer/CP; 228 PhotoDisc; 229 Tom & Dee Ann McCarthy/Firstlight.ca; 232 Ariel Skelley/Firstlight.ca; 235 PhotoDisc; 238 Mark Tuschman/Firstlight.ca; 246 Greg Vandermeulen/Opasquia Times; 247 tl Fred Chartrand/CP, bl Dick Hemingway, r John Henley/Firstlight.ca; 248 Andrew Vaughan/CP; 250 Esbin-Anderson/Firstlight.ca; 252 Larry Williams/Firstlight.ca; 255 Fred Chartrand/CP; 261 John Fowler/Valan Photos; 265 CORBIS RF/MAGMA; 267 © V.C.L./Getty Images/FPG International; 269 Dick Hemingway; 270 Victoria Times-Colonist/Bruce Stotesbury/CP; 273 AP Photo; 274 Dr. Yorgos Nikas/Phototake; 276 Everett Collection/Magma; 278 AP Photo/Nick Ut/CP; 280 Dave McCord/CP; 262 Courtesy of Professor Parin Dossa; 287 Calgary Herald/Mike Sturk/CP; 299 t John Feingersh/Firstlight.ca, b © Bettmann/CORBIS/MAGMA; 300 Richard Nowitz/Valan Photos; 302 John Henley/Firstlight.ca; 305 © Lewis Alan/CORBIS SYGMA/MAGMA; 307 © Bettmann/CORBIS/MAGMA; 309 Everett Collection/MAGMA; 308 AP Photo/Santiago Lyon/CP; 313 Al Harvey/The Slide Farm; 314 Courtesy of Professor Elliot Aronson; 318 © Lawrence Miqdale/Getty Images/Stone; 317 Toronto Star/Paul Irish/CP; 324 La Presse/Bernard Brault/CP; 328 CP; 331 Dick Hemingway; 332 Everett Collection/MAGMA; 334 George Schiavone/Firstlight.ca; 338 V. Wilkinson/Valan Photos; 341 Renzo Gostoli/AP Photo/CP; 342 Everett Collection/MAGMA; 348 © Barrett & MacKay Photography; 349 **Bottom** Tom & Dee Ann McCarthy/Firstlight.ca; 351 CP; 352 Charles Gupton/Firstlight.ca; 354 Phil Snel/Maclean's/CP